HUMAN TRAFFICKING LAW AND POLICY

HUMAN TRAFFICKING LAW AND POLICY

Bridgette Carr
Clinical Professor of Law
Director Human Trafficking Clinic
University of Michigan Law School

Anne Milgram
Senior Fellow and Adjunct Professor
NYU School of Law

Kathleen Kim
Professor of Law
Loyola Law School Los Angeles

Stephen Warnath
Chief Executive Officer, The Warnath Group, LLC
Founder and President, NEXUS Institute

Carolina Academic Press
Durham, North Carolina

ISBN: 978-1-5310-1897-9 (Print)
ISBN: 978-0-32717-970-2 (eBook)

Library of Congress Cataloging-in-Publication Data

Carr, Bridgette, author.
　Human trafficking law and policy / Bridgette Carr, Clinical Professor of Law, Director of Human Trafficking Clinic, University of Michigan Law School; Anne Milgram, Senior Fellow and Adjunct Professor, NYU School of Law; Kathleen Kim, Professor of Law, Loyola Law School, Los Angeles; Stephen Warnath, Chief Executive Officer, the Warnath Group, LLC Founder and President, Nexus Institute.
　　pages cm
Includes index.
ISBN 978-1-4224-8903-1
1. Human trafficking--United States. 2. Human trafficking victims — Legal status, laws, etc. — United States. 3. Slavery — Law and legislation — United States. 4. United States. Mann Act of 1910. I. Milgram, Anne (Professor of law), author. II. Kim, Kathleen (Professor of law), author. III. Warnath, Stephen, author. IV. Title.
　KF9449.C37 2014
　345.73'025—dc23
　　　　　　　　　　　　　　　　　　　　　　　　　　　　　　　　　　　2014003883

This publication is designed to provide authoritative information in regard to the subject matter covered. It is sold with the understanding that the publisher is not engaged in rendering legal, accounting, or other professional services. If legal advice or other expert assistance is required, the services of a competent professional should be sought.

Copyright © 2014 Carolina Academic Press, LLC
All Rights Reserved

No copyright is claimed in the text of statutes, regulations, and excerpts from court opinions quoted within this work.

Carolina Academic Press, LLC
700 Kent Street
Durham, North Carolina 27701
Telephone (919) 489-7486
Fax (919) 493-5668
www.caplaw.com

Printed in the United States of America

Dedications

To Jeff, Elliott, and Owen, thank you for filling my life with joy, laughter, and love, and to my parents Vince and Nondus Carr, my work on behalf of victims of human trafficking is because of your support and guidance, thank you for everything.

To Manuel, the love of my life and my everything, and to Evelyn Gleason and Gail and Bill Milgram, who gave me the courage to fight and the strength to believe that we may one day know a world without trafficking.

To all the human trafficking survivors and anti-trafficking advocates that inspire us and guide our work.

For my parents, Maxine and Charles Warnath, thank you for all of your love and support. You taught me to see injustice and to act against it. For victims and survivors of human trafficking — an injustice of unfathomable depth — you are the inspiration for this work and the writing of this book.

Acknowledgements

This book would not have been possible without the assistance and support of the following: Sheila Berman, Elizabeth Campbell, Lawrence Dabney, Christine DiDomenico, Karin Dryhurst, Darren Geist, Heather Gregorio, Andy Hall, Jane Khodarkovsky, Jane Kim, Loyola Law School Los Angeles, Erica Matson, Julie Mecca, Christina Parello, Meg Powers, Lauren Radebaugh Lee, Stephanie Richard, Suellyn Scarnecchia, Andrea Sitar, Charles Song, Sandy Springer, Patrick Thronson, University of Michigan Law School Librarians, Daniel Werner, Nick Whitaker, Megan Williams, Tristram Wolf, Alicia Yass, Shelly Yoo. And last, but definitely not least, Patrick Barry thank you for helping us find and cross the finish line.

Introduction

Labor trafficking touches many aspects of our daily lives. It touches, through supply chains, the T-shirts we wear, the cell phones we use, and the chocolate we eat and share with others. Moreover, sex trafficking intertwines with much of the global sex industry, whether through the sale of young males into brothels in Bangalore, the sale of young women into strip clubs in San Diego, or the forced prostitution of both males and females, of all ages, in states across the country and countries across the world.

Yet 20 years ago a casebook on either of these criminal activities — which are often linked together under the term "human trafficking" — would have been unthinkable. That's because 20 years ago there was no Palermo Protocol, the international agreement adopted by the United Nations in 2000 to combat human trafficking internationally; and 20 years ago there was no Trafficking Victims Protection Act, the landmark statute Congress passed the same year as the Palermo Protocol to combat human trafficking domestically. In fact, 20 years ago the term "human trafficking" had not even entered the legal lexicon. Lawyers and judges did not think in terms of human trafficking. Nor did politicians and police officers.

Said differently, 20 years ago there was no human trafficking law.

But now there is — which is why we have put together this casebook. In it we knit together the ideas and perspectives of four attorneys who have worked in different areas of human trafficking. To the extent possible, we have each written the sections relating to areas with which we have the greatest expertise, whether as practitioners, academics, or policy makers. For Professor Carr, her work in the field and the academy led to a focus on the Trafficking Victims Protection Act, early domestic trafficking laws, approaches to working with victims of trafficking, and immigration issues. Similarly, Professor Kim's scholarly focus and work in the field led to her concentration on victim issues, immigration issues, civil litigation, and involuntary servitude. For Professor Milgram, her work as a prosecutor of federal human trafficking crimes and as a state policy maker, along with her work in the academy, led to her focus on federal criminal prosecutions, agency responses to trafficking, and antebellum slavery and peonage. Finally, Stephen Warnath's experience in international law and policies, including as an advisor to leaders in government and business, led to his focus on the international components of the human trafficking issue and on corporate accountability and transparency.

During the coming years we will edit and improve our work. We anticipate future revisions and welcome feedback from the many committed people working in this field today, from academics to policy makers to practitioners. We know the stories we provide in the following chapters leave out other stories and we hope that what we have omitted will soon be filled in by others who, freed from the constraints of writing a casebook, can give fuller, more nuanced accounts of how "human trafficking" went from a term few people had heard of to a term 130 countries have codified into law.

But for this first edition, we have decided to attempt something more fundamental. We have decided to attempt to bring together, in one place, the cases and statutes that have come to define human trafficking law over the past 20 years, as well as the cases and

Introduction

statutes out of which that law developed, stretching back all the way to before the Civil War.

So in the chapters that follow you will find cases from the 21st century as well as cases from the 19th and 20th centuries, just as you will find statutes ranging from the California Supply Chain Transparency Act of 2010 to the Mann Act of 1910 to the Black Codes of Reconstruction. In our view, to understand "modern-day slavery" it is helpful to understand antebellum slavery, as well as the various forms of slavery, such as peonage and debt bondage, that sprung up in between — particularly because many of these forms have reemerged in places across the globe.

You will also find in-depth discussions of how human trafficking cases are prosecuted in the criminal context, how human trafficking cases are litigated in the civil context, and what role government agencies and NGOs play in each of these contexts, both in the United States and abroad. In other words, you will find the resources to understand who is doing what with whom in the world of human trafficking.

But what you won't find are a lot of statistics. You won't find a lot of statistics because statistics about human trafficking are notoriously unreliable. Some organizations put the number of people currently enslaved in the world at 15 million. Other organizations estimate that number is as high as 27 million. That's a difference of 12 million human beings, or roughly the amount of human beings that were brought to the New World to be enslaved during the over 300-year reign of the Atlantic Slave Trade.

Rather than devote our energy to navigating these numbers, we have instead decided to devote our energy to reducing them. That is, we have decided to devote our energy to collecting and arranging the legal materials that we think can best help human trafficking lawyers help human trafficking victims, as well as the legal materials we think can best help human trafficking policy makers prevent people from being trafficked in the first place. There may be disagreement about the number of people currently enslaved in the world, but there is no disagreement about the state of that number: it is too high and it, ideally, should be cut down to zero.

With this admittedly ambitious goal in mind, we offer the chapters of this casebook, none of which is meant to be an original work of scholarship nor a comprehensive account of a particular subject. Instead we have designed each chapter with a much more strictly pedagogical purpose in mind: we want to teach students how to read cases and interpret statutes as experienced human trafficking lawyers read cases and interpret statutes.

If we can do that, if we can equip students with the background knowledge and analytical framework they'll need to "think like a human trafficking lawyer," then perhaps just as 20 years ago a casebook on human trafficking law would have been unthinkable, 20 years from now this casebook on human trafficking law will have done some good.

***

We have organized this book into five parts:
- Chapters 1–4: Part I introduces the history of slavery, abolition, and peonage, along with the laws most often used to address slavery and compelled service in the U.S. prior to passage of the Trafficking Victims Protection Act.

Introduction

- Chapters 5–8: Part II describes both U.S. and international laws and policies aimed at combating human trafficking.
- Chapters 9–12: Part III provides readers with an in-depth look at how U.S. human trafficking law and policy is implemented.
- Chapters 13–14: Part IV frames some of the debates and issues attorneys and advocates working to combat human trafficking currently face.
- The Appendix: Part V provides supporting material and an overview of state human trafficking laws and prosecutions.

A Note about Definitions

The Palermo Protocol and the TVPA both use the term "trafficking in persons." But for the purposes of this casebook we have decided to use the somewhat more common and succinct term "human trafficking." In other areas, our task has been made more difficult by the fact that many people use two key terms — "domestic trafficking" and "international trafficking" — to mean different things. These phrases can be used as shorthand for the location in which trafficking takes places, whether the trafficking was transnational, the citizenship status of the victims, and the citizenship status of the traffickers. So we have chosen, where necessary, to use these terms as they have been adopted and used by government agencies and others.

We have also chosen to make two additional definitional distinctions. First, we have chosen to use "foreign national" when talking about individuals in the United States who are not U.S. citizens or who do not have permission to enter or remain in the United States. Second, we have chosen to use the term "victim of human trafficking" to describe individuals who have been exploited by traffickers. We hope these choices lend some clarity to an often times linguistically confusing area of law, and we encourage suggestions for how to lend even more clarity in the future.

***

History of Slavery Timeline

1619 The first African slaves arrive in Virginia.

1776 The Declaration of Independence declares that "all men are created equal."

1787 The U.S. Constitution states that Congress may not ban the slave trade until 1808 (art. 1, § 9) and enacts the three-fifths compromise (art. 1, § 2(3)). The Constitution also establishes a property right in slaves (art. 4, § 2(3)). Slavery is also made illegal in the Northwest Territory, which extends from the western border of Pennsylvania through the present-day states of Ohio, Illinois, Indiana, Michigan, Wisconsin, and part of Minnesota.

U.S. Constitution, Article 1, § 9

The migration or importation of such persons as any of the states now existing shall think proper to admit, shall not be prohibited by the Congress prior to the year one thousand eight hundred and eight, but a tax or duty may be imposed on such importation, not exceeding ten dollars for each person.

U.S. Constitution, Article 1, § 2(3)

Representatives and direct Taxes shall be apportioned among the several States which

Introduction

may be included within this Union, according to their respective Numbers, which shall be determined by adding to the whole Number of free Persons, including those bound to Service for a Term of Years, and excluding Indians not taxed, three fifths of all other Persons.

U.S. Constitution, Article 4, § 2(3)

No Person held to Service or Labour in one State, under the Laws thereof, escaping into another, shall, in Consequence of any Law or Regulation therein, be discharged from such Service or Labour, but shall be delivered up on Claim of the Party to whom such Service or Labour may be due.

Northwest Ordinance, Article 6, 22 Journals of Congress 343 (1787)

There shall be neither Slavery nor involuntary servitude in the said territory otherwise than in the punishment of crimes, whereof the party shall have been duly convicted; provided always that any person escaping into the same, from whom labor or service is lawfully claimed in any one of the original States, such fugitive may be lawfully reclaimed and conveyed to the person claiming his or her labor or service as aforesaid.

1793 Eli Whitney invents the cotton gin, which greatly increases the demand for slave labor.

1793 A federal fugitive slave law is enacted to enforce Article 4, § 2 of the Constitution. The law provides for private capture and return of slaves who escape and cross state lines.

1808 The federal ban on importation of African slaves (hereinafter the "1808 Slave Trade statute"), passed in 1803, goes into effect.

1808 Slave Trade Statute: 9 Cong. Ch. 22; 2 Stat. 426

Be it enacted by the Senate and House of Representatives of the United States of America in Congress assembled, That from and after the first day of January, on thousand eight hundred and eight, it shall not be lawful to import or bring into the United States or the territories thereof from any foreign kingdom, place, or country, any negro, mulatto, or person of colour, with intent to hold, sell, or dispose of such negro, mulatto, or person of colour, as a slave, or to be held to service or labour.

1820 The Missouri Compromise bans slavery north of the 36th parallel, except in Missouri.

1831 Nat Turner, an enslaved African American preacher, leads a slave uprising. He and his followers launch a short, bloody, rebellion in Virginia. State and federal troops quell the rebellion, and Turner is eventually hanged.

1831 William Lloyd Garrison publishes the *Liberator*, a weekly paper advocating the complete abolition of slavery. He quickly becomes one of the leading figures in the abolitionist movement.

1841 The Supreme Court decides *United States v. The Amistad*, 40 U.S. 518 (1841), which frees the Amistad captives, finding that the 49 Africans on board were kidnapped in Africa and never held as slaves.

1842 In *Prigg v. Pennsylvania*, 41 U.S. 539 (1842), the Supreme Court declares a Pennsylvania law unconstitutional that prohibits the capture of *any* African-American for

Introduction

return into slavery, except with procedural protections for suspected fugitive slaves. Prigg had captured and arrested an escaped slave in Pennsylvania and brought her back to Maryland without using the procedures in the state law. The Supreme Court found that the state law was both unconstitutional under Article 4, § 2, clause 3 of the Constitution and preempted by the Fugitive Slave Act of 1793. The Court holds that, "[t]he right to seize and retake fugitive slaves, and the duty to deliver them up, in whatever state of the Union they may be found, is, under the constitution, recognised as an absolute positive right and duty . . . uncontrollable by state sovereignty or state legislation." 41 U.S. at 542.

1849 Harriet Tubman escapes from slavery and becomes a leader of the Underground Railroad.

1850 A debate on whether territory won in the Mexican War should be open to slavery is decided in the Compromise of 1850. California is admitted as a free state, the Utah and New Mexico territories are left to decide the issue by popular sovereignty, and Washington, D.C. prohibits the slave trade but does not abolish slavery. Controversially, the Fugitive Slave Law of 1850 is passed, which is a much harsher version of the 1793 fugitive slave law: the new law mandates fines, or imprisonment, for officials who refuse to execute a warrant for a fugitive slave or anyone who aids, harbors, or hides a fugitive slave. Furthermore, a slave's testimony in a proceeding against his claimant is not admissible as evidence; however, to prevail, a claimant had only to offer sworn testimony of ownership.

1854 The Kansas-Nebraska Act becomes law, establishing the territories of Kansas and Nebraska, each of which may determine the slavery issue by popular sovereignty. The law thus repeals the Missouri Compromise of 1820 and renews tensions between anti- and pro-slavery factions.

1857 In the seminal case of *Dred Scott*, 60 U.S. 393 (1857), the United States Supreme Court holds that freed slaves are not citizens of the United States and that Congress does not have the right to ban slavery in the States. Also in 1857, the New Mexico Supreme Court invalidates the practice of using law enforcement to enforce peonage and debt bondage in *Jaremillo v. Romero*, 1 N.M. 190 (N. Mex. 1857).

1859 John Brown and his followers capture the federal arsenal at Harpers Ferry, Virginia (now West Virginia) in an attempted slave revolt.

1860 Abraham Lincoln elected as President of the United States. South Carolina secedes from the United States.

1861 February: The Confederate States of America is founded by the first seven states that secede from the United States (South Carolina, Mississippi, Florida, Alabama, Georgia, Louisiana, Texas). A provisional army is established.

March: The Confederate States Army is founded. Lincoln is sworn in as President.

April: Confederate forces attack the U.S. military installation at Fort Sumter, and the Civil War begins.

1863 On January 1, President Lincoln issues the Emancipation Proclamation, declaring "that all persons held as slaves" within the Confederate States "are, and henceforward shall be, free."

1864 The Senate passes the Thirteenth Amendment to the Constitution.

Introduction

1865 January 31: The House passes the Thirteenth Amendment, sending it to the States for ratification.

April 9: The Confederate Army surrenders at Appomattox Court House, ending the Civil War.

April 14: President Lincoln is assassinated.

December 6: The requisite three-quarters of states ratify the Thirteenth Amendment, abolishing slavery throughout the United States.

U.S. Constitutional Amendment XIII

Section 1. Neither slavery nor involuntary servitude, except as a punishment for crime whereof the party shall have been duly convicted, shall exist within the United States, or any place subject to their jurisdiction.

Section 2. Congress shall have power to enforce this article by appropriate legislation.

1866 March: Southern states enact so-called black codes, which limit the basic civil liberties of "colored people" (an individual with more than 1/8 African American blood). The black codes, most of which include express racial classifications, forbid "colored people" from, among other things, carrying weapons, marrying white people, selling liquor, or being vagrant.

An Act to alter and amend the 4435th Section of the Penal Code of Georgia, Georgia, Title II, No. 240, March 12, 1866.

SECTION 1. All persons wandering or strolling about in idleness, who are able to work, and who have no property to support them; all persons leading and idle, immoral or profligate life, who have no property to support them, and are able to work, and do not work . . . shall be deemed and considered vagrants, and shall be indicted as such; and it shall be lawful for any person to arrest said vagrants, and have them bound over for trial to the next term of the County Court, and upon conviction they shall be fined or imprisoned, or sentenced to work on the public works or roads for no longer than a year, or shall . . . be bound out to some person for a time not longer than one year, upon such valuable consideration as the Court may prescribe, the person giving bond, in a sum not exceeding three hundred dollars, payable to said Court. . . .

April 9: Largely in response to the black codes, and over the veto of President Andrew Johnson, the Civil Rights Act of 1866 is enacted. The Act states that individuals born in the United States are U.S. citizens and enjoy the right to contract, sue, give evidence, purchase and convey property, and are entitled to "the full and equal benefit of all laws and proceedings for the security of person and property," as are enjoyed by white citizens. The right to contract is a precursor to the Fourteenth Amendment.

1867 The Peonage Abolition Act becomes law, eliminating the practice of debt bondage. Debt bondage, or bonded labor, occurs when a debtor pledges his personal labor or services to a lender in payment of his debt, but the reasonable value of his services is not applied to the liquidation of the debt, or the length and nature of the services is not defined.

1870 February 3 — The requisite number of states ratify the Fifteenth Amendment, prohibiting denial of the right to vote based upon race, color, or previous enslavement.

Introduction

U.S. Constitutional Amendment XV

Section 1. The right of citizens of the United States to vote shall not be denied or abridged by the United States or by any State on account of race, color, or previous condition of servitude.

Section 2. The Congress shall have power to enforce this article by appropriate legislation.

May 31 — The Enforcement Act is passed to enforce the Fifteenth Amendment, making it a misdemeanor to refuse to allow otherwise qualified people to complete the "prerequisites" for voting.

1874 The Padrone Statute, aimed at preventing Italian children from being enslaved as street musicians and beggars, prevents the involuntary servitude of all foreign-born individuals.

1875 The Page Act prohibits the importation of "alien" women from Asia for purposes of prostitution. Portions of this act will be used in the White Slave Traffic Act in 1910.

1904 In *United States v. Ah Sou*, 132 F. 878 (N.D. Wash. 1904), a Washington Federal District Court blocks the deportation of a Chinese woman, Ah Sou, because she was forced into sexual servitude. The Ninth Circuit Court of Appeals later reverses, holding that the Thirteenth Amendment does not prohibit the deportation of a slave. *United States v. Ah Sou*, 138 F. 775 (9th Cir. 1905).

1909 Congress removes race from all involuntary servitude and slavery statutes, making all prohibitions against slavery race-neutral for the first time.

1910 The White Slave Traffic Act, later known as the Mann Act, becomes law and criminalizes the interstate transport of women for "prostitution," "debauchery," or "immoral purposes."

1926 League of Nations Convention to Suppress the Slave Trade and Slavery. The first international instrument to provide a definition of slavery is enacted. Article 1 defines slavery as "the status or condition of a person over whom any or all of the powers attaching to the right of ownership are exercised." Article 2 calls upon the Parties to undertake "(a) To prevent and suppress the slave trade" and "(b) To bring about . . . the complete abolition of slavery in all its forms."

1930 Convention Concerning Forced or Compulsory Labour, International Labour Organization Convention No. 29. ILO Convention No. 29 defines forced labor and requires States to criminalize it. The Convention prohibits all forms of forced or compulsory labor, defined as "all work or service which is exacted from any person under the menace of any penalty and for which the said person has not offered himself voluntarily."

1948 Federal criminal law is amended to enact 18 U.S.C. §§ 1581–1588, which ban peonage and involuntary servitude. The amendments are a consolidation of the 1874 Padrone Statute (formerly 18 U.S.C. § 446 (1940 ed.)) and the 1808 Slave Trade statute, as amended in 1909 (18 U.S.C. § 423 (1940 ed.)).

1948 UN General Assembly, *Universal Declaration of Human Rights*. The United Nations adopts the Universal Declaration of Human Rights in 1948 in order to strengthen human rights protection at the international level. Article 4 states: "No one shall be held in slavery

Introduction

or servitude; slavery and the slave trade shall be prohibited in all their forms."

1950 Council of Europe, *European Convention for the Protection of Human Rights and Fundamental Freedoms*, as amended by Protocols Nos. 11 and 14.

Article 4 of the European Convention for the Protection of Human Rights and Fundamental Freedoms provides that: "1. No one shall be held in slavery or servitude" and "2. No one shall be required to perform forced or compulsory labour." In addition to recognizing basic rights and freedoms, this Convention established a framework of enforcement.

1956 Supplementary Convention on the Abolition of Slavery, the Slave Trade, and Institutions and Practices Similar to Slavery. The Convention supplements the 1926 Convention by identifying practices similar to slavery including debt bondage, serfdom, and marriage where the woman is treated as property.

1964 The Civil Rights movement leads to enactment of the Civil Rights Act (Public Law 82-352 (78 Stat. 241)). The Act targeted "Jim Crow laws" in the South that imposed de jure segregation in all public facilities. Thus, the Act prohibited discrimination and segregation on the basis of race, color, and national origin in public accommodations engaged in interstate commerce. 42 U.S.C. § 2000a. It also prohibited discrimination by employers (of more than 25 people) on the basis of race, color, religion, sex, or national origin (§ 2000e ("Title VII")), and discrimination by government agencies that receive federal funds (§ 2000d).

1965 The Voting Rights Act is enacted, outlawing discriminatory voting practices by prohibiting "qualifications" or "prerequisites" to voting that result in a "denial or abridgement of the right of any citizen . . . to vote on account of race or color." Aug. 6, 1965, P.L. 89-110, 79 Stat. 437.

1988 The Supreme Court decides *United States v. Kozminski*, 487 U.S. 931 (1988), holding that "involuntary servitude," as prohibited by 18 U.S.C. §§ 241 and 1584, means a condition of servitude where the victim was forced to work by threat of physical restraint, physical injury, or coercion by the law or legal process. "Involuntary servitude," therefore, does not encompass psychological coercion without physical or legal coercion. *Id.* at 944.

1989 Convention on the Rights of the Child (CRC). The CRC provides that "State Parties shall take all appropriate national, bilateral and multilateral measures to prevent the abduction of, the sale of or traffic in children for any purpose or in any form."

1998 Presidential Memorandum on Steps to Combat Violence Against Women and Trafficking in Women and Girls, 1 PUB. PAPERS 358, 259 (Mar. 11, 1998). This Presidential directive launched U.S. government's comprehensive framework for addressing modern slavery ("3-P's") and created an interagency process to develop domestic and international law and policy on human trafficking.

1999 Convention concerning the Prohibition and Immediate Action for the Elimination of the Worst Forms of Child Labour, International Labour Organization Convention No. 182. ILO Convention No. 182 is aimed at identifying and preventing the worst forms of child labor. Article 3 of Convention 182 prohibits:

(a) all forms of slavery or practices similar to slavery, such as the sale and

Introduction

trafficking of children, debt bondage and serfdom and forced or compulsory labour, including forced or compulsory recruitment of children for use in armed conflict;

(b) the use, procuring or offering of a child for prostitution, for the production of pornography or for pornographic performances;

(c) the use, procuring or offering of a child for illicit activities, in particular for the production and trafficking of drugs as defined in the relevant international treaties;

(d) work which, by its nature or the circumstances in which it is carried out, is likely to harm the health, safety or morals of children.

2000 The Trafficking Victims Protection Act (TVPA), *Public Law 106-386, 114 Stat. 1464*, acknowledges the modern slave trade and provides criminal and civil remedies for victims, including immigration relief and access to social services, in addition to funding for other countries fighting human trafficking. The TVPA also overturns the holding in *Kozminski* and expands the criminal law of human trafficking to acknowledge that subtle forms of coercion, and not just threats of force, actual force, and the legal process, can enslave individuals. The TVPA creates new offenses aimed at the eradication of slavery in the United States, including the crimes of forced labor and sex trafficking.

2000 The Protocol to Prevent, Suppress and Punish Trafficking in Persons, Especially Women and Children, Supplementing the United Nations Convention against Transnational Organized Crime ("Palermo Protocol"). The Protocol achieves global consensus on the scope of the definition and provides a comprehensive framework for addressing human trafficking in countries around the worldwide.

2002 The Rome Statute of the International Criminal Court (Rome Statute) established the first International Criminal Court (ICC) authorized to prosecute crimes of great concern to the international community. Crimes against humanity are defined under Article 7 to include "enslavement," "sexual slavery," "enforced prostitution," and "any other form of sexual violence of comparable gravity."

2003 The TVPA is reauthorized, becoming the Trafficking Victims Prevention Act Reauthorization (TVPRA), *Public Law 108-193, 117 Stat. 2875*, and:

- Expands eligibility for T-visas generally by explicitly providing for law enforcement certification from both federal and state officials that the victim has assisted in the investigation and prosecution of the crime. (Sec. 4(a)(3), 22 U.S.C. § 7105(b)(1)(E)).

- Creates a private right of action for a victim to pursue a civil remedy against his traffickers, including damages and attorneys fees. (Sec. 4, 18 U.S.C. § 1595).

- Expands eligibility for T-visas for children by exempting them from complying with a "Reasonable request for assistance" to law enforcement if they are under 18 years of age. (Sec. 4, 8 U.S.C. § 1101(a)(15)(T)).

- The definition of "sex trafficking of children" is expanded to reach activities "in or affecting" foreign commerce. (Sec. 5, 18 U.S.C. § 1591).

2005 The TVPA is reauthorized, *Public Law 109-164, 119 Stat. 3558*, and:

- Mandates that USAID and the Departments of State and Defense incorporate anti-trafficking and protection measures into their post-conflict and humanitarian emergency assistance activities. (Sec. 101, 22 U.S.C. § 7104).

Introduction

- Creates extraterritorial jurisdiction for trafficking offenses committed by government employees, federal contractors, and subcontractors at any tier. (Sec. 103, 18 U.S.C. § 3271).
- Establishes grant programs to develop and expand assistance to U.S. citizen and foreign national trafficking victims. (Sec. 202, 42 U.S.C. § 14044a).
- Creates a pilot program for residential treatment facilities for trafficked juveniles. (Sec. 203, 42 U.S.C. § 14044b).

2005 Council of Europe Action against Trafficking in Human Beings (CAATH). CAATH mandated stronger protection and assistance provisions than were enacted in the Palermo Protocol. These included a non-punishment provision and reflection/recovery periods for victims of human trafficking.

2008 The TVPA is again reauthorized, *Public Law 110-457, 122 Stat. 5044*, and:

- Charges the State Department with developing an information pamphlet on legal rights and resources for aliens applying for employment or education based nonimmigrant visas, which the applicant must understand before being granted a visa. (Sec. 202, 8 U.S.C. 1375b).
- Strengthens visa application requirements for domestic workers coming into the U.S. with diplomats by requiring a written contract that states wages and vacation days, and the employer agrees to lawful conduct. (Sec. 203, 8 U.S.C. 1375(e)).
- Establishes a program to specifically assist U.S. citizen and Legal Permanent Residents who have been trafficked. (Sec. 213, 22 U.S.C. 7105(f)).
- The definitions of "enticement into slavery" and "sale into involuntary servitude" are broadened to include "obstruction" of enforcement. (Sec. 222, 18 U.S.C. §§ 1583, 1584).
- The definition of "forced labor" is broadened to include force, threats of force, and threats of physical restraint. (Sec. 222, 18 U.S.C. § 1589).
- "Sex trafficking of children" is broadened to include being "in reckless disregard of the fact that means of force, fraud, [or] coercion" will be used to compel commercial sex acts. (Sec. 222, 18 U.S.C. § 1591).
- In a sex trafficking prosecution of a minor, the Government does not have to prove that the defendant knew the minor was under 18 years old if the defendant "had a reasonable opportunity to observe" the minor. (Sec. 222, 18 U.S.C. § 1591).
- Criminalizes "knowingly benefiting," financially or otherwise, from a venture that has committed peonage or trafficking offenses, and "knowing or in reckless disregard" of the fact that these offenses were committed. (Sec. 222, 18 U.S.C. § 1593A).
- Criminalizes fraud in foreign labor contracting. (Sec. 222, 18 U.S.C. § 1351).
- Creates extraterritorial jurisdiction over trafficking crimes abroad when the offender is a U.S. citizen or Legal Permanent Resident, or if the alleged offender is inside the United States. (Sec. 223, 18 U.S.C. § 1596).
- Broadens eligibility for immigration relief for children at risk of being trafficked

Introduction

    by loosening the requirements for Special Immigrant Juvenile status. (Sec. 235, 8 U.S.C. 1101(a)(27)(J)).

- Enacts the Child Soldier Prevention Act, 22 U.S.C. § 2151, which limits assistance to foreign governments that either have government armed forces or government-supported armed groups that recruit use child soldiers.

2010 California Transparency in Supply Chains Act is enacted obligating large manufacturer and retailers to disclose actions to prevent and eradicate human trafficking from their supply chains.

2010 *Rantsev v. Cyprus and Russia.* The European Court of Human Rights issues opinion in Rantsev holding, *inter alia*, that Cyprus and Russia violated affirmative obligations held toward trafficking victim Ms. Rantsev.

2013 The TVPA is again reauthorized, Violence Against Women Reauthorization Act of 2013, § 1202, and:

- Authorizes the Office to Monitor and Combat Trafficking in Persons to provide assistance to countries that enter child protection compacts with the U.S. (Sec. 1202).
- Adds provisions addressing and seeking to prevent child marriage and child soldiers. (Sec. 1207, 1208).
- Strengthens the oversight of government contracts through implementation of a report investigating — among other things — abuses of foreign workers, the role of foreign labor recruiters and brokers, and the role of employers in the U.S. who commission those recruiters and brokers. Furthermore calls for effective policies and laws to ensure that foreign labor recruiters are held criminally and civilly liable for fraudulent recruiting. (Sec. 1204, 1235).
- Amends the RICO Act to include a fraud in foreign labor contracting clause. (Sec. 1211).

    Includes provisions seeking to improve interagency coordination and reporting. (Sec. 1231–36).

- Authorizes appropriations for grants to state and local law enforcement to help combat trafficking, as well as appropriations for grants to help assist trafficking victims. (Sec. 1241–42, 1251–52).

Table of Contents

Chapter 1		SLAVERY	1
I.		INTRODUCTION	1
II.		SLAVERY IN THE COLONIES AND THE EARLY REPUBLIC	1
III.		*DRED SCOTT* AND THE CITIZENSHIP QUESTION	3
		Scott v. Sandford	4
		Notes and Questions	10
IV.		THE CIVIL WAR AND THE EMANCIPATION PROCLAMATION	11
		The Emancipation Proclamation	13
V.		THE THIRTEENTH AMENDMENT: ABOLITION OF SLAVERY	15
		U.S. Constitutional Amendment XIII (1865)	16
VI.		THE THIRTEENTH AMENDMENT AND *AH SOU*	17
		United States v. Ah Sou	18
		Notes and Questions	20
VII.		CONCLUSION	20

Chapter 2		PEONAGE	21
I.		OVERVIEW: FROM PROCLAMATION TO PEONAGE	21
II.		PEONAGE IN THE SOUTHWEST	22
		Jaremillo v. Romero	22
		Notes and Questions	25
III.		PEONAGE IN THE AMERICAN SOUTH	26
	A.	The Peonage System	27
	B.	An Example	27
IV.		CHALLENGING THE PEONAGE SYSTEM: FINDING AND ENFORCING FEDERAL LAW	28
	A.	Anti-Peonage Act of 1867	28
	B.	The First Court Test — *US v. Clyatt*	29
		Clyatt v. United States	29
		Notes and Questions	31
V.		*BAILEY* AND *REYNOLDS*: TWO ADDITIONAL CHALLENGES TO PEONAGE	33
	A.	The *Bailey* Case	33
		Bailey v. Alabama	33
		Notes and Questions	38
	B.	The *Reynolds* Case	38
		United States v. Reynolds	39
		Notes and Questions	41
VI.		CONCLUSION	41

Table of Contents

Chapter 3	**INVOLUNTARY SERVITUDE**	43
I.	INTRODUCTION	43
	United States v. Ingalls	43
	Notes and Questions	46
II.	THE INVOLUNTARY SERVITUDE STATUTE	47
III.	INTERPRETING 18 U.S.C. § 1584: THE CIRCUIT COURT SPLIT	48
	United States v. Shackney	48
	Notes and Questions	59
	U.S. v. Mussry	60
	Notes and Questions	66
	United States v. Kozminski	67
	Notes and Questions	85

Appendix to Chapter 3 90

Chapter 4	**IMMIGRATION STATUTES AND THE MANN ACT**	95
I.	IMMIGRATION STATUTES	95
	Notes and Questions	96
II.	THE MANN ACT	97
A.	Legislative History	97
B.	The Mann Act as Passed in 1910	98
C.	Constitutionality of the Mann Act	99
	Hoke v. United States	100
	Notes and Questions	102
D.	Scope of the Mann Act	103
	Caminetti v. United States	104
	Notes and Questions	106
E.	Decline of the Mann Act	106
F.	Victim's Perspective	107
III.	MODERN-DAY MANN ACT	108

Chapter 5	**TVPA: THE TRAFFICKING VICTIMS PROTECTION ACT**	109
I.	POLICY HISTORY	109
A.	El Monte	110
B.	From El Monte to a Multi-Pronged Approach	111
II.	THE LEGISLATIVE HISTORY OF THE TRAFFICKING VICTIMS PROTECTION ACT	112
A.	Criminal Provisions	113
1.	Forced Labor	113

Table of Contents

		United States v. Kaufman	115
		Notes and Questions	120
	2.	Sex Trafficking	120
		Notes and Questions	122
	3.	Trafficking, Document Servitude, and Attempt	122
		Notes and Questions	124
B.		Restitution and Civil Relief	127
C.		Social Service Provisions	128

Chapter 6   THE PALERMO PROTOCOL 129

I.		INTRODUCTION	129
II.		ANATOMY OF A DEFINITION	130
A.		Overview	130
B.		Dissecting the Three Elements	131
	1.	*The "Recruitment, Transportation, Transfer, Harbouring or Receipt of Persons"*	132
	2.	*"By Means of the Threat or Use of Force or Other Forms of Coercion, of Abduction, of Fraud, of Deception, of the Abuse of Power or of a Position of Vulnerability or of the Giving or Receiving of Payments or Benefits to Achieve the Consent of a Person Having Control Over Another Person"*	133
	3.	*"for the Purpose of Exploitation"*	134
		Notes and Questions	135
III.		AN UMBRELLA TERM	135
		Notes and Questions	136
IV.		SPECIAL DEFINITIONAL ISSUES	137
A.		Human Trafficking Under the Guise of Adoption	137
		Notes and Questions	137
B.		"Fostering" and "Children in Domesticity"	138
		Notes and Questions	138
C.		Child Brides and Forced Marriage	138
		Notes and Questions	139
D.		Labor Migration	139
		Notes and Questions	139
E.		Exploitation of the Prostitution of Others	139
		Notes and Questions	140
F.		Removal of Organs	140
G.		Consent	140
		Notes and Questions	140
V.		EXTENDING THE SCOPE OF CRIMINAL LIABILITY	141
		Notes and Questions	142

Table of Contents

VI.	OBLIGATION BY COUNTRIES TO CRIMINALIZE	142
	Notes and Questions	143
VII.	EIGHT PRINCIPLES OF GOOD ANTI-TRAFFICKING LEGISLATION	144
1.	Prioritize Victim-Centered Responses	145
2.	Link Provision of Victim Care and Protection to Need in Individual Cases	146
3.	Address All Forms of Human Trafficking and Protect/Assist All Categories of Victims	146
4.	Implement a Comprehensive and Integrated Response	147
5.	Address Root Causes/Contributing Factors	147
6.	Act in the Best Interest of the Child	148
7.	Maximize Cooperation, both International and Domestic	148
8.	Provide Meaningful Legal Remedies: Ensure Access to Justice for Victims; Establish Dissuasive, Proportionate, and Effective Penalties for Traffickers; and Dismantle Criminal Enterprises	149
	Notes and Questions	149

Chapter 7   **AN INTERNATIONAL LEGAL AND POLICY FRAMEWORK** **151**

I.	PREVENTION	152
	Notes and Questions	153
II.	PROTECTION & ASSISTANCE	153
A.	Protecting Physical Safety	154
	Article 24 Protection of witnesses	154
	Notes and Questions	155
B.	Assistance	155
	Article 6 Assistance and protection of victims of trafficking in persons	156
	Article 25 Assistance to and protection of victims	156
	Notes and Questions	156
III.	PROSECUTION	158
	Notes and Questions	159
IV.	SHORTCOMINGS OF THE PROTOCOL	160
V.	EVOLVING LAW AND POLICY SINCE THE PROTOCOL: STRENGTHENING THE PROTOCOL'S PROTECTIONS AND ASSISTANCE	162
	Notes and Questions	164
VI.	LOOKING FORWARD: INTERNATIONAL COURTS AND THE ANTI-TRAFFICKING OBLIGATIONS OF NATIONS	164
	Rantsev v. Cyprus and Russia	165
	Notes and Questions	178

Table of Contents

Chapter 8	**CORPORATE ACCOUNTABILITY AND FEDERAL CONTRACTORS**	**181**
I.	LEGAL LIABILITY FOR COMPANIES	182
	Article 10 Liability of legal persons	182
II.	COUNCIL OF EUROPE CONVENTION ON ACTION AGAINST TRAFFICKING IN HUMAN BEINGS	183
	Article 22 Corporate liability	183
	Article 25 Azerbaijan The Law on the Fight Against Trafficking in Persons, 2005 Liability of legal entities for trafficking in persons	183
	Antigua and Barbuda The Trafficking in Persons (Prevention) Act, 2010	184
	Notes and Questions	184
III.	SPECIAL SUB-GROUP OF CORPORATE ACCOUNTABILITY: FEDERAL CONTRACTORS	185
	Kathryn Bolkovac, DynCorp, and Human Trafficking in Bosnia Herzegovina	186
	Section 3271. Criminal offenses committed by Federal contractors outside the United States	188
IV.	FEDERAL ACQUISITIONS REGULATIONS	189
	Notes and Questions	191
	Notes and Questions	192
	Executive Order 13627: "Strengthening Protections Against Trafficking in Persons in Federal Contracts" & the Ending Trafficking in Government Contracting Act	192
	Notes and Questions	194
	Title XVII — Ending Trafficking in Government Contracting	194
V.	DEPARTMENT OF DEFENSE	197
	Notes and Questions	201
VI.	SPECIAL CASE: THE ROLE OF LABOR RECRUITERS IN HUMAN TRAFFICKING	201
	Optimal Regulatory Approach for Labor Recruiting	202
	Notes and Questions	202
VII.	TRANSPARENCY LAWS	203
	California Transparency in Supply Chains Act	203
	Notes and Questions	205
	Business Transparency in Trafficking and Slavery Act	206
	Notes and Questions	206
	A Practical Example: Transparency and Conflict Minerals	207
	Notes and Questions	208
VIII.	CODES OF CONDUCT AND GUIDING PRINCIPLES	208
	Notes and Questions	209

Table of Contents

Chapter 9		**ANTI-TRAFFICKING AGENCIES AND ORGANIZATIONS** 211
I.		INTRODUCTION 211
II.		THE U.S. GOVERNMENT 211
	A.	The President 211
	B.	The Department of Justice 212
	1.	DOJ Criminal Prosecutions 212
	a.	DOJ Sections: The Criminal Section and the Child Exploitation Section 213
	i.	The Criminal Section 213
	ii.	Child Exploitation Section 213
	b.	United States Attorneys' Offices 214
	c.	Other Partnerships and Coordinated Prosecution Efforts 214
	C.	Federal Law Enforcement and Anti-Trafficking Task Forces 215
	1.	The FBI 215
	a.	Child Sex Tourism Initiative 215
	b.	Innocence Lost Initiative 215
	2.	Anti-Trafficking Task Forces 216
	3.	DOJ Annual Report to Congress 216
	D.	The Department of State 216
	1.	The Trafficking in Persons Report 217
	2.	Foreign Financial Assistance Grants 219
	3.	Public Engagement and Awareness 219
	4.	Additional State Department Offices and Efforts 219
	E.	The Department of Homeland Security 219
	F.	The Department of Health and Human Services 220
	1.	Certification for Foreign Victims of Trafficking 220
	2.	HHS Services Grants 221
	3.	Public-Awareness and Victim-Identification Efforts 221
	G.	The Department of Labor 221
	H.	Other Federal Agencies 222
III.		NON-GOVERNMENTAL ORGANIZATIONS 223
IV.		INTERNATIONAL ORGANIZATIONS 223
	A.	The United Nations 223
	1.	United Nations Office on Drugs and Crime 224
	2.	International Labor Organization 224
	B.	Non-United Nations Organizations 224
	1.	International Organization for Migration 224
	2.	Council of Europe 224
	3.	Organization for Security and Cooperation in Europe 225
V.		CONCLUSION 225

Table of Contents

Chapter 10	**FEDERAL CRIMINAL PROSECUTIONS**	**227**
I.	INTRODUCTION	227
A.	Criminal Prosecutions Under the TVPA	227
1.	Forced Labor	227
2.	Sex Trafficking	228
3.	Other Offenses	228
B.	Evolution of Criminal Prosecutions	228
II.	BASIC PRINCIPLES FOR CRIMINAL OFFENSES UNDER THE TVPA	229
III.	FORCED LABOR	230
A.	Pre-TVPA Forced Labor Cases	231
1.	*United States v. Harris*	231
2.	The *Paoletti* Case	231
3.	*United States v. Kozminski*	232
B.	Post-TVPA Forced Labor Cases	233
1.	*United States v. Bradley*	233
	United States v. Bradley	233
	Notes and Questions	239
2.	Additional Cases That Define and Expand § 1589	240
a.	Non-economic Labor or Services	240
b.	Abuse of the Legal Process as a Form of Coercion	241
c.	Peonage	242
d.	Forced Labor Involving Compelled Sexualized Labor	244
e.	Forced Labor by Military Contractors	245
C.	Domestic Servitude	247
1.	*United States v. Calimlim*	247
	United States v. Calimlim	247
2.	Involuntary Servitude and Domestic Servitude	251
3.	Domestic Servitude and Sexual Abuse	252
4.	Additional Issues: Document Servitude, the Knowledge Requirement Under Forced Labor, and Restitution	253
5.	Domestic Servitude and Diplomatic Immunity	254
IV.	SEX TRAFFICKING	256
A.	International Sex Trafficking	256
1.	Mexican Sex Trafficking Rings	257
	Kate Brumback & Mark Stevenson, *Mexican Women Forced into U.S. Prostitution by Pimps*	257
2.	An Example: *United States v. Jimenez-Calderon*	261
	United States v. Jimenez-Calderon	261
B.	Domestic Sex-Trafficking	263
1.	An Example: *United States v. Pipkins*	263

Table of Contents

		United States v. Pipkins	263
	2.	Other Issues: Conspiracy, the Definition of Commercial Sex Act, and Interstate Commerce	265
	3.	Reasonable Opportunity to Observe	267
	4.	Exclusion of Victims' Prior Sexual Behavior	268
	C.	Other Examples of Sex Trafficking in the United States	269
	D.	The PROTECT Act of 2003 and the Constitutionality of § 2423(c)	271
V.		CONCLUSION	272

Chapter 11		**CIVIL LITIGATION**	**273**
I.		INTRODUCTION	273
		Kathleen Kim & Kusia Hreshchyshyn, *Human Trafficking Private Right of Action: Civil Rights for Trafficked Persons in the United States*	274
		Notes and Questions	278
II.		18 U.S.C. § 1595: THE TRAFFICKING PRIVATE RIGHT OF ACTION	279
		Rosa Romero Hernandez, Plaintiff v. Samad Attisha; and Yvonne Attisha, Defendants	279
		Notes and Questions	284
III.		SCOPE OF DEFENDANTS UNDER § 1595	285
		John Roe I v. Bridgestone Corp.	286
		Notes and Questions	294
IV.		IMMIGRATION RELIEF UNDER § 1595	294
		Garcia v. Audubon Cmtys. Mgmt., LLC	295
		Notes and Questions	298
V.		STATE TRAFFICKING CIVIL REMEDIES	300
VI.		THE ALIEN TORT CLAIMS ACT ("ATCA")	301
		Notes and Questions	306
VII.		FEDERAL RACKETEER INFLUENCED AND CORRUPT ORGANIZATIONS ACT ("RICO")	307
		Notes and Questions	312
VIII.		FAIR LABOR STANDARDS ACT ("FLSA")	313
	A.	Wage and Hour Protections	313
	B.	Employment Relationship	315
		Notes and Questions	318
IX.		ADDITIONAL CAUSES OF ACTION	320
	A.	Discrimination Claims	320
	1.	Title VII of the Civil Rights Act ("Title VII")	320
	2.	42 U.S.C. § 1981	320
	3.	Conspiracy to Interfere with Civil Rights ("Section 1985")	321
	B.	Torts and Contracts Claims	321

Table of Contents

	Notes and Questions	322

Chapter 12		IMMIGRATION RELATED PROTECTIONS FOR VICTIMS OF TRAFFICKING	323
I.		T VISA REQUIREMENTS	323
	A.	How to Apply for a T Visa	324
	B.	Interpreting and Applying the T Visa Requirements	326
	1.	Interpreting Criteria One: Victim of a "Severe Form" of Human Trafficking	326
	2.	Interpreting Criteria Two: Physical Presence	328
	3.	Interpreting Criteria Three: Compliance with Law Enforcement	329
	4.	Interpreting Criteria Four: Extreme Hardship Involving Severe and Unusual Harm	331
	5.	An Additional Consideration: Admissibility	332
II.		DERIVATIVE VISAS	332
III.		CAPS ON T VISA AND DERIVATIVE VISAS	333
		Notes and Questions	333
IV.		CHALLENGES TO OBTAINING A T VISA	333
	A.	Lack of Access to Legal Services	338
	B.	Definitional Barriers	339
	1.	Are You a "Victim" if You Escape?	339
	2.	Can an Individual Agree to be a Slave?	339
	3.	Does Human Trafficking Require Transportation?	340
V.		BENEFITS FOR TRAFFICKING VICTIMS AND DERIVATIVES	340
VI.		OTHER FORMS OF IMMIGRATION RELIEF	342
	A.	U Visa	342
	B.	Asylum	344
	C.	Violence Against Women Act	346
	D.	Special Immigrant Juvenile Status	349
	E.	S Visa	350
		Notes and Questions	352

Chapter 13		THEORETICAL AND DEFINITIONAL CHALLENGES	353
I.		SEX TRAFFICKING AND PROSTITUTION	353
		Catharine A. MacKinnon, *Trafficking, Prostitution, and Inequality*	354
		Ann Jordan, *Sex Trafficking: The Abolitionist Fallacy*	359
		Notes and Questions	362
		DKT International, Inc., v. United States Agency for International Development	365
		Notes and Questions	368

xxvii

Table of Contents

II.	LABOR-FOCUSED APPROACHES	369
	Melynda Barnhart, *Sex and Slavery: An Analysis of Three Models of State Human Trafficking Legislation*	370
	Notes and Questions	372
	Notes and Questions	373
III.	CONSENT vs. COERCION	374
	Kathleen Kim, *The Coercion of Trafficked Workers*	376
	Notes and Questions	379
IV.	CONCLUSION	379

Chapter 14   **SPECIAL ISSUES RELATED TO SPECIFIC TRAFFICKED POPULATIONS** **381**

I.		IMMIGRATION ENFORCEMENT AND UNDOCUMENTED WORKERS	381
	A.	Undocumented Workers	381
	B.	Immigration Reform and Control Act	383
		Notes and Questions	385
		Notes and Questions	387
II.		VICTIMS OF SEX TRAFFICKING	390
		Notes and Questions	391
	A.	Reconciling State Laws on Sex Trafficking and Prostitution	392
		In Re B.W.	392
		Notes and Questions	399
III.		DOMESTIC WORKERS	400
		United States v. Djoumessi	401
		Notes and Questions	405
IV.		AGRICULTURAL WORKERS	405
		Notes and Questions	407

APPENDIX 1	**STATE AND LOCAL HUMAN TRAFFICKING LAWS AND PROSECUTIONS**	**409**
APPENDIX 2	**18 USCS § 1589**	**439**
TABLE OF CASES		**TC-1**
INDEX		**I-1**

Chapter 1

SLAVERY

I. INTRODUCTION

Human trafficking is frequently described as "modern-day slavery," a label that provides a helpful link between what we think of today as human trafficking — the compelled acquisition of labor, services, or commercial sex against the will of women, men, and children worldwide — and what is often referred to in the United States as antebellum slavery: the legally sanctioned system of labor in which millions of individuals of African descent were enslaved on American soil between 1619 and 1865. The link stands on firm ground, for at their core, both human trafficking and antebellum slavery share a common theme: a lack of freedom for millions of people brought about through differing means of oppression and subjugation.

That said, slavery and human trafficking do differ in several ways, as Kevin Bales and Ron Soodalter discuss in one of the seminal books on human trafficking, *The Slave Next Door*. *First*, slavery was legally sanctioned, whereas trafficking is illegal in the United States and throughout most of the world. *Second*, while slavery conveyed a form of social status to slave holders and was publicly displayed, traffickers today strive to keep trafficking hidden from public view. *Third*, while slavery in the United States involved only Africans and African-Americans, trafficking today discriminates against no one; worldwide, people of every race, national origin, gender, and age are trafficked. And, *fourth*, a slave in 1850 in the United States would have cost over $40,000 in current dollars, whereas victims of trafficking today are estimated to cost no more than a few hundred dollars, and in many cases much less than that. Indeed, the value placed on modern trafficking victims is so low that they are often referred to as "disposable.'"

It would be difficult to understand human trafficking in the United States without understanding, in at least some small way, the history of slavery, emancipation, and abolition. Accordingly, this chapter will provide an overview of these historical issues and identify links between slavery and human trafficking today. To simplify a vast amount of historical information that has been well documented elsewhere, each of the following sections is preceded by a short timeline of historical events.

II. SLAVERY IN THE COLONIES AND THE EARLY REPUBLIC

1619　　The first African slaves arrive in Virginia.

1641	Massachusetts is the first colony to legalize slavery.
1682	Virginia declares that all imported black servants are slaves for life.
1776	The Declaration of Independence declares that "all men are created equal."
1787	The U.S. Constitution is adopted by the Constitutional Convention.
1789	The U.S. Constitution is ratified by 11 states, and becomes the foundation of government in the United States.
1790	First Census: U.S. slave population reaches 680,000. Total U.S. population reaches 3.9 million.
1793	The Fugitive Slave Act provides for private capture and return of slaves who escape and cross state lines.
1794	Eli Whitney patents the cotton gin, which greatly increases the demand for slave labor.
1810	Third Census: U.S. slave population reaches 1.1 million. Total U.S. population reaches 5.9 million.

Slavery began almost immediately after colonization of the New World and quickly became an integral part of the American economy. Slavery itself was lawful and accepted as a means of procuring cheap and abundant labor. At first, the number of slaves in the colonies was small; for example, in 1625 the Virginia colony had only 23 slaves. Yet these numbers grew rapidly as the demand for labor increased and slave labor became the backbone of the Southern tobacco industry. So by 1650, the Virginia colony had 300 slaves and by 1700 an additional 1,000 African slaves were being brought to the Virginia colony every year. By 1860, there were nearly four million slaves in the United States, making up over 12% of the country's population. At that time, a total of 25% of white Southerners were believed to have owned slaves.

Slavery in the 18th and 19th centuries in the United States took many forms, but the predominant form was that of Southern slavery. While slaves in the North were primarily household servants and skilled laborers, agricultural work predominated in the South. And while some slaves were domestics and skilled laborers as in the North, the majority of slaves in the South worked on cotton plantations.

The life of a slave was often brutal and short. Slaves were beaten and punished for not working hard or fast enough and were subjected to torture, whipping, mutilation, imprisonment, and even murder. Female slaves were subjected to sexual assault and exploitation. Slaves lived in constant fear of being sold as property and separated from family members. Furthermore, the Slave Codes legalized the oppression of slaves and ensured that they would be treated as lesser in the eyes of the law, codifying the status of African-Americans as property without any basic rights. They could not make contracts. They could not testify in court. They could not gather without a white person present or own guns or engage in trade. Killing a slave was not murder, and the rape of a female slave was considered merely "trespass."

The depth to which slavery was legally accepted in the United States is reflected in the language of the U.S. Constitution, adopted in 1787. The Constitution established a property right in slaves, adopted a three-fifths compromise so that slaves were counted as three-fifths of a person, and outlawed slavery in the Northwest Territory. Through the Migration and Importation Clause in Article I, the Constitution declared that Congress could not prohibit "the Migration or Importation of such Persons as any of the States now existing shall think proper to admit" until 1808. "Such Persons" referred to the slave trade and meant that Congress could not ban the importation of slaves into the country for at least 21 years.

Congress banned the importation of slaves from foreign countries beginning on January 1, 1808 by making it illegal to "import or bring into the United States . . . any negro, mulatto, or person of colour" from a foreign place with "intent to hold, sell, or dispose" of such person as a slave. Although this was an important step toward the end of slavery, it was a small one. The ban on importation did not eliminate slavery or end its spread within the United States through the birth of children into bondage and the sale of slaves.

III. *DRED SCOTT* AND THE CITIZENSHIP QUESTION

1820	The *Missouri Compromise* bans slavery north of the 36th parallel, except in Missouri.
1831	Nat Turner, an enslaved African American preacher, leads a slave uprising. He and his followers launch a short, bloody rebellion in Virginia. State and federal troops quell the rebellion, and Turner is eventually hanged.
1831	William Lloyd Garrison publishes *The Liberator*, a weekly paper advocating the complete abolition of slavery. He quickly becomes one of the leading figures in the abolitionist movement.
1841	The Supreme Court decides *The Amistad*, 40 U.S. (15 Pet.) 518 (1841), which frees the Amistad captives, finding that the 49 Africans on board were kidnapped in Africa and never held as slaves.
1842	In *Prigg v. Pennsylvania*, 41 U.S. (16 Pet.) 539 (1842), the Supreme Court declares a Pennsylvania law unconstitutional that prohibits the capture of any African-American for return into slavery, except with procedural protections for suspected fugitive slaves. Prigg had captured and arrested an escaped slave in Pennsylvania and brought her back to Maryland without using the procedures in the state law. The Supreme Court found that the state law was both unconstitutional under Article 4, § 2, clause 3 of the Constitution and preempted by the Fugitive Slave Act of 1793. The Court holds that "[t]he right to seize and retake fugitive slaves, and the duty to deliver them up, in whatever state of the Union they may be found, is, under the constitution, recognized as an absolute positive right and duty . . . uncontrollable by state sovereignty or state legislation.".
1849	Harriet Tubman escapes from slavery and becomes a leader of the Underground Railroad.

1850	A debate on whether territory won in the Mexican War should be open to slavery is decided in the Compromise of 1850. California is admitted as a free state, the Utah and New Mexico territories are left to decide the issue by popular sovereignty, and Washington, D.C. prohibits the slave trade but does not abolish slavery. Controversially, the Fugitive Slave Law of 1850 is passed, which is a much harsher version of the 1793 Fugitive Slave Law: the new law mandates fines or imprisonment for officials who refuse to execute a warrant for a fugitive slave or anyone who aids, harbors, or hides a fugitive slave. Furthermore, a slave's testimony in a proceeding against his claimant is not admissible as evidence; however, to prevail, a claimant had only to offer sworn testimony of ownership.
1850	Seventh Census: U.S. slave population reaches 3.2 million. Total U.S. population reaches 23 million.
1854	The Kansas-Nebraska Act becomes law, establishing the territories of Kansas and Nebraska, each of which may determine the slavery issue by popular sovereignty. The law thus repeals the Missouri Compromise of 1820 and renews tensions between anti- and pro-slavery factions.

Although Congress banned the importation of slaves to the country after 1808, courts continued to uphold the legality of slavery as an institution. This can be seen clearly in the 1857 U.S. Supreme Court decision in the *Dred Scott* case. In its ruling, the Supreme Court held that freed slaves and slaves living in free states were not citizens of the United States and that Congress did not have the right to ban slavery. The decision was a tremendous setback to efforts to attain freedom for slaves. However, it also set clear battle lines between pro- and anti-slavery forces that eventually led to the Emancipation Proclamation, the Civil War, and ratification of the Thirteenth Amendment prohibiting slavery.

The facts of *Dred Scott* centered upon Scott's journey from birth in a slave state to residence, while still a slave, in free territories and states, including Illinois and Wisconsin. While living in the slave state of Missouri, Scott sued for his freedom in Missouri state court. After the state court rejected Scott's claim for freedom, Scott sued in federal court in Missouri. The federal court deferred to the state court decision and rejected Scott's claim. Scott appealed to the U.S. Supreme Court.

SCOTT v. SANDFORD
60 U.S. 393 (1857)

Mr. Chief Justice Taney delivered the opinion of the court.

[The Court begins with a discussion of the question of jurisdiction, finding that it has jurisdiction to hear the case, and proceeds to the second question before it, whether Scott is a citizen of the United States.]

The question is simply this: Can a negro, whose ancestors were imported into this country, and sold as slaves, become a member of the political community formed and brought into existence by the Constitution of the United States, and as such become entitled to all the rights, and privileges, and immunities, guaranteed by that instrument to the citizen? One of which rights is the privilege of suing in a court of the United States in the cases specified in the Constitution.

It will be observed, that the plea applies to that class of persons only whose ancestors were Negroes of the African race, and imported into this country, and sold and held as slaves. The only matter in issue before the court, therefore, is, whether the descendants of such slaves, when they shall be emancipated, or who are born of parents who had become free before their birth, are citizens of a State, in the sense in which the word citizen is used in the Constitution of the United States. . . .

The words "people of the United States" and "citizens" are synonymous terms, and mean the same thing. They both describe the political body who, according to our republican institutions, form the sovereignty, and who hold the power and conduct the Government through their representatives. . . . The question before us is, whether the class of persons described in the plea in abatement compose a portion of this people, and are constituent members of this sovereignty? We think they are not, and that they are not included, and were not intended to be included, under the word 'citizens' in the Constitution, and can therefore claim none of the rights and privileges which that instrument provides for and secures to citizens of the United States. On the contrary, they were at that time considered as a subordinate and inferior class of beings, who had been subjugated by the dominant race, and, whether emancipated or not, yet remained subject to their authority, and had no rights or privileges but such as those who held the power and the Government might choose to grant them. . . .

In discussing this question, we must not confound the rights of citizenship, which a State may confer within its own limits, and the rights of citizenship as a member of the Union. It does not by any means follow, because he has all the rights and privileges of a citizen of a State, that he must be a citizen of the United States. He may have all of the rights and privileges of the citizen of a State, and yet not be entitled to the rights and privileges of a citizen in any other State. For, previous to the adoption of the Constitution of the United States, every State had the undoubted right to confer on whomsoever it pleased the character of citizen, and to endow him with all its rights. But this character of course was confined to the boundaries of the State, and gave him no rights or privileges in other States beyond those secured to him by the laws of nations and the comity of States. . . .

It is very clear, therefore, that no State can, by any act or law of its own, passed since the adoption of the Constitution, introduce a new member into the political community created by the Constitution of the United States. It cannot make him a member of this community by making him a member of its own. And for the same reason it cannot introduce any person, or description of persons, who were not intended to be embraced in this new political family, which the Constitution brought into existence, but were intended to be excluded from it.

The question then arises, whether the provisions of the Constitution, in relation to the personal rights and privileges to which the citizen of a State should be entitled, embraced the negro African race, at that time in this country, or who might afterwards be imported, who had then or should afterwards be made free in any

State; and to put it in the power of a single State to make him a citizen of the United States, and endue him with the full rights of citizenship in every other State without their consent? Does the Constitution of the United States act upon him whenever he shall be made free under the laws of a State, and raised there to the rank of a citizen, and immediately clothe him with all the privileges of a citizen in every other State, and in its own courts?

The court think the affirmative of these propositions cannot be maintained. And if it cannot, the plaintiff in error could not be a citizen of the State of Missouri, within the meaning of the Constitution of the United States. . . .

In the opinion of the court, the legislation and histories of the times, and the language used in the Declaration of Independence, show, that neither the class of persons who had been imported as slaves, nor their descendants, whether they had become free or not, were then acknowledged as a part of the people, nor intended to be included in the general words used in that memorable instrument.

. . . .

They had for more than a century before been regarded as beings of an inferior order, and altogether unfit to associate with the white race, either in social or political relations; and so far inferior, that they had no rights which the white man was bound to respect; and that the negro might justly and lawfully be reduced to slavery for his benefit

. . . .

[The Court surveys state laws that demonstrate the subordination of African-Americans at the time the Constitution was adopted.]

. . . .

The language of the Declaration of Independence is equally [c]onclusive:

It begins by declaring that, "when in the course of human events it becomes necessary for one people to dissolve the political bands which have connected them with another, and to assume among the powers of the earth the separate and equal station to which the laws of nature and nature's God entitle them, a decent respect for the opinions of mankind requires that they should declare the causes which impel them to the separation."

It then proceeds to say: "We hold these truths to be self-evident: that all men are created equal; that they are endowed by their Creator with certain unalienable rights; that among them is life, liberty, and the pursuit of happiness; that to secure these rights, Governments are instituted, deriving their just powers from the consent of the governed."

The general words above quoted would seem to embrace the whole human family, and if they were used in a similar instrument at this day would be so understood. But it is too clear for dispute, that the enslaved African race were not intended to be included, and formed no part of the people who framed and adopted this declaration; for if the language, as understood in that day, would embrace them, the conduct of the distinguished men who framed the Declaration of Independence would have been utterly and flagrantly inconsistent with the principles they asserted; and instead of the sympathy of mankind, to which they so confidently appealed, they would have deserved and received universal rebuke and reprobation.

. . . .

And upon a full and careful consideration of the subject, the court is of opinion, that, upon the facts stated in the plea in abatement, Dred Scott was not a citizen of Missouri within the meaning of the Constitution of the United States, and not entitled as such to sue in its courts. . . .

We proceed, therefore, to inquire whether the facts relied on by the plaintiff entitled him to his freedom.

. . . .

In considering this part of the controversy, two questions arise: 1. Was he, together with his family, free in Missouri by reason of the stay in the territory of the United States hereinbefore mentioned? And 2. If they were not, is Scott himself free by reason of his removal to Rock Island, in the State of Illinois, as stated in the above admissions?

. . . .

The act of Congress, upon which the plaintiff relies, declares that slavery and involuntary servitude, except as a punishment for crime, shall be forever prohibited in all that part of the territory ceded by France, under the name of Louisiana, which lies north of thirty-six degrees thirty minutes north latitude, and not included within the limits of Missouri. And the difficulty which meets us at the threshold of this part of the inquiry is, whether Congress was authorized to pass this law under any of the powers granted to it by the Constitution; for if the authority is not given by that instrument, it is the duty of this court to declare it void and inoperative, and incapable of conferring freedom upon any one who is held as a slave under the laws of any one of the [s]tates.

. . . .

. . . [I]t may be safely assumed that citizens of the United States who migrate to a Territory belonging to the people of the United States, cannot be ruled as mere colonists, dependent upon the will of the General Government, and to be governed by any laws it may think proper to impose. The principle upon which our Governments rest, and upon which alone they continue to exist, is the union of States, sovereign and independent within their own limits in [60 U.S. 393, 448] their internal and domestic concerns, and bound together as one people by a General Government, possessing certain enumerated and restricted powers, delegated to it by the people of the several States, and exercising supreme authority within the scope of the powers granted to it, throughout the dominion of the United States.

. . . .

But the power of Congress over the person or property of a citizen can never be a mere discretionary power under our Constitution and form of Government. The powers of the Government and the rights and privileges of the citizen are regulated and plainly defined by the Constitution itself. And when the Territory becomes a part of the United States, the Federal Government enters into possession in the character impressed upon it by those who created it. It enters upon it with its powers over the citizen strictly defined, and limited by the Constitution, from which it derives its own existence, and by virtue of which alone it continues to exist and act as a Government and sovereignty. . . .

Upon these considerations, it is the opinion of the court that the act of Congress which prohibited a citizen from holding and owning property of this kind in the territory of the United States north of the line therein mentioned, is not warranted by the Constitution, and is therefore void; and that neither Dred Scott himself, nor any of his family, were made free by being carried into this territory; even if they had been carried there by the owner, with the intention of becoming a permanent resident. . . .

Upon the whole, therefore, it is the judgment of this court, that it appears by the record before us that the plaintiff in error is not a citizen of Missouri, in the sense in which that word is used in the Constitution; and that the Circuit Court of the United States, for that reason, had no jurisdiction in the case, and could give no judgment in it. Its judgment for the defendant must, consequently, be reversed, and a mandate issued, directing the suit to be dismissed for want of jurisdiction.

Mr. Justice Curtis, dissenting.

I dissent from the opinion pronounced by the Chief Justice, and from the judgment which the majority of the court think it proper to render in this case. . . .

[U]nder the allegations contained in this plea, and admitted by the demurrer, the question is, whether any person of African descent, whose ancestors were sold as slaves in the United States, can be a citizen of the United States. If any such person can be a citizen, this plaintiff has the right to the judgment of the court that he is so; for no cause is shown by the plea why he is not so, except his descent and the slavery of his ancestors.

The first section of the second article of the Constitution uses the language, "a citizen of the United States at the time of the adoption of the Constitution." One mode of approaching this question is, to inquire who were citizens of the United States at the time of the adoption of the Constitution. Citizens of the United States at the time of the adoption of the Constitution can have been no other than citizens of the United States under the Confederation. By the Articles of Confederation, a Government was organized, the style whereof was, "The United States of America." This Government was in existence when the Constitution was framed and proposed for adoption, and was to be superseded by the new Government of the United States of America, organized under the Constitution. When, therefore, the Constitution speaks of citizenship of the United States, existing at the time of the adoption of the Constitution, it must necessarily refer to citizenship under the Government which existed prior to and at the time of such adoption . . . it may safely be said that the citizens of the several States were citizens of the United States under the Confederation. . . .

To determine whether any free persons, descended from Africans held in slavery, were citizens of the United States under the Confederation, and consequently at the time of the adoption of the Constitution of the United States, it is only necessary to know whether any such persons were citizens of either of the States under the Confederation, at the time of the adoption of the Constitution.

Of this there can be no doubt. At the time of the ratification of the Articles of Confederation, all free native-born inhabitants of the States of New Hampshire, Massachusetts, New York, New Jersey, and North Carolina, though descended from African slaves, were not only citizens of those States, but such of them as had the other necessary qualifications possessed the franchise of electors, on equal terms with other citizens. . . .

[Justice Curtis examines cases within the enumerated states showing that all free persons born within a state were citizens of the state.]

. . . .

The fourth of the fundamental articles of the Confederation was as follows: "The free inhabitants of each of these States, paupers, vagabonds, and fugitives from justice, excepted, shall be entitled to all the privileges and immunities of free citizens in the several States."

The fact that free persons of color were citizens of some of the several States, and the consequence, that this fourth article of the Confederation would have the effect to confer on such persons the privileges and immunities of general citizenship, were not only known to those who framed and adopted those articles, but the evidence is decisive, that the fourth article was intended to have that effect, and that more restricted language, which would have excluded such persons, was deliberately and purposely rejected.

On the 25th of June, 1778, the Articles of Confederation being under consideration by the Congress, the delegates from South Carolina moved to amend this fourth article, by inserting after the word "free," and before the word "inhabitants," the word "white," so that the privileges and immunities of general citizenship would be secured only to white persons. Two States voted for the amendment, eight States against it, and the vote of one State was divided. The language of the article stood unchanged, and both by its terms of inclusion, "free inhabitants," and the strong implication from its terms of exclusion, "paupers, and the strong implication from its terms of exclusion, "paupers, vagabonds, and fugitives from justice," who alone were excepted, it is clear, that under the Confederation, and at the time of the adoption of the Constitution, free colored persons of African descent might be, and, by reason of their citizenship in certain States, were entitled to the privileges and immunities of general citizenship of the United States.

Did the Constitution of the United States deprive them or their descendants of citizenship?

. . . .

. . . [C]onfining our view to free persons born within the several States, we find that the Constitution has recognized the general principle of public law, that allegiance and citizenship depend on the place of birth; that it has not attempted practically to apply this principle by designating the particular classes of persons who should or should not come under it; that when we turn to the Constitution for an answer to the question, what free persons, born within the several States, are citizens of the United States, the only answer we can receive from any of its express provisions is, the citizens of the several States are to enjoy the privileges and immunities of citizens in every State, and their franchise as electors under the Constitution depends on their citizenship in the several States. Add to this, that the Constitution was ordained by the citizens of the several States; that they were "the people of the United States," for whom and whose posterity the Government was declared in the preamble of the Constitution to be made; that each of them was "a citizen of the United States at the time of the adoption of the Constitution," within the meaning of those words in that instrument; that by them the Government was to be and was in fact organized; and that no power is conferred on the Government of the Union to discriminate between them, or to disfranchise any of them — the necessary conclusion is, that those persons born within the several States, who, by force of their respective Constitutions and laws, are citizens of the State, are thereby citizens of the United States. . . .

[Determining that the Supreme Court had jurisdiction to hear the case, Justice Curtis then reaches the merits of the case, and determines that (1) Dred Scott became free upon moving to the Wisconsin Territory where slavery had been banned by Congress, and (2) the Congressional abolition of slavery in the Wisconsin Territory (through the Missouri Compromise) was constitutional.]

. . . In my opinion, the judgment of the Circuit Court should be reversed, and the cause remanded for a new trial.

* * *

NOTES AND QUESTIONS

1. Peter Blow, a son of Dred Scott's original owner, bought Scott and his family and freed them. Within a year, Scott died of tuberculosis. Justice Curtis resigned from the Court after the *Dred Scott* decision, noting at the time that he doubted his usefulness on the Court in its "present state." GEORGE TICKNOR CURTIS, A MEMOIR OF BENJAMIN ROBBINS CURTIS, LL.D. 249–51 (Benjamin R. Curtis ed., Nabu Press 2010) (1879). Curtis' dissent, despite the presence of three other dissents in the case, had lasting impact. Abolitionists widely circulated the Curtis dissent, and Lincoln's speeches often echoed its analysis.

2. In addition to holding that freed slaves are not citizens of the United States, the Court also held that anti-slavery statutes, including the Missouri Compromise, were unconstitutional. Should the Court have even reached this conclusion given its jurisdictional holding? The suit was only properly in federal court if a "citizen" of one State was suing a "citizen" of another state and the Court held that Dred Scott was not a citizen of Missouri and thus there was no diversity of citizenship for the purposes of federal jurisdiction. Why do you think that the Court took the liberty of reaching the merits of the case, that is, the question of whether Dred Scott was free and the Missouri Compromise constitutional?

3. Even Justice Curtis, in his lengthy and vigorous dissent, limited the acquisition of citizenship to "every free person born on the soil of a State." Consider why Justice Curtis was not ready to declare that *all* African-Americans were

citizens of the United States.

4. Interestingly, Justice Curtis distinguished between being a citizen of the United States and acquiring accompanying privileges and immunities, such as the right to vote. This answered a common objection at the time that allowing freed slaves to be citizens meant that they would have the right to vote.

5. Frederick Douglas and the Declaration of Independence. The Court argued that the Declaration of Independence demonstrates that slaves "were not acknowledged as a part of the people, nor intended to be included in the general words used in that memorable instrument." In 1852, Frederick Douglas was asked to give a speech commemorating the signing of the Declaration of Independence. Douglas used the speech to argue strongly against slavery and in favor of abolition. Compare Douglass's view of the Declaration of Independence and Independence Day with that of the Court in *Dred Scott*:

> What, to the American slave, is your 4th of July? I answer; a day that reveals to him, more than all other days in the year, the gross injustice and cruelty to which he is the constant victim. To him, your celebration is a sham; your boasted liberty, an unholy license; your national greatness, swelling vanity; your sounds of rejoicing are empty and heartless; your denunciation of tyrants, brass fronted impudence; your shouts of liberty and equality, hollow mockery; your prayers and hymns, your sermons and thanksgivings, with all your religious parade and solemnity, are, to Him, mere bombast, fraud, deception, impiety, and hypocrisy — a thin veil to cover up crimes which would disgrace a nation of savages. There is not a nation on the earth guilty of practices more shocking and bloody than are the people of the United States, at this very hour.

Frederick Douglass. *What to the Slave Is the Fourth of July?* Extract from an ORATION, at Rochester, July 5, 1852, as presented in FREDERICK DOUGLASS, MY BONDAGE AND MY FREEDOM 340 (Penguin Classics 2003) (1855).

IV. THE CIVIL WAR AND THE EMANCIPATION PROCLAMATION

1859	John Brown and his followers capture the federal arsenal at Harpers Ferry, Virginia (now West Virginia) in an attempted slave revolt.
1860	Abraham Lincoln elected as President of the United States. South Carolina secedes from the United States.
1860	Eighth Census: U.S slave population reaches 4 million. Total U.S. population reaches 31 million.
1861 (February)	The Confederate States of America is founded by the first seven states that secede from the United States (South Carolina, Mississippi, Florida, Alabama, Georgia, Louisiana, Texas). A provisional army is established.
1861 (April)	Confederate forces attack the U.S. military installation at Fort Sumter, and the Civil War begins.

1863 On January 1, President Lincoln issues the Emancipation Proclamation, declaring "that all persons held as slaves" within the Confederate States "are, and henceforward shall be, free."

The *Dred Scott* decision was a catalyst in the movement for the abolition of slavery. As Frederick Douglass put it, the case "awaken[ed]" America.

The decision may have also paved the way for Lincoln's presidential nomination. Predictably, the response to *Dred Scott* was polarized along Northern and Southern lines. The South embraced the ruling and President Buchanan referred favorably to the opinion during his Inaugural Address. The North, however, was outraged. *The New York Herald Tribune* termed the holding "wicked" and "atrocious." Another observer wrote that, if "epithets and denunciations could sink a judicial body, the Supreme Court . . . would never be heard of again."

Although scholars debate the extent to which the *Dred Scott* decision directly caused the events that followed, there can be no doubt that events unfolded rapidly after the Court ruling in 1857. In 1859, John Brown led an unsuccessful slave revolt at Harpers Ferry, Virginia. In 1861, the Union garrison at Fort Sumter surrendered following bombardment by Confederate forces. Shortly after, the Civil War began, pitting abolitionists against supporters of slavery. In 1861 and 1862, the First and Second Confiscation Acts were enacted into law, allowing the government to seize property belonging to rebels. Also in 1862, President Lincoln signed legislation freeing all slaves in the District of Columbia. And then, in 1863, Lincoln issued the Emancipation Proclamation, declaring that all slaves within the confederate states were free.

Coming during the third year of the Civil War, the Emancipation Proclamation made it a war for freedom, designating the end of slavery as the only acceptable outcome for the North. The Proclamation also permitted the acceptance of African Americans into the Union Army and Navy.[1] Many freed slaves in the Confederate States subsequently fought on behalf of the Union and, by the war's end, more than 200,000 African Americans had fought for the Union. The Emancipation Proclamation also sanctioned the use of military and naval forces to maintain the freedom of the former slaves. This allowed the military units, fighting in the South, to use force both to liberate slaves and to maintain their freedom.

Despite its broad language, and its importance as a battle cry for freedom, the Emancipation Proclamation was limited in significant ways. It freed only those slaves residing in the Confederate states. It did not apply to Northern or border states. This meant that slavery was not illegal, since the Proclamation applied only to those territories that had formally declared rebellion.[2]

---

[1] By the time of the Emancipation Proclamation, emancipation was being used effectively as a weapon of war. Countries had frequently used the law of war to emancipate slaves, such as Britain did during the American Revolution. Under the law of war, slaves were accepted as a form of property that could be seized and liberated as a weapon of war — to both harm the economy and military capabilities of an enemy state and to gain potential allies.

[2] The sweeping power of the Emancipation Proclamation was legally grounded in the law of war. The law of war was applicable because of the dual nature of the conflict. Being both foreign and domestic, the

IV.   THE CIVIL WAR AND THE EMANCIPATION PROCLAMATION

Yet, although limited in ways, the Emancipation Proclamation was nevertheless critical in making abolition a central goal of the Civil War. The Proclamation was also historic in that it freed slaves in states where the Union did not have control, and furthermore, it made these slaves *"forever* free." Thus, although the Emancipation Proclamation had limits, it played a key role in moving the country toward the complete legal abolition of slavery.

Immediately after the Emancipation Proclamation was issued, a debate ensued over its legality. In the Proclamation itself Lincoln did not state a constitutional basis for it. He may have been unwilling to publicly acknowledge that the Union was applying the law of war since this recognized the Confederacy as having *de facto* independence. Instead, in explaining the legal basis for the Proclamation, Lincoln emphasized its grounding in the law of war. In a letter read in his absence to an Illinois rally in 1863, Lincoln explained:

> You dislike the emancipation proclamation; and, perhaps, would have it retracted. You say it is unconstitutional — I think differently. I think the constitution invests its Commander-in-chief, with the law of war, in time of war. The most that can be said, if so much, is, that slaves are property. Is there — has there ever been — any question that by the law of war, property, both of enemies and friends, may be taken when needed? . . .

> . . . [S]ome of the commanders of our armies in the field who have given us our most important successes believe the emancipation policy and the use of the colored troops constitute the heaviest blow yet dealt to the Rebellion, and that at least one of these important successes could not have been achieved when it was but for the aid of black soldiers . . .

THE EMANCIPATION PROCLAMATION
January 1, 1863

By the President of the United States of America:

A Proclamation.

. . . .

That on the first day of January, in the year of our Lord one thousand eight hundred and sixty-three, all persons held as slaves within any State or designated part of a State, the people whereof shall then be in rebellion against the United States, shall be then, thenceforward, and forever free; and the Executive Government of the United States, including the military and naval authority thereof, will

---

Union treated the Confederacy as having *de facto* independence (meaning the law of war was applicable), but not *de jure* independence (meaning they were not recognized as a foreign country and could be treated as traitors). Lincoln believed that the power to use the law of war was reserved to the president as Commander-in-Chief. Furthermore, because it was grounded in the law of war, slaves would be treated as a form of property subject to confiscation. Lastly, Lincoln would free slaves based on military necessity — "a necessity indispensable to the maintenance of the government." Abraham Lincoln, *The Emancipation Proclamation* (Jan. 1, 1863), *available at* http://www.archives.gov/exhibits/featured_documents/emancipation_proclamation/transcript.html.

recognize and maintain the freedom of such persons, and will do no act or acts to repress such persons, or any of them, in any efforts they may make for their actual freedom.

That the Executive will, on the first day of January aforesaid, by proclamation, designate the States and parts of States, if any, in which the people thereof, respectively, shall then be in rebellion against the United States; and the fact that any State, or the people thereof, shall on that day be, in good faith, represented in the Congress of the United States by members chosen thereto at elections wherein a majority of the qualified voters of such State shall have participated, shall, in the absence of strong countervailing testimony, be deemed conclusive evidence that such State, and the people thereof, are not then in rebellion against the United States.

Now, therefore I, Abraham Lincoln, President of the United States, by virtue of the power in me vested as Commander-in-Chief, of the Army and Navy of the United States in time of actual armed rebellion against the authority and government of the United States, and as a fit and necessary war measure for suppressing said rebellion, do, on this first day of January, in the year of our Lord one thousand eight hundred and sixty-three, and in accordance with my purpose so to do publicly proclaimed for the full period of one hundred days, from the day first above mentioned, order and designate as the States and parts of States wherein the people thereof respectively, are this day in rebellion against the United States, the following, to wit:

Arkansas, Texas, Louisiana, (except the Parishes of St. Bernard, Plaquemines, Jefferson, St. John, St. Charles, St. James Ascension, Assumption, Terrebonne, Lafourche, St. Mary, St. Martin, and Orleans, including the City of New Orleans) Mississippi, Alabama, Florida, Georgia, South Carolina, North Carolina, and Virginia, (except the forty-eight counties designated as West Virginia, and also the counties of Berkley, Accomac, Northampton, Elizabeth City, York, Princess Ann, and Norfolk, including the cities of Norfolk and Portsmouth[)], and which excepted parts, are for the present, left precisely as if this proclamation were not issued.

And by virtue of the power, and for the purpose aforesaid, I do order and declare that all persons held as slaves within said designated States, and parts of States, are, and henceforward shall be free; and that the Executive government of the United States, including the military and naval authorities thereof, will recognize and maintain the freedom of said persons.

And I hereby enjoin upon the people so declared to be free to abstain from all violence, unless in necessary self-defence; and I recommend to them that, in all cases when allowed, they labor faithfully for reasonable wages.

And I further declare and make known, that such persons of suitable condition, will be received into the armed service of the United States to garrison forts, positions, stations, and other places, and to man vessels of all sorts in said service.

And upon this act, sincerely believed to be an act of justice, warranted by the Constitution, upon military necessity, I invoke the considerate judgment of mankind, and the gracious favor of Almighty God.

In witness whereof, I have hereunto set my hand and caused the seal of the United States to be affixed.

Done at the City of Washington, this first day of January, in the year of our Lord one thousand eight hundred and sixty three, and of the Independence of the United States of America the eighty-seventh.

By the President: ABRAHAM LINCOLN

V. THE THIRTEENTH AMENDMENT: ABOLITION OF SLAVERY

1864	The Senate passes the Thirteenth Amendment to the U.S. Constitution.
1865 (January 31)	The House passes the Thirteenth Amendment, sending it to the States for ratification.
1865 (April 9)	The Confederate Army surrenders at Appomattox Court House, ending the Civil War.
1865 (April 14)	President Lincoln is assassinated.
1865 (December 6)	The requisite three-quarters of states ratify the Thirteenth Amendment, abolishing slavery throughout the United States.

The Emancipation Proclamation was the first critical step towards nationwide abolition of slavery. But it was not the last. After *Dred Scott*, it was understood that legally abolishing slavery would require a constitutional amendment.

Although President Lincoln became one of the most vocal and powerful advocates for the Thirteenth Amendment, he initially opposed it. In fact, prior to the war Lincoln supported a constitutional amendment that would have prohibited the federal government from banning slavery or from intervening in any way. Lincoln supported this constitutional amendment based on his belief that the correct way to end slavery was through individual state action, not through federal government prohibition. Indeed, at his inaugural address in 1861, Lincoln emphasized that he had neither the power nor the inclination to interfere with slavery where it existed, in an attempt to allay southern fears of ending slavery.[3]

In addition to Lincoln's early reticence, many others hoped that the Civil War would end slavery without the need for a constitutional amendment. Indeed, early in the Civil War the Thirteenth Amendment was by no means inevitable. Yet the battle lines were clearly drawn, with abolitionists arguing that true victory in the Civil War could not be had without the legal end of slavery. Frederick Douglass declared, "If the Union can only be maintained by new concessions to the slaveholders, let the Union perish." And Lyman Trumbull, a Senator from Illinois and an influential anti-slavery member of Congress, proclaimed, "If this struggle ends with slavery still in existence, the Battle of Liberty has been only half fought."

---

[3] Eric Foner, The Story of American Freedom 158 (W.W. Norton & Co. 1998).

By 1864, Lincoln was a supporter of the Thirteenth Amendment. Lincoln's thinking had evolved as the Civil War raged on, and he came to believe that the Thirteenth Amendment was necessary to end slavery. He also believed that passage of the Thirteenth Amendment would hasten an end to the Civil War.

Efforts to abolish slavery gained significant traction during the late 1850s and early 1860s. By mid-1864, over 400,000 signatures had been gathered in support of an amendment abolishing slavery. Meanwhile, Congress worked on draft amendments. When the draft amendment of what would later become the Thirteenth Amendment was introduced to the Senate in February 1864, there was no consensus about its fate. In fact, when the Thirteenth Amendment was first put forward for a vote in 1864, it failed to get the requisite two-thirds majority in the House needed to pass such an amendment.

The election of 1864 was a turning point. Lincoln won re-election and pro-Thirteenth Amendment legislators strengthened their control of Congress. After his re-election, Lincoln made passage of the Thirteenth Amendment a top priority. The first task of the new Congress was to reconsider the House vote during the previous June, when the Amendment failed. Republicans now had a majority in Congress, and with the extra pressure of border representatives, and the threat of a special session of Congress the following year should the vote fail, the Thirteenth Amendment finally passed on January 31, 1865.

U.S. Constitutional Amendment XIII (1865)

Section 1. Neither slavery nor involuntary servitude, except as a punishment for crime whereof the party shall have been duly convicted, shall exist within the United States, or any place subject to their jurisdiction.

Section 2. Congress shall have power to enforce this article by appropriate legislation.

Lincoln described the Thirteen Amendment as "a King's cure for all the evils. It winds the whole thing up." In other words, the amendment did what the Emancipation Proclamation was unable to do, in that the Proclamation did not cover slaves who did not come within Union lines and also may not have covered the children of slaves. Still, the Thirteenth Amendment had to pass muster in the states to become part of the Constitution. Lincoln insisted that the Southern states be counted so as not to legitimize secession, thus requiring 27 votes out of the 36 states. Illinois was the first to ratify the Thirteenth Amendment, and by December of 1865, the requisite three-fourths of the states had ratified it, making slavery wholly illegal. The Thirteenth Amendment was now part of the U.S. Constitution.

VI. THE THIRTEENTH AMENDMENT AND *AH SOU*

1866 (March) Southern states enact so-called Black Codes, which limit the basic civil liberties of "colored people" (an individual with more than 1/8 African-American blood). The Black Codes, most of which include express racial classifications, forbid "colored people" from, among other things, carrying weapons, marrying white people, selling liquor, or being vagrant. Georgia's Code read:

An Act to alter and amend the 4435th Section of the Penal Code of Georgia, Georgia, Title II, No. 240, March 12, 1866 SECTION 1. All persons wandering or strolling about in idleness, who are able to work, and who have no property to support them; all persons leading and idle, immoral or profligate life, who have no property to support them, and are able to work, and do not work . . . shall be deemed and considered vagrants, and shall be indicted as such; and it shall be lawful for any person to arrest said vagrants, and have them bound over for trial to the next term of the County Court, and upon conviction they shall be fined or imprisoned, or sentenced to work on the public works or roads for no longer than a year, or shall . . . be bound out to some person for a time not longer than one year, upon such valuable consideration as the Court may prescribe, the person giving bond, in a sum not exceeding three hundred dollars, payable to said Court. . . .

1866 (April 9) Largely in response to the Black Codes, and over the veto of President Andrew Johnson, the Civil Rights Act of 1866 is enacted. The Act states that individuals born in the United States are U.S. citizens and enjoy the right to contract, sue, give evidence, purchase and convey property, and are entitled to "the full and equal benefit of all laws and proceedings for the security of person and property" as are enjoyed by white citizens. The right to contract is a precursor to the Fourteenth Amendment.

1867 The Peonage Abolition Act becomes law, eliminating the practice of debt bondage. Debt bondage, or bonded labor, occurs when a debtor pledges his personal labor or services to a lender in payment of his debt, but the reasonable value of his services is not applied to the liquidation of the debt, or the length and nature of the services is not defined.

1868 The Fourteenth Amendment to the U.S. Constitution is adopted. The Amendment overrules *Dred Scott* by declaring that all people born or naturalized in the country are citizens of the United States, and it further provides for due process and the equal protection of the laws by stating, "nor shall any state deprive any person of life, liberty, or property, without due process of law; nor deny to any person within its jurisdiction the equal protection of the laws."

1870 (February 3)	The requisite number of states ratify the Fifteenth Amendment, prohibiting denial of the right to vote based upon race, color, or previous enslavement.
1870 (May 31)	The Enforcement Act is passed to enforce the Fifteenth Amendment, making it a misdemeanor to refuse to allow otherwise qualified people to complete the "prerequisites" for voting.
1874	The Padrone Statute, aimed at preventing Italian children from being enslaved as street musicians and beggars, prevents the involuntary servitude of all foreign-born individuals.

Dred Scott, the Emancipation Proclamation, and the Thirteenth Amendment all dealt with slavery in its antebellum form as experienced by African slaves on plantations in the South. Subsequent court cases explored the boundaries of slavery and the protections of the Thirteenth Amendment.

One 1905 case, *United States v. Ah Sou*, dealt with whether the Thirteenth Amendment prohibited deportation of a Chinese girl who had been held as a sexual slave in the United States and was certain to face a life of continued sexual slavery if returned to her home in China. The Ninth Circuit Court of Appeals held that the statute mandating deportation controlled and that the Thirteenth Amendment was not implicated where the potential for future slavery would not occur on U.S. soil.

This case is important not only for the court's ruling that the Thirteenth Amendment did not apply but also for the documentation it provides that sexual slavery — which today would be called sex trafficking — was occurring in the United States in 1905 in an almost identical manner to what we see today.

UNITED STATES v. AH SOU
138 F. 775 (9th Cir. 1905)

GILBERT, CIRCUIT JUDGE.

On January 1, 1904, the appellee, a Chinese girl, was apprehended for being unlawfully in the United States, and, upon examination before a United States Commissioner, was adjudged to be unlawfully in the United States, and ordered to be deported to China, whence she came. . . . The testimony shows that the appellee was brought to the United States for purposes of prostitution, but that she entered the United States ostensibly as the minor daughter of Moy Sam, a Chinese merchant residing at Tacoma, Wash. She was not the daughter of Moy Sam, but was the slave of a Chinaman by the name of Ah Bun . . . , her master, [who] compelled her to enter upon a life of prostitution.

. . . .

The trial court found that the appellee should be deported to China, whence she came, except for one thing; and that was that, in his opinion, her deportation would in fact be remanding her to a life of perpetual slavery and degradation.

The appellee has moved to dismiss the appeal on the ground that the sole question involved is the application of the thirteenth amendment to the Constitution of the United States, and that therefore the appellate jurisdiction of the Supreme Court is exclusive. We do not see that the decision of the appeal involves the construction or application of the thirteenth amendment.

. . . .

The true ground of the decision, from the language of the opinion, would appear to have been that compliance with the statute would be a barbarous proceeding, equivalent to remanding the appellee to perpetual slavery and degradation. The court said:

> "If sent back to her own country, where she was by her own kindred sold to a cruel master, she must abandon hope, and it is shocking to contemplate that the laws of our country require the court to use its process to accomplish such an unholy purpose."

The court, arguendo, proceeded to observe that it was proper to consider that by the *thirteenth amendment* it is ordained that neither slavery nor involuntary servitude, except as a punishment for crime, whereby the party shall have been duly convicted, shall exist within the United States or any place subject to their jurisdiction, and said:

> This article is a part of the supreme law of this land, whereby all branches of the government must be controlled," and that if was "a mandate from the highest authority, requiring the exercise of all the force necessary for the protection of the liberty of any and every individual whose right to liberty has not been forfeited by conviction of crime.

The court said in conclusion:

> The effort which the appellant has made to escape from thraldom and to rise from her condition of degradation entitles her to humane consideration, and, because I can see no other way in which to emancipate her from actual slavery, I direct that an order be entered vacating the order for her deportation.

In so ruling the court did not, as we understand it, hold that the *thirteenth amendment*, prohibiting slavery within the United States or in any place subject to their jurisdiction by its terms prohibited the deportation of the appellee; nor is it contended on this appeal that by virtue of an order of deportation her condition as a slave would be recognized, or that she would be sent into slavery at any place within the United States or within its jurisdiction. The case is one which, from its nature, enlists the sympathy of the court, and we regret that the law is so written that it does not permit us, as we view it, to yield to the humane considerations which actuated the court below.

We see no escape from the conclusion that the judgment of the trial court must be reversed, and the appellee remanded to the country whence she came. It is so ordered.

NOTES AND QUESTIONS

1. If the facts of *Ah Sou* were to happen today, how would the outcome be different? Would the victim be deported? What potential criminal charges might be brought against her trafficker? What impact would the age of the victim have upon the evidence required for potential charges?

2. To what extent might political and public policy concerns have influenced the Ninth Circuit decision? Remember this decision was issued during the time of the Chinese Exclusion Acts of the 19th and 20th centuries. Could those Acts have influenced the court's decision?

VII. CONCLUSION

Although the Thirteenth Amendment became the law of the land, the struggle to end slavery was still in its nascent phase following the Amendment's passage. Many supporters of abolition understood that slavery would quickly return in other forms without Reconstruction or greater constitutional protections, such as a guaranteed right to vote. Added to this equation was a desperate Southern need for cheap and readily available labor to replace former slaves. From this emerged widespread Southern peonage, a condition akin to slavery — but more subtle. And, thus, the struggle to end all forms of slavery, and to abolish peonage in the South, continued on. The following chapter will examine these developments.

Chapter 2

PEONAGE

I. OVERVIEW: FROM PROCLAMATION TO PEONAGE

The Emancipation Proclamation in 1863 and the ratification of the Thirteenth Amendment in 1865 formally ended slavery in the United States. Yet, many acts and conditions akin to slavery continued well into the 20th century. In fact, the formal abolition of slavery led to the expansion of a different, more subtle form of oppression and servitude: peonage.

Defined as forced labor in payment of a debt, peonage was common in the American Southwest during the time when slavery predominated in the American Southeast. But following the end of the Civil War, when the American Southeast was left economically devastated and plantations and other industries faced a new demand for low-cost labor, peonage quickly spread. Indeed, peonage was the predominant way that many businesses filled the labor void left by newly emancipated slaves.

The peonage model varied slightly from business to business and industry to industry. But in general, it involved business owners first having African Americans arrested on fabricated criminal charges, and then levying fines against the African Americans that the African Americans could not pay. These "peons" were then leased out and forced to work in lumber camps, plantations, coal mines, brickyards, railroads, and quarries to pay off their debts.[1] The conditions of this work were grim, particularly on the plantations. As Booker T. Washington observed — having been born a slave himself in 1856 — plantation peonage was "in one sense as bad as the slavery of antebellum days."

Peonage spread throughout the South at the same time that the post-Civil-War Reconstruction occurred. Reconstruction was complex and brought with it both good and bad for so-called "freedmen," who transitioned from slavery to freedom while the South adjusted to a new reality. Among the difficulties faced by freedmen, who were emancipated but not yet full citizens, were what came to be known as "Black Codes." These were laws that granted freedmen some basic rights — such as the right to marry and own property — but denied them the right to vote, participate in juries, serve in the militia, or testify against white people. By 1865, every Southern state had enacted them.

---

[1] A slightly different version of this model also existed, known as "convict leasing." The main difference between peonage and convict leasing arose from the fact that convict leasing did not rely solely on debt but rather involved a system where state prisons leased out people convicted on all types of offenses to work as forced laborers in different industries.

At the federal level, a law prohibiting peonage was enacted as part of the formal legal architecture of Reconstruction in 1867. Still, efforts to combat peonage faced many challenges, in practice and in the courts. On top of Black Codes, many states passed restrictive contract and labor laws that reinforced the peonage system. One example of these laws can be found in the case of *U.S. v. Bailey*, discussed later in this chapter, where an Alabama labor law was enacted that made failure to perform a contract prima facie evidence of an intent to defraud.

Viewed in a broader historical context, peonage can be seen as the bridge between antebellum slavery and what we now identify as human trafficking, or "modern-day slavery." Despite the formal end of slavery, many indicia and elements of involuntary servitude and slavery existed in forms of peonage that occurred between the late 1860s and the late 1940s. Among these forms is something called "debt peonage," where victims of peonage were compelled to provide labor or services in exchange for payment of a debt. This form of peonage continues today in human trafficking cases worldwide.

II. PEONAGE IN THE SOUTHWEST

Jaremillo v. Romero, an 1857 opinion from the Supreme Court of New Mexico, struck down efforts to enforce an alleged peonage arrangement in New Mexico and provides insight into the peonage system in the American Southwest.

JAREMILLO v. ROMERO
1 N.M. 190 (1857)

BENEDICT, J.

This is an appeal from a justice of the peace to the district court in the first district, and from thence to this court. It has become our duty for the first time in this tribunal to examine and construe the laws of this territory, declaring the rights and defining the relations of masters and servants. . . . It includes what is commonly called the peon system of this country. It is that system to which we so frequently see reference (and sometimes in high places in our republic) as maintaining here similar relations between masters and servants as are found to be established between the master and his slave in different states of the union. . . .

[T]he justice describes Mariana as a servant who had abandoned the work or service of her master while owing the sum of fifty-one dollars and seventy-five cents, before advanced to her. The transcript shows that at the time of trial Mariana did not appear, and that, upon the motion of the plaintiff, the justice rendered judgment against Mariana for twenty-six months of work as a servant, *o el equivalente*, fifty-one dollars and seventy-five cents, *in dinero* (or for fifty-one dollars and seventy-five cents, the equivalent in money), as also for interest and all costs. In the district court the case was tried *de novo*, and the court adjudged "that the plaintiff recover of the said defendant, Mariana Jaremillo, and of Domingo Fernandez Luz Jaremillo and Juan Miguel Ortego, the securities on her appeal bond, the sum of fifty-six dollars and twenty-one cents; and also the costs of this suit to be taxed, and in default of payment hereof that she be held to serve her said master, Jose de la

Cruz Romero, as a peon until said sum of money is paid." The error assigned by the appellant is this judgment, to reverse which she has appealed to this court. . . .

Upon the entry of the power of the United States within this territory in 1846, and establishing their rule and government, there was found a large class of persons commonly designated in the language of the country by the name of peons. They were not of any particular color, race, or caste of the inhabitants. They appeared as servants, menials, or domestics, "bound" to some kind of "service" to their masters. Generally they had none or small amounts of property. . . . Many had been raised from childhood within the households of such families. One fact existed universally: all were indebted to their masters. . . . Upon entering the new service, or while continuing therein, the peon was held rigorously to fulfill his pledge and render his labor so long as his debts remained, or an additional one was incurred. He could not abandon the service; and if he did, his master pursued, reclaimed, and reduced him to obedience and labor again . . . .

We turn now to inquire for the legislative act which established these rules between peon and master. . . .

[The court proceeds to examine the history of peonage in Spain and Mexico (as New Mexico became a U.S. territory in 1846 after the Mexican-American War), looking to Spanish statutory authority and treatises to determine that "the consent of the parties was invariably the foundation upon which a servant became bound to service," and was bounded by contract. The court also notes that the civil law of Spain and Mexico prohibited a man's selling of his liberty, though he could sell his services for a limited time, and the heirs of a servant were not bound to finish his work upon his death.]

. . . .

In 1846, the political relations of this country were changed from Mexico to the United States. . . .

The same course of proceeding was left a master to recover his debt from his servant or peon, as in the ordinary way from another debtor, nor was any summary process provided, when the peon had left his master's service, to compel him to return. The mode of summoning a debtor was plainly marked out, as also every succeeding step to be taken in the cause, and the alcaldes were bound to conform thereto. . . .

The prefect of Santa Fe, as it appears by the certificate made by him, stated that Romero had presented himself before him claiming a servant, that her name was Mariana, and that her father had taken her from his service, and that there was due him the sum of fifty-one dollars and seventy-five cents. The purpose of the process or document was to assist Romero in demanding the money or girl of her father. Nothing shows that either the girl or her father was ever before the prefect to adjust the accounts or claims with Romero, or that any notice had been given either to appear. . . . To hold that such judgment possessed any force, that it proved anything against Mariana or her father, would be setting at open defiance the known and long-observed rules of evidence and opening the doors to irresistible and measureless wrongs and frauds. . . .

If the going to the prefect by Romero and making his *ex parte* representations, adjudicated Mariana's case with him, proved her a debtor and bound to service, and has given a master a right to reclaim or reduce her to bondage, it is easy to perceive how any person whosoever within the territory may be made a debtor and sent into servitude, should an unscrupulous man and an ignorant and faithless prefect or probate judge devise mischief together. . . . The parties must be present by themselves or agents. It is not a trial; it is a mutual agreement of the parties as to the contract or account. The magistrate is the official witness and he attests the facts agreed upon. . . . In the cause at bar there is no proof of any mutual adjustment between the parties before any magistrate, nor does any certify to the correctness of any accounts owned by Mariana. Nothing appears beyond the representations made by Romero. The paper issued by the prefect says that Mariana's father had brought her away, and the document was given in order that Romero might demand his servant or money from her father. So far as this shows anything, it suggests strongly that the debt, if any, was due by the father, and not the girl. He took control of his daughter, and Romero obtained the action of the prefect against him. The inference is patent that the girl was a minor, and, if held for a debt, it was her father's. . . . If it was upon her father's account, as doubtless it was, she has passed, it may be well-inferred, beyond her minority, and if so, can not, against her own consent, be held bound to service by reason of her father's indebtedness.

We think proper, in this place, to notice the further legislation of this territory upon the subject of master and servant. In 1852 an act provided as follows:

> Section 1. All contracts, voluntarily entered into between masters and servants, agreeing and designating the kind of service, the salary, and the time such service shall continue, whether any money shall have been given or received in advance or not, both parties shall be compelled to comply with the contract without power to rescind it, except in the following cases: 1. By mutual consent; 2. For sufficient motive having been given by one party to the other, such as having grievously injured him; 3. If the master keeps the accounts in an ambiguous manner, so that the servant can not understand them. In these three cases the contract may be rescinded by paying the amount due from one party to the other, as the case may be; but if such motives should not be proven, the contract shall be complied with, and the judge or court of any precinct shall order it to be carried into effect, imposing upon the party failing to comply with the contract, and who shall persevere in doing so, that he indemnify the other party for the injuries resulting therefrom, or which may follow; and all resistance shall be punished by fine or imprisonment . . . .
>
> Section 2. If a servant shall refuse to comply with the contract, and he should owe any part of the money to the master, and he refuses or can not pay it, the justice of the peace, judge of probate, or district court will compel him to pay *numerata pecunia* the entire principal and legal interest for all the time it may remain unpaid, it being the duty of the judge or court, in case of difficulty, to order the sheriff to contract the services of said person to the highest bidder for the purpose of recovering the debt. The

same proceeding shall be had when the master owes the servant any sum of money for services rendered, and shall refuse to pay him for the same.

. . . .

We see in this section the exertions of the legislature to make more strict and multiply the remedies for the enforcement of these descriptions of contracts. They modify in some respect the act of 1851. By that the servant could leave his master whenever he willed by paying his debt. By this he must abide by and fulfill his agreement according to its terms, whether he owes or does not owe, pays or does not pay. Unless he can get his master's consent to rescind or prove some one of the causes specified to procure a cancellation, he may be prosecuted for a failure, and so may the master, and the servant compelled to a compliance by a fine and imprisonment. . . . It appears clear that the legislators were determined that by no means should either of the parties escape the consequences of their own voluntary engagements. . . . No authority is given the tribunal in this course to adjudicate the servant to the master upon giving the latter judgment for his debt.

We find here no support to that portion of the judgment of the district court which adjudged Mariana to the service of Romero as a peon, in default of her or her securities paying the money. The compulsory process of fine and imprisonment in case the servant refuses to perform his agreement, and the extent to which it may be exerted, to enforce obedience, would seem to furnish ample means to secure him to service. A still further remedy is added in the proceeding. The master may proceed in the ordinary form for the collection of his debt, and in the execution for the sale of the servant's services. The act is in some respects loose and indefinite in its language, yet not so much so that an intelligent court cannot find the rule for its guidance.

. . . In the common use of language the term peon is now used in this country as synonymous with servant. . . . A peon or servant loses none of his rights as a citizen by contracting with a master to serve him. He is under no political disqualifications; he votes at all elections if otherwise legally qualified; his servitude does not render him under our laws ineligible to the offices of the precinct, the county, the legislature, or delegate in congress.

Such are some of the features which the peon system (as commonly called) presents in this territory. In pronouncing upon the testimony in the cause we are required to determine, we are of the opinion that the writ *exhorto*, or letters requisitorial, possessed no legal force as evidence of indebtedness from Mariana to Romero. . . . Their utter insufficiency to prove Mariana's contract of service or any indebtedness to Romero, on her part, obligates this court to reverse the judgment of the court below, with costs against Romero.

* * *

NOTES AND QUESTIONS

Judge Benedict gives three reasons for not returning Jaremillo to Romero. *First*, Jaremillo was denied due process. The Court concluded that Jaremillo received no notice of the proceedings against her. Thus, the Justice of the Peace who adjudicated the claim did not have personal jurisdiction over her. *Second*, the Justice of the Peace exceeded his power in what he was allowed to do to resolve the dispute. Summoning Jaremillo to return to her master was outside of his authority. *Third*, the district court itself erred in its decision. The 1852 legislation cited by the Court regarding masters and peons enumerated the remedies available to masters should their servants stop short of their contracted service. But bonded service to their master — that is, service to pay off a debt — was not one of the options. Notice, however, that another type of service in payment of the debt *was* permitted. The sheriff could "contract the services of said person to the highest bidder for the purpose of recovering the debt." The difference here is that the servant presumably would be paid for her services and pay down the debt to her master this way, rather than through merely providing labor or services to the master.

III. PEONAGE IN THE AMERICAN SOUTH

Following the end of the Civil War, peonage spread rapidly throughout the American South, touching multiple industries and implicating some of the largest companies and families in the South.[2] According to historian Pete Daniel,

> [P]eonage that existed throughout the American South was most obvious in three patterns. First, the cotton belt from the Carolinas to Texas and including the Mississippi Delta supplied most peonage complaints, a testimony to the enduring plantation system. Second, the turpentine areas of northern Florida, southern Georgia, Alabama, and Mississippi furnished numerous peonage complaints. Third, for a relatively brief time railroad construction camps became the scene of peonage.

SHADOW OF SLAVERY: PEONAGE IN THE SOUTH 1901–69, 21 (1990).

In some ways, peonage was as brutal and destructive as antebellum slavery. The conditions in which peons were held were deplorable: camps had rampant disease and most did not have sanitation systems. At one major company, Sloss-Sheffield, which operated the Coalburg mine, a state prison inspector estimated the death rate to be 30 percent per year. The inspector reported that between 1888 and 1889, 34 percent of the 648 forced laborers at the mine died.

Although peonage resembled slavery in many ways, it differed considerably in the subtle manner in which it operated. Peons were not held in chains nor typically whipped as a form of punishment. Instead the coercion used on them was much less visible and more economic. They were forced to buy equipment they couldn't afford. They were saddled with interest rates that kept their debt perpetual. Essentially, they were indentured servants under the guise of "freedom of contract."

---

[2] Many large Southern companies relied on slaves, including Tennessee Coal Iron & Railroad (TCI), Sloss-Sheffield, and Pratt Consolidated Coal. Following the abolition of slavery, labor from peonage and convict-leasing proved a substantial part of their work product. Pratt Mines, which was owned by TCI, had at one time over 1,000 forced laborers. DOUGLAS A. BLACKMON, SLAVERY BY ANOTHER NAME: THE RE-ENSLAVEMENT OF BLACK AMERICANS FROM THE CIVIL WAR TO WORLD WAR II 295 (2009).

Moreover, in some respects, elements of peonage were worse than that of chattel slavery, in that the labor arrangement was shorter and less certain. Both of these conditions increased the likelihood that a peon's health and welfare would be disregarded. Holders of slaves had a strong economic incentive to keep slaves healthy. Slaves were a form of property, an "investment" that rewarded being protected. But the same incentive did not apply to holders of peons, since peons, unlike slaves, did not hold any value *as* peons. They were not a form of property. They did not reward investment. Their only value was the labor they produced, which meant that, in many cases, they would be quite literally worked to death.

A. The Peonage System

Peonage relied on local law enforcement and judges to uphold a system of legally enforced debt bondage arrangements that were often grounded in fictional or contrived debt. As noted, local law enforcement would typically arrest able-bodied African Americans and accuse them of having committed a petty crime. This could include violation of vagrancy laws, failure to pay a debt, or a more serious crime. A justice of the peace would sentence the individual to a small fine that the individual could not afford to pay. A third party would arrive to pay the debt and require that the prisoner sign a contract in return. The prisoner would then be bound by a contract, which effectively stripped them of rights and required them to work for a designated employer for an extended period of time to pay off the debt. In *Slavery by Another Name*, Douglas Blackmon's comprehensive study of the peonage system and its 80-year history, Blackmon describes the manner in which men were compelled into peonage:

> By the dawn of the twentieth century, peonage in the Southern cotton belt was a confusing mass of customs, legalities, and pseudo-legalities. Nearly every Southern state legislature had passed a contract-labor measure that in many ways resembled the black codes of Reconstruction. Under such laws. . . a laborer who signed a contract and then abandoned his job could be arrested for a criminal offense. Ultimately his choice was simple: he could either work out his contract or go to the chain gang.

DOUGLAS A. BLACKMON, SLAVERY BY ANOTHER NAME: THE RE-ENSLAVEMENT OF BLACK AMERICANS FROM THE CIVIL WAR TO WORLD WAR II 25 (2009).

Because of the considerable authority of local courts and law enforcement, thousands of African Americans were easily arrested, tried, and forced to labor to pay down a debt. Moreover, once within the system, laborers would incur more debts than they made in wages, and ended up in an endless cycle of debt, which was enforced by local law enforcement officials.

B. An Example

Justices of the peace played a crucial role in peonage, as the story of Justice James M. Kennedy illustrates. Kennedy assisted a prominent family in Alabama, the Cosby family, to obtain forced laborers through peonage. The Cosby family owned a large plantation in Alabama. Blackmon details how the Cosby family obtained a supply of workers:

When the Cosby family wanted to take control of a particular black man, one of the Cosbys would order an employee to swear out an affidavit accusing the African-American of a crime — usually failure to pay for goods, breaking a contract to work for the entire planting season, or a charge as generic as "fighting.". . .

. . . [T]he Cosbys seized the black man and took him and their affidavit to Pace's farm, where Kennedy would hold the semblance of a trial . . . . The defendant was always found guilty and ordered to pay a fine he could not produce, usually $5 plus the costs of the arrest and trial . . . . The Cosbys, who had seized the black man to begin with, would claim to pay . . . the ostensible fine and fees, and force the prisoner to sign a labor contract agreeing to work a year or more to pay them back.

Id. at 136–38.

IV. CHALLENGING THE PEONAGE SYSTEM: FINDING AND ENFORCING FEDERAL LAW

Opponents of peonage struggled to define why it was illegal and how they might end this widespread practice. At a local level, many claimed that peonage was legal, since it was frequently grounded in state laws on contracts and debts, and enforced by law enforcement and the courts. In 1901, Fred Cubberly, a 31-year-old U.S. Commissioner, witnessed what he believed to be peonage when he observed an African-American man, George Huggins, being threatened at gunpoint to return to a turpentine farm. Cubberly believed that this practice, as Blackmon puts it, "stood outside of the law, but Cubberly could think of no state or federal law that applied. But unlike countless others who had passively observed such incidents, he began searching the federal statutes." Cubberly's search bore fruit. He found an 1867 statute passed to deal with peonage in New Mexico, whose language covered the whole United States. The relevant sections of that statute appear below.

A. Anti-Peonage Act of 1867

The Anti-Peonage Act, ch. 187, 14 Stat. 546 (1867), prohibited compulsory labor in payment of a debt. It stated:

SEC. 1990. The holding of any person to service or labor under the system known as peonage is abolished and forever prohibited in the Territory of New Mexico, or in any other Territory or State of the United States; and all acts, laws, resolutions, orders, regulations, or usages of the Territory of New Mexico, or of any other Territory or State, which have heretofore established, maintained, or enforced, or by virtue of which any attempt shall hereafter be made to establish, maintain, or enforce, directly or indirectly, the voluntary or involuntary service or labor of any persons as peons, in liquidation of any debt or obligation, or otherwise, are declared null and void.

SEC. 5526. Every person who holds, arrests, returns, or causes to be held, arrested, or returned, or in any manner aids in the arrest or return of any person to a condition of peonage, shall be punished by a fine of not less than one thousand nor more than five thousand dollars, or by imprisonment not less than one year nor more than five years, or by both.

B. The First Court Test — *US v. Clyatt*

After finding a statute to enforce, Cubberly contacted local U.S. Attorney John Eagan. Together, Cubberly and Eagan sought a test case for the peonage statute, hoping to prove that the statute prohibited the conduct Cubberly had witnessed. In early 1901, Cubberly alerted Eagan about an incident in which Samuel M. Clyatt, accompanied by a Deputy Sherriff, raided a camp in Florida in search of his former employees, alleging that they had left Georgia owing him money. This would become the first test case of the Anti-Peonage Act, *U.S. v. Clyatt*.

Clyatt involved an 1891 Florida law that permitted imprisonment of a laborer for leaving a job while owing money. The warrant was issued in Georgia but served in Florida without extradition proceedings. Clyatt was allowed to cuff his former employees and load them onto a train to Tifton, Georgia to work out their debt. Clyatt said he wanted "to take the men to Georgia in order to make an example of them; that he always went after men who ran away from him."[3]

CLYATT v. UNITED STATES
197 U.S. 207 (1905)

Mr. Justice Brewer delivered the opinion of the court.

The constitutionality and scope of sections 1990 and 5526 present the first questions for our consideration. They prohibit peonage. . . . That which is contemplated by the statute is compulsory service to secure the payment of a debt. Is this legislation within the power of Congress? . . .

. . . The prohibitions of the Fourteenth and Fifteenth Amendments are largely upon the acts of the States; but the Thirteenth Amendment names no party or authority, but simply forbids slavery and involuntary servitude, grants to Congress power to enforce this prohibition by appropriate legislation. . . .

. . . It is not open to doubt that Congress may enforce the Thirteenth Amendment by direct legislation, punishing the holding of a person in slavery or in involuntary servitude except as a punishment for crime. In the exercise of that power Congress has enacted these sections denouncing peonage, and punishing one who holds another in that condition of involuntary servitude. This legislation is not limited to the territories or other parts of the strictly national domain, but is operative in the states and wherever the sovereignty of the United States extends. We entertain no doubt of the validity of this legislation, or its applicability to the case of any person holding and wherever the sovereignty of the United whether there be a municipal ordinance or state law sanctioning such holding. It operates directly on every citizen of the Republic, wherever his residence may be. . . .

---

[3] Douglas A. Blackmon, Slavery By Another Name: The Re-Enslavement of Black Americans from the Civil War to World War II 5–6 (2009).

... Section 5526 punishes "every person who holds, arrests, returns, or causes to be held, arrested, or returned." Three distinct acts are here mentioned — holding, arresting, returning. The disjunctive "or" indicates the separation between them and shows that either one may be the subject of indictment and punishment. A party may hold another in a state of peonage without ever having arrested him for that purpose. He may come by inheritance into the possession of an estate in which the peon is held, and he simply continues the condition which was existing before he came into possession. He may also arrest an individual for the purpose of placing him in a condition of peonage, and this whether he be the one to whom the involuntary service is to be rendered or simply employed for the purpose of making the arrest. Or he may, after one has fled from a state of peonage, return him to it, and this whether he himself claims the service or is acting simply as an agent of another to enforce the return.

The indictment charges that the defendant did "unlawfully and knowingly return one Will Gordon and one Mose Ridley to a condition of peonage, by forcibly and against the will of them, the said Will Gordon and the said Mose Ridley, returning them, the said Will Gordon and the said Mose Ridley, to work to and for Samuel M. Clyatt."

Now a "return" implies the prior existence of some state or condition. Webster defines it "to turn back; to go or come again to the same place or condition." . . .

It was essential, therefore, under the charge in this case to show that Gordon and Ridley had been in a condition of peonage, to which, by the act of the defendant, they were returned. We are not at liberty to transform this indictment into one charging that the defendant held them in a condition or state of peonage, or that he arrested them with a view of placing them in such condition or state. . . .

The testimony discloses that the defendant with another party went to Florida and caused the arrest of Gordon and Ridley on warrants issued by a magistrate in Georgia for larceny, but there can be little doubt that these criminal proceedings were only an excuse for securing the custody of Gordon and Ridley and taking them back to Georgia to work out a debt. At any rate, there was abundant testimony from which the jury could find that to have been the fact. While this is true, there is not a scintilla of testimony to show that Gordon and Ridley were ever theretofore in a condition of peonage. That they were in debt and that they had left Georgia and gone to Florida without paying that debt, does not show that they had been held in a condition of peonage, or were ever at work willingly or unwillingly for their creditor. We have examined the testimony with great care to see if there was anything which would justify a finding of the fact, and can find nothing. No matter how severe may be the condemnation which is due to the conduct of a party charged with a criminal offense, it is the imperative duty of a court to see that all the elements of his crime are proved, or at least that testimony is offered which justifies a jury in finding those elements. Only in the exact administration of the law will justice in the long run be done, and the confidence of the public in such administration be maintained.

We are constrained, therefore, to order a reversal of the judgment, and remand the case for a new trial.

Mr. Justice Harlan, concurring and dissenting:

I concur with my brethren in holding that the statutes in question relating to peonage are valid under the Constitution of the United States. . . .

But I cannot agree in holding that the trial court erred in not taking the case from the jury. Without going into the details of the evidence, I care only to say that, in my opinion, there was evidence tending to make a case within the statute. The opinion of the court concedes that there was abundant testimony to show that the accused with another went from Georgia to Florida to arrest the two negroes, Gordon and Ridley, and take them against their will back to Georgia to work out a debt. And they were taken to Georgia by force. It is conceded that peonage is based upon the indebtedness of the peon to the master. The accused admitted to one of the witnesses that the negroes owed him. In any view, there was no motion or request to direct a verdict for the defendant. The accused made no objection to the submission of the case to the jury, and it is going very far to hold in a case like this, disclosing barbarities of the worst kind against these negroes, that the trial court erred in sending the case to the jury.

NOTES AND QUESTIONS

1. Before *Clyatt*, three seminal cases marked the legal landscape in the aftermath of emancipation. *First*, the *Slaughterhouse Cases*, 83 U.S. (16 Wall.) 36 (1873), in which the Supreme Court narrowly interpreted the privileges and immunities clause of the Fourteenth Amendment as limited to those privileges and immunities articulated in the Constitution and not including additional rights provided by individuals states. *Second*, the *Civil Rights Cases*, 109 U.S. 3 (1883), which struck down the prohibition of racial discrimination by private individuals and organizations as outside congressional power under the enforcement power of the Fourteenth Amendment. And, *third*, *Plessy v. Ferguson*, 163 U.S. 537 (1896), which established "separate but equal" as a constitutionally acceptable standard for segregated railroad cars and was quickly extended to permit segregation in all areas of public life.

What did these three decisions mean for freedmen and other African Americans in the United States? Did they have any impact on efforts to combat peonage? Note that the first indictment under the Anti-Peonage Act was brought significantly after the Act became law in 1867.

2. Consider the dissent in the *Civil Rights Cases* by Justice John Marshall Harlan, who also dissented in various peonage decisions, including *Clyatt* and the case we will discuss next, *U.S. v. Bailey*. In the *Civil Rights Cases*, Justice Harlan wrote:

> My brethren say, that when a man has emerged from slavery, and by the aid of beneficent legislation has shaken off the inseparable concomitants of that state, there must be some stage in the progress of his elevation when he takes the rank of a mere citizen, and ceases to be the special favorite of the laws, and when his rights as a citizen, or a man, are to be protected in the ordinary modes by which other men's rights are protected. It is, I

submit, scarcely just to say that the colored race has been the special favorite of the laws. What the nation, through Congress, has sought to accomplish in reference to that race is, what had already been done in every state in the Union for the white race, to secure and protect rights belonging to them as freemen and citizens; nothing more. The one underlying purpose of congressional legislation has been to enable the black race to take the rank of mere citizens. The difficulty has been to compel a recognition of their legal right to take that rank, and to secure the enjoyment of privileges belonging, under the law, to them as a component part of the people for whose welfare and happiness government is ordained.

109 U.S. 3, 61 (1883) (Harlan, J., dissenting).

3. The government successfully defended the constitutionality of the peonage statute, but the *Clyatt* case was ultimately remanded for a new trial on the basis that the indictment's charges had not been proved. The case was never retried, since the two identified victims, Will Gordon and Mose Ridley, could not be found. Eventually, more than eight years after the original indictment in *Clyatt*, then-United States Attorney Fred Cubberly asked and received permission from the Department of Justice to dismiss the case. That Clyatt never went to jail and that the witnesses disappeared during the case typified peonage prosecutions in the United States.

4. The case led to many other peonage cases being charged in the South. Yet although the case upheld the constitutionality of the statute, it also set a high bar for proving peonage, as Justice Harlan's dissent noted. Contrast the historical importance attached to the *Clyatt* case with Blackmon's view of the complex history of peonage prosecutions in the United States:

> In 1909, an internal review of all peonage prosecutions in Alabama in the first decade of the century found that of forty-three indictments issued . . . all ended in acquittals, dismissals, suspended sentences, or presidential pardons. A total of $300 in fines had been collected from the defendants; four of those convicted served short periods in jail.
>
> . . . [I]ndictments grew rare. More and more often, federal officials — citing a highly technical reading of the peonage statute — asserted that they had jurisdiction only in cases in which a slave was being held specifically to repay a debt. Adopting the same legal rationale put forward by the defense lawyers in the trials of 1903, officials increasingly took the position that merely forcing a man or woman to labor for nothing — or buying them for that purpose — was not a federal crime.

DOUGLAS A. BLACKMON, SLAVERY BY ANOTHER NAME: THE RE-ENSLAVEMENT OF BLACK AMERICANS FROM THE CIVIL WAR TO WORLD WAR II 355–56 (2009).

V. *BAILEY* AND *REYNOLDS*: TWO ADDITIONAL CHALLENGES TO PEONAGE

A. The *Bailey* Case

Legal efforts to end peonage continued in Alabama in the case of Alonzo (Lonzo) Bailey, where what was at stake was not defending the peonage statute or another round of prosecutions but rather the ability to undermine the legal infrastructure that facilitated peonage. Across the South, contract-labor laws were being amended to enable the prosecution of laborers for fraud, providing the basis for longer sentences, which in turned facilitated the leasing system at the core of peonage.

A black agricultural worker and peon, Lonzo Bailey was convicted in the Montgomery City Court under an Alabama labor law providing that prima facie evidence of a laborer's intent to injure or defraud his employer existed when a laborer took money and subsequently failed to pay back his employer. Moreover, Alabama's rules of evidence prohibited Bailey from testifying in court about his reasons for leaving his employer. Bailey challenged the Alabama law as a violation of the Thirteenth Amendment, on the grounds that the effect of the statute was to establish a condition of involuntary servitude. He also challenged the statute as violating the Fourteenth Amendment's due process and equal protection guarantees.

Following a complex procedural history, in which the Alabama Supreme Court upheld the constitutionality of the state labor law and the U.S. Supreme Court remanded the case for a jury trial, the U.S. Supreme Court heard arguments on Bailey's Thirteenth Amendment challenge. Ultimately, the Court struck down the Alabama labor law that made entering into a contract prima facie evidence of intent to defraud if non-payment occurred, finding that the state statute facilitated involuntary servitude in violation of the Thirteenth Amendment.

BAILEY v. ALABAMA
219 U.S. 219 (1911)

[This case involved the legality of the Alabama Code of 1896, which was amended to make failure to perform a contract, without just cause, prima facie evidence of an intent to defraud.]

JUSTICE CHARLES EVANS HUGHES delivered the opinion of the Court

. . . .

[The statute in question reads:]

> Any person, who with intent to injure or defraud his employer, enters into a contract in writing for the performance of any act of service, and thereby obtains money or other personal property from such employer, and with like intent, and without just cause, and without refunding such money, or paying for such property, refuses or fails to perform such act or service,

must on conviction be punished by a fine in double the damage suffered by the injured party, but not more than $300, one-half of said fine to go to the county and one-half to the party injured; and any person, who with intent to injure or defraud his landlord, enters into any contract in writing for the rent of land, and thereby obtains any money or other personal property from such landlord, and with like intent, without just cause, and without refunding such money, or paying for such property, refuses or fails to cultivate such land, or to comply with his contract relative thereto, must on conviction be punished by fine in double the damage suffered by the injured party, but not more than $300, one-half of said fine to go to the county and one-half to the party injured. And the refusal or failure of any person, who enters into such contract, to perform such act or service or to cultivate such land, or refund such money, or pay for such property without just cause shall be prima facie evidence of the intent to injure his employer or landlord or defraud him. That all laws and parts of laws in conflict with the provisions hereof be and the same are hereby repealed.

There is also a rule of evidence enforced by the courts of Alabama which must be regarded as having the same effect as if read into the statute itself, that the accused, for the purpose of rebutting the statutory presumption, shall not be allowed to testify "as to his uncommunicated motives, purpose or intention." *Bailey v. State*, 161 Ala. 77, 78 (1909).

. . . Bailey, the plaintiff in error, was committed for detention on the charge of obtaining fifteen dollars under a contract in writing with intent to injure or defraud his employer. . . .

. . . On December 26, 1907, Bailey entered into a written contract with the Riverside Company, which provided:

> That I Lonzo Bailey for and in consideration of the sum of Fifteen Dollars in money, this day in hand paid to me by said The Riverside Co., the receipt whereof, I do hereby acknowledge, I, the said Lonzo Bailey do hereby consent, contract and agree to work and labor for the said Riverside Co. as a farm hand on their Scotts Bend Place in Montgomery County, Alabama, from the 30 day of Dec. 1907, to the 30 day of Dec. 1908, at and for the sum of 12.00 per month.
>
> And the said Lonzo Bailey agrees to render respectful and faithful service to the said The Riverside Co. and to perform diligently and actively all work pertaining to such employment, in accordance with the instructions of the said The Riverside Co., or ag't."

And the said The Riverside Co. in consideration of the agreement above mentioned of the said Lonzo Bailey hereby employs the said Lonzo Bailey as such farm hand for the time above set out, and agrees to pay the said Lonzo Bailey the sum of $10.75 per month.

. . . .

The jury found the accused guilty . . . .

. . . .

We pass then to the consideration of the amendment, through the operation of which under the charge of the trial court this conviction was obtained.... By this amendment it was provided, in substance, that the refusal or failure to perform the service contracted for, or to refund the money obtained, without just cause, should be prima facie evidence of the intent to injure or defraud.

. . . .

. . . It is not sufficient to declare that the statute does not make it the duty of the jury to convict, where there is no other evidence but the breach of the contract and the failure to pay the debt. The point is that, in such a case, the statute authorizes the jury to convict. It is not enough to say that the jury may not accept that evidence as alone sufficient; for the jury may accept it, and they have the express warrant of the statute to accept is as a basis for their verdict. And it is in this light that the validity of the statute must be determined.

While in considering the natural operation and effect of the statute, as amended, we are not limited to the particular facts of the case at the bar, they present an illuminating illustration. We may briefly restate them. Bailey made a contract to work for a year at $12 a month. He received $15 and he was to work this out, being entitled monthly only to $10.75 of his wages. No one was present when he made the contract but himself and the manager of the employing company. There is not a particle of evidence of any circumstance indicating that he made the contract or received the money with any intent to injure or defraud his employer. On the contrary, he actually worked for upwards of a month. . . .

. . . We cannot escape the conclusion that, although the statute in terms is to punish fraud, still its natural and inevitable effect is to expose to conviction for crime those who simply fail or refuse to perform contracts for personal service in liquidation of a debt, and judging its purpose by its effect that it seeks in this way to provide the means of compulsion through which performance of such service may be secured. The question is whether such a statute is constitutional.

. . . .

In the present case it is urged that the statute as amended, through the operation of the presumption for which it provides, violates the Thirteenth Amendment of the Constitution of the United States and the act of Congress passed for its enforcement. . . .

. . . While the Amendment was self-executing, so far as its terms were applicable to any existing condition, Congress was authorized to secure its complete enforcement by appropriate legislation. As was said in the Civil Rights cases: "By its own unaided force and effect it abolished slavery, and established universal freedom. Still, legislation may be necessary and proper to meet all the various cases and circumstances to be affected by it, and to prescribe proper modes of redress for its violation in letter or spirit." . . .

. . . .

The . . . [Anti-Peonage Act of 1867] was a valid exercise of this express authority. *Clyatt v. United States*, 197 U.S. 207. It declared that all laws of any State, by virtue of which any attempt should be made 'to establish, maintain, or enforce, directly or indirectly, the voluntary or involuntary service or labor of any persons as peons, in liquidation of any debt or obligation, or otherwise," should be null and void.

Peonage is a term descriptive of a condition which has existed in Spanish America, and especially in Mexico. The essence of the thing is compulsory service in payment of a debt. A peon is one who is compelled to work for his creditor until his debt is paid. And in this explicit and comprehensive enactment, Congress was not concerned with mere names or manner of description, or with a particular place or section of the country. It was concerned with a fact, wherever it might exist; with a condition, however named and wherever it might be established, maintained or enforced.

The fact that the debtor contracted to perform the labor which is sought to be compelled does not withdraw the attempted enforcement from the condemnation of the statute. The full intent of the constitutional provision could be defeated with obvious facility if, through the guise of contracts under which advances had been made, debtors could be held to compulsory service. It is the compulsion of the service that the statute inhibits, for when that occurs the condition of servitude is created, which would be not less involuntary because of the original agreement to work out the indebtedness. The contract exposes the debtor to liability for the loss due to the breach, but not to enforced labor. This has been so clearly stated by this court in the case of *Clyatt, supra,* that discussion is unnecessary. . . .

. . . If the statute in this case had authorized the employing company to seize the debtor and hold him to the service until he paid the fifteen dollars, or had furnished the equivalent in labor, its invalidity would not be questioned. It would be equally clear that the State could not authorize its constabulary to prevent the servant from escaping and to force him to work out his debt. . . .

What the State may not do directly it may not do indirectly. If it cannot punish the servant as a criminal for the mere failure or refusal to serve without paying his debt, it is not permitted to accomplish the same result by creating a statutory presumption which upon proof of no other fact exposes him to conviction and punishment. Without imputing any actual motive to oppress, we must consider the natural operation of the statute here in question (*Henderson v. Mayor,* 92 U.S. p. 268), and it is apparent that it furnishes a convenient instrument for the coercion which the Constitution and the act of Congress forbid; an instrument of compulsion peculiarly effective as against the poor and the ignorant, its most likely victims. There is no more important concern than to safeguard the freedom of labor upon which alone can enduring prosperity be based. . . . [W]e conclude that § 4730 as amended, of the Code of Alabama, in so far as it makes the refusal or failure to perform the act or service, without refunding the money or paying for the property received, prima facie evidence of the commission of the crime which the section defines, is in conflict with the Thirteenth Amendment and the legislation authorized by that Amendment, and is therefore invalid.

. . . .

Reversed and cause remanded for further proceedings not inconsistent with this opinion.

MR. JUSTICE HOLMES, with whom concurred MR. JUSTICE LURTON, dissenting.

We all agree that this case is to be considered and decided in the same way as if it arose in Idaho or New York. Neither public document nor evidence discloses a law which by its administration is made something different from what it appears on its face, and therefore the fact that in Alabama it mainly concerns the blacks does not matter. *Yick Wo v. Hopkins*, 118 U.S. 356, does not apply. I shall begin then by assuming for the moment what I think is not true and shall try to show not to be true, that this statute punishes the mere refusal to labor according to contract as a crime, and shall inquire whether there would be anything contrary to the Thirteenth Amendment or the statute if it did, supposing it to have been enacted in the State of New York. I cannot believe it. The Thirteenth Amendment does not outlaw contracts for labor. That would be at least as great a misfortune for the laborer as for the man that employed him. For it certainly would affect the terms of the bargain unfavorably for the laboring man if it were understood that the employer could do nothing in case the laborer saw fit to break his word. But any legal liability for breach of a contract is a disagreeable consequence which tends to make the contractor do as he said he would. Liability to an action for damages has that tendency as well as a fine. If the mere imposition of such consequences as tend to make a man keep to his promise is the creation of peonage when the contract happens to be for labor, I do not see why the allowance of a civil action is not, as well as an indictment ending in fine. Peonage is service to a private master at which a man is kept by bodily compulsion against his will. But the creation of the ordinary legal motives for right conduct does not produce it. Breach of a legal contract without excuse is wrong conduct, even if the contract is for labor, and if a State adds to civil liability a criminal liability to fine, it simply intensifies the legal motive for doing right, it does not make the laborer a slave.

But if a fine may be imposed, imprisonment may be imposed in case of a failure to pay it. Nor does it matter if labor is added to the imprisonment. Imprisonment with hard labor is not stricken from the statute books. On the contrary, involuntary servitude as a punishment for crime is excepted from the prohibition of the Thirteenth Amendment in so many words. Also the power of the States to make breach of contract a crime is not done away with by the abolition of slavery. But if breach of contract may be made a crime at all, it may be made a crime with all the consequences usually attached to crime. There is produced a sort of illusion if a contract to labor ends in compulsory labor in a prison. But compulsory work for no private master in a jail is not peonage. If work in a jail is not condemned in itself, without regard to what the conduct is it punishes, it may be made a consequence of any conduct that the State has power to punish at all. I do not blink the fact that the liability to imprisonment may work as a motive when a fine without it would not, and that it may induce the laborer to keep on when he would like to leave. But it does not strike me as an objection to a law that it is effective. If the contract is one that ought not to be made, prohibit it. But if it is a perfectly fair and proper contract, I can see no reason why the State should not throw its weight on the side of performance. There is no relation between its doing so in the manner supposed and allowing a private master to use private force upon a laborer who wishes to leave.

. . . .

. . . To sum up, I think that obtaining money by fraud may be made a crime as well as murder or theft; that a false representation, expressed or implied, at the time of making a contract of labor that one intends to perform it and thereby obtaining an advance, may be declared a case of fraudulently obtaining money as well as any other; that if made a crime it may be punished like any other crime, and that an unjustified departure from the promised service without repayment may be declared a sufficient case to go to the jury for their judgment; all without in any way infringing the Thirteenth Amendment or the statutes of the United States.

NOTES AND QUESTIONS

1. Consider Justice Holmes's approach to peonage. Dissenting in both *Clyatt* and *Bailey*, Justice Holmes displays an arguably cynical, non-idealistic, and technocratic interpretation of peonage law. To him, peonage is not more than a manifestation of "the freedom to contract." Do you find merit in this interpretation?

2. The repercussions of *Bailey* were significant, both for the decision's supporters and for its opponents. For *Bailey*'s supporters, it was a huge victory because it meant that that no state could permit peonage through its system of contract and labor laws. For *Bailey*'s opponents, it was a resounding defeat, one that led many in the South to echo the lament in Justice Holmes's dissent.

3. Consider what impact cases like *Clyatt* and *Bailey* had on ending peonage:

> The results of *Bailey* case were not spectacular, but they were nevertheless significant. Future court battles regarding civil rights often came from large, organized efforts. Despite the persistence of peonage and even spectacular exposes in the 1920s and 1940s, however, neither the Justice Department nor a civil rights or labor group finished what Bailey's supporters began in 1911. Peonage continued to the 1940s and beyond, and the legal basis for the practice endured thirty years after the precedent-setting *Bailey* case had been decided.

DOUGLAS A. BLACKMON, SLAVERY BY ANOTHER NAME: THE RE-ENSLAVEMENT OF BLACK AMERICANS FROM THE CIVIL WAR TO WORLD WAR II 355–56 (2009).

B. The *Reynolds* Case

Like *Bailey*, *U.S. v. Reynolds* also involved — and struck down — an Alabama law. In *Reynolds*, the defendants acted as sureties on the laborers' fines for criminal convictions and imposed more onerous contractual terms than would have been permitted under Alabama's laws. The Supreme Court held that this added element of contractual coercion violated the Thirteenth Amendment, because it allowed individuals convicted of criminal offenses to confess judgment to a third-party surety, who the individuals then had to reimburse through compelled labor. Under the state law, if a laborer violated a contract with a surety, the surety had authority to have the laborer arrested, and the cycle of debt bondage became self-perpetuating.

UNITED STATES v. REYNOLDS
235 U.S. 133 (1914)

Mr. Justice Day delivered the opinion of the court.

. . . .

The facts to be gathered from the indictments and pleas, upon which the court below decided the cases and determined that no offense was charged against the statutes of the United States as above set forth, are substantially these: In No. 478, one Ed Rivers, having been convicted in a court of Alabama of the offense of petit larceny, was fined $15, and costs $43.75. The defendant Reynolds appeared as surety for Rivers, and a judgment by confession was entered up against him for the amount of the fine and costs, which Reynolds afterwards paid to the State. On May 4, 1910, Rivers, the convict, entered into a written contract with Reynolds to work for him as a farm-hand for the term of nine months and twenty-four days, at the rate of six dollars per month, to pay the amount of fine and costs. The indictment charges that he entered into the service of Reynolds, and under threats of arrest and imprisonment if he ceased to perform such work and labor, he worked until the sixth day of June, when he refused to labor. Thereupon he was arrested upon a warrant issued at the instance of Reynolds from the County Court of Alabama, on the charge of violating the contract of service. He was convicted and fined the sum of one cent for violating this contract, and additional costs in the amount of $87.05, for which he again confessed judgment with G. W. Broughton as surety, and entered into a similar contract with Broughton to work for him as a farm-hand at the same rate, for a term of fourteen months and fifteen days.

In No. 479, the case against Broughton, E. W. Fields, having been convicted in an Alabama state court, at the July, 1910, term, of the offense of selling mortgaged property, was fined fifty dollars and costs, in the additional sum of $69.70. Thereupon Broughton, as surety for Fields, confessed judgment for the sum of fine and costs, and afterwards paid the same to the State. On the eighth day of July, 1910, a contract was entered into, by which Fields agreed to work for Broughton as a farm and logging hand for the term of nineteen months and twenty-nine days, at the rate of six dollars per month, to pay the fine and costs. He entered into the service of Broughton, and, it was alleged, under threats of arrest and imprisonment if he ceased to labor, he continued so to do until the fourteenth day of September, 1910, when he refused to labor further. Thereupon Broughton caused the arrest of Fields upon a charge of violating his contract, and upon a warrant issued upon this charge, Fields was again arrested. . . .

[The Court discusses a number of Alabama statutes and then proceeds to examine Section 6846 of the Alabama Code, which permitted the formation of contracts between individuals convicted of misdemeanors and third-party sureties who assumed the fines and costs owed by the individuals. The statute allowed contracts between sureties and convicted individuals to require performance of labor or services to satisfy the debt.]

. . . .

... [T]he question for consideration is, [w]ere the defendants well charged with violating the provisions of the Federal [Anti-Peonage Act], notwithstanding they undertook to act under the Alabama laws, particularly under the provisions of § 6846 of the Alabama Code, authorizing sureties to appear and confess judgment and enter into contracts such as those we have described? . . .

. . . The actual situation is this: The convict instead of being committed to work and labor as the statute provides for the State, when his fines and costs are unpaid, comes into court with a surety, and confesses judgment in the amount of fine and costs, and agrees with the surety, in consideration of the payment of that fine and costs, to perform service for the surety after he is released because of the confession of judgment.

. . . .

. . . [W]e are to decide the question whether the labor of the convict, thus contracted for, amounted to involuntary service for the liquidation of a debt to the surety, which character of service it was the intention of the acts of Congress to prevent and punish. When thus at labor, the convict is working under a contract which he has made with his surety. He is to work until the amount which the surety has paid for him the sum of the fine and costs is paid. The surety has paid the State and the service is rendered to reimburse him. This is the real substance of the transaction. The terms of that contract are agreed upon by the contracting parties, as the result of their own negotiations. The statute of the State does not prescribe them. It leaves the making of contract to the parties concerned, and this fact is not changed because of the requirement that the judge shall approve of the contract. When the convict goes to work under this agreement, he is under the direction and control of the surety, and is in fact working for him. If he keeps his agreement with the surety, he is discharged from its obligations without any further action by the State. This labor is performed under the constant coercion and threat of another possible arrest and prosecution in case he violates the labor contract which he has made with the surety, and this form of coercion is as potent as it would have been had the law provided for the seizure and compulsory service of the convict. Compulsion of such service by the constant fear of imprisonment under the criminal laws renders the work compulsory, as much so as authority to arrest and hold his person would be if the law authorized that to be done. *Bailey v. Alabama*, 219 U.S. 219, 244; *Ex parte Hollman*, 60 S. E. Rep. 19, 24.

Under this statute, the surety may cause the arrest of the convict for violation of his labor contract. He may be sentenced and punished for this new offense, and undertake to liquidate the penalty by a new contract of a similar nature, and, if again broken, may be again prosecuted, and the convict is thus kept chained to an ever-turning wheel of servitude to discharge the obligation which he has incurred to his surety, who has entered into an undertaking with the State or paid money in his behalf. . . .

Nor is the labor for the surety by any means tantamount to that which the State imposes if no such contract has been entered into, as these cases afford adequate illustration. In the case against Reynolds, Rivers was sentenced to pay $15 fine and $43.75 costs. Under the Alabama Code, he might have been sentenced to hard labor for the county for ten days for the non-payment of the fine, and assuming that he could be sentenced for non-payment of costs under § 7635 of the Alabama Code, he could have worked it out at the rate of seventy-fine cents per day, an additional 58 days might have been added, making 68 days as his maximum sentence at hard labor. Under the contract now before us, he was required to labor for nine months and twenty-four days, thus being required to perform a much more onerous service than if he had been sentenced under the statute, and committed to hard labor. Failing to perform the service he may be again re-arrested, as he was in fact in this case, and another judgment confessed to pay a fine of one cent and $87.75 costs, for which the convict was bound to work for another surety for the term of fourteen months and seventeen days. In the case against Broughton, Fields was fined $50 and $69.70 costs. Under the law he might have been condemned to hard labor for less than four months. By the contract described, he was required to work for Broughton for a period of nineteen months and twenty-nine days.

. . . .

. . . On our opinion, this system is in violation of rights intended to be secured by the Thirteenth Amendment, as well as in violation of the statutes to which we have referred, which the Congress has enacted for the purpose of making that amendment effective.

It follows that the judgment of the District Court must be reversed.

Judgment accordingly.

Mr. Justice Holmes, concurring.

There seems to me nothing in the Thirteenth Amendment or the Revised Statutes that prevents a State from making a breach of contract, as well a reasonable contract for labor as for other matters, a crime and punishing it as such. But impulsive people with little intelligence or foresight may be expected to lay hold of anything that affords a relief from present pain even though it will cause greater trouble by and by. The successive contracts, each for a longer them than the last, are the inevitable, and must be taken to have been the contemplated outcome of the Alabama laws. On this ground I am inclined to agree that the statutes in question disclose the attempt to maintain service that the Revised Statutes forbid.

NOTES AND QUESTIONS

1. Contrast Justice Holmes's concurrence here with his dissent in *Bailey*. Why does Justice Holmes side with the Court this time?

2. Can you distinguish the statutes in question in these two cases?

VI. CONCLUSION

The peonage cases were an important step in the struggle to end the practice of compelled labor in the South. Coming after the Emancipation Proclamation, the Thirteenth Amendment, and the laws and amendments enacted during Reconstruction, the peonage cases established important legal precedents in efforts to combat newer, subtle forms of forced labor and oppression.

But despite efforts to end peonage, the practice continued in the United States until the 1940s when President Franklin Delano Roosevelt mandated that the Justice Department root out all forms of slavery. Building upon President Roosevelt's renewed commitment to ending slavery, President Truman's Committee on Civil Rights recommended that Congress pass a new law prohibiting involuntary servitude, which Congress eventually did in 1948. This law, which entered the U.S. Code as Title 18 Section 1584, makes it illegal to compel an individual to work against his or her will through the use of force, the threat of force, or the threat of legal coercion sufficient to compel labor or service. It is discussed in more detail in the following chapter.

Chapter 3
INVOLUNTARY SERVITUDE

I. INTRODUCTION

Although the Thirteenth Amendment prohibited chattel slavery, new manifestations of unfree labor continued to emerge. Courts recognized the reach of the Thirteenth Amendment to address not only the "badges and incidents" of historic chattel slavery, but also "involuntary servitude," perpetrated by private actors, who held others in slave-like working conditions. Involuntary servitude did not involve state-sanctioned slavery, peonage, or debt bondage, but rather an employer's coercive conduct intended to compel the labor of another against his or her will. The following case illustrates the expansion of the Thirteenth Amendment's application to involuntary servitude, a more modern form of slavery that could take place within a private employment arrangement even in the absence of direct physical or legal restraint.

UNITED STATES v. INGALLS
73 F. Supp. 76 (S.D. Cal. 1947)

WEINBERGER, DISTRICT JUDGE.

The defendant Elizabeth Ingalls, having been convicted by a jury, and now moving for a new trial, is charged in Count 1 of an indictment as follows:

"On or about October 11, 1946, defendants, Elizabeth Ingalls and Alfred Wesley Ingalls, did entice persuade and induce another person, namely, Dora L. Jones, to go from Berkeley, Alameda County, California, to Coronado, San Diego, County, California, within the Southern Division of the Southern District of California, with the intent that said other person, namely, Dora L. Jones, be held as a slave."

The motion for a new trial challenges the sufficiency of the evidence and also asserts that the Court erroneously defined "slave" to the jury.

There is an abundance of evidence which establishes that for many years prior to the date charged in the indictment, defendant Elizabeth Ingalls kept one Dora L. Jones, a negro woman, in her household as a servant during a period in excess of twenty-five years. There is evidence that during an uninterrupted period of in excess of twenty-five years said servant was required to arise at an early hour in the morning and perform practically all of the household labor in connection with the maintenance of the Ingalls household. She was forbidden to leave the household except for the commission of errands and performed drudgery of the most menial and laborious type, without compensation. She had no days off from her work, no vacation. Her quarters were among the poorest in the several homes occupied by the defendant during this period of years. There is evidence that the food furnished to her by defendant was of a substantially lower standard than that common to servants generally. She was denied the right to have friends and was required to send away a relative who called upon her. There is evidence that she was physically abused on several occasions. When she protested and asserted that she would leave the service of defendant Elizabeth Ingalls, that defendant reminded her of an adulterous relationship which had existed intermittently over a period of three years between the first husband of Mrs. Ingalls and Dora Jones, and of an abortion to which Dora Jones had submitted because of a pregnancy resulting from said relationship; that on such occasion Mrs. Ingalls would threaten to have Dora Jones committed to prison because of the former existence, about 38 years ago, of such relationship, and because of such abortion. Dora Jones had come into the service of the defendant at the age of seventeen years, her earlier life having been spent in Athens, Alabama. She testified that she believed the defendant could and would execute the threat frequently made and have her committed to prison if she left the defendant's service. She testified further that the defendant told her she was not bright, mentally, and could not make her way in the competitive world and would — if not sent to prison — be committed to a mental institution. It appears that these threats and numerous others acted effectively upon the servant to hold her against her free will in the service of the defendant until the early morning of October 11, 1946, on which date a daughter of the defendant induced the servant to leave the family automobile in which she was required to sleep during a cross-country trip. Thereafter on the same day, in the presence of a member of the Berkeley, California, Police Department, the defendant renewed to the servant the threat that she could, and would, have her placed in prison if she persisted in leaving her, and also made other threats of retaliation, not only to the victim but concerning those who had aided her in escape. The servant testified that because she feared these threats would be executed, she left the Police Station in custody of the defendant and her husband and returned to their service. That night she was required to sleep on the floor of a hotel room although there were rooms available and the hotel had no restriction against providing such rooms to a person of the negro race. The defendant took the servant with her to an exclusive hotel at Coronado, California. This hotel had accommodations for the housing of servants of its guests, but the defendant made no application in behalf of Dora Jones therefor, and while the defendant enjoyed the commodious facilities of the hotel in her own behalf, she required the servant to sleep in the family automobile parked upon the public streets for the period of about a month, during which time the servant subsisted upon meager meals brought to her in the car and on occasions fed her in the defendant's room. Thereafter, when the defendant moved into a house, at Coronado, California, the servant again did all of the household work without compensation, and on at least one occasion when she rendered a small outside service to another for compensation, the defendant took that compensation from her.

These facts, gleaned from a great mass of other evidence of similar treatment, compel the conclusion that the servant, Dora L. Jones, was a person wholly subject to the will of defendant; that she was one who had no freedom of action and whose person and services were wholly under the control of defendant and who was in a state of enforced compulsory service to the defendant.

The Court, in charging the jury, instructed it as follows:

"The indictment charges the defendants with the intent to hold Dora L. Jones as a slave. I shall, therefore define the word "slave" for you.

"A slave is a person who is wholly subject to the will of another, one who has no freedom of action and whose person and services are wholly under the control of another, and who is in a state of enforced compulsory service to another."

It must be borne in mind that many definitions of slavery were formulated at a time when slavery was lawful in the United States, and that the Thirteenth Amendment not only abolished slavery of persons of the negro race, but empowered the Congress to enact legislation prohibiting slavery. There is, therefore, no de jure slavery in the United States, and there was none at the time of the enactment of Section 443 of Title 18, U.S. Code, 18 U.S.C.A. § 443, the statute under which this prosecution was had, Dictionary definitions published even before the Thirteenth Amendment was enacted, recognized that there were many shades of meaning of the word, which did not include all the incidentals of lawful slavery in the United States, as it applied to negro slaves who were bought and sold as chattels and whose issue were the property of their owner.

Noah Webster's "American Dictionary of English Language," published in 1850, defines, "slave" as follows:

1. The noun 'slave,' a person who is wholly subject to the will of another, one who has no freedom of action but whose person and services are wholly under the control of another. In the early state of the world and to this day, among some barbarous nations, prisoners of war are considered and treated as slaves. The slaves of modern times are more generally purchased like horses and oxen.

2. One who has lost the power of resistance; or one who surrenders himself to any power whatever; as, a slave to passion, to lust, or to ambition. (Waller)

3. 'A mean person, one in the lower state of life.

4. 'Is a drudge, one who labors like a slave.'

A dictionary published in London, written by Stormouth in 1886, gives the following definition:

A slave supposed to be taken from Sclavi, the name of the Sclavonian race, a common source for slaves in early times; old Dut. slavven (a slave, anyone held as a bond-servant for life; a human being wholly the property of another; one who surrenders himself wholly to any power, as to an appetite, or to the influence of another; a drudge; v. to drudge; to toil unremittingly.

The Permanent Edition of Words and Phrases, vol. 39, gives the following definition of 'slavery':

"A state of entire subjection of one person to the will of another . . . a condition of enforced compulsory service of one to another."

The term "slave" received judicial construction in the unreported District Court case tried in 1907 in the Southern District of New York, *United States v. Sabbia*. There the Court stated:

> I prefer to consider the act as framed Section 443 of Title 18, U.S.C.A. for post-bellum conditions, in the light of the war amendments, and as using the word slave as meaning a person in a state of enforced or extorted servitude to another.

The question was also presented in *United States v. Peacher*, decided in the United States District Court for the Eastern District of Arkansas in 1937. Although unreported, an examination of the records of that case discloses that it was the Government's contention that "slave," as used in Section 443, meant one held in a state of involuntary servitude in the post-civil war sense, and that an indictment which disclosed that contention was held good as against demurrer.

In *Hodges v. United States*, 203 U.S. 1, at page 16, 27 S. Ct. 6, at page 8, 51 L. Ed. 65, decided in 1905, the Supreme Court defined slavery as 'a condition of enforced compulsory service of one to another.

On page 17 of the same opinion in 203 U.S., 27 S. Ct. 8, 51 L. Ed. 65, we find the following:

> A reference to the definitions in the dictionaries of words whose meaning is so thoroughly understood by all seems an affection, yet in Webster 'slavery' is defined as 'the state of entire subjection of one person to the will of another.' Even the secondary meaning given recognizes the fact of subjection, as 'one who has lost the power of resistance; one who surrenders himself to any power whatever; as a slave to passion, to lust, to strong drink, to ambition,' and 'servitude' is by the same authority declared to be 'the state of voluntary or compulsory subjection to a master.

The Court arrived at its definition which was embodied in the instruction on slavery after a consideration of the authorities hereinbefore mentioned.

The evidence was sufficient to warrant the jury in finding that the defendant Elizabeth Ingalls did entice, persuade and induce Dora L. Jones to go from Berkeley, Alameda County, California, to Coronado, San Diego County, California, with the intent that Dora L. Jones be held as a slave, as charged in Count One of the indictment.

The motion for new trial is denied.

NOTES AND QUESTIONS

1. How did the *Ingalls* court define slavery? Is it different from chattel slavery? What is involuntary servitude? Is it different than slavery? Why did the *Ingalls* court find that Dora Jones was a slave? What facts indicate that she did not have the freedom to leave the Ingalls's home?

2. Professor Kathleen Kim has argued that *Ingalls* did not involve direct physical force or legal restraint. Instead, the victim, Dora Jones, had been compelled to work through a variety of nonphysical threats and verbal abuse:

> The court concluded that Ingalls's overall treatment of Jones subverted Jones's free will, forcing her to comply with the deplorable working conditions. The court further opined that Jones's apparent opportunities to escape did not preclude a finding of involuntary servitude. Rather, the fact that Jones did not leave the highly exploitive work situation emphasized her lack of meaningful "freedom of action."

The Coercion of Trafficked Workers 96 IOWA L. REV. 409, 421 (2011). Do you agree with this assessment? Professor Risa Goluboff explains that to understand the impact of the threats and abuse on Dora Jones, the *Ingalls* court considered Jones's subjective perception of the mistreatment, "rather than any objective harm that would come to her." *The Thirteenth Amendment and the Lost Origins of Civil Rights*, 50 DUKE L.J. 1609, 1667 (2001).

II. THE INVOLUNTARY SERVITUDE STATUTE

One year after the *Ingalls* decision, in 1948, Congress enacted 18 U.S.C. § 1584, pursuant to its Thirteenth Amendment, section two enforcement power. Section 1584 criminalized involuntary servitude:

> (a) Whoever knowingly and willfully holds to involuntary servitude or sells into any condition of involuntary servitude, any other person for any term, or brings within the United States any person so held, shall be fined under this title or imprisoned not more than 20 years, or both. If death results from the violation of this section, or if the violation includes kidnapping or an attempt to kidnap, aggravated sexual abuse or the attempt to commit aggravated sexual abuse, or an attempt to kill, the defendant shall be fined under this title or imprisoned for any term of years or life, or both.

> (b) Whoever obstructs, attempts to obstruct, or in any way interferes with or prevents the enforcement of this section, shall be subject to the penalties described in subsection (a).

Section 1584 did not specifically define involuntary servitude. It was derived from older antislavery statutes that addressed slavery-like practices beyond chattel slavery. Some courts viewed it as broadening the scope of involuntary servitude to cover all persons laboring against their will to benefit another under some type of coercion. These courts interpreted § 1584 to prohibit not only the physical and legal coercion that characterized chattel slavery and peonage, but also psychological coercion. Other courts rejected this broad view of § 1584 and interpreted the statute narrowly, confining involuntary servitude to the historic parameters defined by its predecessors: chattel slavery and peonage. These courts found nonphysical and nonlegal forms of coercion insufficient for a violation of involuntary servitude, as in the following case.

III. INTERPRETING 18 U.S.C. § 1584: THE CIRCUIT COURT SPLIT

UNITED STATES v. SHACKNEY
333 F.2d 475 (2d Cir. 1964)

Friendly, Circuit Judge.

In July, 1962, a grand jury in the District Court for Connecticut returned a nine count indictment charging David I. Shackney with violations of 18 U.S.C. §§ 1581(a) and 1584. The former section makes it a crime, punishable by a fine of not more than $5,000, or imprisonment of not more than five years, or both, to hold or return 'any person to a condition of peonage' or to arrest 'any person with the intent of placing him in or returning him to a condition of peonage.' The latter section subjects to similar punishment 'Whoever knowingly and willfully holds to involuntary servitude or sells into any condition of involuntary servitude, any other person for any term, or brings within the United States any person so held . . . .' The first two counts of the indictment charged the holding of Luis Oros and his wife, Virginia Oros, in a condition of peonage in Middlefield, Conn., from July 12, 1961, to March 3, 1962. The other seven counts charged the holding to involuntary servitude of Luis, Virginia, their four daughters and their son, at the same place and for the same time. Trial before Judge Blumenfeld and a jury began late in January, 1963, and continued until mid-March. At the end of the Government's case the court granted a motion for acquittal on the two counts relating to the wife; later, on being required to elect between the peonage count and the involuntary servitude count as to the husband, the Government consented to dismissal of the former. Reserving decision on a motion for acquittal on the remaining six counts, all under § 1584, relating to Luis and the five children, the judge submitted the case to the jury, which rendered verdicts of guilty on all. Subsequently the judge denied Shackney's motions for an acquittal and for a new trial and entered the judgment of conviction whence this appeal is taken. We hold that the Government did not show commission of the crime defined by § 1584.

Taking the evidence most favorably to the Government, we summarize this, noting only a few of the many items that were contradicted.

Shackney, who had been ordained as a rabbi in Poland, came to the United States with his wife in 1941. During the period charged in the indictment he taught afternoon classes at the B'nai Jacob School near New Haven, where his wife also taught; on two evenings a week he lectured on the Talmud to adult audiences in Middletown and New Haven. In addition, under the name of Maytav Kosher Packing Corporation, of which he was president, he operated a chicken farm adjacent to his home in Middlefield.

Shackney had found it hard to get American farm laborers who would accommodate themselves to the hens' annoying disregard for week-ends. Having seen an advertisement in a trade journal as to the availability of Mexican workers, he went to Mexico City in late June 1960, and hired two families, the Chavez' and the Olguins. One evening he hailed a taxi to take him to a theatre. The taxi was driven by Oros, then 40, who had been a Mexico City taxi driver for some eleven years. Oros had been in the United States as a railroad worker for nine months in 1944 in Wilmington, Delaware, and again in 1945-46 in Nevada. Talk in the taxi led, according to Oros, to Shackney's saying he needed still another family for the farm and Oros' offering his own. Shackney made it plain that Oros would have to sign a two-year contract, during which he was never to drink or to leave the farm. Undeterred, Oros took Shackney to his house to meet the family; Shackney said he had a house like it on his farm. The family being away, Oros later brought them to Shackney's hotel. Shackney, who was leaving the next morning, told Oros to prepare his immigration papers and to communicate with him.

After developments unnecessary to detail, Oros, his wife and his eldest daughter Maria Elena signed a contract, in Spanish, to work on Shackney's farm. This provided, among other things, that the contract should have a two-year term beginning August 15, 1961; that together with another couple the three Oros' would care for 20,000 laying hens; that the hours of work were to be from 6:30 A.M. until the work was completed, with three breaks; that "because of the fact that our work will be handling living things which must be carefully cared for, this work must be done every day, 7 days a week and 365 days a year with no exception"; that they were to receive a furnished place to live, with heat, electricity and gas for cooking, and sufficient food; and that their combined salary should be $160 per month for the first year and $240 for the second, half of which was to be deposited in a joint bank account as security for their performing their obligations.

Since Oros had encountered difficulty in obtaining visas, he asked Shackney to come to Mexico City to help. It was apparently on this occasion that Shackney allegedly made two statements much emphasized by the Government:

> You have contract, if you break this contract, I deport you and you never come back to the United States, not you, not your son, and not your grandsons, nobody, because I have lot of friends in Mexico and the United States, too, and I have lot of money, and money is money here or any place.

In contrast,

> If you are nice man and you work in my farm the two years like say the contract, after two years you are American citizen and then you can go any place, you are free, you go to work in taxi-cab or you go to California if feel you want to go. You want stay in my farm, you can stay.

It developed that Oros had no money to pay for his visas or transportation save for $80 which he had borrowed and turned over to Shackney. The latter arranged for funds to be provided but insisted on the signing by Oros of twelve promissory notes for $100 each, payable monthly, and their co-signing by a friend, Rosalio, who owned his own home. The next day Shackney made Oros sign six additional $100 notes, allegedly explaining merely 'You have confidence in me, you sign, and that's all.' According to Oros, Shackney paid only $350 for bus tickets and $210 for expenses in connection with the visas. Shackney claimed the $1200 notes had covered $500 for the expense of procuring visas and other documents, and $700 for plane tickets, which Oros had wrongfully diverted to the payment of his debts, and that the $600 notes covered another $380 that had to be paid for bus tickets, $40 for spending money for Oros and a contribution toward the expense of Shackney's own trip. After four days and five nights of travel the Oros' reached the farm in the morning of July 12, 1961, and were immediately put to work.

They found the conditions of life less attractive and the work more arduous than they had pictured. Their dwelling was a four-room half of a Quonset hut, set upon wooden pilings; the walls were of corrugated cardboard; and there were holes in the floor which Shackney told Oros to cover. Two of the rooms were bedrooms, with a total of two beds and a cot for the family of seven, there was a bathroom, and the other room contained kitchen facilities, an automatic hot water heater, a large television set and later a radio as well. The dwelling was heated by a wood stove. There was some criticism of the food, but the Government does not make this a serious item of complaint. Shackney gave the Oros' used clothing, and also furnished them with some new clothes, toilet articles and postage stamps which he said would ultimately have to be paid for. Although the contract called only for the services of the parents and the eldest daughter, all seven of the family worked, the two youngest children, aged 9 and 7, starting their labors at 10:00 A.M. instead of 6:30 A.M. when the others began. There is dispute whether so many would have had to labor so long if Oros had worked diligently, the defense claiming the television set had proved unduly distracting. Shackney raised the monthly salary for the parents and Maria Elena to $180 and also drew monthly checks of $20 to Maria Teresa and Sergio, the second and third eldest children. However, the Oros' received no cash since Shackney would get them to endorse the checks and would tear up two $100 notes each month; the only cash they obtained during the entire period was $10 which Shackney gave them at the request of a purchaser of chickens whom they had helped.

None of the Oros children went to school. Oros claimed that Shackney had said that the school was too far away, that the Oros' had no money to pay for the school, the school bus and clothing, and that the children could not speak English; Shackney countered that he had urged Oros to send the children to school but that Oros had objected. Oros also testified that a request for permission to attend the movies and a few requests to go to church were denied. Oros left the farm on only four occasions, Shackney going along on all save one. Until the latter months of the Oros' stay on the farm, all outgoing letters from the Oros' were given for posting to Shackney, who supplied the stamps; all incoming letters for the farm were placed in a rural post box and letters to the Oros' were delivered by him. There was evidence from which the jury could find that Shackney censored the Oros' mail, although he stoutly denied this. Oros testified that Shackney had instructed him not to talk with persons who came to the farm and to send them away if Shackney was not there, and that he was reprimanded when he violated these instructions.

Oros and Maria Elena testified that from the first day they had come to the farm they wished to leave it because the house was so different from what had been represented. It is admitted that none of the Oros' ever communicated this desire to Shackney, and that they were never restrained from leaving either by force or the threat of force. The farm is not in open country. It is on School Street in Middlefield, fourtenths [*sic*] of a mile west of a main highway connecting Meriden and Middletown, which is nearby. There is a house about 500' east of Shackney's residence and there are four others between the latter and the highway; a considerable housing development is near enough that the Oros' could hear the sounds from it. The driveway from the road passes Shackney's house and then winds back to the Oros' hut. At all times a truck was kept near the hut, with the keys in the ignition; at times Oros drove it. There were long periods every week, both daytime and evening, when the Oros' were left alone while the Shackneys were away on their teaching duties. Once a week a man came on the farm with feed for the chickens, egg pickups were made twice weekly, and other helpers were coming and going.

The Government's case was that the Oros' did not dare avail themselves of the easy methods of release admittedly available because their wills were overborne by fear which Shackney had engendered. Oros and Maria Elena testified they were always afraid. Of prime importance was the fear of deportation if they left. Here the Government linked the conversation in Mexico in July, 1961, that if Oros broke his contract he would be deported, with incidents in which Shackney spoke of deportation for other causes. A notable one occurred around September or October; Oros quoted Shackney's description how a 'man he say is too lazy and don't do everything, and say sometime he's drunk, too, so is bad man; and sometime he do something Mr. Shackney don't like, and this time Mr. Shackney say are very mad, and take him from the chicken coop, and send back to Mexico in half hour.' Also the Government linked the reference to powerful friends in the Mexican [sic] statement with Shackney's saying to Oros while on the farm that 'all the neighbors, the Post Office man, the policeman, and- well, he say everybody is a friend, the neighbors, police, and Post Office, and everybody is. When another time he say have money and money is money everywhere.' The young son, Sergio, testified that on one occasion Shackney had become irritated and 'told to my family that I am irresponsible boy. If I don't do the work, he going to send back to Mexico, then I have to go. Then I went to the bathroom and I was crying right there and then he told me not to cry any more; that I made him feel very bad to think he had made us cry. Then he took me to his home and he gave me a small package of candies, and he told me if I would go on being his friend, and I said 'Yes.' That was it.' On other occasions Shackney threatened that if any of the Oros' became ill, they would be sent back. A further fear-engendering factor was a threat in February, 1962, that unless Oros paid the notes that Rosalio had co-signed, 'somebody take my friend's house, and this thing I know when I sign the notes, and this is where I am scared to leave the farm.'[1]

The first and, in our view, dispositive issue is the reach of the language of 18 U.S.C. § 1584, 'Whoever knowingly and willfully holds to involuntary servitude . . ..' 'The Government suggests in effect that this is equivalent to 'Whoever knowingly and willfully holds to service by duress.' To test the consequences of such a reading, appellant's brief put a series of cases, starting with that of a man chained to his work bench and kept under restraint at all times, and ranging through the instant case to others where an employer threatens an employee who wishes to leave his service with blackballing in the industry, revealing a crime to the police, or preventing the employee's son from achieving a much desired admission to Yale. The Government

---

[1] [FN 7] The testimony as to this threat having been made in February, 1962, is somewhat hard to reconcile with Oros' admission that by that time the twelve notes co-signed by Rosalio had been surrendered to him. Of course, Oros might have been mistaken as to the date or have feared such action without any express threat.

manfully answered that all these cases constitute a holding to involuntary servitude, although also denying 'that the outer limits of that statute need be explored in this case.' With the most profound respect for the illustrious university at New Haven, we cannot believe that retention of an employee by a threat to prevent his son's admission there was quite what Congress had in mind when, in the great words of the 13th Amendment, it forbade a holding in involuntary servitude; and a court does not discharge its duty by saying that although it cannot tell just what a penal statute does forbid, it is confident that the case sub judice falls within it. When criminal statutes use 'abstractions of common certainty,' E. Freund, The Use of Indefinite Terms in Statutes, 30 Yale L.J. 437 (1921), courts must give what has been aptly called 'a pointing definition- a direction which attaches them to that one object to which they refer,' if the statute is to escape condemnation as void for vagueness. Connally v. General Construction Co., 269 U.S. 385, 391, 46 S.Ct. 126, 70 L.Ed. 322 (1926).

Our endeavor to construe the statute had best begin with its history. There is an initial puzzlement why the Criminal Code should contain two provisions, one relating to peonage, § 1581, and the other to involuntary servitude, § 1584, since any case that could be reached under the former section could also be reached under the latter.[2]

The section with respect to peonage is a century old, deriving from the Act of March 2, 1867, 14 Stat. 546, a prompt exercise of the power granted Congress by § 2 of the 13th Amendment, which had become effective December 18, 1865, 'to enforce this article by appropriate legislation.' In its original form, entitled 'An Act to abolish and forever prohibit the System of Peonage in the Territory of New Mexico and other Parts of the United States,' § 1 of this Act provided:

> That the holding of any person to service or labor under the system known as peonage is hereby declared to be unlawful, and the same is hereby abolished and forever prohibited in the Territory of New Mexico, or in any other Territory or State of the United States; and all acts, laws, resolutions, orders, regulations, or usages of the Territory of New Mexico, or of any other Territory or State of the United States, which have heretofore established, maintained, or enforced, or by virtue of which any attempt shall hereafter be made to establish, maintain, or enforce, directly or indirectly, the voluntary or involuntary service or labor of any persons as peons, in liquidation of any debt or obligation, or otherwise, be, and the same are hereby, declared null and void; and any person or persons who shall hold, arrest, or return, or cause to be held, arrested, or returned, or in any manner aid in the arrest or return of any person or persons to a condition of peonage, shall, upon conviction, be punished by fine not less than one thousand nor more than five thousand dollars, or by imprisonment not less than one nor more than five years, or both, at the discretion of the court.

In contrast, § 1584 is a relative newcomer to the statute book. It dates only from

---

[2] [FN 9] Peonage involves the additional element that the involuntary servitude is tied to the discharge of an indebtedness. *Clyatt v. United States*, 197, U.S.207, 215 (1905).

1948, although, as the Reviser's Notes tell us, it supposedly represents a 'consolidation' of two much older statutes. One was a part of the series of enactments of the first quarter of the nineteenth century dealing with the African slave trade, other portions of which survive, in somewhat altered form, as 18 U.S.C. §§ 1582 and 1585-1587; this statute, Act of April 20, 1818, c. 91, § 6, 3 Stat. 452, was directed at 'Every person who brings within the jurisdiction of the United States, in any manner whatsoever, any negro, mulatto, or person of color, from any foreign kingdom or country, or from sea, or holds, sells, or otherwise disposes of, any negro, mulatto, or person of color so brought in, as a slave, or to be held to service or labor. The other parent was the Act of June 23, 1874, 18 Stat. 251, 'An act to protect persons of foreign birth against forcible constraint or involuntary servitude.' This provided that 'whoever shall knowingly and willfully bring into the United States, or the Territories thereof, any person inveigled or forcibly kidnapped in any other country, with intent to hold such person so inveigled or kidnapped in confinement or to any involuntary service, and whoever shall knowingly and willfully sell, or cause to be sold, into any condition of involuntary servitude, any other person for any term whatever, and every person who shall knowingly and wilfully hold to involuntary service any person so sold and bought, shall be deemed guilty of a felony. 'This statute was aimed at abuses practiced against Italian children who were being recruited to perform as street musicians. It was said in the House, 'this bill is intended to prevent the practice of enslaving, buying, selling, or using Italian children' Cong.Record, 43 Cong. 1 Sess. 4443 (1874), a purpose not adequately served by a prior act of May 21, 1866 'to prevent and punish Kidnapping,' 14 Stat. 50, since this applied only to those who participated in or aided in the kidnapping, enticing, or carrying away of 'any other person, whether negro, mulatto, or otherwise, with the intent that such other person shall be sold or carried into involuntary servitude' and did not necessarily apply to the person who exacted the servitude. The peonage statute also was evidently thought insufficient to cope with this problem because it required proof that the involuntary service was to work out a debt. Although broader than the peonage statute in that respect, the Act of 1874 was narrower in others; it applied only if the person had been 'inveigled or kidnapped' or had been sold.

The Reviser's statement that 18 U.S.C. § 1584 simply 'consolidated' these sections with changes of phraseology necessary to effect consolidation, was thus quite inaccurate. The two statutes, neither of which would cover the instant case, had purposes and effects different from each other and from their 'consolidation.' Since, in contrast to Title 18 of the 1926 Code, the 1948 enactment of Title 18 constitutes 'positive law,' 62 Stat. 683, our search must be for the meaning of 1584 rather than of its two parents. But the history, along with the statement of a consultant to the revisers 'In general, with a few exceptions, the Code does not attempt to change existing law,' Holtzoff, Preface to Title 18 U.S.C.A. vi, at least forbids any view that Congress considered § 1584 to be staking out important new ground. We read its reference to involuntary servitude as covering the same type of compulsory holding as was proscribed by its parent statutes, comparable to the holding which was a necessary element of the crime of peonage.

For illumination as to what kinds of holding were so prohibited we turn initially to Supreme Court decisions under the peonage statute, all reviewed in Pollock v.

Williams, 322 U.S. 4, 64 S.Ct. 792, 88 L.Ed. 1095 (1944). In [these cases] the peonage statute was used, in Mr. Justice Jackson's phrase, 'as a shield'- namely, to invalidate convictions under state laws making it a crime for servants owing debts or other types of debtors to leave their employment; by their very nature these decisions can shed little light on our problem since the obligation to serve was enforced by the criminal laws of the state. Two cases in which the statute was used 'as a sword' are not much more helpful. In United States v. Reynolds, 235 U.S. 133, 35 S.Ct. 86, 59 L.Ed. 162 (1914), an employer had a laborer convicted under an Alabama statute making it a crime for a convict 'working out' a fine paid by the surety to refuse to labor further. United States v. Gaskin, 320 U.S. 527, 64 S.Ct. 318, 88 L.Ed. 287 (1944), arose on a demurrer to an indictment charging that defendant had forcibly arrested a debtor, detained him against his will, and transported him with intent to cause him to perform labor in satisfaction of the debt. The decision was simply that the district court had erred in dismissing the indictment for failure to allege that services had in fact been rendered after the arrest. Language in Clyatt v. United States, 197 U.S. 207, 25 S.Ct. 429, 49 L.Ed. 726 (1905), is more enlightening for our purposes, although the decision itself is not. The case came before the Court on an indictment charging that defendant did 'unlawfully and knowingly return one Will Gordon and one Mose Ridley to a condition of peonage, by forcibly and against the will of them, returning them to work to and for Samuel M. Clyatt to work out a debt claimed to be due.' The evidence showed that Clyatt had gone from Georgia to Florida to have Gordon and Ridley arrested and brought back. Defining peonage 'as a status or condition of compulsory service, based upon the indebtedness of the peon to the master,' equating 'compulsory service' with 'involuntary servitude,' and distinguishing this from 'the voluntary performance of labor or rendering of services in payment of a debt' where 'no law or force compels performance or a continuance of the service,' 197 U.S. at 215-216, 25 S.Ct. at 430, the Court held that although there was abundant evidence that the Florida criminal proceedings were only an excuse 'for securing the custody of Gordon and Ridley, and taking them back to Georgia to work out a debt,' there was no evidence that Gordon and Ridley had previously been in a condition of peonage to which they were being returned- the offense specified in the indictment. 'That they were in debt, and that they had left Georgia and gone to Florida without paying that debt, does not show that they had been in a condition of peonage, or were even at work, willingly or unwillingly, for their creditor.' 197 U.S. at 222, 25 S.Ct. at 433.

Failing to find a clear answer in these Supreme Court cases under the peonage act, we explore the earlier history of the term 'involuntary servitude.' A draft of the Northwest Ordinance drawn in 1784, almost certainly by Thomas Jefferson, contained a provision 'That, after the year 1800 of the Christian era, there shall be neither slavery nor involuntary servitude in any of the said states, otherwise than in the punishment of crimes whereof the party shall have been duly convicted to have been personally guilty.' It seems reasonably plain that what Jefferson meant to ban by the words 'involuntary servitude' was the legal enforcement of 'conditional servitude under indentures or covenants' such as had long existed in Virginia, at least to the extent that such indentures were not entered into voluntarily without the compulsion of a previously existing debt or obligation. Although this provision was not enacted in 1784, § 14, Article VI of the Ordinance of 1787, which replaced the version of three years earlier, provided 'There shall be neither slavery nor

III. INTERPRETING 18 U.S.C. § 1584   55

involuntary servitude in the said territory, otherwise than in the punishment of crimes, whereof the party shall have been duly convicted'. . . .

Hence it was natural that these historic words should be used in the 13th Amendment — 'Neither slavery nor involuntary servitude, except as a punishment for crime whereof the party shall have been duly convicted, shall exist within the United States, or any place subject to their jurisdiction.' . . .

The first judicial interpretation of this phrase in the 13th Amendment that we have found is in Tyler v. Heidorn, 46 Barb. 439, 458 (Albany General Term, 1866). The court there said:

> The term involuntary servitude, in my opinion, is substantially synonymous with slavery, though it may perhaps be regarded as slightly more comprehensive, and as embracing every thing under the name of servitude, though not denominated slavery, which gives to one person the control and ownership of the involuntary and compulsory services of another against his will and consent.

Not long after came the more authoritative statement in Mr. Justice Miller's opinion in the Slaughter-House Cases, 16 Wall. (83 U.S. 36, 69, 21 L.Ed. 394 (1873):

> The exception of servitude as a punishment for crime gives an idea of the class of servitude that is meant. The word 'servitude' is of larger meaning than 'slavery,' as the latter is popularly understood in this country, and the obvious purpose was to forbid all shades and conditions of African slavery. It was very well understood that in the form of apprenticeship for long terms, as it had been practiced in the West India Islands, on the abolition of slavery by the English government, or by reducing the slaves to the condition of serfs attached to the plantation, the purpose of the article might have been evaded, if only the word 'slavery' had been used.

Important material is found in Hodges v. United States, 203 U.S. 1, 16-17, 27 S.Ct. 6, 8, 51 L.Ed. 65 (1906), a case which, although heavily relied upon by the Government, is rather more helpful to appellant. The Court said that 'All understand by these terms (Slavery and involuntary servitude) a condition of enforced compulsory service of one to another,' and referred to dictionary definitions of slavery as 'the state of entire subjection of one person to the will of another' and of servitude as 'the state of voluntary or compulsory subjection to a master.' The first Mr. Justice Harlan's dissent characterized peonage as 'the compulsory holding of one individual by another individual for the purpose of compelling the former, by personal service, to discharge his indebtedness to the latter,' and stated its disagreement with the majority by saying that 'One who is shut up by superior or overpowering force, constantly present and threatening, from earning his living in a lawful way of his own choosing, is as much in a condition of involuntary servitude as if he were forcibly held in a condition of peonage.' 203 U.S. at 34, 27 S.Ct. at 16. The final datum is Butler v. Perry, 240 U.S. 328, 332, 36 S.Ct. 258, 259, 60 L.Ed. 672 (1916), where the Court said, in language reminiscent of the Slaughter-House opinion:

> This (13th) Amendment was adopted with reference to conditions existing since the foundation of our government, and the term 'involuntary servi-

tude' was intended to cover those forms of compulsory labor akin to African slavery which, in practical operation, would tend to produce like undesirable results.

This survey indicates to us that the prime purpose of those who outlawed 'involuntary servitude' in the predecessors of the 13th Amendment, in the Amendment itself, and in statutes enacted to enforce it, was to abolish all practices whereby subjection having some of the incidents of slavery was legally enforced, either directly, by a state's using its power to return the servant to the master, as had been the case under the peonage system in New Mexico, [ ] or indirectly, by subjecting persons who left the employer's service to criminal penalties. Rather plainly, however, the term goes farther. The 13th Amendment, unlike the 14th, is not addressed solely to state action, and it would be grotesque to read 'involuntary servitude' as not covering a situation where an employee was physically restrained by guards, as in Davis v. United States, 12 F.2d 253 (5 Cir.), cert. denied, 271 U.S. 688, 46 S.Ct. 639, 70 L.Ed. 1153 (1926); [ ] or, coming closer to this case, if the Oros' had been isolated in a secluded farm with barbed wire fences and locked gates. Various combinations of physical violence, of indications that more would be used on any attempt to escape, and of threats to cause immediate legal confinement, whether for the escape or some other reason, have also been held sufficient. [ ]. But we see no basis for concluding that because the statute can be satisfied by a credible threat of imprisonment, it should also be considered satisfied by a threat to have the employee sent back to the country of his origin, at least absent circumstances which would make such deportation equivalent to imprisonment or worse.[3] A credible threat of deportation might well constitute such duress as to invalidate any agreement made under its influence, as, for example, if on the completion of the Oros' contract Shackney had threatened to have them deported unless they made another; very likely, also, if something was sought or obtained for withdrawing such a threat, the maker could be successfully prosecuted under state blackmail or extortion statutes. But a holding in involuntary servitude means to us action by the master causing the servant to have, or to believe he has, no way to avoid continued service or confinement, in Mr. Justice Harlan's language, 'superior and overpowering force, constantly present and threatening,' 203 U.S. at 34, 27 S.Ct. at 16- not a situation where the servant knows he has a choice between continued service and freedom, even if the master has led him to believe that the choice may entail consequences that are exceedingly bad. This seems to us a line that is intelligible and consistent with the great

---

[3] [FN 17] The judge rightly instructed the jury to disregard 'any threat to enforce the payment of notes signed by Luis Oros and to proceed legally against the Oros' friend as endorser of those notes in order to obtain payment,' as it is within the rights of a mortgagee to threaten to enforce the security which the contract gives him for nonperformance. In fact, Oros' testimony that desire to protect his friend was a motivating factor works against the view that his will was overcome by the threats of deportation which the Government claims to come within the prohibition of the statute. The evidence as to threats of deportation for inefficiency or illness seems to have been relevant only to show further assertions by Shackney of power to cause deportation; threats of that sort alone would plainly not meet the statutory test.

III. INTERPRETING 18 U.S.C. § 1584

purpose of the 13th Amendment; to go beyond it would be inconsistent with the language and the history, both pointing to the conclusion that 'involuntary servitude' was considered to be something 'akin to African slavery,' Butler v. Perry, supra, 240 U.S. at 332, 36 S.Ct. at 259, although without some of the latter's incidents. While a credible threat of deportation may come close to the line, it still leaves the employee with a choice, and we do not see how we could fairly bring it within § 1584 without encompassing other types of threat, quite as devastating in the particular case as that of deportation may have been to the Oros', whose inclusion would make the statute an easy tool for blackmail and other serious abuse. Friction over employment punctuated by hotheaded threats is well known and inevitable. But the subjugation of another's will through such threats is more easily accused than accomplished. There must be 'law or force' that 'compels performance or a continuance of the service,' Clyatt v. United States, supra, 197 U.S. at 215-216, 25 S.Ct. at 430, for the statute to be violated.

Whether or not the 13th Amendment would permit passing this line, we are not convinced Congress has done so. If a makeweight were needed for our construction that the statute applies only to service compelled by law, by force or by the threat of continued confinement of some sort, the rule as to interpreting a statute to avoid 'grave and doubtful constitutional questions,' United States v. Delaware & Hudson Co., 213 U.S. 366, 407-408, 29 S.Ct. 527, 53 L.Ed. 836 (1909), would afford one. Another would be the equally established canon that 'When Congress leaves to the Judiciary the task of imputing to Congress an undeclared will' with respect to a criminal statute, 'the ambiguity should be resolved in favor of lenity.' Bell v. United States, 349 U.S. 81, 83, 75 S.Ct. 620, 622, 99 L.Ed. 905 (1955).

It goes without saying that if defendant's conduct was what the Oros' testified and the jury evidently believed, this would have been highly reprehensible. But before deciding to make such conduct a felony, punishable with up to five years' imprisonment, a legislator would wish to weigh the advantages to society in providing deterrence and retribution where the conduct had in fact occurred against the risk that innocent employers might be victimized by disgruntled employees able to convince prosecutors, and ultimately juries, of their story, and the consequent possible preferability of dealing with the evil by less drastic means. The most ardent believer in civil rights legislation might not think that cause would be advanced by permitting the awful machinery of the criminal law to be brought into play whenever an employee asserts that his will to quit has been subdued by a threat which seriously affects his future welfare but as to which he still has a choice, however painful. Before we would assume that Congress meant to encompass such cases or consider whether it would have the power to do so, we would require clearer evidence of legislative purpose than repetition of the history-laden term, 'holds to involuntary servitude.'

The judgment of conviction is reversed, with instructions to dismiss the indictment.

DIMOCK, DISTRICT JUDGE (concurring).

As I read the majority opinion, the distinction that it draws is between the servitor's belief that he is being confined, by law, by force or by threat of force and his submitting to continued service because of a threat of another kind. I cannot find this distinction between different means of confinement to be implied by the statute.

The opinion rejects what I would consider the plain and intended meaning of 'involuntary' as dealing only with the will of the servitor. That word raises the question of whether the will of the servitor has been subjugated, i.e., whether he has been rendered incapable of making a rational choice, and not the question of what were the means by which the servitude was imposed. It is impossible to generalize the means by which the will of man can be subjugated. What to one man is a paralyzing threat is to another merely a harsh alternative. Threats of force are the most extreme of threats to most of us but there are many who can brave this risk and will crumble in the face of others. To a drug addict the threat of deprivation of his supply is certainly more overbearing than the threat of almost any kind of force, yet it is a means falling outside of the majority's guilt criterion.

On the other hand cases may be supposed within the majority's guilt criterion where the servitude would not be involuntary. Take the case of United States v. Ingalls, D.C.S.D.Cal.S.D., 73 F.Supp. 76, cited by the majority. There was there a threat of prosecution and consequent imprisonment by the employer of a maidservant. All that my brethren would require in that case would be that she believe that the threat would be carried out. The Ingalls opinion, however, went into great detail as to the domination exercised by the employer and reached the conclusion [ ] that the servant 'was a person wholly subject to the will of defendant; that she was one who had no freedom of action and whose person and services were wholly under the control of defendant.' The mere belief of a threat of imprisonment is not, to my mind, enough to satisfy the requirement of the statute. The victim must also have such fear of the consequences as to deprive him of will power.

The servitude may be voluntary though imposed by a means falling within the majority's guilt criterion and may be involuntary though imposed by a means falling without that criterion.

The 'void for vagueness' doctrine does not compel us to substitute for the statutory test of involuntariness an arbitrary classification of means. To have an arbitrary classification which will resolve with equal facility all of the cases that would arise under the statute is indeed a tempting prospect. It is much harder to have to work under a statute which will raise difficult questions in the borderline cases inevitable wherever the application of a statute depends upon an appraisal of the state of the human mind. Statutes are not, however, void for vagueness because they raise difficult questions of fact. They are void for vagueness only where they fail to articulate a definite standard. I should not have thought that a statute fixing involuntariness as a standard would fall within that class.

Where the subjugation of the will of the servant is so complete as to render him incapable of making a rational choice, the servitude is involuntary within the terms of the statute and it is only where there is such subjugation that the servitude is involuntary. Where a master 'willfully' thus subjugates a servant's will, he has violated section 1584 of Title 18 of the United States Code. Unless he does so, there is no such violation. There is no evidence in the record from which the jury could have found willful subjugation of a servant's will. I concur in the result.

NOTES AND QUESTIONS

1. What is the definition of involuntary servitude according to the prosecution? The court? According to the majority, is a violation of involuntary servitude based on the nature of an employer's threats or the working conditions experienced by the alleged victims of involuntary servitude? Why did the majority find that Shackney did not hold the Oros' in involuntary servitude?

2. The majority determines the definition of involuntary servitude from a close historical reading of the statutes from which § 1584 was derived. Is their analysis persuasive?

3. Professor Kim finds that "despite egregious work conditions in any given case [of involuntary servitude], if the victim submitted to the labor by his or her own free will, courts could not find a violation of § 1584. Thus, the central focus was not on the *conditions* of the alleged servitude, but on whether the *means* of coercion were severe enough to render the victim with *no alternative* but to perform the labor." *Psychological Coercion in the Context of Modern-Day Involuntary Labor: Revisiting* United States v. Kozminski *and Understanding Human Trafficking*, 38 U. TOL. L. REV. 941, 947–48 (2007). Based on this analysis, do threats of deportation suffice for a violation of involuntary servitude according to the *Shackney* majority?

4. Writing for the majority, Judge Friendly determined that only the direct or threatened use of physical force or legal coercion were sufficiently "superior and overpowering" to subjugate the will of another. Other means of coercion, while perhaps entailing "consequences that are exceedingly bad," still left the worker with a choice. Why should this be the case? Is there a discernible line between direct or threatened physical or legal coercion and other forms of coercion? Is the former necessarily more severe than the latter?

5. The concurrence by Judge Dimock provides an alternative definition of involuntary servitude — what is it? Is Judge Dimock's definition broader or narrower than the majority's definition?

6. A number of other circuit courts ruled similarly to the Second Circuit in *Shackney*, finding that involuntary servitude required evidence of threatened or direct physical harm or legal restraint. *See United States v. Harris*, 701 F.2d 1095, 1100 (4th Cir. 1983) (relying on the employers' "reign of physical terror" over their farm laborers, which included beatings and positioning guards outside their doors at night, to sustain their convictions); *United States v. Booker*, 655 F.2d 562, 566–67 (4th Cir. 1981) (affirming convictions under § 1584, finding that beatings, assaults, and threats of the same were sufficient to categorize the employment as involuntary); *United States v. Bibbs*, 564 F.2d 1165, 1168 (5th Cir. 1977) (affirming defendants' convictions under § 1584 and defining coercion under the statute as any situation in which an employer places his employee "in such fear of physical harm that the victim is afraid to leave, regardless of the victim's opportunities for escape").

The following case illustrates a broader interpretation of § 1584, one that contemplated violations of involuntary servitude even in the absence of direct or threatened physical force or legal restraint.

U.S. v. MUSSRY
726 F.2d 1448 (9th Cir. 1984)

REINHARDT, CIRCUIT JUDGE.

The defendants were indicted on charges of holding individuals in peonage and involuntary servitude. The district court dismissed most of the counts. It concluded that those counts failed to sufficiently charge the defendants with a "holding" in involuntary servitude under 18 U.S.C. §§ 1581, 1583, and 1584 (1982) because they failed to allege that the defendants used or threatened to use law or force. We hold that a violation of the peonage and involuntary servitude statutes may occur through conduct other than the use or threatened use of law or force and that all of the counts are sufficient to charge the defendants with the crimes enumerated. Accordingly, we reverse.

The defendants are charged with violating 18 U.S.C. §§ 1581 (holding in peonage), 1583 (enticement into involuntary servitude), 1584 (holding in involuntary servitude), and 371 (conspiracy). The indictment and bill of particulars allege that the defendants unlawfully held poor, non-English speaking Indonesian servants against their will by enticing them to travel to the United States, paying them little money for their services, and withholding their passports and return airline tickets, while requiring them to work off, as servants, the debts resulting from the costs of their transportation. The government claims that the defendants' conduct effectively coerced the workers into remaining in their service and therefore constituted a holding in involuntary servitude.

According to the indictment and bill of particulars: The Indonesian servants were required to work up to 15 hours per day seven days a week. The defendants routinely denied all requests for vacations. Most of the servants cleaned the defendants' houses, cooked meals for the defendants, massaged them, and served them in a variety of other ways. Some did landscaping and gardening and engaged in household construction for the defendants. All of the servants lived in the defendants' homes.

The district court dismissed all counts under 18 U.S.C. §§ 1581, 1583, and 1584 which failed to allege that the defendants used, or threatened to use, law or force to hold the workers against their will. The district court also deleted all references to involuntary servitude, peonage, and slavery from the conspiracy count.

The government contends that the district court misconstrued the law when it concluded that a "holding" in involuntary servitude can be accomplished only through the use, or threatened use, of law or physical force. Accordingly, the government urges that the district court erred in holding that the indictment and bill of particulars are not sufficient to charge the defendants with violations of the statutes.

"Holding" in Involuntary Servitude

We have jurisdiction to review the dismissal of the substantive counts and the partial dismissal of the conspiracy count under 18 U.S.C. § 3731 (1982).

18 U.S.C. § 1584, in relevant part, provides that "[w]hoever knowingly and willfully holds to involuntary servitude . . . any other person for any term . . . shall be fined . . . or imprisoned . . . or both."[4] The question of what is sufficient to constitute a "holding" under 18 U.S.C. §§ 1581, 1583, and 1584 is a question of law that we address *de novo*. Because we are reviewing a dismissal of the charges, we need only decide whether the indictment and bill of particulars are sufficient to *charge* the defendants with a criminal offense, rather than whether sufficient facts have been adduced to *prove* that the defendants committed a crime.

The 13th amendment and its enforcing statutes are designed to apply to a variety of circumstances and conditions. Neither is limited to the classic form of slavery. Both apply to contemporary as well as to historic forms of involuntary servitude. The amendment and statutes were intended

> not merely to end slavery but to maintain a system of completely free and voluntary labor throughout the United States . . . . [I]n general, the defense against oppressive hours, pay, working conditions, or treatment is the right to change employers. When the master can compel and the laborer cannot escape the obligation to go on, there is no power below to redress and no incentive above to relieve a harsh overlordship or unwholesome conditions of work.

Pollock v. Williams, 322 U.S. 4, 17-18, 64 S.Ct. 792, 799, 88 L.Ed. 1095 (1944); Because of that purpose, it has long been recognized that "[t]he words involuntary servitude have a 'larger meaning than slavery.'" *Bailey v. Alabama*, 219 U.S. at 241, 31 S.Ct. at 151 (quoting *The Slaughter-House Cases*, 83 U.S. (16 Wall.) 36, 69, 21 L.Ed. 394 (1872)).

In deciding the issues before us, we must consider the realities of modern economic life: yesterday's slave may be today's migrant worker or domestic servant.[5]

---

[4] [FN 2] 18 U.S.C. § 1581, in relevant part, provides that "[w]hoever holds or returns any person to a condition of peonage . . . shall be fined . . . or imprisoned . . . or both."

18 U.S.C. § 1583, in relevant part, provides that "[w]hoever kidnaps or carries away any other person, with the intent that such other person be sold into involuntary servitude, or held as a slave . . . [s]hall be fined . . . or imprisoned . . . or both."

The government concedes that, because peonage is involuntary servitude for the purpose of liquidating a debt, it must establish a holding in involuntary servitude in order to charge the defendants with violating section 1581. The defendants' sole objection to the indictment and bill of particulars is that the government does not sufficiently charge them with a holding in involuntary servitude. Therefore, in reviewing the dismissal of all of the counts, we need only decide whether the indictment and bill of particulars are sufficient to charge the defendants with a holding in involuntary servitude.

Hereafter, we refer to all three statutes collectively as the involuntary servitude statutes.

[5] [FN 3] The most recent applications of the involuntary servitude statutes have involved migrant farm laborers. The reason is evident. As the Fourth Circuit noted, [t]he statutes [were designed to]

Today's involuntary servitor is not always black; he or she may just as well be Asian, Hispanic, or a member of some other minority group. Also, the methods of subjugating people's wills have changed from blatant slavery to more subtle, if equally effective, forms of coercion.

The question of what forms of coercion may serve as the basis for a finding of a violation of the involuntary servitude statutes is not a simple one. In *United States v. Shackney*, 333 F.2d 475, 487 (2d Cir.1964), the Second Circuit held that "[t]here must be 'law or force' that 'compel[led] performance or a continuance of the service'" in order for there to be such a finding. (*quoting Clyatt v. United States, 197 U.S. 207, 215-16, 25 S.Ct. 429, 430, 49 L.Ed. 726 (1905)*). Relying on *Shackney*, the defendants claim that, because the indictment and bill of particulars do not allege the use, or threatened use, of law or *physical* force, the district court was correct in dismissing the charges.

We agree with the defendants that the most reasonable interpretation of *Shackney* is that a holding in involuntary servitude may occur only when there is the use, or threatened use, of law or physical force. However, while a test that looks to the use of law or physical force attempts to draw a clear line between lawful and unlawful conduct and has the apparent advantage of simplicity, it is too narrow to fully implement the purpose of the 13th amendment and its enforcing statutes. That a broader test is required was recognized in Judge Dimock's concurring opinion:

> [The] meaning of "involuntary"... deal[s] only with the will of the servitor. That word raises the question of whether the will of the servitor has been subjugated, i.e., whether he has been rendered incapable of making a rational choice, and not the question of what were the means by which the servitude was imposed.... Where the subjugation of the will of the servant is so complete as to render him incapable of making a rational choice, the servitude is involuntary within the terms of the statute....

Shackney, 333 F.2d at 487-88 (Dimock, J., concurring).

The essence of a holding in involuntary servitude is the exercise of control by one individual over another so that the latter is coerced into laboring for the former. The use, or threatened use, of law or physical force is the most common method of forcing another to enter into or remain in a state of involuntary servitude. However, "the means or method of coercion" is not the determinative factor in deciding whether there is a holding. *Pierce v. United States*, 146 F.2d 84, 86 (5th Cir.1944).

Conduct other than the use, or threatened use, of law or physical force may, under some circumstances, have the same effect as the more traditional forms of coercion-or may even be more coercive; such conduct, therefore, may violate the 13th amendment and its enforcing statutes. The crucial factor is whether a person

---

protect[ ] persons similarly situated to the migrant workers of our own time. They were persons without property and without skills save those in tending the fields. With little education, little money and little hope, they easily fell prey to the tempting offers of "powerful and unscrupulous" individuals ... who would soon assert complete control over their lives.... [T]he statute must be read not only to render criminal the evil Congress sought to eradicate so long ago but, as well, its Twentieth Century counterpart. *United States v. Booker*, 655 F.2d 562, 566 (4th Cir.1981).

intends to and does coerce an individual into his service by subjugating the will of the other person. A holding in involuntary servitude occurs when an individual coerces another into his service by improper or wrongful conduct that is intended to cause, and does cause, the other person to believe that he or she has no alternative but to perform the labor.

In determining the question of involuntariness, the court should consider whether the challenged conduct would have had the claimed effect upon a reasonable person of the same general background and experience. Thus, the particular individual's background is relevant in deciding whether he or she was coerced into laboring for the defendant.

We recognize that economic necessity may force persons to accept jobs that they would prefer not to perform or to work for wages they would prefer not to work for. Such persons may feel coerced into laboring at those jobs. That coercion, however, results from societal conditions and not from the employer's conduct. Only improper or wrongful conduct on the part of an employer subjects him to prosecution. To illustrate this point further, an employer who truthfully informs an individual that there are no other available jobs in the market, merely provides an opportunity for a person to work for low wages, or simply takes advantage of circumstances created by others is not guilty of an offense. An employer who has not engaged in improper or wrongful conduct has not violated the law. It is the act of the employer, as well as the effect upon the worker, that the 13th amendment and its enforcing statutes address.

Here, the bill of particulars alleges that the Indonesian servants generally had almost no education, were unskilled, spoke little, if any, English, and had never been outside Indonesia. Although they received higher wages in the United States than they had received in Indonesia, their wages were far below the minimum wage. Most of the workers were in the United States illegally. They were brought here by the defendants. The defendants allegedly compelled the servants to surrender their passports and return airplane tickets, and required them to work in their employ in order to repay the costs of their transportation to the United States. In short, the government claims that [the defendants] knowingly placed [the Indonesian servants] in a strange country where [they] had no friends, had nowhere to go, did not speak English, had no work permit, social security card, or identification, no passport or return airline ticket to return to Indonesia, [were] here as . . . illegal alien[s] [sic], with no means by which to seek other employment, and with insufficient funds to break [their] contract[s] by paying back to defendant[s] the alleged expenses incurred in getting . . . here.

Given these allegations, and particularly those relating to the retention of the passports and airline tickets, we cannot (for purposes of a motion to dismiss the indictment) view the defendants as "innocent" parties to the traditional employer-employee relationship.[6]

---

[6] [FN 6] The defendants suggest that, because the Indonesian servants voluntarily contracted to work for higher wages than they earned in Indonesia, the allegations are not sufficient to charge a holding in involuntary servitude. We disagree. Even though a person may come to a job voluntarily, subsequent coerced service constitutes involuntary servitude. In addition, 18 U.S.C. § 1581, which

The indictment and bill of particulars allege conduct that, if proved, is sufficient to demonstrate improper or wrongful acts by the defendants that were intended to coerce the Indonesian servants into performing service for the defendants. The indictment sufficiently alleges that the conduct had the intended effect. Although the bill of particulars also indicates that some of the servants left the defendants' homes without apparent retaliation by the defendants, that is merely relevant evidence which could be introduced to rebut the government's case if the defendants claim that their conduct was not such as would have caused a reasonable person to become an involuntary servitor. The opportunity to escape, and even successful escape, is not enough in and of itself to preclude a finding that a person was held in involuntary servitude. All counts of the indictment, including those relating to the servants who left the defendants' homes, must stand.

The Vagueness Challenge

The defendants assert that if we conclude that a holding in involuntary servitude may be accomplished absent the use, or threatened use, of law or physical force, the statutes would be rendered so vague that they would violate the due process clause of the fourteenth amendment. We disagree.

In order to survive a vagueness challenge, "a penal statute [must] define the criminal offense with sufficient definiteness [so] that ordinary people can understand what conduct is prohibited and in a manner that does not encourage arbitrary and discriminatory enforcement." *Kolender v. Lawson*, 461 U.S. 352, 103 S.Ct. 1855, 1858, 75 L.Ed.2d 903 (1983) "[N]o individual [may] be forced to speculate, at peril of indictment, whether his conduct is prohibited." *Dunn v. United States*, 442 U.S. 100, 112, 99 S.Ct. 2190, 2197, 60 L.Ed.2d 743 (1979) (*citing Grayned v. City of Rockford, 408 U.S. 104, 108, 92 S.Ct. 2294, 2298, 33 L.Ed.2d 222 (1972)*).

However, "[i]t is well established that vagueness challenges to statutes which do not involve First Amendment freedoms must be examined in the light of the facts of the case at hand." *United States v. Mazurie*, 419 U.S. 544, 550, 95 S.Ct. 710, 714, 42 L.Ed.2d 706 (1975) (quoted in *United States v. Bohonus*, 628 F.2d 1167, 1173 (9th Cir.). We therefore need only decide whether the defendants had fair notice that the conduct that they allegedly engaged in was prohibited.

To give fair notice of what constitutes a criminal offense, a statute need not be drafted as precisely as it possibly could have been:

> [F]ew words possess the precision of mathematical symbols, most statutes must deal with untold and unforeseen variations in factual situations, and the practical necessities of discharging the business of government inevitably limit the specificity with which legislators can spell out prohibitions. Consequently, no more than a reasonable degree of certainty can be demanded.

Boyce Motor Lines, Inc. v. United States, 342 U.S. 337, 340, 72 S.Ct. 329, 330, 96 L.Ed. 367 (1952). Accordingly, a penal statute should not be so narrowly "construed

---

prohibits the holding of another in involuntary servitude for purposes of liquidating a debt, limits the ability to enforce a contract for labor.

III. INTERPRETING 18 U.S.C. § 1584

as to interfere with the federal government's ability to efficiently administer its criminal laws." *In re Subpoena of Persico*, 522 F.2d 41, 64 (2d Cir.1975) (quoted in *United States v. Prueitt*, 540 F.2d 995, 1002 (9th Cir.1976), *cert. denied sub nom., Temple v. United States, 429 U.S. 1063, 97 S.Ct. 790, 50 L.Ed.2d 780 (1977)).*

The language of 18 U.S.C. §§ 1581, 1583, and 1584 is not the most precise. But the breadth in that language was necessary in order to prohibit new forms of compulsory labor that might arise-rather than just the type that existed in the ante-bellum South. The language is not so opaque that ordinary people would not have notice that the conduct allegedly engaged in by the defendants was prohibited. Although close questions may arise in interpreting the language of a criminal statute, that alone does not render a statute unconstitutionally vague. Nor is the language so broad as to create the potential for arbitrary law enforcement.

"[T]he constitutionality of a vague statutory standard is closely related to whether that standard incorporates a requirement of *mens rea.*" *Colautti v. Franklin*, 439 U.S. 379, 395, 99 S.Ct. 675, 685, 58 L.Ed.2d 596 (1979). The fact that the statute requires that an individual must have acted with the intent of coercing another into his service goes a long way toward alleviating any vagueness problems. It is difficult to argue that a person did not have notice that certain conduct was illegal when the offense requires that the conduct be improper or wrongful and that the actor intend that the conduct have a coercive effect.

An inquiry into whether a "reasonable person" would be coerced into the service of another does not by itself create the potential for arbitrary and discriminatory enforcement. *See Coates v. City of Cincinnati, 402 U.S. 611, 613 & n. 3, 91 S.Ct. 1686, 1688 & n. 3, 29 L.Ed.2d 214 (1971).*

We expect that criminal prosecutions under the involuntary servitude and peonage statutes will occur only in rare circumstances. Here, the defendants had fair notice that their conduct, which, allegedly, was designed to have and did have an unlawful effect, was prohibited. The absence of a requirement that coercion be accomplished by means of physical force or law does not render the statutes unconstitutionally vague.

Conclusion

For purposes of 18 U.S.C. §§ 1581, 1583, and 1584, the use, or threatened use, of law or physical force is not an essential element of a charge of "holding" in involuntary servitude. Other forms of coercion may also result in a violation of the involuntary servitude statutes. The allegations that the defendants engaged in specific improper or wrongful conduct with the intent to coerce the Indonesian servants into performing services for them involuntarily, and that the conduct had the intended effect, are sufficient to preclude dismissal. All counts in the indictment must stand.

The order of the district court dismissing the substantive counts and partially dismissing the conspiracy count is reversed and the case is remanded.

Reversed and Remanded.

NOTES AND QUESTIONS

1. In contrast to the Second Circuit decision in *Shackney*, the Ninth Circuit in *Mussry* decided unanimously on a broader test for involuntary servitude. How did the *Mussry* court define involuntary servitude? How did this broader definition of involuntary servitude overcome the vagueness challenges by the defense? How did the court establish the defendant employer's intent to hold the workers in involuntary servitude?

2. The court notes that the domestic workers in *Mussry* were poor, non-English speaking and, uneducated Indonesian men and women. Did these characteristics help to support a finding of involuntary servitude?

3. Judge Reinhardt's opinion recognizes that "the realities of modern economic life" could compel labor by less overt methods. Thus, certain methods of non-physical coercion, such as cultural and linguistic isolation, could be just as powerful, if not more powerful, than physical or legal coercion to induce a worker to perform services involuntarily. Do you agree or disagree? What would Judge Friendly, who wrote the majority opinion in *Shackney*, think?

4. The *Mussry* court recognized that

> yesterday's slave may be today's migrant worker or domestic servant. Today's involuntary servitor is not always black; he or she may just as well be Asian, Hispanic, or a member of some other minority group. Also, the methods of subjugating people's wills have changed from blatant slavery to more subtle, if equally effective, forms of coercion. *Id.* at 1451–52.

Similarly, some commentators have discussed the "evolutive" nature of the Thirteenth Amendment and that it was intended to capture evolving forms of slavery. *See* Baher Azmy, *Unshackling the Thirteenth Amendment: Modern Slavery and a Reconstructed Civil Rights Agenda*, 71 FORDHAM L. REV. 981 (2002); Tobias Barrington Wolff, *The Thirteenth Amendment and Slavery in the Global Economy*, 102 COLUM. L. REV. 973 (2002).

5. The *Mussry* decision reinforces the Thirteenth Amendment origins of § 1584's prohibition of involuntary servitude suggesting that it was necessary to consider forms of non-physical coercion to ensure the Thirteenth Amendment's guarantee of a system of "free and voluntary labor." Did the Thirteenth Amendment prohibit slavery or advance a vision of free labor? Are they different or one and the same? For discussions of the Thirteenth Amendment, a free labor principle, see James Gray Pope, *Labor's Constitution of Freedom*, 106 YALE L.J. 941 (1997); Lea S. VanderVelde, *The Labor Vision of the Thirteenth Amendment*, 138 U. PA. L. REV. 437, 438 (1989) (finding evidence in the congressional record and the history of the Thirteenth Amendment that it stood for "a much broader idea of employee autonomy and independence").

6. In addition to *Mussry*, the Eleventh Circuit in *United States v. Warren*, 772 F.2d 827 (11th Cir. 1985), provided a broad interpretation of § 1584 in a case

involving the forced labor of migrant agricultural workers. While the facts of *Warren* included acts of direct physical violence upon the workers, the court held that "[v]arious forms of coercion may constitute a holding in involuntary servitude" and only that "[t]he use, or threatened use, of physical force to create a climate of fear is the most grotesque example of such coercion." The court discussed the recruitment and abuse of migrant laborers, including misrepresented opportunities of good jobs that later turn into compelled work through threats that "create a climate of fear which intimidates the workers and prevents them from leaving the camp." As in *Ingalls*, the court emphasized that chances of escape did not preclude a finding of involuntary servitude since the defendants' conduct had effectively placed the workers in such fear of harm that they were afraid to leave.

In 1988, the Supreme Court resolved the circuit-court split on the interpretation of § 1584 in the following case.

UNITED STATES v. KOZMINSKI
487 U.S. 931 (1988)

JUSTICE O'CONNOR delivered the opinion of the Court.

This case concerns the scope of two criminal statutes enacted by Congress to enforce the Thirteenth Amendment. Title 18 U.S.C. § 241 prohibits conspiracy to interfere with an individual's Thirteenth Amendment right to be free from "involuntary servitude." Title 18 U.S.C. § 1584 makes it a crime knowingly and willfully to hold another person "to involuntary servitude." We must determine the meaning of "involuntary servitude" under these two statutes.

I.

In 1983, two mentally retarded men were found laboring on a Chelsea, Michigan, dairy farm in poor health, in squalid conditions, and in relative isolation from the rest of society. The operators of the farm — Ike Kozminski, his wife Margarethe, and their son John — were charged with violating 18 U.S.C. § 241 by conspiring to "injure, oppress, threaten, or intimidate" the two men in the free exercise and enjoyment of their federal right to be free from involuntary servitude. The Kozminskis were also charged with knowingly holding, or aiding and abetting in the holding of, the two men to involuntary servitude in violation of 18 U.S.C. § 1584 and § 2. The case was tried before a jury in the United States District Court for the Eastern District of Michigan. The Government's evidence is summarized below.

The victims, Robert Fulmer and Louis Molitoris, have intelligence quotients of 67 and 60 respectively. Though chronologically in their 60's during the period in question, they viewed the world and responded to authority as would someone of 8 to 10 years. Margarethe Kozminski picked Fulmer up one evening in 1967 while he was walking down the road, and brought him to work at one of the Kozminski farms. He was working on another farm at the time, but Mrs. Kozminski simply left a note telling his former employer that he had gone. Molitoris was living on the streets of Ann Arbor, Michigan, in the early 1970's when Ike Kozminski brought him to work on the Chelsea farm. He had previously spent several years at a state mental hospital.

Fulmer and Molitoris worked on the Kozminskis' dairy farm seven days a week, often 17 hours a day, at first for $15 per week and eventually for no pay. The Kozminskis subjected the two men to physical and verbal abuse for failing to do their work and instructed herdsmen employed at the farm to do the same. The Kozminskis directed Fulmer and Molitoris not to leave the farm, and on several occasions when the men did leave, the Kozminskis or their employees brought the men back and discouraged them from leaving again. On one occasion, John Kozminski threatened Molitoris with institutionalization if he did not do as he was told.

The Kozminskis failed to provide Fulmer and Molitoris with adequate nutrition, housing, clothing, or medical care. They directed the two men not to talk to others and discouraged the men from contacting their relatives. At the same time, the Kozminskis discouraged relatives, neighbors, farm hands, and visitors from contacting Fulmer and Molitoris. Fulmer and Molitoris asked others for help in leaving the farm, and eventually a herdsman hired by the Kozminskis was concerned about the two men and notified county officials of their condition. County officials assisted Fulmer and Molitoris in leaving the farm and placed them in an adult foster care home.

In attempting to persuade the jury that the Kozminskis held their victims in involuntary servitude, the Government did not rely solely on evidence regarding their use or threatened use of physical force or the threat of institutionalization. Rather, the Government argued that the Kozminskis had used various coercive measures — including denial of pay, subjection to substandard living conditions, and isolation from others — to cause the victims to believe they had no alternative but to work on the farm. The Government argued that Fulmer and Molitoris were "psychological hostages" whom the Kozminskis had "brainwash[ed]" into serving them. Tr. 15, 23.

At the conclusion of the evidence, the District Court instructed the jurors that in order to convict the Kozminskis of conspiracy under § 241, they must find (1) the existence of a conspiracy including the Kozminskis, (2) that the purpose of the conspiracy was to injure, oppress, threaten, or intimidate a United States citizen in the free exercise or enjoyment of a federal right to be free from involuntary servitude, and (3) that one of the conspirators knowingly committed an overt act in furtherance of that purpose. The court further instructed the jury that § 1584 required the Government to prove (1) that the Kozminskis held the victims in involuntary servitude, (2) that they acted knowingly or willfully, and (3) that their actions were a necessary cause of the victims' decision to continue working for them. The court delivered the following instruction on the meaning of involuntary servitude under both statutes:

Involuntary servitude consists of two terms.

Involuntary means 'done contrary to or without choice' — 'compulsory' — 'not subject to control of the will.'

Servitude means '[a] condition in which a person lacks liberty especially to determine one's course of action or way of life' — 'slavery' — 'the state of being subject to a master.'

Involuntary servitude involves a condition of having some of the incidents of slavery.

It may include situations in which persons are forced to return to employment by law.

It may also include persons who are physically restrained by guards from leaving employment.

It may also include situations involving either physical and other coercion, or a combination thereof, used to detain persons in employment.

In other words, based on all the evidence it will be for you to determine if there was a means of compulsion used, sufficient in kind and degree, to subject a person having the same general station in life as the alleged victims to believe they had no reasonable means of escape and no choice except to remain in the service of the employer. App. to Pet. for Cert. 109a-110a.

So instructed, the jury found Ike and Margarethe Kozminski guilty of violating both statutes. John Kozminski was convicted only on the § 241 charge. Each of the Kozminskis was placed on probation for two years. In addition, Ike Kozminski was fined $20,000 and was ordered to pay $6,190.80 in restitution to each of the victims. John Kozminski was fined $10,000.

A divided panel of the Court of Appeals for the Sixth Circuit affirmed the convictions. After rehearing the case en banc, however, the Court of Appeals reversed the convictions and remanded the case for a new trial. The majority concluded that the District Court's definition of involuntary servitude, which would bring cases involving general psychological coercion within the reach of § 241 and § 1584, was too broad. The court held that involuntary servitude exists only when

> (a) the servant believes that he or she has no viable alternative but to perform service for the master (b) because of (1) the master's use or threatened use of physical force, or (2) the master's use or threatened use of state-imposed legal coercion (i. e., peonage), or (3) the master's use of fraud or deceit to obtain or maintain services where the servant is a minor, an immigrant or one who is mentally incompetent. 821 F. 2d, at 1192 (footnote omitted).

The dissenting judges charged that the majority had "rewritten rather than interpreted" § 1584. *Id.*, at 1213. They argued that involuntary servitude may arise from whatever means the defendant intentionally uses to subjugate the will of the victim so as to render the victim "'incapable of making a rational choice.'" *Id.*, at 1212-1213 (quoting *United States v. Shackney*, 333 F. 2d 475, 488 (CA2 1964) (Dimock, J., concurring)).

The Court of Appeals' definition of involuntary servitude conflicts with the definitions adopted by other Courts of Appeals. Writing for the Second Circuit in

United States v. Shackney, supra, Judge Friendly reasoned that

> a holding in involuntary servitude means to us action by the master causing the servant to have, or to believe he has, no way to avoid continued service or confinement, . . . not a situation where the servant knows he has a choice between continued service and freedom, even if the master has led him to believe that the choice may entail consequences that are exceedingly bad. *Id.,* at 486.

Accordingly, Judge Friendly concluded that § 1584 prohibits only "service compelled by law, by force or by the threat of continued confinement of some sort." *Id.,* at 487. The Ninth Circuit, in contrast, has not limited the reach of § 1584 to cases involving physical force or legal sanction, but has concluded that

> [a] holding in involuntary servitude occurs when an individual coerces another into his service by improper or wrongful conduct that is intended to cause, and does cause, the other person to believe that he or she has no alternative but to perform labor. *United States v. Mussry,* 726 F. 2d 1448, 1453 (1984).

We granted the Government's petition for a writ of certiorari, to resolve this conflict among the Courts of Appeals on the meaning of involuntary servitude for the purpose of criminal prosecution under § 241 and § 1584.

II.

Federal crimes are defined by Congress, and so long as Congress acts within its constitutional power in enacting a criminal statute, this Court must give effect to Congress' expressed intention concerning the scope of conduct prohibited. Congress' power to enforce the Thirteenth Amendment by enacting § 241 and § 1584 is clear and undisputed. The scope of conduct prohibited by these statutes is therefore a matter of statutory construction.

The Court of Appeals reached its conclusions regarding the meaning of involuntary servitude under both § 241 and § 1584 based solely on its analysis of the language and history of § 1584. A reading of these statutes, however, reveals an obvious difference between them. Unlike § 1584, which by its terms prohibits holding to involuntary servitude, § 241 prohibits conspiracies to interfere with rights secured "by the Constitution or laws of the United States," and thus incorporates the prohibition of involuntary servitude contained in the Thirteenth Amendment. The indictment in this case, which was read to the jury, specifically charged the Kozminskis with conspiring to interfere with the "right and privilege secured . . . by the Constitution and laws of the United States *to be free from involuntary servitude as provided by the Thirteenth Amendment of the United States Constitution.*" App. 177 (emphasis added). Thus, the indictment clearly specified a conspiracy to violate the Thirteenth Amendment. The indictment cannot be read to charge a conspiracy to violate § 1584 rather than the Thirteenth Amendment, because the criminal sanction imposed by § 1584 does not create any individual "right or privilege" as those words are used in § 241. The Government has not conceded that the definition of involuntary servitude as used in the Thirteenth Amendment is limited by the meaning of the same phrase in § 1584. To the contrary, the Government argues (1) that the Thirteenth Amendment should be broadly construed, and (2) that Congress did not intend § 1584 to have a narrower scope. Brief for United States 22-32. The District Court defined involuntary servitude broadly under both § 241 and § 1584. The Court of Appeals reversed the convictions under both counts because it concluded that the definition of involuntary servitude given for each count was erroneous. Since the proper interpretation of each statute is squarely before us, we construe each statute separately to ascertain the conduct it prohibits.

A.

Section 241 authorizes punishment when

> "two or more persons conspire to injure, oppress, threaten, or intimidate any citizen in the free exercise or enjoyment of any right or privilege secured to him by the Constitution or laws of the United States, or because of his having so exercised the same."

This Court interpreted the purpose and effect of § 241 over 20 years ago in United States v. Guest, and United States v. Price. Section 241 creates no substantive rights, but prohibits interference with rights established by the Federal Constitution or laws and by decisions interpreting them. Congress intended the statute to incorporate by reference a large body of potentially evolving federal law. This Court recognized, however, that a statute prescribing criminal punishment must be interpreted in a manner that provides a definite standard of guilt. The Court resolved the tension between these two propositions by construing § 241 to prohibit only intentional interference with rights made specific either by the express terms of the Federal Constitution or laws or by decisions interpreting them.

The Kozminskis were convicted under § 241 for conspiracy to interfere with the Thirteenth Amendment guarantee against involuntary servitude. Applying the analysis set out in Price and Guest, our task is to ascertain the precise definition of that crime by looking to the scope of the Thirteenth Amendment prohibition of involuntary servitude specified in our prior decisions.

The Thirteenth Amendment declares that "[n]either slavery nor involuntary servitude, except as a punishment for crime whereof the party shall have been duly convicted, shall exist within the United States, or any place subject to their jurisdiction." The Amendment is "self-executing without any ancillary legislation, so far as its terms are applicable to any existing state of circumstances," *Civil Rights Cases*, 109 U.S. 3, 20 (1883), and thus establishes a constitutional guarantee that is protected by § 241. The primary purpose of the Amendment was to abolish the institution of African slavery as it had existed in the United States at the time of the Civil War, but the Amendment was not limited to that purpose; the phrase "involuntary servitude" was intended to extend "to cover those forms of compulsory labor akin to African slavery which in practical operation would tend to produce like undesirable results." *Butler v. Perry*, 240 U.S. 328, 332 (1916).

While the general spirit of the phrase "involuntary servitude" is easily comprehended, the exact range of conditions it prohibits is harder to define. The express exception of involuntary servitude imposed as a punishment for crime provides some guidance. The fact that the drafters felt it necessary to exclude this situation indicates that they thought involuntary servitude includes at least situations in which the victim is compelled to work by law. Moreover, from the general intent to prohibit conditions "akin to African slavery," see *Butler v. Perry, supra*, at 332-333, as well as the fact that the Thirteenth Amendment extends beyond state action, we readily can deduce an intent to prohibit compulsion through physical coercion.

This judgment is confirmed when we turn to our previous decisions construing the Thirteenth Amendment. Looking behind the broad statements of purpose to the actual holdings, we find that in every case in which this Court has found a condition of involuntary servitude, the victim had no available choice but to work or be subject to legal sanction. In *Clyatt v. United States*, 197 U.S. 207 (1905), for example, the Court recognized that peonage — a condition in which the victim is coerced by threat of legal sanction to work off a debt to a master — is involuntary servitude under the Thirteenth Amendment. Similarly, in *United States v. Reynolds*, 235 U.S. 133 (1914), the Court held that "[c]ompulsion of . . . service by the constant fear of imprisonment under the criminal laws" violated "rights intended to be secured by the Thirteenth Amendment." *Id.*, at 146, 150. In that case the Court struck down a criminal surety system under which a person fined for a misdemeanor offense could contract to work for a surety who would, in turn, pay the convict's fine to the State. The critical feature of the system was that that breach of the labor contract by the convict was a crime. The convict was thus forced to work by threat of criminal sanction. The Court has also invalidated state laws subjecting debtors to prosecution and criminal punishment for failing to perform labor after receiving an advance payment. The laws at issue in these cases made failure to perform services for which money had been obtained prima facie evidence of intent to defraud. The Court reasoned that "the State could not avail itself of the sanction of the criminal law to supply the compulsion [to enforce labor] any more than it could use or authorize the use of physical force." [*Bailey v. Alabama*, 219 U.S. 219, 244 (1911).]

Our precedents reveal that not all situations in which labor is compelled by physical coercion or force of law violate the Thirteenth Amendment. By its terms the Amendment excludes involuntary servitude imposed as legal punishment for a crime. Similarly, the Court has recognized that the prohibition against involuntary servitude does not prevent the State or Federal Governments from compelling their citizens, by threat of criminal sanction, to perform certain civic duties. Moreover, in *Robertson v. Baldwin*, 165 U.S. 275 (1897), the Court observed that the Thirteenth Amendment was not intended to apply to "exceptional" cases well established in the common law at the time of the Thirteenth Amendment, such as "the right of parents and guardians to the custody of their minor children or wards," *id.*, at 282, or laws preventing sailors who contracted to work on vessels from deserting their ships.

Putting aside such exceptional circumstances, none of which are present in this case, our precedents clearly define a Thirteenth Amendment prohibition of involuntary servitude enforced by the use or threatened use of physical or legal coercion. The guarantee of freedom from involuntary servitude has never been interpreted specifically to prohibit compulsion of labor by other means, such as psychological coercion. We draw no conclusions from this historical survey about the potential scope of the Thirteenth Amendment. Viewing the Amendment, however, through the narrow window that is appropriate in applying § 241, it is clear that the Government cannot prove a conspiracy to violate rights secured by the Thirteenth Amendment without proving that the conspiracy involved the use or threatened use of physical or legal coercion.

B.

Section 1584 authorizes criminal punishment of

"[w]hoever knowingly and willfully holds to involuntary servitude or sells into any condition of involuntary servitude any other person for any term."

This is our first occasion to consider the reach of this statute. The pivotal phrase, "involuntary servitude," clearly was borrowed from the Thirteenth Amendment. Congress' use of the constitutional language in a statute enacted pursuant to its constitutional authority to enforce the Thirteenth Amendment guarantee makes the conclusion that Congress intended the phrase to have the same meaning in both places logical, if not inevitable. In the absence of any contrary indications, we therefore give effect to congressional intent by construing "involuntary servitude" in a way consistent with the understanding of the Thirteenth Amendment that prevailed at the time of § 1584's enactment. See *United States v. Shackney*, 333 F. 2d 475 (CA2 1964) (Friendly, J.).

Section 1584 was enacted as part of the 1948 revision to the Criminal Code. At that time, all of the Court's decisions identifying conditions of involuntary servitude had involved compulsion of services through the use or threatened use of physical or legal coercion. By employing the constitutional language, Congress apparently was focusing on the prohibition of comparable conditions.

The legislative history of § 1584 confirms this conclusion and undercuts the Government's claim that Congress had a broader concept of involuntary servitude in mind. No significant legislative history accompanies the 1948 enactment of § 1584; the statute was adopted as part of a general revision of the Criminal Code. The 1948 version of § 1584 was a consolidation, however, of two earlier statutes: the Slave Trade statute, as amended in 1909, formerly 18 U.S.C. § 423 (1940 ed.), and the 1874 Padrone statute, formerly 18 U.S.C. § 446 (1940 ed.). There are some indications that § 1584 was intended to have the same substantive reach as these statutes. Whether or not § 1584 was intended to track these earlier statutes exactly, it was most assuredly not intended to work a radical change in the law. We therefore review the legislative history of the Slave Trade statute and the Padrone statute to inform our construction of § 1584.

The original Slave Trade statute authorized punishment of persons who "hold, sell, or otherwise dispose of any . . . negro, mulatto, or person of colour, so brought [into the United States] as a slave, or to be held to service or labour." Act of Apr. 20, 1818, ch. 91, § 6, 3 Stat. 452. This statute was one of several measures passed in the early 19th century for the purpose of ending the African slave trade. A 1909 amendment removed the racial restriction, extending the statute to the holding of "any person" as a slave. This revision, however, left unchanged that portion of the statute describing the condition under which such persons were held. See 42 Cong. Rec. 1114 (1908). The Government attempts to draw a contrary conclusion from a comment by Senator Heyburn to the effect that the 1909 amendment was intended to protect vulnerable people who were brought into the United States for labor or for immoral purposes. *Id.*, at 1115. This comment is inconclusive, however. Other Senators expressly disagreed with the view that the elimination of the racial restriction changed the meaning of the word "slavery." *See id.*, at 1114-1115. Moreover, the 1909 reenactment of the Slave Trade statute was part of a general codification of the federal penal laws, which Senator Heyburn himself stated was "in no instance to change the practice of the law." *Id.*, at 2226. Thus, we conclude that nothing in the history of the Slave Trade statute suggests that it was intended to extend to conditions of servitude beyond those applied to slaves, i.e., physical or legal coercion.

The other precursor of § 1584, the Padrone statute, reflects a similarly limited scope. The "padrones" were men who took young boys away from their families in Italy, brought them to large cities in the United States, and put them to work as street musicians or beggars. Congress enacted the Padrone statute in 1874 "to prevent [this] practice of enslaving, buying, selling, or using Italian children." 2 Cong. Rec. 4443 (1874) (Rep. Cessna). The statute provided that

> whoever shall knowingly and willfully bring into the United States . . . any person inveigled or forcibly kidnapped in any other country, with intent to hold such person . . . in confinement or to any involuntary service, and whoever shall knowingly and willfully sell, or cause to be sold, into any condition of involuntary servitude, any other person for any term whatever, and every person who shall knowingly and willfully hold to involuntary service any person so sold and bought, shall be deemed guilty of a felony. Act of June 23, 1874, ch. 464. 18 Stat. 251.

This statute, too, was aimed only at compulsion of service through physical or legal coercion. To be sure, use of the term "inveigled" indicated that the statute was intended to protect persons brought into this country by other means. But the statute drew a careful distinction between the manner in which persons were brought into the United States and the conditions in which they were subsequently held, which are expressly identified as "confinement" or "involuntary servitude." Our conclusion that Congress believed these terms to be limited to situations involving physical or legal coercion is confirmed when we examine the actual physical conditions facing the victims of the padrone system. These young children were literally stranded in large, hostile cities in a foreign country. They were given no education or other assistance toward self-sufficiency. Without such assistance, without family, and without other sources of support, these children had no actual means of escaping the padrones' service; they had no choice but to work for their masters or risk physical harm. The padrones took advantage of the special vulnerabilities of their victims, placing them in situations where they were physically unable to leave.

The history of the Padrone statute reflects Congress' view that a victim's age or special vulnerability may be relevant in determining whether a particular type or a certain degree of physical or legal coercion is sufficient to hold that person to involuntary servitude. For example, a child who is told he can go home late at night in the dark through a strange area may be subject to physical coercion that results in his staying, although a competent adult plainly would not be. Similarly, it is possible that threatening an incompetent with institutionalization or an immigrant with deportation could constitute the threat of legal coercion that induces involuntary servitude, even though such a threat made to an adult citizen of normal intelligence would be too implausible to produce involuntary servitude. But the Padrone statute does not support the Court of Appeals' conclusion that involuntary servitude can exist absent the use or threatened use of physical or legal coercion to compel labor. Moreover, far from broadening the definition of involuntary servitude for immigrants, children, or mental incompetents, § 1584 eliminated any special distinction among, or protection of, special classes of victims.

Thus, the language and legislative history of § 1584 both indicate that its reach should be limited to cases involving the compulsion of services by the use or threatened use of physical or legal coercion. Congress chose to use the language of the Thirteenth Amendment in § 1584 and this was the scope of that constitutional provision at the time § 1584 was enacted.

C.

The Government has argued that we should adopt a broad construction of "involuntary servitude," which would prohibit the compulsion of services by any means that, from the victim's point of view, either leaves the victim with no tolerable alternative but to serve the defendant or deprives the victim of the power of choice. Under this interpretation, involuntary servitude would include compulsion through psychological coercion as well as almost any other type of speech or conduct intentionally employed to persuade a reluctant person to work.

This interpretation would appear to criminalize a broad range of day-to-day activity. For example, the Government conceded at oral argument that, under its interpretation, § 241 and § 1584 could be used to punish a parent who coerced an adult son or daughter into working in the family business by threatening withdrawal of affection. It has also been suggested that the Government's construction would cover a political leader who uses charisma to induce others to work without pay or a religious leader who obtains personal services by means of religious indoctrination. As these hypotheticals suggest, the Government's interpretation would delegate to prosecutors and juries the inherently legislative task of determining what type of coercive activities are so morally reprehensible that they should be punished as crimes. It would also subject individuals to the risk of arbitrary or discriminatory prosecution and conviction.

Moreover, as the Government would interpret the statutes, the type of coercion prohibited would depend entirely upon the victim's state of mind. Under such a view, the statutes would provide almost no objective indication of the conduct or condition they prohibit, and thus would fail to provide fair notice to ordinary people who are required to conform their conduct to the law. The Government argues that any such difficulties are eliminated by a requirement that the defendant harbor a specific intent to hold the victim in involuntary servitude. But in light of the Government's failure to give any objective content to its construction of the phrase "involuntary servitude," this specific intent requirement amounts to little more than an assurance that the defendant sought to do "an unknowable something." *Screws v. United States*, 325 U.S., at 105.

In short, we agree with Judge Friendly's observation that

> [t]he most ardent believer in civil rights legislation might not think that cause would be advanced by permitting the awful machinery of the criminal law to be brought into play whenever an employee asserts that his will to quit has been subdued by a threat which seriously affects his future welfare but as to which he still has a choice, however painful. *United States v. Schackney*, 333 F. 2d., at 487.

Accordingly, we conclude that Congress did not intend § 1584 to encompass the broad and undefined concept of involuntary servitude urged upon us by the Government.

Justice Brennan would hold that § 1584 prohibits not only the use or threatened use of physical or legal coercion, but also any means of coercion "that actually succeeds in reducing the victim to a condition of servitude resembling that in which slaves were held before the Civil War." This formulation would be useful if it were accompanied by a recognition that the use or threat of physical or legal coercion was a necessary incident of pre-Civil War slavery and thus of the "'slavelike' conditions of servitude Congress most clearly intended to eradicate." Instead, finding no objective factor to be necessary to a "slavelike condition," Justice Brennan would delegate to prosecutors and juries the task of determining what working conditions are so oppressive as to amount to involuntary servitude.

Such a definition of involuntary servitude is theoretically narrower than that advocated by the Government, but it suffers from the same flaws. The ambiguity in the phrase "slavelike conditions" is not merely a question of degree, but instead concerns the very nature of the conditions prohibited. Although we can be sure that Congress intended to prohibit "'slavelike' conditions of servitude," we have no indication that Congress thought that conditions maintained by means other than by the use or threatened use of physical or legal coercion were "slavelike." Whether other conditions are so intolerable that they, too, should be deemed to be involuntary is a value judgment that we think is best left for Congress.

Justice Stevens concludes that Congress intended to delegate to the Judiciary the inherently legislative task of defining "involuntary servitude" through case-by-case adjudication. Neither the language nor the legislative history of § 1584 provides an adequate basis for such a conclusion. Reference to the Sherman Act does not advance Justice Stevens' argument, for that Act does not authorize courts to develop standards for the imposition of criminal punishment. To the contrary, this Court determined that the objective standard to be used in deciding whether conduct violates the Sherman Act — the rule of reason — was evinced by the language and the legislative history of the Act. *Standard Oil Co. v. United States*, 221 U.S. 1, 60 (1911). It is one thing to recognize that some degree of uncertainty exists whenever judges and juries are called upon to apply substantive standards established by Congress; it would be quite another thing to tolerate the arbitrariness and unfairness of a legal system in which the judges would develop the standards for imposing criminal punishment on a case-by-case basis.

Sound principles of statutory construction lead us to reject the amorphous definitions of involuntary servitude proposed by the Government and by Justices Brennan and Stevens. By construing § 241 and § 1584 to prohibit only compulsion of services through physical or legal coercion, we adhere to the time-honored interpretive guideline that uncertainty concerning the ambit of criminal statutes should be resolved in favor of lenity. The purposes underlying the rule of lenity — to promote fair notice to those subject to the criminal laws, to minimize the risk of selective or arbitrary enforcement, and to maintain the proper balance between Congress, prosecutors, and courts — are certainly served by its application in this case.

III.

Absent change by Congress, we hold that, for purposes of criminal prosecution under § 241 or § 1584, the term "involuntary servitude" necessarily means a condition of servitude in which the victim is forced to work for the defendant by the use or threat of physical restraint or physical injury, or by the use or threat of coercion through law or the legal process. This definition encompasses those cases in which the defendant holds the victim in servitude by placing the victim in fear of such physical restraint or injury or legal coercion. Our holding does not imply that evidence of other means of coercion, or of poor working conditions, or of the victim's special vulnerabilities is irrelevant in a prosecution under these statutes. As we have indicated, the vulnerabilities of the victim are relevant in determining whether the physical or legal coercion or threats thereof could plausibly have compelled the victim to serve. In addition, a trial court could properly find that evidence of other means of coercion or of extremely poor working conditions is relevant to corroborate disputed evidence regarding the use or threatened use of physical or legal coercion, the defendant's intention in using such means, or the causal effect of such conduct. We hold only that the jury must be instructed that compulsion of services by the use or threatened use of physical or legal coercion is a necessary incident of a condition of involuntary servitude.

The District Court's instruction on involuntary servitude, which encompassed other means of coercion, may have caused the Kozminskis to be convicted for conduct that does not violate either statute. Accordingly, we agree with the Court of Appeals that the convictions must be reversed and the case remanded for a new trial.

We disagree with the Court of Appeals to the extent it determined that a defendant could violate § 241 or § 1584 by means other than the use or threatened use of physical or legal coercion where the victim is a minor, an immigrant, or one who is mentally incompetent. But because we believe the record contains sufficient evidence of physical or legal coercion to enable a jury to convict the Kozminskis even under the stricter standard of involuntary servitude that we announce today, we agree with the Court of Appeals that a judgment of acquittal is unwarranted.

The judgment of the Court of Appeals is affirmed, and the case is remanded for further proceedings consistent with this opinion.

It is so ordered.

JUSTICE BRENNAN, with whom JUSTICE MARSHALL JOINS, concurring in the judgment.

I agree with the Court that the construction given 18 U.S.C. § 1584 by the District Court and the Government either sweeps beyond the intent of Congress or fails to define the criminal conduct with sufficient specificity, and that a new trial under different instructions is therefore required. I cannot, however, square the Court's decision to add a physical or legal coercion limitation to the statute with either the statutory text or legislative history, and would adopt a different statutory construction that, I think, defines the crime with sufficient specificity but comports better with the evident intent of Congress.

I.

It is common ground among the parties and all the courts and Justices that have interpreted § 1584[7] that it encompasses, at a minimum, the compulsion of labor via the use or threat of physical or legal coercion. That much need not be belabored, for the use of the master's whip and the power of the State to compel one human to labor for another were clearly core elements of slavery that the Thirteenth Amendment and its statutory progeny intended to eliminate. As the Government points out, however, the language of both the Thirteenth Amendment and § 1584 simply prohibits "involuntary servitude" and contains no words limiting the prohibition to servitude compelled by particular methods. "[The Thirteenth] amendment denounces a status or condition, irrespective of the manner or authority by which it is created." *Clyatt v. United States*, 197 U.S. 207, 216 (1905).

If as a factual matter the use or threat of physical or legal coercion were the only methods by which a condition of involuntary servitude could be created, then the constitutional and statutory text might provide some support for the Court's conclusion. But the Court does not dispute that other methods can coerce involuntary labor — indeed it is precisely the broad range of nonphysical private activities capable of coercing labor that the Court cites as the basis for its vagueness concerns. I address those concerns below, but the point here is only that those concerns, however serious, are not textual concerns, for the text suggests no grounds for distinguishing among different means of coercing involuntary servitude. Nor do I know of any empirical grounds for assuming that involuntary

---

[7] [FN 1] The District Court instructed the jury to incorporate the definition of "involuntary servitude" from § 1584 into 18 U.S.C. § 241. The parties did not challenge this incorporation either below or in this Court, but rather argued only that the § 1584 definition the District Court incorporated was incorrect. I therefore believe it appropriate to address only the proper construction of § 1584. I note also that the § 241 count of the indictment charged a conspiracy to interfere with the "free exercise and enjoyment of the right and privilege secured to [the victims] by the Constitution *and laws* of the United States to be free from involuntary servitude as provided by the Thirteenth Amendment of the United States Constitution." App. 177 (emphasis added). Thus, the parties may have assumed that § 1584 is a "la[w] of the United States" specifying the content of the constitutional right to be free from involuntary servitude, [ ]and that accordingly if respondents' actions violated § 1584, the conspiracy to engage in those actions would necessarily constitute a violation of § 241. Such an assumption does not strike me as at all unreasonable. At any rate, for whatever reason the parties never raised the argument that the definition of "involuntary servitude" under § 241 should differ from that under § 1584, and I think it imprudent to decide that issue in the first instance in this Court and without briefing.

servitude can be coerced only by physical or legal means. To the contrary, it would seem that certain psychological, economic, and social means of coercion can be just as effective as physical or legal means, particularly where the victims are especially vulnerable, such as the mentally disabled victims in this case. Surely threats to burn down a person's home or business or to rape or kill a person's spouse or children can have greater coercive impact than the mere threat of a beating, yet the coercive impact of such threats turns not on any direct physical effect that would be felt by the laborer but on the psychological, emotional, social, or economic injury the laborer would suffer as a result of harm to his or her home, business, or loved ones. And drug addiction or the weakness resulting from a lack of food, sleep, or medical care can eliminate the will to resist as readily as the fear of a physical blow. Hypnosis, blackmail, fraud, deceit, and isolation are also illustrative methods — but it is unnecessary here to canvas the entire spectrum of nonphysical machinations by which humans coerce each other. It suffices to observe that one can imagine many situations in which nonphysical means of private coercion can subjugate the will of a servant.

Indeed, this case and others readily reveal that the typical techniques now used to hold persons in slavelike conditions are not limited to physical or legal means. The techniques in this case, for example, included disorienting the victims with frequent verbal abuse and complete authoritarian domination; inducing poor health by denying medical care and subjecting the victims to substandard food, clothing, and living conditions; working the victims from 3 a.m. to 8:30 p.m. with no days off, leaving them tired and without free time to seek alternative work; denying the victims any payment for their labor; and active efforts to isolate the victims from contact with outsiders who might help them.[8]

Without considering these techniques (and their particular effect on a mentally disabled person), one would hardly have a complete picture of whether the coercion inflicted on the victims was sufficient to make their servitude involuntary. Other involuntary servitude cases have also chronicled a variety of nonphysical and nonlegal means of coercion including trickery; isolation from friends, family, transportation or other sources of food, shelter, clothing, or jobs; denying pay or creating debt that is greater than the worker's income by charging exorbitant rates for food, shelter, or clothing; disorienting the victims by placing them in an unfamiliar environment, barraging them with orders, and controlling every detail of their lives; and weakening the victims with drugs, alcohol, or by lack of food, sleep, or proper medical care. See, e.g., *United States v. Warren*, 772 F. 2d 827 (CA11 1985); *United States v. Mussry*, 726 F. 2d 1448 (CA9 1984); *United States v. Ingalls*, 73 F. Supp. 76 (SD Cal. 1947). One presumes these methods of coercion would not

---

[8] [FN 3] Although not detailed by the Court, the Government introduced evidence that the Kozminskis (1) ripped a phone off the wall in the barn when one of the victims was caught using it, and did not simply "discourage" contact with relatives but falsely told relatives who asked to speak to the victims that the victims did not want to see them and falsely told the victims that their relatives were not interested in them; (2) falsely told neighbors that the victims were in their custody as wards of the State; and (3) refused to allow the victims to seek medical care, even when one was gored by a bull and the tip of the other's thumb was cut off (both victims eventually became very ill while serving the Kozminskis). The Court also neglects to mention that the Government has conceded that the victims were not forcibly held to work on the farm.

reappear with such depressing regularity if they were ineffective.

My reading of the statutory language as not limited to physical or legal coercion is strongly bolstered by the legislative history. Section 1584 was created out of the consolidation of the Slave Trade statute and the Padrone statute. I agree with the Government that the background of both those statutes suggests that Congress intended to protect persons subjected to involuntary servitude by forms of coercion more subtle than force. The Padrone statute, for example, was designed to outlaw what was known as the "padrone system" whereby padrones in Italy inveigled from their parents young boys whom the padrones then used without pay as beggars, bootblacks, or street musicians. Once in this country, without relatives to turn to, the children had little choice but to submit to the demands of those asserting authority over them, yet this form of coercion was deemed sufficient — without any evidence of physical or legal coercion — to hold the boys in "involuntary servitude." See *United States v. Ancarola*, 1 F. 676, 682-684 (CC SDNY 1880). Given the nature of the system the Padrone statute aimed to eliminate, the statute's use of the words "involuntary servitude" demonstrates not that the statute was "aimed only at compulsion of service through physical or legal coercion," but that Congress understood "involuntary servitude" to cover servitude compelled through other means of coercion. Indeed, the official title of the Padrone statute was "An act to protect persons of foreign birth against forcible constraint *or* involuntary servitude," Act of June 23, 1874, ch. 464, 18 Stat. 251 (emphasis added); 2 Cong. Rec. 4443 (1874), and the legislative history describes the statute as broadly "intended to prevent the practice of enslaving, buying, selling, *or using* Italian children," ibid. (Rep. Cessna) (emphasis added).

In light of this legislative history, the Court of Appeals below concluded that § 1584 must at least be construed to criminalize nonphysical means of private coercion used to obtain the services of particularly vulnerable victims such as minors, immigrants, or the mentally disabled. 821 F. 2d 1186, 1190-1192 (CA6 1987). I agree with the Court, however, that this creation of specially protected classes of victims is both textually unsupported and inconsistent with Congress' decision to eliminate such distinctions in enacting § 1584, and thus turn to the task of defining what I regard as the proper construction of the statute.

II.

Based on an analysis of the statutory language and legislative history similar to that set forth in Part I, the Government concludes that § 1584 criminalizes any conduct that intentionally coerces involuntary service. It is of course not easy to articulate when a person's actions are "involuntary." In some minimalist sense the laborer always has a choice no matter what the threat: the laborer can choose to work, or take a beating; work, or go to jail. We can all agree that these choices are so illegitimate that any decision to work is "involuntary." But other coercive choices, even if physical or legal in nature, might present closer questions. Happily, our task is not to resolve the philosophical meaning of free will, but to determine what coercion Congress would have regarded as sufficient to deem any resulting labor "involuntary" within the meaning of § 1584.

The Government concludes that the statute encompasses any coercion that either leaves the victim with "no tolerable alternative" but to serve the defendant or deprives the victim of "the capacity for rational calculation." As the Court notes, however, such a statutory construction potentially sweeps in a broad range of conduct that Congress could not have intended to criminalize. The Government attempts to avoid many of these problems by stressing that a victim does not lack "tolerable alternatives" when he simply has "no attractive or painless options"; the alternatives must be as bad for the victim as physical injury. One can, however, imagine troublesome applications of that test, such as the employer who coerces an employee to remain at her job by threatening her with bad recommendations if she leaves, the religious leader who admonishes his adherents that unless they work for the church they will rot in hell, or the husband who relegates his wife to years of housework by threatening to seek custody of the children if she leaves. Surely being unable to work in one's chosen field, suffering eternal damnation, or losing one's children can be far worse than taking a beating, but are all these instances of involuntary servitude? The difficulty with the Government's test is that although nonphysical forms of private coercion can indeed be as traumatic as physical force, their coercive impact is more highly individualized than that of physical and legal threats. I thus agree with the Court that criminal punishment cannot turn on a case-by-case assessment of whether the alternatives confronting an individual are sufficiently intolerable to render any continued service "involuntary." Such an approach either renders the test hopelessly subjective (if it relies on the victim's assessment of what is tolerable) or delegates open-ended authority to prosecutors and juries (if it relies on what a reasonable person would consider intolerable). Similarly, I agree with the Court that the difficulty of distinguishing the victim deprived of "the capacity for rational calculation" from the victim influenced by love, charisma, persuasive argument, or religious fervor is sufficiently great that the standard fails to define the criminal conduct with sufficient specificity.

The solution, however, lies not in ignoring those forms of coercion that are perhaps less universal in their effect than physical or legal coercion, but in focusing on the "slavelike" conditions of servitude Congress most clearly intended to eradicate. That the statute prohibits "involuntary servitude" rather than "involuntary service" provides no small insight into the central evil the statute unambiguously aimed to eliminate. For "servitude" generally denotes a relation of complete domination and lack of personal liberty resembling the conditions in which slaves were held prior to the Civil War. Thus, in 1910 and 1949, Webster's defined "servitude" as the "[c]ondition of a slave; slavery; serfdom; bondage; state of compulsory subjection to a master. . . . In French and English Colonies of the 17th and 18th centuries, the condition of transported or colonial laborers who, under contract or by custom, rendered service with temporary and limited loss of political and personal liberty." Webster's New International Dictionary of the English Language. And in 1913 and 1944 Funk and Wagnalls defined "servitude" as "[t]he condition of a slave; a state of subjection to a master or to arbitrary power of any kind" and cited the same colonial practice. Funk and Wagnalls, New Standard Dictionary of the English Language. Our cases have expressed the same understanding. "The word servitude is of larger meaning than slavery, as the latter is popularly understood in this country, and the obvious purpose was to forbid all shades and conditions of African slavery." *Slaughter-House Cases*, 16 Wall. 36, 69 (1873). "[T]he term involuntary servitude was intended to cover those forms of compulsory labor akin to African slavery which in practical operation would tend to produce like undesirable results." *Butler v. Perry*, 240 U.S. 328, 332 (1916).

I thus conclude that whatever irresolvable ambiguity there may be in determining (for forms of coercion less universal than physical or legal coercion) the degree of coercion Congress would have regarded as sufficient to render any resulting labor "involuntary" within the meaning of § 1584, Congress clearly intended to encompass coercion of any form that actually succeeds in reducing the victim to a condition of servitude resembling that in which slaves were held before the Civil War. While no one factor is dispositive, complete domination over all aspects of the victim's life, oppressive working and living conditions, and lack of pay or personal freedom are the hallmarks of that slavelike condition of servitude. Focusing on such a slavelike condition not only accords with the type of servitude Congress unambiguously intended to eliminate but also comports well with the policies behind the statute, for the concern that coerced laborers will be unable to relieve themselves from harsh work conditions by changing employers is less likely to be implicated if that laborer has a normal job with time off, personal freedom, and some money, and has contact with other people.

This focus on the actual conditions of servitude also provides an objective benchmark by which to judge either the "intolerability" of alternatives or the victim's capacity for "rational" thought: the alternatives can justifiably be deemed intolerable, or the victim can justifiably be deemed incapable of thinking rationally, if the victim actually felt compelled to live in a slavelike condition of servitude. True, in marginal cases it may well be difficult to determine whether a slavelike condition of servitude existed, but the ambiguity will be a matter of degree on a factual spectrum, not, as in the "no tolerable alternative" or "improper or wrongful conduct" tests, a matter of value on which one would expect wide variation among different prosecutors or jurors. The risk of selective or arbitrary enforcement is thus minimized, and the defendant who, as a result of intentional coercion, employs persons in conditions resembling slavery has fair notice regarding the applicability of the criminal laws. And many of the more troublesome applications of the Government's openended test would be avoided. For example, § 1584 would not encompass a claim that a regime of religious indoctrination psychologically coerced adherents to work for the church unless it could also be shown that the adherents worked in a slavelike condition of servitude and (given the intent requirement) that the religious indoctrination was not motivated by a desire to spread sincerely held religious beliefs but rather by the intent to coerce adherents to labor in a slavelike condition of servitude.

This restrictive construction of limiting the statute to slavelike conditions, although necessary to comply with the rule of lenity given the inherent ambiguity of the statute where the coercion is neither physical nor legal, is not, however, necessary where the defendant compels involuntary service by the use or threat of legal or physical means. Because the coercive impact of legal or physical coercion is less individualized than other forms of coercion, we need be less concerned about selective or arbitrary enforcement; and the defendant who intentionally employs physical or legal means to coerce labor has fair notice his acts may be criminal. The ambiguity justifying a restrictive reading is, moreover, not present when the means of coercion are those at the heart of the institution of slavery, and it seems clear that

Congress would have regarded a victim working under a legal or physical threat as serving in a condition of servitude, however limited in time or scope.

III.

In sum, I conclude that § 1584 reaches cases where the defendant intentionally coerced the victim's labor by the use or threat of legal or physical means or the defendant intentionally coerced the victim into a slavelike condition of servitude by other forms of coercion or by rendering the defendant incapable of rational choice. I therefore concur in the judgment.

JUSTICE STEVENS, with whom JUSTICE BLACKMUN JOINS, concurring in the judgment.

No matter what we write, this case must be remanded for a new trial because the Court of Appeals held that expert testimony was erroneously admitted and the Government has not asked us to review that holding. My colleagues' opinions attempting to formulate an all-encompassing definition of the term "involuntary servitude" demonstrate that this legislative task is not an easy one. They also persuade me that Congress probably intended the definition to be developed in the common-law tradition of case-by-case adjudication, much as the term "restraint of trade" has been construed in an equally vague criminal statute.

In rejecting an argument that the Sherman Act was unconstitutionally vague, Justice Holmes wrote:

> But apart from the common law as to restraint of trade thus taken up by the statute the law is full of instances where a man's fate depends on his estimating rightly, that is, as the jury subsequently estimates it, some matter of degree. If his judgment is wrong, not only may he incur a fine or a short imprisonment, as here; he may incur the penalty of death. 'An act causing death may be murder, manslaughter, or misadventure according to the degree of danger attending it' by common experience in the circumstances known to the actor. 'The very meaning of the fiction of implied malice in such cases at common law was, that a man might have to answer with his life for consequences which he neither intended nor foresaw.' Commonwealth v. Pierce, 138 Massachusetts, 165, 178 [(1884)]. Commonwealth v. Chance, 174 Massachusetts, 245, 252 [(1899)]. 'The criterion in such cases is to examine whether common social duty would, under the circumstances, have suggested a more circumspect conduct.' [1 E. East, Pleas of the Crown 262 (1803)]." *Nash v. United States*, 229 U.S. 373, 377 (1913).

A similar approach to the statute before us in this case was expressed by Judge Guy in his dissenting opinion in the Court of Appeals:

> It is clear that 18 U.S.C. § 1584 is lacking in definitional precision when it makes criminal the holding of one in 'involuntary servitude.' Whether this is the genius of this section or a deficiency to be cured by judicial legislation is not so clear. The majority apparently concludes it is a deficiency and

proceeds to cure it by substituting an arbitrary definition that raises more questions than it answers. In discussing this specific section, Judge Dimock, who concurred in Shackney, prophetically wrote:

" 'To have an arbitrary classification which will resolve with equal facility all of the cases that would arise under the statute is indeed a tempting prospect. It is much harder to have to work under a statute which will raise difficult questions in the borderline cases inevitable whenever the application of a statute depends upon an appraisal of the state of the human mind. 333 F. 2d at 488.

This is not an easy definitional question and it is one on which reasonable minds and federal circuits might differ. I write in dissent, however, primarily because I believe the majority has rewritten rather than interpreted 18 U.S.C. § 1584." 821 F. 2d 1186, 1212-1213 (CA6 1987)'".

I have a similar reaction to both Justice O'Connor's opinion for the Court and to Justice Brennan's concurrence. They are both unduly concerned with hypothetical cases that are not before the Court and that, indeed, are far removed from the facts of this case. Although these hypothetical cases present interesting and potentially difficult philosophical puzzles, I doubt that they have any significant relationship to real world decisions that will be faced by possible defendants, prosecutors, or jurors.

The text of § 1584 identifies three components of this criminal offense. First, the defendant must have acted "knowingly and willfully." As the District Court instructed the jury, the Government has the burden of proving that the defendants had "the specific intent" to commit the offense. Second, they must have imposed an "involuntary" condition upon their victims. As the District Court correctly stated, the term "involuntary" means " 'done contrary to or without choice'— 'compulsory' — 'not subject to control of the will.' " Third, the condition that must have been deliberately imposed on the victims against their will must have been a condition of "servitude." As the District Court explained, the term "servitude" means "'[a] condition in which a person lacks liberty especially to determine one's course of action or way of life' — 'slavery' — 'the state of being subject to a master.' " The judge further instructed the jury that the defendants could not be found guilty unless they had used "a means of compulsion . . . sufficient in kind and degree, to subject a person having the same general station in life as the alleged victims to believe they had no reasonable means of escape and no choice except to remain in the service of the employer."

I agree with Justice Brennan that the reach of the statute extends beyond compulsion that is accompanied by actual or threatened physical means or by the threat of legal action. The statute applies equally to "physical or mental restraint," cf. *Chatwin v. United States*, 326 U.S. 455, 460 (1946), and I would not distinguish between the two kinds of compulsion. However, unlike Justice Brennan, I would not impose the additional requirement in cases involving mental restraint that the victim be coerced into a "slavelike condition of servitude." To the extent the phrase "slavelike condition of servitude" simply mirrors the term "involuntary servitude," I see no reason for imposing this additional level of definitional complexity. In my view, individuals attempting to conform their conduct to the rule of law, prosecutors, and jurors are just as capable of understanding and applying the term "involuntary servitude" as they are of applying the concept of "slavelike condition." Moreover, to the extent "slavelike condition of servitude" means something less than "involuntary servitude," I see no basis for reading the statute more narrowly than written. Instead, in determining whether the victims' servitude was "involuntary," I would allow the jury to consider the "totality of the circumstances" just as we do when it is necessary to decide whether a custodial statement is voluntary or involuntary, see, e.g., *Mincey v. Arizona*, 437 U.S. 385, 401 (1978). In this case, however, the burden is of course on the Government to prove that the victims did not accept the terms of their existence voluntarily.

In sum, taking the evidence in the light most favorable to the Government, I am persuaded that the statute gave the defendants fair notice that their conduct was unlawful and that the trial court's instructions, read as a whole, adequately informed the jury as to the elements of the crime. I think they were fairly convicted.

Nevertheless, as I stated at the outset, I must concur in the Court's judgment.

NOTES AND QUESTIONS

1. In a five-four opinion authored by Justice O'Connor, the Supreme Court in *Kozminski* settled widespread judicial inconsistency by providing a final definition of involuntary servitude under § 1584. What was this definition and how did the Court derive it?

2. Similar to the Second Circuit in *Shackney*, the Supreme Court's definition of involuntary servitude was drawn in part from the historical roots of the Thirteenth Amendment and in part from § 1584's antecedents of chattel slavery and peonage. What sources of Thirteenth Amendment doctrine did the majority opinion draw from to determine the plain meaning of involuntary servitude?

3. The Court also addressed whether § 1584 had broadened the scope of involuntary servitude to reach forms of coercion beyond physical or legal coercion. Finding no indication of § 1584's scope in the statute's text, the Court considered legislative history to derive the statute's original intent. Section 1584 was a revision of the criminal code consolidating two earlier statutes, the Slave Trade statute of 1909 and the Padrone statute of 1874. These statutes are included in the appendix at end of this chapter. What did the Court surmise from its analysis of these statutes? How did these statutes inform the Court as to the range of coercion that constituted involuntary servitude?

4. What was the prosecution's chief argument? According to the government, what were the primary means of coercion that the Kozminskis used to hold Molitoris and Fulmer in involuntary servitude? Why did the majority reject the prosecution's argument?

5. Joined by Justice Marshall, the concurrence by Justice Brennan focused on the existence of "slave-like conditions" of the alleged servitude. According to Brennan, what was the range of coercive means sufficient for a finding of involuntary servitude? In a separate concurrence joined by Justice Blackmun, Justice Stevens proposed that Congress intended judicial interpretation of the

definition of involuntary servitude on a case-by-case basis. According to Stevens, how might a jury determine violations of involuntary servitude? Are either of the concurring approaches preferable to the majority's approach?

6. The majority relied on the rule of lenity to reject the arguments of the government and concurring Justices. The rule of lenity[9] or strict construction directs courts to interpret ambiguous criminal statutes conservatively "to promote fair notice to those subject to the criminal laws, to minimize the risk of selective or arbitrary enforcement, and to maintain the proper balance between Congress, prosecutors, and courts." *Kozminski*, 487 U.S. 931, 952 (1988). The rule of lenity has guided courts to construe vague criminal statutes in a manner favorable to criminal defendants. Rarely invoked in modern cases, courts reserve the rule for those situations in which "a reasonable doubt persists about a statute's intended scope even *after* resort to 'the language and structure, legislative history, and motivating policies' of the statute." *Moskal v. United States*, 498 U.S. 103, 108 (1990) (citing *Bifulco v. United States*, 447 U.S. 381, 387 (1980)). The *Kozminski* majority reasoned that any interpretation of involuntary servitude that encompassed psychological coercion would be too amorphous to be consistent with lenity's maxims of fair notice and legislative supremacy. According to the majority, how would the government's approach violate the principles of lenity? How would Brennan's concurrence? How would Stevens's concurrence?

7. Professor Kim has suggested that a closer reading of the *Kozminski* majority opinion reveals the Court's normative preference for evidence of physical coercion over psychological coercion to substantiate violations of involuntary servitude, based on the assumption that evidence of physical coercion is "objective" while psychological coercion is "subjective":

> The Court contended that the history of Thirteenth Amendment related enforcement clearly supported physical and legal coercion as criminal. Yet, the Court's perspective on physical coercion in the context of the Padrone system evidences little similarity to any conventional understanding of physical coercion. [I]nstead of hitting or beating as examples of physical coercion, the Court regarded the cultural isolation and economic dependence of the victims of the Padrone system as physical coercion . . . As Justice Brennan remarked in his concurrence, the majority's notion of physical coercion in the context of the Padrone system was tenuous at best. . . .
>
> Second, the Court argued that legislative supremacy demanded a narrow interpretation of § 1584. A more flexible reading of the statute invited prosecutors and courts to enforce actions beyond the statute's original intent. However, the Court failed to recognize that its own restrictive definition of involuntary servitude may have impeded legislative desires, rather than advanced them. Section 1584 was part of a general revision of

---

[9] *See* United States v. Bass, 404 U.S. 336, 348 (1971) (explaining that the rule of lenity provides "a fair warning . . . to the world in language that the common world will understand, of what the law intends to do if a certain line is passed") (quoting McBoyle v. United States, 283 U.S. 25, 27 (1931)).

the criminal code consolidating the Slave Trade statute of 1909 and the Padrone statute of 1874.

The consolidation simplified the language of the older statutes by eliminating the words bought, sold, or imported as a necessary element of involuntary servitude. The resulting broadly worded § 1584 may indicate congressional intent to prohibit *any* condition of involuntary servitude, regardless of the specific means that created it.

Moreover, given the diverse characteristics of modern-day involuntary servitude cases, the open-endedness of § 1584 may reflect legislative desire to delegate to the courts case-by-case adjudication to capture the evolving manifestations of involuntary servitude. As Justice Stevens remarked in his concurrence, the majority's preoccupation with difficult hypothetical cases posed uncertainties best resolved by the adjudication of real cases. No legal rule, no matter how strict, produced certainty, including the "seemingly unambiguous rule adopted by the majority."

As an abstract matter, the Court's resistance to broader interpretations of involuntary servitude is somewhat persuasive when considering its numerous hypothetical examples. For instance, the Court noted that it sought to prevent the criminalization of everyday activities, such as parents pressuring their adult children to work for the family business. However, the Court's affirmative creation of a bright-line rule limiting the scope of involuntary servitude to prevent these imaginary circumstances was inapt for the actual facts presented by *Kozminski*. As explained in Justice Brennan's concurrence, the majority opinion took lightly the psychological abuse that the workers underwent. According to Brennan, such conditions clearly indicated servitude of the kind that the Thirteenth Amendment prohibited regardless of the methods implemented.

According to the Court, any definition of involuntary servitude that included psychological coercion was improperly subjective and reliant on the victim's state of mind. Such subjective determinations opened the door for individuals to erroneously assert that their "'will to quit ha[d] been subdued by a threat which seriously affect[ed] his future welfare but as to which he still ha[d] a choice, however painful.'"

38 U. TOL. L. REV. 941 (2007) [internal citations omitted]. Do you find this analysis persuasive? Why or why not?

Although the *Kozminski* decision prescribed a narrow interpretation of involuntary servitude, it opened the possibility for more expansive definitions. First, the majority opinion recognized that the "special vulnerabilities" of victims such as their "minor" or "immigrant" status might be relevant to determining involuntary servitude violations. Second, the Court suggested that a broader view of the range of means sufficient to establish involuntary servitude would be appropriate given a subsequent congressional mandate.

Professor Kim explains the limits of the *Kozminski* definition of involuntary servitude and the push, within the Department of Justice, to encourage Congress to act to broaden its definition:

Beginning in the mid-1990s, momentum within the government spurred the development of new legislation addressing human trafficking. Reports from the Department of Justice to Congress emphasized the need for a new standard of coercion in the laws addressing modern-day involuntary servitude. In his testimony to Congress in 2000, then-Deputy Assistant Attorney General William Yeomans provided an example of a case that he considered forced labor, yet was unprosecutable under *Kozminski*. The case involved a domestic worker in a Midwestern private home. She worked sixteen hours per day, seven days a week and was provided with little food. Her employers threatened to have her deported when she complained about the working conditions. They prevented her from leaving the home unaccompanied by threatening that they would have her arrested. Yeomans explained that despite the worker's exploitation, "it is unlikely that we can prosecute this case because *psychological and economic coercion* was the method used to keep the victim trapped in a condition of involuntary servitude."

Yeomans emphasized the unique vulnerabilities of trafficked immigrants, who "are particularly susceptible to coercion because of their unfamiliarity with our language, laws and customs." He also recognized that means of coercion varied from case to case and that physical force would not be necessary in situations characterized by great differentials in power:

> We have also had situations where the use of physical force is really unnecessary. For instance, when people are brought in from societies with a caste system, and when lower-class people are used to accepting orders and they will accept those orders, under conditions that simply would not be tolerated in this country.

He contended that *Kozminski*'s narrow definition of involuntary servitude could not adequately reach the cases of subtle coercion that the Department of Justice was encountering with more frequency:

> [W]e must expand the types of coercion that can be used to demonstrate involuntary servitude and peonage under Federal law. One of the biggest enforcement hurdles we face is that the U.S. Supreme Court requires a showing that the defendant used actual force, threat of force, or threat of legal coercion to enslave the victim. As a result, Federal law suffers from gaps in coverage. Law enforcement cannot reach and prosecute those who intentionally use more subtle, but no less heinous, forms of coercion that wrongfully keep the victim from leaving his or her labor or service.

Kathleen Kim, *The Coercion of Trafficked Workers*, 96 IOWA L. REV. 409, 435–36 (2011) [internal citations omitted]; for statement by William Yeomans, see *International Trafficking in Women and Children: Hearings Before the Subcomm. on Near E. and S. Asian Affairs of the S. Comm. on Foreign Relations*, 106th Cong. 80 (2000) (statement of William R. Yeomans, Chief of Staff, Civil Rights Div., Dep't of Justice).

Congress heard the call for new legislation that could capture modern forms of slavery left unaddressed by the *Kozminski* definition of involuntary servitude. The Trafficking Victims Protection Act would soon be enacted.

Appendix to Chapter 3

The Slave Trade Statute
18 U.S.C. § 423 (1940 ed.)

Whoever brings within the jurisdiction of the United States, in any manner whatsoever, any person from any foreign kingdom or country, or from sea, or holds, sells, or otherwise disposes of, any person so brought in, as a slave, or to be held to service or labor, shall be fined not more than $10,000, one-half to the use of the United States and the other half to the use of the party who prosecutes the indictment to effect; and moreover, shall be imprisoned for not more than seven years. (Mar. 4, 1909, ch. 321 § 248, 35 Stat. 1139)

Act of Apr. 20, 1818, ch. 91, 3 Stat. 450–53.

Chap. XCI — *An Act in addition to "An act to prohibit the introduction (importation) of slaves into any port or place within the jurisdiction of the United States, from and after the first day of January, in the year of our Lord on thousand eight hundred and eight," and to repeal certain parts of the same.*

Be it enacted by the Senate and House of Representatives of the United States of America, in Congress assembled, That from and after the passing of this act, it shall not be lawful to import or bring, in any manner whatsoever, into the United States, or territories thereof, from any foreign kingdom, place, or country, any negro, mulatto, or person of colour[sic], with intent to hold, sell, or dispose of, any such negro, mulatto, or person of colour[sic], as a slave, or to be held to service or labour[sic]; and any ship, vessel, or other water craft, employed in any importation as aforesaid, shall be liable to seizure, prosecution, and forfeiture, in any district in which it may be found; one half thereof to the use of the United States, and the other half to the use of him or them who shall prosecute the same to effect.

Sec 2. *And be it further enacted,* That no citizen or citizens of the United States, or any other person or persons, shall, after the passing of this act, as aforesaid, for himself, themselves, or any other person or persons whatsoever, either as master, factor, or owner, build, fit equip, load, or otherwise prepare, any ship or vessel, in any port or place within the jurisdiction of the United States, nor cause any such ship or vessel to sail from any port or place whatsoever, within the jurisdiction of the same, for the purpose of procuring any negro, mulatto, or person of colour[sic], from any foreign kingdom, place, or country, to be transported to any port or place whatsoever, to be held, sold, or otherwise disposed of, as slaves, or to be held to service or labour[sic]; and if any ship or vessel shall be so built, fitted out, equipped, laden, or otherwise prepared, for the purpose aforesaid, every such ship or vessel, her tackle, apparel, furniture, and lading shall be forfeited, one moiety to the use of the United States, and the other to the use of the person or persons who shall sue for said forfeiture, and prosecute the same to effect; and such ship or vessel shall be liable to be seized prosecuted, and condemned, in any court of the United States having competent jurisdiction.

Sec 3. *And be it further enacted,* That every person or persons so building, fitting out, equipping, loading, or otherwise preparing, or sending away, or causing any of the acts aforesaid to be done, with intent to employ such ship or vessel in such trade or business, after the passing of this act, contrary to the true intent and meaning thereof, or who shall, in any wise, be aiding or abetting therein, shall, severally, on conviction thereof, by due course of law, forfeit and pay a sum of not exceeding five thousand dollars, nor less than one thousand dollars, one moiety to the use of the United States, and the other to the use of the person or persons who shall sue for such forfeiture and prosecute the same to effect, and shall moreover be imprisoned for a term not exceeding seven years, nor less than three years.

Sec 4. *And be it further enacted*, That if any citizen or citizens of the United States, or other person or persons resident within the jurisdiction of the same, shall, from and after the passing of this act, take on board, receive, or transport, from any of the coasts or kingdoms of Africa, or from any other foreign kingdom, place, or country, or from sea, any negro, mulatto, or person of colour[sic], not being an inhabitant, nor held to service by the laws of either of the states or territories of the United States, and in any ship, vessel, boat, or other water craft, for the purpose of holding, selling, or otherwise disposing of, such person as a slave, or to be held to service or labour[sic], or be aiding or abetting therein, every such person or persons, so offending, shall, on conviction, by due course of law, severally forfeit and pay a sum not exceeding five thousand, nor less than one thousand dollars, one moiety to the use of the United States, and the other to the use of the person or persons who shall sue for such forfeiture and prosecute the same to effect; and, moreover, shall suffer imprisonment, for a term not exceeding seven years nor less than three years; and every ship or vessel, boat, or other water craft, on which such negro, mulatto, or person of colour[sic], shall have been taken on board, received, or transported, as aforesaid, her tackle, apparel, and furniture, and the goods and effects which shall be found on board the same, or shall have been imported therein in the same voyage, shall be forfeited, one moiety to the use of the United States, and the other to the use of the person or persons who shall sue for and prosecute the same to effect; and every such ship or vessel shall be liable to be seized, prosecuted, and condemned, in any court of the United States having competent jurisdiction.

Sec 5. *And be it further enacted*, That neither the importer or the importees, nor any person or persons claiming from or under him or them, shall hold any right, interest, or title whatsoever, in or to any negro, mulatto, or person of colour[sic], nor to the service or labour[sic] thereof who may be imported or brought into the United States or the territories thereof in violation of the provisions of this act, but the same shall remain subject to any regulations, not contravening said provisions, which the legislatures of the several states or territories may at any time heretofore have made, or hereafter may make, for disposing of any such negro, mulatto, or person of colour[sic].

Sec 6. *And be it further enacted*, That if any person or persons whatsoever shall, from and after the passing of this act, bring within the jurisdiction of the United States, in any manner whatsoever, any negro, mulatto, or person of colour[sic], from any foreign kingdom, place, or country, or from sea, or shall hold, sell, or otherwise dispose of, any such negro, mulatto, or person of colour[sic], so brought in, as a slave, or to be held to service or labour[sic], or be in any wise aiding or abetting therein, every person so offending shall, on conviction thereof by due course of law, forfeit and pay, for every such offence, a sum not exceeding ten thousand nor less than one thousand dollars, one moiety to the use of the United States, and the other to the use of the person or persons who shall sue for such forfeiture, and prosecute the same to effect; and, moreover, shall suffer imprisonment, for a term not exceeding seven years nor less than three years.

Sec 7. *And be it further enacted*, That if any person or persons whatsoever shall hold, purchase, sell, or otherwise dispose of, any negro, mulatto, or person of colour[sic], for a slave or to be held to service or labour[sic], who shall have been imported or brought, in any way, from any foreign kingdom, place, or country, or from the dominions of any foreign state immediately adjoining to the United States, into any port or place within the jurisdiction of the United States, from and after the passing of this act, every person so offending, and every person aiding or abetting therein, shall severally forfeit and pay, for every negro, mulatto, or person of colour[sic], so held, purchased, sold, or disposed of, one thousand dollars, one moiety to the use of the United States, and the other to the use of the person or persons who may sue for such forfeiture, and prosecute the same to effect, and to stand committed until the said forfeiture be paid: *Provided*, That the aforesaid forfeiture shall not extend to the seller or purchaser of any negro, mulatto, or person of colour[sic], who may be sold or disposed of in virtue of any regulations which have been heretofore, or shall hereafter be, lawfully made by any legislature of any state or territory in pursuance of this act and the constitution of the United States.

Sec 8. *And be it further enacted*, That in all prosecutions under this act, the defendant or defendants shall be holden[sic] to prove that the negro, mulatto, or person of colour[sic], which he or they shall be charged with having brought into the United States, or with purchasing, holding, selling, or otherwise disposing of, and which, according to the evidence in such case, the said defendant or defendants shall have brought in aforesaid, or otherwise disposed of, was brought into the United States at least five years previous to the commencement of such prosecution, or was not brought in, holden[sic], purchased, or otherwise disposed of, contrary to the provisions of this act; and in failure thereof, the said defendant or defendants shall be adjudged guilty of the offence of which he or they may stand accused.

Sec. 9. *And be it further enacted*, That any prosecution, information, or action, may be sustained, for any offence under this act, at any time within five years after such offence shall have been committed, any law to the contrary notwithstanding.

Sec. 10. *And be it further enacted*, That the first six sections of the act to which this is in addition, shall be and the same are hereby repealed: *Provided*, That all offences committed under the said sections of the act aforesaid, before the passing of this act, shall be prosecuted and punished, and any forfeitures which have been incurred under the same shall be recovered and distributed, as if this act had not been passed.

[1909 Amendment removed the racial restriction, extending the statute to the holding of "any person" as a slave.

42 Cong. Rec. 1114 (1908); *U.S. v. Kozminski*, 487 U.S. 931, 946 (1988).]

Padrone Statute

formerly — 18 U.S.C. § 446 (1940)

§ 446 (Criminal Code, Section 271.) Bringing kidnaped[sic] person into United States.

Whoever shall knowingly and willfully bring into the United States or any place subject to the jurisdiction thereof, any person inveigled or forcibly kidnaped[sic] in confinement or to any involuntary servitude; or whoever shall knowingly and willfully sell or cause to be sold, into any condition of involuntary servitude, any other person for any term whatever; or whoever shall knowingly and willfully hold to involuntary servitude any person so brought or sold, shall be fined not more than $5,000 and imprisoned not more than five years. (Mar. 4, 1909, ch. 321, § 271, 35 Stat. 1142)

Act of June 23, 1874, ch. 464, 18 Stat. 251.

An Act to protect persons of foreign birth against forcible constraint or involuntary servitude.

Be it enacted by the Senate and House of Representatives of the United States of America in Congress assembled, That whoever shall knowingly and wilfully[sic] bring into the United States, or the Territories thereof, any person inveigled or forcibly kidnapped in any other country, with intent to hold such person so inveigled or kidnapped in confinement or to any involuntary service, and whoever shall knowingly and wilfully[sic] sell, or cause to be sold, into any condition of involuntary servitude, any other person for any term whatever, and every person who shall knowingly and wilfully[sic] hold to involuntary service any person so sold and bought, shall be deemed guilty of a felony, and, on conviction thereof be imprisoned for a term not exceeding five years and pay a fine not exceeding five thousand dollars.

Sec. 2. That every person who shall be accessory to any of the felonies herein declared, either before, or after the fact, shall be deemed guilty of a felony, and on conviction thereof be imprisoned for a term not exceeding five years and pay a fine not exceeding one thousand dollars.

Chapter 4

IMMIGRATION STATUTES AND THE MANN ACT

Although legislation using the phrase "human trafficking" would not be enacted in the United States until 2000, concern about a subset of human trafficking cases — those involving compelled prostitution — was present in the passage of immigration laws in the late 1800s and was the central inspiration for the passage of the Mann Act in 1910.

I. IMMIGRATION STATUTES

Early attempts to regulate what, in certain cases, would now be called human trafficking focused on the transportation of foreign national women into the United States for prostitution.

Passed on March 3, 1875, the Page Act, ch. 141, 18 Stat. 477, prohibited the importation of "alien" women from Asia for purposes of prostitution. This Act was superseded by the 1903 Immigration Act, ch. 1012, 32 Stat. 1213 and 1907 Immigration Act, ch. 1134, 34 Stat. 898. The 1907 Immigration Act is excerpted below. The major changes made by the 1903 and 1907 Immigration Acts to the Page Act are discussed after the excerpt.

> SEC. 3. That the importation into the United States of any alien woman or girl for the purpose of prostitution, or for any other immoral purpose, is hereby forbidden; and whoever shall, directly or indirectly, import or attempt to import, into the United States, any alien woman or girl for the purpose of prostitution, or for any other immoral purpose, or whoever shall hold or attempt to hold any alien woman or girl for any such purpose in pursuance of such illegal importation, or whoever shall keep, maintain, control, support, or harbor in any house or other place, for the purpose of prostitution, or for any other immoral purpose, any alien woman or girl, within three years after she shall have entered the United States, shall in every such case, be deemed guilty of a felony, and on conviction thereof be imprisoned not more than five years and pay a fine of not more than five thousand dollars; and any alien woman or girl who shall be found an inmate of a house of prostitution or practicing prostitution, at any time within three years after she shall have entered the United States, shall be deemed to be unlawfully within the United States and shall be deported as provided by sections twenty and twenty-one of this act.

In 1875, the Page Act only regulated the importation of women; it did not mention girls. It also had a *mens rea* requirement of "knowingly and willfully." But by 1903, this requirement was eliminated. In its place came a more general prohibition against importing, holding, or attempting to hold "any woman or girl

. . . in pursuance of such illegal importation," regardless of whether you did so knowingly or willingly.

In this way, the amendments leading up to and including the 1907 amendments began to signal what was to come three years later in the Mann Act. In addition to forbidding the importation of "alien" women or girls for the purpose of prostitution, these amendments also criminalized the importation of these individuals for "any other immoral purpose." Moreover, they established, for the first time, that individuals who were involved only indirectly in these illegal acts could be charged. And they also created a brand new provision covering those who "keep, maintain, control, support, or harbor in any house or other place, for the purpose of prostitution or for any other immoral purpose, any alien woman or girl."

Such innovations are a significant change from the original focus of the 1875 Act, which had restricted its scope to individuals directly involved in importing foreign women for the purpose of prostitution.

NOTES AND QUESTIONS

1. In *Keller v. United States*, 213 U.S. 138 (1909), the plaintiffs were convicted of harboring an alien for the purpose of prostitution under the following section of the 1907 Immigration Act statute:

> [Criminal liability is assigned to] whoever shall keep, maintain, control, support, or harbor in any house or other place, for the purpose of prostitution, or for any other immoral purpose any alien woman or girl, within three years after she shall have entered the United States.

This section of the 1907 Immigration Act was found unconstitutional because it criminalized acts happening solely within a state. The Court ruled that Congress could not regulate such acts. In dicta the Court noted the narrowness of its holding and signaled the future focus of congressional lawmaking on involuntary prostitution:

> It is unnecessary to determine how far Congress may go in legislating with respect to the conduct of an alien while residing here, for there is no charge against one; nor to prescribe the extent of its power in punishing wrongs done to an alien, for there is neither charge nor proof of any such wrong. So far as the statute or the indictment requires, or the testimony shows, she was voluntarily living the life of a prostitute, and was only furnished a place by the defendants to follow her degraded life. While the keeping of a house of ill-fame is offensive to the moral sense, yet that fact must not close the eye to the question whether the power to punish therefor is delegated to Congress or is reserved to the state. Jurisdiction over such an offense comes within the accepted definition of the police power. Speaking generally, that power is reserved to the states, for there is in the Constitution no grant thereof to Congress.

Keller, 213 U.S. at 144.

2. The 1907 amendments to the Immigration Act included a section authorizing the deportation of any alien woman or girl "found [to be] an inmate of a house of

prostitution or practicing prostitution, at any time within three years after she . . . entered the United States." Modern day immigration law still reflects this focus today.[1]

II. THE MANN ACT

A. Legislative History

Ostensibly immigration laws, the Page Act, and the 1903 and 1907 Immigration Acts also involved issues of morality — issues Congress took up more directly when it passed the Mann Act in 1910. This Act grew out of concern for a phenomenon known as "white slavery." (Indeed, the Mann Act was originally called the "White Slave Act.")

Unfortunately the term "white slavery" suffered from a proliferation of meanings. Some people used the term to mean "coerced, imprisoned women"; others used it to mean "psychological bondage"; still others used it to mean "purely voluntary prostitution."[2] Because of this confusion, the scope of "white slavery" prior to the passage of the Mann Act is hard to estimate.[3] To make matters worse, advocates combating the white slave trade seldom cited concrete numbers when discussing the trade itself. Instead these advocates relied heavily on anecdotal evidence, individual stories, and approximate estimates of scale based on interviews with victims.

What is clear, however, is that members of Congress took up the issue with moral fervor. For example, during a debate of a proposed amendment to the 1907 Immigration Act on the floor of the House of Representatives, Representative Oscar Gillespie of Texas condemned this practice as the "meanest, blackest crime that was ever instilled into the human heart" adding that it was the work of "the devil himself." Other members of Congress echoed Gillespie's sentiment, including both Representative William Cox of Indiana, who railed against white slavery as "this evil traffic," and Representative James Mann of Illinois, the congressman for whom the Mann Act was eventually named. In Mann's view, "all of the horrors

---

[1] Foreign nationals who engage in prostitution may be deported under two different grounds. *See* Immigration and Nationality Act § 237(a) (1)(A), (a)(2)(A)(i)(I), 8 U.S.C. § 1227(a)(1)(A), (a)(2)(A)(i)(I) (2012).

[2] *See* DAVID J. LANGUM, CROSSING OVER THE LINE: LEGISLATING MORALITY AND THE MANN ACT 34 (John C. Fout ed., 1994) (citing Daniel J. Leab, *Women and the Mann Act*, 21 AMERIKASTUDIEN/AM. STUD. 55, 57 (1976) and Roy Lubove, *The Progressives and the Prostitute*, 34 HISTORIAN 308, 314–15 (1962)).

[3] The estimates for females coerced into prostitution vary widely. One scholar estimates that as little as 5% of prostitutes were coerced. *See* WALTER C. RECKLESS, VICE IN CHICAGO 42, 45 (1969) (arguing from a Chicago case study that there was very little evidence for an organized system of men trapping and selling women into literal captive sexual slavery). Apart from this estimate, however, most writers and scholars at the time spoke largely in terms of numbers and generalities as opposed to percentages. In James Mann's 1909 Report from the House of Representatives, Representative Mann writes of "panderers and procurers . . . compelling thousands of women and girls against their will and desire to enter and continue in the life of prostitution." The White Slavery problem is described as one of "widespread dimensions," which is "systematic and extensive." Mann claimed that one Chicago syndicate imported an average of 2,000 women a year, though more global estimates were not offered. JAMES MANN, WHITE SLAVE TRAFFIC, H.R. Rep. No. 61-47, at 10–12 (1909).

which have ever been urged, either truthfully or fancifully, against the black-slave traffic pale into insignificance as compared with the horrors of the so-called white slave traffic."[4]

All of these statements suggest that what lawmakers during the time of the Mann Act lacked in definitional precision and empirical data they made up for in righteous indignation. This combination of incomplete evidence and outrage is still with us today, as we will see in the comments made by some members of Congress surrounding the passage of the Trafficking Victims Protection Act. (*See* Chapter 5)

B. The Mann Act as Passed in 1910

The debate surrounding the passage of the Mann Act focused on the coerced prostitution of white women and girls. But the language of the Act itself allowed for a much wider application in that the Act criminalized the transportation of women or girls for the "purpose of prostitution or debauchery, *or for any other immoral purpose*" (emphasis added). This language echoes the 1907 Immigration Act by referencing only women and girls and by including immoral purposes in its scope. Relevant excerpts from the White-Slave Traffic (Mann) Act, ch. 395, 36 Stat. 825, as passed by the Sixty-First Congress on June 25, 1910:

> CHAP. 395 — An Act to further regulate interstate and foreign commerce by prohibiting the transportation therein for immoral purposes of women and girls, and for other purposes.
>
> SEC. 2. That any person who shall knowingly transport or cause to be transported, or aid or assist in obtaining transportation for, or in transporting, in interstate or foreign commerce, or in any Territory or in the District of Columbia, any woman or girl for the purpose of prostitution or debauchery, or for any other immoral purpose, or with the intent and purpose to induce, entice, or compel such woman or girl to become a prostitute or to give herself up to debauchery, or to engage in any other immoral practice; or who shall knowingly procure or obtain, or cause to be procured or obtained, or aid or assist in procuring or obtaining, any ticket or tickets, or any form of transportation or evidence of the right thereto, to be used by any woman or girl in interstate or foreign commerce, or in any Territory or the District of Columbia, in going to any place for the purpose

---

[4] It is important to note that the concern over the White Slave Traffic Act was exactly and primarily that — a concern over *white* slaves. Representative Mann's comments to the House of Representatives are not unique in their invocation of comparative racial slavery. Strains of racial anxiety underlying the issue of "white slavery" are clearly visible in the congressional record, as evidenced by statements of lawmakers of the day. During one floor debate, Representative Russell quoted from an article on the white slave trade, in which the author claimed that "some weeks ago a negro who signed himself 'John Frankling' wrote me . . . a letter in which he stated that he had a white wife whom he had bought out of a group of twenty-five that were offered for sale in Chicago, and that she was the third white 'wife' that he had purchased. Upon making inquiry of prominent men in Chicago, I was told that there was reason to believe that the negro had told the truth." 45 Cong. Rec. 821 (1910) (statement of Representative Russell). Similarly, Representative Cox remarked during debate that "It is indeed appalling to know that, in this day of enlightenment, we have had for several years a species of slavery a thousand times worse and more degrading in its consequences and effects upon humanity than any species of human slavery that ever existed in this country." 45 Cong. Rec. 547 (1910) (statement of Representative Cox).

of prostitution or debauchery, or for any other immoral purpose, or with the intent or purpose on the part of such person to induce, entice, or compel her to give herself up to the practice of prostitution, or to give herself up to the practice of debauchery, or any other immoral practice, whereby any such woman or girl shall be transported in interstate or foreign commerce, or in any Territory or the District of Columbia, shall be deemed guilty of a felony, and upon conviction thereof shall be punished by a fine not exceeding five thousand dollars, or by imprisonment of not more than five years, or by both such fine and imprisonment, in the discretion of the court.

SEC. 3. That any person who shall knowingly persuade, induce, entice, or coerce, or cause to be persuaded, induced, enticed, or coerced, or aid or assist in persuading, inducing, enticing or coercing any woman or girl to go from one place to another in interstate or foreign commerce or in any Territory or the District of Columbia, for the purpose of prostitution or debauchery, or for any other immoral purpose, or with the intent and purpose on the part of such person that such woman or girl shall engage in the practice of prostitution or debauchery, or any other immoral practice, whether with or without her consent, and who shall thereby knowingly cause or aid or assist in causing such woman or girl to go and to be carried or transported as a passenger upon the line or route of any common carrier or carriers in interstate or foreign commerce, or any Territory or the District of Columbia, shall be deemed guilty of a felony and on conviction thereof shall be punished by a fine of not more than five thousand dollars, or by imprisonment for a term not exceeding five years, or by both such fine and imprisonment, in the discretion of the court.

SEC. 4. That any person who shall knowingly persuade, induce, entice or coerce any woman or girl under the age of eighteen years from any State or Territory or the District of Columbia to any other State or Territory or the District of Columbia, with the purpose and intent to induce or coerce her, or that she shall be induced or coerced to engage in prostitution or debauchery, or any other immoral practice, and shall in furtherance of such purpose knowingly induce or cause her to go and to be carried or transported as a passenger in interstate commerce upon the line or route of any common carrier or carriers, shall be deemed guilty of a felony, and on conviction thereof shall be punished by a fine of not more than ten thousand dollars, or by imprisonment for a term not exceeding ten years, or by both such fine and imprisonment, in the discretion of the court.

C. Constitutionality of the Mann Act

Such broad language — in particular, the language that criminalized acts connected to "prostitution or debauchery, or for any other immoral purpose" — raised questions about the Mann Act's constitutionality: Was this act within the power of the federal government or was it instead an encroachment into the police power reserved to the states? *See Keller v. United States*, 213 U.S. 138 (1909). In *Hoke v. United States*, the Supreme Court began to form an answer.

HOKE v. UNITED STATES
227 U.S. 308 (1913)

[Effie Hoke and Basile Economides had been convicted under the Mann Act for enticing females from New Orleans to travel to Beaumont, Texas for the purposes of prostitution.]

* * *

The power of Congress under the commerce clause of the Constitution is the ultimate determining question. If the statute be a valid exercise of that power, how it may affect persons or states is not material to be considered. It is the supreme law of the land, and persons and states are subject to it.

Congress is given power "to regulate commerce with foreign nations and among the several states." The power is direct; there is no word of limitation in it, and its broad and universal scope has been so often declared as to make repetition unnecessary. And, besides, it has had so much illustration by cases that it would seem as if there could be no instance of its exercise that does not find an admitted example in some one of them. Experience, however, is the other way, and in almost every instance of the exercise of the power differences are asserted from previous exercises of it and made a ground of attack. The present case is an example.

Commerce among the states, we have said, consists of intercourse and traffic between their citizens, and includes the transportation of persons and property. There may be, therefore, a movement of persons as well as of property; that is, a person may move or be moved in interstate commerce. And the act under consideration was drawn in view of that possibility. What the act condemns is transportation obtained or aided, or transportation induced, in interstate commerce, for the immoral purposes mentioned. But an objection is made and urged with earnestness. It is said that it is the right and privilege of a person to move between states, and that such being the right, another cannot be made guilty of the crime of inducing or assisting or aiding in the exercise of it, and "that the motive or intention of the passenger, either before beginning the journey, or during or after completing it, is not a matter of interstate commerce." The contentions confound things important to be distinguished. It urges a right exercised in morality to sustain a right to be exercised in immorality. It is the same right which attacked the law of Congress which prohibits the carrying of obscene literature and articles designed for indecent and immoral use from one [s]tate to another. 29 Stat. at L. 512, chap. 172, U. S. Comp. Stat. 1901, p. 3180; *United States v. Popper*, 98, Fed. 423. It is the same right which was excluded as an element as affecting the constitutionality of the act for the suppression of lottery traffic through national and interstate commerce. *Lottery Case (Champion v. Ames)* 188 U.S. 321, 357, 47 L.ed. 492, 501, 23 Sup. Ct. Rep. 321, 13 Am. Crim. Rep. 561. It is the right given for beneficial exercise which is attempted to be perverted to and justify baneful exercise, as in the instances stated, and which finds further illustration in *Reid v. Colorado*, 187 U.S. 137, 47 L. ed. 108, 23 Sup. Ct. Rep. 92, 12 Am. Crim. Rep. 506. This constitutes the supreme fallacy of plaintiffs' error. It pervades and vitiates their contentions.

Plaintiffs in error admit that the states may control the immoralities of its citizens. Indeed, this is their chief insistence; and they especially condemn the act under review as a subterfuge and an attempt to interfere with the police power of the states to regulate the morals of their citizens, and assert that it is in consequence an invasion of the reserved powers of the states. There is unquestionably a control in the states over the morals of their citizens, and, it may be admitted, it extends to making prostitution a crime. It is a control, however, which can be exercised only within the jurisdiction of the states, but there is a domain which the states cannot reach and over which Congress alone has power; and if such power be exerted to control what the states cannot, it is an argument for — not against — its legality. Its exertion does not encroach upon the jurisdiction of the states. We have examples; others may be adduced. The pure food and drugs act is a conspicuous instance. In all of the instances a clash of national legislation with the power of the states was urged, and in all rejected.

Our dual form of government has its perplexities, [s]tate and [n]ation having different spheres of jurisdiction, as we have said; but it must be kept in mind that we are one people; and the powers reserved to the states and those conferred on the nation are adapted to be exercised, whether independently or concurrently, to promote the general welfare, material and moral. This is the effect of the decisions; and surely, if the facility of interstate transportation can be taken away from the demoralization of lotteries, the debasement of obscene literature, the contagion of diseased cattle or persons, the impurity of food and drugs, the like facility can be taken away from the systematic enticement to and the enslavement in prostitution and debauchery of women, and, more insistently, of girls.

This is the aim of the law, expressed in broad generalization; and motives are made of determining consequence. Motives executed by actions may make it the concern of government to exert its powers. Right purpose and fair trading need no restrictive regulation, but let them be transgressed, and penalties and prohibitions must be applied. We may illustrate again by the pure food and drugs act. Let an article be debased by adulteration, let it be misrepresented by false branding, and Congress may exercise its prohibitive power. It may be that Congress could not prohibit the manufacture of the article in a state. It may be that Congress could not prohibit in all of its conditions its sale within a state. But Congress may prohibit its transportation between the states, and by that means defeat the motive and evils of its manufacture. How far-reaching are the power and the means which may be used to secure its complete exercise we have expressed in *Hipolite Egg Co. v. United States*, 220 U.S. 45, 31 Sup. Ct. Rep. 364, 55 L. ed. 364. There, in emphasis of the purpose of the law, are denominated adulterated articles as 'outlaws of commerce,' and said that the confiscation of them enjoined by the law was appropriate to the right to bar them from interstate transportation, and completed the purpose of the law by not merely preventing their physical movement, but preventing trade in them between the states. It was urged in that case, as it is urged here, that the law was an invasion of the power of the states.

Of course it will be said that women are not articles of merchandise, but this does not affect the analogy of the cases; the substance of the congressional power is the same, only the manner of its exercise must be accommodated to the difference in its objects. It is misleading to say that men and women have rights. Their rights cannot fortify or sanction their wrongs; and if they employ interstate transportation as a facility of their wrongs, it may be forbidden to them to the extent of the act of July 25, 1910, and we need go no farther in the present case.

The principle established by the cases is the simple one, when rid of confusing and distracting considerations, that Congress has power over transportation 'among the several [s]tates'; that the power is complete in itself, and that Congress, as an incident to it, may adopt not only means necessary but convenient to its exercise, and the means may have the quality of police regulations. *Gloucester Ferry Co. v. Pennsylvania*, 114 U.S. 196, 215, 29 L. ed. 158, 166. 1 Inters. Com. Rep. 382, 5 Sup. Ct. Rep. 826; Cooley, Const. Lim. 7th ed. 856. We have no hesitation, therefore, in pronouncing the act of June 25, 1910, a legal exercise of the power of Congress.

NOTES AND QUESTIONS

1. Notably absent from the Court's opinion in *Hoke* is a focus on the horror of the "white-slave traffic" described by James Mann and the other early advocates of the Mann Act. In the Court's view, the Mann Act is simply an extension of a long line of federal laws based in Congress's power over "transportation 'among the several states.'" Similar laws cover topics such as "the contagion of diseased cattle or persons" or "the impurity of food and drugs." In other words, the Mann Act isn't about slavery. It's about the Commerce Clause. Do you agree with this perspective? Does it matter?

2. Having held the Mann Act constitutional in *Hoke*, the Court again encountered the Mann Act in *Wilson v. United States*, 232 U.S. 563, 571 (1914), a case that asked whether the Mann Act only criminalized the transportation of women and girls when an illegal purpose was actually carried out, or whether it criminalized the transportation of women and girls even in cases when there was simply an intent to carry out an illegal purpose. According to the Court, intent was sufficient:

> It is argued that the end and object of the act is to prevent immorality and trafficking in girls, and not the mere act of transportation. But we think that by the plain language of the statute, the offense is complete when "any such woman or girl shall be transported in interstate or foreign commerce, or in any territory or the District of Columbia" as a result of any of the criminal acts previously described. The suggestion that the law contemplates a *locus penitentice* for defendant, after the journey is ended and the woman or girl has been brought to the intended destination within the walls of a house of prostitution, is obviously untenable.

Id. at 571.

3. Contrast the outcome of *Wilson* with that of *Mortensen v. United States*, 322 U.S. 369 (1944), in which two Nebraska brothel owners were prosecuted and convicted of violating the Mann Act because they had taken two women who worked in their brothel across state lines for a vacation in Nevada, even though the transportation was not for an immoral purpose. There, the Supreme Court reversed the conviction of the brothel owners on the grounds that, although the defendants had transported the two women across state lines, the entire purpose of the trip was

innocent, legal, and thus beyond the "immoral purposes" scope of the Mann Act. The Court wrote:

> An intention that the women or girls shall engage in the conduct outlawed by [the Mann Act] must be found to exist before the conclusion of the interstate journey and must be the dominant motive of such interstate movement. And the transportation must be designed to bring about such result. Without that necessary intention and motivation, immoral conduct during or following the journey is insufficient to subject the transporter to the penalties of the Act.
>
> . . . Our examination of the record in this case convinces us that there was a complete lack of relevant evidence from which the jury could properly find or infer, beyond a reasonable doubt, that petitioners transported the girls in interstate commerce "for the purpose of prostitution or debauchery" within the meaning of the Mann Act.
>
> . . . What Congress has outlawed by the Mann Act, however, is the use of interstate commerce as a calculated means for effectuating sexual immorality. In ordinary speech an interstate trip undertaken for an innocent vacation purpose constitutes the use of interstate commerce for that innocent purpose. Such a trip does not lose that meaning when viewed in light of a criminal statute outlawing interstate trips for immoral purposes.

Mortensen, 322 U.S. at 374–75.

D. Scope of the Mann Act

In *Hoke*, the Court describes the purpose of the Mann Act as prohibiting the "systematic enticement to and the enslavement in prostitution and debauchery of women, and, more insistently, of girls." This framing echoes the focus of James Mann and the House and Senate Committee reports, which state that the Mann Act was written to criminalize only coerced prostitution:

> [The Mann Act] does not attempt to regulate the practice of voluntary prostitution, but aims solely to prevent panderers and procurers from compelling thousands of women and girls against their will and desire to enter and continue in a life of prostitution. . . . The characteristic which distinguishes "the white-slave trade" from immorality in general is that the women who are the victims of the traffic are unwillingly forced to practice prostitution. The term "white slave" includes only those women and girls who are literally slaves — those women who are owned and held as property and chattels — whose lives are lives of involuntary servitude; those who practice prostitution as a result of the activities of the procurer, and who, for a considerable period at least, continue to lead their degraded lives because of the power exercised over them by their owners. In short, the white-slave trade may be said to be the business of securing white women and girls and of selling them outright, or of exploiting them for immoral purposes.

H.R. Rep. No. 61-47, at 10–11 (1909).

Yet despite these apparently narrow intentions, the plain language of the Mann Act allowed its reach to quickly broaden, as further demonstrated by the Court's opinion in *Caminetti v. United States*. Two things are important to consider when reading *Caminetti*, particularly in terms of the case's relationship to the increasingly complicated history of the Mann Act. First, the Court acknowledges the legislative history of the Mann Act and its narrow focus on commercialized vice. Second, the Court relies on the 1907 Immigration Act (*See* Immigration Statutes Section above) to interpret the Mann Act's "immoral purpose" clause, highlighting the connection between these acts.

CAMINETTI v. UNITED STATES
242 U.S. 470 (1917)

[Three cases, Caminetti, Diggs, and Hays were all argued together and the court rendered a single opinion. Mr. Caminetti was found guilty of transporting and causing to be transported and aiding and assisting in obtaining transportation for a woman from California to Nevada to become his mistress and concubine. Mr. Diggs was found guilty of the same as well as two charges for assisting in the transportation and procurement of a ticket for both Mr. Diggs's and Mr. Caminetti's mistress and concubine. Mr. Hays was found guilty of persuading, inducing, enticing, and coercing an unmarried minor to travel from Oklahoma to Kansas for the purpose of inducing and coercing her to engage in prostitution, debauchery, and other immoral purposes. Mr. Hays was also found guilty of procuring the tickets needed for the trip. The Court then turned to the scope of the Mann Act.]

It is contended that the act of Congress is intended to reach only "commercialized vice," or the traffic in women for gain, and that the conduct for which the several petitioners were indicted and convicted, however reprehensible in morals, is not within the purview of the statute when properly construed in the light of its history and the purposes intended to be accomplished by its enactment. In none of the cases was it charged or proved that the transportation was for gain or for the purpose of furnishing women for prostitution for hire, and it is insisted that, such being the case, the acts charged and proved, upon which conviction was had, do not come within the statute.

It is elementary that the meaning of a statute must, in the first instance, be sought in the language in which the act is framed, and if that is plain, and if the law is within the constitutional authority of the law-making body which passed it, the sole function of the courts is to enforce it according to its terms. *Lake County v. Rollins*, 130 U.S. 662, 670, 671; *Bate Refrigerating Co. v. Sulzberger*, 157 U.S. 1, 33; *United States v. Lexington Mill and Elevator Co.*, 232 U.S. 399, 409; *United States v. Bank*, 234 U.S. 245, 258.

Where the language is plain and admits of no more than one meaning the duty of interpretation does not arise and the rules which are to aid doubtful meanings need no discussion. *Hamilton v. Rathbone*, 175 U.S. 414, 421. There is no ambiguity in the terms of this act. It is specifically made an offense to knowingly transport or cause to be transported, etc., in interstate commerce, any woman or girl for the purpose of prostitution or debauchery, or for "any other immoral purpose," or with the intent and purpose to induce any such woman or girl to become a prostitute or to give herself up to debauchery, or to engage in any other immoral practice.

Statutory words are uniformly presumed, unless the contrary appears, to be used in their ordinary and usual sense, and with the meaning commonly attributed to them. To cause a woman or girl to be transported for the purposes of debauchery, and for an immoral purpose, to-wit, becoming a concubine or mistress, for which Caminetti and Diggs were convicted; or to transport an unmarried woman, under eighteen years of age, with the intent to induce her to engage in prostitution, debauchery and other immoral practices, for which Hays was convicted, would seem by the very statement of the facts to embrace transportation for purposes denounced by the act, and therefore fairly within its meaning.

While such immoral purpose would be more culpable in morals and attributed to baser motives if accompanied with the expectation of pecuniary gain, such considerations do not prevent the lesser offense against morals of furnishing transportation in order that a woman may be debauched, or become a mistress or a concubine from being the execution of purposes within the meaning of this law. To say the contrary would shock the common understanding of what constitutes an immoral purpose when those terms are applied, as here, to sexual relations.

In *United States v. Bitty*, 208 U.S. 393, it was held that the act of Congress against the importation of alien women and girls for the purpose of prostitution "and any other immoral purpose" included the importation of an alien woman to live in concubinage with the person importing her. In that case this court said:

> All will admit that full effect must be given to the intention of Congress as gathered from the words of the statute. There can be no doubt as to what class was aimed at by the clause forbidding the importation of alien women for purposes of 'prostitution.' It refers to women who for hire or without hire offer their bodies to indiscriminate intercourse with men. The lives and example of such persons are in hostility to "the idea of the family, as consisting in and springing from the union for life of one man and one woman in the holy estate of matrimony; the sure foundation of all that is stable and noble in our civilization; the best guaranty of that reverent morality which is the source of all beneficent progress in social and political improvement." *Murpher v. Ramsey* 114 U.S. 15, 45 . . . . Now the addition in the last statute of the words, "or for any other immoral purpose," after the word "prostitution," must have been made for some practical object. Those added words show beyond question that Congress had in view the protection of society against another class of alien women other than those who might be brought here merely for purposes of "prostitution." In forbidding the importation of alien women "for any other immoral purpose," Congress evidently thought that there were purposes in connection with the importations of alien women which, as in the case of importations for prostitution, were to be deemed immoral. It may be admitted that in accordance with the familiar rule of *ejusdem generis*, the immoral purpose referred to by the words any other immoral purpose, must be one of the same general class or kind as the particular purpose of "prostitution" specified in the same clause of the statute. 2 Lewis' Sutherland Stat. Const.,

§ 423, and authorities cited. But that rule cannot avail the accused in this case; for, the immoral purpose charged in the indictment is of the same general class or kind as the one that controls in the importation of an alien woman for the purpose strictly of prostitution. The prostitute may, in the popular sense, be more degraded in character than the concubine, but the latter none the less must be held to lead an immoral life, if any regard whatever be had to the views that are almost universally held in this country as to the relations which may rightfully, from the standpoint of morality, exist between man and woman in the matter of sexual intercourse.

This definition of an immoral purpose was given prior to the enactment of the act now under consideration, and must be presumed to have been known to Congress when it enacted the law here involved.

But it is contended that though the words are so plain that they cannot be misapprehended when given their usual and ordinary interpretation, and although the sections in which they appear do not in terms limit the offense defined and punished to acts of "commercialized vice," or the furnishing or procuring of transportation of women for debauchery, prostitution or immoral practices for hire, such limited purpose is to be attributed to Congress and engrafted upon the act in view of the language of § 8 and the report which accompanied the law upon its introduction into and subsequent passage by the House of Representatives.

In this connection, it may be observed that while the title of an act cannot overcome the meaning of plain and unambiguous words used in its body, [internal citations omitted] the title of this act embraces the regulation of interstate commerce "by prohibiting the transportation therein for immoral purposes of women and girls, and for other purposes." It is true that § 8 of the act provides that it shall be known and referred to as the "White-slave traffic Act," and the report accompanying the introduction of the same into the House of Representatives set forth the fact that a material portion of the legislation suggested was to meet conditions which had arisen in the past few years, and that the legislation was needed to put a stop to a villainous interstate and international traffic in women and girls. Still, the name given to an act by way of designation or description, or the report which accompanies it, cannot change the plain import of its words. If the words are plain, they give meaning to the act, and it is neither the duty nor the privilege of the courts to enter speculative fields in search of a different meaning.

NOTES AND QUESTIONS

Is "immoral purpose" the term we would use today to describe the facts of *Caminetti*? Note that this phrase still appears in some state laws on prostitution today. *See* MICH. COMP. LAWS § 750.448 (2002).

E. Decline of the Mann Act

Gradually, there was a shift away from noncommercial prosecutions, like *Caminetti*, under the Mann Act. "No bell rang, no memo can be quoted, and no precise date can be specified, but a definite shift in Mann Act prosecutions took place at the end of the 1920s. The morals crusade ended, and with it so did noncommercial prosecutions where no aggravating circumstances existed. A big exception was made where a specific defendant was politically unpopular with the federal government or where his activities were of a type despised by the federal authorities."[5]

For example, the heavyweight champion boxer John Arthur "Jack" Johnson was convicted of violating the Mann Act in 1913 after arranging and paying for the transportation of a woman across state lines. The woman was Johnson's lover, and a significant amount of the controversy surrounding the case was due to the fact that Johnson was African-American and the woman in question was white, as was every member of the jury.

The racial reverberations from this case have continued to the present day. In May 2011, resolutions were introduced in the House and Senate "expressing the sense of Congress that John Arthur 'Jack' Johnson should receive a posthumous pardon for the racially motivated conviction in 1913 that diminished the athletic, cultural, and heroic significance of Jack Johnson and unduly tarnished his reputation."

In 1944, Charlie Chaplin was prosecuted under the Mann Act in a case stemming from a paternity suit involving the actress Joan Barry. Chaplin was tried under the Mann Act after he bought his young mistress, and mother of his six-month-old child, a train ticket back to New York after she came to visit him for "immoral purposes." Commentators have argued that the FBI charged Chaplin because of his politics and ethnicity and not his relationship with Joan Barry.[6] Chaplin was eventually acquitted of the charges.

F. Victim's Perspective

So far, all of the cases discussed have focused on the transporters, usually men, who violate the Mann Act. The voices of those being transported, usually women and girls, have been silent.

When the Mann Act was created, the plight of these women and girls seemed to be paramount. The Act's passage was supposed to guarantee their protection. But the reality for some of these women and girls, once the Mann Act was implemented, was much different. Rather than being protected, they were prosecuted, or at least threatened with prosecution so that they would cooperate with law enforcement officials.

In 1915, such threats were ostensibly sanctioned by the Supreme Court when it held in *Holte v. United States* that, in certain situations, the woman being transported could be charged with conspiracy. This holding was later limited in 1932 in *Gebardi v. United States*. There, the Court held that a female's consent to the transportation and its immoral purpose did not constitute a violation of the Mann Act, nor could she be punished as a co-conspirator.

---

[5] DAVID J. LANGUM, CROSSING OVER THE LINE: LEGISLATING MORALITY AND THE MANN ACT 161 (John C. Fout ed., 1994).

[6] *See* Lisa R. Seville, *The Mann Act: Anatomy of a Law*, THE CRIME REPORT, Apr. 2, 2012, http://www.thecrimereport.org/news/inside-criminal-justice/from-the-archives.

Yet, 17 years after *Gebardi*, the FBI continued to endorse the old approach of using charges of conspiracy as a way to force cooperation. Specifically, a 1949 memo titled "Memorandum Policy and Procedure White Slave Traffic Act" advises FBI agents to "discuss with the U.S. Attorney the possibility of holding the victim in custody," to ensure her availability as a witness, and to use conspiracy charges against uncooperative witnesses.

III. MODERN-DAY MANN ACT

Since 1910 the Mann Act has been amended significantly. In 1986, Congress recognized that males could also be transported for commercialized vice by removing the Act's exclusive focus on females; the Act now refers to "individuals" rather than "women and girls." But certain themes remain. For example, the framing from *Hoke* means these cases are still Commerce Clause cases, with a focus on commercialized vice in interstate or foreign commerce or both. James Mann's call to rescue slaves is eerily absent, and the focus on prostitution regardless of compulsion rings loudly.

The scope of the modern-day Mann Act is defined as "prostitution, or in any sexual activity for which any person can be charged with a criminal offense." This language replaced almost all of the references to "immoral purposes" used to prosecute noncommercial cases.[7]

Violations of the Mann Act did not stop making headlines after Jack Johnson and Charlie Chaplin. The high-profile case of former New York Governor Eliot Spitzer is a case in point. In 2008, Spitzer was discovered to be a client of an escort service. As part of a liaison with an escort provided by the Emperor's Club Escort service, Spitzer paid for the escort's travel and accommodations across state lines. Ultimately, Spitzer was not charged with criminal conduct, but for a time there was intense speculation over the possibility of criminal charges under the Mann Act. *See* Danny Hakim & William K. Rashbaum, *Spitzer Is Linked to Prostitution Ring*, N.Y. TIMES, Mar. 10, 2008, http://www.nytimes.com/2008/03/10/nyregion/10cnd-spitzer.html.

---

[7] The phrase still remains in one section of the Mann Act. Section 2424 titled "Filing Factual Statement About Alien Individual" requires anyone who:

> [M]aintains, controls, supports, or harbors in any house or place for the purpose of prostitution, or *for any other immoral purpose*, any individual, knowing or in reckless disregard of the fact that the individual is an alien, shall file with the Commissioner of Immigration and Naturalization a statement in writing setting forth the name of such individual, the place at which that individual is kept, and all facts as to the date of that individual's entry into the United States, the port through which that individual entered, that individual's age, nationally, and parentage, and concerning that individuals procuration to come to this country within the knowledge of such person.

18 U.S.C. § 2424 (2012) (emphasis added). The punishment for failure to file the statement is a fine or imprisonment with a maximum sentence of 10 years. This provision is still in use. (*See* U.S. v. Hernandez, 2006 U.S. App. LEXIS 22960 (11th Cir. Sept. 8, 2006).)

Chapter 5

TVPA: THE TRAFFICKING VICTIMS PROTECTION ACT

As discussed in the previous chapter, neither the early Immigration Statutes nor the Mann Act could reach the range of cases defined as human trafficking today, even with perfect application. That's because today's victims of human trafficking include not just women and girls who are sex trafficked but also men and boys who are sex trafficked and also because human trafficking extends beyond simply sex trafficking or "compelled prostitution" — it also includes labor trafficking. In fact, in 2012, there were an estimated 14.2 million victims of labor trafficking, a number that is more than three times the amount of victims of sex trafficking. Chapters 1–3 highlighted the gaps in protection for these labor trafficking victims under the slavery, involuntary servitude and peonage laws in the United States.

The reality of modern-day slavery in the United States required new tools to combat human trafficking. The United States, in step with the international movement against trafficking of all persons, enacted the Trafficking Victims Protection Act of 2000 (TVPA) on October 28, 2000.[1] The TVPA created the first comprehensive federal legislation that addresses human trafficking. This chapter provides an overview of the criminal, civil, and social service provisions of that landmark legislation — accounting for the four times the TVPA has been amended and reauthorized since 2000: first in 2003, next in 2005 and 2008, and most recently in 2013.

I. POLICY HISTORY

Human trafficking cases were prosecuted prior to the TVPA, for example under involuntary servitude or peonage laws. However, often these cases faced three persistent problems: (1) the laws on which the cases were brought were not comprehensive enough to give adequate relief to victims, (2) the victims were often criminalized themselves, and (3) the victims were rarely given access to the kind of services they needed to recover from being enslaved.

---

[1] The stated purpose of the TVPA of 2000 was to combat human trafficking, to protect victims, and to guarantee the punishment of traffickers. Trafficking Victims Protection Act of 2000 § 102(a), 22 U.S.C. § 7101(a) (2000). The TVPA of 2000 further noted that "[a]t least 700,000 persons annually, primarily women and children, are trafficked within or across international borders. Approximately 50,000 women and children are trafficked into the United States each year." *Id.* (b)(1), 22 U.S.C. § 7101(b)(1) (2000).

A. El Monte

All three of these problems are evident in what is known as the "El Monte Sweatshop Case" — a case that marked a turning point in combatting human trafficking. As Luis CdeBaca, Ambassador-at-Large in the Office to Monitor and Combat Trafficking in Persons, explains, "[t]he 'El Monte sweatshop case' was a landmark incident that taught so many of us what had to happen in order to thwart modern-day slavery: multiple law enforcement jurisdictions, nongovernmental service providers, and community-based organizations working together to craft an emergency response, to investigate and prosecute the traffickers, and to assist the victims."

El Monte was the result of a police raid on a garment factory in El Monte, California on August 2, 1995. During the raid, the police discovered 72 workers who were being held captive in a wire-ringed building and forced to stitch garments for an average of 84 hours a week. All of these workers were Thai nationals; some of them had been held captive for over seven years.

The workers had been promised jobs in the United States. But when they arrived, they were confined in a compound and threatened with physical harm both to themselves and to their families in Thailand if they failed to comply with the demands of the traffickers. Those demands included working for less than 70 cents per hour for up to 18 hours a day, seven days a week.

Immediately after the raid, the workers were taken into custody by the Immigration and Naturalization Service (INS).[2] But the INS was designed to deal with people working in the United States without authorization; it was not designed to deal with people working in the United States under the threat of physical harm. In other words, the INS was not designed to deal with victims of human trafficking, a label that did not even exist in U.S. law when the El Monte case was discovered.

This disconnect helps explain why the El Monte workers were detained for nine days by the INS and essentially treated as criminals before ultimately being recognized as victims. It also helps explain the ad hoc solution the INS came up with. Without any statutes or case law to guide them, the INS released the workers and gave them temporary permission to remain in the United States as material witnesses in the criminal case against the traffickers. Because there was no federal benefits structure for these victims, the government had to rely on community organizations to provide housing and basic services to the victims.

The lesson of El Monte is not that the INS mishandled the Thai workers. Rather, the lesson of El Monte is that the INS was not equipped to handle the Thai workers because at the time there was no comprehensive law on human trafficking to guide the INS (or any other government agency or organization), there was no real understanding that victims of human trafficking were victims and not criminals, and there was no support system in place to provide those victims with

---

[2] Immigration and Naturalization Service (INS) functions were transferred from the Department of Justice to three new components within the newly formed Department of Homeland Security (DHS) on March 1, 2003.

the services needed to recover from the experience of being enslaved.

In fact, one way to understand the current multi-prong approach to combating human trafficking is, in part, a response to El Monte. What was lacking then has become a priority now: comprehensive laws that at once prosecute traffickers, protect current victims, and prevent future victimization. The specific development of this multi-pronged approach is discussed in the next section. For a more detailed account of the El Monte case, see SWEATSHOP USA 57–59 (Daniel E Bender & Richard A. Greenwald eds., 2003); Scott L. Cummings, *Hemmed in: Legal Mobilization in the Los Angeles Anti-Sweatshop Movement*, 30 BERKELEY J. EMP. & LAB. L. 1, 22 (2009).

B. From El Monte to a Multi-Pronged Approach

The federal government first developed a multi-pronged approach to combating human trafficking when President Clinton issued an anti-trafficking directive on March 11, 1998, two and a half years after the El Monte raid. The Clinton Directive focused on the "three Ps" — prosecution, protection, and prevention — and within a year, several similarly multi-pronged anti-trafficking bills were introduced in the House and Senate.[3]

For example, on November 8, 1999, Representative Chris Smith, who has become one of the leading anti-trafficking legislators, introduced, with Representative Sam Gejdenson and other Democrat and Republican members of Congress, the bipartisan Trafficking Victims Protection Act of 1999, H.R. 3244 containing the Clinton Administration's "3-Ps" framework. This bill passed the House seven months later, on May 9, 2000. But before making its way to the Senate, Representative Smith's bill was revised and many provisions protecting victims of human trafficking were eliminated. In light of the substantial differences between the House version of the bill and the Senate version of the bill, these versions had to be reconciled and were sent to a conference committee. The

---

[3] *See* Jayashri Srikantiah, *Perfect Victims and Real Survivors: The Iconic Victim in Domestic Human Trafficking Law*, 87 B.U. L. REV. 157, 168 n.62 (2007). In March 1999, Senator Paul Wellstone (D-Minn.) and Representative Louise Slaughter (D-N.Y.) introduced identical bills entitled the International Trafficking of Women and Children Victim Protection Act of 1999. S. 600, 106th Cong. (1999); H.R. 1238, 106th Cong. (1999). On March 25, 1999, Representative Christopher Smith (R-N.J.) introduced the Freedom from Sexual Trafficking Act of 1999. H.R. 1356, 106th Cong. (1999), a bill that was limited exclusively to addressing sex trafficking. On October 27, 1999, Representative Sam Gejdenson (D-Conn.) introduced the Comprehensive Anti-trafficking in Persons Act of 1999, based upon a comprehensive legislative proposal originating with the President's Interagency Council on Women's General Counsel's office that addressed all forms of trafficking in persons and incorporated the multi-pronged integrated elements of the Administration's "3-Ps" framework, and on November 2, 1999, Senator Wellstone introduced an identical bill in the Senate. H.R. 3154, 106th Cong. (1999); S. 1842, 106th Cong. (1999). Selected provisions from Congressman Smith's sex trafficking bill and the more comprehensive and expansive trafficking in persons bill originating with the Clinton Administration, improved and introduced by Congressmen Gejdenson, were brought together and, finally, on November 8, 1999, Representative Smith introduced the bipartisan bill that was later enacted into law as the Trafficking Victims Protection Act. H.R. 3244, 106th Cong. (1999). Around the same time, Senator Sam Brownback (R-Kan.) sponsored a similar bill in the Senate. S. 2449, 106th Cong. (2000). Prior to the introduction of this legislation, the House and Senate had passed several resolutions condemning trafficking and urging the State Department to take action. *See, e.g.*, H.R. Con. Res. 239, 105th Cong. (1998); S. Con. Res. 82, 105th Cong. (1998); S. Con. Res. 12, 104th Cong. (1995); H.R. Con. Res. 21, 104th Cong. (1995).

conference committee recommended a compromise that returned some but not all of the original victim protections of the House version of the bill. This compromise was passed by the House 371 to 1 and then approved by the Senate 95 to 0. A few weeks later it became law when President Clinton signed what is now known as the TVPA.

While the TVPA provides certain victim protections, a number of important victim protections from the House bill were eliminated by the conference committee, most notably a private right of action for victims of human trafficking and asset forfeiture. Neither of these provisions made it into the TVPA in 2000.[4]

II. THE LEGISLATIVE HISTORY OF THE TRAFFICKING VICTIMS PROTECTION ACT

While the TVPA was hailed as the first comprehensive federal legislation to combat human trafficking, the legislative history reads like a chapter out of the creation of the Mann Act (*See* Chapter 4). In other words, to listen to legislators explain the need for the TVPA one might think that human trafficking only happened to women and girls from other countries and that it only involved sex trafficking, not labor trafficking.

For example, when introducing the TVPA in a committee hearing, Congressman Chris Smith, whose own legislative proposals prior to the bipartisan TVPA addressed only sex trafficking, stressed that "Each year . . . up to a million innocent victims, of whom the overwhelming majority are women and children, are brought by force and/or fraud into the international commercial sex industry." In a separate hearing, Congresswoman Cynthia McKinney similarly focused on how "[w]omen and children are forced into the illegal commercial sex trade." But neither Smith nor Mckinney made any mention of how men are also forced into the illegal commercial sex trade or noted that victims of both sexes are forced into the illegal commercial labor trade. The next year, Senator Paul Wellstone perpetuated the same narrow focus when he spoke in support of TVPA on the Senate floor. "I rise today to address the serious and widespread problem of international trafficking in persons, particularly women and children, for the purposes of sexual exploitation."

By then, Wellstone's words had come to fit a familiar pattern: words offered in support of the TVPA in Congress were focused almost entirely on sexual exploitation and sex trafficking, while barely touching the subject of labor trafficking. Moreover, the purposes and findings of the TVPA did not even mention men, boys,

---

[4] While the loss to victims of the private right of action and asset forfeiture has been acknowledged, less noticed is the impact of the adoption of the Senate version on the incarceration of victims. The House version of the TVPA recognized the risk of incarceration for victims of human trafficking by including an explicit prohibition on not fining or jailing victims of severe forms of trafficking. H.R. REP. No. 106-487, at 7 (1999) (Conf. Rep.). The conference agreement adopts the Senate approach of prohibiting the detention of victims in facilities inappropriate to their status as crime victims. S. 3244, 106th Cong. § 7(c) (2000). While the language of the TVPA is from the Senate version of the bill, the House approach is assumed: "The conferees believe that the House provision with respect to jailing, fining, or otherwise penalizing victims of serious crimes on account of their status as crime victims or on account of conduct committed under duress incident to such status restates existing criminal law and is therefore unnecessary." H.R. REP. No. 106-939, at 93 (1999).

or U.S. citizens as possible victims. The focus was on women and girls with the implication that all victims of human trafficking were foreign nationals.

That said, the actual language of the TVPA is more inclusive — to a point. The TVPA restricts the receipt of victim protections such as social services and immigration relief to victims of "severe forms of human trafficking," which, according to the TVPA, can be one of two things. First, a severe form of human trafficking can be "sex trafficking in which a commercial sex act is induced by force, fraud, or coercion, or in which the person induced to perform such act has not attained 18 years of age." In other words, it can be the sex trafficking of adults through compulsion or simply sex trafficking of children. Second, a severe form of human trafficking can be what we know simply as labor trafficking — specifically, "the recruitment, harboring, transportation, provision, or obtaining of a person for labor or services, through the use of force, fraud, or coercion for the purpose of subjection to involuntary servitude, peonage, debt bondage, or slavery."

If victims do not fall into either of these categories, they are not eligible for benefits under the TVPA.[5] And even if victims do fall into either of these categories, there is still a chance, particularly if the victims are U.S. citizens, that they will not receive benefits under the TVPA because the majority of benefits under the TVPA are for victims that are foreign nationals.

A. Criminal Provisions

The TVPA recognized, for the first time, the specific offense of trafficking in persons. To prosecute and punish traffickers the TVPA increased sentences for existing criminal violations, statutorily defined involuntary servitude, and added provisions for the crimes of (a) forced labor; (b) sex trafficking of children or by force, fraud, or coercion; (c) trafficking with respect to peonage, slavery, involuntary servitude, or forced labor; and (d) unlawful conduct with respect to documents.

Prior to the TVPA, human trafficking cases were prosecuted under the peonage, slavery, and involuntary servitude statutes within U.S. law. But these statutes could only be used in a subset of human trafficking cases. The TVPA strengthened the criminal penalties of these existing statutes in two ways. First, it increased the term of imprisonment from 10 years up to 20 years. Second, it made a life sentence possible in cases in which a violation of the peonage, slavery, or involuntary servitude statutes results in death or includes "kidnapping, an attempt to kidnap, aggravated sexual abuse, or an attempt to kill."

1. Forced Labor

Recognizing that peonage, slavery, and involuntary servitude statutes may not apply in cases involving only psychological coercion, the TVPA includes a criminal provision on forced labor: 18 U.S.C. § 1589 (Section 1589). The purpose of this

---

[5] According to the TVPA, a victim of trafficking who is not a victim of a severe form of trafficking would be someone who was recruited, harbored, transported, provided, or obtained for the purpose of a commercial sex act. *See* 22 U.S.C. §§ 7102 (9) & (13)–(14) (2008).

forced labor provision is outlined in The Joint Explanatory Statement of the Committee of Conference (Joint Statement) for the TVPA, which notes that Congress intended for Section 1589 to be a tool for prosecutors to use in cases that do not fall within the parameters of involuntary servitude:

> Section 1589 is intended to address the increasingly subtle methods of traffickers who place their victims in modern-day slavery, such as where traffickers threaten harm to third persons, restrain their victims without physical violence or injury, or threaten dire consequences by means other than overt violence. Section 1589 will provide federal prosecutors with the tools to combat severe forms of worker exploitation that do not rise to the level of involuntary servitude as defined in *Kozminski*. Because provisions within section 1589 only require a showing of a threat of 'serious harm,' or of a scheme, plan, or pattern intended to cause a person to believe that such harm would occur, federal prosecutors will not have to demonstrate physical harm or threats of force against victims. The term 'serious harm' as used in this Act refers to a broad array of harms, including both physical and nonphysical, and section 1589's terms and provisions are intended to be construed with respect to the individual circumstances of victims that are relevant in determining whether a particular type or certain degree of harm or coercion is sufficient to maintain or obtain a victim's labor or services, including the age and background of the victims.
>
> For example, it is intended that prosecutors will be able to bring more cases in which individuals have been trafficked into domestic service, an increasingly common occurrence, not only where such victims are kept in service through overt beatings, but also where the traffickers use more subtle means designed to cause their victims to believe that serious harm will result to themselves or others if they leave, as when a nanny is led to believe that children in her care will be harmed if she leaves the home. In other cases, a scheme, plan, or pattern intended to cause a belief of serious harm may refer to intentionally causing the victim to believe that her family will face harms such as banishment, starvation, or bankruptcy in their home country. Section 1589 will in certain instances permit prosecutions where children are brought to the United States and face extreme nonviolent and psychological coercion (e.g. isolation, denial of sleep, and other punishments). A claim by an adult of a false legal relationship with a child in order to put the child in a condition of servitude may constitute a scheme, plan or pattern that violates the statute, if there is a showing that such a scheme was intended to create the belief that the victim or some other person would suffer serious harm.

H.R. REP. NO. 106-939, at 101 (2000). Section 1589 is an expansive tool that allows prosecutors to reach more subtle forms of trafficking and instances of trafficking with or without physical violence. Although Section 1589 does not require force, threats of force, or threats of the abuse of the legal process, in many cases today the statute is charged when these elements are found. But its reach was unclear because when the TVPA criminalized "whoever knowingly provides or obtains the *labor or services* of a person,"[6] the phrase "labor or services" was not defined.

In absence of a statutory definition, courts have looked to other sources to define the phrase, including history, legislative intent, and relevant case law — a three-part approach that is well captured in the Tenth Circuit's opinion in *United States v. Kaufman* excerpted below.

UNITED STATES v. KAUFMAN
546 F.3d 1242 (10th Cir. 2008)

HENRY, CHIEF JUDGE.

In November 1999, Butler County, Kansas, deputy sheriffs observed two men working in the nude on a farm outside the town of Newton. As the deputies approached, the defendant, Arlan Kaufman, a doctor of social work who owned the farm and was fully clothed, directed the two workers into a nearby van, where they put on their clothes. Dr. Kaufman explained that the workers were residents of the Kaufman House Residential Care Treatment Center (the Kaufman House), an unlicensed group home for the mentally ill that he owned and operated with his wife, the defendant Linda Kaufman, a licensed nurse.

The deputies' discovery led to an extended investigation of the Kaufman House by county, state, and federal authorities. They learned that, over a period of more than fifteen years, the Kaufmans had directed the severely mentally ill residents of the Kaufman House to perform sexually explicit acts and farm labor in the nude while maintaining that these acts constituted legitimate psychotherapy for the residents' mental illnesses. Moreover, the Kaufmans billed Medicare and the residents' families for the therapy.

In 2005, a federal grand jury charged the Kaufmans with violating the involuntary servitude and forced labor statutes, health care fraud, mail fraud, and obstructing a federal audit. The government also sought forfeiture of the Kaufmans' assets. A jury convicted each of the Kaufmans of the following offenses: conspiracy (under 18 U.S.C. § 371); two counts of forced labor (under 18 U.S.C. § 1589); three counts of involuntary servitude (under 18 U.S.C. § 1584); sixteen counts of health care fraud (under 18 U.S.C. § 1347); nine counts of mail fraud (under 18 U.S.C. § 1341); one count of obstructing a federal audit (under 18 U.S.C. § 1516); and one count of criminal forfeiture (under 18 U.S.C. § 982). The jury convicted Dr. Kaufman of an additional count of submitting a false document to Medicare (under 18 U.S.C. § 1035).

The district court sentenced Dr. Kaufman to 360 months imprisonment, upwardly varying from the Guideline range of 160-210 months. In contrast, the court sentenced Mrs. Kaufman to eighty-four months imprisonment, a downward variance from a Guideline range of 135-168 months. In support of that decision, the court reasoned that Mrs. Kaufman had probably been convicted as an aider and abettor rather than a principal, that she had a dependent personality disorder, and that she had accepted responsibility for the offenses.

---

[6] 18 U.S.C. § 1589(a) (emphasis added).

[*On appeal the Kaufmans argued that the jury should have been instructed to limit the definition of "labor or services" to "work in an economic sense."*]

Next, the Kaufmans argue that the district court erred in defining "labor" and "services" when it instructed the jury on the involuntary servitude and forced labor counts. At issue here are counts 2-5 of the indictment. Counts 2 and 3 alleged violations of the forced labor statute, 18 U.S.C. § 1589, with regard to labor or services provided by Kaufman House residents Mary and Barbara respectively. Counts 4 and 5 alleged violations of the involuntary servitude statute, 18 U.S.C. § 1584, as to the same two residents.

In assessing the Kaufmans' argument, we begin with the terms of the relevant statutes. The involuntary servitude statute, 18 U.S.C. § 1584, establishes an offense for "knowingly and willfully hold[ing] to involuntary servitude or sell[ing] into any condition of involuntary servitude, any other person for any term." The forced labor statute, 18 U.S.C § 1589, provides, in part:

[*Section 1589 has been amended since the publication of this decision. The amendments do not affect the analysis or holding in this decision.*]

> Whoever knowingly provides or obtains the labor or services of a person—
>
> (1) by threats of serious harm to, or physical restraint against, that person or another person;
>
> (2) by means of any scheme, plan, or pattern intended to cause the person to believe that, if the person did not perform such labor or services, that person or another person would suffer serious harm or physical restraint; or
>
> (3) by means of the abuse or threatened abuse of law or the legal process, shall be fined under this title or imprisoned not more than 20 years, or both.

Neither statute defines the terms "involuntary servitude," "labor," or "services." However, Instruction 14C, which explained the involuntary servitude counts, stated that:

> The term "involuntary servitude" means a condition of compulsory service in which the alleged victim is compelled to perform labor or services against the victim's will for the benefit of a defendant due to the use or threat of physical restraint or physical injury, or by the use or threat of coercion through law or the legal process.

Rec. vol. 5, doc. 305, instr. 14C.

Instruction 16 informed the jury that, in deciding whether the Kaufmans had violated the forced labor statute,

> [Y]ou must decide whether the defendant obtained the labor or services of another person, namely, the alleged victim named in that particular count of the indictment. "Obtain" means to gain, acquire, or attain. "Labor"

means the expenditure of physical or mental effort. "Services" means conduct or performance that assists or benefits someone or something

Id. instr. 16.

Instruction 14C did not contain a separate definition of "labor" or "services," and we therefore assume, as do the parties, that the jury applied the definitions set forth in instruction 16 to the involuntary servitude offenses as well.

The Kaufmans did not object to either instruction at trial. Nevertheless, they now maintain that the district court committed plain error because the definitions of "labor" and "services" were too broad. In their view, the definitions allowed them to be convicted for inducing the nudity and the sexual acts recorded on the videotapes. According to the Kaufmans, the involuntary servitude and forced labor statutes apply only to "labor or services" that constitute "work in an economic sense," Dr. Kaufman's Aplt's Br. at 60, and the acts on the videotapes cannot be fairly characterized as such work.

The Kaufmans reason that, as to 18 U.S.C. § 1584, Congress borrowed the phrase "involuntary servitude" from the Thirteenth Amendment. In the Supreme Court's view, the phrase was intended to cover "'compulsory labor akin to African slavery, which in practical operation would tend to produce like undesirable results.'" Dr. Kaufman's Aplt's Br. at 62 (quoting *United States v. Kozminski*, 487 U.S. 931, 942, 108 S. Ct. 2751, 101 L. Ed. 2d 788 (1988) (other internal quotation marks omitted)). The Kaufmans maintain that the Supreme Court decisions applying the Thirteenth Amendment generally involve "work that was economic in nature." Dr. Kaufman's Aplt's Br. at 63. In their view, the same limitation applies to the "labor" and "services" covered by § 1589.

We are not persuaded by the Kaufmans' arguments. First, as the government observes, the jury instructions' definitions of "labor" and "services" set forth the ordinary meaning of those terms. *See* 8 Oxford English Dictionary 559 (2d ed. 1989) (defining "labour" as "[e]xertion of the faculties of the body or mind, esp. when painful or compulsory; bodily or mental toil"); 15 Oxford English Dictionary 34, 36 (2d ed. 1989) (defining "service" as "[t]he condition of being a servant; the fact of serving a master" and as "[t]he action of serving, helping, or benefitting; conduct tending to the welfare or advantage of another"); *see also Hackwell v. United States*, 491 F.3d 1229, 1233-34 (10th Cir. 2007) (relying on the Random House Dictionary of the English Language's definition of services as "the performance of any duties or work for another").

Moreover, the authorities on which the Kaufmans rely do not establish that "labor" and "services" under the involuntary servitude and forced labor statutes are limited to "work in an economic sense." In *Kozminski*, 487 U.S. at 945, the Supreme Court considered the "involuntary" component of the phrase "involuntary servitude" in *§ 1584*. The Court concluded that Congress had borrowed the phrase from the Thirteenth Amendment, and it therefore interpreted the statute "in a way consistent with the understanding of the Thirteenth Amendment that prevailed at the time of § 1584's enactment." *Id.* at 945. Rejecting the government's argument, the Court held that "compulsion of services by the use or threatened use of physical coercion is a necessary incident of a condition of involuntary servitude." *Id.* at 952.

Kozminski thus addressed the means by which services are coerced, but it did not determine what kinds of services are covered by § 1584. *See id.* at 942 (stating that "while the general spirit of the phrase 'involuntary servitude' is easily comprehended, the exact range of conditions it prohibits is harder to define").

As to the forced labor statute, § 1589, we note that Congress enacted it as part of the Trafficking Victims Protection Act of 2000, a subset of the Victims of Trafficking and Violence Protection Act of 2000, Pub. L. No. 106-386, 114 Stat. 1464 (2000). *See United States v. Bradley*, 390 F.3d 145, 150 (1st Cir. 2004) (discussing § 1589). The stated purpose of the Trafficking Victims Protection Act is to "combat trafficking in persons, a contemporary manifestation of slavery whose victims are predominantly women and children, to ensure just and effective punishment of traffickers, and to protect their victims." 22 U.S.C. § 7101(a).

The legislative history reveals that, in enacting § 1589, Congress sought to expand *Kozminski's* limited definition of coercion under § 1584, stating that "[s]ection 1589 will provide federal prosecutors with the tools to combat severe forms of worker exploitation that do not rise to the level of involuntary servitude as defined in *Kozminski*." See H.R. Conf. Rep. No. 106-939, at 101, *as reprinted in* 2000 U.S.C.C.A.N. 1380, 1393. There is no indication that Congress sought to limit the scope of "labor or services" in the manner suggested by the Kaufmans.

We acknowledge that many cases invoked by the Kaufmans and interpreting the Thirteenth Amendment, § 1584, and § 1589 involve "work that was economic in nature" and describe slavery and involuntary servitude in economic terms. *See, e.g., Pollock v. Williams*, 322 U.S. 4, 17, 64 S. Ct. 792, 88 L. Ed. 1095 (1944) ("The undoubted aim of the Thirteenth Amendment as implemented by the Antipeonage Act was not merely to end slavery but to maintain a system of completely free and voluntary labor throughout the United States."). Nevertheless, the authorities invoked by the Kaufmans also describe slavery and involuntary servitude in a broader fashion. For example, in *Bailey v. Alabama*, 219 U.S. 219, 31 S. Ct. 145, 55 L. Ed. 191 (1911), the Court stated that

> [t]he words involuntary servitude [in the 13th Amendment] have a larger meaning than slavery. . . . The plain intention was to abolish slavery *of whatever name and form and all its badges and incidents*; to render impossible any state of bondage; to make labor free, by prohibiting that control by which the personal service of one man is disposed of or coerced for another's benefit, which is the essence of involuntary servitude

Id. at 241 (emphasis added) (internal quotation marks omitted).

Moreover, the fact that these various authorities describe slavery in economic terms does not mean that was all there was to the institution or that the Thirteenth Amendment and the subsequent legislation implementing it apply only to economic relationships. Indeed, scholars have discerned a broader meaning in the condition of slavery and the legislation that abolished it. In Professor Amar's assessment, "many slaves were in fact the victims of sadism and torture rather than being put in the fields[,] . . . and yet they were surely covered by the core of the Thirteenth Amendment." Akhil Reed Amar, *Remember the Thirteenth*, 10 Const. Comment. 403, 405 (1993); Neal Kumar Katyal, *Men Who Own Women: A Thirteenth*

Amendment Critique of Forced Prostitution, 103 YALE L.J. 793, 796, 811 (1993) (observing that "the context of coerced prostitution, which involves compelled sexual chores, surrounds the Thirteenth Amendment's prohibition against forced labor"). That analysis supports the government's contention that §§ 1584 and 1589 are applicable here. In our view, if an antebellum slave was relieved of the responsibility for harvesting cotton, brought into his master's house, directed to disrobe and then engage in the various acts performed by the Kaufman House residents on the videotapes (e.g., masturbation and genital shaving), his or her condition could still be fairly described as one of involuntary servitude and forced labor.

The Fourth Circuit's recent decision in *United States v. Udeozor*, 515 F.3d 260 (4th Cir. 2008), supports that conclusion. There, the government charged a physician and her husband with conspiring to hold a fourteen-year-old girl in involuntary servitude, as defined in § 1584. The evidence at trial revealed that the defendants had required the girl to care for their children, to clean their house, to cook for them, and to work in the physician's medical office, all without compensation. Additionally, the girl testified that the husband had forced her to have sexual intercourse with him.

In affirming the conviction, the Fourth Circuit stated that the sexual abuse was "*a badge and incident of servitude* which is distressingly common, not just historically, but for young women who find themselves in coercive circumstances today." *Id.* at 266 (emphasis added). That statement that suggests that sexual acts that have been coerced by other means are covered by the involuntary servitude statute.

Moreover, in *United States v. Marcus*, 487 F. Supp. 2d 289 (E.D. N.Y. 2007), *vacated on other grounds*, 538 F.3d 97 (2d Cir. 2008), a district court relied on the ordinary meaning of the terms "labor" and "services" in rejecting a similar challenge to a forced labor conviction. *See id.* at 300 (citing the definition of "labor" as "an 'expenditure of physical or mental effort especially when fatiguing, difficult, or compulsory' " and the definition of "services" as " 'useful labor that does not produce a tangible commodity' ") (quoting Webster's Third New International Dictionary Unabridged (2002)). The Marcus court also supported its holding by considering the legislative history of § 1589, stating that "while the legislative history does not address situations where traffickers have intimate relationships with their victims, the court's survey of the [Trafficking Victims Protection Act's] legislative history reveals no expressed intention to preclude criminal liability in those contexts." *Id.* at 301.

In light of those authorities, we are persuaded that the involuntary servitude and forced labor statutes apply to coerced acts other than "work in an economic sense." Accordingly, the district court did not plainly err in instructing the jury as to the definitions of "labor" and "services" covered by those provisions.

NOTES AND QUESTIONS

1. Note the direct linkage made by the *Kaufman* court between the TVPA and the Thirteenth Amendment. Do you agree with the linkage made by the court? Is the following analogy by the court persuasive: "In our view, if an antebellum slave was relieved of the responsibility for harvesting cotton, brought into his master's house, directed to disrobe and then engage in the various acts performed by the Kaufman House residents on the videotapes (e.g., masturbation and genital shaving), his or her condition could still be fairly described as one of involuntary servitude and forced labor"?

2. Should forced labor be limited to labor and services that can be directly tied to "work in an economic sense"?

3. The *Kaufman* court relies on an outdated version of Section 1589. Please read the updated Section 1589 in Appendix 2.

2. Sex Trafficking

In addition to Section 1589, the TVPA added other criminal provisions including 18 U.S.C. § 1591 (Section 1591). This section divides its focus between the sex trafficking of adults and the sex trafficking of children.

To be convicted of sex trafficking an adult, three elements must be met. The first element is a "process" element: it requires that an adult victim be recruited, enticed, harbored, transported, provided, obtained, or maintained. The second element is a "means" element: it requires "force, threats of force, fraud, coercion . . . or any combination of such means" be used to compel the adult victim. And the third element is an "ends" element: it requires that the adult victim be caused to "engage in a commercial sex act."

But to be convicted of sex trafficking of children only two of these elements must be met — the "process" element and the "ends" element. The "means" element is not part of the equation, meaning when children are involved in a commercial sex act there is no requirement to prove force, fraud, or coercion.

With these distinctions in mind, read Section 1591 below and pay particular attention to both the *mens rea* requirement and the definition of coercion.

Section 1591. Sex trafficking of children or by force, fraud, or coercion

(a) Whoever knowingly—

(1) in or affecting interstate or foreign commerce, or within the special maritime and territorial jurisdiction of the United States, recruits, entices, harbors, transports, provides, obtains, or maintains by any means a person; or

(2) benefits, financially or by receiving anything of value, from participation in a venture which has engaged in an act described in violation of paragraph (1), knowing, or in reckless disregard of the fact, that means of force, threats of force, fraud, coercion described in subsection (e)(2), or any combination of such means will be used to cause the person to engage in a

commercial sex act, or that the person has not attained the age of 18 years and will be caused to engage in a commercial sex act, shall be punished as provided in subsection (b).

(b) The punishment for an offense under subsection (a) is—

(1) if the offense was effected by means of force, threats of force, fraud, or coercion described in subsection (e)(2), or by any combination of such means, or if the person recruited, enticed, harbored, transported, provided, or obtained had not attained the age of 14 years at the time of such offense, by a fine under this title and imprisonment for any term of years not less than 15 or for life; or

(2) if the offense was not so effected, and the person recruited, enticed, harbored, transported, provided, or obtained had attained the age of 14 years but had not attained the age of 18 years at the time of such offense, by a fine under this title and imprisonment for not less than 10 years or for life.

(c) In a prosecution under subsection (a)(1) in which the defendant had a reasonable opportunity to observe the person so recruited, enticed, harbored, transported, provided, obtained or maintained, the Government need not prove that the defendant knew that the person had not attained the age of 18 years.

(d) Whoever obstructs, attempts to obstruct, or in any way interferes with or prevents the enforcement of this section, shall be fined under this title, imprisoned for a term not to exceed 20 years, or both.

(e) In this section:

(1) The term "abuse or threatened abuse of law or legal process" means the use or threatened use of a law or legal process, whether administrative, civil, or criminal, in any manner or for any purpose for which the law was not designed, in order to exert pressure on another person to cause that person to take some action or refrain from taking some action.

(2) The term "coercion" means—

(A) threats of serious harm to or physical restraint against any person;

(B) any scheme, plan, or pattern intended to cause a person to believe that failure to perform an act would result in serious harm to or physical restraint against any person; or

(C) the abuse or threatened abuse of law or the legal process.

(3) The term "commercial sex act" means any sex act, on account of which anything of value is given to or received by any person.

(4) The term "serious harm" means any harm, whether physical or nonphysical, including psychological, financial, or reputational harm, that is sufficiently serious, under all the surrounding circumstances, to compel a reasonable person of the same background and in the same circumstances to perform or to continue performing commercial sexual activity in order to avoid incurring that harm.

(5) The term "venture" means any group of two or more individuals associated in fact, whether or not a legal entity.

NOTES AND QUESTIONS

1. In the 2008 reauthorization of the TVPA, the *mens rea* requirement in Section 1591 was amended to include "reckless disregard" rather than just "knowing." At the same time part (c) was added: "In a prosecution under subsection (a)(1) in which the defendant had a reasonable opportunity to observe the person so recruited, enticed, harbored, transported, provided, obtained or maintained, the Government need not prove that the defendant knew that the person had not attained the age of 18 years." Why might these provisions have been added? Should lack of knowledge about an individual's age be a defense to Section 1591?

2. Traffickers often prey on the vulnerabilities of their victims in order to exploit them. The 2008 reauthorization of the TVPA recognized this tactic by traffickers and included a broad definition for "serious harm." This definition acknowledges an individual's unique circumstances and vulnerabilities. Re-read § 1591(e)(4). If you were a prosecutor, how might you use this tool?

3. Section 1591 criminalizes both the person who "recruits, entices, harbor, transports, provides, obtains, or maintains" the victim and anyone who "benefits, financially or by receiving anything of value, from participation in a venture which has engaged" in such acts. Why do you think Congress criminalized anyone who "financially benefits"? Are you comfortable that someone who financially benefits might simply have "reckless disregard" of the fact that adults are being compelled or that children are involved but be held criminally liable?

3. Trafficking, Document Servitude, and Attempt

In addition to criminalizing forced labor and sex trafficking of children or by force, fraud, or coercion, the TVPA includes criminal provisions prohibiting trafficking, document servitude, and attempt. Reread Section 1589 and then read 18 U.S.C. § 1590, the trafficking provision below:

Section 1590. Trafficking with respect to peonage, slavery, involuntary servitude, or forced labor

(a) Whoever knowingly recruits, harbors, transports, provides, or obtains by any means, any person for labor or services in violation of this chapter shall be fined under this title or imprisoned not more than 20 years, or both. If death results from the violation of this section, or if the violation includes kidnapping or an attempt to kidnap, aggravated sexual abuse, or the attempt to commit aggravated sexual abuse, or an attempt to kill, the defendant shall be fined under this title or imprisoned for any term of years or life, or both.

(b) Whoever obstructs, attempts to obstruct, or in any way interferes with or prevents the enforcement of this section, shall be subject to the penalties under subsection (a).

Note the difference in scope between Sections 1590 and 1589. Section 1589 focuses on someone who "provides or obtains" forced labor, while Section 1590 criminalizes a broader range of actions such as knowingly recruiting, harboring, or transporting a victim of peonage, slavery, involuntary servitude, or forced labor.

Traffickers often try to exploit victims by controlling their immigration or identification documents such as passports, driver's license, and birth certificates. So under 18 U.S.C. § 1592 (Section 1592), the TVPA criminalizes taking control of such documents in order to compel someone into service, regardless of whether the documents are real or fraudulent. The inclusion of fraudulent documents recognizes something important: that victims with fraudulent documents may be even more vulnerable to exploitation, since traffickers may threaten to turn those documents over to the police if the victims do not comply with their demands. (The penalty for using fraudulent documents can be up to 15 years in prison.)

Section 1592. Unlawful conduct with respect to documents in furtherance of trafficking, peonage, slavery, involuntary servitude, or forced labor

(a) Whoever knowingly destroys, conceals, removes, confiscates, or possesses any actual or purported passport or other immigration document, or any other actual or purported government identification document, of another person—

(1) in the course of a violation of section 1581, 1583, 1584, 1589, 1590, 1591, or 1594(a);

(2) with intent to violate section 1581, 1583, 1584, 1589, 1590, or 1591; or

(3) to prevent or restrict or to attempt to prevent or restrict, without lawful authority, the person's liberty to move or travel, in order to maintain the labor or services of that person, when the person is or has been a victim of a severe form of trafficking in persons, as defined in section 103 of the Trafficking Victims Protection Act of 2000,

shall be fined under this title or imprisoned for not more than five years, or both.

(b) Subsection (a) does not apply to the conduct of a person who is or has been a victim of a severe form of trafficking in persons, as defined in Section 103 of the Trafficking Victims Protection Act of 2000, if that conduct is caused by, or incident to, that trafficking.

(c) Whoever obstructs, attempts to obstruct, or in any way interferes with or prevents the enforcement of this section, shall be subject to the penalties described in subsection (a).

On paper, Section 1592 seems to be a powerful tool to combat human trafficking; however, its reach might be limited in practice. The scope of Section 1592 depends on whether it is a derivative crime, which requires a finding of peonage, slavery, involuntary servitude, or forced labor, or whether the section stands alone. According to the Second Circuit in *U.S. v. Sabhnani*, 599 F.3d 215, 244–45 (2d Cir. 2010), the answer is somewhere in between: the section is not a stand alone crime, but it also does not require the finding of a derivative crime. Rather, what it requires is simply the *intent* to commit the derivative crime:

As already noted, [Defendant] does not directly challenge the sufficiency of the evidence to support his convictions for document servitude and conspiracy to commit document servitude. Instead, he argues that, because the evidence was insufficient to support his forced labor and peonage convictions, he necessarily cannot be guilty of the "derivative" offense of document servitude. [Defendant's]Br. 64. [Defendant's] argument is based on a fundamental misreading of the document servitude statute. . . . [Defendant] continually refers to this crime as an offense that is merely "derivative" of the forced labor and peonage crimes. This is incorrect: a defendant may be convicted under § 1592 for knowingly concealing immigration documents merely "with intent to violate" the forced labor or peonage statutes.

18 U.S.C. § 1592(a)(2).

Finally, in addition to creating all of the crimes discussed above, the TVPA made an attempt to commit all of these crimes, except Section 1592, "punishable in the same manner as a completed violation" 18 U.S.C. § 1594(a). This provision covers both crimes found in the TVPA and attempts to commit peonage, slavery, and involuntary servitude.

NOTES AND QUESTIONS

1. Building on Section 1592's focus on the use of immigration documents, the 2013 reauthorization of the TVPA added the following section, 18 U.S.C. § 1597:

Section 1597. Unlawful conduct with respect to immigration documents

(a) Destruction, concealment, removal, confiscation, or possession of immigration documents. It shall be unlawful for any person to knowingly destroy, conceal, remove, confiscate, or possess, an actual or purported passport or other immigration document of another individual—

(1) in the course of violating section 1351 of this title [18 U.S.C.§ 1351] or section 274 of the Immigration and Nationality Act (8 U.S.C. § 1324);

(2) with intent to violate section 1351 of this title [18 U.S.C. § 1351] or section 274 of the Immigration and Nationality Act (8 U.S.C. § 1324); or

(3) in order to, without lawful authority, maintain, prevent, or restrict the labor of services of the individual.

(b) Penalty. Any person who violates subsection (a) shall be fined under this title, imprisoned for not more than one year, or both.

(c) Obstruction. Any person who knowingly obstructs, attempts to obstruct, or in any way interferes with or prevents the enforcement of this section, shall be subject to the penalties described in subsection (b).

Why do you think this provision was added in 2013? What situations would it apply to that Section 1592 would not? What is the reach of this provision? Said differently, how might Section 1597(a)(3) be interpreted?

(Note 18 U.S.C. § 1351 criminalizes fraud in foreign labor contracting for both — work inside and outside of the United States.)

2. The TVPA has been lauded in some circles as groundbreaking and ambitious legislation. *See* Kara C. Ryf, *The First Modern Anti-Slavery Law: The Trafficking Victims Protection Act of 2000*, 34 CASE W. RES. J. INT'L L. 45, 47 (2002). But other scholars critique the TVPA for only making minimal steps towards protecting exploited workers, especially undocumented migrants. *See* Jennifer M. Chacon, *Misery and Myopia: Understanding the Failures of U.S. Efforts to Stop Human Trafficking*, 74 FORDHAM L. REV. 2977 (2006); Jennifer M. Chacon, *Tensions and Trade-offs: Protecting Trafficking Victims in the Era of Immigration Enforcement*, 158 U. PA. L. REV. 1609 (2010); *see also* Stephanie M. Berger, *No End in Sight: Why the "End Demand" Movement Is the Wrong Focus for Efforts to Eliminate Human Trafficking*, 35 HARV. J.L. & GENDER 523 (2012); Dina Francesca Haynes, *(Not) Found Chained to a Bed in a Brothel: Conceptual, Legal, and Procedural Failures to Fulfill the Promise of the Trafficking Victims Protection Act*, 21 GEO. IMMIGR. L.J. 337, 338–40 (2007); Julie Marie Lopiccolo, *Where Are the Victims? The New Trafficking Victims Protection Act's Triumphs and Failures in Identifying and Protecting Victims of Human Trafficking*, 30 WHITTIER L. REV. 851, 852 (2009); April Rieger, *Missing the Mark: Why the Trafficking Victims Protection Act Fails to Protect Sex Trafficking Victims in the United States*, 30 HARV. J.L. & GENDER 231, 233 (2007).

3. One of the more powerful critiques of the implementation of the TVPA is that corporations are rarely charged criminally with human trafficking. In, *Misery and Myopia: Understanding the Failures of U.S. Efforts to Stop Human Trafficking*, Professor Chacon provides two explanations for the lack of corporate defendants in human trafficking prosecutions:

> At least two prominent corporations have recently been involved in cases alleging workplace exploitation that might be viewed as trafficking. First, a 2001 indictment of Tyson Foods included allegations that the company paid coyotes to recruit ongoing streams of undocumented workers for its plants in Arkansas, Indiana, Missouri, North Carolina, Tennessee, Texas, and Virginia. These immigrants allegedly were subject to higher production demands and less humane working conditions than legal workers. The case was closely observed by immigration lawyers and labor leaders because they viewed methods used by Tyson Foods in recruiting and employing its undocumented workers as exemplifying the practices in many large food processing companies. Although the charges against Tyson Foods were premised on the notion that the company exploited its workers' vulnerable legal status to coerce them into working in substandard conditions, no trafficking violations were alleged.
>
> Second, following a four-year investigation, federal immigration officials detained more than 250 undocumented immigrants working at sixty Wal-Mart stores around the country in October of 2003. The employees in question alleged that they had been subjected to severely substandard employment conditions. One worker explained that he worked fifty-six hours a week making $6.25 an hour, 363 nights a year. Wal-Mart's labor

practices allegedly included physically locking workers inside stores overnight - a practice also commonly used with immigrant workers in New York area supermarkets. Nevertheless, no charges of trafficking were raised against either Wal-Mart or its subcontractors. Instead, Wal-Mart was charged with violations of smuggling laws, and those charges were dropped after Wal-Mart agreed to pay the government $11 million.

The alleged actions of these corporations apparently would have justified trafficking charges. The companies, or at the very least their subcontractors, did not simply hire undocumented workers in violation of immigration laws. These companies also used the threat of legal sanction to force those undocumented workers to labor harder, longer, and under more demeaning conditions than legal workers. Such acts should be publicly labeled "trafficking," but they are not. Mainstream corporate employers are seldom even charged with general immigration violations, and of the few companies that have been so charged, none have been charged with violating the TVPA. These companies also continue to shield themselves from liability for other labor and immigration law violations by arguing that they were unaware of the violations committed by their subcontractors

At the same time that Wal-Mart and Tyson Foods faced and settled or defeated smuggling charges, the government was also prosecuting the case of *United States v. Kil Soo Lee* under the provisions of the TVPA. That case involved two hundred Vietnamese and Chinese nationals, mostly young women, who had been forced to work in a Daewoosa garment factory in American Samoa. The workers were held in a guarded compound and were threatened with confiscation of their passports, false arrest, and other economic and legal punishments. On February 21, 2003, a jury convicted Lee, the owner of the factory, on nearly all counts.

Kil Soo Lee is the most significant trafficking case to date, both in terms of the number of victims assisted, and the degree of publicity the case has received as a successful TVPA prosecution. It involved foreign defendants operating a factory outside of the U.S. The cases involving Wal-Mart and Tyson Foods also included allegations of the exploitation of immigrant labor, particularly through the use of threats of legal punishment. But those companies were never even charged with, let alone convicted of, trafficking. Why were the actions of the Kil Soo Lee corporate defendants readily identified as trafficking, while the actions of the Tyson Foods and Wal-Mart corporate defendants were not?

There are two related explanations. First, the harsh sentences and political rhetoric surrounding the TVPA may actually operate to limit prosecutions under the Act, even in cases where the conduct in question seems to violate the letter of the TVPA. Since the enactment of the TVPA, a trafficking charge carries a particular stigma, one that seems best reserved for the worst of the worst offenders. The lengthy prison sentences required for "trafficking" are harsher than those designed for smugglers and much harsher than those designed for violations of wage and hour or other labor laws. Because most people in the United States are not conditioned to view the general exploitation of migrant labor as an evil on par with sex trafficking, prosecutors may be reluctant to attach the harsh penalties and high stigma of the TVPA to all but the most unpopular and politically powerless offenders

Ironically, it is thus possible that the very success of the TVPA in generating the social notion that trafficking is, as President Bush has said, a "special evil," may actually explain why mainstream companies and high-profile actors are never charged with trafficking. As trafficking has been linked in the public imagination with child prostitution and sex tourism, it has been decoupled from workplace abuses that may indeed amount to peonage and involuntary servitude. Congress's failure to discuss the possible expansion of the Thirteenth Amendment and Commerce Clause-based remedies to undocumented migrants cemented the idea that, rather than operating on a continuum, the abuse of laborers fell into two clear camps: virtual or actual enslavement, particularly sexual slavery, and "common" workplace violations unworthy of substantial new criminal punishment or victim remedies.

Second, noncitizens are easier targets for harsh sanctions such as those required by the TVPA than are U.S. citizens or U.S corporations. U.S. law has already dehumanized noncitizens. They have been criminalized in popular rhetoric. The tendency to conflate noncitizens and criminals has become even more common on in the wake of September 11, 2001, as immigrants are increasingly depicted as a security threats. In the face of popular assumptions that "aliens" are "criminals," accusing such individuals of the "special evil" of trafficking does not seem like such a leap. President Bush's linkage of the trafficking problem with antiterrorism efforts also feeds the stereotype of the trafficker as a foreigner.

Jennifer M. Chacon, *Misery and Myopia: Understanding the Failures of U.S. Efforts to Stop Human Trafficking*, 74 FORDHAM L. REV. 2977, 3033–36 (2006) (internal citations omitted).

B. Restitution and Civil Relief

Restitution is mandatory under the TVPA. This means that convicted traffickers are ordered to pay for the victim's losses resulting from the trafficking. In trafficking cases, restitution must cover "the full amount of the victim's losses." Restitution is not a civil cause of action. Instead it must be requested by the prosecutor in a criminal trafficking case. When it is requested, it can be requested for both lost income and out-of-pocket losses that are a direct result of the trafficking.

The TVPA recognized victims would be exploited in both legal and illegal industries. As a result, lost income can be computed as either "the greater of the gross income or value to the defendant of the victim's services or labor or the value of the victim's labor as guaranteed under the minimum wage and overtime guarantees of the Fair Labor Standards Act." A restitution award does not preclude a civil damages award.

Civil damages were not available for victims under the TVPA until 2003, when a private right of action was added by the 2003 TVPA reauthorization. Individuals who were victims of crimes under Section 1589, 1590, or 1591 could now bring a civil action to recover damages and reasonable attorney's fees.[7] In 2008, this provision was amended again. The 2008 amendments clarified that the private right of action under this section is now available for victims of any violation in the TVPA, not just Section 1589, 1590, or 1591. In addition, victims can recover damages and attorney's fees from both the perpetrator and "whoever knowingly benefits, financially or by receiving anything of value from participation in a venture which that person knew or should have known has engaged in act in violation" of the criminal provisions of the TVPA. For example, a victim of human trafficking who was forced to work in a strip club may be able to go after the owners of the club under this provision. The 2008 amendments also created a statute of limitations for civil claims: a civil case must be "commenced not later than 10 years after the cause of action arose." Civil actions under this provision are stayed if there is a criminal investigation or prosecution.[8] For additional information about civil litigation for trafficking victims please see Chapter 11.

C. Social Service Provisions

The TVPA provides certain benefits for foreign national trafficking victims who have been the victim of a "severe form of human trafficking."[9] Chapter 12 has an in-depth discussion of benefits for these victims. The 2005 TVPA reauthorization recognized for the first time in its purposes and findings section that U.S. citizens were at a risk of human trafficking.[10] With this reality in mind, the reauthorization included funding for a pilot program in three cities to provide benefits such as shelter, psychological counseling, and life skills training to juveniles who have been subjected to trafficking.[11] Individuals eligible for these benefits must meet three requirements. First, they must be U.S. citizens or legal permanent residents who are victims of trafficking or victims of a severe form of human trafficking. Second, they must have been the victim of trafficking somewhere in the United States. And third, they must not yet be 18 years of age.

---

[7] 18 U.S.C. § 1595(a) (2006) (amended 2008).

[8] 18 U.S.C. § 1595(b) (2012).

[9] *See generally* 22 U.S.C. § 7102(9) (2012).

[10] Trafficking Victims Protection Reauthorization Act of 2005, Pub. L. No. 109-164 § 2(4)-(6), 119 Stat. 3558, 3558–59.

[11] *Id.* at § 102(b), 119 Stat. at 3561–62.

Chapter 6

THE PALERMO PROTOCOL

I. INTRODUCTION

In 1998 and 1999, delegations consisting of high-level government officials from over 100 countries convened in Vienna, Austria. The goal of the delegations was to develop a global response to the growing problem of human trafficking. The end result was a pair of international agreements that helped transform human trafficking from a little known issue into a robust body of international law.

The first of these agreements is the United Nations Convention against Transnational Organized Crime ("Convention"). The second agreement, which supplemented the first and has become known as "Palermo Protocol" after the Italian city where it was ceremonially opened for signatures in December of 2000, is the Protocol to Prevent, Suppress and Punish Trafficking in Persons, Especially Women and Children. The discussion in this Chapter focuses on the Palermo Protocol. Please see Chapter 7 for a discussion of provisions in the Convention that contribute to the larger international framework for combating human trafficking.

The multi-year negotiations involving these agreements was a complex undertaking because it meant getting the countries of the world to adopt a new conceptual framework for thinking about human trafficking, a new set of represented obligations for dealing with human trafficking, and perhaps most difficult of all, a new definition of what constitutes "human trafficking."

This chapter provides an introductory guide to the scope and elements of the definition agreed to by the delegations in Vienna. The delegations hoped that reaching agreement on a definition and associated strategic framework would produce many key benefits for combating human trafficking. Among the desired benefits of an international instrument harmonizing treatment of the issue were:

> • *A global consensus harmonizes criminal provisions*: A common conception of human trafficking as a crime means fewer safe havens for traffickers to operate with impunity.

> • *A global consensus helps identify victims who would not have previously been identified as victims and also helps establish a standard of how these victims should be treated*: A common conception of human trafficking provides a common understanding of who is a victim of that crime and also provides a starting point for treating these individuals as victims rather than as, for example, migrants illegally in a country, prostitutes, or criminals themselves.

- *A global consensus aids research, analysis, and understanding*: A common conception of human trafficking gives researchers a common vocabulary of terms and metrics for collecting and analyzing data. This data can then be shared by governments around the world to compare and share effective approaches to combating human trafficking.

In addition to offering a guide to the Palermo Protocol's definition, this chapter also provides a list of eight guiding principles to help evaluate international and national human trafficking laws and best practices arising from the implementation of those laws.

II. ANATOMY OF A DEFINITION

A. Overview

The Palermo Protocol's Article 3(a) defines "trafficking in persons" in the following way:

> "Trafficking in persons" shall mean the recruitment, transportation, transfer, harbouring or receipt of persons, by means of the threat or use of force or other forms of coercion, of abduction, of fraud, of deception, of the abuse of power or of a position of vulnerability or of the giving or receiving of payments or benefits to achieve the consent of a person having control over another person, for the purpose of exploitation. Exploitation shall include, at a minimum, the exploitation of the prostitution of others or other forms of sexual exploitation, forced labor or services, slavery or practices similar to slavery, servitude or the removal of organs.

At its most basic level, this definition describes situations when a person is acquired for, held in, or used for some form of compelled activity. The following chart entitled "The Scope of Human Trafficking: The Palermo Protocol Definition" illustrates a breakdown of the component elements of this definition.[1]

---

[1] This chart is used to aid international training of government officials, prosecutors, lawyers, and others by The Warnath Group, LLC (www.WarnathGroup.com).

II. ANATOMY OF A DEFINITION

		The Warnath Group **The Scope of Human Trafficking** Anatomy of the Palermo Protocol Definition		
		The essence of human trafficking is gaining control of one or more individuals and using that power to exploit them		
ACTION (Expansive range of conduct)	**+**	**MEANS** (Ways of gaining control)	**+**	**The Trafficking** **END – PURPOSE** (The End-Purpose is the Manifestation of Slavery or Slavery-Like Exploitation Against the Victim)
AT LEAST ONE OF THE FOLLOWING: Harboring Transferring Receiving Transportation Recruitment	A N D	AT LEAST ONE OF THE FOLLOWING: Actual or Threatened: Coercion Abduction Fraud Deceit Deception Abuse of Power Abuse of a Position of Vulnerability Buying or selling control of a person (e.g. parents of a child)	A N D	AT LEAST ONE OF THE FOLLOWING: Exploitation of Prostitution Sexual Exploitation Forced Labor/Forced Services Servitude Debt Bondage Slavery Practices Similar to Slavery (Int'l Def.) Slavery-like & Analogous Practices Removal of Organs Other Forms of Exploitation may be Specified in a Country's Anti-Trafficking Law
* * * * * * *There should not be zones of impunity due to gaps in the types of participation or types of conduct included in the national legislation* *Complicity, aiding and abetting trafficking = criminal liability* *Corporations and other legal persons, subcontractors and employees associated with trafficking equals liability*		* * * * * * *For a child: No means is required* *Consent: For adults, consent of victim is irrelevant if one of the Means in this column is employed. For children, "consent" is always irrelevant.* *Physical, psychological, legal, debt bondage or other means used to compel the person.*		* * * * * * *Forced labor may or may not involve a formal labor sector or employment relationship* *Although "sexual exploitation" is not defined, it should be interpreted to include sexual slavery or servitude not requiring showing of a commercial transaction* © the Warnath Group, LLC

B. Dissecting the Three Elements

As the chart illustrates, the Protocol's definition has three elements. The following discusses these elements.

1. The "Recruitment, Transportation, Transfer, Harbouring or Receipt of Persons"

The first clause of the definition describes the types of "actions" presenting a human trafficking scenario. In a case of human trafficking, any of these actions may be present individually or they may occur in some combination. And any actor in a trafficking case may be involved in one or more of these activities. But, importantly, the existence of only one of these actions is needed to satisfy this element of the crime.

Some of the possible roles of perpetrators that are included in the crime are the "lover-boy" recruiter who offers a promise of marriage and other false promises to ensnare a targeted victim in a trafficking scheme; the labor recruiter who deceptively makes representations about the nature of the work and/or charges exorbitant fees leading to debt bondage; the driver who knowingly hands victims off to an enforcer who "breaks" or "grooms" them; and the exploiter who holds or "harbours" the victims of trafficking in whatever form of exploitation the victims are subjected to in the particular case.

This element of the definition is meant to describe the expansive range of possible participants in trafficking as well as the broad spectrum of possible kinds of participation. In other words, the activities of "recruitment, transportation, transfer, harboring or receipt of persons" were envisioned to be broadly encompassing: anyone acting with the *mens rea* linked to the end-purpose of enslavement, servitude, or other forms of exploitation involving control over another human being may be legally culpable for the crime of human trafficking.

The definition's listing of activities does not mean that it requires a linear chain of these events to exist for there to be a case of human trafficking. A trafficking scheme may, but need not necessarily, link several of these activities sequentially from recruitment to transfer, receipt and harboring a person. As described above, demonstrating that an accused trafficker has engaged in a single one of these activities is sufficient to satisfy this element of the crime.

Another potential area of confusion is that the definition of human trafficking is equivalent solely to the "process," comprised of the activities listed in this element, by which a person ends up in slavery or forced labor, as if the essence of human trafficking law and policy is about the logistics of recruiting and transporting of an individual. But human trafficking is not a crime of transport and logistics. Instead, the core conception of human trafficking — and the nature of human trafficking reflected in the Protocol — was born out of a need to create a new body of law and policy, one that would more effectively address the complex challenges presented by modern slavery and slavery-like conduct than the law and policy existing at that time allowed. Thus, it follows that the third element of the human trafficking definition — "for the purpose of exploitation" — discussed more below, rather than any "process" by which victims end up in slavery or forced labor that represents the core transgression of this crime.

A final common misunderstanding of the definition is that movement is a necessary legal element of the trafficking crime. But the plain meaning of the Protocol language makes clear that movement is not required. The use of the disjunctive "or" shows that the definition does not demand proof by prosecutors in a trafficking case of transportation or any specific enumerated act as a requisite element of trafficking — any one of the acts listed will suffice. Any erroneous focus on transportation, movement, or crossing borders is perhaps the result of the lingering historical remnants of the word "trafficking" combined with the somewhat clumsy structure of the definition. Nevertheless, under the Protocol, neither movement nor crossing borders is a legal requirement of the crime.

2. *"By Means of the Threat or Use of Force or Other Forms of Coercion, of Abduction, of Fraud, of Deception, of the Abuse of Power or of a Position of Vulnerability or of the Giving or Receiving of Payments or Benefits to Achieve the Consent of a Person Having Control Over Another Person"*

The element of "means" outlines the range of ways in which one person coerces or controls another person. The intent of this element was, in large part, to overcome the limitations of existing law (e.g., requiring showing physical coercion or ownership) in order to reach all forms of modern slavery. The "means" element was drafted essentially to include any form of behavior that is intended to achieve control over another person. As a result, the "means" may be physical coercion, psychological coercion, or legal coercion. It also includes abusing power or a position of vulnerability. It may also involve providing benefits or paying money to secure consent. It may even extend to fraud and deceit. The force or coercion may be actual or threatened.

Moreover, this coercive behavior does not have to be present at the beginning of the trafficking; it may start at any moment during the trafficking scheme. It may occur during the exploitation itself, or it may occur during the conduct preceding the exploitation, such as the recruitment or transportation of the victim — in cases where there is movement of the victim. The key point, and the thing that all cases of human trafficking share, is that there has been some effort by a person to control another person, regardless of whether that is by coercion, force, fraud, or deceit. The specific form used by a trafficker is not the salient characteristic. Debt bondage, for example, is one common means of compelling service. But less common means are used as well. There are cases, for example, where traffickers have used a victim's fear of voodoo to secure compliance.[2]

The "means" element does not apply when the victim is a minor. Article 3(c) of the Protocol states that, in these instances, a showing of means is not required. That is because for anyone under the age of 18 when the trafficking began, lack of agency is presumed by law. And without agency, the law would also not recognize the possibility of consent.

---

[2] *See, e.g.*, BBC News, *Spain holds "voodoo" traffickers*, (May 22, 2009), *available at* http://news.bbc.co.uk/go/em/fr/-/2/hi/europe/8063205.stm.

3. "for the Purpose of Exploitation"

The element of "exploitation" is the focal point of the human trafficking violation. Particularly when read together with the "means" element, it defines the kind of treatment that is the essence of the crime: subjugating another person to slavery or slave-like conditions.

Specifically, Article 3 states that:

> Exploitation shall include, at a minimum, the exploitation of the prostitution of others or other forms of sexual exploitation, forced labor or services, slavery or practices similar to slavery, servitude or the removal of organs.

This description contains a combination of precision and ambiguity. Some of the terms — such as "slavery" and "forced labor" — are themselves defined in international law and many national laws.[3] But other terms — such as "sexual exploitation" — remain undefined in the Protocol.

One reason for the intentional ambiguity of the term "exploitation" was to provide a degree of flexibility to countries in tailoring the parameters of the human trafficking crime in their laws. Thus, the list of the forms of exploitation is not meant to be exhaustive. The phrase "at a minimum" signals that countries are free to expand the list, consistent with the nature and severity of the enumerated exploitations that may be encountered within their national experience. For example, some countries have included specific forms such as debt bondage, forced begging, forced marriage, or child soldiers in the exploitation element of their national anti-trafficking law.

This definitional flexibility permits countries to (1) identify specific categories of application within the broader legal concepts (e.g., forced begging that is otherwise covered in the general category of forced labor) or (2) fill in the interstitial space between existing legal definitions within their own specific national contexts (e.g., criminalizing conduct amounting to slavery without requiring showing of legal ownership, or servitude without requiring a showing of physical coercion). And, finally, flexibility was incorporated into the definition to ensure that future laws could reach all forms of human trafficking, even new manifestations that could not be anticipated at the time of the Protocol deliberations.

The absence of definitions for "exploitation of the prostitution of others" or "other forms of sexual exploitation" hints at deep ideological battles that swirled around the negotiations. Leaving these terms undefined was intentional. It reflected — especially in the case of "sexual exploitation" — the realities of negotiating and reaching consensus on an international instrument among countries with different laws on the selling and buying of sex involving adults. As the *Legislative Guides for the Implementation of the United Nations Convention Against Transnational Organized Crime and the Protocol Thereto* explains: "Dealing with prostitution and related matters outside the scope of trafficking in persons is specifically reserved

---

[3] *E.g.*, "forced labour" is defined in international law as "all work or service which is exacted from any person under the menace of any penalty and for which the said person has not offered himself voluntarily." International Labour Organization, Forced Labour Convention, art. 2, May 1, 1932.

for the laws and policies of individual States parties."[4] By leaving the term "sex exploitation" undefined, the Protocol reflects a recognition that countries had different approaches to prostitution, some where prostitution was criminalized while other countries did not prosecute adult sellers and purchasers of sex as criminals.[5]

NOTES AND QUESTIONS

1. What types of exchanges do you think are addressed by the words "giving or receiving of payments or benefits to achieve the consent of a person having control over another person"? Such language seems aimed at exchanges between parents and traffickers for the parents' children. But could it apply to any exchange in which a person is bought and sold?

2. Threats involving voodoo is mentioned above as an example of a non-physical form of coercion. What other forms of non-physical coercion can you think of?

3. In what contexts have you used the term "exploitation"? How do these contexts match up with the context of human trafficking? For example, under the Palermo Protocol, would substandard working conditions or wages satisfy the "exploitation" element? In what ways is the scope of "exploitation" for the purposes of human trafficking ultimately limited by the "means" requirement that force, coercion, fraud, or other similar conduct be present for the case to be a trafficking crime?

4. The "means" element of the Protocol's definition is required when a victim is over the age of 18 but it is not required when the victim is under the age of 18. What are the pros and cons of setting the dividing line at this age?

5. How might conflicting interpretations of the definition of human trafficking affect real-world responses to trafficking? Compare, for example, the response of a country that requires proof that a border was crossed and generally focuses on the "process" by which victims are enslaved with the response of a country that responds to human trafficking based upon the scope of the Protocol's language?

III. AN UMBRELLA TERM

Just as the TVPA was intended to recalibrate the application and scope of existing domestic laws in order to respond to contemporary forms of slavery in the United States, the Protocol aimed to recalibrate the application and scope of

---

[4] *Legislative Guides for the Implementation of the United Nations Convention Against Transnational Organized Crime and the Protocol Thereto*, at 268 n.15 (citing the interpretive notes of the U.N. OFFICE ON DRUGS AND CRIME TRAVAUX PRPARATOIRES OF NEGOTIATIONS FOR THE ELABORATION OF THE UNITED NATIONS CONVENTION AGAINST TRANSNATIONAL ORGANIZED CRIME AND THE PROTOCOLS THERETO, SALES NO. E.06.V.5 (2006), at 64).

[5] The definition is "without prejudice to how State parties address prostitution in their respective domestic laws." U.N. OFFICE ON DRUGS AND CRIME TRAVAUX PRPARATOIRES OF NEGOTIATIONS FOR THE ELABORATION OF THE UNITED NATIONS CONVENTION AGAINST TRANSNATIONAL ORGANIZED CRIME AND THE PROTOCOLS THERETO, SALES NO. E.06.V.5 (2006), at 347; *see also* ANNE T. GALLAGHER, THE INTERNATIONAL LAW OF HUMAN TRAFFICKING 39 (Cambridge Univ. Press 2010).

existing international laws in order to respond to contemporary forms of slavery worldwide. In both cases, the objective was the same: close the legal gaps, inherited from 19th- and 20th-century notions of slavery, servitude, forced labor, practices similar to slavery or slavery-like practices and related violations that 21st-century traffickers would be able to exploit and 21st-century victims would be left unprotected by.

The scope of the term "trafficking in persons," the term used in the Protocol — or, alternatively, "human trafficking" — accomplishes this objective by creating an overarching definitional "umbrella," one which not only encompasses practices covered by pre-existing legal frameworks such as slavery and forced labor, but also practices that fall outside of those frameworks. For example, in those jurisdictions where the legal definition of "slavery" reached only cases where property-like "ownership" of another existed, the human trafficking definition was meant to reach cases of slavery that did not involve property ownership of a human being — in other words, to reach "modern slavery."

Thus, the new human trafficking definition did not simply gather the traditional legal concepts together to create a bundled package of pre-existing international or national laws. Instead, human trafficking focused on all of the ways that people could be enslaved without legal ownership, physical force, absolute physical control, complete control of movement, kidnapping, abduction, domination, or other indicia of total physical control, etc. Human trafficking would recognize the full spectrum of enslavement and severe exploitation based upon non-physical coercion and control. Thus, the overarching umbrella of the Protocol definition called on countries to reform their laws to also reach the range of additional cases that these traditional concepts did not always reach.

In sum, the umbrella term "trafficking in persons" was designed not just so that old forms of slavery would be covered but to make sure that new forms of slavery would be covered as well — a point nicely captured in a United Nations guide created to help government officials draft their own national laws on trafficking:

> It must be borne in mind that the Trafficking in Persons Protocol does not limit trafficking in persons to slavery as traditionally defined. While certain forms of trafficking may entail ownership and buying and selling of persons, in most cases the victim is merely under the control, influence or domination of another person.[6]

NOTES AND QUESTIONS

1. Do you think it is accurate to call human trafficking "modern slavery"? What are the advantages of using this term? On the other hand, are there potential costs involved?

2. Is it possible for a country to comply with the letter and spirit of Article 3 without adopting a new criminal provision called "human trafficking"?

---

[6] *See* INTER-PARLIAMENTARY UNION & U.N. OFFICE ON DRUGS & CRIME, Combating Trafficking in Persons: A Handbook for Parliamentarians No. 16-2009, 17–18 (2009).

3. Human trafficking is often described in the media as the abduction or forced migration of a person for prostitution. Given the language in the Protocol, how accurate is this description?

IV. SPECIAL DEFINITIONAL ISSUES

Human trafficking may appear in many forms. This can present a number of definitional issues about whether a particular case is one of trafficking or not. The examples in this section illustrate how some of these challenging issues may arise.

A. Human Trafficking Under the Guise of Adoption

Concerns about the heightened vulnerabilities of children and their risk of being trafficked are regularly expressed after natural disasters, such as the earthquake in Haiti or the tsunami striking Indonesia. The possibilities of obtaining and transferring a child illicitly seem ripe with opportunities for traffickers. Recognizing this, some countries have included adoption as one of the explicitly identified exploitations that, when combined with the requisite "means" element, constitutes trafficking.

NOTES AND QUESTIONS

1. Under what circumstances do you think that the Protocol applies to an illicit adoption situation? Consider the first scenario: if an infant or child is "adopted" for the intended purpose of exploiting the child.[7] But does there have to be the purpose of exploitation of the child (or a practice similar to slavery) for it to be trafficking? Can a case of trafficking exist based upon the exploitation of the natural family — the parents, brothers, and sisters — if the child is deceptively or perhaps coercively acquired (regardless of the prospects for the unknown future life that the child will lead)? What if the child is raised in a happy and loving home by his or her adoptive parents? What are the arguments for and against the latter case being human trafficking under the Protocol definition?

2. If you think that the child must be transferred for the purpose of exploitation for there to be trafficking, consider the case of trafficking for the removal of organs. In that case the exploited individual is the coerced individual providing the organ and there is no requirement to show that the purpose was to exploit the organ. Do you find this analogy that associates the exploitation with the coerced individual persuasive? Why or why not?

3. Should parents be charged with human trafficking if they sell their child to a trafficker for "adoption"? Would it be a factor in your decision if the parents did not have the financial resources to take care of the child? What if the sum received

---

[7] U.N. Office on Drugs and Crime Travaux Prparatoires of Negotiations for the Elaboration of the United Nations Convention against Transnational Organized Crime and the Protocols Thereto, Sales No. E.06.V.5 (2006), at 347. (The Travaux's interpretive note posits that "illegal adoption" constitutes an exploitative end-purpose when it amounts to a "practice similar to slavery as defined in article 1, paragraph (d), of the Supplementary Convention on the Abolition of Slavery, the Slavery Trade, and Institutions and Practices Similar to Slavery.")

would help support the basic survival costs of the child's siblings for a year?

4. Could it be trafficking if a child is abducted from an orphanage to sell to the highest bidding "adoption agency"?

5. For any scenario that you think should be a case of trafficking, who could or should be charged with a trafficking crime?

B. "Fostering" and "Children in Domesticity"

In a number of countries some children live with a family other than their own for a period of time. Different names and variations for this practice include fostering[8] and children in domesticity[9]. Sometimes the family is related to the child, but not always. Parents are often told that the child will live with the family, help occasionally with small chores around the house in exchange for care and an education. However, there is a large range of experiences faced by children in these situations. Not all cases constitute human trafficking, but based upon the facts of individual cases, many arguably do. Often the children are required to put in long and hard hours of toil, cleaning, taking care of the family's children, and doing other tasks and chores. It may involve walking miles to obtain water for the family each day. Not infrequently there is sexual abuse. Often the promise of an education is an illusion.

NOTES AND QUESTIONS

1. When children provide help around the house for a family, under what circumstances is it acceptable and when is it trafficking? What if the child is not physically harmed but is forced to work long hours every day, kept out of school, and treated differently than other children in the house?

2. How much should a country's historical and cultural context be taken into account in determining whether it is trafficking?

C. Child Brides and Forced Marriage

Around the world there are countries in which children are wed to much older men. UNICEF estimates that over 60 million young women were married as girls. Adult women in some places are also forced into marriage. Violence, abuse, and rape are common in forced marriages. In this modern world, these practices persist.

---

[8] "Fostering" — a practice found in West Africa and elsewhere — refers to the temporary placement of a child with a foster or temporary family who provides care and support (basic needs, education, etc.). This often occurs when a family is without the means to adequately support the child and places her/him temporarily in a foster environment for her/his well-being.

[9] "Children in domesticity" refers to the practice of child labor in homes. Haitian children living with other families in this situation are commonly referred to as "restaveks," which may be considered a derogatory term.

NOTES AND QUESTIONS

1. Would you argue that these practices constitute human trafficking? If not, what is the missing element? Would there be facts that constitute "recruitment"? Can a husband "harbor" a wife in satisfaction of the first element of the crime of trafficking?

2. Recall that for a child bride, the "means" element would not be required.

3. Even if forcing girls to marry men is human trafficking, do you think that such practices should be respected and deferred to because they are part of a country's or group's cultural heritage?

D. Labor Migration

Labor migrants, both those who have migrated legally and illegally (or "irregularly"), are often exploited. Their economic exploitation may involve wages, hours, and safety protections, for example. Migrants also often face acts of violence, and abuse against them. Such violence can be severe and even life-threatening.

NOTES AND QUESTIONS

1. Do wage and hour exploitation or harsh conditions of employment constitute human trafficking under the Protocol? Describe what other factors you think need to be present in a work environment to constitute trafficking?

2. If a smuggler requires an individual (and/or her family) to pay a fee that is so large that it requires the family to repay the debt after the individual is smuggled into the country, does that transform the case into human trafficking?

3. If migrants smuggled across the border are held or harbored in a guarded warehouse while an exorbitant payment is demanded to release them and they are beaten to increase the level of fear, would that transform the smuggling into a trafficking case?

4. If a migrant incurs an exorbitant debt to a smuggler, and after crossing the border must pay the money back in full — but can work anywhere to earn the money to pay it back, is that a trafficking case?

5. If a migrant incurs an exorbitant debt to a smuggler, and after crossing the border is told where he or she will work and is only permitted to work at that one place until the debt is repaid in full, is that a trafficking case?

E. Exploitation of the Prostitution of Others

The Protocol includes as one end-purpose the "exploitation of the prostitution of others." During the negotiations, alternative language was proposed: i.e., "use in prostitution," but this language was declined in favor of "exploitation of the prostitution of others."

NOTES AND QUESTIONS

1. Consider what difference there might be between the legal scope of "exploitation of the prostitution of others" in contrast to "use in prostitution"?

2. For prosecuting a case of human trafficking, would there be a difference in the showing required in a country where selling and buying sex is illegal versus a country where prostitution is not a crime?

F. Removal of Organs

The inclusion of "removal of organs" seems, on its face, to be out of place among slavery, servitude, and the nature of these other crimes. At the urging of some countries late in the negotiations, human trafficking for the purpose of organ removal was included in the definition. Organ removal in the Protocol does not refer to the illegal organ trade whereby organs are simply obtained illegally or outside normal channels. Instead, it refers to cases where people are subjected to treatment that satisfies all of the elements of trafficking with the end-purpose of illicitly obtaining one or more of the person's organs. The crime is not trafficking in organs and it is not referring to the transport of a person for the purpose of removing organs or the mere transport of organs. While some cases have been reported since the Protocol negotiations, this still remains a relatively rare form of trafficking.

G. Consent

Can a person consent to being trafficked? Is it a defense to the charge of human trafficking that an individual consented to his or her treatment? Article 3(b) of the Protocol states:

> "The consent of a victim of trafficking in persons to the intended exploitation set forth in subparagraph (a) of this article shall be irrelevant where any of the means set forth in subparagraph (a) have been used."

This addresses a concern that a case could boil down to a "he said, she said" credibility contest. In the absence of corroborating evidence to support victim-witness testimony, it was feared that a prosecution could be easily stymied. Article 3(b) of the Protocol seeks to minimize the prospect of this by clarifying that once the elements of a trafficking case are evident then consent is irrelevant. In this way, the Protocol seeks to effectively remove the defense of consent in human trafficking cases.

This provision is not relevant to cases involving children. Because no proof of "means" is required to establish a case of child trafficking, no consent issue arises.

NOTES AND QUESTIONS

1. Do you think that a person's initial consent to migrate (in transnational cases), where the person ends up trapped in domestic servitude or as a victim of sex trafficking precludes that person from being treated as a victim of trafficking? Would it make a difference if the migration is by legal or illegal means?

2. The possibility of a "he said/she said" defense during trial is not the only way the issue of consent — or the related concept of denial of being trafficked — arises. Law enforcement, NGOs and others report that individuals found at the scene of a suspected case of trafficking will often deny being a victim of trafficking or any crime. This can happen in the midst of a rescue, when all signs — based upon investigation and the totality of the circumstances — point to the existence of a trafficking case. It happens when traffickers are on location and the individual feels intimidated. It also happens in the so-called "lover-boy" situation.[10] Interestingly, a variation of this issue arises in trafficking cases involving men. Research shows that men sometimes do not want to self-identify and be classified as a "victim" of human trafficking.[11] This can be due to concerns about stigma in general. But, in addition, where human trafficking is equated with sex trafficking some men resist self-identification to avoid being misperceived in their home communities as having been trafficked for prostitution.[12] Article 3(b) does not provide easy answers to these difficult real-world situations. It does, however, highlight that countries should approach identification of victims recognizing that because it is a complex challenge it requires multi-layered procedures (effective identification cannot be based on a snapshot impression) conducted by properly trained personnel.

3. One impetus for including language about consent came from some of the NGOs attending the deliberations. These NGOs advocated for language making consent irrelevant in order to extend the definition of "human trafficking" to all prostitution rather than forced or coerced prostitution. They argued that selling one's body can never be voluntary or consented to.

V. EXTENDING THE SCOPE OF CRIMINAL LIABILITY

The Protocol makes clear that criminal liability does not attach solely to those leading, organizing, or directing the end-purpose itself. The spectrum of activities (recruitment, transfer, harboring, etc.) for which there is liability also serves to point to the extended range of actors that might otherwise be overlooked in investigating and prosecuting the trafficking crime. While not every case of trafficking is transnational, for those that are, this provides an explicit reminder of the connections among the potentially larger group of actors (whether formally or loosely organized).

Article 2(a), (b), & (c) also extends the sphere of responsibility to accomplices, those who attempt the crime and those who organize or direct other persons to commit the crime of human trafficking. And the Protocol and Convention call upon

---

[10] In a typical "lover-boy" situation, the trafficker presents himself as a potential boyfriend and courts the victim with professions of love and promises of a bright future together. He convinces the victim to move with him to another location in order to establish their life there. Once they relocate and the trafficker isolates the victim from her support network, he claims that in order to sustain their life together, the victim must prostitute herself. The trafficker becomes the dominant person in the victim's life and it is not uncommon for the victim to develop an emotional bond with the trafficker.

[11] This phenomenon is described in research by the NEXUS Institute. *See* Rebecca Surtees, *Trafficking of Men — A Trend Less Considered: The Case of Belarus and Ukraine* 91–95 (IOM 2008), available at www.NEXUSInstitute.net.

[12] *Id.*

countries to ensure that companies (legal persons) are also made liable for acts of human trafficking.

NOTES AND QUESTIONS

1. Despite the steady progress in the number of trafficking cases prosecuted in countries around the world, international organizations have expressed concern about whether those who control larger trafficking enterprises may too often escape prosecution. While human trafficking enterprises are organized in different ways, the question posed is whether the perpetrators who make the consequential decisions involving the criminal enterprise and make the bulk of the profit are as likely to be arrested, prosecuted, and convicted as the operatives or functionaries, such as enforcers, bartenders, drivers, or others who are, for example, physically at the location at the time of an enforcement raid.

2. When you review articles and reports about transnational human trafficking cases, especially larger transnational cases, see if you can determine whether or not the defendants include the central figures of the trafficking enterprise.

3. If you were the head of a country's anti-trafficking enforcement task force — and your country's criminal code included the legal tools of the Convention and Protocol — how would you plan to investigate, arrest, and prosecute the full range of culpable individuals in a large human trafficking case to better disrupt and dismantle a human trafficking network?

4. Trafficking cases are complex and often require a significant investment of resources to investigate and prosecute. They may involve criminal actors and crime scenes in different jurisdictions. What other challenges might you face in successfully developing your case?

VI. OBLIGATION BY COUNTRIES TO CRIMINALIZE

By ratifying the Convention and Protocol, countries obligate themselves to criminalize the conduct described in Article 3 of the Protocol. National laws adopted pursuant to Article 5 of the Protocol must criminalize all forms of trafficking: sex trafficking, labor trafficking, and other forms that may defy facile classification. National laws should address cases that are both transnational and domestic (often referred to as "internal") trafficking. And, as just described, national laws must reach all of those complicit in a trafficking enterprise and create liability for both natural and legal persons.

Many countries now have new laws, structures, and institutional mechanisms in place to combat human trafficking. Many countries have governmental inter-ministerial committees and National Plans of Action and other measures and mechanisms to organize and coordinate their national and international anti-trafficking efforts and work in collaboration with civil society.[13]

---

[13] *See, e.g.*, Stephen Warnath, *Efforts to Combat Trafficking in Human Beings in the OSCE Area: Co-ordination and Reporting Mechanisms: 2008 Annual Report of the OSCE Special Representative*

NOTES AND QUESTIONS

1. The achievement of over 130 countries having laws to combat human trafficking has occurred due to a number of factors. One has been the effectiveness of implementation of the Protocol's mandate to criminalize human trafficking in each country's laws. Another critical element has been the U.S. State Department's Office to Monitor and Combat Trafficking in Persons, established in 2000 by the TVPA, which has prioritized and monitored the enactment of legislation around the world since that time. At the same time, civil society — especially international organizations and NGOs — have made significant contributions to ensuring that countries have the legislation in place to address this problem.

2. To the greatest degree possible, the criminal provision of a country's human trafficking law should be drafted to guide criminal justice actors and to provide clear elements to prove criminal conduct within the scope described by Article 3. This will make investigations and prosecutions more targeted and therefore, more effective than is possible by incorporating the Article 3 language verbatim into a country's penal code. The United Nations and others have made this point clear[14]:

> Therefore, in drafting legislation, care should be taken not to incorporate verbatim parts of the text but to reflect the spirit and meaning of the various articles.[15]

And

> it is important that the meaning of the Protocol, rather than the actual language used, should be reflected in national law. Generally simple incorporation of the definition and criminalization elements into national

---

and Co-ordinator for Combating in Trafficking in Human Beings (Organization for Security and Cooperation in Europe 2008).

[14] Domestic legislation need not follow the language of the Palermo Protocol precisely, but should be adapted in accordance with domestic legal systems to give effect to the concepts contained in the Protocol. U.N. OFFICE ON DRUGS AND CRIME, TOOLKIT TO COMBAT TRAFFICKING IN PERSONS, at 3, U.N. SALES NO. E.08.V.14 (2008). "Parliamentarians must have a firm understanding of the concept of trafficking in persons if they are to develop and implement effective national legislation to combat the phenomenon. The Palermo Protocol provides them with an internationally agreed definition, which they are to use as a basis to define the crime of trafficking in domestic legislation." U.N. OFFICE ON DRUGS, AND CRIME, COMBATING TRAFFICKING IN PERSONS: A HANDBOOK FOR PARLIAMENTARIANS, at 12, U.N. SALES NO. E.09.V.5 (2009).

[15] *See* U.N. OFFICE ON DRUGS AND CRIME, LEGISLATIVE GUIDE FOR THE IMPLEMENTATION OF THE UNITED NATIONS CONVENTION AGAINST ORGANIZED CRIME AND THE PROTOCOL THERETO, at 249 PARA. 13, SALES NO. E.0000000n (2004).

> 13. It is recommended that drafters of legislation check for consistency with other offences, definitions, and other legislative uses before relying on formulations or terminology of the Organized Crime Convention, which was drafted for general purposes and addressed to Governments. Thus, the level of abstraction is higher than that necessary for domestic legislation.
>
> Therefore, in drafting legislation, care should be taken not to incorporate verbatim parts of the text but to reflect the spirit and meaning of the various articles. To assist in that process, interpretative notes will be cited throughout the legislative guide, providing context and insight into the intent and concerns of the negotiators of the Organized Crime Convention and its Protocols.

law will not be sufficient; given the nature and complexity of trafficking and other forms of transnational organized crime, drafters of legislation and legislators are advised to consider, draft and adopt the criminal offences and related provisions with great care.[16]

3. The scope of the definition of the human trafficking crime has an impact on the application of a country's law from who gets prosecuted to who may or may not be identified as a victim to who is eligible for protection and assistance.

4. Imagine that you are leading your country's legislative drafting committee, keeping in mind the meaning and spirit of the Protocol, how would you draft a criminal code provision and other significant non-criminal provisions (e.g., protection/assistance)?

VII. EIGHT PRINCIPLES OF GOOD ANTI-TRAFFICKING LEGISLATION

Despite progress evidenced by the number of laws enacted, the 2012 Trafficking in Persons Report produced by the State Department's Office to Monitor and Combat Trafficking in Persons identifies over 55 countries as either not having legislation or needing to strengthen their legislation. The Report identifies areas of improvement needed for national laws ranging from strengthening legal tools for law enforcement to protecting the rights of victims.

What are the hallmarks of a good anti-trafficking law?

Stephen Warnath, an advisor to government leaders on the development and implementation of their human trafficking laws has set out a framework comprised of eight guiding principles that can help in drafting legislation, reviewing a country's law, and evaluating the implementation of a law.[17] The following summarizes these guiding principles. This is not a comprehensive overview of the specific provisions or language that should be included in a piece of national law as there are many excellent resources that provide that information.[18]

---

[16] U.N. OFFICE ON DRUGS AND CRIME, LEGISLATIVE GUIDE FOR IMPLEMENTATION OF THE PROTOCOL TO PREVENT, SUPPRESS AND PUNISH TRAFFICKING IN PERSONS, ESPECIALLY WOMEN AND CHILDREN SUPPLEMENTING THE UNITED NATIONS CONVENTION ON TRANSNATIONAL ORGANIZED CRIME, at 270, SALES No. E. 0000000n (2004).

[17] Adapted from Stephen Warnath, *Eight Principles of Good Anti-Trafficking Legislation* (2013), available at www.WarnathGroup.com.

[18] In addition to referencing the specific mandates and guidance of the Convention, Palermo Protocol and applicable regional and other international instruments, there are many resources that provide good overviews to the content and drafting of human trafficking legislation. A small illustrative sample includes generally, U.N. OFFICE ON DRUGS AND CRIME TRAVAUX PREPARATOIRES OF NEGOTIATIONS FOR THE ELABORATION OF THE UNITED NATIONS CONVENTION AGAINST TRANSNATIONAL ORGANIZED CRIME AND THE PROTOCOLS THERETO, SALES NO. E.06.V.5 (2006); U.N. OFFICE ON DRUGS AND CRIME, LEGISLATIVE GUIDES FOR THE IMPLEMENTATION OF THE UNITED NATIONS CONVENTIONS AGAINST TRANSNATIONAL ORGANIZED CRIME AND PROTOCOL THERETO, SALES NO. E.0000000n (2004); U.N. OFFICE ON DRUGS AND CRIME, TOOLKIT TO COMBAT TRAFFICKING IN PERSONS, SALES NO. E.08.V.14 (2008); U.N. OFFICE ON DRUGS AND CRIME, COMBATING TRAFFICKING IN PERSONS: HANDBOOK FOR PARLIAMENTARIANS, U.N. SALES No. E.09.V.5 (2009); U.N. OFFICE ON DRUGS AND CRIME, MODEL LAW ON TRAFFICKING IN PERSONS, SALES No. E.09.V.8 (2009); Anne T. Gallagher, *Commentary to the Recommended Principles and Guidelines on Human Rights and Human Trafficking*, Office of the UN High Commissioner for Human Rights (2010), available at http://works.bepress.com/anne_

VII. EIGHT PRINCIPLES OF GOOD ANTI-TRAFFICKING LEGISLATION

1. Prioritize Victim-Centered Responses

A victim-centered (or human rights-centered) response is a central element of human trafficking law and policy. This principle refers to crafting and implementing a country's laws and policies in ways that will promote victims' interests. The minimum imperative of the victim-centered principle is straightforward: protect from harm and do no further harm.

Of course an appropriate victim-centered response involves doing more than the minimum. In practice, actions by governments, organizations, and others interacting with a victim must be guided by their legal obligations under international, national, and other applicable laws. Beyond that, according to this principle, all actions should be guided, to the greatest extent possible, by what is in the best interest for each individual victim (consulting with each individual victim) such that his or her rights and other interests are protected and advanced. When the victim is a child, the child's special needs must be considered and his or her best interests must drive all actions and decisions regarding their treatment. (*see* Principle 6 below)

This principle applies to how a government treats victims throughout its engagement with them. It starts during rescue efforts, to interviewing a presumptive victim, to the process used to refer to and collaborate with NGO service providers or other caregivers, to the provision of assistance and protection, to investigation of the case, to court and post-court treatment, and to his or her reintegration into society. Where more than one country is involved (e.g., a country of destination and a home country), this principle extends to the treatment afforded to each victim by all countries involved.

One of the central aspects of this principle is, in the first instance, identifying and treating individuals who have been trafficked as victims and not as perpetrators of a crime.

The victim-centered principle guides countries to recognize that victim safety is paramount. The justification for protection extends to all victims, not only those who agree to be witnesses at trial. It requires protecting the privacy, location, and identity of victims of trafficking and those who are close to them. All of these are critical to minimize the risk of retribution, intimidation, and stigmatization. The principle drives very specific application in court proceedings, including making video testimony available and making legal proceedings confidential. It affirms that providing for victim safety needs to be based upon a credible risk assessment: protecting the safety of individuals only during the criminal justice process and not after that even when the safety of the trafficked person remains in jeopardy is inconsistent with the victim-centered principle. In other words: Protect from harm and do no further harm.

---

gallagher/15. *See also* ANNE T. GALLAGHER, THE INTERNATIONAL LAW OF HUMAN TRAFFICKING (2010).

2. Link Provision of Victim Care and Protection to Need in Individual Cases

The principle to link victim care and protection to a victim's needs in individual cases overlaps with the general principle of providing a victim-centered response, but its importance calls for specific attention. This principle asks whether the provision of care in a country matches the needs of individual victims.[19]

Victims need care to begin to heal and to support their recovery. Sometimes the support only needs to be for a short time, but many times the needs are more severe and the care needs to be longer-term.

There are many aspects to adequate and appropriate care: flexible accommodation (not just shelter-based), food, medical care, mental health counseling, social counseling, legal aid, employment skills, work authorization, and help with job placement. Eligibility in the law and availability in practice are needed for a victim to have a chance at recovery and to minimize the victim's chances of being re-trafficked.

Research shows that victims decline assistance that does not respond to their needs or is available in a manner that is impossible to accept.[20] One example is when a victim has to work to support her or his family but the country of destination makes her ineligible for a work permit. Another example is when the victim is a mother with children, but the government runs a closed residential shelter with eligibility to stay in the shelter limited to single women or women without children while, at the same time, the only assistance provided is linked to living in the shelter. A final example is when assistance is only available in the city while the victim lives with family at home in the countryside. Assistance programs should be designed with beneficiary input and their real-world recovery needs at the forefront of implementation.[21]

3. Address All Forms of Human Trafficking and Protect/Assist All Categories of Victims

An aim of the Protocol is to reach, not exclude, the multitude of forms of human trafficking. Thus, the Protocol requires that countries, for example, address all forms of human trafficking, not only sex trafficking.[22] This principle is so funda-

---

[19] The Protocol does not mandate the provision of services. Rather, it obligates countries to consider implementing measures for the provision of services and recognizes the existence of victims' needs for assistance: "Trafficked persons have a wide range of assistance needs and the duty to consider provision of care and support extends to both receiving countries and victims' countries of origin." Article 6(3). Other instruments — such as the Council of Europe Convention Against Trafficking in Human Beings (CAATH) — and national legislations mandate the provision of protection and assistance.

[20] *See, e.g.*, Anette Brunovskis & Rebecca Surtees, *Leaving the Past Behind: When Victims of Trafficking Decline Assistance* (2012, Fafo & NEXUS Institute); Anette Brunovskis & Rebecca Surtees, *A Fuller Picture: Addressing Trafficking-Related Assistance Needs and Socio-economic Vulnerabilities* (2012, Fafo & NEXUS Institute), *available at* www.NEXUSInstitute.net.

[21] *Id.*

[22] Including all forms of trafficking and not excluding types of cases or categories of victims is also part of having a comprehensive approach (Principle 4).

mental to the spirit of the Protocol that it provides additional definitional flexibility to enable countries to explicitly tailor their laws to adequately address forms of trafficking that may be country-specific.[23]

A law addressing all forms of trafficking includes a definition that clearly expresses that all forms of coercion, including psychological and legal, as well as physical coercion, satisfy the "means" element.

The Protocol's definitional flexibility was intended to enable broadening not limiting the scope of the definition. Including requirements such as crossing borders is inconsistent with international standards and results in having otherwise comparable cases of modern slavery lead to different outcomes.

Even when a country's definition addresses all forms of human trafficking, it may be limited in practice. For example, the legislation may state that "victims of trafficking" shall be provided appropriate accommodation and assistance. But in reality shelter and assistance may only be available for young women subjected to sex trafficking. In this way male victims may be effectively excluded from the definition. Female victims who are mothers may be similarly excluded from care. And sometimes there are disparities between the treatment of citizens and non-citizens. There may be other limitations or discriminations that preclude care for those who have suffered the same injuries and violations against them as human beings as those who receive care. These types of limitations to eligibility or access to care differentiating among survivor categories are *de facto* limitations on the scope of the definition.

4. Implement a Comprehensive and Integrated Response

To comply with international standards, national legislation must include more than a provision criminalizing human trafficking. National legislation should be comprehensive in the sense that it reflects an integrated, broad, and holistic approach that strategically marshals and coordinates every tool available to prevent trafficking; incarcerate traffickers for terms reflecting the severity of the crime; and provide needed care and support for trafficking victims.

5. Address Root Causes/Contributing Factors

The Protocol urges countries to address the contributing factors of human trafficking. There are many factors that contribute to trafficking.[24] These "root causes" include economic, social, and cultural environments in which human trafficking exists. Demand for goods and services also contributes to trafficking in persons, as would demand for commercial sex in contexts involving human trafficking. Accordingly, a country's legislation should include initiatives that target those factors that are empirically demonstrated to contribute to human trafficking in that country.

---

[23] Although countries may wish to explicitly reference these and other specific forms, such conduct would nevertheless fall within the general categories identified in the "exploitation" element of the Protocol's definition (e.g., slavery, servitude, forced labor, etc.).

[24] *See* Stephen Warnath, Best Practices in Trafficking Prevention in Europe and Eurasia (USAID 2009).

6. Act in the Best Interest of the Child

Good legislation is not one-size-fits-all. The differentiation required to provide relevant assistance for the different needs of victims includes, especially, recognizing the special needs of child victims of trafficking. Sheltering needs are different. Procedures in court may need to be different for providing testimony when children are the victims. And unaccompanied children may require appointment of a guardian.

The Protocol sought global consensus to unify the treatment of minors by declaring that for the purposes of human trafficking, a child includes anyone under 18 years of age. This is established as a matter of law by the Protocol's Article 3(c). Whether or not a case is classified as one of child trafficking has important implications. This determination triggers, or should trigger, a number of important, substantive, and procedural rights.

7. Maximize Cooperation, both International and Domestic

An underlying premise of the Convention and Protocol is that no country can adequately address human trafficking alone. Therefore, the instruments promote international cooperation in a number of ways, including: transnational law enforcement cooperation such as mutual legal assistance and extradition as well as governmental cooperation for return and reintegration of victims by countries of destination and countries of origin. Cooperation should not be limited to law enforcement operations. Governments should pro-actively seek to coordinate, cooperate, collaborate, and consult with civil society. In particular, this includes non-governmental groups who work to provide care and support for victims of trafficking to recover and rebuild their lives. As part of this outreach it is important to seek the input of those who have survived being trafficked. Transnational referral mechanisms to coordinate victim care within countries and across borders are an important means of organizing and institutionalizing cooperation among governments and NGOs.

Legislation should institutionalize effective mechanisms of both domestic and international cooperation. The Convention and Protocol sought primarily to foster transnational cooperation. However, the rationale applies equally to fostering cooperation and collaboration within a country among governmental actors and between governments and civil society stakeholders. In the United States, in addition to coordinating bodies in the federal government, task forces of multiple levels of government and NGOs have been set up around the country. Increasingly, development of public/private partnerships among government agencies, the business community, and NGOs to work together, leverage and build upon the strengths of the actors in each of these sectors is being viewed as a significant new opportunity to address human trafficking.

8. Provide Meaningful Legal Remedies: Ensure Access to Justice for Victims; Establish Dissuasive, Proportionate, and Effective Penalties for Traffickers; and Dismantle Criminal Enterprises

Victims of trafficking should have avenues to seek justice for the harm perpetrated against them. This includes the right to civil redress through a private right of action or equivalent. A victim should have ways to initiate seeking justice on their own behalf with the assistance of (pro bono) legal counsel who vigorously represents their interests. Remedies available for human trafficking should include the range of compensatory to punitive damages. Victims have a right to the information they need regarding court proceedings so that they can protect their rights during those proceedings. No statute of limitations should apply to crimes related to human trafficking.

The principle of meaningful remedies, when applied to establishing sentences for conviction for trafficking, is that the sentence should reflect the gravity of this serious crime. The sentences should be sufficient to serve as a deterrent. They should be "effective and proportionate."

One way to consider the sufficiency of a country's penalty for the crime of human trafficking is to compare the penalties with sentences for crimes of rape, murder, servitude, or the country's other most serious crimes. Alternatively, how do the sentences compare with punishment for the country's vice crimes or migration violations.

A mature system of penalties and punishment also includes appropriate criminal and civil remedies against legal persons. Forfeiture of assets of enterprises involved in human trafficking should be available.

NOTES AND QUESTIONS

1. The victim-centered principle presents difficult issues when victim interests appear to conflict with other desired objectives. An example of this is when temporary residency or eligibility for benefits or shelter accommodations are conditioned on whether or not a victim cooperates in the investigation and prosecution of the trafficker. Among other things, this results in similarly situated victims being treated differently when only a few individuals out of a larger group of those who were victimized are needed to help with an investigation or serve as witnesses at trial against the traffickers. Victim cooperation, however, is very important to law enforcement because victims are frequently in the best position to provide testimony against the trafficker. In many cases, without victim testimony, it can be difficult to secure convictions. Placing conditions on benefits such as temporary residency likely improves the number of successful prosecutions against traffickers. And this advances an important State interest and seeing that justice is achieved against traffickers is generally something that victims desire as well.

2. Should a government condition the receipt of any benefit for a victim who has been trafficked? What if a victim wants to testify but is too afraid of the traffickers? Is this inconsistent with a victim-centered approach?

3. What do you think about the argument that making benefits dependent on victim testimony is justified because prosecuting traffickers is in the interests of victims and is therefore part of a "victim-centered" response?

Chapter 7

AN INTERNATIONAL LEGAL AND POLICY FRAMEWORK

Although the Protocol to Prevent, Suppress and Punish Trafficking in Persons, Especially Women and Children ("Palermo Protocol") is rightfully known most for providing a unifying definition of human trafficking for the first time, it also provides, in tandem with the United Nations Convention against Transnational Organized Crime ("Convention") that it supplements, a holistic framework that extends well beyond agreement on the scope of countries' criminal provisions. Article 2 articulates the Protocol's multi-pronged purpose: "to prevent and combat trafficking in persons"; "to protect and assist the victims of such trafficking"; and "to promote cooperation among States Parties in order to meet those objectives." These purposes echo the conceptual and strategic framework[1] known as the "3Ps" (standing for Prevention, Protection, and Prosecution) combined with a recognition that this complex work requires international cooperation and partnership because no country can effectively combat human trafficking alone.

Many countries now have new laws, structures, and institutional mechanisms in place to combat human trafficking. Many countries also have governmental inter-ministerial committees, National Plans of Action, National Rapporteurs (to gather and analyze data on human trafficking), and other mechanisms to organize and coordinate their national and international anti-trafficking efforts and work in collaboration with civil society.[2] While the specifics of country responses differ, most are organized around this guiding framework of the "3Ps."

This framework has begun to be elaborated and strengthened by instruments such as the Council of Europe Convention on Action Against Trafficking in Human Beings ("CAATH")[3] and other regional and inter-governmental instruments, as well as the early development of international law affirming rights and obligations in cases such as the European Court of Human Rights' decision in *Rantsev v. Cyprus and Russia* "*Rantsev*."[4]

---

[1] ANTHONY M. DESTEFANO, THE WAR ON HUMAN TRAFFICKING: U.S. POLICY ASSESSED xx (2008); LeRoy G. Potts, Jr., Note, *Global Trafficking in Human Beings: Assessing the Success of the United Nations Protocol to Prevent Trafficking in Persons*, 35 GEO. WASH. INT'L L. REV. 227, 239 (2003).

[2] *See, e.g.*, Stephen Warnath, *Efforts to Combat Trafficking in Human Beings in the OSCE Area: Co-ordination and Reporting Mechanisms: 2008 Annual Report of the OSCE Special Representative and Co-ordinator for Combating in Trafficking in Human Beings* (Organization for the Security and Cooperation of Europe, 2008).

[3] Council of Europe Convention on Action Against Trafficking in Human Beings, *opened for signature* May 16, 2005, 20 C.E.T.S. 197. Helpful associated material can be found at http://www.conventions.coe.int/Treaty/EN/Treaties/Html/197.htm.

[4] Rantsev v. Cyprus and Russia, App. No. 25965/04, Eur. Ct. H.R. (2010).

This chapter starts with an introduction to the Protocol's treatment of the elements of this framework. The chapter then turns to considering future developments in international law and policy of human trafficking signaled by CAATH and *Rantsev*.

I. PREVENTION

In general, prevention activities include any intervention aimed at reducing or eliminating the likelihood of human trafficking and re-trafficking. Prevention programs are typically divided into five categories:

- Changing the overall context or environment in which trafficking in persons [TIP] occurs (e.g., social, cultural, economic, political/legal);
- Addressing one or more factors that may contribute to a heightened risk or vulnerability of an individual (e.g., lack of information, family crisis, economic problems);
- Targeting the criminals, disrupting trafficking enterprises, and establishing deterrence in the form of an effective justice system addressing human trafficking cases;
- Reducing demand for human trafficking where it occurs in supply chains and in the commercial sex industry; and
- Increasing identification of potential cases prior to the occurrence of TIP exploitation and to enable appropriate intervention.

The Protocol requires countries to implement prevention programs. Article 9(1) states:

> 1. States Parties shall establish comprehensive policies, programs, and other measures:
>
> (a) To prevent and combat trafficking in persons.

Article 9(2) focuses on addressing social and economic factors and awareness campaigns. It also alludes to the need to anchor prevention efforts upon the findings of empirical research:

> States Parties shall endeavor to undertake measures such as research, information, and mass media campaigns and social and economic initiatives to prevent and combat trafficking in persons.

And Article 9(4) specifically mandates countries to take affirmative steps to address root causes that are contributing factors to human trafficking:

> States Parties shall take or strengthen measures . . . to alleviate the factors that make persons . . . vulnerable to trafficking, such as poverty, underdevelopment and lack of equal opportunity.

Finally, Article 9(5) requires taking additional mandatory prevention actions, including educational, social or cultural measures, to discourage demand:

> States Parties shall adopt or strengthen legislative or other measures, such as educational, social or cultural measures, including through bilateral and

multilateral cooperation, to discourage the demand that fosters all forms of exploitation of persons, especially women and children, that leads to trafficking.

Prevention of trafficking also refers to prevention of re-trafficking. Article 9(1)(b) reminds countries that effective prevention involves a continuous process that includes implementing strategies that reduce the risks of former victims being revictimized as a result of being re-trafficked. It states:

1. States Parties shall establish comprehensive policies, programs and other measures:

(a) . . . .

(b) To protect victims of trafficking in persons, especially women and children, from revictimization.

The Protocol also calls for measures at borders to prevent human trafficking. Article 11(1) states: "Without prejudice to international commitments in relation to the free movement of people, State Parties shall strengthen, to the extent possible, such border controls as may be necessary to prevent and detect trafficking in persons."

NOTES AND QUESTIONS

1. Imagine that you are in the role of lawyer/policy advisor in a federal government interagency human trafficking task force and are assigned to establish comprehensive policies, programs, and other measures to prevent trafficking in persons. What would you recommend should be the elements that make up that prevention initiative? What other federal departments would you collaborate with and how would they be involved in implementing prevention measures within their respective roles and jurisdictions? How would you prioritize budget expenditures for the program's component parts (e.g., awareness campaigns, reducing root causes, strengthening border controls, etc.)?

2. Many significant societal issues are considered "root causes" of human trafficking (e.g., family violence, lack of employment opportunities, discrimination, etc.). How do you think these large-scale societal issues should be addressed, if you do, to advance anti-trafficking prevention?

3. Article 11 calls for strengthening prevention efforts at country border and entry points. What are the challenges for border officials to identify a case of human trafficking at a country's borders? How would you assess the potential prevention impact of border control techniques to identify human trafficking cases versus the potential prevention impact of other methods?

II. PROTECTION & ASSISTANCE

Protection and assistance refers to a range of care and support needed to provide a victim with the best opportunity for recovery and restoration of his or her life, and, to the greatest extent possible, to be able to reintegrate back into society.

Protection encompasses ensuring physical safety of victims. Viewed through the human rights lens of human trafficking law and policy, it also refers to protection of a person's rights.

A. Protecting Physical Safety

Unless victims of trafficking feel safe, their prospects for recovery may be impeded. They are also less likely to be helpful in investigating and prosecuting the traffickers. The Protocol and Convention therefore address protecting the physical safety of victims, including protection against actual or threatened retaliation or intimidation.

Article 6(5) of the Protocol states:

> Each State Party shall endeavor to provide for the physical safety of victims of trafficking in persons while they are within its territory.

Article 9(1)(b), which was mentioned previously regarding measures to prevent re-trafficking, links protection to reducing the risk of revictimization:

> 1. States Parties shall establish comprehensive policies, programs and other measures:
>
> (a) . . . .
>
> (b) To protect victims of trafficking in persons, especially women and children, from revictimization.

The Protocol seeks to protect victims in several additional ways. It calls on countries to take steps to prevent disclosure of personal information about the victim that could expose their identity or location. Article 6(1) provides:

> . . . to the extent possible under its domestic law each State Party shall protect the privacy and identity of victims of trafficking in persons, including, *inter alia*, by making legal proceedings relating to such trafficking confidential.

Article 24 of the Convention reinforces the Protocol's obligation to "endeavor" to protect all victims of trafficking within a country's borders by mandating protective measures for victims serving as witnesses:

Article 24
Protection of witnesses

1. Each State Party shall take appropriate measures within its means to provide effective protection from potential retaliation or intimidation for witnesses in criminal proceedings who give testimony concerning offences covered by this Convention and, as appropriate, for their relatives and other persons close to them.

2. The measures envisaged in Paragraph 1 of this article may include, *inter alia*, without prejudice to the rights of the defendant, including the right to due process:

> (a) Establishing procedures for the physical protection of such persons, such as, to the extent necessary and feasible, relocating them and permit-

ting, where appropriate, non-disclosure or limitations on the disclosure of information concerning the identity and whereabouts of such persons;

(b) Providing evidentiary rules to permit witness testimony to be given in a manner that ensures the safety of the witness, such as permitting testimony to be given through the use of communications technology such as video links or other adequate means.

3. States Parties shall consider entering into agreements or arrangements with other States for the relocation of persons referred to in paragraph 1 of this article.

4. The provisions of this article shall also apply to victims insofar as they are witnesses.

Thus, the Convention and Protocol require countries to take a number of affirmative steps to provide for the safety of victims and witnesses.

NOTES AND QUESTIONS

1. Reading the Convention and Protocol together, what protection is mandatory for victims? What protection is mandatory for victims serving as witnesses?

2. The purpose of the Protocol's Article 6(1)'s protection of the privacy and identity of victims of trafficking is two-fold: first, to avoid aiding traffickers who would use this personal information to locate the individual to intimidate, retaliate, or attempt to re-traffic the individual, and second, to protect the victim's privacy by not disclosing sensitive information and thereby not "outing" the individual as having been trafficked, risking stigmatization and/or ostracism by family or community. Do you think that there should be criminal liability for leaking identifying information about a trafficked victim who has escaped or been rescued?

3. If you are representing a victim of trafficking, what procedures would you request to protect him or her pursuant to the Convention's Article 24 during the prosecution of the traffickers (assuming the availability of needed procedural and/or evidentiary rules)?

4. Contrast the privacy protections found in the Convention and the Protocol with the manner in which U.S. courts address cases involving adult victims of trafficking. Can you protect the identity of an adult victim in a U.S. criminal prosecution? What are the strengths and weaknesses of approaches available to protect victims' identities?

B. Assistance

The Convention and Protocol were the first international agreements to address the concept that victims of human trafficking should be eligible for a range of protection and assistance measures. Together they identify a range of specific types of care and support that might be needed. However, at least in part because of the give and take of international negotiations needed to reach consensus, most of these provisions for care and assistance are not mandatory. The Protocol's key assistance provisions are contained in Article 6.

Article 6
Assistance and protection of victims of trafficking in persons

1. [. . .]

2. Each State Party shall ensure that its domestic legal or administrative system contains measures that provide to victims of trafficking in persons, in appropriate cases:

(a) Information on relevant and administrative proceedings;

(b) Assistance to enable their views and concerns to be presented and considered at appropriate stages of criminal proceedings against offenders, in a manner not prejudicial to the rights of the defence.

3. Each State Party shall consider implementing measures to provide for the physical, psychological and social recovery of victims of trafficking in persons, including, in appropriate cases, in cooperation with non-governmental organizations, other relevant organizations and other elements of civil society, and, in particular, the provision of:

(a) Appropriate housing;

(b) Counseling and information, in particular as regards their legal rights, in a language that the victims of trafficking in persons can understand;

(c) Medical, psychological and material assistance; and

(d) Employment, educational and training opportunities.

4. Each State Party shall take into account, in applying the provisions of this article, the age, gender and special needs of victims of trafficking in persons, especially the special needs of children, including appropriate housing, education and care.

5. [. . .]

6. Each State Party shall ensure that its domestic legal system contains measures that offer victims of trafficking in persons the possibility of obtaining compensation of damage suffered.

The Protocol's Article 6, however, needs to be considered with Article 25 of the Convention, which contains more mandatory language and states in relevant part:

Article 25
Assistance to and protection of victims

1. Each State Party shall take appropriate measures within its means to provide assistance . . . to victims of offences covered by this Convention . . . .

NOTES AND QUESTIONS

1. Reading Article 25 of the Convention and Article 6(3) of the Protocol together, where would you draw the line between mandatory and discretionary assistance? Can you make an argument that certain specific forms of assistance are mandated and, if so, what forms of assistance?

2. The Protocol obligates countries to address the special needs of victims, especially the special needs of children in Article 6(4). What types of special needs of child victims of trafficking can you think of?

3. Assuming the provision of assistance, does the Protocol signal that there should be any differentiations in the provision of protection and assistance among categories of trafficking victims? E.g., victim of transnational trafficking vs. victim of trafficking entirely within a country? Citizen vs. non-citizen vs. stateless individual? Male vs. female? Sex trafficking vs. labor trafficking? Undocumented immigrant vs. immigrant legally in a country?

4. Providing protection and assistance in transnational cases requires collaborative responses. This calls for cooperation involving governments with other governments and governments with NGOs, as well as NGOs with other NGOs. Consider what some victims of trafficking [VOTs] face when returned to their home countries:

> The return of a trafficked individual to his or her country of origin potentially places him or her at risk of being re-trafficked. VoTs often return to an environment that has remained unchanged, if not worsened. The experience of being trafficked will often exacerbate issues that existed previously, including some that may have contributed to being trafficked in the first place. Additionally, returning VoTs commonly face new issues of stigma and discrimination in their home communities and even by their families.[5]

Considering this, what should the government of a victim's home country do to provide protection and assistance? Should this be connected to protection and assistance that a victim may have received in the country where he or she was a victim of trafficking? What cooperative agreements and/or other actions between countries would be helpful to formalize processes for provision of protection and assistance to provide continuity for victims to assist in their reintegration back home (e.g., provisions in bi-lateral or multi-lateral treaties, memoranda of understanding, etc.)?

5. What obligations should a country have to foreign national victims of trafficking? How might the manner in which the country treats these victims (i.e., grants of legal status, financial assistance, immediate deportation) impact that country's ability to prosecute traffickers and disrupt criminal trafficking operations?

6. What do you think are the respective roles and responsibilities of governments and NGOs in securing protection and assistance for victims of trafficking?

7. Protocol Article 6(6) does not mandate State Parties to provide victims with compensation for damage suffered, but rather speaks of offering victims the possibility of accessing compensation. Why do you think the drafters chose this

---

[5] STEPHEN WARNATH, U.S. AGENCY FOR INT'L DEV., BEST PRACTICES IN TRAFFICKING PREVENTION IN EUROPE AND EURASIA 17 (2009).

language? Do you think this should be done differently?

8. What compensation is appropriate for someone who has been enslaved in domestic servitude or working underground in a gold mine? Only lost wages? Or also pain and suffering? Should the formula for adequate compensation be different for a victim of sex trafficking than for a victim of labor trafficking?

9. The opportunity to seek compensation is an important part of accessing justice for victims of trafficking.[6] But this opportunity is hollow in practice unless the traffickers have funds or other assets and it is possible to reach them. Because profits from a trafficking enterprise may or may not be located in the same country or countries where the primary exploitation is located, this is an area where the international cooperation among countries called for by the Convention and the Protocol is of paramount importance.

10. Since victims' needs for assistance and support, as well as the States' interest in providing assistance and support to help prosecute traffickers, was recognized at the time of drafting the Protocol, why didn't the Protocol make care for victims mandatory? There appear to be two main reasons: At the time some countries were concerned that offering assistance to victims of trafficking would be a magnet that would increase illegal immigration and lead to fraudulent claims by migrants that they had been trafficked. Other countries were concerned with the potential cost — especially because they were not certain about the number of victims of trafficking they might have in their country that would need support.

III. PROSECUTION

The "prosecution" component of the Protocol has been alluded to in the previous chapter in the discussion about criminalizing the scope of the Article 3 definition and the range of criminal liability. As was discussed, the Protocol obligates each country to criminalize, at a minimum, the scope of trafficking described, although it does not require adoption of specific language.

"Prosecution" involves more than enacting a criminal provision. This component is shorthand for the full range of an effective criminal justice response needed to end the impunity of traffickers: e.g., conducting pro-active investigations, engaging in international cooperation in investigations, extradition and mutual legal assistance, prosecution, judgment/conviction, and establishing penalties that reflect the seriousness of the crime of trafficking.

The measures contained in the Convention and Protocol call upon countries to enact or strengthen their laws to make available the panoply of legal tools needed to investigate and prosecute human trafficking cases. Among the other prosecution-related measures for combating perpetrators of human trafficking that the Convention includes are:

Art. 6 — Criminalization of the laundering of proceeds of crime;

Art. 7 — Measures to combat money-laundering;

---

[6] *See* U.N. Office of the High Comm'r for Human Rights, July 1, 2002–July 26 2002,13, U.N. Doc. E/2002/68/Add. 1(May 20, 2002).

Art. 8 — Criminalization of corruption;

Art. 10 — Liability of legal persons;

Art. 11 — Prosecution, adjudication and sanctions;

Art. 12 — Confiscation and seizure;

Art. 13 — International cooperation for purposes of confiscation;

Art. 15 — Jurisdiction;

Art. 16 — Extradition;

Art. 18 — Mutual legal assistance;

Art. 19 — Joint investigations;

Art. 23 — Criminalization of obstruction of justice;

Art. 24 — Protection of witnesses;

Art. 27 — Law enforcement cooperation.

Thus, the Convention directs countries to enact a comprehensive criminal justice framework to combat human trafficking that includes: national legislation and other measures to prosecute traffickers (whether natural or legal persons), extend jurisdiction, track the money, identify and seize assets, protect witnesses, increase international cooperation in criminal justice efforts (e.g., for confiscation of assets, extradition, mutual legal assistance, joint investigations, etc.) and impose sanctions for perpetrators.

NOTES AND QUESTIONS

1. The "prosecution" component of the "3Ps" framework contains a strong multi-agency, multidisciplinary element. Many different actors — front line law enforcement, investigators, prosecutors, victim/witness coordinators, experts in organized crime, asset forfeiture, money laundering, and others — have potential roles. In addition, different levels of government have roles in successful prosecutions of these cases. Multiple government actors and stakeholders need to work together to achieve results in criminal prosecutions. Given this, how should criminal justice efforts be organized by local, regional, and national actors to most effectively identify, investigate, and prosecute human trafficking cases?

2. When you read reports of human trafficking cases, note how a case was identified. Was pro-active investigation by law enforcement involved? After initial identification of a potential case, what was the scope of the investigation that followed to identify all possible perpetrators involved and to develop evidence that could corroborate testimony by victims? What types of evidence would you want to locate to corroborate victim testimony so that a case does not rest solely on their testimony? In a transnational case, what evidence would likely be found in the location of the victims' exploitation and what evidence might be located in the victims' home country or somewhere else? In addition to evidence with a physical location, what evidence might be found on the cloud (i.e., in cyberspace)?

IV. SHORTCOMINGS OF THE PROTOCOL

Under the auspices of the United Nations, the Protocol (supplementing the Convention's overarching transnational organized crime measures) provided a vehicle for countries to collectively achieve a global consensus and begin reform of international and national law, policies, and practices on human trafficking.

As the seminal international instrument, the Protocol is a significant legal document. But, at the same time, some scholars and practitioners have challenged the Protocol as flawed in several significant ways. Commentators have focused primarily on the fact that the Protocol's protection and assistance provisions were not comprehensive and were, in too many cases, non-mandatory. Critiques also have pointed to undesirable consequences produced by the Protocol's implementation arising from its addressing human trafficking within a criminal law context rather than a human rights or "human dimension" context.

Some of the primary criticisms of the Palermo Protocol, referred to in the excerpts below as the "Trafficking Protocol," have been identified as:

> The Protocol outlines victim services that are meant to assist and protect victims of trafficking. Despite this commitment to assisting and protecting trafficking victims, the provisions providing for implementation are weak. Each of these provisions begins with . . . permissive language . . . .
>
> [. . .]
>
> The Protocol contains several additional shortcomings. First, there is no explicit protection from prosecution for the acts victims are forced to perform. Therefore, a victim could be prosecuted for a crime they were coerced into committing, such as prostitution, working without a permit, or having false identification documents. Moreover, it is possible victims will be summarily deported for these violations. Second, because victim assistance is discretionary, victims who remain in a country in order to be witnesses for the prosecution could be detained for months without critical services or employment. Many victims may be unwilling to offer testimony without these provisions, which works to the detriment of the prosecutor and undermines the law enforcement objectives of the Protocol. Victims who are not witnesses are still at risk of physical harm from their traffickers. Third, there is no mention of "reintegration," or providing services upon repatriation to ensure that a victim is able to re-enter society. The Protocol only refers to cooperation between State Parties to ensure safe repatriation of victims to their countries of origin. The victims are, in effect, then delivered back into the same conditions from which they were trafficked and are at risk of revictimization.[7]

And:

---

[7] Kelly E. Hyland, *The Impact of the Protocol to Prevent Suppress and Punish Trafficking in Persons, Especially Women and Children*, HUM. RTS. BRIEF, Winter 2001, at 30; *see also* Kelly E. Hyland, *Protecting Human Victims of Trafficking: An American Framework*, 16 BERKELEY WOMEN'S L.J. 29 (2001).

IV. SHORTCOMINGS OF THE PROTOCOL

> . . . The Trafficking Protocol is most commonly criticized for being overly focused on criminal investigation and prosecution. In particular, it is said that the accord fails meaningfully to protect the victims of human trafficking, which normally are granted access only to discretionary relief under processes that may not be explained to them. Indeed only a minority of states has adopted mechanisms even to consider the protection of trafficked persons, and these programs generally offer no more than strictly provisional assistance. The Trafficking Protocol's drafters, moreover, rejected a proposal to require that repatriation of trafficked persons be 'voluntary' in favor of a duty on the part of countries of origin to 'facilitate and accept' their trafficked citizens back 'without undue or unreasonable delay,' albeit 'with due regard for the safety of that person.' Similar inattention to the human dimension of trafficking is said also to be evident in the . . . Protocol's failure to move beyond rhetorical support for efforts to address the social and economic phenomena that make people vulnerable to traffickers in the first place.[8]

Another legal commentator, one who participated in the Vienna negotiations on behalf of the United Nations High Commissioner for Human Rights, places these shortcomings in broader perspective:

> . . . [I]n relation to the Trafficking Protocol, the final agreement was better than most had hoped. After fractious debate, the first international legal definition of trafficking proved to be sufficiently broad to embrace all but a very small range of situations in which individuals are severely exploited for private profit. Importantly, the Trafficking Protocol's general obligation to criminalize trafficking would, in practice, apply to exploitative practices taking place within as well as between national borders. States also agreed to a limitations clause maintaining the application of recognized rights and obligations. It was in relation to specific commitments of protection and support for victims that the Trafficking Protocol disappointed. The flaw, however, was not considered to be a fatal one. International human rights law already provided substantial, if underutilized protections, and subsequent legal developments, particularly at the regional level, were expected to provide ample authority to fill any remaining gaps. . . . [T]hat optimism was not misplaced. The Trafficking Protocol proved to be only the first step in the development of a comprehensive international legal framework comprising regional treaties, abundant interpretive guidance, a range of policy instruments, and a canon of state practice. This framework is truly remarkable — not just in the speed of its development, but also in its uniformity and relatively high level of consistency with international standards.[9]

---

[8] James C. Hathaway, *The Human Rights Quagmire of "Human Trafficking,"* 49 VA. J. INT'L L. 1, 2–3 (2008) (internal citations omitted); *cf.* Anne T. Gallagher. *Human Rights and Human Trafficking: Quagmire or Firm Ground? A Response to James Hathaway*, 49 VA. J. INT'L L. 789 (2009).

[9] Anne T. Gallagher. *Human Rights and Human Trafficking: Quagmire or Firm Ground? A Response to James Hathaway*, 49 VA. J. INT'L L. 789, 791 (2009).

V. EVOLVING LAW AND POLICY SINCE THE PROTOCOL: STRENGTHENING THE PROTOCOL'S PROTECTIONS AND ASSISTANCE

As a result of the failure of the Protocol to make the provision of needed protection and assistance mandatory, the future development of the law and policy of human trafficking will likely continue a trend that has emerged since the Protocol came into force to strengthen protection and assistance for victims of trafficking.

A number of regional and other international and intergovernmental instruments have been negotiated and adopted since the Protocol's enactment. Among the most influential of these instruments is the 2005 Council of Europe Convention on Action Against Trafficking in Human Beings ("CAATH").[10] Under the auspices of the Council of Europe, CAATH was negotiated and enacted, in large part, to strengthen measures in support of victims.

CAATH begins by incorporating the Protocol's Article 3(a) definition. Much of the rest of CAATH focuses on augmenting States' legal obligations to victims of trafficking. For example, while the Protocol's Article 6 provides that State Parties "shall consider implementing measures to provide for the physical, psychological and social recovery of victims of trafficking in persons," CAATH's Article 12(1) obligates State Parties to adopt measures as may be necessary to assist victims in their recovery and elaborates more specifically that the assistance to victims shall include at least:

- standards of living capable of ensuring their subsistence, through such measures as: appropriate and secure accommodation, psychological and material assistance;
- access to emergency medical treatment;
- translation and interpretation services, when appropriate;
- counseling and information, in particular as regards their legal rights and the services available to them, in a language that they can understand;
- assistance to enable their rights and interests to be presented and considered at appropriate stages of criminal proceedings against offenders;
- access to education for children.

Another important contribution made by CAATH is that it contains a non-punishment provision for victims. Article 26 obligates State Parties to "provide for the possibility of not imposing penalties on victims for their involvement in unlawful activities, to the extent that they have been compelled to do so." This protection against punishment addresses situations whereby victims may otherwise be prosecuted for crimes committed while under the influence of traffickers.

CAATH also specifies additional measures to provide for the special needs of children and to protect and to promote the rights of child victims. With respect to prevention measures, CAATH's Article 5(5) states "Each Party shall take specific

---

[10] Convention on Action Against Trafficking in Human Beings, *supra* note 3.

measures to reduce children's vulnerability to trafficking, notably by creating a protective environment for them." With reference to identification, Article 10(3) of CAATH states that where there is uncertainty whether the victim is a child (i.e., under the age of 18) "he or she shall be presumed to be a child and shall be accorded special protection measures pending verification of his/her age." CAATH's Article 10(4)(a–c) also details procedures for assisting unaccompanied minors who have been trafficked. Additionally, under Article 28(3) of CAATH, child victims who serve as witnesses "shall be afforded special protection measures taking into account the best interests of the child."

As has been discussed in other chapters, victims are instrumental in helping the government to build cases against their traffickers and prosecutors rely on victim testimony. As a result, a number of countries condition a victim's eligibility for assistance and/or the ability to stay in the country on his or her willingness to cooperate in the investigation and prosecution of the trafficker. CAATH recognizes that there can be an inherent tension between victim recovery versus the needs of the prosecution and provides victims with a recovery and reflection period of at least 30 days. Article 13(1) provides:

> Each Party shall provide in its internal law a recovery and reflection period of at least 30 days, when there are reasonable grounds to believe that the person concerned is a victim. Such a period shall be sufficient for the person concerned to recover and escape the influence of traffickers and/or to take an informed decision on cooperating with the competent authorities. During this period it shall not be possible to enforce any expulsion order against him or her. This provision is without prejudice to the activities carried out by the competent authorities in all phases of the relevant national proceedings, and in particular when investigating and prosecuting the offences concerned. During this period, the Parties shall authorise the persons concerned to stay in their territory.

Article 14(1)(a–b) elaborates broad victim eligibility for obtaining a renewable residence permit at the end of the reflection period, including, for example, his or her needs for recovery, personal situation such as risk to his or her safety, or if he or she needs to stay in order to cooperate in a criminal investigation.

Finally, Article 35 recognizes and affirms the critical role of civil society in achieving anti-trafficking objectives, including the provision of protection and assistance:

> Each Party shall encourage state authorities and public officials, to co-operate with non-governmental organizations, other relevant organizations and members of civil society, in establishing strategic partnerships with the aim of achieving the purpose of this Convention.

These are some of the examples of the stronger protection and assistance measures provided by CAATH to address gaps in the Protocol. With its stronger protections and assistance language for victims than is found in the Protocol, CAATH is an important reference that reveals the evolving direction of post-Protocol international standards.

NOTES AND QUESTIONS

1. What do you think are the practical implications for victims of adding such protections and assistance as the non-punishment provision and the reflection and recovery period?

2. Is adopting a non-punishment provision consistent with the "means" element of the trafficking crime?

3. Why is adopting a reflection and recovery period consistent with the serious nature of the crime? What is the relationship between mandatory reflection and recovery periods and the trauma suffered by many victims of trafficking?

4. Do you think that these stronger protection and assistance provisions are helpful, harmful, or inconsequential for law enforcement in human trafficking cases?

VI. LOOKING FORWARD: INTERNATIONAL COURTS AND THE ANTI-TRAFFICKING OBLIGATIONS OF NATIONS

The law and policy of human trafficking are still, relatively speaking, in their formative years. The full breadth of the Protocol's influence is yet to be seen. Certainly, legal reform, in terms of enactment and improvements of national legislations, will continue. Improvements in victim protections and assistance will be made. But, in addition, the body of human trafficking law will be further developed and refined by international courts such as the European Court of Human Rights and the International Criminal Court. International courts have just begun to wrestle with questions of how to address human trafficking within long-existing legal frameworks informed by new legal concepts and approaches that human trafficking law provides.

The 2010 European Court of Human Rights[11] case, *Rantsev v. Cyprus and Russia*[12], for example, is a landmark in the jurisprudence of human trafficking. The case addressed, for the first time, the issue of human trafficking framed as a modern legal phenomenon. In this case, Ms. Oxana Rantseva, a young Russian woman, arrived in Cyprus in 2001 and obtained temporary residence and a work permit allowing her to work as a cabaret artiste. Within weeks, after deciding to leave the cabaret, Ms. Rantseva was found dead on the street below a balcony of an apartment of a cabaret employee where she had been taken after being interviewed by police officers.

Ms. Rantseva's father subsequently brought a complaint to the European Court of Human Rights (ECHR), under the Convention for the Protection of Human Rights and Fundamental Freedoms, asserting the lack of a sufficient investigation

---

[11] The European Court of Human Rights, located in Strasbourg, is an international court established in 1959. It rules on individual or State applications alleging violations of the civil and political rights set out in the European Convention on Human Rights. In this way the Court enforces government human rights obligations in the 47 Council of Europe member States. *See generally* European Court of Human Rights, www.echr.coe.int (last visited July 4, 2013).

[12] Rantsev, App. No. 25965/04, Eur. Ct. H.R. (2010).

into the death of his daughter, the lack of adequate protection of his daughter by the Cypriot police while she was still alive, and the failure of the Cypriot authorities to take steps to punish those responsible for his daughter's death. He also complained of the failure of Russian authorities to investigate his daughter's alleged trafficking and subsequent death or to take steps to protect her from the risk of trafficking.

The ECHR addressed the question of whether countries have positive obligations regarding human trafficking within the human rights mandates found in Article 4 of the European Human Rights Convention[13] (prohibiting slavery, servitude, and forced or compulsory labor) and, if so, whether the respective responses of Cyprus and Russia in the circumstances of Oxana Rantseva violated those affirmative duties.

The ECHR found that although the 1950 European Convention did not mention human trafficking, the scope of Article 4 included human trafficking. The ECHR unanimously found that Cyprus and Russia had affirmative legal obligations toward Ms. Rantseva. In the case of Cyprus, the ECHR found that circumstances gave rise to a credible suspicion that Ms. Rantseva might have been trafficked or exploited and, in the face of that awareness, Cypriot authorities failed to take measures to protect Ms. Rantseva. The ECHR found that this failure violated Article 4.

Looking beyond *Rantsev*, further elaboration by international courts concerning the nature of obligations held by countries toward victims or apparent victims of trafficking will become a critical factor in strengthening national and international responses — especially relating to protecting and assisting victims of trafficking in concrete ways — and may come to represent an important new phase in the future direction of the law and policy of human trafficking.

RANTSEV v. CYPRUS and RUSSIA
Application No. 25965/04
Judgment of the European Court of Human Rights (2010)

I. THE CIRCUMSTANCES OF THE CASE

* * *

A. The Background Facts

15. Oxana Rantseva arrived in Cyprus on 5 March 2001. On 13 February 2001, X.A., the owner of a cabaret in Limassol, had applied for an "artiste" visa and work permit for Ms Rantseva to allow her to work as an artiste in his cabaret (see further

---

[13] Article 4 (1) of the European Convention on Human Rights states: "No one shall be held in slavery or servitude." Convention for the Protection of Human Rights and Fundamental Freedoms art. 4(1), Nov. 4, 1950, 213 U.N.T.S. 221; Article 4(2) of the Convention states: "No one shall be required to perform forced or compulsory labour[0]." *Id.* art. 4(2). The European Convention on Human Rights is an international treaty under which the member States of the Council of Europe promise to secure fundamental, civil, and political rights, not only to their own citizens but also to everyone within their jurisdiction. The Convention, which was signed on November 4, 1950 in Rome, entered into force in 1953. THE COURT IN BRIEF, EUR. CT. H.R., www.echr.coe.int.

paragraph 115 below). The application was accompanied by a copy of Ms. Rantseva's passport, a medical certificate, a copy of an employment contract (apparently not yet signed by Ms Rantseva) and a bond, signed by [X.A.] Agencies [*The contract was in English. Language from the contract that followed in opinion has been omitted*] . . .

[. . .]

16. Ms Rantseva was granted a temporary residence permit as a visitor until 9 March 2001. She stayed in an apartment with other young women working in X.A.'s cabaret. On 12 March 2001 she was granted a permit to work until 8 June 2001 as an artiste in a cabaret owned by X.A. and managed by his brother, M.A. She began work on 16 March 2001.

17. On 19 March 2001, at around 11a.m., M.A. was informed by the other women living with Ms Rantseva that she had left the apartment and taken all her belongings with her. The women told him that she had left a note in Russian saying that she was tired and wanted to return to Russia. On the same date M.A. informed the Immigration Office in Limassol that Ms Rantseva had abandoned her place of work and residence. According to M.A.'s subsequent witness statement, he wanted Ms Rantseva to be arrested and expelled from Cyprus so that he could bring another girl to work in the cabaret. However, Ms Rantseva's name was not entered on the list of persons wanted by the police.

B. The Events of 28 March 2001

18. On 28 March 2001, at around 4 a.m., Ms Rantseva was seen in a discotheque in Limassol by another cabaret artiste. Upon being advised by the cabaret artiste that Ms Rantseva was in the discotheque, M.A. called the police and asked them to arrest her. He then went to the discotheque together with a security guard from his cabaret. An employee of the discotheque brought Ms Rantseva to him.

[. . .]

19. The police officers then contacted the duty passport officer at his home and asked him to look into whether Ms Rantseva was illegal. After investigating, he advised them that her name was not in the database of wanted persons. He further advised that there was no record of M.A.'s complaint of 19 March 2001 and that, in any case, a person did not become illegal until 15 days after a complaint was made. The passport officer contacted the person in charge of the AIS (Police Aliens and Immigration Service), who gave instructions that Ms Rantseva was not to be detained and that her employer, who was responsible for her, was to pick her up and take her to their Limassol Office for further investigation at 7 a.m. that day. The police officers contacted M.A. to ask him to collect Ms Rantseva. M.A. was upset that the police would not detain her and refused to come and collect her. The police officers told him that their instructions were that if he did not take her they were to allow her to leave. M.A. became angry and asked to speak to their superior. The police officers provided a telephone number to M.A. The officers were subsequently advised by their superior that M.A. would come and collect Ms Rantseva. Both officers, in their witness statements, said that Ms Rantseva did not appear drunk.

[. . .]

20. According to M.A.'s witness statement, when he collected Ms Rantseva from the police station, he also collected her passport and the other documents which he had handed to the police when they had arrived. He then took Ms Rantseva to the apartment of M.P., a male employee at his cabaret. The apartment M.P. lived in with his wife, D.P., was a split-level apartment with the entrance located on the fifth floor of a block of flats. According to M.A., they placed Ms Rantseva in a room on the second floor of the apartment.

[. . .]

21. M.A. said that M.P. and his wife went to sleep in their bedroom on the second floor and that he stayed in the living room of the apartment where he fell asleep. The apartment was arranged in such a way that in order to leave the apartment by the front door, it would be necessary to pass through the living room.

[. . .]

22. At around 6.30 a.m. on 28 March 2001, Ms Rantseva was found dead on the street below the apartment. Her handbag was over her shoulder. The police found a bedspread looped through the railing of the smaller balcony adjoining the room in which Ms Rantseva had been staying on the upper floor of the apartment, below which the larger balcony on the fifth floor was located.

II. REPORTS ON THE SITUATION OF "ARTISTES" IN CYPRUS

A. *Ex Officio* report of the Cypriot Ombudsman on the regime regarding entry and employment of alien women as artistes in entertainment places in Cyprus, 24 November 2003

23. In November 2003, the Cypriot Ombudsman published a report on "artistes" in Cyprus. In her introduction, she explained the reasons for her report as follows (all quotes are from a translation of the report provided by the Cypriot Government):

[. . .]

24. The Ombudsman's report considered the history of the employment of young foreign women as cabaret artistes, noting that the word "artiste" in Cyprus has become synonymous with "prostitute." Her report explained that since the mid-1970s, thousands of young women had legally entered Cyprus to work as artistes but had in fact worked as prostitutes in one of the many cabarets in Cyprus. Since the beginning of the 1980s, efforts had been made by the authorities to introduce a stricter regime in order to guarantee effective immigration monitoring and to limit the "well-known and commonly acknowledged phenomenon of women who arrived in Cyprus to work as artistes." However, a number of the measures proposed had not been implemented due to objections from cabaret managers and artistic agents.

[. . .]

25. As regards the living and working conditions of artistes, the report stated:

The majority of the women entering the country to work as artistes come from poor families of the post socialist countries. Most of them are educated . . . Few are the real artistes. Usually they are aware that they will be compelled to prostitute themselves. However, they do not always know about the working conditions under which they will exercise this job. There are also cases of alien women who come to Cyprus, having the impression that they will work as waitresses or dancers and that they will only have drinks with clients ("consomation"). They are made by force and threats to comply with the real terms of their work. . . .

Alien women who do not succumb to this pressure are forced by their employers to appear at the District Aliens and Immigration Branch to declare their wish to terminate their contract and to leave Cyprus on ostensible grounds . . . Consequently, the employers can replace them quickly with other artistes. . . .

The alien artistes from the moment of their entry into the Republic of Cyprus to their departure are under constant surveillance and guard of their employers. After finishing their work, they are not allowed to go wherever they want. There are serious complaints even about cases of artistes who remain locked in their residence place. Moreover, their passports and other personal documents are retained by their employers or artistic agents. Those who refuse to obey are punished by means of violence or by being imposed fees which usually consist in deducting percentages of drinks, "consommation" or commercial sex. Of course these amounts are included in the contracts signed by the artistes.

[. . .] Generally, artistes stay at one or zero star hotels, flats or guesthouses situated near or above the cabarets, whose owners are the artistic agents or the cabaret owners. These places are constantly guarded. Three or four women sleep in each room. According to reports given by the Police, many of these buildings are inappropriate and lack sufficient sanitation facilities.

[. . .] Finally, it is noted that at the point of their arrival in Cyprus alien artistes are charged with debts, for instance with travelling [sic] expenses, commissions deducted by the artistic agent who brought them in Cyprus or with commissions deducted by the agent who located them in their country etc. Therefore, they are obliged to work under whichever conditions to pay off at least their debts."

[. . .]

272. The first question which arises is whether the present case falls within the ambit of Article 4. The Court recalls that Article 4 makes no mention of trafficking, proscribing "slavery", "servitude" and "forced and compulsory labour."

[. . .]

[*The Court considered the Siliadin case in which the Court there applied a "classic" definition of "slavery". Then the Court observes that the International Criminal Tribunal for the Former Yugoslavia concluded that the traditional concept of*

VI. INTERNATIONAL COURTS & ANTI-TRAFFICKING OBLIGATIONS

"slavery" has evolved to encompass various contemporary forms of slavery based on the exercise of any or all of the powers attaching to the right of ownership. And the Court articulates its understanding of the essence of human trafficking.]

276. In *Siliadin*, considering the scope of "slavery" under Article 4, the Court referred to the classic definition of slavery contained in the 1926 Convention, which required the exercise of a genuine right of ownership and reduction of the status of the individual concerned to an "object" (internal citation omitted). With regard to the concept of "servitude", the Court has held that what is prohibited is a particularly serious form of denial of freedom (citations omitted). For "forced or compulsory labour" to arise, the Court has held that there must be some physical or mental constraint, as well as some overriding of the person's will (citations omitted).

277. The absence of an express reference to trafficking in the Convention is unsurprising. The Convention was inspired by the Universal Declaration of Human Rights, proclaimed by the General Assembly of the United Nations in 1948, which itself made no mention of trafficking. In its Article 4, the Declaration prohibited "slavery and the slave trade in all their forms". However, in assessing the scope of Article 4 of the Convention, sight should not be lost of the Convention's special features or of the fact that it is a living instrument which must be interpreted in the light of present-day conditions. The increasingly high standards required in the area of the protection of human rights and fundamental liberties correspondingly and inevitably require greater firmness in assessing breaches of the fundamental values of democratic societies (citations omitted).

278. The Court notes that trafficking in human beings as a global phenomenon has increased significantly in recent years (see paragraphs 89, 100, 103 and 269 above). In Europe, its growth has been facilitated in part by the collapse of former Communist blocs. The conclusion of the Palermo Protocol in 2000 and the Anti-Trafficking Convention in 2005[14] demonstrate the increasing recognition at international level of the prevalence of trafficking and the need for measures to combat it.

279. The Court is not regularly called upon to consider the application of Article 4 and, in particular, has had only one occasion to date to consider the extent to which treatment associated with trafficking fell within the scope of that Article (*Siliadin*, cited above). In that case, the Court concluded that the treatment suffered by the applicant amounted to servitude and forced and compulsory labour, although it fell short of slavery. In light of the proliferation of both trafficking itself and of measures taken to combat it, the Court considers it appropriate in the present case to examine the extent to which trafficking itself may be considered to run counter to the spirit and purpose of Article 4 of the Convention such as to fall within the scope of the guarantees offered by that Article without the need to assess which of the three types of proscribed conduct are engaged by the particular treatment in the case in question.

280. The Court observes that the International Criminal Tribunal for the Former

---

[14] This refers to the Council of Europe Convention on Action Against Trafficking in Human Beings, opened for signature May 16, 2005.

Yugoslavia concluded that the traditional concept of "slavery" has evolved to encompass various contemporary forms of slavery based on the exercise of any or all of the powers attaching to the right of ownership (see paragraph 142 above). In assessing whether a situation amounts to a contemporary form of slavery, the Tribunal held that relevant factors included whether there was control of a person's movement or physical environment, whether there was an element of psychological control, whether measures were taken to prevent or deter escape and whether there was control of sexuality and forced labour (see paragraph 143 above).

281. The Court considers that trafficking in human beings, by its very nature and aim of exploitation, is based on the exercise of powers attaching to the right of ownership. It treats human beings as commodities to be bought and sold and put to forced labour, often for little or no payment, usually in the sex industry but also elsewhere (see paragraphs 101 and 161 above). It implies close surveillance of the activities of victims, whose movements are often circumscribed (see paragraphs 85 and 101 above). It involves the use of violence and threats against victims, who live and work under poor conditions (see paragraphs 85, 87 to 88 and 101 above). It is described by Interights and in the explanatory report accompanying the Anti-Trafficking Convention as the modern form of the old worldwide slave trade (see paragraphs 161 and 266 above). The Cypriot Ombudsman referred to sexual exploitation and trafficking taking place "under a regime of modern slavery" (see paragraph 84 above).

282. There can be no doubt that trafficking threatens the human dignity and fundamental freedoms of its victims and cannot be considered compatible with a democratic society and the values expounded in the Convention. In view of its obligation to interpret the Convention in light of present-day conditions, the Court considers it unnecessary to identify whether the treatment about which the applicant complains constitutes "slavery", "servitude" or "forced and compulsory labour". Instead, the Court concludes that trafficking itself, within the meaning of Article 3(a) of the Palermo Protocol and Article 4(a) of the Anti-Trafficking Convention, falls within the scope of Article 4 of the Convention. The Russian Government's objection of incompatibility *ratione materiae* is accordingly dismissed.

2. General principles of Article 4

283. The Court reiterates that, together with Articles 2 and 3, Article 4 enshrines one of the basic values of the democratic societies making up the Council of Europe (*Siliadin*, cited above, § 82). Unlike most of the substantive clauses of the Convention, Article 4 makes no provision for exceptions and no derogation from it is permissible under Article 15 § 2 even in the event of a public emergency threatening the life of the nation.

284. In assessing whether there has been a violation of Article 4, the relevant legal or regulatory framework in place must be taken into account (see, *mutatis mutandis, Nachova and Others v. Bulgaria* [GC], nos. 43577/98 and 43579/98, § 93, 2005VII). The Court considers that the spectrum of safeguards set out in national legislation must be adequate to ensure the practical and effective protection of the rights of victims or potential victims of trafficking. Accordingly, in addition to

criminal law measures to punish traffickers, Article 4 requires member States to put in place adequate measures regulating businesses often used as a cover for human trafficking. Furthermore, a State's immigration rules must address relevant concerns relating to encouragement, facilitation or tolerance of trafficking (see, *mutatis mutandis, Guerra and Others v. Italy*, 19 February 1998, §§ 58 to 60, *Reports of Judgments and Decisions* 1998I; *Z and Others v. the United Kingdom* [GC], no. 29392/95, §§ 73 to 74, ECHR 2001V; and *Nachova and Others*, cited above, §§ 96 to 97 and 99-102).

285. In its *Siliadin* judgment, the Court confirmed that Article 4 entailed a specific positive obligation on member States to penalise and prosecute effectively any act aimed at maintaining a person in a situation of slavery, servitude or forced or compulsory labour (cited above, §§ 89 and 112). In order to comply with this obligation, member States are required to put in place a legislative and administrative framework to prohibit and punish trafficking. The Court observes that the Palermo Protocol and the Anti-Trafficking Convention refer to the need for a comprehensive approach to combat trafficking which includes measures to prevent trafficking and to protect victims, in addition to measures to punish traffickers (see paragraphs 149 and 163 above). It is clear from the provisions of these two instruments that the Contracting States, including almost all of the member States of the Council of Europe, have formed the view that only a combination of measures addressing all three aspects can be effective in the fight against trafficking (see also the submissions of Interights and the AIRE Centre at paragraphs 267 and 271 above). Accordingly, the duty to penalise and prosecute trafficking is only one aspect of member States' general undertaking to combat trafficking. The extent of the positive obligations arising under Article 4 must be considered within this broader context.

286. As with Articles 2 and 3 of the Convention, Article 4 may, in certain circumstances, require a State to take operational measures to protect victims, or potential victims, of trafficking (see, *mutatis mutandis, Osman*, cited above, § 115; and *Mahmut Kaya v. Turkey*, no. 22535/93, § 115, ECHR 2000III). In order for a positive obligation to take operational measures to arise in the circumstances of a particular case, it must be demonstrated that the State authorities were aware, or ought to have been aware, of circumstances giving rise to a credible suspicion that an identified individual had been, or was at real and immediate risk of being, trafficked or exploited within the meaning of Article 3(a) of the Palermo Protocol and Article 4(a) of the Anti-Trafficking Convention. In the case of an answer in the affirmative, there will be a violation of Article 4 of the Convention where the authorities fail to take appropriate measures within the scope of their powers to remove the individual from that situation or risk (see, *mutatis mutandis, Osman*, cited above, §§ 116 to 117; and *Mahmut Kaya*, cited above, §§ 115 to 116).

287. Bearing in mind the difficulties involved in policing modern societies and the operational choices which must be made in terms of priorities and resources, the obligation to take operational measures must, however, be interpreted in a way which does not impose an impossible or disproportionate burden on the authorities (see, *mutatis mutandis, Osman*, cited above, § 116). It is relevant to the consideration of the proportionality of any positive obligation arising in the present case that the Palermo Protocol, signed by both Cyprus and the Russian Federation in 2000,

requires States to endeavour to provide for the physical safety of victims of trafficking while in their territories and to establish comprehensive policies and programmes to prevent and combat trafficking (see paragraphs 153 to 154 above). States are also required to provide relevant training for law enforcement and immigration officials (see paragraph 155 above).

288. Like Articles 2 and 3, Article 4 also entails a procedural obligation to investigate situations of potential trafficking. The requirement to investigate does not depend on a complaint from the victim or next-of-kin: once the matter has come to the attention of the authorities they must act of their own motion (see, *mutatis mutandis*, *Paul and Audrey Edwards v. the United Kingdom*, no. 46477/99, § 69, ECHR 2002II). For an investigation to be effective, it must be independent from those implicated in the events. It must also be capable of leading to the identification and punishment of individuals responsible, an obligation not of result but of means. A requirement of promptness and reasonable expedition is implicit in all cases but where the possibility of removing the individual from the harmful situation is available, the investigation must be undertaken as a matter of urgency. The victim or the next-of-kin must be involved in the procedure to the extent necessary to safeguard their legitimate interests (see, *mutatis mutandis*, *Paul and Audrey Edwards*, cited above, §§ 70 to 73).

289. Finally, the Court reiterates that trafficking is a problem which is often not confined to the domestic arena. When a person is trafficked from one State to another, trafficking offences may occur in the State of origin, any State of transit and the State of destination. Relevant evidence and witnesses may be located in all States. Although the Palermo Protocol is silent on the question of jurisdiction, the Anti-Trafficking Convention explicitly requires each member State to establish jurisdiction over any trafficking offence committed in its territory (see paragraph 172 above). Such an approach is, in the Court's view, only logical in light of the general obligation, outlined above, incumbent on all States under Article 4 of the Convention to investigate alleged trafficking offences. In addition to the obligation to conduct a domestic investigation into events occurring on their own territories, member States are also subject to a duty in cross-border trafficking cases to cooperate effectively with the relevant authorities of other States concerned in the investigation of events which occurred outside their territories. Such a duty is in keeping with the objectives of the member States, as expressed in the preamble to the Palermo Protocol, to adopt a comprehensive international approach to trafficking in the countries of origin, transit and destination (see paragraph 149 above). It is also consistent with international agreements on mutual legal assistance in which the respondent States participate in the present case (see paragraphs 175 to 185 above).

[. . .]

VI. INTERNATIONAL COURTS & ANTI-TRAFFICKING OBLIGATIONS

3. Application of the general principles to the present case

a. Cyprus

i. Positive obligation to put in place an appropriate legislative and administrative framework

290. The Court observes that in Cyprus legislation prohibiting trafficking and sexual exploitation was adopted in 2000 (see paragraphs 127 to 131 above). The law reflects the provisions of the Palermo Protocol and prohibits trafficking and sexual exploitation, with consent providing no defence to the offence. Severe penalties are set out in the legislation. The law also provides for a duty to protect victims, *inter alia* through the appointment of a guardian of victims. Although the Ombudsman criticised the failure of the authorities to adopt practical implementing measures, she considered the law itself to be satisfactory (see paragraph 90 above). The Council of Europe Commissioner also found the legal framework established by Law 3(1) 2000 to be "suitable" (see paragraph 92 above). Notwithstanding the applicant's complaint as to the inadequacy of Cypriot trafficking legislation, the Court does not consider that the circumstances of the present case give rise to any concern in this regard.

291. However, as regards the general legal and administrative framework and the adequacy of Cypriot immigration policy, a number of weaknesses can be identified. The Council of Europe Commissioner for Human Rights noted in his 2003 report that the absence of an immigration policy and legislative shortcomings in this respect have encouraged the trafficking of women to Cyprus (see paragraph 91 above). He called for preventive control measures to be adopted to stem the flow of young women entering Cyprus to work as cabaret artistes (see paragraph 94 above). In subsequent reports, the Commissioner reiterated his concerns regarding the legislative framework, and in particular criticised the system whereby cabaret managers were required to make the application for an entry permit for the artiste as rendering the artiste dependent on her employer or agent and increasing her risk of falling into the hands of traffickers (see paragraph 100 above). In his 2008 report, the Commissioner criticised the artiste visa regime as making it very difficult for law enforcement authorities to take the necessary steps to combat trafficking, noting that the artiste permit could be perceived as contradicting the measures taken against trafficking or at least as rendering them ineffective (see also the report of the U.S. State Department at paragraphs 105 and 107 above). The Commissioner expressed regret that, despite concerns raised in previous reports and the Government's commitment to abolish it, the artiste work permit was still in place (see paragraph 103 above). Similarly, the Ombudsman, in her 2003 report, blamed the artiste visa regime for the entry of thousands of young foreign women into Cyprus, where they were exploited by their employers under cruel living and working conditions (see paragraph 89 above).

292. Further, the Court emphasizes that while an obligation on employers to notify the authorities when an artiste leaves her employment (see paragraph 117 above) is a legitimate measure to allow the authorities to monitor the compliance of immigrants with their immigration obligations, responsibility for ensuring compli-

ance and for taking steps in cases of non-compliance must remain with the authorities themselves. Measures which encourage cabaret owners and managers to track down missing artistes or in some other way to take personal responsibility for the conduct of artistes are unacceptable in the broader context of trafficking concerns regarding artistes in Cyprus. Against this backdrop, the Court considers that the practice of requiring cabaret owners and managers to lodge a bank guarantee to cover potential future costs associated with artistes which they have employed (see paragraph 115 above) particularly troubling. The separate bond signed in Ms Rantseva's case is of equal concern (see paragraph 15 above), as is the unexplained conclusion of the AIS that M.A. was responsible for Ms Rantseva and was therefore required to come and collect her from the police station (see paragraph 20 above).

293. In the circumstances, the Court concludes that the regime of artiste visas in Cyprus did not afford to Ms Rantseva practical and effective protection against trafficking and exploitation. There has accordingly been a violation of Article 4 in this regard.

ii. Positive obligation to take protective measures

294. In assessing whether a positive obligation to take measures to protect Ms Rantseva arose in the present case, the Court considers the following to be significant. First, it is clear from the Ombudsman's 2003 report that here has been a serious problem in Cyprus since the 1970s involving young foreign women being forced to work in the sex industry (see paragraph 83 above). The report further noted the significant increase in artistes coming from former Soviet countries following the collapse of the USSR (see paragraph 84 above). In her conclusions, the Ombudsman highlighted that trafficking was able to flourish in Cyprus due to the tolerance of the immigration authorities (see paragraph 89 above). In his 2006 report, the Council of Europe's Commissioner for Human Rights also noted that the authorities were aware that many of the women who entered Cyprus on artiste's visas would work in prostitution (see paragraph 96 above). There can therefore be no doubt that the Cypriot authorities were aware that a substantial number of foreign women, particularly from the ex-USSR, were being trafficked to Cyprus on artistes visas and, upon arrival, were being sexually exploited by cabaret owners and managers.

295. Second, the Court emphasises that Ms Rantseva was taken by her employer to Limassol police station. Upon arrival at the police station, M.A. told the police that Ms Rantseva was a Russian national and was employed as a cabaret artiste. Further, he explained that she had only recently arrived in Cyprus, had left her employment without warning and had also moved out of the accommodation provided to her (see paragraph 19 above). He handed to them her passport and other documents (see paragraph 21 above).

296. The Court recalls the obligations undertaken by the Cypriot authorities in the context of the Palermo Protocol and, subsequently, the Anti-Trafficking Convention to ensure adequate training to those working in relevant fields to enable them to identify potential trafficking victims (see paragraphs 155 and 167 above). In particular, under Article 10 of the Palermo Protocol, States undertake to provide or

strengthen training for law enforcement, immigration and other relevant officials in the prevention of trafficking in persons. In the Court's opinion, there were sufficient indicators available to the police authorities, against the general backdrop of trafficking issues in Cyprus, for them to have been aware of circumstances giving rise to a credible suspicion that Ms Rantseva was, or was at real and immediate risk of being, a victim of trafficking or exploitation. Accordingly, a positive obligation arose to investigate without delay and to take any necessary operational measures to protect Ms Rantseva.

297. However, in the present case, it appears that the police did not even question Ms Rantseva when she arrived at the police station. No statement was taken from her. The police made no further inquiries into the background facts. They simply checked whether Ms Rantseva's name was on a list of persons wanted by the police and, on finding that it was not, called her employer and asked him to return and collect her. When he refused and insisted that she be detained, the police officer dealing with the case put M.A. in contact with his superior (see paragraph 20 above). The details of what was said during M.A.'s conversation with the officer's superior are unknown, but the result of the conversation was that M.A. agreed to come and collect Ms Rantseva and subsequently did so.

298. In the present case, the failures of the police authorities were multiple. First, they failed to make immediate further inquiries into whether Ms Rantseva had been trafficked. Second, they did not release her but decided to confide her to the custody of M.A.. Third, no attempt was made to comply with the provisions of Law 3(1) of 2000 and to take any of the measures in section 7 of that law (see paragraph 130 above) to protect her. The Court accordingly concludes that these deficiencies, in circumstances which gave rise to a credible suspicion that Ms Rantseva might have been trafficked or exploited, resulted in a failure by the Cypriot authorities to take measures to protect Ms Rantseva. There has accordingly been a violation of Article 4 in this respect also.

iii. Procedural obligation to investigate trafficking

299. A further question arises as to whether there has been a procedural breach as a result of the continuing failure of the Cypriot authorities to conduct any effective investigation into the applicant's allegations that his daughter was trafficked.

300. In light of the circumstances of Ms Rantseva's subsequent death, the Court considers that the requirement incumbent on the Cypriot authorities to conduct an effective investigation into the trafficking allegations is subsumed by the general obligation arising under Article 2 in the present case to conduct an effective investigation into Ms Rantseva's death (see paragraph 234 above). The question of the effectiveness of the investigation into her death has been considered above in the context of the Court's examination of the applicant's complaint under Article 2 and a violation has been found. There is therefore no need to examine separately the procedural complaint against Cyprus under Article 4.

b. Russia

i. Positive obligation to put in place an appropriate legislative and administrative framework

301. The Court recalls that the responsibility of Russia in the present case is limited to the acts which fell within its jurisdiction (see paragraphs 207 to 208 above). Although the criminal law did not specifically provide for the offence of trafficking at the material time, the Russian Government argued that the conduct about which the applicant complained fell within the definitions of other offences.

302. The Court observes that the applicant does not point to any particular failing in the Russian criminal law provisions. Further, as regards the wider administrative and legal framework, the Court emphasises the efforts of the Russian authorities to publicise the risks of trafficking through an information campaign conducted through the media (see paragraph 262 above).

303. On the basis of the evidence before it, the Court does not consider that the legal and administrative framework in place in Russia at the material time failed to ensure Ms Rantseva's practical and effective protection in the circumstances of the present case.

ii. Positive obligation to take protective measures

304. The Court recalls that any positive obligation incumbent on Russia to take operational measures can only arise in respect of acts which occurred on Russian territory (see, *mutatis mutandis*, *AlAdsani*, above, §§ 38 to 39).

305. The Court notes that although the Russian authorities appear to have been aware of the general problem of young women being trafficked to work in the sex industry in foreign States, there is no evidence that they were aware of circumstances giving rise to a credible suspicion of a real and immediate risk to Ms Rantseva herself prior to her departure for Cyprus. It is insufficient, in order for an obligation to take urgent operational measures to arise, merely to show that there was a general risk in respect of young women travelling to Cyprus on artistes' visas. Insofar as this general risk was concerned, the Court recalls that the Russian authorities took steps to warn citizens of trafficking risks (see paragraph 262 above).

306. In conclusion, the Court does not consider that the circumstances of the case were such as to give rise to a positive obligation on the part of the Russian authorities to take operational measures to protect Ms Rantseva. There has accordingly been no violation of Article 4 by the Russian authorities in this regard.

iii. Procedural obligation to investigate potential trafficking

307. The Court recalls that, in cases involving cross-border trafficking, trafficking offences may take place in the country of origin as well as in the country of destination (see paragraph 289 above). In the case of Cyprus, as the Ombudsman pointed out in her report (see paragraph 86 above), the recruitment of victims is

usually undertaken by artistic agents in Cyprus working with agents in other countries. The failure to investigate the recruitment aspect of alleged trafficking would allow an important part of the trafficking chain to act with impunity. In this regard, the Court highlights that the definition of trafficking adopted in both the Palermo Protocol and the Anti-Trafficking Convention expressly includes the recruitment of victims (see paragraphs 150 and 164 above). The need for a full and effective investigation covering all aspects of trafficking allegations from recruitment to exploitation is indisputable. The Russian authorities therefore had an obligation to investigate the possibility that individual agents or networks operating in Russia were involved in trafficking Ms Rantseva to Cyprus.

308. However, the Court observes that the Russian authorities undertook no investigation into how and where Ms Rantseva was recruited. In particular, the authorities took no steps to identify those involved in Ms Rantseva's recruitment or the methods of recruitment used. The recruitment having occurred on Russian territory, the Russian authorities were best placed to conduct an effective investigation into Ms Rantseva's recruitment. The failure to do so in the present case was all the more serious in light of Ms Rantseva's subsequent death and the resulting mystery surrounding the circumstances of her departure from Russia.

309. There has accordingly been a violation by the Russian authorities of their procedural obligation under Article 4 to investigate alleged trafficking.

FOR THESE REASONS, THE COURT UNANIMOUSLY

[. . .]

8. *Holds* that there has been a violation of Article 4 of the Convention by Cyprus by not affording to Ms Rantseva practical and effective protection against trafficking and exploitation in general and by not taking the necessary specific measures to protect her;

9. *Holds* that there is no need to examine separately the alleged breach of Article 4 concerning the continuing failure of the Cypriot authorities to conduct an effective investigation;

10. *Holds* that there has been no breach by Russia of its positive obligations under Article 4 of the Convention to take operational measures to protect Ms Ranseva against trafficking;

11. *Holds* that there has been a violation of Article 4 of the Convention by Russia of its procedural obligations to investigate the alleged trafficking;

[. . .]

13. *Holds*

> (a) that the Cypriot Government is to pay the applicant, within three months from the date on which the judgment becomes final in accordance with Article 44 § 2 of the Convention, EUR 40,000 (forty thousand euros) in respect of non-pecuniary damage and EUR 3,150 (three thousand one hundred and fifty euros) in respect of costs and expenses, plus any tax that may be chargeable to the applicant on these amounts;

(b) that the Russian Government is to pay the applicant, within three months from the date on which the judgment becomes final in accordance with Article 44 § 2 of the Convention, EUR 2,000 (two thousand euros) in respect of non-pecuniary damage, to be converted into Russian roubles at the rate applicable at the date of settlement, plus any tax that may be chargeable to the applicant on this amount;

(c) that from the expiry of the above-mentioned three months until settlement simple interest shall be payable on the above amounts at a rate equal to the marginal lending rate of the European Central Bank during the default period plus three percentage points;

[. . .]

Done in English, and notified in writing on 7 January 2010, pursuant to Rule 77 §§ 2 and 3 of the Rules of Court.

Søren Nielsen
Registrar

Christos Rozakis
President

NOTES AND QUESTIONS

1. Do you agree with the ECHR decision and rationale for Cyprus? Do you agree with the ECHR decision and reasoning for Russia?

2. What facts would be sufficient to trigger a State's positive obligations?

3. What facts would be sufficient to constitute awareness or "credible suspicion"?

4. The employment contract that was filed by Ms. Rantseva's employer with Cypriot authorities was unsigned by Ms. Rantseva and was in English. If Ms. Rantseva was not fluent in English, is this an additional indicia of a potential trafficking situation?

5. Do you think that the reasoning or outcome of this case depends, at least in part, upon an assumption that Ms. Rantseva was killed by her traffickers? Do you think that Ms. Rantseva was killed by her traffickers?

6. What are the positive obligations of States regarding human trafficking that the Court finds arise pursuant to Article 4? In considering the concrete steps implicated by these positive obligations, consider the range of categories of a State's potential anti-trafficking activity, including:

- Enacting legislation and other measures
- Prevention (economic, social, cultural factors, etc.)
- Protection and Assistance for victims (in country of destination and country of origin)
- Investigation
- Prosecution (and ensuring those found guilty serve their sentence)

7. Based upon the reasoning of *Rantsev*, what should be the parameters of State obligation for the conduct of private individuals and legal entities who perpetrate trafficking?

8. How could the *Rantsev* decision/reasoning apply to other cases and fact patterns? In the cases you've read in this book and for this course, where might countries face a risk of a similar decision against them (assuming this case or analysis is applicable to the country)?

9. As you review research reports of human trafficking within selected countries, consider which countries are at risk of violating their obligations (assuming the decision and rationale of *Rantsev* were applicable precedent for that country).

10. For an excellent legal analysis of State obligations in human trafficking, see ANNE T. GALLAGHER, THE INTERNATIONAL LAW OF HUMAN TRAFFICKING 218–75 (1st ed. 2010). *See also* Jean Allain, Rantsev v. Cyprus and Russia: *The European Court of Human Rights and Trafficking as Slavery*, 10 HUM. RTS. L. REV. 546 (2010); Roza Pati, *States' Positive Obligations with Respect to Human Trafficking: The European Court of Human Rights Breaks New Ground in* Rantsev v. Cyprus and Russia, 29 B.U. INT'L L.J. 79 (2011).

Chapter 8

CORPORATE ACCOUNTABILITY AND FEDERAL CONTRACTORS

The business community has a central role to play in ending human trafficking; companies are among the best-positioned of actors to do so. Human trafficking may exist within a company's labor force, sometimes facilitated by unscrupulous labor recruiters and employment agencies, or enabled by a company's subcontractor. Human trafficking may appear in the global supply chain of goods that a company produces. Many people are unaware of the prevalence of human trafficking in the extraction of raw materials and the production, manufacture, processing, and distribution of many of the products and services they regularly consume.[1]

The goods and services tainted by human trafficking touch every aspect of our lives. The list includes agricultural products, seafood, cotton, computers, cell phones, electronics, chocolate, rugs, garments, gold, and diamonds. To provide an idea of the scope of the human trafficking problem in production, consider that in 2012 the U.S. Department of Labor identified a total of 134 goods, from 74 countries that were produced by child or forced labor.[2]

Cases involving companies implicated in human trafficking are not limited to the production of goods. Other cases involve the commercial sex industry, or the provision of labor and services, including security work, construction, domestic services, and food services.

The framework of legislation, regulations, and other measures needed to engage companies in the eradication of human trafficking within their supply chains — and to hold accountable those that do not — is still in the early stages of development. But governments, nongovernmental organizations, and consumers are increasingly turning their attention toward accountability in the business sector. The legal framework to secure private sector accountability appears poised to grow in the coming years, and is likely to demand ever-increasing time and attention from

---

[1] *See generally* Slavery Footprint, http://www.slaveryfootprint.org (last visited June 30, 2013) (online survey entitled "How Many Slaves Work for You?").

[2] U.S. Dep't of Labor's Bureau of Int'l Labor Affairs Office of Child Labor, Forced Labor, and Human Trafficking, *List of Goods Produced by Child Labor or Forced Labor* (2012), http://www.dol.gov/ilab/programs/ocft/2012TVPRA.pdf. These numbers are conservative because the Department noted that its list included only goods that it could document or there is reason to believe were produced by child labor or forced labor. The Labor Department's Bureau of International Labor Affairs' (ILAB) Office of Child Labor, Forced Labor, and Human Trafficking develops and publishes an annual List of Goods Produced by Child Labor or Forced Labor, pursuant to the Trafficking Victims Protection Reauthorization Act (TVPRA) of 2005, Section 105(b). http://www.dol.gov/ilab/programs/ocft/tvpra.htm. *See also* U.S. Dep't of State, *Trafficking in Persons Report* (2013), http://www.state.gov/j/tip/rls/tiprpt/2013/index.htm.

corporate counsel, business sustainability professionals, government contract compliance officials, and others.

This chapter introduces the law and policy relevant to the private sector and its role in the fight against human trafficking.

I. LEGAL LIABILITY FOR COMPANIES

During the drafting of the Palermo Protocol, negotiating countries recognized the need to impose accountability on businesses implicated in cases of human trafficking.

The Palermo Protocol's parent instrument, the UN Transnational Organized Crime Convention (Convention), requires countries to establish liability for legal entities' roles in transnational organized crime[3] and render companies accountable through meaningful criminal and non-criminal sanctions:

Article 10   Liability of legal persons

1. Each State Party shall adopt such measures as may be necessary, consistent with its legal principles, to establish the liability of legal persons for participation in serious crimes involving an organized criminal group and for the offences established in accordance with articles 5, 6, 8 and 23 of this Convention.[4]

2. Subject to the legal principles of the State Party, the liability of legal persons may be criminal, civil or administrative.

3. Such liability shall be without prejudice to the criminal liability of the natural persons who have committed the offences.

4. Each State Party shall, in particular, ensure that legal persons held liable in accordance with this article are subject to effective, proportionate and dissuasive criminal or non-criminal sanctions, including monetary sanctions.[5]

Beyond this, Article 12 of the Convention provides for seizure and confiscation of assets associated with crimes covered by Convention, such as human trafficking. This language is primarily aimed at disabling and dismantling organized criminal enterprises, but it could apply equally to any entity complicit in human trafficking crimes. Seizing and confiscating assets of the criminal enterprise generally serves at least one of the following purposes: 1) striking a financial blow against the

---

[3] "Legal persons" or "legal entities" refers to a non-human entity that is treated as a person for limited legal purposes — corporations, for example. Legal persons can sue and be sued, own property, and enter into contracts.

[4] Convention, art. 5 (*Criminalization of participation in an organized group*), art. 6 (*Criminalization of the laundering of proceeds of crime*), art. 8 (*Criminalization of corruption*), art. 23 (*Criminalization of obstruction of justice*).

[5] Article 5(2)(c) of Protocol states, "Each State Party shall also adopt such legislative and other measures as may be necessary to establish as criminal offenses: Organizing or directing other persons to commit an offense established in accordance with paragraph 1 of this article."

criminal enterprise and 2) reaching assets that can help support victims in their recovery and compensation.

These and associated measures in the Convention[6] provide the framework for countries to track funds, identify and seize assets, and/or withdraw business licenses within the jurisdiction.

II. COUNCIL OF EUROPE CONVENTION ON ACTION AGAINST TRAFFICKING IN HUMAN BEINGS

The Council of Europe Convention on Action Against Trafficking in Human Beings (CAATH) reinforces the obligation of State Parties to adopt laws that will ensure the liability of a legal entity.

Article 22   Corporate liability

* * *

2. Apart from the cases already provided for in paragraph 1, each Party shall take the measures necessary to ensure that a legal person can be held liable where the lack of supervision or control by a natural person referred to in paragraph 1 has made possible the commission of a criminal offence established in accordance with this Convention for the benefit of that legal person by a natural person acting under its authority.

Thus, countries that have ratified the Convention and/or the CAATH are obligated to establish criminal and noncriminal liability for legal entities in cases of human trafficking.

The following excerpts illustrate provisions for criminal liability for corporate entities and other legal persons within each country's respective human trafficking law:

Article 25   Azerbaijan
The Law on the Fight Against Trafficking in Persons, 2005
Liability of legal entities for trafficking in persons

25.1. A legal entity (its branch or representative) functioning in the territory of the Azerbaijan Republic can be closed down in accordance with legislation of the Azerbaijan Republic for its links to trafficking in persons.

25.2. Once a legal entity engaged in trafficking in persons is identified and abolished, all its property shall be transferred to the funds on assisting the victims of trafficking in persons.

---

[6] *E.g.*, Convention, art. 7 (*Measures to combat money-laundering*), art.13 (*International cooperation for purposes of confiscation*), art. 14 (*Disposal of confiscated proceeds of crime or property*) ("State Parties shall . . . give priority consideration to returning the confiscated proceeds of crime or property to the requesting State Party so that it can give compensation to the victims of the crime or return such proceeds of crime or property to their legitimate owners.").

Antigua and Barbuda
The Trafficking in Persons (Prevention) Act, 2010

Article 69. Offence by body corporate

Where an offence against a provision of this Act has been committed by a body corporate, a person who at the time of the commission of the offence was—

(a) a director or manager or other similar officer of the body corporate;

(b) purporting to act in the capacity of a director or manager or other similar officer of the body corporate, or was in any manner responsible for the management of any of the affairs of such body corporate or was assisting in such management; shall also be liable for that offence unless he proves that the offence was committed without his knowledge, consent or connivance, and that he exercised all such diligence to prevent the commission of the offence as he ought to have exercised, having regard to the nature of his functions in that capacity and to all the circumstances.

Article 70. Offence by employee or agent

(1) In order to establish the liability of an employer or principal for an offence under Part III, the conduct of an employee or agent of or any other person acting on behalf of the employer or principal may be attributed to the employer or principal if that person was acting—

(a) within the scope of his employment;

(b) within the scope of his actual or apparent authority; or

(c) with the consent, whether express or implied, of a director, member or partner of the employer or principal.

(2) Subsection (1) does not exclude the liability of an employee or agent of or any other person acting on behalf of the employer or principal for committing the offence of trafficking in persons.

(3) The court may, upon convicting an employer or principal of an offence under Part III, make an order revoking the license or registration of the employer or principal to operate the business in the course of which the offence was committed.

NOTES AND QUESTIONS

1. CAATH establishes liability for legal entities when the trafficking crime is committed "for the benefit" of that legal entity. Consider different human trafficking scenarios involving companies, their subcontracted supply chain, and employees: do you think this "for the benefit" language sets the right threshold for accountability or does it establish a scope of liability for legal entities that is too restrictive?

2. Countries frequently set up funds for the statutorily prescribed dispersal of assets acquired from traffickers in these cases. Azerbaijan's anti-trafficking law, in

addition to creating liability for legal entities, also directs that a legal entity's property shall be utilized to assist the victims of the crime. How might this be helpful for the possibility of having resources available to provide victim support? What potential negative consequences may result if a country's victim support is entirely dependent on the recovered assets of traffickers?

3. For Antigua and Barbuda's anti-trafficking law, consider the scope of liability for corporate officials once an offense has been established. If you represented an officer of a company that was found to have committed a trafficking offence, what evidence and arguments would you make on behalf of your client, insofar as the law states that a "director or manager or other similar officer of the corporate body [. . .] shall also be liable for that offence unless he proves that the offence was committed without his knowledge, consent or connivance, and that he exercised all such diligence to prevent the commission of the offence as he ought to have exercised, having regard to the nature of his functions in that capacity and to all the circumstances . . . "? If you were the corporate counsel of a company doing business in Antigua and Barbuda, what type of policies and standard operating procedures regarding human trafficking would you recommend be adopted by the company?

III. SPECIAL SUB-GROUP OF CORPORATE ACCOUNTABILITY: FEDERAL CONTRACTORS

One category of business that has drawn specific government attention on the issue of human trafficking is federal contractors with the U.S. government.

The U.S. government is the largest single purchaser of goods and services in the world. It also deploys an immense global labor force in military, diplomatic, and civilian roles.[7] Many of these are U.S. government employees but, increasingly, much of this labor force is supplied by federal contractors.

> States and international organizations have, over the past ten years, shifted a surprising range of foreign policy function to private contractors. While they have done so quietly and with little fanfare, the extent of this shift is truly breathtaking: working for both for-profit companies and nonprofit organizations, these contractors are delivering aid, negotiating peace settlements, and fighting wars.[8]

Some of these contractors, or their subcontractors or employees, working on behalf of the U.S. government and expending funds provided by U.S. taxpayers, have been implicated in cases of human trafficking.

* * *

---

[7] There were more than 225,000 laborers employed by private contractors by mid-2009. LAURA A. DICKINSON, OUTSOURCING WAR & PEACE 3 (2011) (citing U.S. Gov't Accountability Office, GAO-10-1, *Contingency Contracting: DOD, State, and USAID Continue to Face Challenges in Tracking Contractor Personnel and Contracts in Iraq and Afghanistan* (2009), http://www.gao.gov/products/GAO-10-1).

[8] *Id.*

One of the earliest reported cases linking a federal contractor to human trafficking arose before the finalization of the Palermo Protocol and the TVPA. As the following describes, this is a case of trafficking by a contractor's employees, whose mission was to train police in post-war Bosnia Herzegovina. The story was uncovered by a small group of determined individuals, including a whistleblower, Kathryn Bolkovac, who figured prominently in uncovering the shocking discoveries that were made.

Kathryn Bolkovac, DynCorp, and Human Trafficking in Bosnia Herzegovina

Kathryn Bolkovac was a former police officer from Nebraska. In 2000, she was working as United Nations [UN] International Police Task Force (IPTF) human rights gender officer in post-war Bosnia for DynCorp, a contractor for the U.S. Department of State. Dyncorp was providing American personnel for the UN Mission in Bosnia.

> [O]ne day the body of a skimpily dressed Ukrainian girl came floating down the River Bosna. Soon after, a Moldovan girl was found wandering the river banks. Bolkavac attempted to interview her but only understood one word, "Florida," the name of a nightclub where she'd often see UN vehicles parked.
>
> When she arrived the club was deserted. She found stacks of American dollars and foreign passports in a safe and, behind a locked door, seven girls. . . . They were afraid to talk. One of them pointed to the river outside. "We don't want to end up floating."
>
> Dozens of girls began turning up at Bolkovac's station with "eerily similar" stories: they'd taken a job abroad as a waitress or cleaner or nanny, but during the journey everything had gone wrong. They were taken somewhere else, forcibly stripped and sold to someone who humiliated, beat and raped them into submission. Now they were imprisoned in brothels in Bosnia.[9]

Bolkovac and another DynCorp employee, Ben Johnston, later discovered that some of their colleagues in the UN IPTF were complicit in the trafficking. Some were taking advantage of the trafficked victims sexually, while others were on the traffickers' payroll. "They were paid to give warnings on raids, return girls who escaped or, when rescued girls were repatriated ('dumped somewhere near the border,' according to Bolkovac), let the traffickers know where they could collect them so that they could be 'recycled back into the system. Free access to the girls was an added perk.'"[10] Ms. Bolkovac notified her supervisors and UN officials.

Mr. Johnston characterized what he found this way: "At that time I heard you could purchase women, that they knew a way . . . they falsified their passports or that they would get them falsified . . . a lot of people said you can buy a woman and

---

[9] Nisha Lilia Diu, *Unsilent Witness*, THE TELEGRAPH, Jan. 29, 2012. *See generally* Martina Vandenberg, *Hopes Betrayed: Trafficking of Women and Girls to Post-Conflict Bosnia and Herzegovina for Forced Prostitution* (Human Rights Watch 2002), *available at* http://www.hrw.org/reports/2002/bosnia/.

[10] Diu, *supra* note 9.

how good it is to have a sex slave at home."[11]

In April 2001, DynCorp terminated Bolkovac, alleging that she had falsified timesheets.[12] She sued London-based DynCorp through an employment tribunal in the United Kingdom, claiming she had been unfairly dismissed. The tribunal ruled in her favor, and awarded her $173,000.

The Department of Defense subsequently began an inquiry into the allegations, but ultimately ceased its investigation because DynCorp's contract was with the Department of State.[13]

* * *

This and other reports of involvement in human trafficking by U.S. government personnel and federal contractors — including U.S. military personnel in South Korea — caught the attention of U.S. government leaders.

In response to concerns about these incidents, on December 16, 2002, President George W. Bush signed a National Security Presidential Directive mandating a "zero tolerance" policy toward human trafficking by members of the U.S. armed services, civilian government employees, and civilian contractors.

Congress also moved to address federal contractor involvement in trafficking through their reauthorizations of the TVPA. In Section 106(g)(1) of the 2003 Reauthorization, Congress established accountability for contractors by requiring that any grant, contract, or cooperative agreement provided or entered into by a Federal department or agency shall include a condition that authorizes the department or agency to terminate the grant, contract, or cooperative agreement, without penalty, if the contractor or any subcontractor (i) engages in severe forms of trafficking of persons or has procured a commercial sex act during the period of time that the grant, contract, or cooperative agreement is in effect, or (ii) uses forced labor in the performance of the grant, contract, or cooperative agreement.[14]

Congress, in the TVPA's 2005 Reauthorization, articulated a compelling national interest rationale for holding accountable any entity or person representing the United States who facilitates human trafficking:

> (10) The involvement of employees and contractors of the United States Government and members of the Armed Forces in trafficking in persons,

---

[11] Vandenberg, *supra* note 9, at 65–66. Ben Johnston had filed a statement with the Criminal Division of Investigation of the U.S. Army in Bosnia and Herzegovina. The U.S. army placed him in protective custody and DynCorp subsequently terminated him. According to his termination letter, he had brought "discredit" to DynCorp and the U.S. army. DynCorp eventually settled the case with Mr. Johnston for an undisclosed amount in August 2002.

[12] *Id.* at 54–55.

[13] Dana Liebelson, *Interview: Kathryn Bolkovac of "The Whistleblower" on Human Trafficking Scandal, New Film*, PROJECT ON GOVERNMENT OVERSIGHT (POGO) BLOG (Oct. 12, 2011, 5:25 PM), http://pogoblog.typepad.com/pogo/2011/10/interview-kathryn-bolkovac-of-the-whistleblower-discusses-trafficking-scandal-new-film.html.

[14] Trafficking Victims Protection Reauthorization Act of 2003, Pub. L. No. 108-7, 114 Stat. 1536, codified at 22 U.S.C. § 7104(g) (prior to the 2013 amendment in the Trafficking Victims Protection Reauthorization Act of 2013, Pub. L. No. 113 sec. 201(c)(1)–(2), 127 Stat. 54 (2013)).

facilitating the trafficking in persons, or exploiting the victims of trafficking in persons is inconsistent with United States laws and policies and undermines the credibility and mission of United States Government programs in post-conflict regions.[15]

Through this statement, Congress affirmed that trafficking is not only a serious crime and human rights violation, but that facilitating or engaging in trafficking-related activities by U.S. employees, members of the Armed Services, and contractors or subcontractors also harms the national interest of the United States. Although this finding specifically refers to the context of operations in post-conflict regions, the underlying rationale that such conduct "undermines the credibility and mission of the United States Government" is generally applicable in all international settings.

Congress underscored the need to strengthen accountability and deter such practices by holding U.S. personnel and contractors criminally liable.

(11) Further measures are needed to ensure that United States Government personnel and contractors are held accountable for involvement with acts of trafficking in persons, including by expanding United States criminal jurisdiction to all United States Government contractors abroad.[16]

Accordingly, Congress authorized the exercise of extraterritorial criminal jurisdiction to prosecute contractors and U.S. government employees for trafficking crimes committed outside the United States:[17] Title 1, Section 103 of the 2005 reauthorization extends extra-territorial jurisdiction over federal contractors (by amending Title 18 of the United States Code (U.S.C.) §§ 3271 and 1596), and provides for punishment as if the offense were committed inside the United States:

Section 3271. Criminal offenses committed by Federal contractors outside the United States

(a) Whoever, while an extraterritorial Federal contractor, engages in conduct outside the United States that would constitute an offense punishable by imprisonment for more than 1 year if the conduct had been engaged in within the special maritime and territorial jurisdiction of the United States shall be punished as provided for that offense.

By making involvement in human trafficking a criminal offense for federal contractors, while simultaneously extending jurisdictional reach, Congress established a high level of risk for contractors associated with trafficking in persons, using forced labor, or whose employees or subcontractors' employees have procured commercial sex.

---

[15] Trafficking Victims Protection Reauthorization Act of 2005, Pub. L. No. 109-164, sec. 1, § 2(10), 119 Stat. 3558, 3559.

[16] Trafficking Victims Protection Reauthorization Act of 2005, Pub. L. No. 109-164, sec. 1, § 2(11), 119 Stat. 3558, 3559.

[17] *Id.* at § 103, 119 Stat. at 3562–63; William Wilberforce Trafficking Victims Protection Reauthorization Act of 2008, Pub. L. No. 110-457, tit. II, § 223, 122 Stat. 5044, 5071–72.

IV. FEDERAL ACQUISITIONS REGULATIONS

Following the enactment of statutory measures like those above, federal regulations, guidance, and instructions have been promulgated to advance the objective of ending human trafficking in the context of federal contracts.

Primary among these are Federal Acquisitions Regulation (FAR)[18] Subpart 22.17 and Clause 52.222-50,[19] which together articulate how to implement the TVPA reauthorization language.[20] The FAR reiterates U.S. policy and prohibits contractors, subcontractors, and their employees from engaging in human trafficking during the period of performance:

(b) *Policy.* The United States Government has adopted a zero tolerance policy regarding trafficking in persons. Contractors and contractor employees shall not—

(1) Engage in severe forms of trafficking in persons during the period of performance of the contract;

(2) Procure commercial sex acts during the period of performance of the contract; or

(3) Use forced labor in the performance of the contract.[21]

FAR 52.222-50 further articulates the ways that contractors can fulfill their obligations in compliance with the zero tolerance policy:

(c) *Contractor requirements.* The Contractor, if other than an individual, shall establish policies and procedures for ensuring that its employees do not engage in or support severe forms of trafficking in persons, procure commercial sex acts, or use forced labor in the performance of this contract. At a minimum, the Contractor shall—

(1) Publish a statement notifying its employees of the United States Government's zero tolerance policy described in paragraph (b) of this clause and specifying the actions that will be taken against employees for violations of this policy. Such actions may include, but are not limited to, removal from the contract, reduction in benefits, or termination of employment;

(2) Establish an awareness program to inform employees about—

(i) The Contractor's policy of ensuring that employees do not engage in severe forms of trafficking in persons, procure commercial sex acts, or use forced labor;

---

[18] The FAR provides uniform policies and procedures for acquisition for all Executive branch agencies.

[19] Part 52 (Solicitation Provision and Contract Clauses).

[20] Subpart 22.17 (Combating Trafficking in Persons) prescribes policy for implementing 22 U.S.C. § 7104.

[21] FAR 52.222-50; in addition, Subpart 22.1703 declares: "The United States Government has adopted a zero tolerance policy regarding trafficking in persons."

(ii) The actions that will be taken against employees for violation of such policy;

(iii) Regulations applying to conduct if performance of the contract is outside the U.S., including—

(A) All host country Government laws and regulations relating to severe forms of trafficking in persons, procurement of commercial sex acts, and use of forced labor; and

(B) All United States laws and regulations on severe forms of trafficking in persons, procurement of commercial sex acts, and use of forced labor which may apply to its employees' conduct in the host nation, including those laws for which jurisdiction is established by the Military Extraterritorial Jurisdiction Act of 2000 (18 U.S.C. 3261–3267), and 18 U.S.C. 3271, Trafficking in Persons Offenses Committed by Persons Employed by or Accompanying the Federal Government Outside the United States;

(3) Provide all employees directly engaged in performance of the contract with a copy of the statement required by paragraph (c)(1) of this clause and obtain written agreement from the employee that the employee shall abide by the terms of the statement; and

(4) Take appropriate action, up to and including termination, against employees or subcontractors that violate the policy in paragraph (b) of this clause.

The remedies available against those contractors that violate the zero-tolerance policy include the loss of the government contract or subcontract, and removal or termination of the employee(s) involved:

(e) *Remedies.* In addition to other remedies available to the Government, the Contractor's failure to comply with the requirements of paragraphs (c) or (d) of this clause may render the Contractor subject to—

(1) Required removal of a Contractor employee or employees from the performance of the contract;

(2) Required subcontractor termination;

(3) Suspension of contract payments;

(4) Loss of award fee for the performance period in which the Government determined Contractor non-compliance;

(5) Termination of the contract for default, in accordance with the termination clause of this contract; or

(6) Suspension or debarment.

These sanctions are not inconsequential. Suspension or disbarment of a company poses the possibility of not only discontinuing an existing contract, but also losing opportunities for future business with the federal government. On the other hand, criminal and administrative enforcement of these rules against federal contractors has so far been minimal.[22] Consequently, the next step for this area of human trafficking policy will be to transform a "zero-tolerance" policy into effective action against prohibited conduct.

NOTES AND QUESTIONS

1. What do you think "zero-tolerance" should mean in the context of enforcing human trafficking laws, and the actions of contractors, subcontractors, and their employees?

2. What legal measures, if any, would you recommend be enacted to strengthen the prohibition on human trafficking in the context of federal contracting?

3. How effective do you think a contractor's oversight of its subcontractor can be on matters related to human trafficking?

4. How much accountability should contractors have for subcontractors' conduct?

In February 2011, the Office of Inspector General (OIG) for the U.S. Department of State released a report assessing contractor practices at four embassies and two consulates general in Kuwait, Oman, Saudi Arabia, and the United Arab Emirates (U.A.E.). These contractors supplied gardeners, maids, cooks and local guards to work at these U.S. posts. The OIG identified the presence of a number of indicators of human trafficking in its investigation:

- All the contractors surveyed held the passports of the workers.
- More than three-quarters of the workers told investigators that they had to pay recruitment fees to get their jobs. The fees were exorbitant, equaling more than a year's salary for more than twenty-five percent of those interviewed.
- Deceptive recruitment practices were used, involving abuse of the workers' lack of language familiarity and local or general knowledge.
- Wages were withheld.
- More than seventy percent of the laborers interviewed said they lived in overcrowded, unsafe, or unsanitary conditions. Twenty occupied quarters with less personal space than is required to be provided to inmates at minimum security prisons in the United States.

---

[22] *See Legal Options to Stop Human Trafficking: Hearing Before the Subcomm. On Human Rights and the Law, S. Comm. on the Judiciary*, 110th Cong. 83 (2007) (prepared statement of Martina E. Vandenberg, Att'y, Jenner & Block) ("With zero prosecutions, zero tolerance has zero credibility."); AMERICAN CIVIL LIBERTIES UNION AND ALLARD K. LOWENSTEIN INTERNATIONAL HUMAN RIGHTS CLINIC, YALE LAW SCHOOL, VICTIMS OF COMPLACENCY: THE ONGOING TRAFFICKING AND ABUSE OF THIRD COUNTRY NATIONALS BY U.S. GOVERNMENT CONTRACTORS 57 (2012), http://www.aclu.org/files/assets/hrp_traffickingreport_web_0.pdf ("Although the TVPRA and the Federal Acquisition Regulations require [U.S. Government] contracts to mandate compliance with the prohibition against trafficking, U.S. contracting agencies have yet to implement this requirement in any meaningful way.").

OIG report[23] concluded that there was no evidence that department-funded contractors had violated the TVPA or the FAR clause 52.222-50 (Combating Trafficking in Persons).

NOTES AND QUESTIONS

1. What combination of the indicia identified above by the OIG report do you think would need to exist to constitute a violation of the TVPA?

2. What combination of the indicia identified above do you think would need to exist in a case to constitute a violation of the FAR?

3. If no combination of the identified indicia would constitute a violation of the TVPA or the FAR, what further questions would you ask to determine whether or not a violation existed?

* * *

Executive Order 13627: "Strengthening Protections Against Trafficking in Persons in Federal Contracts" & the Ending Trafficking in Government Contracting Act

Recognizing the need for additional legal force, and the limitations of the implementation of the zero tolerance policy, both Congress and the Executive Branch have moved to strengthen measures to combat human trafficking in federal contracting. In particular, the range of prohibited trafficking-related activities by a federal contractor has been expanded.

On September 25, 2012, President Barack Obama issued Executive Order [E.O.] 13627[24], entitled "Strengthening Protections Against Trafficking in Persons in Federal Contracts", further addressing the responsibilities of federal contractors. In concert with the legislation addressing human trafficking implicating federal contractors, the E.O. puts companies doing business with the U.S. government on clear notice that there would be consequences for those involved with human trafficking or trafficking-related activities.

The E.O. augments existing law by spelling out, in detail, a range of prohibited trafficking-related activities. These include:

    1) misleading or fraudulent recruitment practices;

    2) charging employees recruitment fees;

    3) destroying or confiscating an employee's identity documents, such as a passport or a driver's license; and

    4) failing to pay return transportation costs upon the end of employment for non-national employees.

---

[23] U.S. Office of Inspector General, *Report No. MERO-1-11-06- Performance Evaluation of Dept. of State Contracts to Assess Risk of TIP Violations in Gulf States* (2011).

[24] Exec. Order No. 13,627, 77 Fed. Reg. 60029 (Sept. 25, 2012).

To provide a greater certainty of deterrence, the E.O. seeks to end practices frequently associated with human trafficking without requiring that all of the other elements of human trafficking be established. For example, it prohibits misleading or fraudulent recruitment practices, even where the conduct may not, on its own, constitute a trafficking crime.

In addition, the E.O. requires federal contractors and subcontractors to certify to the federal government that they have an appropriate compliance program in place. This program must include:

> (ii) a process for employees to report, without fear of retaliation, any activity that would justify termination under section 106(g) of the TVPA, or is inconsistent with the requirements of this order, or any other applicable law or regulation establishing restrictions on trafficking in persons, the procurement of commercial sex acts, or the use of forced labor;

> (iii) a recruitment and wage plan that only permits the use of recruitment companies with trained employees, prohibits charging recruitment fees to the employee, and ensures that wages meet applicable host country legal requirements or explains any variance;

> (iv) a housing plan, if the contractor or subcontractor intends to provide or arrange housing, that ensures that the housing meets host country housing and safety standards or explains any variance; and

> (v) procedures to prevent subcontractors at any tier from engaging in trafficking in persons, including those trafficking-related activities described in subsection (a)(1)(A) of this section, and to monitor, detect, and terminate any subcontractors or subcontractor employees that have engaged in such activities; and

(B) that each such contractor and subcontractor shall certify, prior to receiving an award and annually thereafter during the term of the contract or subcontract, that:

> (i) it has the compliance plan referred to in subsection (a)(2)(A) of this section in place to prevent trafficking-related activities described in section 106(g) of the TVPA and this order; and

> (ii) either, to the best of its knowledge and belief, neither it nor any of its subcontractors has engaged in any such activities; or, if abuses have been found, the contractor or subcontractor has taken the appropriate remedial and referral actions;

The E.O. is a powerful addition to anti-trafficking efforts, not only for the anti-trafficking measures it contains, but also as an expression of high-level political will condemning and committing to end these practices.

NOTES AND QUESTIONS

As seen above in the OIG report, a number of the activities prohibited by the E.O. are not uncommon practices for companies, in certain contexts.[25]

1. For each of the prohibited activities, standing on its own, would you consider it to be an inherently exploitative act?

2. For each of the prohibited activities, standing on its own, under what circumstances do you think the activity could occur for a purpose other than to exploit a worker?

3. For each of the prohibited activities, what other facts would you want to know to determine if the activity is occurring as part of a case of human trafficking?

* * *

Soon after the Executive Order was issued, on January 2, 2013, Congress passed, and President Obama signed, the National Defense Authorization Act for Fiscal Year 2013. The Act contained Title XVII, entitled Ending Trafficking in Government Contracting.[26] While Title XVII contains a number of provisions analogous to the Executive Order, it also strengthens certain measures to combat trafficking (and related or associated conduct) among contractors, their subcontractors, and their employees.

TITLE XVII — ENDING TRAFFICKING IN GOVERNMENT CONTRACTING

SEC. 1703. COMPLIANCE PLAN AND CERTIFICATION REQUIREMENT.

(a) Requirement. — The head of an executive agency may not provide or enter into a grant, contract, or cooperative agreement if the estimated value of the services required to be performed under the grant, contract, or cooperative agreement outside the United States exceeds $500,000, unless a duly designated representative of the recipient of such grant, contract, or cooperative agreement certifies to the contracting or grant officer prior to receiving an award and on an annual basis thereafter, after having conducted due diligence, that—

(1) the recipient has implemented a plan to prevent the activities described in section 106(g) of the Trafficking Victims Protection Act of 2000 (22 U.S.C. § 7104(g)), as amended by section 1702, and is in compliance with that plan;

---

[25] *See, e.g.*, Office of Inspector General, *supra* note 23 (all the contractors surveyed held the passports of the workers, many of whom are from South and Southeast Asia, a practice that is barred in each of the four countries; deception in recruitment practices occurred — more than three quarters of the workers told investigators that they had to pay recruitment fees to get their jobs; the fees were exorbitant, equaling more than a year's salary for more than 25% of those interviewed); Matthew Lee, *State Dep't Watchdog Says Contract Workers at Embassies in Gulf at Risk of Exploitation*, Star Trib., Feb. 7, 2011, http://www.startribune.com/templates/Print_This_Story?sid=115519794.

[26] National Defense Authorization Act for Fiscal Year 2013, Pub. L. No. 112-239, tit. XVII, 126 Stat. 1632, 2092–98.

(2) the recipient has implemented procedures to prevent any activities described in such section 106(g) and to monitor, detect, and terminate any subcontractor, subgrantee, or employee of the recipient engaging in any activities described in such section; and

(3) to the best of the representative's knowledge, neither the recipient, nor any subcontractor or subgrantee of the recipient or any agent of the recipient or of such a subcontractor or subgrantee, is engaged in any of the activities described in such section.

SEC. 1704. MONITORING AND INVESTIGATION OF TRAFFICKING IN PERSONS.

(a) Referral and Investigation.—

(1) Referral. — If the contracting or grant officer of an executive agency for a grant, contract, or cooperative agreement receives credible information that a recipient of the grant, contract, or cooperative agreement; any subgrantee or subcontractor of the recipient; or any agent of the recipient or of such a subgrantee or subcontractor, has engaged in an activity described in section 106(g) of the Trafficking Victims Protection Act of 2000 (22 U.S.C. § 7104(g)), as amended by section 1702, including a report from a contracting officer representative, an auditor, an alleged victim or victim's representative, or any other credible source, the contracting or grant officer shall promptly refer the matter to the agency's Office of Inspector General for investigation. The contracting officer may also direct the contractor to take specific steps to abate an alleged violation or enforce the requirements of a compliance plan implemented pursuant to section 1703.

(2) Investigation. — An Inspector General who receives a referral under paragraph (1) or otherwise receives credible information that a recipient of the grant, contract, or cooperative agreement; any subgrantee or subcontractor of the recipient; or any agent of the recipient or of such a subgrantee or subcontractor, has engaged in an activity described in section 106(g) of the Trafficking Victims Protection Act of 2000 (22 U.S.C. § 7104(g)), as amended by section 1702, shall promptly review the referral or information and determine whether to initiate an investigation of the matter. In the event that an Inspector General does not initiate an investigation, the Inspector General shall document the rationale for the decision not to investigate.

(3) . . . .

(b) Report. — Upon completion of an investigation under subsection (a), the Inspector General shall submit a report on the investigation to the head of the executive agency that awarded the contract, grant, or cooperative agreement. The report shall include the Inspector General's conclusions regarding whether or not any allegations that the recipient of a grant, contract, or cooperative agreement; any subcontractor or subgrantee of the recipient; or any agent of the recipient or of such a subcontractor or subgrantee, engaged in any of the activities described in section 106(g) of the Trafficking Victims Protection Act of 2000 (22 U.S.C. § 7104(g)), as amended by section 1702, are substantiated.

(c) Remedial Actions.—

(1) In general. — Upon receipt of an Inspector General's report substantiating an allegation that the recipient of a contract, grant, or cooperative agreement; any subgrantee or subcontractor of the recipient; or any agent of the recipient or of a subgrantee or subcontractor, engaged in any of the activities described in section 106(g) of the Trafficking Victims Protection Act of 2000 (22 U.S.C. § 7104(g)), as amended by section 1702, or notification of an indictment, information, or criminal complaint for an offense under subsection (a)(3), the head of agency shall consider taking one or more of the following remedial actions:

(A) Requiring the recipient to remove an employee from the performance of work under the grant, contract, or cooperative agreement.

(B) Requiring the recipient to terminate a subcontract or subgrant.

(C) Suspending payments under the grant, contract, or cooperative agreement until such time as the recipient of the grant, contract, or cooperative agreement has taken appropriate remedial action.

(D) Withholding award fees, consistent with the award fee plan, for the performance period in which the agency determined the contractor or subcontractor engaged in any of the activities described in such section 106(g).

(E) Declining to exercise available options under the contract.

(F) Terminating the contract for default or cause, in accordance with the termination clause for the contract.

(G) Referring the matter to the agency suspension and debarment official.

(2) Savings clause.— Nothing in this subsection shall be construed as limiting the scope of applicable remedies available to the Federal Government.

(3) . . . .

These are potentially powerful tools. In particular, Section 1703's mandate that the contractor provide certification of pro-active monitoring, plans, and procedures to prevent human trafficking, is significant. Section 1704(a)(1)'s mandated referral of potential cases to a Department's Office of Inspector General is equally important. If the Inspector General decides not to investigate an alleged violation, Section 1704(a)(2) mandates that a rationale be provided. Finally, Section 1704(c) authorizes a range of remedial actions, including termination of the contract and referral of the matter for suspension and debarment. With this piece of legislation, Congress greatly enhanced the tools available to end participation of U.S. government contractors, subcontractors, and employees in human trafficking.

V. DEPARTMENT OF DEFENSE

A significant subset of U.S. federal contracts are awarded through, and administered by, the Department of Defense (DOD). This is partially because, to an ever-growing degree, the United States has outsourced security, military-related, and war zone jobs to private contractors.[27] Companies that operate in conflict and post-conflict zones conduct their work in environments particularly conducive to human trafficking. A war zone may be the unexpected destination of a trafficking victim, as the following case demonstrates:

Kellogg, Brown and Root and Daoud & Partners and the Nepali workers

Kellog, Brown and Root (KBR) is an American services, engineering and construction company that has served as a war contractor to the U.S. government in Iraq. Daoud & Partners (Daoud) is a Jordanian company that has performed numerous contracts for the U.S. government and has also served as a subcontractor of KBR.

> Thirteen Nepali laborers, men between the ages of 18 and 27, were recruited in Nepal believing that they would work in hotel and restaurant kitchens in Amman, Jordan. Some of the men were told that they would be working in an American camp, and though there was no indication that they were told where the camp would be, many of the laborers' family members believed that the base would be in the United States.[28] Their families incurred debt to arrange the promised employment.[29] However, when the men arrived in Jordan, agents of Daoud seized their passports and told them that they were being sent to work at a United States Air Base in western Iraq. As the twelve men were being transported to Iraq by Daoud, in a convoy of civilian vehicles, the car was stopped by a group of insurgents who posed as Iraqi police. The twelve men were taken hostage and executed by the insurgents, who filmed and posted the executions on the Internet. One of the Nepali men, Plaintiff Gurung, was being transported at the same time as the other twelve men but his van was not captured by the insurgents and he arrived in Al Asad as scheduled.[30] He was supervised by KBR in his duties as a warehouse loader/unloader.[31] When he learned of the death of the other twelve men, he requested that he be returned home. He was told both by Daoud and KBR that he could not leave until his work in Iraq was complete. Only after fifteen months, in very harsh conditions and where he experienced frequent mortar fire without protection, he was permitted to return to Nepal.[32]

---

[27] *See generally* DICKINSON, *supra* note 7.

[28] Amended Complaint at ¶ 63, Adhikari v. Daoud & Partners, No. 4:09-cv-01237 (S.D. Tex. Dec. 22, 2008), ECF No. 58.

[29] *Id.* at ¶¶ 64–65. The men were promised a salary of approximately $500 per month.

[30] *Id.* at ¶ 93.

[31] *Id.*

[32] *Id.* at ¶¶ 95–96.

Thus, the passports and means of identification of these men were taken from them and they were transported to a country that was not familiar to them (often not knowing where exactly they were).[33] Once in the country, they did not speak the language, had no access to those who could represent their interests, and were forced to work long hours in exhausting and dangerous conditions, all the while being told that they owed large sums of money to their labor contractors.[34]

In August 2008, a lawsuit was filed on behalf of the families of the Nepali trafficking victims and the one trafficking survivor in federal court in Los Angeles. The Plaintiffs' complaint alleged violations of the Trafficking Victims Protection Reauthorization Act (TVPRA)[35]; the Racketeering Influenced and Corrupt Organizations Act (RICO)[36]; the Alien Tort Statute (ATS)[37] and various common law claims against Defendant Daoud and Defendant KBR.[38] [39]

Defendant Daoud entered into a number of contracts with the United States for the provision of services at military bases, including the Al Asad Air Base in Iraq.[40] And Defendant KBR is a business conglomerate, which included a parent corporation with a principal place of business in Houston, Texas.[41] The Complaint sought, "among other things, compensation for the injuries suffered by both the trafficked laborers and their families,[42] as well as civil penalties and punitive damages against the defendants for having engaged in and benefited from a human trafficking enterprise."[43]

The case was transferred to federal court in Houston, Texas, pursuant to the defendants' motion. KBR moved to dismiss the complaint on grounds that the court lacked jurisdiction to hear the claims under the principle of extraterritoriality and that the plaintiffs failed to state a complaint under which relief could be granted. The Court ruled that 18 U.S.C. Section 1596 granted it jurisdiction over offenses which comprise the substantive

---

[33] Claudia D'estre, *Voices from Victims and Survivors of Human Trafficking, in* HUMAN TRAFFICKING: EXPLORING THE INTERNATIONAL NATURE, CONCERNS, AND COMPLEXITIES 79, 89 (John Winterdyk, Benjamin Perrin & Philip L. Reichel eds., 2012).

[34] *Id.*

[35] 18 U.S.C. § 1595.

[36] 18 U.S.C. § 1962(c).

[37] 28 U.S.C. § 1350.

[38] Adhikari v. Daoud & Partners, No. 2:08-cv-05626 (C.D. Cal. Aug. 27, 2008). *See generally* Cam Simpson, *Pipeline to Peril: Desperate for Work, Lured into Danger*, CHI. TRIB., Oct. 9–10, 2005 (multi-part series on the journey and exploitation of Nepali men in Iraq underpinning war effort).

[39] *Adhikari, supra* note 30, at ¶¶ 103–210.

[40] *See Id.* at ¶ 52.

[41] *Id.* at ¶ 23.

[42] Adhikari v. Daoud & Partners, CV- 09-1237 (S.D. Tex. Dec. 12, 2011)

[43] Matthew Handley & Molly McOwen, *Combating Human Trafficking in Iraq:* Adhikari v. Daoud, INT'L L. NEWS, Winter 2009, at 24, 26.

provisions of the TVPRA.[44] The Court ruled that the complaint sufficiently alleged violations under the TVPRA, the ATS and RICO, but dismissed the plaintiffs' negligence claims against KBR on statute of limitations grounds.[45] On March 5, 2012, after multiple appeals and cross-motions, the federal court upheld its jurisdiction over Daoud & Partners. On August 23, 2013, after another review of the evidence the federal court ordered KBR and Daoud & Partners to proceed to trial and set a trial date for April 4, 2014.[46]

The DOD has increased scrutiny of potential trafficking-related activities by its contractors, subcontractors, and their employees, as well as by foreign companies providing services on U.S. military bases. On November 18, 2011, DOD regulations were amended to require contract administrators to be affirmatively responsible for overseeing trafficking in persons requirements for all DOD service contracts. Contract administrators are charged to enforce obligations in FAR 52.222-50 that prohibit contractors, subcontractors, and their employees from engaging in a "severe form of trafficking" or the use of forced labor in the performance of the contract, as well as the procurement of commercial sex acts by employees of contractors or subcontractors.

For contracts performed in Iraq and Afghanistan, DOD has imposed additional layers of protections against human trafficking and other abuses.[47] These additional requirements were described in congressional testimony by Richard T. Ginman, Director, Defense Procurement and Acquisition Policy:

> [A]ll services and construction contracts which require performance in Iraq and Afghanistan, [must] incorporate into the associated solicitations and contracts, a local clause 'Prohibition Against Human Trafficking, Inhumane Living Conditions, and Withholding of Employee Passports.' This clause provides additional requirements that contractors must follow to protect its employees and subcontractors at all tiers. This includes:
>
> (a) Reminding contractors of the prohibition contained in Title 18, United States Code, Section 1592, against knowingly destroying, concealing, removing, confiscating, or possessing any actual or purported passport or other immigration document, or any other actual or purported government identification document, of another person, to prevent or restrict or to attempt to prevent or restrict, without lawful authority, the person's liberty to move or travel, in order to maintain the labor or services of that person.

---

[44] Memorandum and Order at 19–20, Adhikari v. Daoud & Partners, No. 4:09-cv-01237 (S.D. Tex. Dec. 12, 2011), ECF No. 273.

[45] Memorandum and Order, Adhikari v. Daoud & Partners, No. 4:09-cv-01237 (S.D. Tex. Nov. 3, 2009), ECF No. 168.

[46] Memorandum and Order, Adhikari v. Daoud & Partners, 2012 U.S. Dist. LEXIS 28394 (S.D. Tex. Mar. 5, 2012), ECF No. 290; for other proceeding documents, see https://www.docketalarm.com/cases/Texas_Southern_District_Court/4--09-cv-01237/Adhikari_et_al_v._Daoud_%26_Partners_et_al/; *see also* http://kbrlitigation.com/kbr-ordered-to-stand-trial-in-human-trafficking-case/ (last accessed Jan. 24, 2014).

[47] *Hearing on CCCRA*, *supra* note 45, at 56 (statement of Richard T. Ginman, Director, Defense Procurement and Acquisition Policy).

(b) Requiring contractors to comply with the following provisions: 1) Hold employee passports and other identification documents discussed above only for the shortest period of time reasonable for administrative processing purposes; 2) Provide all employees with a signed copy of their employment contract, in English as well as the employee's native language that defines the terms of their employment/compensation; 3) Do not utilize unlicensed recruiting firms, or firms that charge illegal recruiting fees; 4) Provide adequate living conditions (sanitation, health, safety, living space) for their employees. Fifty square feet is the minimum acceptable square footage of personal living space per employee. Upon contractor's written request, contracting officers may grant a waiver in writing in cases where the existing square footage is within 20% of the minimum, and the overall conditions are determined by the contracting officer to be acceptable. A copy of the waiver approval shall be maintained at the respective life support area; 5) Incorporate checks of life support areas to ensure compliance with the requirements of this Trafficking in Persons Prohibition into their Quality Control program, which will be reviewed within the Government's Quality Assurance process; and 6) Comply with International and Host Nation laws regarding transit/exit/entry procedures, and the requirements for visas and work permits.

(c) Advising the Contracting Officer if they learn of their employees violating the human trafficking and inhumane living conditions provisions contained herein. Put on notice that contracting officers and/or their representatives will conduct random checks to ensure contractors and subcontractors at all tiers are adhering to the law on human trafficking, humane living conditions and withholding of passports.

(d) Requiring incorporation of the substance of this clause, including this paragraph, in all subcontracts under this contract.[48]

The lawyers representing the Nepali workers killed traveling to Iraq recognized that some laws, not specific to trafficking, may apply to human trafficking cases and may be helpful in pursuing results. They turned to the Defense Base Act (DBA), enacted in 1941,[49] just before the United States entered World War II. The DBA was passed to cover overseas civilian workers, both U.S. and foreign nationals, working on government contracts. The act applies to injuries and deaths that arise out of, and in the course of, their employment.

The DBA claims resulted in awards of between $130 and $297 a month to the families of 10 of the victims, for the rest of their lives.[50] Clearly, the DBA does not afford a comprehensive response to the harm inflicted by human trafficking, and is an unsatisfactory tool in terms of financial deterrence for a company's misconduct. But it may be an effective partial remedy:

---

[48] *Hearing on Labor Abuses*, *supra* note 45, at 31–32 (statement of Richard T. Ginman, Director, Defense Procurement and Acquisition Policy).

[49] Defense Base Act, 42 U.S.C.§§ 1651–54.

[50] Handley & McOwen, *supra* note 43, at 26. The other two deceased victims did not have living spouse, parents, or children and so no award was made.

Because recovery under the DBA requires no allegations of wrongdoing, DBA claims for injury or death while in the employment of a U.S. contractor are often an efficient remedy. Such a remedy does not, however, compensate victims for the physical and economic injuries they suffered as a result of the trafficking; the DBA compensates them only for a fraction of lost wages arising from workplace injuries.

. . . Accordingly, a combined approach of DBA and TVPA claims is currently the best means to compensate individuals for both trafficking-related and work-related injuries and to deter future abuses. Thirteen Nepali families are demonstrating that this approach can work. As the U.S. war in Iraq thunders on, the *Adhikari* plaintiffs stand to make a significant contribution to a quieter battle being waged in the courtroom — the war against human trafficking.[51]

NOTES AND QUESTIONS

1. In what ways, if any, might the measures described by Director Ginman have been helpful in protecting the Nepali workers (or future workers in similar circumstances)?

2. If all of the policies described in this testimony are implemented, how effective do you think they would be in reducing the frequency of human trafficking? What other steps, if any, would you require contractors to take to address human trafficking?

3. As illustrated by the use of the DBA, lawyers should think broadly in considering how to advance the interests of their clients. What other potential legal theories can you think of that may be available to argue a trafficking case? For example, in what ways might kick-backs or bribes be part of a case, if labor recruiters are involved?

VI. SPECIAL CASE: THE ROLE OF LABOR RECRUITERS IN HUMAN TRAFFICKING

Unscrupulous labor recruiters often play a critical role in human trafficking cases. Their involvement can be the beginning of a chain of events leading to severe exploitation, violence, and abuse. Some of these cases constitute human trafficking. These cases occur both in and outside of the context of federal contracting. While most employment agencies are reputable and have nothing to do with human trafficking, reports of widespread abuses by some labor recruiters, including luring and trapping individuals into trafficking schemes, have drawn the attention of U.S. government officials.

Congress moved to end federal contractors' use of unscrupulous labor recruiters by providing for a fine and/or up to five years imprisonment for materially false or fraudulent pretenses, representations, or promises regarding employment to be performed on a U.S. government contract. This includes work performed outside

---

[51] *Id.*

the United States, on a U.S. military installation or mission outside the United States, or on other property or premises outside the United States owned or controlled by the U.S. government.[52]

In its 2011 Trafficking in Persons Report by the Office to Monitor and Combat Trafficking in Persons, the U.S. Department of State provided guidance on "best practices" to end the complicity of labor recruiters in human trafficking, regardless of whether those using the recruiters were federal contractors.

Optimal Regulatory Approach for Labor Recruiting

- Ensure that private recruitment agencies have a recruitment fee limit in an amount that can cover minimal expenses. For example no more than one month's wages abroad for a 12-month contract, or 4.2 percent of the wages expected to be earned under a 24-month contract.

- Ensure competition among private recruitment agencies to foster the lowest recruitment fees and the best services offered to potential migrants.

- Enact criminal laws that penalize fraudulent recruitment or usurious fees.

- Impose sanctions on private recruitment agencies that break the law and include compensation mechanisms for the affected workers.

- Vigorously investigate and prosecute recruitment agencies or brokers who willfully do not register in order to avoid worker protections.

- Establish adequate complaint procedures to identify and examine allegations of violations, including representative employers', workers', and migrants' organizations in the complaint process.[53]

NOTES AND QUESTIONS

1. What anti-trafficking measures presented in this chapter do you think could be used to prosecute the labor recruitment companies, and/or to assist victims to obtain legal remedies?

2. A 2011 BBC News article[54] reported that an employment agency recruited Ugandan women representing to them that they would be working in shops on a U.S. military base in Iraq but they were instead forced into domestic servitude in homes in Iraq (with sexual violence occurring in some cases). The recruitment agency, which was identified in the article as the Uganda Veterans Development Ltd., denied knowledge of what happened to the women in Iraq. The agency's Managing Director said: "They are not our employees. . . . We recruit them and they make a contract with the companies on the other side (in Iraq). We look after them and see that they are being treated well, but really the contract is between the agents and the girls." Fourteen of the Ugandan women were rescued from their

---

[52] H.R. Rep. No. 112-705, tit. XVII, § 1706, at 468–69 (2012) (Conf. Rep.).

[53] U.S. Dept. of State, Trafficking in Persons Rep. (2011), http://www.state.gov/j/tip/rls/tiprpt/2011/164224.htm#7.

[54] Anna Cavell, *Ugandan Women Tricked into Domestic Slavery in Iraq*, BBC News (Mar. 31, 2011, 4:55 AM), http://www.bbc.co.uk/news/world-12887018.

servitude. Over a hundred other Ugandan women recruited in 2009 reportedly are unaccounted for. The recruitment agency's license was revoked for a time but then was reinstated. The recruitment agency, Uganda Veterans Development Ltd., was neither a federal contractor nor a subcontractor in this case (it is not clear from reports whether it contracts or subcontracts with the U.S. government on any other matters). Can you think of a way to reach the perpetrators in Uganda or Iraq? What if some of the homes in which the women ended up in were residences of employees of a federal contractor?

3. Are there other actions that you would add to the U.S. Department of State's Office to Monitor and Combat Trafficking in Persons' list that could help victims in any of the cases described in this chapter or other cases of human trafficking involving labor recruiters?

4. What is the legal significance if someone is trafficked when there is:

- no written contract for employment?
- a written contract but terms are not complied with (e.g., wage paid is much lower, etc)?
- a written contract, but that contract was replaced by a later signed written contract indicating lower wage, different hours, etc?
- a signed written contract, but it is in a language other than one spoken by the worker?

VII. TRANSPARENCY LAWS

California Transparency in Supply Chains Act

This chapter has thus far focused primarily on company accountability and liability for human trafficking. Another approach focuses on corporate transparency. The next wave of initiatives to combat human trafficking will almost certainly include new disclosure requirements for companies' supply chains. In 2010, California passed a law that aimed to empower individuals to combat human trafficking by providing greater product supply chain transparency, which could inform purchasing decisions. By providing this information to consumers, the law aimed to create market incentives that would reward companies that ensure there is no human trafficking in their supply chains, while negatively impacting companies that do not do so. The California legislature expressed the need for these disclosures in this way:

> (f) Legislative efforts to address the market for goods and products tainted by slavery and trafficking have been lacking, the market being a key impetus for these crimes.
>
> [. . .]
>
> (i) Absent publicly available disclosures, consumers are at a disadvantage in being able to distinguish companies on the merits of their efforts to supply products free from the taint of slavery and trafficking. Consumers are at a

disadvantage in being able to force the eradication of slavery and trafficking by way of their purchasing decisions.

(j) It is the policy of this state to ensure large retailers and manufacturers provide consumers with information regarding their efforts to eradicate slavery and human trafficking from their supply chains, to educate consumers on how to purchase goods produced by companies that responsibly manage their supply chains, and, thereby, to improve the lives of victims of slavery and human trafficking.[55]

The requirement to publicly disclose efforts to eradicate human trafficking from their supply chains applies to all retail sellers and manufactures doing business in California with world-wide gross receipts exceeding $100 million. The following disclosures must be posted on the company's website, through a conspicuous and easily understood link:[56]

(c) The disclosure described in subdivision (a) shall, at a minimum, disclose to what extent, if any, that the retail seller or manufacturer does each of the following:

(1) Engages in verification of product supply chains to evaluate and address risks of human trafficking and slavery. The disclosure shall specify if the verification was not conducted by a third party.

(2) Conducts audits of suppliers to evaluate supplier compliance with company standards for trafficking and slavery in supply chains. The disclosure shall specify if the verification was not an independent, unannounced audit.

(3) Requires direct suppliers to certify that materials incorporated into the product comply with the laws regarding slavery and human trafficking of the country or countries in which they are doing business.

(4) Maintains internal accountability standards and procedures for employees or contractors failing to meet company standards regarding slavery and trafficking.

(5) Provides company employees and management, who have direct responsibility for supply chain management, training on human trafficking and slavery, particularly with respect to mitigating risks within the supply chains of products.[57]

Retailers and manufacturers are *not* mandated by the California law to take any particular steps to seek out or eradicate human trafficking — they are only obligated to disclose what they are or are not doing to that end.[58]

---

[55] 2010 Cal. Legis. Serv. 556 (S.B. 657) (West).

[56] CAL. CIV. CODE § 1714.43(b) (West 2012). "In the event the retail seller or manufacturer does not have an Internet Web site, consumers shall be provided the written disclosure within 30 days of receiving a written request for the disclosure from a consumer." *Id.*

[57] *Id.* at (c).

[58] The law itself provides for only one form of remedy: "The exclusive remedy for a violation of this

Approximately 3200 retailers and manufacturers are required to make annual disclosures pursuant to the new California law. The first disclosures were required to be placed on companies' websites on January 1, 2012. An initial review of these statements found many to be lacking in substance, and prompted a coalition of anti-trafficking nongovernmental organizations to call for companies to improve their statements going forward. It recommended that companies:

> move beyond pronouncements about how they are against trafficking and take immediate and effective steps to implement anti-trafficking policies (e.g. through audits, management and internal accountability processes, training, partnerships, stakeholder engagement, public policy advocacy, worker empowerment, etc.) Furthermore, those steps must be backed by information about how companies measure the impact of their performance and descriptions of how they feed results and lessons learned back into future policy revision and implementation.[59]

The law is still at an early stage of implementation. Specificity and clarity in the business communities' disclosures will be critical to realizing the law's intended purpose.

NOTES AND QUESTIONS

1. As a vehicle for change in the private sector and an anti-trafficking tool, what are the prospects of consumer empowerment through disclosure requirements?

2. What kind of content do you think would satisfy the disclosure requirements, consistent with the letter and spirit of the law? After reviewing a sample of company websites to see what level of detail they provide, which ones do you think provide sufficient information for consumers to make informed decisions about the companies' actions against human trafficking?

3. What is the relationship between public access to company disclosures and the likely effectiveness of this law? Go to the websites of companies with disclosure requirements under this law. Did you find the link to the required information to be conspicuous and easily identifiable, as required by the statute?

4. If you were drafting a transparency disclosure bill, would you enlarge the pool of companies beyond retailers and manufacturers? Is $100 million in gross global receipts the right line for activating the reporting requirement? If you were a lawmaker, would you place the line at a higher or lower figure?

5. How much should the costs or difficulty of monitoring a company's global supply chain impact what can reasonably be expected?

6. Should companies be required to provide information beyond what they have provided for forced or child labor to comply with this new law? If a company already made public disclosure about its training, codes of conduct, and audits for forced

---

section shall be an action brought by the Attorney General for injunctive relief. Nothing in this section shall limit remedies available for a violation of any other state or federal law." *Id.* at (d).

[59] ALLIANCE TO END SLAVERY & TRAFFICKING, BEYOND SB 657: HOW BUSINESSES CAN MEET AND EXCEED CALIFORNIA'S REQUIREMENTS TO PREVENT FORCED LABOR IN SUPPLY CHAINS 3 (2013).

labor and child labor, would that previous statement also be sufficient disclosure about their efforts against human trafficking?

* * *

Business Transparency in Trafficking and Slavery Act

There are signs that the approach adopted in California may spread.[60] Federal legislation, for example, was introduced in 2011, but not passed. The Business Transparency on Trafficking and Slavery Act[61] is an example of the type of bill that might eventually come from the U.S. Congress. The proposed bill expressed Congress' intention, stating, in part:

> (2) the legislative and regulatory framework to prevent goods produced through forced labor, slavery, human trafficking, and the worst forms of child labor from passing into the stream of commerce in the United States is gravely inadequate; and

> (3) legislation is necessary to provide the information that the public demands, recognizing that businesses can be part of the solution to these problems when they transparently provide information to consumers and investors, and subsequently respond to consumer and investor demands for business reasons, rather than solely reacting to governmental prescription on how to conduct their business.[62]

The bill shares many of the characteristics of the California law, but has several crucial differences. It would expand its scope of application to include all companies required to file reports with the [SEC]. In addition to posting on their websites, as required by the California law, companies would be required to include disclosures in their filings with the SEC (thus directly engaging the companies' investors). In addition, the bill called for audits of labor recruiters, and for companies to report on their efforts to provide remediation to identified victims.

NOTES AND QUESTIONS

1. What are the implications of requiring companies to include disclosures in their SEC filings?

2. What do you think of expanding the scope to include all companies required to file reports with the SEC? Would you expand the coverage further still?

3. The momentum for greater private sector transparency appears to have gained a beachhead internationally, as well. In the United Kingdom, Parliament has been deliberating the "Transparency in UK Company Supply Chains (Eradication of Slavery) Bill." Much of the language of this bill mirrors the language of its U.S. counterparts. In contrast to the California law, however, the UK bill applies not only

---

[60] *See generally* STEPHEN WARNATH, BRIEFING ON TRANSPARENCY IN SUPPLY CHAIN LAWS FOR CORPORATE GENERAL COUNSEL (2013), Warnath Group, LLC, *available from the Warnath Group, LLC*.

[61] Business Transparency on Trafficking and Slavery Act, H.R. 2759, 112th Cong. (2011).

[62] *Id.* at § 1(c).

to the manufacturing and retail sectors, but also to service industries. Furthermore, if specific cases are found in a company's supply chain, it creates an obligation for companies to "take action necessary and appropriate to assist people who have been victims. . . . "[63]

* * *

A Practical Example: Transparency and Conflict Minerals

A specific U.S. example of the transparency approach is the SEC "Wall Street Reform and Consumer Protection Act," ("Dodd-Frank") which targets conflict minerals from the Democratic Republic of Congo (DRC).[64] Conflict minerals are frequently mined by forced and/or child labor, and the proceeds help finance further armed violence in the region. These minerals, some mined by victims of trafficking, are used by some companies in the production of computers, phones, and other electronic products. In an approach echoed by the proposed Business Transparency on Trafficking and Slavery Act described above, Dodd-Frank is designed to use securities law disclosure requirements to enable consumers and investors to make more informed decisions about companies potentially using conflict minerals.

Section 1502 of the Act (the "Conflict Minerals Statutory Provision") requires that a "person described"[65] disclose annually whether any "conflict minerals" that "are necessary to the functionality or production of a product manufactured by such person" originated in the countries identified in the statute, and to make that disclosure publicly available on the person's website.[66] If those conflict minerals originated in a country covered by the statute, that person must submit a report to the SEC that includes a description of the measures taken by the person to monitor the minerals' source and chain of custody.[67] Measures taken to monitor the supply chain "shall include an independent private sector audit" of the report.[68]

---

[63] Transparency in UK Company Supply Chains (Eradication of Slavery) Bill, 2012–13, H.C. Bill [26] cl. 3. The comparable language in the U.S. federal proposal is that companies are to report the extent to which, "[i]n cases where forced labor, slavery, human trafficking, and the worst forms of child labor have been identified within the supply chain[, they ensure] that remediation is provided to those who have been identified as victims." Business Transparency on Trafficking and Slavery Act, H.R. 2759, 112th Cong. § 2 (2011).

[64] The term "conflict mineral" is defined in Section 1502(e)(4) of the Act as "(A) columbite-tantalite(coltan) [the metal ore from which tantalum is extracted], cassiterite [the metal ore from which tin is extracted], gold, wolframite [the metal ore from which tungsten is extracted]; or their derivatives; or (B) any other mineral or its derivatives determined by the Secretary of State to be financing conflict in the Democratic Republic of Congo or an adjoining country." Dodd-Frank Wall Street Reform & Consumer Protection Act, Pub. L. No. 111-203, § 1502(e)(4), 124 Stat. 1376, 2218 (2010) [hereinafter Dodd-Frank Act].

[65] This means a legal person. The Dodd-Frank Act amends Section 13(p)(2) of the Securities Exchange Act of 1934 to define a "person described" as one who is required to file reports under Section 13(p)(1)(A) of that Act, and for whom the "conflict minerals are necessary to the functionality or production of a product manufactured by such person." Dodd-Frank Act, *supra* note 64, at tit. XV, sec. 1502(b), § 13(p)(2), 124 Stat. at 2214.

[66] Dodd-Frank Act, *supra* note 64, at tit. XV, sec. 1502(b), § 13(p)(1)(E), 124 Stat. at 2214.

[67] Dodd-Frank Act, *supra* note 64, at tit. XV, sec. 1502(b), § 13(p)(1)(A)(i), 124 Stat. at 2214.

[68] *Id.*

NOTES AND QUESTIONS

1. What are the pros and cons of requiring companies to be transparent regarding their efforts to combat human trafficking? Is disclosure enough? How effective do you think disclosure can be as a means of changing human trafficking activities of subcontractors? Should there only be disclosure (as in the California law), or should there be an obligation to take action if trafficking is discovered (as the proposed U.S. and UK bills seek)?

2. Do you think including affirmative obligations to help identified victims are likely to increase or hinder private sector involvement in uncovering human trafficking in their supply chains?

3. How reasonable do you think it is to require companies to know what all of their suppliers and subcontractors are doing on this issue?

VIII. CODES OF CONDUCT AND GUIDING PRINCIPLES

Codes of Conduct are a staple of corporate social responsibility. Companies associate themselves with codes of conduct in areas ranging from sustainability, to the environment, to forced and child labor. Some of these are drafted by corporate associations, while others are produced by outside groups who invite companies to sign on.

These codes are guided by companies' legal obligations, corporate social responsibility policies, and ethical codes. The first concerted effort by the business community in this area was the Athens Ethical Principles, adopted in 2006. The Athens Principles state:

> The Athens Ethical Principles were adopted by business companies in Athens on 23 January 2006, to combat human trafficking worldwide by focusing on seven main areas:
>
> We, Members of the business community,
>
> [. . .]
>
> will:
>
> 1. Demonstrate the position of zero tolerance towards trafficking in human beings, especially women and children for sexual exploitation (Policy Setting).
>
> 2. Contribute to prevention of trafficking in human beings including awareness- raising campaigns and education (Public Awareness-Raising).
>
> 3. Develop a corporate strategy for an anti-trafficking policy which will permeate all our activities (Strategic Planning).
>
> 4. Ensure that our personnel fully comply with our anti-trafficking policy (Personnel Policy Enforcement).
>
> 5. Encourage business partners, including suppliers, to apply ethical principles against human trafficking (Supply Chain Tracing).

6. In an effort to increase enforcement it is necessary to call on governments to initiate a process of revision of laws and regulations that are directly or indirectly related to enhancing anti-trafficking policies (Government Advocacy).

7. Report and share information on best practices (Transparency).[69]

So far, more than 12,000 companies have pledged to abide by the Athens Principles. These principles were elaborated in 2010 at an international forum in Luxor, Egypt. The resulting "Luxor Implementation Guidelines to the Athens Ethical Principles: Comprehensive Compliance Programme for Businesses," provides guidance to companies wanting to incorporate those principles into their own policies, procedures, and practices.[70]

NOTES AND QUESTIONS

1. In what ways do you think Codes of Conduct can be helpful for companies that are already motivated to root out human trafficking in their supply chains or by their employees and subcontractors?

2. Can you think of any ways that Codes of Conduct can be helpful with regard to companies that are *not* inclined to root out human trafficking in their supply chains or by their employees and subcontractors?

3. When reviewing Codes of Conduct to reduce human trafficking consider the scope of concrete anti-trafficking action that a Code calls upon a company to undertake.

---

[69] END HUMAN TRAFFICKING NOW!, THE ATHENS ETHICAL PRINCIPLES (2006), http://www.endhumantraffickingnow.com.

[70] END HUMAN TRAFFICKING NOW!, LUXOR IMPLEMENTATION GUIDELINES TO THE ATHENS ETHICAL PRINCIPLES: COMPREHENSIVE COMPLIANCE PROGRAMME FOR BUSINESSES (2010), http://www.unglobalcompact.org/docs/issues_doc/human_rights/Resources/Luxor_Implementation_Guidelines_Ethical_Principles.pdf.

Chapter 9

ANTI-TRAFFICKING AGENCIES AND ORGANIZATIONS

I. INTRODUCTION

Before the TVPA was enacted in 2000, anti-trafficking efforts in the United States were confined to a small number of federal government agencies and non-governmental organizations. But since then, the anti-trafficking efforts of the federal government and its component agencies have expanded dramatically, as have the number of nongovernmental organizations devoted to the issue. The most important of these agencies and organizations are described in the first eight sections of this chapter, after which a short ninth section identifies some of the major international institutions involved in the fight to end human trafficking. As a result of increased global awareness, human trafficking is today considered a systemic problem requiring worldwide coordination of governmental and non-governmental resources.

II. THE U.S. GOVERNMENT

The TVPA created a comprehensive federal framework for combating human trafficking, an issue that had largely been addressed — when addressed at all — by limited efforts on the part of the Department of Justice and the Department of Labor. In particular, the TVPA engaged much more of the executive branch by calling on the president to create an Interagency Task Force to Monitor and Combat Trafficking, and by delegating specific duties to several other governmental agencies — not just the Department of Justice and the Department of Labor. These agencies include the Department of Homeland Security and the Department Health and Human Services, each of which has, along with the Department of Justice and the Department of Labor, a different task related to the statute's three explicit goals, known as the "3Ps": (1) *prosecuting* the crime of human trafficking, (2) *protecting* victims, and (3) *preventing* future incidents of human trafficking.

A. The President

The TVPA was the first piece of legislation to make the president specifically responsible for combating trafficking. Under the Act, the president is required to create an "Interagency Task Force to Monitor and Combat Trafficking," whose purpose is to implement the TVPA.

In 2002, President George W. Bush complied with this requirement by issuing an executive order creating the Task Force. The Chair of this task force is the

Secretary of State. Other members include the Attorney General, the Secretary of Health and Human Services, and the Secretary of Homeland Security. This Interagency Task Force was later expanded to include the Federal Bureau of Investigation (FBI) and other federal agencies.

More recently, President Barack Obama spoke out against human trafficking in a speech at the Clinton Global Initiative on September 25, 2012, describing it as a "debasement of our common humanity" and something that should concern the whole world:

> When a man, desperate for work, finds himself in a factory or on a fishing boat or in a field, working, toiling, for little or no pay, and beaten if he tries to escape — that is slavery. When a woman is locked in a sweatshop, or trapped in a home as a domestic servant, alone and abused and incapable of leaving — that's slavery.
>
> When a little boy is kidnapped, turned into a child soldier, forced to kill or be killed — that's slavery. When a little girl is sold by her impoverished family — girls my daughters' age — runs away from home, or is lured by the false promises of a better life, and then imprisoned in a brothel and tortured if she resists — that's slavery. It is barbaric, and it is evil, and it has no place in a civilized world.

In that speech, President Obama also made new commitments to strengthen the United States' response to trafficking. These commitments include: (1) evaluating human trafficking in the United States, (2) improving training for law enforcement, teachers, and others on identification of human trafficking victims, (3) developing safer online technology for young people, and (4) improving the federal government's response to victims of trafficking.

Additionally, the president signed an executive order addressing human trafficking in federal contracts and emphasized that "American tax dollars must never, ever be used to support the trafficking of human beings." While prohibitions against the use of forced labor by U.S. contractors already existed, the executive order strengthened those provisions and instituted new measures to enhance compliance.

B. The Department of Justice

Today, the Department of Justice (DOJ) plays two key roles when it comes to implementing the TVPA. First, as the lead federal prosecution agency, the DOJ maintains primary responsibility for prosecuting trafficking under federal criminal statutes. Second, as required by the Trafficking Victims Protection Reauthorization Act (TVPRA) of 2003, the DOJ prepares an annual report to Congress that details how different federal agencies are implementing the TVPA.

1. DOJ Criminal Prosecutions

As the lead federal prosecution agency, the DOJ holds the primary responsibility for prosecuting federal crimes under the TVPA. To facilitate these prosecutions, the TVPA created a number of new federal crimes, including federal crimes for forced labor and for sex trafficking. Although the new TVPA statutes are the primary offenses charged in human trafficking cases today, in many cases the DOJ prosecutes defendants under both the newer statutes and the old, pre-TVPA involuntary servitude statutes.

With these additional federal crimes at its disposal, the DOJ significantly increased its criminal prosecutions of human trafficking in the decade following the passage of the TVPA. For example, in 2001 the DOJ only prosecuted 10 human trafficking cases, for a total of just 23 convictions. But by 2011, that yearly conviction total had jumped to 151, as a result of the DOJ increasing the number of cases it prosecuted to 125. Some of these cases involved forced labor; others involved sex trafficking of adults by force, fraud, and coercion; and still others involved sex trafficking of minors — all of which are crimes specifically created by the TVPA.[1]

a. DOJ Sections: The Criminal Section and the Child Exploitation Section

The two DOJ sections tasked with enforcing the TVPA and other involuntary servitude and slavery provisions are the Criminal Section in the Civil Rights Division (Criminal Section) and the Child Exploitation and Obscenity Section in the Criminal Division (Child Exploitation Section). In prosecuting human trafficking offenses prior to the TVPA, the Criminal Section enforced involuntary servitude and slavery statutes, and the Child Exploitation section enforced laws addressing child pornography, online sexual predators, child sex tourism, and other forms of child exploitation. But in the post-TVPA world, the responsibilities of both sections have expanded dramatically, as outlined below.

i. The Criminal Section

The Criminal Section holds primary responsibility for prosecuting crimes of labor trafficking and sex trafficking of adults involving force, fraud, and coercion, and it also runs a specialized unit — the Human Trafficking Prosecution Unit — that investigates and prosecutes human trafficking offenses nationwide. Although the Criminal Section prosecutes cases involving both foreign national and domestic victims of trafficking, a significant number of its cases involve foreign national victims and traffickers.

ii. Child Exploitation Section

The Child Exploitation Section enforces laws prohibiting the sex trafficking of minors. Like the Criminal Section, the Child Exploitation Section handles cases with both foreign national and domestic victims. However, unlike the Criminal Section, the majority of its cases involve domestic victims and traffickers.

---

[1] *Att'y Gen. Ann. Rep. to Cong. & Assessment of U.S. Gov't Activities to Combat Trafficking Persons* 62 (2010).

b. United States Attorneys' Offices

All DOJ investigations and prosecutions of human trafficking are closely coordinated with other DOJ entities, including the 94 local U.S. Attorneys' Offices. The U.S. Attorneys' Offices have formed strong partnerships with the two specialized Sections at DOJ and frequently prosecute cases jointly. To ensure that federal human trafficking laws are appropriately and uniformly enforced, any U.S. Attorneys' Office that begins a human trafficking criminal investigation must notify the Criminal Section and, in cases involving child sex trafficking, the Child Exploitation Section. This notification requirement ensures that the DOJ Sections will be able to share expertise, provide resources for victim assistance, and help coordinate efforts by multiple law enforcement and prosecution agencies, which may be targeting the same or related criminal networks.

c. Other Partnerships and Coordinated Prosecution Efforts

In many instances, the two DOJ sections will assist or partner with local or state law enforcement. Other times, the sections assist with international criminal prosecution efforts. In an effort to combat transnational trafficking networks, the Criminal Section has worked with foreign governments. One example of this kind of international cooperation has been the U.S.-Mexico Bilateral Human Trafficking Enforcement Initiative. Confronting the problem of human trafficking criminal networks operating across the border in the United States and Mexico, both DOJ sections collaborated with Mexican law enforcement. The goal was to build prosecutorial capacity and develop joint U.S. and Mexican investigations and prosecutions of trafficking networks operating on both sides of the border. The resulting initiative has produced "bilateral prosecutions charging members of sex trafficking networks under both U.S and Mexican laws."

Similarly, the Child Exploitation Section has worked with other governmental entities across the United States and internationally. For example, the 2011 prosecution of James Mozie in the Southern District of Florida was the result of a partnership between the Child Exploitation Section and other federal law enforcement agencies to combat child sex trafficking. Mozie had recruited seven minor victims, many of whom were runaways. According to the victims' testimony, Mozie forced the children to engage in prostitution in his house, which he operated as a brothel. Moreover, "[s]everal of the minor victims testified that Mozie required them to have sex with him as part of their 'orientation,' which he explained was his way of 'testing the merchandise.'" To advertise his business, Mozie took sexually explicit pictures of the victims and sent them via text messages to prospective clients. The Child Exploitation Section, the U.S. Attorneys' Office for the Southern District of Florida, and the FBI joined forces with a local law enforcement task force to investigate and prosecute the case. As a result of these efforts, Mozie was found guilty on 10 counts including sex trafficking of minors, conspiracy to commit sex trafficking of minors, and child pornography. In May 2012, he was sentenced to life in prison.

C. Federal Law Enforcement and Anti-Trafficking Task Forces

The vast majority of human trafficking investigations nationwide are conducted by two federal law enforcement agencies: the FBI and Immigration and Customs Enforcement (ICE). The FBI is housed within the Department of Justice and ICE is housed within the Department of Homeland Security. (ICE will be discussed in greater detail in the Department of Homeland Security section below.)

1. The FBI

The FBI is the DOJ's primary investigative arm and plays a vital role in efforts to combat human trafficking. The FBI has several major initiatives dedicated to eradicating the exploitation of children, two of which focus specifically on the sex trafficking of children: the Child Sex Tourism Initiative and the Innocence Lost Initiative.

a. Child Sex Tourism Initiative

The Child Sex Tourism Initiative addresses the problem of individuals traveling from the United States to "procure children in other countries for sexual purposes." The goal is to prevent the commercial sexual exploitation of minor victims in other countries by U.S. citizens. The FBI shares intelligence to identify potential offenders and assist with criminal prosecutions in the host country or in the United States.

b. Innocence Lost Initiative

The Innocence Lost Initiative began in 2003 as a joint effort by the FBI, the Child Exploitation Section, and the National Center for Missing & Exploited Children to address domestic sex trafficking of children. As a result of this initiative, there are presently 47 task forces and working groups around the country focused on child sex trafficking. These task forces include federal, state, and local law enforcement agencies that work closely with U.S. Attorneys' Offices. Over the last nine years, their efforts have led to the rescue of approximately 2,100 children from child trafficking and the conviction of more than 1,000 pimps and others who sexually exploit children. In a press release following a successful 2010 national Innocence Lost Initiative enforcement action, the FBI described the Task Force operations:

Task Force operations usually begin as local actions, targeting such places as truck stops, casinos, street "tracks," and Internet websites, based on intelligence gathered by officers working in their respective jurisdictions. Initial arrests are often violations of local and state laws relating to prostitution or solicitation. Information gleaned from those arrests often uncovers organized efforts to prostitute women and children across many states. FBI agents further develop this information in partnership with U.S. Attorneys' Offices and the Child Exploitation Section and file federal charges where appropriate.

2. Anti-Trafficking Task Forces

Based on the strong need for cooperation with state and local law enforcement, the DOJ funds task forces around the country composed of victim service providers as well as federal, state, and local law enforcement investigators.[2] At its high point in 2011, the DOJ funded 40 task forces across the United States; however, the number decreased to 29 funded task forces by the end of the 2011 fiscal year, when some of the federal funding expired.[3]

Although the task forces have reportedly improved coordination between the federal government and state and local law enforcement agencies, critics have observed that "state law enforcement participation mainly continued pre-existing programs to combat commercial vice," and that the task forces had not achieved consistent success.

3. DOJ Annual Report to Congress

As specified by the TVPRA, the DOJ's annual report to Congress must include the following human trafficking statistics from the previous fiscal year:

i. The number of persons who received federal government benefits.
ii. The number of persons who have been granted continued presence to remain in the United States.
iii. The number of persons who have applied for, been granted, or been denied a trafficking-related visa.
iv. The number of persons who have been charged or convicted and the sentences given to them under federal trafficking-related offenses.
v. Information on trafficking-related grants.
vi. Training conducted.
vii. The activities of the Senior Policy Operating Group.

In particular, the report evaluates the efforts of federal agencies during the prior fiscal year, makes recommendations for the next fiscal year, and explains what steps federal agencies have taken to comply with recommendations from the previous report. For example, the DOJ's report to Congress for the 2010 fiscal year addressed benefits and services given to trafficking victims by federal agencies, immigration benefits for trafficking victims, investigations and prosecutions of traffickers, international grants to combat trafficking administered by the U.S. government, and domestic and international training and outreach.

D. The Department of State

The Department of State acts as the United States' authority on human trafficking worldwide. Several offices within the Department contribute to its response to global trafficking: the Office to Monitor and Combat Trafficking in

---

[2] U.S. Dep't of State, *Trafficking in Persons Report* 373 (2011).
[3] U.S. Dep't of State, *Trafficking in Persons Report* 361 (2012).

Persons (J/TIP); the Bureau of Democracy, Human Rights, and Labor; the Bureau of Population, Refugees and Migration; and the Bureau of Diplomatic Security.

The Office to Monitor and Combat Trafficking in Persons

The Office to Monitor and Combat Trafficking in Persons (J/TIP) stands at the forefront of the U.S. government's efforts to combat human trafficking worldwide. Created by the TVPA in 2000, J/TIP is responsible for "bilateral and multilateral diplomacy, targeted foreign assistance, and public engagement on trafficking in persons."[4] It encourages the international adoption of the "3Ps" approach of *protecting* victims, *preventing* trafficking, and *prosecuting* traffickers.

1. The Trafficking in Persons Report

J/TIP engages foreign governments on the issue of human trafficking by issuing a yearly report on Trafficking in Persons (Report). The Report measures human trafficking worldwide and monitors countries' progress in addressing human trafficking. Mandated by the TVPA, the Report annually rates individual countries and is considered to be, in the words of the State Department, "the world's most comprehensive resource of governmental anti-human trafficking efforts."[5]

The 2012 Report evaluated 186 countries — including the United States, which appeared in the report for the first time in 2010. In accordance with the TVPA's requirements, the Report categorizes countries into the following four tiers based on governments' efforts to comply with the TVPA's minimum standards for eliminating human trafficking:

- Tier 1 countries fully comply with minimum standards for the elimination of trafficking.

- Tier 2 countries do not fully comply with minimum standards but are making significant efforts to do so.

- Tier 2 Watch List countries do not fully comply with minimum standards but are making significant efforts to do so but have additional aggravating factors, such as:

    - a) A significant or increasing number of victims of severe forms of trafficking.

    - b) A failure to provide evidence of increasing efforts to combat severe forms of trafficking in persons from the previous years.

    - c) The determination that a country is making significant efforts to bring itself into compliance with minimum standards was based on commitments by the country to take additional steps over the next year.

- Tier 3 countries whose governments do not fully comply with the TVPA's

---

[4] U.S. Dep't of State, *Office to Monitor and Combat Trafficking in Persons: About Us*, available at http://www.state.gov/j/tip/about/index.htm (last visited Nov. 17, 2012).

[5] U.S. Dep't of State, *Trafficking in Persons Report*, available at http://www.state.gov/j/tip/rls/tiprpt/index.htm (last visited Nov. 17, 2012).

minimum standards and are not making significant efforts to do so.

In 2012, the report ranked 33 countries in Tier 1, 93 countries in Tier 2, 42 countries on the Tier 2 Watch List, and 17 countries in Tier 3.

The minimum standards used to evaluate countries' anti-trafficking efforts include the following four duties: First, governments should prohibit severe forms of trafficking and punish traffickers. Second, governments should impose significant penalties for child sex trafficking comparable to existing penalties for sexual-assault offenses. Third, governments should impose serious penalties for severe forms of human trafficking. Fourth, governments should attempt to eliminate severe forms of trafficking.

J/TIP uses a broad range of resources to gather information for the Report. Relevant information comes from government entities in the United States and abroad, non-governmental organizations, publicly available media, research trips, and public comment. The factors considered by J/TIP when ranking countries are focused on governmental action and are closely tied to the 3Ps paradigm. For example, the Report considers government actions related to prosecution (such as criminalizing severe forms of trafficking in persons and vigorously prosecuting traffickers), protection (such as the extent to which governments ensure that victims have access to shelter, health care, and legal services), and prevention (such as government efforts to curtail labor practices that contribute to trafficking). But the Report rankings do not take into account anti-trafficking work by nongovernmental groups. Nor do they consider other government efforts that are not concretely related to the 3Ps paradigm.

To strongly encourage foreign governments to make efforts to comply with the minimum standards, the TVPA lays out penalties for countries in Tier 3. These penalties include economic sanctions by the United States: the U.S. government may withhold non-humanitarian, non-trade-related financial assistance from Tier 3 countries. Additionally, the United States may oppose assistance to those countries from the International Monetary Fund, the World Bank, and other international financial institutions (with an exception for humanitarian, trade-related, and some development-related aid).

The penalties attached to a Tier 3 categorization mean that countries have much at stake when it comes to being identified as either Tier 2 or Tier 3. As a result, special procedures surround this decision. A country that appears on the Tier 2 Watch List for two years in a row, and would appear on the Tier 2 Watch List for a third year, is automatically downgraded to Tier 3. However, there are a limited number of exceptions through which a country may prevent imposition of sanctions or an automatic downgrade from the Tier 2 Watch List to Tier 3.

2. Foreign Financial Assistance Grants

J/TIP administers foreign financial assistance grants to help other countries prosecute traffickers, protect victims, and prevent human trafficking.[6] To select projects for funding, J/TIP runs an annual competition. As part of that competition, J/TIP solicits proposals and selects projects for funding.[7] J/TIP receives many applications: in 2010 and 2011, a total of 998 applicants competed for funding.[8] In fiscal year 2010, J/TIP awarded 97 grants totaling $33 million, and in fiscal year 2012, J/TIP awarded 69 grants totaling almost $24 million. Today, J/TIP administers $64 million of grants that fund 168 projects in 70 countries worldwide.

3. Public Engagement and Awareness

J/TIP also provides information about human trafficking to members of the U.S. government and civil society. An example of a public awareness project funded through a J/TIP grant is the Slavery Footprint website: slaveryfootprint.org. The website greets visitors with the question, "How many slaves work for you?" and guides them through a series of detailed questions about their lifestyle and consumption habits to determine their total slavery footprint. The total slavery footprint is defined by the website as "the number of forced laborers that were likely to be involved in creating and manufacturing the products you buy." Since the Slavery Footprint's September 2011 launch, the website has attracted millions of visitors from 200 countries.

4. Additional State Department Offices and Efforts

Other offices within the State Department contribute to anti-trafficking efforts. The Bureau of Democracy, Human Rights, and Labor focuses on forced labor worldwide. The Bureau of Population, Refugees, and Migration contributes funding to the Return, Reintegration, and Family Reunification Program for Victims of Trafficking in the United States. This program helps families of trafficking victims obtain T Visas to travel to the United States, and assists trafficking victims who choose not to remain in the United States to return home and reintegrate into their communities. Finally, the Bureau of Diplomatic Security provides anti-trafficking training to its agents.

E. The Department of Homeland Security

The Department of Homeland Security (DHS) also assists the federal government's anti-trafficking efforts. DHS launched the Blue Campaign in 2010 to coordinate these efforts and to focus on the 3Ps of prevention, prosecution, and protection. The Blue Campaign coordinates efforts by different components of DHS, including: ICE, Customs and Border Protection, Citizenship and Immigration Services, and the Federal Law Enforcement Training Center.

---

[6] U.S. Dep't of State, *International Grant Programs*, available at http://www.state.gov/j/tip/intprog/index.htm (last visited Feb. 27, 2013).

[7] *Id.*

[8] *Id.*

Within DHS, ICE is primarily responsible for investigating human trafficking, child sex tourism, and forced child labor both within the United States and internationally. With offices in more than 40 countries around the world, ICE coordinates domestic and international investigations with foreign law enforcement. The agency also trains foreign law enforcement partners.

In the 2010 fiscal year, ICE initiated 651 investigations connected to human trafficking. The table below reflects the number of investigations, arrests, indictments, and convictions reported by ICE as having a nexus to human trafficking between 2005 and 2010. It is important to note that although these cases were identified by ICE as having a trafficking nexus, trafficking offenses were not charged by federal prosecutors in all instances.

ICE Cases with a Nexus to Human Trafficking				
FISCAL YEAR	INVESTI-GATIONS	ARRESTS	INDICT-MENTS	CONVIC-TIONS
2005	274	101	58	10
2006	299	184	130	102
2007	348	164	107	91
2008	432	189	126	126
2009	566	388	148	165
2010	651	300	151	144

In addition to ICE, several other components of DHS work to combat human trafficking. Customs and Border Protection conducts public awareness campaigns centered on human trafficking and evaluates unaccompanied alien children to determine if they are victims of human trafficking. Citizenship and Immigration Services provides two types of immigration relief to trafficking victims: T Visas (T Nonimmigrant Status) and U Visas (U Nonimmigrant Status). It also provides training to its officers, NGOs, and law enforcement agencies on recognizing potential victims of trafficking. The Federal Law Enforcement Training Center "provides human trafficking training to federal, state, local, campus, and tribal law enforcement officers throughout the United States."

F. The Department of Health and Human Services

The Department of Health and Human Services (HHS) is the only federal agency with the authority to certify adult foreign victims of human trafficking and give eligibility letters to minor foreign victims of trafficking so that those victims may receive federal benefits and services. Other anti-trafficking efforts by HHS include grants to assist trafficking victims and a public awareness campaign

1. Certification for Foreign Victims of Trafficking

HHS's certification for adults and eligibility letters for children give victims access to federally funded benefits and services to the same extent as provided to refugees. An adult trafficking victim may only be certified if he or she (1) has been subjected to a severe form of trafficking in persons, (2) will assist in the investigation and prosecution of the trafficking case, or cannot assist because of physical or psychological trauma, (3) and has been granted continued presence by DHS to remain in the United States during the pendency of the case, or has been told that a pending T Visa application is "bona fide or approved." In contrast, child foreign victims of trafficking do not need to assist in the prosecution of their traffickers or have either a T Visa or continued presence status to receive an eligibility letter for benefits. During the 2010 fiscal year, HHS issued certifications to 449 foreign national adults and eligibility letters to 92 foreign national children. In fiscal year 2011, these numbers increased to 463 certifications for adults and 101 eligibility letters for children.

2. HHS Services Grants

HHS funds case management services to potential and certified foreign trafficking victims. In fiscal year 2011, HHS awarded $4.7 million to three NGOs — Tapestri, Heartland Human Care Services, and the U.S. Committee for Refugees and Immigrants — that in turn funded NGO sub-awardees nationwide to provide victim services. This program operates on a per capita reimbursement system: NGOs that receive sub-grants from the three designated NGOs provide victim services such as shelter, legal assistance, job training, and health care to trafficking victims. They are subsequently reimbursed with HHS funding subject to a monthly maximum per victim for up to 12 months. Through this program, HHS funded 122 NGO service providers who provided trafficking victim assistance to 366 potential foreign national victims and 341 certified foreign national victims.

3. Public-Awareness and Victim-Identification Efforts

While most of HHS's work related to human trafficking focuses on victim protection and services, the Department also conducts public-awareness and victim-identification efforts. HHS's human trafficking public-awareness campaign has established 24 community action groups across the country, consisting of NGOs, law enforcement, academics, and students.[9]

G. The Department of Labor

The Department of Labor's (DOL) anti-trafficking efforts include researching and publishing reports on international instances of forced labor, funding projects to combat child trafficking and other forms of exploitative child labor, and participating in investigative and law enforcement efforts.

The DOL publishes three yearly reports relating to human trafficking and forced labor: *Findings on the Worst Forms of Child Labor*, which documents child labor and governmental responses to it in 144 countries; *List of Goods Produced by Child Labor or Forced Labor*, which counts 130 goods from 71 countries; and the *List of Products Produced by Forced or Indentured Child Labor*, which counts 31 products from 23 countries.

---

[9] Dep't of Health & Hum. Services, *Office of Refugee Resettlement: About Anti-Trafficking in Persons, U.S.*, available at http://www.acf.hhs.gov/programs/orr/programs/anti-trafficking/about (last visited Feb. 27, 2013).

The DOL also currently funds three projects to address child labor trafficking and other forms of exploitative child labor. Each of these projects includes an anti-trafficking component. One addresses the "worst forms of child labor" in Nigeria. Another focuses on child labor in cocoa growing communities in Ghana and Cote D'Ivoire. And the third targets child labor in Thailand's shrimp and seafood processing areas.

Along with its research efforts and project funding, DOL also contributes to federal efforts to detect and enforce laws against human trafficking within the United States. DOL participates in task forces nationwide and has also increased its efforts to protect temporary foreign workers within the United States by enforcing existing labors protections for these workers more aggressively.

H. Other Federal Agencies

Several other federal agencies also contribute to the government's response to human trafficking.

The Department of Defense (DOD) policy on human trafficking states that it "[opposes] prostitution, forced labor, and [related activities including coercion, commercial sex acts, and debt bondage] that may contribute to the phenomenon of TIP [trafficking in persons] as inherently harmful and dehumanizing."[10] It is also the Department's stated policy to "[d]eter activities of DOD Service members [and other employees] that would facilitate or support TIP, domestically and overseas. This includes activities such as pandering, prostitution, and patronizing a prostitute even though such activities may be legal within a host nation country."

The Department of Agriculture has begun to address the use of forced labor and child labor in the production of agricultural goods imported by the United States. The 2008 Farm Bill created a Consultative Group to Eliminate the Use of Child Labor and Forced Labor in Imported Agricultural Products that is charged with developing recommended practices for the Department. The Department of Transportation formed a partnership with Amtrak and DHS, announced in October 2012, to train and educate Amtrak employees on how to identify victims of human trafficking.

The Department of Education addresses human trafficking by working to provide school districts and educators with information about human trafficking and the commercial sexual exploitation of children. The Department disseminates a fact sheet to schools on human trafficking of children; the fact sheet includes information on identifying trafficking victims and available services for victims of trafficking.

The Agency for International Development funds international anti-trafficking and victim assistance programs and provides training for law enforcement and criminal justice personnel in other countries to support prosecutions of traffickers. The Agency also combats trafficking by funding "programs that support economic

---

[10] U.S. Dep't of Defense, Instruction No. 2200.01 § 4 (Sept. 15, 2010), *available at* http://www.dtic.mil/whs/directives/corres/pdf/220001p.pdf.

development, child protection, women's empowerment, good governance, education, health, and human rights."[11]

III. NON-GOVERNMENTAL ORGANIZATIONS

Non-governmental organizations (NGOs) play a critical role in efforts to combat human trafficking in the United States and worldwide. Since the TVPA was enacted, the number of organizations committed to fighting human trafficking has grown significantly. Some provide direct services in the form of legal assistance and support services to victims of human trafficking. Others focus on advocacy, awareness, and policy reform. Some organizations focus exclusively on combating human trafficking, while others incorporate those efforts into broader agendas. Immigrant-rights organizations, human-rights organizations, workers'-rights organizations, and religious organizations all contribute to efforts to combat human trafficking.

Human trafficking victims often require various forms of direct services. Legal services organizations assist victims in applying to the U.S. government for immigrant visas and work authorization, filing civil claims against traffickers, securing public benefits, and resolving family law issues. Some organizations focus on other forms of support, such as counseling and psychological services, health services, education, housing, employment training and support, and case management.

Advocacy organizations often work at the local, state, national, and international levels. These organizations advocate for victims' rights, promote public awareness and community outreach, support legislation, and provide training and technical assistance to law enforcement, public officials, and other NGOs. Other organizations focus on improving corporate and consumer awareness of the risk of human trafficking in supply chains.

IV. INTERNATIONAL ORGANIZATIONS

In addition to nongovernmental NGOs in the United States that are focused on addressing human trafficking, a number of international organizations work to combat human trafficking. Some organizations operate as arms of larger international organizations, such as the United Nations. Others were formed as the result of international agreements. Still others are intergovernmental partnerships among national governments seeking to address issues of common concern. Some organizations are worldwide, while others work in particular countries or regions.

A. The United Nations

Many of the key international organizations that have led efforts to combat human trafficking are subsidiary bodies of the United Nations, including the United Nations Office on Drugs and Crime, the International Labor Organization,

---

[11] U.S. Dep't of State, *U.S. Government Entities Combating Human Trafficking*, available at http://www.state.gov/j/tip/rls/fs/2010/143237.htm (last visited Feb. 27, 2013).

the Office of the United Nations High Commissioner for Human Rights, and the United Nations Children's Fund. These organizations, along with the International Organization for Migration and the Organization for Security and Cooperation in Europe, work together as part of a campaign called the U.N. Global Initiative to Fight Human Trafficking.

1. United Nations Office on Drugs and Crime

The United Nations Office on Drugs and Crime oversees the implementation of the United Nations Convention on Transnational Organized Crime and its protocols, which include the Protocol to Prevent, Suppress, and Punish Trafficking in Persons, Especially Women and Children (the Palermo Protocol). The U.N. Office on Drugs and Crime runs global awareness campaigns and issues research reports; assists countries in drafting laws and developing strategies to strengthen criminal justice responses; encourages governments to provide victim assistance; and has developed an online database of international prosecutions and convictions of human traffickers.

2. International Labor Organization

The International Labour Organization was formed in 1919 as part of the Treaty of Versailles following World War I to address the exploitation of workers occurring in industrializing nations at the time. The organization brings together representatives of government, workers, and business to develop international standards regulating the payment and treatment of workers and to draft both binding conventions and non-binding recommendations on a number of issues, including hours of work, regulation of the labor supply, protection of women and children, and freedom of association. The International Labour Organization addresses forced labor and labor exploitation through research and reports and through guidelines for labor inspections. The Organization also provides member countries with technical assistance in achieving labor standards.

B. Non-United Nations Organizations

1. International Organization for Migration

The International Organization for Migration is an intergovernmental organization that provides assistance to governments and migrants. This organization, which has historically focused more on migration than on trafficking, conducts research into human trafficking routes and trends, causes and consequences, and behaviors of criminal organizations. It also provides victims of trafficking with options for return to their home countries, resettlement, and reintegration and direct assistance such as shelter, medical and psychological services, and employment training.

2. Council of Europe

The Council of Europe promoted adoption in 2005 of the "Convention on Action Against Trafficking in Human Beings" and organized a monitoring mechanism to monitor compliance with obligations under the convention. Comprised of a multi-disciplinary panel of experts and a committee of parties to the convention, the monitoring mechanism conducts country evaluations and adopts recommendations for implementation.

3. Organization for Security and Cooperation in Europe

The Organization for Security and Cooperation in Europe has adopted an action plan to combat trafficking in humans. The action plan provides recommendations to participating countries on the implementation of commitments to combat human trafficking and specific tasks to assist with implementation.

V. CONCLUSION

A significant number of agencies and organizations — from the U.S. government to NGOs operating in the United States and abroad — work to combat human trafficking today. Since the TVPA was enacted in 2000, an expanded legal framework to combat trafficking has developed, along with an increased global awareness of the problem. Consequently, the number of agencies and organizations devoted, in whole or in part, to combating human trafficking has increased significantly during the past decade, a trend that will likely continue.

Chapter 10

FEDERAL CRIMINAL PROSECUTIONS

I. INTRODUCTION

Since 1865, when the Thirteenth Amendment officially outlawed slavery and involuntary servitude in the United States, federal prosecution has played an indispensable role in combating these unlawful practices.[1] Federal prosecutors traditionally relied on a variety of statutes to enforce the prohibition on slavery and involuntary servitude, such as the anti-peonage act and the involuntary servitude law. These prosecutors have also charged human trafficking suspects under a number of statutes that do not explicitly address slavery, peonage, or involuntary servitude, but nonetheless serve as powerful tools in trafficking cases. These statutes include the Mann Act, the Travel Act, and the Federal Kidnapping Act.

A. Criminal Prosecutions Under the TVPA

The passage of the Trafficking Victims Protection Act (TVPA) in 2000 established the framework for combating human trafficking worldwide as being centered upon the 3Ps: prevention, protection, and prosecution. As such, the TVPA prioritized criminal prosecutions as one of the three key components to combating trafficking. The law significantly changed the legal landscape by creating new offenses to combat modern forms of trafficking. Most important among these were the offenses of "forced labor" and "sex trafficking."

1. Forced Labor

The forced labor statute, 18 U.S.C. § 1589, specifically answered the call by the Supreme Court in *Kozminski* for Congress to pass a statute that reached non-physical and non-legal forms of coercion in trafficking cases. In other words, the forced labor statute expanded the law beyond the limitations of the existing involuntary servitude statute by criminalizing more subtle forms of coercion. While labor trafficking may involve instances of physical violence, threats, or threats of deportation, that is not always the case. So the TVPA recognized that traffickers often operate through threats against third parties, psychological forms of oppression and coercion, and the creation of "a climate of fear" that makes victims believe that if they do not provide labor or services, they or someone else will suffer harm. Since traffickers often employ only the amount of coercion needed to overcome the

---

[1] In recent years, state and local prosecutors have brought cases pursuant to state human trafficking criminal laws and other offenses. However, despite a recent increase in local prosecutions, the number of state and local prosecutions remains very small. Indeed, the overwhelming majority of human trafficking cases have been brought by the federal government.

will of a victim — be that coercion physical, legal, or psychological — the creation of the forced labor statute, with provisions to capture these more subtle forms of trafficking, has greatly expanded the reach of the law. Thus, law enforcement officials are able to legally address the manner in which traffickers operate today.

2. Sex Trafficking

The TVPA also established the offense of sex trafficking, and so for the first time created a separate federal offense to address one of the most common forms of trafficking: the forced prostitution of women and the prostitution of children in the United States. Although sex trafficking offenses could previously be brought under the involuntary servitude statute and the Mann Act, the creation of this new offense has greatly expanded the reach of the law and, as a result, has profoundly enhanced the ability of law enforcement and prosecutors to bring these cases.

3. Other Offenses

Today, after various amendments, the TVPA now contains provisions not only addressing forced labor (18 U.S.C. § 1589) and sex trafficking (18 U.S.C. § 1591) but also peonage, slavery, involuntary servitude, and forced labor (§ 1590); the confiscation or destruction of documents in furtherance of a trafficking offense (§ 1592); restitution for victims (§ 1593); attempts and conspiracies to commit a trafficking offense (§ 1594), and obstruction of a trafficking investigation (§§ 1583(a)(3), 1584(b), and 1592(c)). Additionally, the TVPA has strengthened provisions addressing peonage (18 U.S.C. § 1581), enticement into slavery (§ 1583), and sale into involuntary servitude (§ 1584).

B. Evolution of Criminal Prosecutions

Since passage of the TVPA, criminal prosecutions have had a significant impact on efforts to combat human trafficking in the United States. According to the DOJ, 52 human trafficking cases were charged by its Civil Rights Division and U.S. Attorneys Offices in 2010, compared to just three in 2000, the year before passage of the TVPA.[2] Moreover, a National Criminal Justice Reference Service study identified 268 federal cases prosecuted under the TVPA between the enactment of the TVPA in 2000 and December 2007.[3] The study found that California (26%) and New York (20%) prosecuted the most cases, with an overall breakdown, among all the states, of 55% of cases involving forced labor offenses and 43% involving sex trafficking with 33% of all cases involving child victims.

In addition to an increased number of prosecutions nationwide, the federal criminal law on human trafficking has evolved in two additional ways. First, the TVPA has been re-authorized on multiple occasions. These re-authorizations have established new offenses and clarified legal standards. Second, federal courts have established precedent by issuing legal opinions in cases brought under the TVPA

---

[2] UNITED STATES DEPARTMENT OF JUSTICE CIVIL RIGHTS DIVISION, REPORT ON THE TENTH ANNIVERSARY OF THE TRAFFICKING VICTIMS PROTECTION ACT 6 (2010).

[3] HEATHER J. CLAWSON, NICOLE DUTCH, SUSAN LOPEZ & SUZANNA TIAPULA, PROSECUTING HUMAN TRAFFICKING CASES: LESSONS LEARNED AND PROMISING PRACTICES ii–iii, 13 (2008).

provisions. Notably, the vast majority of court decisions on trafficking have been handed down by federal district and circuit courts. Since *Kozminski*, the U.S. Supreme Court has not spoken on trafficking in a significant way.

In this chapter, separate consideration will be given to forced labor, domestic servitude (a unique type of forced labor), and sex trafficking cases. Although these cases share many common themes — most notably the effort by traffickers to compel victims to provide labor or services against their will — there are significant factual and legal differences between these types of offenses that merit separate discussion.

II. BASIC PRINCIPLES FOR CRIMINAL OFFENSES UNDER THE TVPA

Criminal offenses in the TVPA are guided by four basic principles. First, the TVPA requires proof of a prohibited means of compelling a victim's labor, such as force, fraud, or coercion, unless the case involves a minor trafficked in commercial sexual exploitation, in which case such proof is not required. Second, the TVPA does not require transportation or any form of physical movement for an offense to have been committed. Although a victim may have been transported across a border, movement is not a required element of any of the TVPA offenses. Third, the forced labor and sex trafficking statutes may be charged together in the same case. Indeed, forced prostitution constitutes a type of "service" under the language of the forced labor statute, 18 U.S.C. § 1589. Fourth, additional offenses under the re-authorizations of the TVPA, such as obstruction and conspiracy, have expanded the scope of the trafficking statutes in critical ways.

These legal issues are discussed in detail by federal prosecutors Pamela Chen and Monica Ryan:

> The key element to any forced labor or sex trafficking charge, except where the victim is a minor, is the use of a prohibited means, such as force, threats, fraud, coercion, physical restraint and abuse or threatened abuse of legal process, to compel a person's labor. In sex trafficking cases involving minor victims, compulsion is not required. Rather, the government need only show that the defendant knew that the victim was a minor *or* that the defendant "had a reasonable opportunity to observe" the minor victim.
>
> A common misconception is that forced labor and sex trafficking must involve the transportation or smuggling of the victim across a state line or international border. In fact, neither Section 1589 nor 1591 has such a requirement, and Section 1589 does not even require a nexus to "interstate commerce." Indeed, the crime of forced labor under Section 1589 can be a purely domestic or local activity. And while Section 1591 requires that the sex trafficking conduct "affect interstate or foreign commerce," this element can be met without a showing that the victim traveled interstate or internationally as part of the crime . . . .
>
> . . . .

In addition to forced labor and sex trafficking, the [TVPA] criminalizes other trafficking-related conduct, including, *inter alia*, confiscating a person's identification documents as part of a trafficking offense (18 U.S.C. § 1592), attempts or conspiracies to commit a trafficking offense (18 U.S.C. §§ 1594(a)-(c)), and obstruction of a trafficking investigation (18 U.S.C. §§ 1583(a)(3), 1584(b), 1591(d) and 1592(c)). The significance of the conspiracy offense, which was created as part of the 2008 TVPRA, is that it carries the same maximum sentence as the underlying substantive offense — life for sex trafficking and twenty years for forced labor — as compared to the five-year statutory maximum available under the general conspiracy statute, 18 U.S.C. § 371. Also, the new trafficking-specific obstruction offenses appear to offer an advantage over general obstruction laws, which require proof that the defendant sought to obstruct or interfere with a federal investigation or judicial proceeding. *See, e.g.*, 18 U.S.C. §§ 1512, 1515 and 1519. So, for example, under the 2008 TVPRA, it might now be possible to prosecute a trafficker who lies to local, as opposed to federal, authorities about trafficking activity.

Pamela Chen & Monica Ryan, *Federal Prosecution of Human Traffickers*, in LAWYER'S MANUAL ON HUMAN TRAFFICKING: PURSUING JUSTICE FOR VICTIMS 273–75 (Jill Laurie Goodman & Dorchen A. Liedholdt eds., 2011)

III. FORCED LABOR

Forced labor is broadly defined in the TVPA as knowingly providing or obtaining a person's labor or services by illegal means such as force, fraud, or coercion. The phrase "labor or services" has been interpreted to cover a wide range of activities, and defendants have been convicted of trafficking people for agricultural labor, construction labor, cleaning services, hotel and restaurant labor, salon work, domestic servitude, and sexualized labor such as work in strip clubs or on pornographic websites.

The cases in this section demonstrate common issues arising in forced labor cases. Among these are:

- the legal definition of "serious harm"
- payment for work done
- what constitutes a climate of fear
- consent of the victim to some of the terms or conditions of his or her treatment; lack of refusal to work
- lack of attempt to flee
- targeting vulnerable victims
- threats against others
- a significant imbalance of power between the trafficker and the victim.

A. Pre-TVPA Forced Labor Cases

Before passage of the TVPA in 2000, forced labor cases were prosecuted under existing statutes such as 18 U.S.C. § 1584 (involuntary servitude), civil rights statutes, and other criminal laws. Pre-TVPA cases paved the way for the legislation in a variety of ways, both by foreshadowing the TVPA's standards and by reaching conclusions that the TVPA would seek to supersede.

1. *United States v. Harris*

One example of a typical pre-TVPA forced labor case is *United States v. Harris*. In *Harris*, the defendants were convicted of holding a number of migrant farm workers in involuntary servitude, and of conspiracy to violate the laborers' rights to be free from slavery. Defendants were managers of a migrant labor farm in North Carolina and recruited their workers by methods that ranged from deception to kidnapping. After expenses such as meals, cigarettes, and alcohol were deducted from the workers' wages, evidence showed that the workers only received $5.00 every two weeks on paydays. Additionally,

> The evidence also showed that workers were guarded at night and any who tried to flee were picked up and returned by Harris or others. There was proof of actual and threatened physical violence to prevent workers from leaving or to force them to work faster. A house, called the "jail," was used to confine workers who had tried to run away or for other punishment. Harris and Dennis Warren each carried a piece of rubber hose and beat laborers with them. Workers who complained of illness or injuries were denied medical assistance.
>
> On September 13, 1981, Robert Anderson, a migrant worker from Philadelphia, died in a bus to which he had been taken after collapsing in the fields. Two autopsies established that the primary cause of death was heat stroke. His death and reports of civil rights violations at the farm precipitated an investigation of conditions at the camp by the FBI which ultimately ripened into these prosecutions.

United States v. Harris, 701 F.2d 1095, 1098 (4th Cir. 1983)

In holding that there was sufficient evidence to convict defendants of involuntary servitude, the court pointed to, among other things, the physical beatings of victims, physical beatings that victims observed defendants impose upon others, and threats of bodily harm when workers spoke about leaving. One defendant was sentenced to life imprisonment. Another was sentenced to 20 years in prison.

2. The *Paoletti* Case

Another pre-TVPA case — and perhaps the most well-known trafficking case prosecuted prior to the TVPA — is *Paoletti*, better known in the media as the "Deaf Mexican Case." In 1998, 18 defendants, including the Paoletti family, were successfully prosecuted for forcing 57 deaf Mexicans to come to New York to sell trinkets like key chains and pencils in the streets and subways for 18 hours per day,

7 days per week.⁴ Although the phrase "human trafficking" was not yet used to describe such instances of labor trafficking, the conditions of the forced labor in the *Paoletti* case mirror many common themes of forced labor cases today — namely (1) long hours (2) sale quotas (3) victims being unlawfully smuggled into the United States (4) compelled work beatings and physical and sexual abuse (5) enforced rules of conduct (6) and fear by the victims based upon a lack of knowledge of their surroundings and their unlawful immigration status.

The following article excerpt details some of the facts of the case:

> The police discovered fifty-seven of these recruits, twelve of whom were children, crammed within two apartments in Queens, New York, along with several identification cards and $35,000 in cash. The money was part of the hard-earned profits that the deaf-mute Mexicans had earned for the Paolettis in their new jobs — peddling trinkets in New York City's subway cars for eighteen hours a day, seven days a week. They worked the long hours in order to satisfy a $600 weekly quota, which was enforced with heavy sanctions including beatings, electrocution, mental abuse, and sexual molestation, which they endured because they had nowhere else to go. Many of the deaf-mute workers were smuggled into the country, and leaving entailed risking the consequences of illegal immigration. Others, even if they accepted that gamble, needed their government documents, which were confiscated upon their arrival.

Developments in the Law — Jobs and Borders: II. The Trafficking Victims Protection Act, 118 HARV. L. REV. 2180, 2181 (2005).

3. *United States v. Kozminski*

As previously noted, the case of *United States v. Kozminski*, 487 U.S. 931, 952 (1988), led directly to passage of the TVPA. *Kozminski* limited the definition of involuntary servitude to "a condition of servitude in which the victim is forced to work for the defendant by the use or threat of *physical* restraint or *physical* injury or by the use or threat of coercion *through law or the legal process*" (emphasis added). The Court thus explicitly excluded non-physical coercion from the definition. Most critical to an understanding of human trafficking statutes today is that Congress passed § 1589 with the explicit intention that it would supersede *Kozminski* and broaden the definition of involuntary servitude to include non-physical threats and non-legal coercion.

By expanding the definition of threats and coercion beyond that laid down in *Kozminski*, the TVPA gave the crime of forced labor a broader reach and allowed the law to reach the subtle forms of coercion that are often used by traffickers. This change was most likely one of the primary reasons that in the years following the

---

⁴ More than 18 defendants pleaded guilty by 1998. Jose Paoletti-Moreda and his son Renato Paoletti-Lemus spent eight years in prison in Mexico before pleading guilty in the Eastern District of New York to extortion in 2006, agreeing to five-year prison sentences and $1.4 million in restitution. *See* Joseph Goldstein, *Two Plead Guilty in Decade-Old Slavery Case*, N.Y. SUN, June 29, 2006, http://www.nysun.com/new-york/two-plead-guilty-in-decade-old-slavery-case/35266/ [internal citations omitted].

passage of the TVPA, there was a significant increase in the number of forced labor cases prosecuted in the United States.

B. Post-TVPA Forced Labor Cases

1. *United States v. Bradley*

In one of the first post-TVPA cases to be heard on appeal, *United States v. Bradley*, 390 F.3d 145 (1st Cir. 2004), the First Circuit addressed the definition of "serious harm" under the forced labor statute and other issues related to the new law. Since *Bradley* was one of the first cases to charge § 1589 under the TVPA, many questions existed at that time about the scope of the law. Did it cover instances where workers were paid something, although not what they were promised? Did it encompass situations when workers could come and go, even occasionally visiting a nightclub in the town where they resided? What constitutes a climate of fear? And how would courts handle vulnerabilities of the victims and prior bad acts of the defendants?

Bradley addressed many of these core questions. Indeed, it contained many themes that are common to forced labor prosecutions today, including: the meaning of serious harm; the objective nature of the test of undue pressure and special vulnerabilities; the opportunity to flee by victims; and payment received by victims.

UNITED STATES v. BRADLEY
390 F.3d 145 (1st Cir. 2004)

BOUDIN, CHIEF JUDGE.

Timothy H. Bradley and Kathleen Mary O'Dell appeal from convictions for forced labor and related crimes. The gist of the charges was that the defendants lured Jamaican laborers to New Hampshire through fraud, mistreated them during their employ and coerced them to stay. From the evidence presented at trial, the jury could reasonably have found that the following events occurred.

In 1999, Bradley and O'Dell traveled to Jamaica to recruit seasonal workers for Bradley Tree Service, a tree removal company that they operated in New Hampshire. In Jamaica, the defendants convinced two men — Livingston Wilson and Garth Clarke — to come to work for them in the United States. The men were promised wages of $15-20 per hour and lodging in one of two houses on Bradley and O'Dell's property.

When Wilson and Clarke arrived in New Hampshire to begin their work, they were provided a camping trailer — initially without running water, electricity or heat. Both Jamaicans were paid $7 per hour rather than the $15-20 they had been promised. At work, yells, curses and intimidation were directed at them. After a week, Clarke fled to New York where he received a phone call from O'Dell, who threatened to "kick his ass" — as well as call the police, the FBI, and the immigration service — if he did not return.

Bradley stated in front of Wilson that he planned to "take his gun and go to New

York and look for [Clarke]." After Clarke's departure, the defendants also seized Wilson's passport and plane tickets. Bradley frequently got angry and yelled at Wilson on the job site, occasionally pushing him down. Clarke never returned to New Hampshire but instead went on from New York to Jamaica. Wilson eventually returned to Jamaica when his work visa expired in October 2000.

Shortly after Wilson's departure, the defendants again traveled to Jamaica and recruited Martin Sadler, Andrew Flynn and David Hutchinson to work for Bradley Tree Service from April to October 2001, promising each of the latter two men wages of at least $11 per hour. When the men arrived in New Hampshire, O'Dell took all three of their passports, explaining that in the previous year a worker had run away — and that Bradley would hire someone in Jamaica to "destroy" that man. Flynn and Hutchinson were both frightened by this statement, believing that murder for hire was quite feasible in Jamaica.

As with their predecessors, the three men were badly housed and ill-treated. They were paid $8 per hour rather than the $11 promised and were charged $50 a week in rent. When Hutchinson argued with Bradley about pay and rent, he was told that he only needed to stay and work long enough to repay $1,000 allegedly spent on his ticket — money that Hutchinson did not have. The defendants hindered the men when they sought treatment for injuries or medical care, and O'Dell kept tabs on the men's whereabouts although they traveled on their own in the neighborhood and elsewhere.

In September 2001, the local police visited in response to an anonymous tip that Jamaican laborers were being held against their will. When interviewed, Flynn and Hutchinson complained about their treatment; O'Dell told the officers that the men were free to leave but would have to pay for their return tickets. When the police left, Bradley browbeat the men and pushed one of them, seeking to learn who had called the police.

During this encounter Bradley grabbed Hutchinson by the neck and started to choke him. Flynn fled to a neighbor's house. O'Dell reported this to Bradley and then herself began to hit Hutchinson. After a struggle with Bradley and O'Dell, Hutchinson also fled to the neighbor's house; from there both men went to the police and spent the evening in a shelter. They remained in the United States until the time of Bradley and O'Dell's trial, working at other jobs and apparently receiving assistance from the government.

. . . .

After trial in August 2003, the jury convicted the defendants on all counts except for the false statement charge and the attempted forced labor charges (which the jury did not consider after convicting on the underlying offenses). . . .

. . . .

We begin with the jury instructions. The main statute under which the defendants were charged is captioned "Forced Labor"; so far as relevant here, the statute makes it a criminal act for anyone "knowingly" to "provide[] or obtain[] the labor or services of a person"

(1) by threats of serious harm to, or physical restraint against, that person or another person; [or]

(2) by means of any scheme, plan, or pattern intended to cause the person to believe that, if the person did not perform such labor or services, that person or another person would suffer serious harm or physical restraint.

18 U.S.C. § 1589.

The defendants' first challenge is to the district court's instruction defining "serious harm," which read as follows:

The term "serious harm" includes both physical and non-physical types of harm. Therefore, a threat of serious harm includes threats of any consequences, whether physical or non-physical, that are sufficient under all of the surrounding circumstances to compel or coerce a reasonable person in the same situation to provide or to continue providing labor or services.

Bradley and O'Dell claim that this definition expands the meaning of serious harm beyond the limits contemplated by 18 U.S.C. § 1589.

Section 1589 is a recent addition to the chapter that makes criminal acts of slavery, peonage and holding to involuntary servitude, 18 U.S.C. §§ 1581–1594 (2000). Adopted in 2000 as part of a broader set of provisions — the Victims of Trafficking and Violence Protection Act of 2000, 114 Stat. 1464 — section 1589 was intended expressly to counter *United States v. Kozminski*, 487 U.S. 931, 108 S. Ct. 2751, 101 L. Ed. 2d 788 (1988). *See* H.R. Conf. Rep. No. 106-939, at 100-01 (2000). In *Kozminski*, the Supreme Court had interpreted the pre-existing ban on "involuntary servitude" in section 1584 to prohibit only conduct involving the use or threatened use of *physical* or *legal* coercion. 487 U.S. at 949-52.

In glossing the new statute, the conference report said "serious harm" was intended to encompass not only physical violence, but also more subtle psychological methods of coercion — "such as where traffickers threaten harm to third persons, restrain their victims without physical violence or injury, or threaten dire consequences by means other than overt violence." H.R. Conf. Rep. No. 106-939, at 101. It continued: "The term 'serious harm' as used in this Act refers to a broad array of harms, including both physical and nonphysical . . . ." *Id*.

Bradley and O'Dell argue that the conference report's reference to "dire consequences" stands in sharp contrast to the district court's instruction, which states that serious harm can include "any consequences." They further claim that the district court's definition could apply to a broad range of innocent conduct, such as employers who legitimately convince their "victims" to continue working, for example, by threatening to withhold *future* pay that is sorely needed by a worker.

Starting with the *extent* of pressure, we note that Congress did not use "dire consequences" in the statute; it said "serious harm" and the district court properly charged in those words. We read the instruction's reference to "any consequences" as explaining that non-physical as well as physical consequences should be considered. Instructions must be read as a whole, *see United States v. Serino*, 835

F.2d 924, 930 (1st Cir. 1987), and no jury, taking the above-quoted paragraph as a whole, could think that trivial consequences would suffice.

We do agree that the phrase "serious harm," as extended to non-physical coercion, creates a potential for jury misunderstanding as to the *nature* of the pressure that is proscribed. Taken literally, Congress' "threats" and "scheme" language could be read to encompass conduct such as the employer's "threat" not to pay for passage home if an employee left early. Depending upon the contract, surely such a "threat" could be a legitimate stance for the employer and not criminal conduct.

Thus, in an appropriate case we think that the court in instructing the jury would be required to draw a line between improper threats or coercion and permissible warnings of adverse but legitimate consequences.

. . . .

There was no plain error here. No evidence was offered at trial that the defendants made "legitimate" threats, so there is no risk that the jury convicted them for such threats. The defendants' arguable threats or coercion involved the taking of passports and mentions of violence, combined with what the jury could have found to be complementary scrutiny of, or restrictions on, the victims' local travel. So even if the instruction was overbroad, it did not "likely" affect the outcome or threaten a miscarriage of justice, as plain error doctrine requires. *See United States v. Sotomayor-Vazquez*, 249 F.3d 1, 19 (1st Cir. 2001).

Bradley and O'Dell also claim that the district court's instructions adopted an overly subjective test for whether Hutchinson and Flynn felt compelled to work by the defendants' actions. In particular, they point to the following statement:

> You may also consider Mr. Hutchinson's and Mr. Flynn's special vulnerabilities, if any. In this regard you may consider whether or not all persons are of the same courage or firmness. You may consider, for example, Mr. Hutchinson's and Mr. Flynn's background, physical and mental condition, experience, education, socioeconomic status, and any inequalities between Mr. Hutchinson and Mr. Flynn and the defendants with respect to these considerations, including their relative stations in life. You may consider and weigh whether or not Mr. Hutchinson and Mr. Flynn were vulnerable in some way so that the actions of the defendant, even if not sufficient to compel another person to work, were enough to compel Mr. Hutchinson and Mr. Flynn to work.

. . . .

The test of undue pressure is an objective one, asking how a reasonable employee would have behaved; to rely upon some hidden emotional flaw or weakness unknown to the employer would raise various problems (*e.g.*, scienter). But, as the defendants concede, known objective conditions that make the victim especially vulnerable to pressure (such as youth or immigrant status) bear on whether the employee's labor was "obtained" by forbidden means. *See* H.R. Conf. Rep. No. 106-939, at 101; *see also Kozminski*, 487 U.S. at 952; *United States v. Alzanki*, 54 F.3d 994, 1000-01 (1st Cir. 1995), *cert. denied*, 516 U.S. 1111, 116 S. Ct. 909, 133 L. Ed. 2d 841 (1996).

Viewed with the rest of the charge, the district court's instruction makes clear that any fear of serious harm on the part of Hutchinson or Flynn needed to be reasonable for an individual with his special vulnerabilities. Nor did the evidence or arguments indicate that there were, or that the jury should consider, any peculiar vulnerabilities of the victims not fairly apparent from their objective circumstances (immigrant status, lack of local ties). There is also no indication that the defendants asked for an instruction to deal with hidden vulnerabilities.

Bradley and O'Dell's third objection is to the district court's instruction on Hutchinson and Flynn's opportunity to flee, which read:

> The government . . . need not prove physical restraint; such as, the use of chains, barbed wire, or locked doors, in order to establish the offense of forced labor. The fact that Mr. Hutchinson or Mr. Flynn may have had an opportunity to flee is not determinative of the question of forced labor if either or both of the defendants placed Mr. Hutchinson or Mr. Flynn in such fear or circumstances that he did not reasonably believe he could leave.

Pointing to the Eleventh Circuit's pattern jury instructions for involuntary servitude, the defendants claim that the opportunity to flee is determinative of forced labor — and that the district court's instruction once again erroneously replaces objective analysis with a subjective standard for coercion.

The Eleventh Circuit's pattern instruction is not in conflict with the charge just quoted; it tells the jury to "consider . . . any reasonable means the person may have had to escape" in deciding whether the person reasonably believed that he was being compelled to serve. *Eleventh Circuit Pattern Jury Instructions (Criminal Cases) 2003* at 365. We see nothing wrong with the pattern instruction; but the defendants did not ask for the pattern instruction and the language that the court used in this case is not erroneous.

The defendants' fourth objection is to the district court's instruction on the payment of wages to victims:

> Whether a person is paid a salary or a wage is not determinative of the question of whether that person has been held in forced labor. In other words, if a person is compelled to labor against his will by any one of the means prohibited by the forced labor statute, such service is forced, even if he is paid or compensated for the work.

Noting that Hutchinson and Flynn were both paid above the minimum wage, Bradley and O'Dell claim that the district court should have instructed the jury to consider whether payment of wages was the reason for the victims' decision to work.

Once again, the instruction given is correct. The defendants were free to ask for their own version as a complement to the charge given but they did not. Of course, they were free to argue to the jury (as they did) that the reason the victims remained was because of pay rather than threats. The charge as a whole made amply clear that the defendants could be convicted only if their threats and abusive conduct reasonably coerced or forced Flynn or Hutchinson to provide labor.

We turn next to an entirely separate claim of error. Over the course of the eight-day trial, slightly over one day of testimony concerned the defendants' treatment of Wilson and Clarke. This included their recruitment by the defendants, their experience at the defendants' hands, and Clarke's flight and the subsequent seizure of Wilson's passport. On this appeal, the defendants claim that the testimony was irrelevant, prejudicial and comprised forbidden character evidence. Fed R. Evid. 401, 403, 404.

The evidence of the recruitment, low wages and bad housing of Wilson and Clarke was plainly relevant to the charges in the indictment that the defendants had defrauded both men. However, no forced labor counts were based upon their treatment [internal citation omitted]. Thus one might fairly ask why certain portions of the testimony as to Wilson and Clarke were relevant — specifically, those parts concerning verbal abuse, the apparent indifference to Wilson and Clarke's medical needs, and the circumstances of Clarke's flight.

Evidence of prior bad acts to show bad character, and so a propensity to commit crimes, is forbidden for reasons of policy; but prior bad acts that are otherwise specially relevant are still permitted so long as prejudice does not substantially outweigh probative value. *See* Fed. R. Evid. 403, 404; *United States v. Van Horn*, 277 F.3d 48, 57 (1st Cir. 2002). Unfortunately for the defendants, most of the key evidence of the treatment of Wilson and Clarke is relevant to the forced labor charges concerning Flynn and Hutchinson — independent of the forbidden inferences as to the defendants' character.

This is assuredly so of what is the most damaging evidence — that Clarke fled, was pursued by threats, and that Wilson's passport was then seized. These circumstances give a malign motive for, and provide the context of, the later seizure of Flynn and Hutchinson's passports and of the initial threat made to them based on Bradley's supposed intention to "destroy" a former worker. Motive evidence is a settled exception to Rule 404's general ban. *See* Fed. R. Evid. 404(b); *United States v. Cintolo*, 818 F.2d 980, 1000 (1st Cir.), *cert. denied*, 484 U.S. 913, 108 S. Ct. 259, 98 L. Ed. 2d 216 (1987).

The abusive treatment of Wilson and Clarke, apart from their bad housing, is closer to the margin. A showing of bad acts is permitted to demonstrate a defendant's intent or plan, *see, e.g.*, *United States v. Spinosa*, 982 F.2d 620, 628 (1st Cir. 1992); *United States v. Wood*, 924 F.2d 399, 401 (1st Cir. 1991), and the intimidation of Wilson and Clarke, including their isolation from medical care, was arguably part of a pattern of intimidation that carried over to Flynn and Hutchinson. Yet bad acts comprising most criminal careers form a pattern so, taken too broadly, the exception could be made to swallow the rule.

Because none of the laborers was held in formal captivity, the government in this case faced inevitable doubts as to whether the defendants were merely abusive employers or deliberately sought to compel forced labor. Arguably the defendants' prior treatment of Wilson and Clarke, so far as it showed efforts to intimidate them and minimize their outside contact, tended to reinforce the inference that the later, similar treatment of Flynn and Hutchinson was part of a deliberate scheme to hold laborers by intimidation. There is certainly precedent for such reasoning.

The main issue, then, is not relevance (over and above propensity) but how much prejudice was added by the less necessary detail as to the abuse suffered by Wilson and Clarke. For the most part, it was not different than the treatment meted out to Flynn and Hutchinson and so was unlikely to inflame the jury. And, of course, Rules 403 and 404 weigh the decision in the government's favor by saying that evidence is excluded only if probative value is substantially outweighed by prejudice. . . .

Affirmed.

NOTES AND QUESTIONS

1. When it was first passed in 2000, the TVPA contained numerous references to "serious harm." But it did not define the term, which helps explain why the Court in *Bradley* struggled to define the boundaries of what would, and what would not, constitute "serious harm." For guidance, the *Bradley* Court looked to Congress and the House of Representatives Conference Report accompanying the TVPA, which explicitly stated that "serious harm" was intended to encompass situations where "traffickers threaten harm to third persons, restrain their victims without physical violence or injury, or threaten dire consequences by means other than overt violence."

In a subsequent reauthorization of the TVPA, the Trafficking Victims Prevention Reauthorization Act of 2008, Congress added language to specifically define "serious harm" as follows: "any harm, whether physical or nonphysical, including psychological, financial, or reputational harm, that is sufficiently serious, under all the surrounding circumstances, to compel a reasonable person of the same background and in the same circumstances to perform or to continue performing labor or services in order to avoid incurring that harm."

Although the added definition of "serious harm" has provided clarity to courts, prosecutors, and defendants, subsequent cases have continued to deal with the issue raised in *Bradley* of where to draw the line between legitimate threats and threats of "serious harm" under § 1589. *See United States v. Dann*, 652 F.3d 1160, 1169–70 (9th Cir. 2011) (holding that a reasonable juror could have found that defendant intended to threaten her immigrant nanny with financial harm, reputational harm, immigration harm and harm to the children in her care if she were to leave, thus affirming a § 1589 conviction); *United States v. Calimlim*, 538 F.3d 706, 712, 714 (7th Cir. 2008).

2. The *Bradley* court made clear that "the test of undue pressure is an objective one, asking how a reasonable employee would have behaved." It also emphasized that "known objective conditions that make the victim especially vulnerable to pressure" bear on whether labor was illegally obtained. Hidden vulnerabilities will not count. The court cited youth and immigration status as examples of some known objective conditions.

Courts have agreed that youth and immigration status are "special vulnerabilities" relevant to a § 1589 offense, and have additionally discussed other factors that fall within this category, such as lack of money and lack of contact with others. *See United States v. Djoumessi*, 538 F.3d 547, 552 (6th Cir. 2008) (finding that victim's age of 14, illegal immigration status, lack of money, and lack of contact with people other than defendants made her particularly susceptible to defendants' threats of deportation and imprisonment).

3. The defendants in *Bradley* also objected to the district court's instruction that, "The government . . . need not prove physical restraint; such as, the use of chains, barbed wire, or locked doors, in order to establish the offense of forced labor. The fact that Mr. Hutchinson or Mr. Flynn may have had an opportunity to flee is not determinative of the question of forced labor if either or both of the defendants placed Mr. Hutchinson or Mr. Flynn in such fear or circumstances that he did not reasonably believe he could leave." Defendants argued that this instruction replaced the Eleventh Circuit's objective standard for "opportunity to flee" with a subjective one. The court rejected this argument, finding that the jury instruction was proper. Other courts have similarly emphasized that an opportunity to flee is not determinative in human trafficking cases. *See United States v. Warren*, 772 F.2d 827, 834 (11th Cir. 1985) (holding that in involuntary servitude case, "[t]hat the worker had the opportunity to escape is of no moment, if the defendant has placed him in such fear of physical harm that he is afraid to leave."); *Ramos v. Hoyle*, 2008 U.S. Dist. LEXIS 102677, at *13 (S.D. Fla. Dec. 19, 2008) (finding the fact that plaintiffs had opportunities to escape and did not take them to be "irrelevant").

4. In addition to the above contentions, defendants in *Bradley* also objected to the district court's instruction that "[w]hether a person is paid a salary or a wage is not determinative of the question of whether that person has been held in forced labor. In other words, if a person is compelled to labor against his will by any one of the means prohibited by the forced labor statute, such service is forced, even if he is paid or compensated for the work." The Court, however, upheld this instruction as proper.

In many trafficking cases, under both § 1589 and § 1591, defendants have pointed to the fact that victims have kept a portion of their wages to demonstrate that they were working for money rather than out of force, fraud, or coercion. However, most courts, like *Bradley*, have held that a person can be a victim of human trafficking despite the fact that he has been allowed to keep a portion of his wages.

2. Additional Cases That Define and Expand § 1589

Following *Bradley*, many other forced labor cases have addressed similar issues. Some have further defined and expanded the scope of § 1589.

a. Non-economic Labor or Services

One subsequent case that expanded the scope of the forced labor statute was *United States v. Kaufman*, 546 F.3d 1242 (10th Cir. 2008). Specifically, the Circuit Court in *Kaufman* expanded the definition of "labor and services" to cover "non-economic" work. The facts of *Kaufman* are remarkable. Defendants Arlan and Linda Kaufman were convicted of numerous charges, including forced labor and involuntary servitude, related to their operation of an unlicensed group home and farm that housed chronically mentally ill residents in Kansas. At trial, the evidence showed that the Kaufmans required residents to farm in the nude and that Arlan

Kaufman instructed residents to engage in sexual acts and videotaped them doing so. The evidence also showed that Kaufman coerced the residents into performing such acts and that he threatened, and sometimes administered, beatings to residents who did not comply with his demands. In discussing the facts, the court noted,

> At trial, an investigator from the Kansas Attorney General's office informed the jury that he had watched forty-eight of the [video] tapes. He reported that forty-four of them contain scenes of the Kaufman House residents appearing in the nude; fourteen tapes show the residents masturbating; six show them massaging one another; and five show them shaving one another's genitals. In several instances, the tapes show Dr. Kaufman touching the genitals of some of the residents (two women and a man). Repeatedly, the camera zooms in on the residents' genitals.

On appeal, the defendants in *Kaufman* argued that the involuntary servitude and forced labor statutes applied only to "labor or services" that constitute "work in an economic sense." The Court, in rejecting this argument, relied upon the dictionary definitions of "labor" and "services," the history of the Thirteenth Amendment, and the legislative history of the TVPA to find that the terms were intended to cover non-economic work:

> In our view, if an antebellum slave was relieved of the responsibility for harvesting cotton, brought into his master's house, directed to disrobe and then engage in the various acts performed by the Kaufman House residents on the videotapes (*e.g.*, masturbation and genital shaving), his or her condition could still be fairly described as one of involuntary servitude and forced labor.

Other courts have agreed with *Kaufman*'s finding that the TVPA statutes and the Thirteenth Amendment extend to actions that are not economic in nature. *See United States v. Udeozor*, 515 F.3d 260, 266 (4th Cir. 2008) (affirming convictions of a husband and wife who held a 14-year-old girl in involuntary servitude and forced her to perform a range of domestic tasks; the court called the girl's sexual abuse by the husband "*a badge and incident of servitude* which is distressingly common, not just historically, but for young women who find themselves in coercive circumstances today") (quoted in *Kaufman*, 546 F.3d at 1262) (emphasis added); *United States v. Beebe*, 807 F. Supp. 2d 1045, 1053 (D.N.M. 2011) (holding that although hate crimes are not economic in nature, they qualify as a "badge or incident of slavery" under the Thirteenth Amendment); *United States v. Marcus*, 487 F. Supp. 2d 289, 300–01 (E.D.N.Y. 2007), *vacated on other grounds*, 538 F.3d 97 (2d Cir. 2008) (rejecting defendant's contention that the TVPA should only be interpreted to cover labor and services for which compensation is ordinarily given).

b. Abuse of the Legal Process as a Form of Coercion

Abuse or threatened abuse of the legal process is one of the prohibited means of coercion under both the involuntary servitude and forced labor statutes. An issue often arises in trafficking cases where victims are unlawfully in the United States and are told by their traffickers that they will be deported if they do not continue to work. As a result, courts have addressed the question of whether truthful threats of adverse immigration consequences that are made by traffickers are prohibited as a threatened abuse of legal process.

The court in *United States v. Garcia*, 2003 U.S. Dist. LEXIS 22088 (W.D.N.Y. Dec. 2, 2003), specifically addressed abuse of the legal process. The defendants in *Garcia* were convicted of forced labor and other offenses for bringing men and boys from Mexico to New York, where they were confined in terrible living conditions and required to work in fields for local growers. The evidence showed that the workers were not paid and were not allowed to leave their housing, except to go to work. The workers were told that they owed large sums of money to the defendants and could not leave until they paid off their debts. They were also told that if they tried to escape they would be "hunted down." Moreover, the defendants threatened their workers with, among other things, being caught and deported by the Immigration and Naturalization Service (INS) if they attempted to leave. The forced labor statute, § 1589(a)(3) specifically prohibits the obtaining of labor "by means of the abuse or threatened abuse of law or legal process." The court in *Garcia* relied in part upon the Black's Dictionary Definition of abuse of legal process as "[t]he improper and tortious use of a legitimately issued court process to obtain a result that is either unlawful or beyond the process's scope" in finding that the defendants' threats of deportation "clearly fall" within "abuse of legal process" as it is used in § 1589.

Other courts have similarly rejected arguments by defendants that threats to workers that they will lose their immigration status do not qualify under § 1589(a)(3). *See Ramos v. Hoyle*, 2008 U.S. Dist. LEXIS 102677, at *10–*11 (S.D. Fla. Dec. 19, 2008) (rejecting the argument that the truthfulness of the statements about illegality disqualify those statements from meeting § 1589(a)(3)); *see also United States v. Calimlim*, 538 F.3d 706, 713 (7th Cir. 2008); *Camayo v. John Peroulis & Sons Sheep*, 2012 U.S. Dist. LEXIS 136100, at *12 (D. Colo. Sept. 24, 2012).

c. Peonage

United States v. Farrell, 563 F.3d 364, 366 (8th Cir. 2009), provides an example of modern-day peonage and bears many of the hallmarks of the debt servitude cases that occurred throughout the South after the Civil War. The defendants in *Farrell*, Robert and Angelita Farrell, owned and operated a Comfort Inn & Suites in South Dakota. They were convicted at trial of four counts of peonage, in violation of 18 U.S.C. § 1581, and conspiracy to commit peonage, in violation of 18 U.S.C. § 371. They brought nine workers from the Philippines to the United States under temporary visas to work as housekeepers at their inn.

The court noted the evidence at trial that the defendants entered into employment contracts with each of the workers:

> [T]he Farrells drafted employment contracts for each of the nine workers they had solicited. As with the Petition, these contracts stated that the Farrells would employ the workers as housekeepers and that the workers would work six days per week for eight hours each day. The

contracts set compensation at $6.05 per hour and also provided for holiday and overtime pay. In addition to these provisions, the contracts stated that the Farrells were responsible for housing the workers and that each worker would reimburse the Farrells $150 per month for this expense. The contracts also provided that the Farrells were responsible for the cost of transportation to and from the United States, as required by law. After the Farrells submitted the Petition and drafted the employment contracts, the workers filed their applications for non-immigrant visas with the U.S. Embassy in Manila, Philippines. The applications reflected the terms of the employment contracts as recounted above, including the promise that the Farrells would pay for the workers' transportation to and from the United States.

As it turned out, the defendants did not honor the terms of the contracts. Rather, when the workers arrived in the United States, they were forced to surrender their passports, visas, and immigration documents, and were told they would be paid $3 per room, or roughly the equivalent of $3 per hour. The workers were each also required to pay a $1200 visa processing fee, although the defendants had only incurred this expense one time, and were charged for transportation to and from work and for personal items that they did not request or desire. The court noted, "[t]hus, once in the United States, the workers' debt increased dramatically while the income with which they anticipated being able to pay down that debt had decreased by at least one-half." The defendants also threatened the workers and required that the workers go get additional jobs, so that they could pay off their mounting debt.

The facts of *Farrell* are strikingly similar to those peonage cases from the early 20th century where individuals were forced to work to pay off ever-mounting debts in a cycle of compelled labor from which they could not escape. Indeed, in upholding the defendants' convictions on the peonage charges, the Court cited to *Bailey* and defined peonage as the equivalent of involuntary servitude:

> Peonage is "compulsory service in payment of a debt." *Bailey v. Alabama, 219 U.S. 219, 242, 31 S. Ct. 145, 55 L. Ed. 191 (1911)*. "[C]ompulsory service" is the equivalent of "involuntary servitude," id. at 243, which the Supreme Court has defined as "a condition of servitude in which the victim is forced to work for the defendant by the use or threat of physical restraint or physical injury, or by the use or threat of coercion through law or the legal process." *United States v. Kozminski, 487 U.S. 931, 952, 108 S. Ct. 2751, 101 L. Ed. 2d 788 (1988)*. 3 Thus, in order to prove peonage, the government must show that the defendant intentionally held a person against his or her will and coerced that person to work in order to satisfy a debt by (1) physical restraint or force, (2) legal coercion, or (3) threats of legal coercion or physical force.

d. Forced Labor Involving Compelled Sexualized Labor

Many forced labor cases involve compelled sexualized labor such as forced work in strip clubs or for pornographic materials. Some of these cases also involve sex trafficking charges. *See United States v. Marcus*, 487 F. Supp. 2d 289 (E.D.N.Y. 2007) (sex trafficking charged); *United States v. Maksimenko*, 2005 U.S. Dist. LEXIS 35087 (E.D. Mich. Apr. 26, 2005) (sex trafficking not charged); and *United States v. Aronov*, 2005 U.S. Dist. LEXIS 35082 (E.D. Mich. Apr. 26, 2005) (sex trafficking not charged).

The case of *United States v. Marcus* is notable for two reasons. First, because it addresses the application of the TVPA to conduct within intimate, domestic relationships. Second, because it defines the "anything of value" language in the sex trafficking statute broadly to include photographs for commercial gain.

In *Marcus*, the defendant was convicted of sex trafficking and forced labor. The facts of *Marcus* involved the defendant's conduct towards a woman with whom he initially engaged in a consensual BDSM relationship.[5] The victim testified at trial that although she entered into a consensual BDSM relationship with the defendant, he "subsequently used force and coercion to prevent her from leaving when she sought to do so." The victim further noted that the defendant photographed his sexual conduct with her and placed the photographs on his website.

Following his conviction for forced labor and sex trafficking, the defendant argued that the TVPA was not intended to apply to conduct taking place within an "intimate, domestic relationship" and thus that the conduct at issue was not "labor or services" under § 1589 or a "commercial sex act" under § 1591.

> According to the defendant, the legislative history demonstrates that these statutes were intended to respond to the "problem of international slave trafficking," which is "a far cry from acts of violence and abuse that take place in the context of an intimate personal relationship."

The Court firmly rejected this argument, pointing to the statutory language and legislative history of the TVPA to find that the conduct at issue fell well within the definitions of both statutes.

This issue is of considerable importance because human trafficking cases commonly involve victims who are in intimate relationships with their traffickers. This is particularly true of human trafficking cases that are sex trafficking cases, as Amy Barasch and Barbara C. Kryszko explain:

> In many cases, perpetrators of trafficking are also boyfriends or husbands of their victims, exacerbating the power dynamics and making disclosure of the trafficking and escape from the trafficker that much more difficult. In these cases, women are simultaneously victims of domestic violence and trafficking. One study found that 44% of victims of domestic sex trafficking indicated that their pimp was their boyfriend, while another

---

[5] BDSM has been defined as bondage, dominance/discipline, submission/sadism, and masochism.

20% said the pimp was "my man." Pimps, one common type of trafficker, prey on vulnerable girls, often from dysfunctional families, offering them — or so it seems at first — a safe place to stay and romance. Pimps waste no time making their victims reliant on them for shelter and economic support as well as for emotional connection, which enables them to turn their victims out into prostitution.

Amy Barasch & Barbara C. Kryszko, *The Nexus Between Domestic Violence and Trafficking for Commercial Sexual Exploitation*, in LAWYER'S MANUAL ON HUMAN TRAFFICKING: PURSUING JUSTICE FOR VICTIMS 87 (Jill Laurie Goodman & Dorchen A. Liedholdt eds., 2011) (citing Jody Raphael and Jessica Ashley, *Domestic Sex Trafficking of Chicago Women and Girls*, DePaul University School of Law and Illinois Criminal Justice Information Authority, at 25 (May 2008), *available at* http://www.enddemandillinois.org/sites/default/files/ICJIA_Research_Jody.pdf); *see also, e.g., United States v. Jimenez-Calderon*, 2006 U.S. App. LEXIS 14313 (3d Cir. June 9, 2006) (Defendants had targeted young girls from low-income areas of Mexico and convinced them to come to the United States with promises of love and marriage).

In *Marcus*, the Court also addressed the "anything of value" language in the sex trafficking statute, 18 U.S.C. § 1591. As discussed in *Marcus*, § 1591 defines a "commercial sex act" as "any sex act, on account of which anything of value is given to or received by any person." On appeal, the defendant argued that the victim had not engaged in a "commercial sex act" within the meaning of § 1591 because "the commercial gain resulted from the depiction of sex acts rather than from the acts themselves." The Court rejected this narrow reading of § 1591, which would have required payment to be for sex acts themselves and instead concluded that "a commercial sex act may include sexual acts that are photographed for commercial gain." *Marcus*, 487 F. Supp. 2d at 306.

The implications of this decision are that § 1591 can be interpreted as covering pornography that is obtained through force, fraud, or coercion. Courts have also subsequently interpreted § 1591 to cover other situations in which there is not a clear exchange of money for a sex act. *See United States v. O'Connor*, 650 F.3d 839, 857 (2d Cir. 2011) (finding that the conditions of § 1591 were satisfied when defendant allowed her landlord to sexually abuse her daughter when she was behind on paying rent.)

e. Forced Labor by Military Contractors

A different type of forced labor involves human trafficking by U.S. military contractors. The U.S. Commission on Wartime Contracting, a bipartisan panel established to investigate contracting waste during the wars in Iraq and Afghanistan, reported to Congress in 2011 that it uncovered evidence of trafficking and exploitation of workers during trips to war zones.[6] Confirming reports by non-governmental organizations (NGOs), the Commission found that foreigners from

---

[6] Transforming Wartime Contracting: Controlling Costs, Reducing Risks, Final Report to Congress (Aug. 2011), at 92–94, *available at* http://www.wartimecontracting.gov/docs/CWC_FinalReport-lowres.pdf.

various countries, labeled Third-Country Nationals, were promised work in Kuwait at good wages. When the workers arrived, they were re-routed to Afghanistan and paid wages lower than promised. The Commission also found that contractors withheld pay from workers until their contracts were completed, preventing them from returning home; that at least one contractor denied the workers vacations they were promised; and that many of the workers' living conditions were substandard. NGOs and reporters have documented a number of instances of sex trafficking, sexual exploitation, and other labor abuses as well. *See* ACLU and Allard K. Lowenstein, International Human Rights Clinic, Yale Law School, *Victims of Complacency: The Ongoing Trafficking and Abuse of Third Country Nationals by U.S. Government Contractors* (June 2012), *available at* http://www.aclu.org/files/assets/hrp_traffickingreport_web_0.pdf; Sarah Stillman, *The Invisible Army: For Foreign Workers on U.S. Bases in Iraq and Afghanistan, War Can Be Hell*, THE NEW YORKER, June 6, 2011, http://www.newyorker.com/reporting/2011/06/06/110606fa_fact_stillman?currentPage=all.

In the aftermath of the report, the U.S. government has taken steps to prohibit federal contractors, contractor employees, subcontractors, and subcontractor employees from using misleading recruitment practices, charging employees recruitment fees, and destroying or confiscating workers' passports.[7] Companies with contracts abroad valued at more than $500,000 must set up a process for employees to report trafficking violations "without fear of retaliation" and must certify that they haven't participated in trafficking.[8] While many view this as a significant first step to addressing trafficking on American military bases abroad, others have argued that it does not go far enough. Indeed, anti-trafficking groups and others have called for passage of a proposed bill, the End Human Trafficking in Government Contracting Act, which would create a new federal crime of foreign labor bondage. *See* Devon Chaffee, *President Issues Executive Order to Stop Human Trafficking in Government Contracts*, ACLU — WASH. MARKUP, Sept. 25, 2012, http://www.aclu.org/blog/human-rights/president-issues-executive-order-stop-human-trafficking-government-contracts; Nick Taborek, *Obama Signs Human Trafficking Order Targeting U.S. Contractors*, Sept. 25, 2012, http://www.businessweek.com/news/2012-09-25/obama-signs-human-trafficking-order-targeting-u-dot-s-dot-contractors ("Darrell Issa, who chairs the House Oversight and Government Reform Committee, said while the executive order 'borrows many components from Congress' legislative effort, it does not include the most important part: expanding the criminal code to encompass foreign labor bondage for work performed outside the U.S. and cracking down on grants and grantees as well as just contractors.' ").

---

[7] In 2012, President Barack Obama signed an executive order entitled "Strengthening Protections Against Trafficking in Persons in Federal Contracts," which ordered the Federal Acquisition Regulatory Council (FAR) to amend the Federal Acquisition Regulation by 77 Fed. Reg. 60,029 Exec. Order No. 13,627, 77 Fed. Reg. 60,029 (Sept. 25, 2012).

[8] *Id.* at 60,030.

C. Domestic Servitude

Although domestic servitude is charged under the forced labor statute, it is in many ways a distinct form of labor trafficking. Unlike larger agricultural, factory, or restaurant forced labor enterprises, domestic servitude cases usually have a single female victim, who is isolated from the outside world and kept hidden away in a household. Many cases of domestic servitude share similar characteristics.

In the classic case of domestic servitude, the victim is a young girl or woman who: comes to the United States to perform household and childcare duties; hails from an impoverished background in a developing country; speaks little or no English; fears deportation by immigration authorities; and believes promises made by her traffickers that she will be given opportunities in the United States, such as the chance to attend school and the opportunity to make money to send to her family at home.

In typical cases, the traffickers also share many similarities. They are often a husband and wife, with the wife serving as the primary trafficker and the enforcer of rules. In many instances, the husband sexually assaults the victim. Traffickers also frequently: pay victims less than promised; commit immigration or visa fraud; are well-established and financially secure; confiscate the victim's immigration documents upon arrival; tell the victim that she is illegally in the United States upon arrival; set rules and conditions; prohibit the victim from leaving the house, or permit the victim to leave only on rare occasions; restrict communication with others; and use all forms of coercion — threats, beatings, deprivation, sexual assault, and psychological manipulation — to compel the victim to work.

1. *United States v. Calimlim*

Many of the characteristics of domestic servitude cases are found in the following case, *United States v. Calimlim.*

UNITED STATES v. CALIMLIM
538 F.3d 706 (7th Cir. 2008)

WOOD, CIRCUIT JUDGE.

At age 16, Irma Martinez began working for the Mendoza family in the Philippines, where it is common for wealthier families to have a live-in housekeeper to attend to the house and children. Her family was poor and depended on the salary she earned. At the urging of Dr. Jovito Mendoza (the father of defendant Elnora Calimlim), Martinez traveled to the United States when she was about 19 years old. She told consular officials that she needed a visa in order to accompany Dr. Mendoza, who was going to the United States for medical treatment, but she really intended to stay in the United States to work. Her visa permitted a two-year stay as long as she departed and re-entered the United States at least once every six months.

When Martinez arrived, Jefferson and Elnora Calimlim confiscated her passport and told her that she would have to reimburse the Mendozas for the cost of her plane ticket. The Calimlims told her she was in the United States illegally from the day after she arrived. Martinez was unable to communicate in English for the first five or six years of her stay.

Martinez worked for the Calimlims, both of whom are physicians, as a live-in housekeeper. Her daily routine usually began at 6:00 a.m. and ended around 10:00 p.m., seven days a week as well as during most vacations. Her duties initially included caring for the Calimlim household and children; eventually they expanded to include the family cars, investment properties, and medical offices. After ten years, the family moved to a more luxurious house, 8,600 square feet in area and equipped with a private tennis court. Martinez provided their only household help.

While she worked for the Calimlims, Martinez was greatly restricted in what she could do. She never walked out the front door of the first house, and only answered the door in the second house once — on Halloween, wearing a mask. She was told not to play outside with the children or leave her room in the basement during social functions, even to go to the bathroom. She was permitted to walk to church (one selected by Elnora), but only via a back path that was well away from possible observation. Elnora did not allow her to go to the same church too many times in a row. When she was driven someplace she had to ride in the back seat with her head down so that nobody could see her. The "house rules" included a phone code that enabled Martinez to answer the phone when the children called, but not when outsiders did. The children were told not to discuss Martinez with anyone outside the family. Martinez was not permitted to seek medical care outside of the house, even for special needs such as dentistry.

The Calimlims allowed Martinez to speak with her family four or five times over the 19 years she was with them, and even then she was surrounded by the Calimlim family while speaking on the phone. Martinez initially had a savings account into which her earnings were deposited, but Elnora closed it one day after Martinez's visa expired. Martinez authorized Elnora to send money to Martinez's family in the Philippines through Elnora's parents' account, but over the entire 19-year period, the total that the Calimlims sent was only 654,412 pesos, or about $19,000. Martinez's "earnings" were nothing but a book entry in the Calimlims' accounts. Martinez was allowed to shop for personal items, but she had to leave the cart in the store (so that Elnora Calimlim could pay) and go wait in the car; she would later "reimburse" the Calimlims for the cost through withheld "wages." Martinez was told repeatedly by the adult Calimlims and their children that if anyone discovered her she could be arrested, imprisoned, and deported, and she would not be able to send any more money back to her family. Fear of that consequence kept her from breaking any of the rules or appearing outside the house.

On September 29, 2004, federal agents, acting on an anonymous tip, executed a search warrant and found a trembling Martinez huddled in the closet of her bedroom. A federal grand jury returned a third superseding indictment on December 6, 2005, charging the Calimlims with obtaining and conspiring to obtain forced labor (Counts 1 and 2), in violation of 18 U.S.C. §§ 371, 1589, and 1594, and harboring and conspiring to harbor an alien for private financial gain (Counts 3 and 4), in violation of 8 U.S.C. § 1324(a)(1). A jury convicted them of all four counts on May 26, 2006. . . .

. . . .

The Calimlims challenge their convictions . . . [on the grounds that] there the forced labor statute is vauge and overbroad and that there was insufficient evidence of financial gain on the harboring counts.

. . . .

Vagueness and Overbreadth

The Calimlims raise two constitutional challenges to the forced labor statute, 18 U.S.C. § 1589. First, they argue that the statute is so vague that it fails to provide notice of what is criminalized, and second, that it is overbroad enough to punish innocent activity. . . .

A vagueness challenge is best described by the evils it seeks to prevent: "Unconstitutionally vague statutes pose two primary difficulties: (1) they fail to provide due notice so that 'ordinary people can understand what conduct is prohibited,' and (2) they 'encourage arbitrary and discriminatory enforcement.' " *United States v. Cherry*, 938 F.2d 748, 753 (7th Cir. 1991) (quoting *Kolender v. Lawson*, 461 U.S. 352, 357, 103 S. Ct. 1855, 75 L. Ed. 2d 903 (1983)). The Calimlims argue that the statute failed to put them on notice that warning Martinez that she was violating the law by being in the country illegally could be construed as violating the forced labor statute. . . .

We find that the forced labor statute provides sufficient notice of what it criminalizes. Under 18 U.S.C. § 1589, it is illegal

>knowingly [to] provide [] or obtain [] the labor or services of a person —
>
>(1) by threats of serious harm to, or physical restraint against, that person or another person;
>
>(2) by means of any scheme, plan, or pattern intended to cause the person to believe that, if the person did not perform such labor or services, that person or another person would suffer serious harm or physical restraint; or
>
>(3) by means of the abuse or threatened abuse of law or the legal process

. . . .

The Government did not allege that the Calimlims made direct threats against Martinez within the scope of § 1589(1); the charges rest on subparts (2) and (3). They kept Martinez under physical restraint and caused her to believe that she might be deported and her family seriously harmed because she would no longer be able to send money. They also implicitly threatened her with deportation proceedings. Looking at those charges, the Calimlims argue that the phrases "serious harm" and "threatened abuse of the law or the legal process" are too vague to support criminal liability. They argue that while they did notify Martinez that a threat existed from other quarters, they did not threaten Martinez that they would take action themselves.

. . . .

We turn, then, to the Calimlims' overbreadth argument. It is tempting to reject this for the simple reason that § 1589 penalizes conduct, whereas overbreadth is a doctrine designed to protect free speech. *See Virginia v. Hicks*, 539 U.S. 113, 118, 123 S. Ct. 2191, 156 L. Ed. 2d 148 (2003). The Calimlims argue that they are focusing, however, on speech associated with the forbidden conduct. They speculate that, in the wake of their convictions, innocent employers who merely warn their workers about the consequences of illegal immigration or a potential loss of health insurance coverage could get caught up by this law. "[T]he overbreadth doctrine permits the facial invalidation of laws that inhibit the exercise of First Amendment rights if the impermissible applications of the law are substantial when 'judged in relation to the statute's plainly legitimate sweep.' ". . .

There are many problems with this argument. As we said, § 1589 does not criminalize any speech; it bans behavior that may involve speech. This blunts any overbreadth attack. . . . Because of the *scienter* requirement, any speech involved must be a threat or else intended to achieve an end prohibited by law.

To the extent that § 1589 raises First Amendment concerns, the *scienter* requirement limits the prohibited speech to unprotected speech. . . .

Taking their vagueness and overbreadth challenges together, the Calimlims are arguing that nothing they said or did to Martinez amounted to a threat. . . . Perhaps another jury might have accepted this story, but the one that heard their case did not. . . .

The evidence showed that the Calimlims intentionally manipulated the situation so that Martinez would feel compelled to remain. They kept her passport, never admitted that they too were violating the law, and never offered to try to regularize her presence in the United States. Their vague warnings that someone might report Martinez and their false statements that they were the only ones who lawfully could employ her could reasonably be viewed as a scheme to make her believe that she or her family would be harmed if she tried to leave. . . .

. . . .

Insufficient Evidence for Harboring Conviction

We next turn to the Calimlims' challenge to the evidence supporting their conviction for harboring an alien for private financial gain under 8 U.S.C. § 1324(a)(1). The statute provides for stricter punishments if the harboring occurs "for the purpose of commercial advantage or private financial gain." 8 U.S.C. § 1324(a)(1)(B)(i). . . .

The Calimlims argue that Congress intended to punish smugglers and coyotes when it doubled the maximum penalty for harboring aliens for private financial gain. They portray themselves as innocent employers who simply bargained for mutual advantage. They struck a fair deal with Martinez for the value of her labor, they claim; they even go so far as to say that she enjoyed a fine lifestyle while she lived with them. Perhaps, they concede, they did take some advantage of the fact that she was present in the country illegally, but they blame the immigration system, not themselves, for that inequity. This was a fair deal, they conclude, from which they reaped no net financial gain.

This argument makes no sense. The Calimlims must have enjoyed some profit, at least on the margin, or else they would not have gone to the trouble of having a live-in housekeeper whom they kept hidden, often through extraordinary measures, from all outsiders. They argue that the value of her labor was offset by 1) the price of her wages, room, and board, and 2) the risk of harboring her, and that the values all balance out. Even accepting this implausible argument and granting that the Calimlims might not have any reason to spend one more dollar on Martinez, they would still have a motive to spend some dollars on her: her labor came at a significantly lower price than a comparable American housekeeper. This is enough of a pecuniary motive by itself to prove financial gain, as we observed in United States v. Fujii, 301 F.3d 535, 539-40 (7th Cir. 2002).

. . . .

We AFFIRM the Calimlims' convictions . . . .

2. Involuntary Servitude and Domestic Servitude

Domestic servitude cases can also be charged under the involuntary servitude statute, 18 U.S.C. § 1584. This is most often done when there is sufficient evidence of threats of physical violence, force, or abuse of the legal process and thus no need for use of the forced labor statute, which reaches more subtle forms of coercion.

One such example is *United States v. Djoumessi*, 538 F.3d 547 (6th Cir. 2008). In this case, a 14-year-old girl from Cameroon was brought to the United States by the defendants, a couple living in a Detroit suburb, to care for their household and their two young children. Despite promises that she would attend school and be provided for by the defendants, the victim found a very different reality when she arrived in Detroit. The Court noted,

> [t]he Djoumessis required the [minor female victim] to perform substantially all of their housework and to provide essentially all of the care for their children. She worked every day from 6:00 a.m. to 10:00 p.m. for no compensation other than room and board, and the Djoumessis never sent her to school. Her housing consisted of a dilapidated, dark and sometimes-flooded space in the Djoumessis' basement. The Djoumessis did not allow her to use any of the working showers in the home, reducing her to collecting hot water from the basement sink in a bucket to clean herself. When [the minor female victim] started her menstrual cycle, Evelyn refused to give her sanitary pads, leaving her to use her clothing instead. The Djoumessis also closely controlled [the minor female victim's] contact with outsiders, rarely allowing her to leave the property except to take the Djoumessis' children to the bus stop or to other events, and telling her that if she ever contacted the police she would go to jail because she was in the country illegally. When the Djoumessis were not satisfied with [the minor female victim's] work, they beat her and threatened her. And on top of all of this, Joseph Djoumessi sexually abused the minor female victim on three occasions.

Id. at 549.

At trial, the victim in *Djoumessi* was asked why she had not objected to the work required by the defendants. The victim "said she had no choice because she was afraid that the Djoumessis would hit her if she did not work. Those fears were not unfounded. Djoumessi once beat her with a belt — severely enough to draw blood — because . . . [the minor female victim] failed to make him breakfast, change the sheets and turn off the Christmas lights."

On appeal, the defendants in *Djoumessi* made a number of arguments frequently used in domestic servitude and other forced labor cases. First, they argued that they had taken custody of the victim under a local tradition in Cameroon known as "take my child," in which a wealthy family agrees to take in and care for a poor child. Second, the defendants stated that the victim's parents consented to allow the defendants to treat her like they did. And, third, they argued that the victim's life was far better in the United States than it was at home in Cameroon. The Court rejected each of these arguments.

3. Domestic Servitude and Sexual Abuse

Evidence of sexual abuse is commonly present in domestic servitude cases. For example, in *United States v. Udeozor*, 515 F.3d 260 (4th Cir. 2008), a couple was convicted of involuntary servitude for subjecting a 14-year-old Nigerian girl to physical, emotional, and sexual abuse. The victim in *Udeozor*, who provided household services and childcare, was also not paid for her services or allowed to go to school.

On appeal, the wife defendant argued that the district court erred in admitting evidence of her husband's sexual abuse of the victim, arguing that the prejudicial effect of such evidence substantially outweighed its probative value. The court rejected this argument, finding that the sexual abuse evidence was "probative of the conspiracy to impress the victim into involuntary servitude." The court further found that the sexual abuse was "one of the forms of force used to keep the minor victim in the condition of involuntary servitude." The Court noted that Dr. Udeozor had been free to challenge the evidence at trial by arguing that she was unaware of and played no part in the sexual abuse, but that the evidence was admissible. *Id.* at 266

Importantly, the *Udeozor* court also noted the prevalence of sexual abuse within domestic servitude situations:

> Sexual coercion and subordination have been among the worst indicia of involuntary servitude. To reverse the trial court's admission of such evidence here would draw us closer to an inadvisable rule of per se inadmissibility with respect to a badge and incident of servitude which is distressingly common, not just historically, but for young women who find themselves in coercive circumstances today. The Udeozors' scheme involved an allegedly noxious brew of physical, psychological, and sexual coercion of its minor victim . . . .

Id.

4. Additional Issues: Document Servitude, the Knowledge Requirement Under Forced Labor, and Restitution

A number of other issues frequently arise in domestic servitude cases. In *United States v. Sabhnani*, 599 F.3d 215 (2d Cir. 2010), the Second Circuit Court of Appeals addressed document servitude, the knowledge requirement under forced labor, and restitution during the appeal of a domestic servitude case wherein the defendants, a couple from Syosset, New York, was convicted of forced labor and other offenses.

In *Sabhnani*, the defendants brought two women from Indonesia to work as servants in their home. Neither of the women spoke English and both were poor and uneducated, seeking to better themselves and provide for their families. The facts of this case are striking for, even in the context of manifest examples of extreme violence and degradation, this case stands out for the violent conduct of the wife defendant towards the victims. The wife defendant poured hot, scalding water over one of the victims on three separate occasions, made the victim eat large quantities of hot chili peppers until she became physically ill, mutilated and cut the victim's head and ear, and regularly deprived her of food.

In addition to convictions for forced labor, harboring aliens, peonage, and conspiracy, the defendants in *Sabhnani* were convicted of document servitude in violation of 18 U.S.C. § 1592(a). Document servitude, a separate statute within the TVPA, prohibits the taking or holding of travel, immigration, or government identification documents during commission of a human trafficking-related crime or in an effort to prevent a person from leaving or to maintain their services.[9] Document servitude is commonly charged alongside forced labor. *See United States v. Farrell*, 563 F.3d 364 (8th Cir. 2009); *United States v. Bradley*, 390 F.3d 145 (1st Cir. 2004).

The court in *Sabhnani* noted that a defendant can be convicted under the document servitude statute "for knowingly concealing immigration documents merely 'with intent to violate' the forced labor or peonage statutes." The evidence in this case showed that the two victims' passports and immigration documents were kept in a locked cupboard in the closet next to defendants' bedroom — evidence that the court found "ample" for conviction. *Sabhnani*, 599 F.3d 215, 245.

The court also rejected a challenge by the husband defendant that there was insufficient evidence to show that he knew about his wife's threats and physical abuse of the victims to sustain his convictions. The court found that the jury had

---

[9] Section 1592. Unlawful conduct with respect to documents in furtherance of trafficking, peonage, slavery, involuntary servitude, or forced labor. (Added Oct. 28, 2000, Pub. L. No. 106-386, Div A, § 112(a)(2), 114 Stat. 1488.) (As amended Dec. 23, 2008, Pub. L. No. 110-457, Title II, Subtitle C, § 222(b)(6), 122 Stat. 5070.) In order to prove document servitude, the government must show that defendants (1) destroyed, concealed, removed, confiscated, or possessed any actual or purported passport or other immigration document, or any other actual or purported government identification document, of another person; (2) did so knowingly, and (3) did so in the course of violating or with intent to violate § 1581, 1583, 1584, 1589, 1590, 1591, or 1594(a) (or to prevent or restrict or to attempt to prevent or restrict, without lawful authority, the person's liberty to move or travel, in order to maintain the labor or services of that person, when the person is or has been a victim of a severe form of trafficking). Section 1592(a). In the cases cited, there is usually concrete evidence of the confiscation, and defendant's knowledge or intent is generally inferred from the circumstances.

"more than ample basis" on which to find that defendant knew about the abuse. The court noted the substantial contact that defendant had with the victims, including many opportunities to observe them with serious injuries from his wife's physical abuse. Additionally, the court found that "[t]here was also sufficient evidence of . . . [the husband defendant's] intent to use . . . [the wife defendant's] threats and maltreatment against the maids in order to obtain their labor," and noted that husband defendant benefitted greatly from their labor. *Id.* at 242–43

This case demonstrates that the knowledge requirements of TVPA statutes may often be inferred in situations in which one defendant did not have a direct role in the force, fraud, or coercion of the victims, but nevertheless played a role in the trafficking enterprise and benefitted from the victims' servitude.

Finally, the court in *Sabhnani* addressed the calculation for mandatory restitution under 18 U.S.C. § 1593 of the TVPA and provided a detailed example of a restitution calculation in a trafficking case. The restitution statute provides that a court shall order restitution to a victim of trafficking for the full amount of the victim's losses, which include the greater of the gross income or value to the defendant of the victim's services, or the value of a victim's labor as guaranteed under minimum wage and overtime laws. Restitution has been awarded in a large percentage of cases brought under the TVPA. *See United States v. Mondragon*, 2009 U.S. App. LEXIS 18244 (5th Cir. Aug. 14, 2009) (defendants ordered to pay $1.7 million in restitution to victims); *United States v. Djoumessi*, 538 F.3d 547, 550 (6th Cir. 2008) (defendant ordered to pay $100,000 in restitution to victims); *United States v. Bradley*, 390 F.3d 145, 150 (1st Cir. 2004) (defendants ordered to pay $13,052 in restitution to victims); *United States v. Abrorkhodja Askarkhodjaev*, 2010 U.S. Dist. LEXIS 107183 (W.D. Mo. Sept. 23, 2010) (defendant ordered to pay $172,000 in restitution to victim); *United States v. Aronov*, 2005 U.S. Dist. LEXIS 35082 (E.D. Mich. Apr. 26, 2005) (defendant ordered to pay over $1 million in restitution to victims); *United States v. Maksimenko*, 2005 U.S. Dist. LEXIS 35087 (E.D. Mich. Apr. 26, 2005) (defendant ordered to pay over $1.5 million to victims).

5. Domestic Servitude and Diplomatic Immunity

A subset of domestic servitude cases involve foreign diplomats,[10] some of whom bring domestic workers to the United States and engage in conduct constituting forced labor.[11] In fact, social services organizations estimate that one-third of all domestic servitude cases implicate diplomats with immunity.

The conduct of foreign diplomats is governed by the Vienna Convention on Diplomatic Relations, which provides that diplomatic agents are immune from

---

[10] Krista Friedrich, Note: *Statutes of Liberty? Seeking Justice Under United States Law When Diplomats Traffic in Persons*, 72 BROOK. L. REV. 1139, 1154–55 (2007) (citing Lena H. Sun, *"Modern-Day Slavery" Prompts Rescue Efforts: Groups Target Abuse of Foreign Maids, Nannies*, WASH. POST, May 3, 2004, at A1) (any employees of international organizations, such as the United Nations and the International Monetary Fund, ambassadors, foreign diplomats, and consular officers bring their own household servants with them while they reside in the United States).

[11] Margaret Murphy, *Modern Day Slavery: The Trafficking of Women to the United States*, 9 BUFF. WOMEN'S L.J. 11, 13 (2000) (approximately 2,000 domestic workers enter the United States each year on visas obtained by diplomatic employers).

criminal, civil, and administrative liability except in three narrow situations: a real action involving private property, an action regarding succession in which the diplomatic agent acts as a private person, and "an action relating to any professional or commercial activity exercised by the diplomatic agent in the receiving State outside his official functions."[12] Diplomats have invoked their immunity against liability for prosecution in a variety of cases, and assertion of this protection has made diplomats' domestic workers particularly vulnerable to forced labor and abuse. *See, e.g.*, Sarah Fitzpatrick, *Diplomatic Immunity Leaves Abused Workers in the Shadows*, WASH. POST, Sept. 20, 2009, at A4; PETRA FOLLMAR, DANIELA HDL & ULRIKE MENTZ-EICKHOFF, FEMALE DOMESTIC WORKERS IN THE PRIVATE HOUSEHOLDS OF DIPLOMATS IN THE FEDERAL REPUBLIC OF GERMANY (Sept. 2003), http://www.ban-ying.de/downloads/cedaw%20engl.pdf

One example is the case of Vishranthamma Swarna, a domestic worker from India who agreed to come to the United States and work in the home of diplomats for an agreed-upon salary of $2,000 per month with vacation time. Instead, she was only paid $200 to $300 per month, had her passport confiscated, was forbidden to leave the apartment or use the telephone to make calls, was verbally insulted, and was physically abused and raped. *See Swarna v. Al-Awadi*, 607 F. Supp. 2d 509, 512–13 (S.D.N.Y.), *reconsideration denied*, 2009 U.S. Dist. LEXIS 47285 (S.D.N.Y. May 29, 2009), *aff'd in part, vacated in part, and remanded*, 622 F.3d 123 (2d Cir. 2010).

Attempts by abused domestic workers to bring cases against their diplomat employers have often been dismissed based on diplomatic immunity. Although this remains the case for diplomats in active service, courts have recently found immunity to be more restricted when the defendant charged with a trafficking offense is a former rather than active diplomat. *See* Emily F. Siedell, *Swarna and Baoanan: Unraveling the Diplomatic Immunity Defense to Domestic Worker Abuse*, 26 MD. J. INT'L L. 173, 192 (2011); *See Swarna and Baoanan v. Baja*, 627 F. Supp. 2d 155 (S.D.N.Y. 2009).

The federal government has also recently enhanced protections under the TVPA for domestic workers, recognizing that this group is particularly vulnerable to exploitation and abuse. To prevent diplomats from exploiting their household help the 2008 reauthorization of the TVPA added a provision that allows the limiting of the issuance of A-3[13] and G-5 visas[14] if there is "credible evidence" of abuse or exploitation within the diplomatic mission or international organization and that the mission or organization tolerated these actions.[15]

---

[12] Vienna Convention on Diplomatic Relations (Apr. 18, 1961) pmbl., 23 U.S.T. 3227, 3230, 3240–41.

[13] A-3 visas allow "personal employees, attendants, cosmetic workers, or servants" of diplomats to have legal status in the United States. U.S. DEPARTMENT OF STATE, VISAS FOR EMPLOYEES OF INTERNATIONAL ORGANIZATIONS AND NATO, http://travel.state.gov/visa/temp/types/types_2638.html.

[14] G-5 visas are for "[p]ersonal employees, attendants, domestic workers, or servants of individuals who hold a valid G-1 through G-4, or NATO-1 through NATO-6 visa." U.S. DEPARTMENT OF STATE, VISAS FOR EMPLOYEES OF INTERNATIONAL ORGANIZATIONS AND NATO, http://travel.state.gov/visa/temp/types/types_2638.html.

[15] TVPRA 2008, Pub. L. No. 110-457, Section 203(a)(2), 122 Stat. 5044.

IV. SEX TRAFFICKING

The sex trafficking statute, 18 U.S.C. § 1591, criminalizes the trafficking of minors, and of adults who have been compelled by force, fraud, or coercion, for the purposes of engaging in a commercial sex act. The statute's application stretches beyond traditional conceptions of trafficking to anyone who knowingly recruits, entices, harbors, transports, provides, obtains, or maintains a trafficking victim for a commercial sex act. The statute can also be violated by someone who benefits from a sex trafficking operation or who knows or acts in reckless disregard of the fact that sex trafficking is taking place.

Certain aspects of the sex trafficking statute bear noting. First, for cases where the victim is under the age of 18, there is no requirement that a commercial sex act be compelled through force, fraud, or coercion. Meaning that the proof required for sex trafficking of juveniles is far less than that required for adults.[16] Second, to prove sex trafficking it must be shown that the trafficking affects interstate or foreign commerce. This jurisdictional standard is easily met and has not been a hurdle to sex trafficking prosecutions. Third, the statute does not require that a defendant knows that a victim is under 18; it is sufficient that the defendant had a "reasonable opportunity to observe" the victim.

Sex trafficking, like labor trafficking, takes many different forms in the United States. Women are recruited from within the United States as well as from many other countries, to work in street prostitution, brothels, motels, or prostitution delivery services. Defendants in these cases are men and women, U.S. citizens, and foreigners. While there are trends in the types of enterprises that operate in this industry, the facts of individual cases differ.

The cases in this chapter address many of the questions that are raised by this statute — what qualifies as a commercial sex act? How much evidence is needed to infer that someone benefitting from trafficking knew about it? What qualifies as affecting interstate commerce? What qualifies as a reasonable opportunity to observe an underage victim?

This chapter will separately discuss international sex trafficking cases and domestic sex trafficking cases. Although many similarities exist between the two types of cases, there are differences that merit independent discussion.

A. International Sex Trafficking

Sex trafficking cases in the United States often involve foreign-born traffickers and victims. The traffickers bring victims to the United States so that they can profit from forced prostitution of the victims. International sex trafficking cases frequently involve a large number of traffickers involved in a criminal organization that more closely resembles an organized crime syndicate or criminal gang.

---

[16] In practice, most cases of juvenile sex trafficking involve force, fraud, or coercion. Yet that evidence is not necessary to sustain a conviction under the law.

1. Mexican Sex Trafficking Rings

There have been many cases over the past decade involving sophisticated Mexican sex trafficking rings. Since many of these instances of sex trafficking have led to successful prosecutions, much has been learned about the manner in which these Mexican trafficking rings operate. A common pattern is for traffickers to lure Mexican girls and women, often poor and uneducated, to the United States using promises of love or non-prostitution work opportunities. Once the victims arrive, the traffickers use a combination of force, fraud, and coercion to compel them to engage in prostitution. *See United States v. Cortes-Meza*, 2011 U.S. App. LEXIS 2109, at *3–*5 (11th Cir. Feb. 1, 2011) (affirming convictions of defendants who enticed "poor teenagers and young women who lived in rural areas of Mexico" to the United States with promises of "legitimate employment and a better way of life," at times acting romantically interested in them or promising to marry them; upon arrival in the United States, defendants would force the women into prostitution); *United States v. Mendez*, 2010 U.S. App. LEXIS 1510, at *2–*3 (6th Cir. Jan. 25, 2010) (affirming convictions of defendants who brought women from Mexico under false pretenses of offering them work in a restaurant); *United States v. Flores Carreto*, 583 F.3d 152, 154–55 (2d Cir. 2009) (affirming convictions of defendants who "seduced" young, poor, and uneducated women from Mexico, brought them to the United States, and used "violence, manipulation, and threats of physical restriction" to force them into prostitution).

Following is an article detailing the purportedly large sex trafficking industry in Tenancingo, Tlaxcala, a town that has received substantial attention for allegations of being a town built by the sex trafficking industry:

Kate Brumback & Mark Stevenson, *Mexican Women Forced into U.S. Prostitution by Pimps*
THE HUFFINGTON POST, August 9, 2010[17]

TENANCINGO, Mexico— In this impoverished town in central Mexico, a sinister trade has taken root: entire extended families exploit desperation and lure hundreds of unsuspecting young Mexican women to the United States to force them into prostitution.

Those who know the pimps of Tlaxcala state — victims, prosecutors, social workers and researchers — say the men from Tenancingo have honed their methods over at least three generations.

They play on all that is good in their victims — love of family, love of husband, love of children — to force young women into near-bondage in the United States.

The town provided the perfect petri dish for forced prostitution. A heavily Indian area, it combines long-standing traditions of forced marriage or "bride kidnapping," with machismo, grinding poverty and an early wave of industrialization in the 1890s that later went bust, leaving a displaced population that would roam, looking for elusive work.

---

[17] Copyright © 2010 by the Associated Press. Reprinted with permission.

Added to that, says anthropologist Oscar Montiel — who has interviewed the pimps about their work — is a tradition of informal, sworn-to-silence male groups. He believes that, in the town of just over 10,000, there may be as many as 3,000 people directly involved the trade. Prosecutors say the network includes female relatives of the pimps, who often serve as go-betweens or supervisors, or who care for the children of women working as prostitutes.

A pimp Montiel identified only by his unprintable nickname said his uncle got him started in the business and that he has since passed the techniques on to his brother and two sons. Federico Pohls, who runs a center that tries to help victims, says established pimps will sometimes bankroll young men who aspire to the profession but lack the clothes, money and cars to impress young women.

Dilcya Garcia, a Mexico City prosecutor who did anti-trafficking work in Tenancingo, confirms that many boys in the town aspire to be pimps.

"If you ask some boys, and we have done this, 'Hey what do you want to be when you grow up?' They reply: 'I want to have a lot of sisters and a lot of daughters to make lots of money.'"

The Tenancingo pimps troll bus stations, parks, stores and high schools in poverty-stricken areas of Mexico, according to prosecutors who have raided their operations in Mexico City — often the "proving ground" where women are tried out as prostitutes before being moved to the U.S.

The pimps use a combination of threats, mistreatment, unkept promises of marriage and jobs, that send their victims on a slippery slope that usually ends in the filthy alleys near Mexico City's La Merced marketplace or at a cheap apartment in metro Atlanta. There, the women are isolated and sometimes forced to service dozens of male clients a day.

Garcia, who has dealt extensively with the victims, says some pimps even show up with fake "parents" to convince women they are serious about commitment.

"The way they fish for their victims is very cruel, very Machiavellian, but very effective," said Garcia. "When somebody is isolated, or unprotected, they are the perfect victim."

A young victim who agreed to speak to The Associated Press fit that profile perfectly. She asked not to be identified because she fears retaliation from her pimp's family.

Miguel Rugerio was charming and sweet when she met him in her impoverished hometown in the gulf coast state of Tabasco, she said.

He wooed her with sweet words and promises — good jobs in the U.S. for both of them with lots of money to send home to build a house in Mexico for their future. He wanted to meet her parents — a sure sign of a serious relationship in Mexico — and said he wanted to marry her.

She couldn't believe her good fortune.

But after he got her to Tenancingo he quickly changed. When the girl, just 17 at the time, wanted to go home for her sister's 15th birthday, he said no.

"I thought he was joking, and he said he wasn't joking, that I couldn't go home," she said. "I told him I would escape, and he said he would find me and make a scene in my hometown."

He got upset and locked her in a room.

"He told me that because I was his woman I had to stay with him," she said.

He finally said she could go home for a day for her sister's party but that if she didn't come right back, he'd hurt her family. When she returned to him after the party, he and his family started to mistreat her — abusing her, humiliating her and making her do all the housework.

A few weeks later, he brought her to Mexico City and forced her to work as a prostitute.

"He told me that if I didn't do it, he was going to hurt my sister and my family," she said. "I was very afraid of him."

A typical scenario, prosecutors say, involves an elaborate sham of a marriage — sometimes with false papers and names — before the pimp feigns a sudden financial crisis that would put the couple out in the street. The pimp then casually mentions a friend whose wife "worked" them out of the problem, noting, "If you love me, you'd do that for me."

Sometimes the tactics are more violent.

Garcia tells of an 18-year-old woman who was picked up by a Tenancingo pimp; her 1 1/2-year-old baby girl was placed in the care of one of his female relatives, and the woman was then taken to a down-at-the-heels Mexico City hotel and made to serve dozens of clients per day, for around 165 pesos ($12) apiece. When she resisted, the pimp told her, "If you don't do what I'm asking you to, you'll never see your daughter. You'll see what we'll do to your daughter."

Mostly, the pimps concentrate on isolating women, lying to them, and breaking down their self-esteem.

The victim who spoke to the AP described it this way: Her pimp, Rugerio, humiliated her, pulled her hair, withheld food and told her that she had to practice sex acts on him so she would perform well with the clients.

"I didn't like it," she said. "I felt ugly and it was very painful."

Rugerio told her he would send her to the U.S. and that he'd join her a bit later. After walking through the desert, she was sent to a nondescript apartment complex in suburban Atlanta, where she was met by two women and a man who, she was told, were related to Rugerio.

One of the women took her shopping for clothes. Even though it was September and starting to get chilly, the woman selected mostly short, tight skirts and tops and told her she'd have to start working the next day.

"I asked them what kind of work I would be doing," the young victim said. "She took out a bag of condoms and then I knew."

Her minders kept her in a small, sparsely furnished apartment, isolated from any other girls and mostly ignored her during the day. Around 4 p.m., a driver would come pick her up to take her to work. In the beginning, she had sex with between five and 10 men a night, but as time went on the number got as high as 40 or 50, mostly Latino men.

"I felt like the worst woman in the world," she said, her voice cracking and tears welling up in her eyes during an interview with the AP three years later. "I felt that if my family found out, they would be so disappointed because of what I was doing."

She thought about escaping many times, she said, but she was afraid because Rugerio had told her that if she left, the police would arrest her and toss her in jail. She also didn't know anyone, didn't have any money and didn't know where to go.

Miraculously, one night, when she got into the car that came to take her to work, a woman from her hometown was inside. She said she had been prostituted by a relative of her pimp but that the driver had helped her escape and they would help her escape too. With the help of the driver, she got away and eventually wound up testifying against her former pimp.

The 28-year-old Rugerio was sentenced in February to five years in federal prison in the U.S. for helping smuggle young women from Mexico to Atlanta and forcing them into prostitution.

But many others aren't caught.

"We've always suspected the problem is larger than we know about," said Brock Nicholson, deputy special agent in charge of the Atlanta division of the federal Department of Immigration and Customs Enforcement. "Oftentimes, victims are very reluctant to come forward."

Those arrested on suspicion of forced prostitution almost never admit it.

Of three suspected pimps captured in raids on Mexico City hotels whose testimony the AP gained access to, all denied the charges against them; they said they were merely guests or employees of the hotel.

And while some in Tenancingo will admit pimps do operate there — resident Josue Reyes says "a few people have given the town a bad name" — others are seemingly in denial, despite the inexplicably luxurious houses that crowd the otherwise dusty, impoverished town.

The three-story homes with elaborate ironwork and Greek-inspired cornices are "safe houses" used by the pimps to awe — and then confine — their victims, said Federico Pohls, a human rights activist who works with victims.

Not so, says Maximino Ramirez, the secretary of the Tenancingo town council.

The structures were "built on hard work," he said, pointing to his own compound of three houses. Indeed, he said, all the palatial homes were built with money sent home by migrants working in restaurants and other businesses in the United States.

He dismissed the claims of the women.

"In this day and age, in the 21st century, are you going to tell me that a woman of 18 or 20 can be tricked?" he asked. "Maybe they went into (prostitution) of their own free will, and then after a while, they say: You know what? They forced me to."

But town residents have another name for the imposing houses. In the local Indian language, they call them "Calcuilchil" — literally, Houses of Ass.

It is an open secret. In 2008, a group of sociologists asked 877 residents of Tlaxcala if they knew of any place where human trafficking was occurring; 132 mentioned Tenancingo and an adjoining village — about 10 times more than any other locality.

How can such a trade flourish without police interference? Bautista, the Mexico City prosecutor, says it would be impossible without corruption.

Tlaxcala police say it is difficult to catch such crimes at their point of origin, because the full gravity of the crime has not yet been realized, even by the victims, when they are in Tenancingo. Some are held or mistreated, but usually by men they believe to be their husbands. Most have not yet been prostituted.

State prosecutors' spokeswoman Judith Soriana says only about a half dozen people have been prosecuted under laws against human trafficking in the last couple of years. She denies it's a particular problem in the state, saying "it has been blown out of proportion."

"There is nothing that indicates it is particularly high in this area," Soriana said. "Pimping isn't a problem exclusive to this state, it happens everywhere in the world."

2. An Example: *United States v. Jimenez-Calderon*

The case of *United States v. Jimenez-Calderon* provides an example of a Mexican sex trafficking ring. The traffickers in the case, the Jimenez-Calderons, resided in the town of Tenancingo in Tlaxcala, Mexico. The facts of this juvenile sex trafficking case are provided below.

UNITED STATES v. JIMENEZ-CALDERON
2006 U.S. App. LEXIS 14313 (3d Cir. June 9, 2006)

ALARCON, CIRCUIT JUDGE.

Appellant Antonia Jimenez-Calderon ("Ms. Jimenez-Calderon") pled guilty to Conspiracy to Promote Sex Trafficking in violation of 18 U.S.C. § 371, and Promoting Sex Trafficking by Force in violation of 18 U.S.C. § 1591(a)(1) . . . .We affirm.

. . . .

On February 22, 2002, police raided a house of prostitution in Plainfield New Jersey. Four minors, young Mexican girls, were discovered and detained. Ms. Jimenez-Calderon and her sister Librada Jimenez-Calderon ("Librada") were arrested in the raid and released on bail. They obtained false birth certificates for the four girls and attempted to gain the girls' release. Ms. Jimenez-Calderon

Antonia and Librada recruited Sergio Farfan, a social worker at the Union County Jail and regular client of the house of prostitution, to deliver the fraudulent birth certificates to the Union County Juvenile Detention Center. Mr. Farfan delivered the documents to the Assistant Director of the Union County Juvenile Detention Center.

Angel Ruiz owned and operated the house of prostitution. Maritzana Lopez helped Mr. Ruiz, and visited the house almost daily to deliver beer and to collect proceeds from the sale of beer and acts of prostitution. In the fall of 2001, Mr. Ruiz and Ms. Lopez recruited Pedro Garcia Burgos to assist in operating the house of prostitution. Mr. Burgos lived at the house. The involvement of Ms. Jimenez-Calderon began when Mr. Burgos brought in Ms. Jimenez-Calderon and Librada to help him run the brothel.

Initially, the prostitutes working at the house were adults. However, in approximately November 2000, the Jimenez-Calderon sisters conspired with their brothers, Delfino and Luis Jimenez-Calderon ("Delfino and Luis"), to lure young girls from Mexico to work at the house. Delfino and Luis targeted girls from extremely impoverished families working in cafes in Mexico. Each of the girls worked far away from their families. They were young, naive, and had a low level of education. Some of the girls were illiterate. Delfino and Luis gave the girls gifts, pretended to be in love with them, and convinced them to go to the United States with them to get married and live a better life.

As part of their plan, Delfino and Luis asked the girls on a date after repeatedly visiting the girls at their place of work. They took the girls away from the towns where they lived and worked, and brought them to a motel, or house, where at least two girls were raped, and one consented to sexual intercourse. The girls were then taken to meet Delfino and Luis's mother. They introduced them as their future brides. The girls were then smuggled into the United States.

After the girls arrived at the brothel in New Jersey, they were handed over to Ms. Jimenez-Calderon and Librada and forced into prostitution. To help control the girls, Ms. Jimenez-Calderon and her siblings falsely represented that the girls were later to be married to Delfino and Luis. All of the money earned from prostitution at the house was turned over to Ms. Jimenez-Calderon. The girls were told that the money they earned would be given to their future husbands. They were told that Delfino and Luis were in Mexico. In reality, Delfino and Luis were in the United States. Ms. Jimenez-Calderon and Librada kept a portion of the money earned. The remainder was divided between Delfino and Luis, Mr. Ruiz, Ms. Lopez, and Mr. Burgos.

Eventually, one of the girls, "AHS," learned that two other girls were also purportedly engaged to Delfino. When Librada discovered that AHS had learned this fact, she hit AHS in the face with a closed fist. Another victim, "GCL," told INS agents that she still considered Luis to be her husband, that she still loved him, and that he had recently bought her jewelry and clothes.

The girls were not allowed to be friendly or establish relationships with the customers, talk to each other, or make any phone calls. The girls were beaten if they broke the rules. On occasion, Ms. Jimenez-Calderon and Librada called Delfino or

Luis to have them talk to the girls about their behavior. Delfino or Luis would yell at the girls and tell them to obey Ms. Jimenez-Calderon and Librada. They were given permission to hit the girls if they did not follow the rules.

B. Domestic Sex-Trafficking

Sex trafficking by U.S.-born traffickers of U.S.-born victims, commonly referred to as domestic sex trafficking, more closely resembles what has been traditionally thought of as the "pimp-prostitute-John" model. It is critical to recognize that in many, if not most, instances this model involves minors or the compelled prostitution of adults through force, fraud, or coercion and thus constitutes sex trafficking under § 1591.

1. An Example: *United States v. Pipkins*

To understand the manner in which domestic sex trafficking rings operate, a portion of the case of *United States v. Pipkins* is included below. *Pipkins* is not notable for its legal precedent; in fact, since the conduct at issue in *Pipkins* ended near the time that the TVPA was first enacted, the case was not charged under the sex trafficking statute. Yet the case provides perhaps the clearest factual explanation for how the criminal enterprise of domestic sex trafficking happens in the United States today.

UNITED STATES v. PIPKINS
378 F.3d 1281 (11th Cir. 2004)

Cox, Circuit Judge.

I. Introduction

In November of 2001, police arrested fifteen Atlanta pimps. A grand jury subsequently returned a 265-count indictment naming these fifteen pimps, involving conduct spanning from 1997 to November, 2001. . . .

. . . .

II. Background and Procedural History

Defendant Pipkins (known as "Sir Charles") and Defendant Moore (known as "Batman") were pimps who operated in southwest Atlanta in an area around Metropolitan Avenue (formerly called Stewart Avenue) known as the "track."

To persuade underage females to prostitute for them, the Defendants (and other pimps charged in the indictment) presented a vision of ostentatious living, promising fame and fortune. Pimps perpetrated this myth with their own flamboyant dress, flashy jewelry, and exotic, expensive cars. To support this apparently extravagant lifestyle, each pimp kept a stable of prostitutes with a well-defined pecking order. At the top of each pimp's organization was his "bottom girl," a trusted and experienced prostitute or female associate. Next in the pimp's chain of command was a "wife-in-law," a prostitute with supervisory duties similar to those of the bottom girl. A pimp's bottom girl or wife-in-law often worked the track in his stead, running interference for and collecting money from the pimp's other prostitutes. The bottom girl also looked after the pimp's affairs if the pimp was out of town, incarcerated, or otherwise unavailable.

The pimps also recognized a hierarchy among their own. "Popcorn pimps," "wanna-bes," and "hustlers" were the least respected, newer pimps. A "guerilla pimp" (as other pimps and prostitutes considered Moore) primarily used violence and intimidation to control his prostitutes. Others were regarded as "finesse pimps," who excelled in the psychological trickery needed to deceive juvenile females and to retain their services. Finally, "players" (apparently, in this case, Pipkins) were successful, established pimps who were well-respected within the pimp brotherhood.

Both pimps and prostitutes generally referred to their activities as "the game." To the pimps, an important component of the game was domination of their females through endless promises and mentally sapping wordplay, physical violence, and financial control. The pimps created a system in which their prostitutes were incapable of supporting themselves or escaping their reliance on the pimp. A prostitute lived either in her pimp's home or in a room at a motel or boarding house paid for by the pimp. The pimp provided clothes for his prostitute, as well as money for the prostitute to fix her hair and nails. The pimp also provided condoms to the prostitute, or money to buy condoms. Also, the pimp frequently used threats of violence to control his prostitutes, or rewarded his prostitutes with drugs for meeting monetary goals. Other times, a pimp dispensed drugs to a prostitute to ensure that she was able to function through the night and into the early morning hours.

The pimping subculture in Atlanta operated under a set of rules, presented in the video called *Really Really Pimpin' in Da South*. This videotape was made in Atlanta by Pipkins and Carlos Glover, a business associate. *Really Really Pimpin' in Da South* featured prominent Atlanta pimps, including Pipkins, explaining the rules of the game. This video, along with its companion piece, *Pimps Up Hoes Down*, outlined the pimp code of conduct, and was repeatedly shown to new pimps and prostitutes alike to concisely explain what was expected of a prostitute. The origin of *Pimps Up Hoes Down* is unknown. In essence, these videos taught that prostitutes were required to perform sexual acts, known as "tricks" or "dates," for money. Prostitutes turned tricks in adult clubs, in parking lots, on mattresses behind local businesses, in cars, in motel rooms, or in rooming houses. A prostitute charged $30 to $80 for each trick, and was required to turn over all of this money to her pimp. Some pimps gave their prostitutes a "quota" to earn over $1,000 a night.

Despite the pimps best efforts to subjugate their prostitutes, the rules allowed a prostitute to move from one pimp to another by "choosing." This was accomplished by the prostitute making her intentions known to the new pimp, and then presenting the new pimp with money, a practice known as "breaking bread." The new pimp would then "serve" the former pimp by notifying him that the prostitute had entered his fold. The former pimp was bound to honor the prostitute's decision to choose her new pimp. A prostitute who frequently moved from pimp to pimp was known as a "Choosey Susie." And, a prostitute might "bounce" from pimp to pimp by moving among different pimps without paying for the privilege of choosing.

Choosing another pimp was not without risk for the prostitute. A prostitute could be punished for merely looking at another pimp; this was considered "reckless eyeballing." Owner pimps apparently were afraid that if their prostitutes were sufficiently impressed with another pimp's vehicle, clothes, and manner, she might choose a new pimp.

Other rules governed a prostitute's conduct. She was required to surrender all of the money from her dates; if she did not, she would be guilty of "cuffing." She was also required to unquestioningly obey her pimp and treat him with respect; if she did not, she was "out of pocket." At the whim of her pimp, a prostitute was obligated to have sexual intercourse with him, another pimp, or even another prostitute.

The pimps sometimes brutally enforced these rules. Prostitutes endured beatings with belts, baseball bats, or "pimp sticks" (two coat hangers wrapped together). The pimps also punished their prostitutes by kicking them, punching them, forcing them to lay naked on the floor and then have sex with another prostitute while others watched, or "trunking" them by locking them in the trunk of a car to teach them a lesson.

The pimps did not service only the Metropolitan Avenue clientele. For example, Pipkins branched out on the Internet, forming a web-based escort service which allowed customers to select a particular prostitute from pictures posted on a website. Also, pimps sometimes sent their prostitutes to Peachtree Street in Midtown Atlanta because patrons paid a premium for prostitutes in that neighborhood. Pipkins entertained members of a municipal police force at his home on at least one occasion, where they engaged in sexual intercourse with his prostitutes.

While all the pimps did not pool their profits from prostitution, some did. And the pimps generally aided each other. Pimps bailed each other's prostitutes out of jail; mentored younger pimps; swapped prostitutes with each other to get a better "fit;" warned other pimps and their prostitutes of the presence of police; provided condoms, rides, and rooms for each other's prostitutes; jointly organized private prostitution parties; recruited juvenile prostitutes together; recruited juvenile prostitutes for each other; divided the track geographically to reduce competition; and traveled out of town together to prostitute females in other cities. Pimps also operated as a price-fixing cartel to regulate the prices that their prostitutes charged for different sexual services.

2. Other Issues: Conspiracy, the Definition of Commercial Sex Act, and Interstate Commerce

In *United States v. Paris*, 2007 U.S. Dist. LEXIS 78418 (D. Conn. Oct. 23, 2007), defendant Dennis Paris and others were convicted of conspiracy and sex trafficking two minor and two adult women in Hartford, Connecticut. All four victims were U.S. born and all were required to give defendant Paris a portion of the money that they received from going on "calls." Paris used violence to maintain control of the women and girls. The victims also knew that Paris brought women back when they left him.

Paris also gave drugs to two of the victims, which further kept them under his control.

One of the victims, Melissa, testified at trial about what happened one time when Paris was angry with her.

> Melissa testified that Paris raped her, handcuffed her, wrapped her in a blanket, called for heroin from another person, and told Melissa that "he was going to get rid of me." Paris then took Melissa's identification and left with Barry Perez, a friend of Melissa's. Melissa testified that "I just made myself deal with the fact that I was going to die." When Paris and Perez returned, Paris had food with him, was laughing and acting "[l]ike it didn't even happen." Melissa was allowed to leave the room. She went back to her own hotel room and called her mother. She told her mother "I don't know what I just got myself into . . . .I can't come home. I'm scared." Melissa testified that she told her mother that she did not want to go home because she was afraid that Paris knew where she lived and that he might harm her younger siblings if she left him.

Id. at 14–15.

On appeal, the court also addressed the definition of "commercial sex act" within § 1591. Under the statute, a commercial sex act is defined as: "any sex act, on account of which anything of value is given to or received by any person." The court in *Paris* rejected defendant's challenge that this definition is unconstitutionally vague, finding that there was "overwhelming evidence of sexual intercourse" in the case at hand, so the conduct was well within the "heartland" of the term "sex act," and therefore the statute gave fair warning that it applied to such conduct. The court therefore did not reach the question of whether it could apply to conduct such as "legitimate modeling or acting in a romantic movie." *Paris*, 2007 U.S. Dist. LEXIS 78418, at *36, *40–*41.

Finally, the *Paris* court dealt with the interstate commerce requirement under the sex trafficking statute. The defendant challenged congressional authority to regulate sex trafficking under § 1591 when the activities in question — "recruiting, enticing, harboring, transporting, providing or obtaining" of the victim — all occur within one state, rather than crossing state lines.[18] The *Paris* court stated that § 1591 satisfied each of the "relevant considerations" for determining whether a law regulates an activity with a substantial effect on interstate commerce.[19]

---

[18] At particular issue was the third prong of the *Lopez* test, which states that, "Congress' commerce authority includes the power to regulate those activities having a substantial relation to interstate commerce, i.e., those activities that substantially affect interstate commerce." *United States v. Lopez*, 514 U.S. 549, 558–59 (1995).

[19] The *Paris* court identified four relevant considerations: first, commercial sex acts are economic in nature. Second, Section 1591 has a jurisdictional element, requiring the jury to find that the activity affected interstate commerce. Third, in enacting the Trafficking Victims Protection Act, Congress found that "Trafficking in persons substantially affects interstate and foreign commerce." 22 U.S.C. § 7101 (b)(12). Fourth, as discussed more fully below, there is a clear nexus between Paris's intrastate recruiting and obtaining of women to commit commercial sex acts, the interstate aspects of Paris's business, and the interstate market for commercial sex. *Paris*, 2007 U.S. Dist. LEXIS 78418, at *23–*24.

The court went on to point to several of defendant's activities that indicated that "Paris's recruiting, enticing, harboring, transporting, providing, or obtaining women had a substantial effect on interstate commerce." In particular, the court referenced defendant's cellular telephone calls, credit card payments, use of hotels frequented by out-of-state guests, and use of condoms manufactured out of state. Additionally, the court also found that defendant's actions contributed to an interstate market in commercial sex. *Paris*, 2007 U.S. Dist. LEXIS 78418, at *23–*24.

Many other cases charged under § 1591 have discussed similar facts to establish a nexus between sex trafficking and interstate commerce. Chen and Ryan discuss some additional examples:

> For example, use of an interstate communication facility, such as pagers, telephones or the internet, should be sufficient to meet the interstate commerce element. . . . The Eleventh Circuit has also held that the use of goods, such as condoms, that were manufactured outside the state where the offense occurred was evidence of interstate commerce. *See United States v. Evans*, 476 F.3d 1176 (11th Cir. 2007); *Pipkins*, 378 F.3d at 1295. Furthermore, the Eleventh Circuit recognized in *Evans* that the requisite effect on interstate commerce can arise from aggregating the effects of purely intrastate commercial or economic activity. 476 F.3d at 1178-79; *see also United States v. Paris*, 2007 WL 3124724, at *8 (D. Conn. 2007) (citing *Evans*).

Pamela Chen & Monica Ryan, *Federal Prosecution of Human Traffickers*, in LAWYER'S MANUAL ON HUMAN TRAFFICKING: PURSUING JUSTICE FOR VICTIMS 273–75 (Jill Laurie Goodman & Dorchen A. Liedholdt eds., 2011).

3. Reasonable Opportunity to Observe

The 2008 reauthorization of the TVPA amended the sex trafficking statute to provide that: "In a prosecution under subsection (a)(1) in which the defendant had a reasonable opportunity to observe the person so recruited, enticed, harbored, transported, provided, obtained or maintained, the Government need not prove that the defendant knew that the person had not attained the age of 18 years." This change widened the net for when prosecutors can charge under the minor sex trafficking provision.

In *United States v. Wilson*, 2010 U.S. Dist. LEXIS 75149 (S.D. Fla. July 27, 2010), defendant Wilson and four others were convicted of sex trafficking minor and adult females at hotels through advertisements featured on an Internet website, backpage.com.

The court in *Wilson* rejected defendant Wilson's argument that § 1591(c) replaces the *mens rea* elements of § 1591(a), making the sex trafficking of minors a strict liability crime with regard to the victim's age. Instead, the court reiterated that, "where the Government elects to proceed under the reckless disregard level of *mens rea*, Section 1591(c) requires the Government to prove beyond a reasonable doubt not only that the defendant acted in reckless disregard, but also that the defendant had a reasonable opportunity to observe the person recruited." *Wilson*,

2010 U.S. Dist. LEXIS 75149, at *17–*19. Some argue, however, that § 1591(c) does essentially make sex trafficking of a minor strict liability with respect to age if there is a reasonable opportunity to observe the victim.

The Second Circuit recently disagreed with the *Wilson* court. In *United States v. Robinson*, 702 F.3d 22 (2d Cir. 2012), the court held that § 1591(c) "imposes strict liability with regard to the defendant's awareness of the victim's age, thus relieving the government's usual burden to prove knowledge or reckless disregard of the victim's underage status under § 1591(a)." The victim, who had been 17 when she worked for the defendant, testified that she had told "everybody" that she was 19. The court rejected defendant's argument for a recklessness standard in line with *Wilson*, and found that "the better reading of § 1591(c) is that the government may prove that the defendant had a reasonable opportunity to view the victim *in lieu of* proving knowledge." *Id.* at *3, *6–*7, *18.

Congress rejected a version of the statute that would have explicitly made age a strict liability element of the offense by including a strict liability clause in § 1591(a). As a result, the exact interaction of § 1591(a), which in final form does not include such a clause, and § 1591(c), which includes the "reasonable opportunity to observe" clause, remains unclear. *See* H.R. 3887, 110th Cong. § 221(a) (2007) ("[T]he Government need not prove that the defendant knew that the person had not attained the age of 18 years.").

Additionally, questions remain about the potential reach of § 1591(c) to people other than traffickers who participate in the sex trafficking operation: Can the statute sweep up liquor distributors or even taxi drivers?

Given the mandatory minimum sentences of § 1591, such application of the statute could have significant consequences. It remains to be seen whether prosecutors will attempt to use the statute for these purposes, and whether courts will allow it.

Until recently, no court had spoken on the scope of the "obtains" language of Section 1591, thus making it unclear whether a customer, or John, who engages in sexual conduct with a victim of sex trafficking could be held liable under 1591 as a trafficker himself. The 8th Circuit addressed this question in *U.S. v. Jungers*, decided on January 7, 2013, *available at* http://media.ca8.uscourts.gov/opndir/13/01/121006P.pdf. In *Jungers*, the court found that two men who had agreed to engage in sexual acts with trafficked minors could be found guilty of attempted sex trafficking under Section 1591. The court interpreted the "obtains" language of § 1591 to include the actions of both suppliers and consumers of trafficking victims. In doing so, the court significantly expanded the scope and reach of the sex trafficking statute to allow for the prosecution of Johns.

4. Exclusion of Victims' Prior Sexual Behavior

The admissibility of evidence of the prior sexual history of victims is frequently at issue in sex trafficking cases. In *United States v. Elbert*, 561 F.3d 771 (8th Cir. 2009), defendant Elbert pleaded guilty to sex trafficking of a minor. On appeal, the Eighth Circuit affirmed the district court's decision to exclude evidence regarding the victims' past acts of prostitution.

The governing legal standard, Federal Rule of Evidence 412, prohibits admission of evidence of a victim's prior sexual conduct except pursuant to clearly defined exceptions. The court in *Elbert* found that none of the exceptions to Rule 412 applied, and that that such acts were irrelevant to Elbert's defense because the girls were minors and thus coercion did not need to be proven under the TVPA. Similarly, in *United States v. Mirna Jeanneth Vasque Valenzuela*, the Ninth Circuit affirmed a district court's decision to exclude evidence about a victim's alleged prior acts of prostitution. 2012 U.S. App. LEXIS 22609 (9th Cir. Nov. 2, 2012).

C. Other Examples of Sex Trafficking in the United States

The cases in this section have thus far dealt primarily with sex trafficking operations that involve Mexican traffickers and victims and American traffickers and victims. However, there have been many cases involving traffickers and victims from other regions of the world.

United States v. Fu Sheng Kuo, 588 F.3d 729 (9th Cir. 2009), involved a sex trafficking operation in American Samoa. Below is an excerpt from the facts of the opinion:

> From December 1998 through September 2006, Defendants induced women to travel to American Samoa from China, Taiwan, and Fiji to engage in prostitution for the financial benefit of Defendants. In January 2006, Wang traveled to China and recruited victims Y.H. and J.C. (collectively "the victims") under the pretense that she would employ them to work as cashiers in her grocery store in American Samoa. Wang told them that she would arrange for their travel and immigration documents for a fee of approximately $1,875 each and would also purchase their airline tickets and secure their visas.
>
> Y.H. and J.C. arrived in American Samoa in March 2006. Defendants immediately confiscated their passports and return tickets. The victims were taken to the Bao Lai, a restaurant and brothel owned by Kuo. The Bao Lai was a three-story structure with locks on each exterior door, making it possible to lock all doors from the outside. Wire covered all of the windows and the exterior staircase of the structure. Wire or plywood also covered most of the balcony area.
>
> The victims were locked in and coerced to work at the Bao Lai as prostitutes, ostensibly to repay Defendants for their travel expenses. Defendants threatened to hit or beat the victims if they did not do as they were told. Wang also told the victims that she knew people in China who would hurt their families if they refused to comply. Additionally, the victims were regularly threatened with food deprivation for refusing to work.
>
> From March 7, 2006, through August 30, 2006, Y.H. and J.C. performed prostitution services every night that fishing vessels were in port. Each victim was forced to have various forms of sexual intercourse with a total of 50 to 70 customers. The victims stated that, from the first night on, they suffered pain, bleeding, bruising, and tearing of their vaginas. They also suffered abrasions, bruising, and pain to their legs and back from certain

sexual demands of customers. Many of the customers did not wear condoms.

The victims were not paid any money for having sex with customers. Customers paid Wang directly at a rate of approximately $100 to $200 per sex act. Wang received 60% of the earnings, supposedly to pay the victims' airfare and room and board, while the remaining 40% went to Kuo. Defendants told the victims that their debt was increasing and had reached $6,000.

After several failed attempts to escape, J.C. successfully cut the wire mesh around her bedroom window, removed the wooden frame, and rolled the wire mesh to create an opening large enough to crawl through. Y.H. used a rope and successfully climbed down the three stories. J.C. followed but slipped and fell to the ground, hurting her head, ankle, arms, hands, and back. The victims were picked up by a taxi driver, who dropped them off in a nearby village. In the village, they met a store owner who spoke Chinese; they explained to him that they had been kept in captivity at the Bao Lai and forced to work as prostitutes. The store owner reported the matter to the police, and the victims were taken to the police station. A Chinese translator assisted the victims in providing a statement to the police.

The defendants in *Fu Sheng Kuo* were convicted and each sentenced to over five years in prison and restitution. *See* Press Release, Department of Justice, Two Chinese Nationals Sentenced for Sex Trafficking Charges in American Samoa (Jan. 4, 2008), *available at* http://www.reuters.com/article/2008/01/04/idUS230567+04-Jan-2008+PRN20080104.

In *United States v. Ae Soon Cho*, 2007 U.S. Dist. LEXIS 81887 (E.D.N.Y. Oct. 31, 2007), defendants were convicted for operating a large massage parlor and brothel business in Queens and using "middlemen" to smuggle Korean women into the country to force them to engage in prostitution.

In *United States v. Telichenko*, 2006 U.S. Dist. LEXIS 98650 (M.D. Fla. Oct. 30, 2006), defendant, a Ukrainian court interpreter, persuaded a 22-year-old Russian woman on a tourist visa to come live with her in Florida. Defendant then told the victim that she would need to have sex with male customers to cover the cost of her room and board. Defendant used psychological coercion, physical abuse, and threats against the victim's family to compel her to engage in prostitution. Defendant pleaded guilty to a forced labor charge and was sentenced to 78 months in prison and three years of supervised release.

In *United States v. Mirna Jeanneth Vasque Valenzuela*, 2012 U.S. App. LEXIS 22609 (9th Cir. Nov. 2, 2012), five defendants were convicted of conspiracy, sex trafficking, and transportation of persons for the purpose of prostitution. Defendants recruited poor girls and women from Guatemala by promising them well-paying jobs in the United States. Defendants forced the victims to engage in prostitution by "using threats of force and witchcraft against the girls and their families, brutal physical and sexual violence, economic and social dependence, as well as lock and key to keep the girls from running away."

D. The PROTECT Act of 2003 and the Constitutionality of § 2423(c)

Although not included in TVPA or pre-TVPA anti-slavery statutes, Congress has enacted laws that criminalize actions by U.S. citizens who travel abroad to engage in what would constitute, on U.S. soil, a commercial sex act with a minor. This is commonly known as sex tourism.[20]

The PROTECT Act of 2003 was enacted to prevent child abduction and the sexual exploitation of children. It contains provisions addressing kidnapping, child sex tourism, rape, a notification and alert system for abducted children, and child obscenity and pornography, among other issues.

In the *United States v. Clark*, 435 F.3d 1100 (9th Cir. 2006), the Ninth Circuit addressed the question of whether Congress has authority under the Foreign Commerce Clause to prohibit U.S. citizens from traveling in foreign commerce to have sexual contact with a minor. The case involved a 71-year-old U.S. citizen, Michael Lewis Clark, who traveled to Southeast Asia to engage in sexual acts with two boys, ages 10 and 13.

The *Clark* court discussed the fact that the PROTECT Act amended 18 U.S.C. § 2423 to include the following provisions, among others:

> (b) Travel With Intent To Engage in Illicit Sexual Conduct. A person who travels in interstate commerce or travels into the United States, or a United States citizen or an alien admitted for permanent residence in the United States who travels in foreign commerce, for the purpose of engaging in any illicit sexual conduct with another person shall be fined under this title or imprisoned not more than 30 years, or both.
>
> (c) Engaging in Illicit Sexual Conduct in Foreign Places. Any United States citizen or alien admitted for permanent residence who travels in foreign commerce, and engages in any illicit sexual conduct with another person shall be fined under this title or imprisoned not more than 30 years, or both.

As discussed in the opinion, one notable aspect of subsection (c), which regulates illicit sexual conduct in other countries, is that it does not contain the phrase "for the purpose of," as opposed to subsection (b), which does contain that phrase. This means that in prosecuting U.S. citizens or permanent residents for illicit sexual conduct abroad, there is no need to prove that the person traveled to another country with the intent to engage in illicit sex acts; it is only necessary to prove that the person did engage in those acts.

The *Clark* court limited its holding to commercial illicit sex acts to avoid deciding a question not at issue (the constitutionality of § 2423(c) as applied to non-commercial illicit sex acts). The court noted that the regulation of foreign commerce has not been subject to the same concerns and limitations as the regulation of interstate commerce, because issues of state sovereignty and federalism do not

---

[20] Note that these cases differ from the majority of sex trafficking prosecutions in the United States, which are brought against traffickers.

apply to the regulation of foreign commerce. Thus, the court found that "the Supreme Court has read the Foreign Commerce Clause as granting Congress sweeping powers" and that "The Court has been unwavering in reading Congress's power over foreign commerce broadly." The court then found that § 2423(c) bore a rational relationship to Congress's foreign commerce powers, noting especially the commercial and economic component of an illicit commercial sex act abroad. *Id. at* 1113.

The *Clark* court's reasoning that the absence of federalism or state sovereignty concerns in the foreign commerce context justify a broad application of foreign commerce powers has drawn criticism from legal scholars, who have questioned the court's reasoning in comparing the foreign commerce clause and the interstate commerce clause. Similarly, the *Harvard Law Review* recently criticized the *Clark* court's reasoning on this same issue, focusing on the troubling implications that could follow if the court's reasoning is applied to other crimes:

> Though the majority's reasoning seems perfectly sound in the context of reaching international child sex travelers, it becomes more troubling when one considers other contexts in which it would apply. . . . Should Congress be given the authority to trot across the globe after Angel Raich, waiting to arrest her upon a legal purchase of marijuana in an Amsterdam cafe? What about arresting American citizens for smoking Cuban cigars in Timbuktu?

Recent Case: Constitutional Law — Foreign Commerce Clause — Ninth Circuit Holds That Congress Can Regulate Sex Crimes Committed by U.S. Citizens Abroad. — United States v. Clark, 435 F.3d 1100 (9th Cir. 2006), 119 Harv. L. Rev. 2612, 2615–17 (2006).

It is also important to note that the *Clark* court explicitly limited its holding to situations involving a commercial sex act.

V. CONCLUSION

The passage of the TVPA and its re-authorizations have significantly altered the investigation and prosecution of human trafficking cases in the United States. Indeed, the addition of the new offenses of forced labor and sex trafficking has allowed law enforcement to reach the more subtle, non-physical forms of coercion commonly used by traffickers. Moreover, the public awareness component of the TVPA has made both law enforcement and the public more knowledgeable of what trafficking in America looks like today. All of these factors have led to an increase in criminal prosecutions. In fact, much of the documented evidence of human trafficking today results from public records created as part of federal trafficking prosecutions.

The cases in this chapter demonstrate the types of federal trafficking cases brought in the United States and provide insight into the legal application of the TVPA statutes, particularly forced labor and sex trafficking. Yet perhaps the most important lesson from the federal criminal cases is the window they provide into the scope and breadth of human trafficking occurring in the United States today.

Chapter 11

CIVIL LITIGATION

I. INTRODUCTION

Codified at 18 U.S.C § 1595, the private right of action under the TVPA provides a significant source of recovery for trafficked persons in addition to other causes of action. Using civil litigation as a strategy for compensating victims of trafficking has emerged as a powerful tool in the United States for addressing the growing problem of modern-day slavery, both at national and at global levels. As of 2013, there had been approximately 80 human trafficking civil actions filed utilizing § 1595. A majority of these cases have proceeded in the absence of criminal prosecution indicating that the civil remedy has served as not only a compensatory tool, but also an important deterrent, filling a gap left by the criminal justice system in those cases in which the government declines to prosecute alleged traffickers.

By suing traffickers pursuant to section 1595, trafficked persons also advance their substantive civil rights, enforcing a remedy that targets the actual harm inflicted upon them — modern-day slavery. Before the civil remedy was amended to the TVPA, trafficked persons relied on various federal and state labor and employment laws and tort laws related to forced labor conditions in order to seek remedies from their traffickers. In addition to these causes of action, trafficked plaintiffs may also utilize the TVPA directly as the basis for a claim against their traffickers. *See generally* DANIEL WERNER & KATHLEEN KIM, CIVIL LITIGATION ON BEHALF OF VICTIMS OF HUMAN TRAFFICKING (3d ed. 2008) (providing an excellent technical assistance guide to practitioners representing human trafficking victims in civil lawsuits against their traffickers).

The following excerpt underscores the unique features of civil litigation in the trafficking context:

Kathleen Kim & Kusia Hreshchyshyn, *Human Trafficking Private Right of Action: Civil Rights for Trafficked Persons in the United States*
16 HASTINGS WOMEN'S L.J. 1, 16–21, 24–26, 34–36 (2004)[1]

THE PROS AND CONS OF CIVIL LITIGATION

Pursuing civil relief gives the trafficked person several advantages over criminal prosecution regarding compensation, accountability, and control over the case. A civil suit provides unique methods by which trafficked persons can recover damages from traffickers while globally deterring trafficking by disabling traffickers financially, thereby reducing the mercurial incentives of the industry. In a criminal prosecution, the TVPA provides for mandatory restitution and criminal forfeiture of assets. However, a restitution award depends largely on the aggressiveness of the prosecutor and the court to inform the criminal defendant that restitution may be an element of the sentence. Since prosecutors are mostly focused on incarceration, restitution is easily forgotten to the detriment of the victim. Civil litigation, in contrast, empowers trafficked persons individually to pursue greater damage awards in the form of compensatory, punitive, and/or pecuniary damages. These damage awards can compensate victims for the physical and psychological injuries they have suffered, unlike limited restitution damages. While a criminal court cannot order non-economic damages, civil litigation can achieve substantial deterrence of trafficking activity through high punitive awards. Finally, in civil litigation, third parties may sometimes be held liable and may be potential sources of payment for the damage awards, which can be particularly useful when the trafficker's assets are difficult to locate. . . . Beyond damage awards, civil suits provide a way for trafficked persons to achieve justice through direct accountability. Defendant traffickers are not just held accountable for crimes against the state; they are directly accountable to their victims.

Procedural differences in civil litigation weigh in favor of successful outcomes for trafficked persons. For instance, the burden of proof is a preponderance of the evidence standard rather than the higher beyond a reasonable doubt standard of criminal proceedings. Plaintiffs can name larger entities as joint employer defendants that may be "unindictable due to the government's burden of proof in a criminal action." Furthermore, in cases where the absence of "hard" evidence weakens a criminal case, a lower burden of proof in civil cases still provides trafficked plaintiffs with avenues for relief. This arises in the domestic servitude context where an individual is kept in a private home and there are few, if any, corroborating witnesses. In the civil context, the testimony of a credible and sympathetic trafficked plaintiff can weigh heavily against the word of the defendant. Finally, evidentiary rules are much more permissive in civil proceedings, thus allowing plaintiffs to successfully rely on evidence of psychological conditions such as post-traumatic stress disorder, rape trauma syndrome, and battered women's syndrome, which is inadmissible in criminal forums.

---

[1] Copyright © 2004 by Hastings Women's Law Journal. Reprinted with permission. Internal citations omitted.

The most important advantage of civil litigation for a trafficked person is that the trafficked person is the one to bring the suit and control the essential decisions shaping the case, in contrast to criminal cases, which are brought by the state and controlled by the prosecutor. In a criminal prosecution, a trafficked person's role is primarily defined as a witness for the prosecution and the prosecutor represents the interests of the state, which may not be coterminous with those of the person who has been trafficked. As a party to a civil suit, the trafficked person cannot be excluded from the courtroom, and always has final approval of settlement proposals. Furthermore, the trafficked person can sue the trafficker regardless of whether the trafficker has been found guilty in criminal proceedings, or even whether the state decides to go forward with any criminal prosecution at all. "Absent an effort from the criminal prosecutors to seek restitution from the traffickers, litigation may provide the only means by which victims of trafficking may be 'made whole.'"

Some of the barriers to civil litigation are similar to those found in prosecutorial efforts. Limited resources and access to information may prevent trafficked persons from seeking legal aid. Threats of retaliatory violence by the traffickers present obstacles to victims coming forward as criminal witnesses or as civil plaintiffs. Potential defendants and their assets may be difficult to locate. Finally, as in criminal cases, civil litigation can be a stressful and lengthy process, which may be particularly difficult for people who have been traumatized and may not have a stable living situation in this country.

Immigration Status: A Pro or a Con to Civil Litigation?

In order to file civil suit within required statute of limitations periods, a trafficked person who has reported a case to law enforcement cannot necessarily wait for the final adjudication of a T visa application. Trafficked persons seeking civil remedies may also be unwilling to cooperate with an investigation or may be otherwise ineligible for the T visa or other forms of immigration relief. Furthermore, because a work permit is conditioned on authorized status, the trafficked person's need for monetary relief may be even more urgent under these circumstances. Consequently, with great courage, trafficked persons have proceeded with civil cases even in the absence of durable status, despite fears that defendants may use this information against them.

Not surprisingly, trafficking civil suits have taken strategic guidance from other cases involving immigrants injured by workplace abuse, where the role of immigration law in regulating employment matters presents significant obstacles in seeking relief. In this context, when faced with a worker complaint, employers may threaten to notify immigration authorities of a worker's undocumented status — at times, this actually occurs. . . . [U]nauthorized work status is grounds for deportation, and workplace raids [and audits] are a key method [of the] U.S. immigration enforcement strategy. . . . The mere threat of exposing a plaintiff's undocumented status has a "serious chilling effect" on those contemplating civil suit and those who have already filed suit. Those who renounce mistreatment and file civil suit against unscrupulous employers frequently face intrusive requests of their current immigration status. Defense attorneys may seek discovery of their status as "relevant" to the merits of the case. This is particularly likely in light of the

Supreme Court's decision in *Hoffman Plastics v. NLRB*, which effectively limited back pay remedies to undocumented workers who asserted their right to organize under the National Labor Relations Act ("NLRA"). Employer-defendants have attempted to use this ruling to curtail plaintiff remedies in even non-NLRA matters such as wage and hour and employment discrimination cases, and even tort cases.

Instruction from these types of cases has provided attorneys representing trafficking victims with strategies to safeguard against the disclosure of a victim's current immigration status. For instance, when faced with intrusive discovery requests, trafficking victims whose employment-based claims generally arise under the Fair Labor Standards Act ("FLSA") can rely on established precedent that undocumented status is irrelevant to a claim of unpaid wages. Thus, courts will generally grant protections against defendants' discovery of this information. Furthermore, where traffickers communicate with immigration authorities in retaliation to a complaint, they subject themselves to penalties as well as high punitive judgments in some jurisdictions for violation of the FLSA's anti-retaliation provisions.

In contrast to employment cases, a trafficked person's immigration status at the time of victimization is fundamental to the merits of the case and therefore information that is not advantageous to conceal. The trafficker generally arranges a trafficked person's migration. This may mean that the trafficked person is smuggled without a visa or that the trafficked person enters this country on a tourist visa, sponsored by the trafficker, which soon expires. A trafficker may apply for a legitimate employment-based temporary visa for the trafficked person. Employment-based visas, however, effectively bind the trafficked person to the trafficker, by denying job portability and limiting labor protections. In all cases, the trafficker often uses the victim's "illegal status" or dominion over their employment-based status to compel the forced labor. Ironically then, there is little reason to keep the trafficked person's past immigration status confidential and many reasons to keep current status protected.

Trafficking civil cases illustrate the way in which immigration controls, and an absence of labor protections in informal industries, intersect to cultivate an environment ripe for egregious human rights abuses. Trafficking cases also show how immigration status may continue to restrict the rights of trafficked persons even after liberation from the traffickers. Despite these logistical complications, trafficked persons who have courageously freed themselves are equally determined to hold their traffickers directly accountable for the abuse. In the end, trafficked persons who assert their civil rights have received successful judgments and have been brought closer to a holistic and fuller recovery. . . .

Before and After the Trafficking Private Right of Action

Prior to the passage of the [trafficking civil remedy], trafficking civil suits were brought primarily under the Fair Labor Standards Act, analogous state employment laws and various state common law torts. Trafficking complaints resembled employment disputes or personal injury claims. Limited by the confines of these laws, trafficking victims were presented with incomplete avenues for relief. For example, victims of forced prostitution are exempt from wage and hour protections under the FLSA since the FLSA covers only legal types of employment. Trafficked persons who may be domestic workers or agricultural workers are exempt from higher overtime pay under the FLSA and the Migrant and Seasonal Worker Protection Act. Relying on employment claims not only deprives trafficked plaintiffs of full monetary relief, but also bases their claim in a law enacted through Congress' commerce power, intended to regulate market relationships, not gross human rights abuses. Defining the relationship of trafficker and trafficking victim as one between an employer and employee presumes a lesser harm that can be corrected by simple calculations of wage and hour discrepancies and does little to vindicate the trafficked person's human rights to be free from slavery.

Although various tort claims such as "intentional infliction of emotional distress" or "false imprisonment" can provide trafficked persons with additional material recovery through punitive damages, these discreet claims address only the "incidental effects" of modern-day slavery. Trafficking lawsuits must plead several torts and prove each independently to even begin to address the full range of injuries suffered by trafficked persons. Finally, state common law torts clearly lack the descriptive power to convey to a court of law that a defendant should be held accountable for committing slavery. . . .

By amending the TVPA to include a private right of action, Congress has provided a mechanism by which trafficked persons can individually enforce a remedy for modern-day slavery. The need for a judicially created remedy has been eliminated, thereby diminishing some of the strategic complexities involved in litigating trafficking cases up until now. The Fair Labor Standards Act no longer poses the risk of mischaracterizing trafficking as primarily an employment matter. Additionally, trafficked persons can seek a complete remedy, rather than the piecemeal approach required by common law torts. By targeting the actual harm suffered by trafficked persons, [trafficking civil remedy] increases the potential for greater material recovery and makes possible the full expression of the trafficked person's experience. . . .

The fuller narrative provided by trafficked persons will expand the very meaning of slavery to include its contemporary manifestations. By asserting [section 1595] in civil courts, the trafficked person can significantly influence interpretation of the TVPA, its definition of trafficking and modern-day slavery, and the application of its enacted criminal statutes. . . .

[B]eyond civil litigation, by conferring a private right to renounce slavery, the [trafficking civil remedy] provides trafficked persons with membership in the greater political community. "'Rights also realize the interests of others, including the construction of a political culture with a specific kind of character.'" Congressional action reflects the values of our political culture. Through laws criminalizing slavery, our society has historically shown broad consensus that slavery is morally reprehensible. The trafficking civil action illustrates that expression of our moral condemnation would be incomplete without the trafficked person's assertion of an expressive remedy.

NOTES AND QUESTIONS

1. What are the procedural and substantive differences between trafficking criminal prosecutions and trafficking civil lawsuits? Is one preferable over the other? Why do you think that a majority of trafficking civil cases have proceeded in the absence of criminal prosecutions?

2. The authors discuss the control in decision-making that a trafficked plaintiff has over the civil legal process and suggest that trafficking civil litigation may be an empowering process for trafficked plaintiffs. Do you agree or disagree? What may impede empowerment in the civil litigation process?

3. In what ways does the immigration status of a trafficked plaintiff play a role in civil litigation? Is undocumented status favorable or unfavorable to a trafficked litigant's civil case? Why or why not? Note that the 2008 amendments to the TVPA provide that a trafficking victim engaged in civil litigation may be granted "continued presence" for the duration of the civil proceedings, discussed further below.

4. As referenced in the above excerpt, legal scholars have discussed the "expressive power" of the law. *See, e.g.*, Baher Azmy, *Unshackling the Thirteenth Amendment: Modern Slavery and a Reconstructed Civil Rights Agenda*, 71 FORDHAM L. REV. 981, 1047 (2002) ("The expressive value of the FLSA and other state common-law remedies are simply a mismatch for the individual harm suffered by the victims of slavery and involuntary servitude or for the collective, social harm inflicted by its perpetrators."); Michael J. Wishnie, *Immigrant Workers and the Domestic Enforcement of International Labor Rights*, 4 U. PA. J. LAB. & EMP. L. 529, 541 (2002) (noting that plaintiffs bringing a civil claim of forced labor can provide a narrative of their experience which can lead to "fuller compensation" and can "spur organizing and public education campaigns"); Elizabeth S. Anderson & Richard H. Pildes, *Expressive Theories of Law: A General Restatement*, 148 U. PA. L. REV. 1503 (2000). How does expressive theory manifest in trafficking civil cases? Is this a benefit to trafficking civil litigation and to the trafficked plaintiff?

5. The authors suggest that before the enactment of § 1595, trafficked plaintiffs who proceeded only upon FLSA and tort claims, could not obtain the "complete" relief now afforded by the addition of the trafficking private right of action. *See also* Azmy at 1039 (explaining that the use of the FLSA in slavery cases "continues an undesirable fiction of grounding human rights protections in the language and theory of the commerce power"). Why not? While advocates consider § 1595 a positive step toward advancing the rights of trafficked workers, some commentators have emphasized the difficulties faced by trafficked plaintiffs in pursuing civil cases against their traffickers. *See* Patricia Medige, *The Labyrinth: Pursuing a Human Trafficking Case in Middle America*, 10 J. GENDER RACE & JUST. 269 (2007) (describing the case of trafficked Chilean sheep herders in Colorado, which represented the first group case to claim violations of the TVPA in the state).

II. 18 U.S.C. § 1595: THE TRAFFICKING PRIVATE RIGHT OF ACTION

The trafficking private right of action allows an individual who is a victim of a trafficking to bring a civil action in a district court to recover damages and reasonable attorneys' fees. A civil action filed under § 1595 shall be stayed during the criminal action arising out of the same occurrence. A claim under § 1595 may be made even in the absence of a criminal investigation or prosecution. While § 1595 was first amended to the TVPA in 2003, subsequent amendments in 2008 broadened the civil remedy in significant ways.

Prior to the 2008 amendments, in order to bring a viable claim under § 1595, the plaintiff must have been a victim of one of three specified trafficking crimes: forced labor, trafficking into servitude, or sex trafficking. After the 2008 amendments, any violation of a trafficking-related crime enumerated within Chapter 77 of Title 18 is grounds for civil relief:

> An individual who is a victim of a violation . . . may bring a civil action against the perpetrator (or whoever knowingly benefits, financially or by receiving anything of value from participation in a venture which that person knew or should have known has engaged in an act in violation of this chapter . . .) in an appropriate district court of the United States and may recover damages and reasonable attorneys fees.

18 U.S.C. § 1595(a) (2012). Thus, a private right of action now exists for every provision in Chapter 77 of Title 18 of the U.S. Code including peonage under § 1581, document theft under § 1592, and even fraud in foreign labor contracting under § 1351. Moreover, the relevant statute of limitations is 10 years. The following case interprets § 1595 in this manner.

ROSA ROMERO HERNANDEZ, PLAINTIFF v. SAMAD ATTISHA; AND YVONNE ATTISHA, DEFENDANTS
2010 U.S. Dist. LEXIS 20235
(S.D. Cal. Mar. 4, 2010)

IRMA E. GONZALEZ, CHIEF JUDGE.

CURRENTLY BEFORE THE Court is Defendants' Motion to Dismiss pursuant to Fed. R. Civ. P. 12(b)(6) the second, third, fifth, sixth, and seventh causes of action in Plaintiff's First Amended Complaint. Having considered the parties' arguments, and for the reasons set forth below, the Court DENIES the motion to dismiss.

I. Factual Background

Plaintiff is a Mexican citizen certified by the U.S. Department of Health and Human Services as a victim of human trafficking under Section 107(b) of the Trafficking Victims Protection Act of 2000 ("TVPA"). She alleges that from at least 2002, Defendants Samad and Yvonne Attisha began searching for a domestic servant through their secretary, Sonia, to serve in their house in San Diego County,

California. Sonia allegedly told Plaintiff that she would be paid $7 per hour to work as a babysitter for Defendants' infant daughter and that she would only be responsible to work from 10 a.m. to 6 p.m. Although Plaintiff did not have a valid working visa, Defendants promised they would "fix her papers." On or about May 18, 2002, Plaintiff entered the United States and began working for Defendants.

Plaintiff alleges that from that time on until approximately July 23, 2008, she was forced to act as a domestic servant to Defendants, performing all household chores and housekeeping duties. Plaintiff made no income in her first year because Defendants took her salary to reimburse Sonia for Plaintiff's transportation to the United States. Plaintiff alleges that during her time with Defendants, she often worked up to 14.5 hours per day for less than California or Federal minimum wage, and that she was subject to constant control of Defendants. Defendants confiscated Plaintiff's passport, made clear to Plaintiff that she was not free to leave, and made her feel that she had to hide if any third parties approached Defendants' residence.

The U.S. Immigration and Customs Enforcement officials rescued Plaintiff from Defendants on July 23, 2008. Plaintiff was then certified by the U.S. Department of Health and Human Services as a victim of human trafficking under Section 107(b) of the TVPA on September 30, 2008. Defendants were subsequently investigated for their human trafficking activities. . . .

DISCUSSION

I. Is there a civil cause of action for violation of Sections 1584 and 1590?

Plaintiff's second cause of action alleges involuntary servitude in violation of 18 U.S.C. § 1584. Plaintiff's third cause of action alleges trafficking with respect to peonage, slavery, involuntary servitude, or forced labor in violation of 18 U.S.C. § 1590(a). Defendants move to dismiss both causes of action because neither provides a basis for a private cause of action. According to Defendants, both statutes were enacted for *criminal* enforcement of the Thirteenth Amendment. Relying on *Buchanan v. City of Bolivar*, 99 F.3d 1352, 1357 (6th Cir. 1996), Defendants allege no private cause of action exists under Section 1584. Defendants make a similar argument with regard to Section 1590. In addition, relying on *Craine v. Alexander*, Defendants argue the third cause of action fails because a claim for peonage requires an allegation of state action. *See* 756 F.2d 1070, 1074 (5th Cir.1985) (concluding that plaintiffs proceedings under the Antipeonage Act, 42 U.S.C. § 1994, "must show some state responsibility for the abuse complained of").

Defendants, however, overlook Section 1595 that explicitly provides a private cause of action for violations of Chapter 77 of Title 18, which includes Sections 1584 and 1590. *See* 18 U.S.C. § 1595(a). Section 1595 is entitled "civil remedy" and provides in pertinent part:

> An individual who is a victim of a violation may bring a civil action against the perpetrator (or whoever knowingly benefits, financially or by receiving anything of value from participation in a venture which that person knew or should have known has engaged in an act in violation of this chapter) in an

appropriate district court of the United States and may recover damages and reasonable attorneys fees.

Id. When initially enacted, Section 1595 applied only to an individual who was "a victim of a violation of section 1589, 1590, or 1591 of this chapter." *See* 18 U.S.C. § 1595 (2006). This language, however, was amended by the Trafficking Victims Protection Reauthorization Act of 2008, which deleted the phrase "of section 1589, 1590, or 1591 of this chapter" after the words "victim of violation." By doing so, Congress in effect expanded the private right of action to any violation under Chapter 77 of Title 18, including violations of Sections 1584 and 1590.[2]

The cases relied upon by Defendants are inapposite. Although Defendants correctly assert that the Sixth Circuit in *Buchanan*, 99 F.3d at 1357, held that no private cause of action exists under Section 1584, that case was decided in 1996 — twelve years before Section 1595 was amended to provide for a private right of action for a violation of Section 1584. Similarly, even though Defendants correctly argue that private causes of action typically cannot be inferred from criminal statutes, that is irrelevant where Congress expressly provides for a private cause of action. Finally, Defendants' reliance on *Craine*, 756 F.2d at 1074, is misplaced because unlike in that case, the statute here is not limited to violations of "acts, laws, resolutions, orders, regulations or usages;" rather, Section 1595 expressly authorizes civil recovery against any "perpetrator." *See* 18 U.S.C. § 1595(a).

Accordingly, because Plaintiff may bring a private right of action, the Court DENIES Defendants' motion to dismiss on this ground.

II. Are Plaintiff's claims pursuant to Sections 1584 and 1590 time-barred?

Defendants next argue Plaintiff's claims under Sections 1584 and 1590 are time-barred. According to Defendants, because neither of the two statutes specifies a statute of limitations, the Court must borrow from the most analogous state action — false imprisonment under California law — which is subject to a one-year statute of limitations.

Defendants once again overlook Section 1595, which provides for a 10-year statute of limitations for any action brought under that section. *See* 18 U.S.C. § 1595(c) ("No action may be maintained under this section unless it is commenced not later than 10 years after the cause of action arose."). In the present case, Plaintiff brought her action on October 13, 2009 — less than two years after she was rescued, and less than eight years after she was first transported to Defendants' home. Accordingly, because Plaintiff's claims under Sections 1584 and 1590 are not barred by the applicable statute of limitations, the Court DENIES Defendants' motion to dismiss on this ground as well.

---

[2] [FN 3] *See* 45 Am. Jur. 2d *Involuntary Servitude and Peonage* § 20 (2009) ("One who is a victim of the crime of forced labor; trafficking with respect to peonage, slavery, involuntary servitude, or forced labor; or sex trafficking of children may bring a civil action against the perpetrator in a district court, and may recover damages, and reasonable attorney's fees." (citing 18 U.S.C. § 1595)); *See also* Kathleen Kim, *The Trafficked Worker as Private Attorney General: A Model for Enforcing the Civil Rights of Undocumented Workers*, 2009 U. Chi. Legal F. 247, 282 (2009). . . .

III. Are Plaintiff's emotional distress claims time-barred?

Plaintiff's fifth and sixth causes of action allege intentional and negligent infliction of emotional distress, respectively. Defendants argue these claims are barred by a two-year statute of limitations under Section 335.1 of the California Code of Civil Procedure because Plaintiff's causes of action accrued in 2002 when she moved into Defendants' home.

Plaintiff makes two arguments in opposition to Defendants' motion to dismiss. First, Plaintiff suffered the emotional distress on a continuing basis through 2008, and therefore the causes of action did not accrue until Plaintiff was rescued in 2008. Second, the statute of limitations period should be equitably tolled because Defendants' actions prevented Plaintiff from bringing suit prior to her rescue.

A. Accrual of Plaintiff's causes of action for emotional distress

Defendants correctly state the general rule that "[i]n ordinary tort and contract actions, the statute of limitations . . . begins to run upon the occurrence of the last element essential to the cause of action." However, as an exception to the general rule, the "continuing tort doctrine" may delay accrual of the action, if the tort involves a continuing wrong, "until the date of the last injury or when the tortious actions cease." Under the continuing tort doctrine in California, liability may still attach to "unlawful employer conduct occurring outside the statute of limitations if it is sufficiently connected to unlawful conduct within the limitations period." Moreover, in a claim for emotional distress, the severity of the emotional distress may be measured by "[b]oth the intensity and duration of the distress suffered." When the conduct complained of is continuing in nature, the point at which it becomes sufficiently outrageous or severe, and whether it in fact continues, are questions of fact.

Plaintiff alleges Defendants' conduct causing her emotional distress was "continuous and systematic." Whether the conduct continued up to the point of Plaintiff's rescue from Defendants' house on July 23, 2008, and whether it constituted "sufficiently connected" conduct to previous incidents of alleged infliction of emotional distress are questions of fact that cannot be resolved at this stage of the proceedings. Accordingly, Plaintiff states claims for which it is plausible the causes of action accrued at the time of her rescue. This is sufficient to survive the motion to dismiss.

B. Equitable tolling of statute of limitations

Claims for both intentional and negligent infliction of emotional distress are governed by a two-year statute of limitations. Although the California Code of Civil Procedure expressly provides for tolling under certain circumstances, none of those sections is directly applicable here. Nonetheless, both federal and California state courts have recognized equitable tolling in cases where the plaintiff is unable to bring suit or exercise an available remedy. *See, e.g., Stoll v. Runyon,* 165 F.3d 1238, 1242 (9th Cir. 1999) (allowing equitable tolling of plaintiff's sexual harassment claim where psychological incapacity prevented her from timely pursuing the claim); *Bureerong v. Uvawas,* 922 F. Supp. 1450, 1463 (C.D. Cal. 1996) (allowing equitable tolling of plaintiffs' various claims where the alleged imprisonment at a garment factory that was the basis of the claims prevented them from filing prior to their release); *Lewis v. Super. Ct.*, 175 Cal. App. 3d 366, 380, 220 Cal. Rptr. 594 (1985) ("Language of statutes of limitation must admit to implicit exceptions where compliance is impossible and manifest injustice would otherwise result.").

In determining whether California's equitable tolling doctrine applies, the Court must balance "'the injustice to the plaintiff occasioned by the bar of his claim against the effect upon the important public interest or policy expressed by the . . . limitations statute.'" Courts have applied equitable tolling in "carefully considered situations to prevent the unjust technical forfeiture of causes of action," but it should not be applied if it is "inconsistent with the text of the relevant statute." Equitable tolling may also be proper "when the plaintiff is prevented from asserting a claim by wrongful conduct on the part of the defendant, or when extraordinary circumstances beyond the plaintiff's control made it impossible to file a claim on time."

Courts have found such "extraordinary circumstances" to exist in cases where the plaintiff had been detained civilly or had been subjected to false imprisonment. *See, e.g.*, Jones, 393 F.3d at 929 (noting the rigid application of the limitations period would shield the act of civil confinement from legal challenge by operation of the very act sought to be challenged); *Bureerong*, 922 F. Supp. at 1463 (holding that equitable tolling was appropriate where plaintiffs were "imprisoned" at a garment-making facility and thus were physically prevented from complying with the statutes of limitations); *see also Stoll, 165 F.3d at 1242* (failing to equitably toll limitations statute would have unjustly allowed the defendants "to benefit from the fact that its own admittedly outrageous acts" left the plaintiff "so broken and damaged that she [could not] protect her own rights").

In the present case, Plaintiff's inability to leave Defendants' home resulted in her total incapacity to file suit or pursue any legal rights, and thus her delay was excusable. Additionally, Defendants' alleged misconduct prevented Plaintiff from complying with the statute of limitations. Strict application of the statute of limitations to Plaintiff's claims would allow Defendants to parlay their wrongful acts into legal immunity — exactly the type of unjust forfeiture equitable tolling is designed to obviate. For those reasons, Plaintiff has pled sufficient facts to support equitable tolling of her claims for intentional and negligent infliction of emotional distress. Accordingly, the Court DENIES Defendants' motion to dismiss Plaintiff's fifth and sixth causes of action.

IV. Is Plaintiff's conversion claim time-barred?

Plaintiff's seventh cause of action alleges conversion based on Defendants' taking and withholding Plaintiff's passport upon her arrival at Defendants' home. Defendants argue Plaintiff's claim for conversion is time-barred by the three-year statute of limitations. *See* Cal. Code Civ. Proc. § 338(c). Defendants contend that Plaintiff alleges the conversion occurred in 2005, and, since Plaintiff did not file her claim until October 13, 2009, the applicable statute of limitations has run on Plaintiff's claim.

Plaintiff argues her claims are not time-barred for two reasons. First, although the initial conversion took place in 2005, the conversion was ongoing because Defendants never returned her passport. Second, equitable tolling should apply to her conversion claim because Plaintiff was confined and unable to pursue legal remedy until her rescue on July 23, 2008.

With regard to Plaintiff's first argument, Plaintiff fails to cite to any cases that would support application of the continuing tort doctrine to a claim for conversion. The continuing tort doctrine is applicable where the conduct is continuing in nature, "where there is 'no single incident' that can 'fairly or realistically be identified as the cause of the significant harm.'" In contrast, the tort of conversion is marked by a discrete event — the taking of the aggrieved party's property — that is incapable of repetition for that particular claim. Based on the foregoing, the Court declines to apply the continuing tort doctrine to Plaintiff's conversion claim.

Nonetheless, the Court agrees that equitable tolling applies to Plaintiff's claim for conversion. As discussed above, equitable tolling of the statute of limitations may be proper where "circumstances effectively render timely commencement of action impossible or virtually impossible." In the present case, Plaintiff alleges she was confined to Defendants' house, unable to leave and, consequently, unable to pursue any legal remedies available to her because of circumstances beyond her control. Plaintiff has alleged her confinement to Defendants' home was total and their control over her continuous. Plaintiff could not pursue her legal remedies until her release from Defendants' control on July 23, 2008. Applying equitable tolling, the present action, filed on October 13, 2009, is well within the three-year statute of limitations. Consequently, the Court DENIES Defendants' motion to dismiss as untimely Plaintiff's seventh cause of action.

CONCLUSION

For the foregoing reasons, the Court DENIES Defendants' motion to dismiss in its entirety.

It is so Ordered.

NOTES AND QUESTIONS

1. As noted by the court in *Hernandez*, neither the Thirteenth Amendment nor § 1584 expressly provided a private right of action for victims of slavery and involuntary servitude. Defendants, thus, argued that the plaintiff had no cause of action available to her under either § 1584 or § 1590. Yet, § 1584's provision of a criminal penalty does not preclude implication of a private cause of action for civil damages. A court may imply a private right of action where Congress intended to create one by implication. Courts that have implied a cause of action have generally done so when "the statute in question . . . prohibited certain conduct or created federal rights in favor of private parties." *Manliguez v. Joseph*, 226 F. Supp. 2d 377, 383 n.7 (E.D.N.Y. 2002) (citing *City of Memphis v. Greene*, 451 U.S. 100, 125 (1981)). The Eastern District of New York in *Manliguez* found a private cause of action under § 1584 based on involuntary servitude, holding that the beneficiaries of § 1584's protection are victims of a constitutionally prohibited practice; the statute

is rooted in the Thirteenth Amendment, which confers the federal right to be protected from involuntary servitude; and a private cause of action would be consistent with § 1584's legislative intent. The *Manliguez* court noted, however, that other circuits have declined to extend civil liability to cases under § 1584. *Id.* at 384 n.8 (citing *Buchanan v. City of Bolivar*, 99 F.3d 1352, 1357 (6th Cir. 1996); *Turner v. Unification Church*, 473 F. Supp. 367, 375 (D.R.I. 1978)).

2. Do you see how procedural concerns such as the relevant statute of limitations can be a crucial factor in the viability of a civil lawsuit? Various circumstances relevant to a trafficked plaintiff's situation may serve to "toll" the statute of limitations. What are they? As previously mentioned, § 1595 provides for a 10-year statute of limitations. Is this sufficient? Are there any fairness concerns for the defendant?

3. Courts have denied the retroactive application of § 1595 when the trafficking activity occurred before December 19, 2003. *See Abraham v. Singh*, 2005 U.S. Dist. LEXIS 17800, slip op. at 13–17 (E.D. La. July 26, 2005). In *Deressa v. Gobena*, the Eastern District of Virginia found no congressional intent to allow for retroactive application. The court further reasoned that retroactive application would impermissibly subject the defendant to a new legal burden of monetary liability with respect to past events. Is there any reason to permit retroactive application of § 1595 in trafficking civil cases? What are the considerations both for and against retroactive application?

4. Section 1595 provides for compensatory and punitive damages and reasonable attorneys' fees. Although most cases settle before trial, a number of trafficked plaintiffs have received large damages awards. For example, in one case involving a trafficked domestic worker from Tanzania, the court ordered $1,059,348.79 in damages and attorneys' fees against the defendant traffickers for approximately four years of work without compensation. *Mazengo v. Mzengi*, 542 F. Supp. 2d 96 (D.D.C. 2008). Another court ordered a default judgment in favor of 12 agricultural laborers of almost $9,000,000 against the defendant tree farm operators. *Aguilar v. Imperial Nurseries*, 2008 U.S. Dist. LEXIS 48404 (D. Conn. May 28, 2008).

III. SCOPE OF DEFENDANTS UNDER § 1595

The 2008 amendments also expand the pool of potential defendants to include not just the direct perpetrators of the trafficking crime, but also those who "knowingly" benefited, financially or otherwise, from the trafficking activity. 18 U.S.C. §§ 1589(b), 1593(a) (2012). However, note that proving "knowledge" is still a requirement to find a defendant liable. The range of defendants is further widened through the 2008 TVPA's extra-territorial provisions which extend liability for trafficking violations to jurisdictions outside the United States where the alleged perpetrator is a U.S. citizen, lawful permanent resident, or present in the United States. 18 U.S.C. § 1596 (2012). Previous to the passage of the 2008 amendments, § 1595 could not be applied extraterritorially as in the following case.

JOHN ROE I v. BRIDGESTONE CORP.
492 F. Supp. 2d 988 (S.D. Ind. 2007)

HAMILTON, DISTRICT JUDGE.

Plaintiffs are adults and children who work on a rubber plantation in the West African nation of Liberia. Based on allegations of forced labor, forced child labor, poor working conditions, and low wages, plaintiffs seek damages from the Japanese, American, and Liberian companies and two individuals that own and control the plantation. Plaintiffs seek relief in the federal courts of the United States. Their twelve-count Complaint asserts claims under international law pursuant to the Alien Tort Statute, 28 U.S.C. § 1350, the Thirteenth Amendment to the United States Constitution, a federal statute authorizing civil actions for criminal forced labor violations, 18 U.S.C. § 1595, and California law. . . .

For the reasons explained in detail below, the defendants' motion to dismiss all claims for lack of subject matter jurisdiction is denied. The motion to dismiss for failure to state a claim is granted with respect to Count One and Counts Three through Twelve and denied with respect to Count Two, the child labor claim under international law.

The adult plaintiffs' principal claim for forced labor in violation of international law is undermined by plaintiffs' own allegations that they are afraid of *losing* the same jobs they claim they are being forced to perform. Forced labor cannot be equated with only low wages and difficult working conditions, which are all too common throughout the world. Some forms of truly forced labor violate specific, universal and obligatory norms of international law, but the circumstances alleged by the adult plaintiffs in this case do not. The Count Two claims of at least some of the child plaintiffs under international law survive the motion to dismiss. Plaintiffs allege that the defendants are actively encouraging parents to require children as young as six, seven, and ten years old to work full-time at heavy and dangerous jobs on defendants' plantation tapping raw latex from rubber trees. As applied to the alleged working conditions for these young children, international law is sufficiently specific, universal, and obligatory to permit relief under the Alien Tort Statute.

I. *The Parties*

The Firestone Rubber Plantation ("the Plantation") near Harbel, Liberia is the world's largest rubber plantation. The Plantation was founded in 1926 under an agreement between the Firestone Tire and Rubber Company and the Liberian government, with what might be called strong encouragement from the United States government. All of the raw latex produced at the Plantation is sold to or otherwise controlled by other Bridgestone Firestone companies

Plaintiffs John Roe I through John Roe XII are adults who work as latex "tappers" on the Plantation. They cut into the rubber trees and collect the raw latex for eventual processing into tires and other rubber products. Plaintiffs James Roe I through James Roe XV and Jane Roe I through Jane Roe VIII are children who have assisted their parents or other family members in work at the Plantation. The child plaintiffs range in age from six to sixteen years old. Plaintiffs seek to represent two plaintiff classes. The first proposed class is all adults who worked as tappers on the Plantation at any time between November 17, 1995 and the present under the conditions described in the Complaint. The second proposed class is all persons who, during the period November 17, 1995 through the present, "were forced as children to work on the Firestone Plantation so that their families could meet their quota and be paid enough to allow the family to avoid starvation." Compl. ¶ 80. . . .

III. *The Factual Allegations*

The Complaint alleges that after the Liberian government leased the Plantation to Firestone Tire and Rubber Company in 1926, indigenous people were forced from their land and were then conscripted to provide forced labor, first planting and cultivating rubber trees and then harvesting latex from the mature trees.. The Complaint alleges that Firestone agreed to pay local chiefs to deliver able-bodied workers to the Plantation, and that the local chiefs conscripted workers at gunpoint. . . . According to the Complaint, plaintiffs and most other current workers on the Plantation are third or fourth generation descendants of those original workers, and these plaintiffs have rarely if ever left the Plantation.

The adult plaintiffs work as tappers on the Plantation. The tappers use a machete to cut a rubber tree to allow the raw latex to drip into a cup mounted on the tree. The tapper collects the latex from the cups and dumps them into a large bucket that weighs 75 pounds when full. When two buckets are full, the tapper hangs one bucket on each end of a branch and carries the 150 pounds of latex to a collection location.. The tappers also apply fertilizers and pesticides to the trees. They do so by hand, without warnings or safety equipment..

The Complaint alleges that payment for the tappers is based on a "task," which is a section of approximately 750 rubber trees. To earn a daily wage equivalent to $3.19 (U.S.), the tapper must tap one complete task of 750 trees and half of a second task, or another 375 trees. If the tapper completes 750 trees but not the additional 375 trees, he is paid only half of the daily wage, or $1.59. Plaintiffs allege that the difference between $3.19 and $1.59 per day is the difference between subsistence and starvation, and they say that earning $3.19 is physically impossible for one adult without unpaid help from children. . . . Plaintiffs allege that the Plantation managers and overseers know that the quotas effectively require child labor and have encouraged plaintiffs who complain about the quotas to use their children to help meet the quotas.

Plaintiffs allege that tappers do not have any days off for worship, family, or other reasons. They receive no paid holidays or sick days. "Because of the relentless production requirements at the Firestone Plantation, even workers who are willing to forgo a day's pay to get a day off are not able to and are told they will be dismissed if they do so. The extremely high unemployment rate in Liberia, in the rural areas above 80%, allows Firestone to say with confidence that anyone who wants to leave can do so and join the ranks of the starving unemployed." ¶ 49.

Plaintiffs also allege that Firestone does not give them any formal letter of employment, so that they can be treated as "casual labor" who can be fired for any reason.. Plaintiffs allege that this is a violation of Liberian law that Firestone uses to keep the workers in line. (The allegation is consistent with the doctrine of employment at will that dominates private employment in Indiana and many other states. See *Meyers v. Meyers*, 861 N.E.2d 704, 706 (Ind. 2007) ("Indiana generally follows the employment at will doctrine, which permits both the employer and the employee to terminate the employment at any time for a 'good reason, bad reason, or no reason at all.' ")

According to the Complaint, Firestone provides medical care in clinics and schools for children on the Plantation. Plaintiffs complain that the clinics are open only three days a week and that the schools charge fees that are deducted from the workers' wages. . . . Company stores sell food and other goods on the Plantation. The plaintiffs complain that after deductions for food and other charges, they are left with virtually nothing at the end of a month. Firestone also provides housing for workers that plaintiffs describe as shacks in shanty-towns, without plumbing or electricity.

In the oral argument on the motion to dismiss, plaintiffs' counsel emphasized the physical isolation of the Plantation, which makes it difficult and dangerous for any Plantation worker to try to leave if he wanted to do so. Liberia does not have much by way of public transportation even if a worker were able to buy a ticket. A worker who wishes to leave the Plantation faces a long and dangerous walk. Plaintiffs argue that defendants have exploited this isolation by refusing to improve wages and working conditions, since workers do not have a practical alternative to continued work at the Plantation.

Liberia experienced a generation of coups d'tat, civil war, and turmoil from approximately 1980 to 2003. Firestone managed to keep the Plantation open and productive through most of that time, but production stopped for several years. The Plantation was certainly affected by the fighting. The Complaint alleges that in 1994, Firestone appointed as the chief of security for the Plantation General Adolphus Dolo, who had been loyal to President Charles Taylor. . . . (Taylor is currently on trial in The Hague, Netherlands, for alleged war crimes in Sierra Leone.) The Complaint alleges that Firestone hired other associates of Taylor and used its shipping facilities to import arms and ammunition for the Taylor regime. . . .

The Complaint summarizes the case as follows:

> 64. As the Firestone Plantation was initially created to allow, the Plantation Workers and the Plantation Child Laborers suffer daily injuries from the extremely exploitative practices on the Plantation. The Plantation Workers are modern day slaves, forced to work by the coercion of poverty, with the prospect of starvation just one complaint about conditions away. They are isolated on the Plantation by design, and are completely dependent upon the Firestone Plantation for access to food and for the only homes they have ever known, the one-room shacks in filthy shanty towns [sic] provided by the company. The paltry net wage the workers receive ensures that they also do not have the resources for transportation to escape the Plantation. The original workforce was captured and forced to work for Firestone. Succeeding generations were kept on the Plantation by poverty, fear, and

ignorance of the outside world, living in a cycle of poverty and raising their children to be the next generation of Firestone Plantation Workers.

65. The Plantation Child Laborers are forced to work to avoid the starvation of their families. These young children have not reached the legal age of consent by any definition, and therefore could not possibly agree to become laborers for the Firestone Plantation. They suffer daily the deprivations of living a slave-like existence, including malnutrition, disease, physical ailments from exposure to chemicals, and the lack of decent educational opportunities.

66. All of the Plantation Workers seek the simple justice of the freedom to choose whether to work, the opportunity to work free of coercion, the security of a proper employment relationship, the benefit of wages that do not leave them in malnourished poverty, and the meager benefits provided under the law of Liberia, including rest days and holidays. Most of all, they seek the cessation of conditions that formed the premise of the Firestone Plantation, and that have left them in the same situation as their own fathers, watching their own children join them as tappers with no future other than the misery they have experienced their entire lives.

The overarching questions in this case are whether the wages and working conditions described in the Complaint violate international law, as well as what role, if any, United States courts might have in addressing such wages and working conditions for employees of foreign subsidiaries of global businesses. The more specific questions in the case are whether the court has jurisdiction over the subject matter and whether plaintiffs have stated claims upon which relief can be granted. The court addresses in turn the plaintiffs' claims under the Thirteenth Amendment, their claims under 18 U.S.C. § 1595, their claims under the Alien Tort Statute, 28 U.S.C. § 1350, and finally their claims under state law. . . .

V. *Thirteenth Amendment Claims*

[I]n Counts Five and Six of the Complaint, plaintiffs allege that defendants have violated the Thirteenth Amendment by knowingly recruiting, harboring, transporting, providing, or obtaining adult and child plaintiffs for the purpose of forcing them to work on the Plantation by means of severe physical and/or mental abuse and restraint, or by schemes and duress intended to induce fear of severe physical and/or mental abuse and restraint, and that defendants acted with a willful and conscious disregard for the plaintiffs' rights. . . .

Defendants argue that the Thirteenth Amendment claims must be dismissed for two reasons: first, the Thirteenth Amendment does not itself provide a private right of action for damages; second, the Thirteenth Amendment itself does not reach conduct outside the United States. The court agrees with defendants on both points without reaching defendants' additional arguments on whether the alleged conditions on the Plantation in Liberia would violate the Thirteenth Amendment if it were located in the United States. . . .

B. *No Extraterritorial Effect*

Even if the Thirteenth Amendment authorized a direct cause of action for damages against a private entity, the Thirteenth Amendment bars slavery and involuntary servitude only "within the United States, or any place subject to their jurisdiction." By its terms, that language does not appear to reach activity in other countries.

Plaintiffs have not come forward with any authority applying the Thirteenth Amendment to activity in foreign nations. They rely on the federal Trafficking Victims Protection Act, 22 U.S.C. § 7101, stating that Congress relied on the Thirteenth Amendment to give some international reach to the statute. The court does not see such reliance in the statute. The House committee report for the 2003 re-authorization of the legislation relied upon the interstate and foreign commerce clause of the Constitution.

Because the Thirteenth Amendment does not create a private right of action for damages and does not directly reach slavery or involuntary servitude outside the territorial jurisdiction of the United States, plaintiffs could not be entitled to relief on Counts Five and Six. Defendants' motion to dismiss is granted with respect to Counts Five and Six.

VI. *Federal Statutory Claims-Extraterritorial Application*

In Counts Seven and Eight of the Complaint, plaintiffs allege that defendants have violated United States criminal statutes, 18 U.S.C. §§ 1589 and 1590, and plaintiffs seek a civil remedy under 18 U.S.C. § 1595. Plaintiffs allege that the same conduct alleged under the Thirteenth Amendment also violates those statutes. . . .

Section 1595 provides a civil damages remedy for violations of several statutes, including section 1589.

Defendants argue that even if the alleged conditions on the Firestone Plantation in Liberia amount to forced labor, section 1589 does not apply to labor conditions outside the United States. Neither side has cited prior case law determining the extent to which section 1589 applies to conduct outside the United States. The court concludes that section 1595 does not provide a remedy for alleged violations of section 1589's standards that occur outside the United States.

"Generally speaking, Congress has the authority to apply its laws, including criminal statutes, beyond the territorial boundaries of the United States, to the extent that extraterritorial application is consistent with the principles of international law." *United States v. Dawn*, 129 F. 3d 878, 882 (7th Cir. 1997). Whether Congress has attempted to legislate beyond those territorial boundaries is a question of statutory interpretation.

In answering the question, the court must be guided by the "longstanding principle of American law 'that legislation of Congress, unless a contrary intent appears, is meant to apply only within the territorial jurisdiction of the United States.'" *E.E.O.C. v. Arabian American Oil Co. ("Aramco")*, 499 U.S. 244, 248, 111 S. Ct. 1227, 113 L. Ed. 2d 274 (1991). This canon of statutory construction "serves to protect against unintended clashes between our laws and those of other nations which could result in international discord." *Id.*

Where Congress has not stated clearly that a statute should apply extraterritorially, it may still be possible to show that Congress intended such application based on the nature of the activity and other relevant indications of Congressional intent. One such rare example is *United States v. Bowman*, 260 U.S. 94, 43 S. Ct. 39, 67 L. Ed. 149 (1922), in which the Supreme Court reversed dismissal of an indictment alleging that three United States citizens had conspired to defraud a corporation in which the United States government owned stock. The alleged conspiracy was hatched on the high seas and was carried out in Brazil by falsifying documents for a purchase of fuel oil for a ship owned by the government-owned corporation. In interpreting the statute, the Court explained:

> Crimes against private individuals or their property . . . must of course be committed within the territorial jurisdiction of the government where it may properly exercise it. If punishment of them is to be extended to include those committed outside of the strict territorial jurisdiction, it is natural for Congress to say so in the statute, and failure to do so will negative the purpose of Congress in this regard.

260 U.S. at 98, 43 S. Ct. 39. Nevertheless, *Bowman* upheld the extraterritorial application of a criminal statute that was silent as to its territorial scope. The Court concluded that the nature of the crime-false claims against the United States and corporations in which the government owned stock-could easily be committed on the high seas and in ports and military bases all over the world. The crime was not against private individuals or their property. The role of the United States government as victim played a key role in persuading the Court to allow extraterritorial application: "Clearly it is no offense to the dignity or right of sovereignty of Brazil to hold [three United States citizens] for this crime against the government to which they owe allegiance." *Id.* at 102, 43 S. Ct. 39.

The *Bowman* approach remains the rare exception for a narrow set of unusual cases. The general presumption remains that a statute will not apply extraterritorially unless Congress has clearly indicated its intent to reach beyond United States boundaries. The Supreme Court has often applied this presumption to United States laws governing employment relationships, including wages and working conditions, where the United States connection to the employment relationships was much stronger than is alleged in this case. Two clear examples are *Aramco* and *Foley Brothers*.

In *Aramco*, the Supreme Court held that Title VII of the Civil Rights Act of 1964 did not apply to alleged discrimination by a *United States* employer against a United States citizen employed in a foreign country. 499 U.S. at 259, 111 S. Ct. 1227. To apply Title VII to *foreign* employers of United States citizens in foreign countries, even stronger and clearer statements of Congressional intent would be needed. *Id.* at 255, 111 S. Ct. 1227. In words that could apply to this case, the Court wrote:

> Without clearer evidence of congressional intent to do so than is contained in the alien-exemption clause, we are unwilling to ascribe to that body a policy which would raise difficult issues of international law by imposing

this country's employment-discrimination regime upon foreign corporations operating in foreign commerce. *Id.*

In *Foley Brothers*, the Court held that the federal "Eight Hour Law" requiring United States government contractors to pay overtime wages to their employees did not apply to a United States contractor that employed a United States citizen in a foreign country. 336 U.S. at 285, 69 S. Ct. 575. Even where the employer was a United States company, the Court viewed the employment relationship in a foreign country as supporting a strong presumption against extraterritorial application, especially where labor conditions (in Iran) were "wholly dissimilar to those in the United States and wholly beyond the control of this nation. An intention so to regulate labor conditions which are the primary concern of a foreign country should not be attributed to Congress in the absence of a clearly expressed purpose." 336 U.S. at 286, 69 S. Ct. 575. This reasoning applies with extra force to the circumstances alleged in this case, where Liberian residents work in Liberia for a Liberian company, which is part of a larger multinational group of corporations.

To avoid the effect of the general presumption against extraterritorial effect, plaintiffs make two arguments. First, they contend that the Victims of Trafficking and Violence Protection Act of 2000, Pub. L. No. 106-386, 114 Stat. 1464, of which 18 U.S.C. § 1589 was a part, also includes "an array of measures to counteract forced labor and trafficking of persons, including provisions for activities overseas." Pl. Mem. at 20. The findings show that Congress understood that forced labor and trafficking are problems with an international dimension. The Act also included several provisions with explicit international dimensions.

The international dimensions of the problems of trafficking and forced labor do not support a departure from the usual presumption against extraterritorial application for section 1589. The other closely related statutes addressing slavery and related practices in Chapter 77 of Title 18 show that Congress has been acquainted with the question of international reach in this context for more than 200 years. Congress knows how to legislate with extraterritorial effect in this field. It has done so expressly when it has intended to do so.

For example, in Chapter 77, section 1581 addresses peonage and contains no territorial language. Sections 1582 to 1588 apply to various aspects of slave trading and include specific language about territorial and extraterritorial application. Section 1586, the first federal anti-slavery statute (passed by Congress in 1800, 2 Stat. 70), includes clear language with extraterritorial effect. It prohibits United States citizens and residents from serving on a slave ship anywhere in the world: "Whoever, being a citizen or resident of the United States, voluntarily serves on board of any vessel employed or made use of in the transportation of slaves from any foreign country or place to another, shall be fined under this title or imprisoned not more than two years, or both." Section 1589, upon which plaintiffs rely in this case, contains no language indicating any intent to have extraterritorial effect. That silence, in the context of these other statutes with explicit extraterritorial language, weighs against giving extraterritorial effect to section 1589.

Plaintiffs' second argument is based on a comparison of the language of section 1589 and section 1591, which addresses sex trafficking of children by any means and of adults by means of force, fraud or coercion. The comparison actually weighs in favor of defendants on the issue of extraterritorial effect. Plaintiffs focus on the phrase "in or affecting interstate or foreign commerce." As first enacted in 2001, section 1591(a)(1) referred only to interstate commerce. Congress amended the provision in 2003 to apply it to activity "in or affecting interstate or foreign commerce, or within the special maritime and territorial jurisdiction of the United States." Trafficking Victims Protection Reauthorization Act of 2003, Pub. L. No. 108-193, § 5(a)(2), 117 Stat. 2875, 2879.

From these statutory differences, plaintiffs infer that the language of section 1591(a)(1) limits its application more narrowly than section 1589. The court does not agree. In amending section 1591 to expand its reach, Congress relied upon its power over both interstate and foreign commerce, and its sovereign power over the special maritime and territorial jurisdiction of the United States. Section 1589, by contrast, is obviously an exercise of Congressional power under Section Two of the Thirteenth Amendment.

Perhaps most illuminating is the provision in section 1591(a)(2) applying to a person who "benefits, financially or by receiving anything of value, from participation in a venture which has engaged in an act described in violation of paragraph (1)." In this case, plaintiffs attempt to impose a similar form of liability on the American affiliates who benefit from exploitive conditions at the Firestone Plantation in Liberia. The problem is that section 1589 does not contain such provisions. If Congress wants to impose such liability, it knows how to do so, just as it knew in 1800 how to prohibit United States citizens and residents from participating in slave trade anywhere in the world. Congress has not taken such steps to impose extraterritorial restrictions on forced labor under section 1589.

Because 18 U.S.C. § 1589 does not apply extraterritorially to conditions on the Plantation in Liberia, plaintiffs could not recover under Counts Seven and Eight of the Complaint. Defendants' motion to dismiss those claims under Rule 12(b)(6) is granted.

[*In the remainder of the opinion, the court considered the plaintiff's claims pursuant to the Alien Tort Claims Act and dismissed the claims based on the forced labor of the adult Liberian workers but permitted the claims on behalf of the child workers to move forward. The application of ATCA in civil trafficking cases is a topic explored further below. The court also dismissed the state common law torts and contracts claims as lacking enforceability in Liberia.*]

CONCLUSION

For the reasons stated above, defendants' motion to dismiss the claims in the complaint is granted with respect to Counts One and Three through Twelve. The motion to dismiss is denied with respect to Count Two. The court will set a status conference in the near future to discuss the next stages of this action.

So ordered.

NOTES AND QUESTIONS

1. In denying the extraterritoriality of the TVPA, the *Roe* court relied on the general presumption derived from Supreme Court precedent that "[u]nless a contrary intent appears, [congressional legislation] is meant to apply only within the territorial jurisdiction of the United States." *Id.* at 1000. The court noted, however, one Supreme Court case that departed from this general presumption due to the "nature of the crime" legislated, as well as indications of congressional intent that inferred extraterritorial application of the statute in question. *Id.* at 1000 (citing *United States v. Bowman*, 260 U.S. 94, 98 (1922)). Why wasn't the court persuaded by the plaintiff's arguments that trafficking was international in dimension and that the TVPA contemplated enforcement of trafficking violations overseas?

2. The *Roe* court recognized the international nature of trafficking, but contended that unless made explicit, section 1589 must be presumed to apply domestically: "The other closely related statutes addressing slavery and related practices in Chapter 77 of Title 18 show that Congress has been acquainted with the question of international reach in this context for more than 200 years. Congress knows how to legislate with extraterritorial effect in this field. It has done so expressly when it has intended to do so." *Id.* at 1002. Thus, the plaintiff's TVPA claims in this case did not survive the motion to dismiss. Do the 2008 amendments to the TVPA, which provide for the extraterritorial reach of the TVPA implicitly suggest that Congress may have intended the extraterritorial application of the TVPA in its original enactment? Does the current extraterritorial reach of the TVPA by statute render the *Roe* decision moot? Why or why not? Would the limitation on extraterritoriality reasoned by the *Roe* court apply to other slavery-based causes of action such as the Thirteenth Amendment?

IV. IMMIGRATION RELIEF UNDER § 1595

Significant among the 2008 amendments is the extension of "continued presence" for certain trafficking victims who pursue civil litigation against their traffickers. 22 U.S.C. § 7105(c)(3) (2012). Previously, continued presence could issued (by DHS through a request from federal law enforcement) to trafficking victims for the duration necessary for the criminal investigation and prosecution of the trafficking criminal activity. DHS may now extend continued presence to allow trafficked persons who have filed a civil action under § 1595 to remain in the United States until the conclusion of their civil case. Continued presence does not allow for adjustment to legal permanent residence, but it does provide work authorization and access to refugee benefits, thereby granting a valuable safety net for trafficked persons engaged in civil suits against their traffickers. Continued presence supplements the two main forms of immigration relief provided by the TVPA: the T visa and the U visa.

As noted previously, a trafficked worker's absence of immigration status can present serious obstacles to accessing civil justice. Fear of deportation may "chill" noncitizen trafficked workers from bringing civil claims against their traffickers. If these workers nonetheless pursue a civil complaint, defendants may attempt to use their lack of immigration status against them. Immigration relief under the TVPA has helped to circumvent these obstacles. Consider the following case involving trafficked undocumented workers in which a federal judge presiding over the civil case granted the plaintiffs "certification" for U visas.

GARCIA v. AUDUBON CMTYS. MGMT., LLC
2008 U.S. Dist. LEXIS 31221
(E.D. La. Apr. 15, 2008)

HELEN G. BERRIGAN, DISTRICT JUDGE.

I. BACKGROUND

The plaintiffs are non-documented workers who have filed suit against their former employer alleging that the Defendants improperly withheld wages. In addition, the Plaintiffs allege claims under the Fair Labor Standards Act ("FLSA") and the Victims of Trafficking Protection Act, 18 U.S.C. § 1581 *et seq.* Specifically, the Plaintiffs allege that the employer-defendants promised housing and weekly salaries in exchange for labor. The Plaintiffs state that they were consistently underpaid, and that complaints were met with threats of eviction. The Plaintiffs note that shortly after they filed this lawsuit to recoup their wages, agents of the Department of Homeland Security and Immigration and Customs Enforcement raided the employer-defendant's workplace and apprehended several of the named plaintiffs. The Plaintiffs now seek U-Visa certifications because the apprehended Plaintiffs have been detained since February 27, 2008, and are facing deportation.

II. LAW & ANALYSIS

According to the regulations promulgated by the Department of Homeland Security, the purpose of the U nonimmigrant classification is to provide a safe-harbor for non-documented victims of qualifying crimes. 72 Fed. Reg. 53014-15. The regulations state:

> Alien victims may not have legal status and, therefore may be reluctant to help in the investigation or prosecution of criminal activity for fear of removal from the United States. In passing this legislation, Congress intended to strengthen the ability of law enforcement agencies to investigate and prosecute cases of domestic violence, sexual assault, trafficking of aliens and other crimes while offering protection to victims of such crimes. See BIWPA,[3] sec. 1513(a)(2)(A). Congress also sought to encourage law enforcement officials to better serve immigrant crime victims.

Id.

There are several criteria in order to obtain U-Visa status. The applicant(s) must demonstrate: (1) that they have suffered substantial physical or mental abuse as a result of having been the victim of qualifying criminal activity; (2) they must possess information concerning the qualifying criminal activity; and (3) the [sic] must have

---

[3] [FN 2] BIWPA stands for the "Battered Immigrant Women Protection Act of 2000."

been helpful, are being helpful, or are likely to be helpful in the investigation or prosecution of the qualifying criminal act. 8 U.S.C. § 1101(a)(15)(U)(i). In addition, applicants must submit Supplement B to Form I918 to file for a U-Visa. Supplement B is also known as "U Nonimmigrant Status Certification," and requires a qualified "certifying official" to affirm:

> the person signing the certificate is the head of the certifying agency, or any person(s) in a supervisory role who has been specifically designated by the head of the certifying agency to issue U nonimmigrant status certifications on behalf of that agency, or is a Federal, State, or local judge; the agency is a Federal, State, or local law enforcement agency, or prosecutor, judge or other authority, that has responsibility for the detection, investigation, prosecution, conviction, or sentencing of qualifying criminal activity; the applicant has been a victim of qualifying criminal activity that the certifying official's agency is investigating or prosecuting; the petitioner possesses information concerning the qualifying criminal activity of which he or she has been a victim; the petitioner has been, is being, or is likely to be helpful to an investigation or prosecution of that qualifying criminal activity; and the qualifying criminal activity violated U.S. law, or occurred in the United States, its territories, its possessions, Indian country, or at military installations abroad.

8 C.F.R. § 214.14(c)(2)(i).

In their motions, the Plaintiffs request that the undersigned act as the "certifying official" for their U-Visa applications. It is undisputed that a federal judge is qualified to "certify" U-Visa applications. 8 U.S.C. § 1101(a)(15)(U)(i)(III); 8 C.F.R. § 214.14(a)(3)(ii).[4] However, the Defendants assert that the Plaintiffs are not eligible for U-Visa status, and thus, the undersigned should not "certify" their applications. Essentially, the Defendants argue that they were not the perpetrators of any of the alleged qualifying criminal activity because outside contractors were responsible for hiring and firing the Plaintiffs. In addition, the Defendants contend that the Plaintiffs have not alleged "substantial physical or mental abuse" as required to obtain U-Visas. Finally, the Defendants assert that the Plaintiffs are not entitled to U-Visa certification because the Plaintiffs' allegations are confined to a civil complaint, instead of criminal charges.

Based on the complaint and the exhibits attached to the Emergency Motions for U-Visa Certification, the Court finds that the Plaintiffs have made a prima facie showing that they have been a victim of qualifying criminal activity,[5] that they possess information concerning the qualifying criminal activity, and that they are likely to be helpful to an investigation or prosecution of that qualifying criminal activity. Specifically, the Plaintiff's statements are evidence that legal coercion was used against the Plaintiffs to continue working without pay. Indeed, the allegations

---

[4] [FN 3] The regulations specifically states, "[j]udges neither investigate crimes nor prosecute perpetrators. Therefore, USCIS believes that the term 'investigation or prosecution' should be interpreted broadly as in the AG Guidelines." 72 Fed. Reg. 53020.

[5] [FN 5] The Plaintiffs assert that they have been victims of several "qualifying crimes," including: Involuntary Servitude and Human Trafficking.

detail a pattern of conduct by the employer-defendants to force the plaintiff-employees to work by taking advantage of the plaintiff-employees undocumented immigration status. The statutory definition of "Involuntary Servitude" states:

> The term "involuntary servitude" includes a condition of servitude induced by means of—
>
> (A) any scheme, plan, or pattern intended to cause a person to believe that, if the person did not enter into or continue in such condition, that person or another person would suffer serious harm or physical restraint; or
>
> (B) the abuse or threatened abuse of the legal process.

22 U.S.C. § 7102(5). In this matter, the Plaintiffs specifically allege that when they complained of failure to remit wages in a timely fashion, they were told that they "didn't have any rights in this county and that we should shut up and keep working if we didn't want [to be deported]." The Plaintiffs allege that their demands for wages were met with the threatened abuse of the legal process. Stated another way, the Plaintiffs allege that their employers used the threat of deportation to force continued labor. Thus, there is sufficient evidence for a prima facie showing of Involuntary Servitude.

Furthermore, the Court notes that on-going criminal investigation may not be necessary to certify a U-Visa application because the regulations contemplate the future helpfulness of the applicant(s):

> USCIS interprets 'helpful' to mean assisting law enforcement authorities in the investigation or prosecution of the qualifying criminal activity of which he or she is a victim . . . The requirement was written with several verb tenses, recognizing that an alien may apply for U nonimmigrant status at different stages of the investigation or prosecution. By allowing an individual to petition for U nonimmigrant status upon a showing that he or she *may be helpful at some point in the future*, USCIS believes that Congress intended for individuals to be eligible for U nonimmigrant status at the very early stages of an investigation. This suggests an ongoing responsibility to cooperate with the certifying official while in U nonimmigrant status.

72 Fed. Reg. 53019 (emphasis added). Indeed, part of the regulations in the CFR state, "U nonimmigrant status certification means Form I-918, Supplement B, 'U Nonimmigrant Status Certification,' which confirms that the petitioner has been helpful, is being helpful, *or is likely to be helpful* in the investigation or prosecution of the qualifying criminal activity of which he or she is a victim." 8 C.F.R. § 214.14(a)(12). Therefore, the Defendants' argument that the Plaintiffs do not qualify for U-Visa certification is unconvincing. The Court concludes that the Plaintiffs are entitled to U-Visa certification because they have provided sufficient evidence to show that they "may be helpful at some point in the future" to an investigation regarding qualifying criminal activity.

The Defendants argument that the Plaintiffs have failed to allege facts sufficient to constitute "substantial physical or mental abuse" is not convincing. The Defendants note that the Plaintiffs have neither alleged that they were victims of "battery or physical violence," nor victims of "extreme cruelty." The Court finds that "physical or mental abuse" is not commensurate with "battery or physical violence." The regulations regarding "substantial physical or mental abuse" state:

> Whether abuse is substantial is based on a number of factors, including but not limited to: The nature of the injury inflicted or suffered; the severity of the perpetrator's conduct; the severity of the harm suffered; the duration of the infliction of the harm; and the extent to which there is permanent or serious harm to the appearance, health, or physical or mental soundness of the victim, including aggravation of pre-existing conditions. No single factor is a prerequisite to establish that the abuse suffered was substantial. Also, the existence of one or more of the factors automatically does not create a presumption that the abuse suffered was substantial. A series of acts taken together may be considered to constitute substantial physical or mental abuse even where no single act alone rises to that level.

8 C.F.R. § 214.14(b)(1). In addition, the regulations state, "[p]hysical or mental abuse means injury or harm to the victim's physical person, or harm to or impairment of the emotional or psychological soundness of the victim." 8 C.F.R. § 214.14(a)(8). In this matter, the Plaintiffs have alleged mental and physical suffering because of the living conditions they were forced to endure. The Plaintiffs state that without steady pay, they had to find food "in the trash." Not only have the Plaintiffs alleged feeling "shameful" and "sad" because they could not afford to buy food; they also allege physical distress from the lack of nourishment. Therefore, the Court finds that the Plaintiffs have made a prima facie showing of substantial mental and physical suffering.

Finally, the Defendants' contention that the Plaintiffs are not entitled to U-Visa certification because the allegations pertain to "the conduct of third parties," not the conduct of Audubon itself, is unconvincing. The regulations state that applicants for U-Visa certification must be victims of qualifying crimes. The regulations do not mandate that a specific entity be the alleged perpetrator of the qualifying crimes. Consequently, at this point in the proceedings, the Plaintiffs have made a prima facie showing that they are entitled to U-Visa certification.

III. CONCLUSION

Accordingly,

The Plaintiffs' Emergency Motions for U-Visa Certification are GRANTED. The Court will certify the Plaintiffs' U-Visa applications by signing the submitted "Supplement B" forms, so long as no additions, deletions, or alterations are made to the "Attachment A" forms.

NOTES AND QUESTIONS

1. Federal judges are not a common source of certifications for T or U Visa relief. Most certifications are obtained from law enforcement officials investigating the trafficking activity. Why kinds of obstacles do you think faced the trafficked

plaintiffs in *Garcia* from obtaining certifications from the traditional law enforcement official sources? Do you think trafficking civil cases provide a promising avenue for facilitating immigration relief for trafficked workers? Why or why not?

2. Note the urgency of immigration relief for the Audobon workers who were in immigration detention facing deportation at the time their civil complaint was filed. Like other cases involving undocumented workers, their employer had informed ICE of their undocumented status after the workers had issued a demand letter to their employer citing violations of the FLSA. ICE raided Audobon Pointe, the construction site, and took into custody the trafficked plaintiffs. While these trafficked plaintiffs successfully established eligibility for U visas, exploited non-citizen workers who do not qualify as trafficking victims may not be able to access TVPA-related immigration relief. Are there nonetheless, important reasons to consider extending immigration relief options to undocumented workers who experience workplace exploitation?

3. In *The Trafficked Worker as Private Attorney General: A Model for Enforcing the Civil Rights of Undocumented Workers*, 2009 U. CHI. LEGAL F. 247. 253–54, 288, 299 (2009), Professor Kathleen Kim refers to the trafficked plaintiff as a private attorney general, who "seeks to obtain not only individual relief, but also accomplishes important public policy goals" through the civil litigation:

> Private attorneys general may be created by statute, judicial decision, or executive order. The basic premise of the private attorney general is that, by empowering private persons with causes of action to sue for their injuries, the individual not only obtains direct relief, but also accomplishes important public policy goals. Interpreting the Civil Rights Act of 1964, the Supreme Court declared that when a plaintiff brings an action and obtains relief "he does so not for himself alone but also as a 'private attorney general,' vindicating a policy that Congress considered of the highest priority." In *City of Riverside v. Rivera*, the Court further explained that this public policy goal is realized even when the private attorney general obtains individual compensatory damages rather than injunctive relief: "[U]nlike most private tort litigants, the civil rights plaintiff seeks to vindicate important civil and constitutional rights that cannot be valued solely in monetary terms. . . . Regardless of the form of relief he actually obtains, a successful civil rights plaintiff often secures important social benefits." . . .
>
> [Trafficking-related] legislative enactments indicate the strong public function served by the trafficked private attorney general to influence policy reform. Augmenting the public function of the trafficked private attorneys general is their role in addressing trafficking violations left unprosecuted by government actors. The precedents generated from trafficking lawsuits enlarge protections to other trafficked workers. And the trafficking litigating itself advances important constitutional and civil rights.

Do you agree? Does trafficking civil litigation achieve not only compensation for the trafficked plaintiff, but also important "social benefits"? If so, what might they be?

Professor Kim also remarks that the "conferral of immigration status to trafficked workers supports their role as private attorneys general while the unlawful status of undocumented workers often takes precedence of their civil claims against abusive employers." She suggests that immigration relief ought to be extended to exploited undocumented workers because "similar to trafficked private attorneys general, they play an important role in the furtherance of substantive legal norms and societal values." Is immigration relief an indication that Congress intended to empower trafficked persons as private attorneys general to pursue civil justice? Should exploited undocumented workers who sue their employers for workplace violations also receive some form of immigration relief to empower them as private attorneys general? Why or why not? If so, should the immigration status be temporary in the form of continued presence or more stable with a pathway to permanent residency such as a U or T visa?

V. STATE TRAFFICKING CIVIL REMEDIES[6]

Despite the national movement toward state anti-trafficking legislation, few states have enacted a state level trafficking private right of action. The first of such state level civil remedies was enacted in California as a result of strong advocacy efforts by the California Anti-Trafficking Initiative,[7] a coalition of non-governmental organizations that closely collaborated with Assemblywoman Sally Lieber, the principal author of the bill, to draft legislation primarily intended to broaden trafficked persons' rights and protections.

AB 22, the California Trafficking Victims Protection Act was signed into law by Governor Schwarzenegger on September 21, 2005. In addition to criminalizing trafficking and providing a trafficking civil cause of action, AB 22 mandates that state and local law enforcement issue an LEA (*Law Enforcement Agency Certification*) within 15 days of encountering a trafficking victim in order to expedite the provision of federally granted social services and immigration relief. AB 22 enacts a trafficking victim-caseworker "privilege" to protect communications between victims and their social services caseworkers from intrusive discovery. AB 22 also provides victims with state crime victim compensation funds and state health and human services.

The California trafficking private right of action was amended as § 52.5 of the California Civil Code. Section 52.5 provides that a trafficking victim may bring a civil action for actual, compensatory and punitive damages, and injunctive relief. Among other things, § 52.5 also provides for treble damages, as well as attorney's fees, costs, and expert witness fees to the prevailing plaintiff. Similar to the federal trafficking private right of action, § 52.5 also provides that a civil action "shall be stayed during the pendency" of a criminal investigation and prosecution arising out of the same set of circumstances. Cal. Civ. Code § 52.5(h). Over a dozen civil lawsuits

---

[6] Portions of the remainder of this chapter are adapted with permission from DANIEL WERNER & KATHLEEN KIM, CIVIL LITIGATION ON BEHALF OF VICTIMS OF HUMAN TRAFFICKING (3d ed. 2008). Copyright © 2008. Southern Poverty Law Center. All Rights Reserved. Reprinted with Permission.

[7] The California Anti-Trafficking Initiative was led by Asian Pacific Islander Legal Outreach, Coalition to Abolish Slavery and Trafficking and Lawyers' Committee for Civil Rights of San Francisco.

have been filed utilizing § 52.5. While some are pending, others have resulted in large damage awards and settlements.

In order to make a claim under § 52.5 of the CA Civil Code, a plaintiff must be trafficked as defined by § 236.1 of the California Penal Code. Section 236.1 of the California Penal Code defines human trafficking as the unlawful deprivation or violation of liberty of another to maintain a felony violation or obtain forced labor or services. Cal. Penal Code § 236.1(a). In 2012, § 236.1 was amended under Proposition 35, a California ballot initiative that among other things increased criminal penalties against human traffickers.

The statute of limitations for adult plaintiffs under § 52.5 of the California civil code is five years from the date when the trafficked person was liberated from the trafficking situation. For trafficked minors, the statute of limitations is eight years from the date that the minor reaches majority age. The statute of limitations may be tolled due to a variety of circumstances including a trafficked individual's disability, minor status, lack of knowledge, psychological trauma, cultural or linguistic isolation, inability to access victim services as well as threatening conduct from a defendant preventing a trafficked individual from bringing a civil action. § 52.5(d)–(e).

Are there benefits or drawbacks to supplementing the federal trafficking private right of action, § 1595, with a state level civil remedy?

VI. THE ALIEN TORT CLAIMS ACT ("ATCA")

The ATCA grants federal jurisdiction for "any civil action by an alien for a tort only, committed in violation of the law of nations or a treaty of the United States." The statute was enacted in 1789 by the first Congress, but was rarely invoked for almost 200 years. It has reemerged as the primary civil litigation tool for addressing international human rights abuses. The Supreme Court in *Sosa v. Alvarez-Machain*, 542 U.S. 692 (2004), upheld ATCA jurisdiction and conferred a cause of action for a narrow class of torts. Additionally, several federal appeals courts have upheld ATCA jurisdiction based on violations of a variety of human rights norms.[8] Still, ATCA litigation has ensued with much judicial scrutiny and the role of courts in adjudicating and enforcing international law continues to be contested.

In order to establish subject matter jurisdiction under the ATCA, a plaintiff must show that defendant violated a "specific, universal and obligatory" norm of international law. *In re Estate of Marcos Human Rights Litig.*, 25 F.3d 1467, 1475 (9th Cir. 1994). Courts have held that the following claims satisfy this standard: torture; forced labor; slavery; prolonged arbitrary detention; crimes against humanity; genocide; disappearance; extrajudicial killing; violence against women; and cruel, inhuman, or degrading treatment. *See Presbyterian Church of Sudan v. Talisman Energy, Inc.*, 244 F. Supp. 2d 289, 305–06 (S.D.N.Y. 2003) (slavery, genocide, extrajudicial killing, torture); *Kadic v. Karadzic*, 70 F.3d 232, 236, 244 (2d

---

[8] The Court, however, has passed on a number of opportunities to grant *certiorari* in ATCA cases. *See, e.g.*, Royal Dutch Petroleum Co. v. Wiwa, 532 U.S. 941 (2001); Karadzic v. Kadic, 518 U.S. 1005 (1996); Estate of Marcos v. Hilao, 513 U.S. 1126 (1995); Tel-Oren v. Libyan Arab Republic, 470 U.S. 1003 (1985).

Cir. 1995) (genocide, war crimes, crimes against humanity); *Forti v. Suarez Mason*, 694 F. Supp. 707, 709–11 (N.D. Cal. 1988) [Forti II] (disappearance); *Forti v. Suarez Mason*, 672 F. Supp. 1531, 1541–42 (N.D. Cal. 1987) [Forti I] (prolonged arbitrary detention, summary execution); *Filartiga v. Pena-Irala*, 630 F.2d 876, 884 (2d Cir. 1980) (torture). However, a number of other serious violations have not met the standard, including forced transborder abduction involving a one-day detention prior to transfer of custody to government authorities. *Sosa*, 542 U.S. at 738.

Plaintiffs hoping to establish subject matter jurisdiction based on other norms of international law must show widespread acceptance of the norm by the community of nations. Such acceptance may be demonstrated by reference to state practice, international treaties, the decisions of international tribunals, and the writings of international law scholars. It should be noted, though, that since international law traditionally applied only to states, there are some restrictions regarding ATCA jurisdiction in cases brought against private individuals or corporations. In such cases, the rule of international law will apply in two contexts: (1) where the rule of international law includes in its definition culpability for private individuals; or (2) where the private actor acted "under color of law." *See Kadic*, 70 F.3d at 239–42, 243–44.

First, the ATCA applies to private actors who violate the limited category of international law violations that do not require state action. These limited violations of customary international law are known as jus cogens norms, "accepted and recognized by the international community of states as a whole as a norm from which no derogation is permitted." *Siderman de Blake v. Republic of Argentina*, 965 F.2d 699, 714 (9th Cir. 1992) (citing the Vienna Convention on the Law of Treaties art. 53, *opened for signature* May 23, 1969, 1155 U.N.T.S. 332). To date, courts have held this category to include war crimes, genocide, piracy, and slavery. Courts have also held that international law is violated where a private individual commits wrongs such as rape, torture or murder in pursuit of genocide, slavery, or violations of the laws of war.

Second, a private individual or entity may also be sued under the ATCA by acting "under color of law" in committing violations of international law norms that only apply to states. In applying this rule, courts have looked to standards developed under 42 U.S.C. § 1983 in suits seeking to redress violations of rights protected by the U.S. Constitution. In general, a defendant has acted under "color of law" where she acted together with state officials or with state aid. *See Kadic*, 70 F.3d at 245.

The ATCA not only creates subject matter jurisdiction for violations of international law, but also provides a cause of action. Once a plaintiff successfully pleads a valid international law violation under the ATCA, she may then proceed to prove her case based on the relevant definition under international law. Where international law does not provide the relevant rules of decision, courts have at various times applied domestic federal common law and statutory law including the TVPA, state law or the law of the foreign nation in which the tort was committed.

In an omitted part of the opinion in *Roe v. Bridgestone*, discussed above, the Southern District of Indiana rejected an ATCA claim based on forced labor brought by plaintiffs who were workers on a rubber plantation in Liberia. The court agreed that a valid ATCA claim could be based on the international law violation of forced labor. However, the court concluded that the working conditions of the plaintiffs in *Roe* did not meet the standard of forced labor as understood under international law. This part of the *Roe* opinion is excerpted below:

> Plaintiffs cite several pre- *Sosa* federal cases holding or stating that "forced labor" violates the law of nations. Those cases show that some forms of forced labor violate the law of nations, but the facts in those cases are so different from the plaintiffs' allegations in this case as to show that the label "forced labor" adds little to the needed analysis.
>
> In *Iwanowa v. Ford Motor Co.*, 67 F. Supp. 2d 424 (D.N.J. 1999), the plaintiff alleged that during World War II, she was literally sold from her home in Russia and transported by Nazi troops to Germany to work for the German subsidiary of Ford under inhuman conditions and without compensation. Then 17 years old, the plaintiff was forced to live with 65 other deportees in a wooden hut without heat, running water, or sewage facilities, and they were locked in at night. She was required to perform heavy labor drilling holes in engine blocks. Company officials, she alleged, used rubber truncheons to beat workers who failed to meet their quotas. In the course of dismissing all of her claims on other grounds, the court stated that "the case law and statements of the Nuremberg Tribunals unequivocally establish that forced labor violates customary international law." *Id.* at 441.
>
> In *In re World War II Era Japanese Forced Labor Litigation*, 164 F. Supp. 2d 1160, 1179 (N.D. Cal. 2001), the court also dismissed all claims as time-barred but stated it was inclined to agree with the *Iwanowa* conclusion that forced labor violates the law of nations. The district court opinion did not dwell on the historical details, but the Ninth Circuit opinion affirming the dismissal described the treatment of the civilians subjected to forced labor by the Japanese military: "[T]hey were all subjected to serious mistreatment, including starvation, beatings, physical and mental torture, being transported in unventilated cargo holds of ships, and being forced to make long marches under a tropical sun without water. Some survived, while others were ultimately executed, or died from disease or physical abuse." *Deutsch v. Turner Corp.*, 324 F.3d 692, 705 (9th Cir. 2003).
>
> In *Jane Doe I v. Reddy*, 2003 U.S. Dist. LEXIS 26120 (N.D. Cal. Aug. 4, 2003), the court denied a motion to dismiss forced labor claims under the ATS.[9] The plaintiffs were young women who alleged they were fraudulently induced to come to the United States with promises of education and employment, but were then forced to work long hours under arduous conditions at illegally low wages, and that they were sexually abused, physically beaten, and threatened. The court found that the allegations stated claims for forced labor, debt bondage, and trafficking actionable under the ATS. In reaching that conclusion, the court relied on the Universal Declaration of Human Rights and the International Covenant on Civil and Political Rights. (As noted above, the Supreme Court later held in

---

[9] Note from authors: The *Roe* court refers to the Alien Tort Claims Act as the Alien Tort Statute or "ATS."

Sosa that both documents were insufficient foundations for ATS claims. 542 U.S. at 734–35, 124 S. Ct. 2739.) . . .

The Complaint in this case uses the same powerful label "forced labor." That conclusory label is not decisive. The court need not take at face value the legal conclusions in a complaint. This case lies at a point on a continuum far from the forced labor of Nazi Germany, Japanese labor camps, or the workers rounded up more recently by the Burmese military. Even if the adult plaintiffs' factual allegations are credited, as the court must, these plaintiffs have not alleged violations of a specific, universal, and obligatory norm of international law. . . .

The question here is what is "forced labor," . . .

[T]he results of recent studies commissioned by the ILO indicated that the national researchers, as well as their respondents, had great difficulty in understanding the concept [of forced labour], and in distinguishing forced labour situations from extremely exploitative, but nonetheless "freely chosen", work.

Even though there are some forms of forced labor (Nazi Germany, for example) that clearly violate international law, these comments signal that the circumstances alleged by the adult plaintiffs in this Complaint do not violate specific, universal, and obligatory norms of international law. . . .

During the hearing on the motion to dismiss, the court asked plaintiffs' counsel what would need to change so that plaintiffs' labor would no longer be forced, in plaintiffs' view. The principal answer was to reduce the daily quota for latex production and thus to raise effective wages on the Firestone Plantation. Plaintiffs' counsel also said that the remedy would include providing information to workers about their rights, upgrading equipment, including safety equipment, and changing the security force. Apart from the comment on the security force, discussed below, those are all clearly matters of wages and working conditions that fall outside any specific, universal, and obligatory understanding of the prohibition against forced labor.

Plaintiffs have not alleged that Firestone fails to pay them. They do not allege that Firestone is using physical force to keep them on the job. They do not allege that Firestone is using legal constraints to keep them on the job. Plaintiffs do not allege that they could not freely quit their jobs if they felt they had better opportunities elsewhere in Liberia. Plaintiffs do not allege that they have been held against their will, tortured, jailed, or threatened with physical harm. Plaintiffs do not allege any form of ownership or trafficking in employees.

Plaintiffs allege instead that they are being kept on the job by the effects of "poverty, fear, and ignorance." As powerful as these forces may be, they are qualitatively different from armed troops keeping kidnapped and deported workers in labor camps. Higher wages, rest days and holidays, and the security of a proper employment relationship, better housing, education, and medical care are all understandable desires. But better wages and working conditions are not the remedy for the forced labor condemned by international law. The remedy for truly forced labor should be termination of the employment and the freedom to go elsewhere. Yet the adult plaintiffs allege in their Complaint that they are afraid of losing the very jobs they say they are forced to perform. . . .

[T]he Complaint does not allege a single incident of physical force, physical threat, or intimidation by those security forces directed against these plaintiffs or other Plantation workers. In the absence of such allegations or other indications of forced labor, the court cannot conclude that the presence of the current security force could transform the alleged circumstances at the Plantation into a violation of a specific, universal, and obligatory international norm against forced labor. . . .

Plaintiffs also argue that they are so isolated on the Plantation that they have no realistic prospect of leaving if they want to do so. Plaintiffs argue that there is no transportation available and that they would starve if they left their jobs. The principal problem with the argument is that those circumstances are not the creation of defendants. Defendants are operating a commercial enterprise in a war-torn nation that is one of the poorest and most dangerous on earth. The court is not aware of a basis in international law for stating that an employer must provide transportation or food or other necessities to a worker who wishes to leave his job.

The court assumes that the plaintiffs do not have better choices available to them as a practical matter. But the absence of those better choices is not the legal responsibility of these defendants. Under the standards of international law, Firestone is not responsible for Liberia's poverty, its history of civil war, or the dangers its people face. This basic distinction between harsh conditions for which an employer is or is not responsible is recognized in the ILO definition of forced labor dating back to ILO Convention 29 in 1930. Forced labor is "work or service which is exacted from any person under the menace of any penalty and for which the said person has not offered himself voluntarily."

The phrase "menace of any penalty" does not refer to the harm a person would suffer if he leaves a job and is unable to earn a living elsewhere. The concept of a penalty is a punishment deliberately inflicted (whether justly or not) by some authority or other actor for some perceived wrongdoing, not the consequences of being homeless and penniless in one of the poorest and most dangerous nations on earth. Without that element of deliberately inflicted harm, the definition of forced labor would expand to reach many people who work at poor jobs to support themselves simply because they have no better alternative. The ILO Director General's 2005 report clearly cautions against such a broad definition: forced labor does not cover "situations of pure economic necessity, as when a worker feels unable to leave a job because of the real or perceived absence of employment alternatives." . . .

In the absence of allegations of physical coercion, this case would reflect an unprecedented expansion of international law, contrary to all the cautionary warnings the Supreme Court posted in *Sosa*. The Court instructed lower courts, when deciding whether a norm of international law is sufficiently definite to support a claim under the ATS, to consider the practical implications of recognizing additional types of claims under the ATS. Those considerations in this case are daunting — far more so than they were in *Sosa*. The merits of this case do not depend at all on the American presence in the chain of corporate ownership. If the working conditions for adults on the Firestone Plantation violate international law, then international law would extend without identifiable boundaries to exploitive working conditions and low wages all over the world. Plaintiffs' basic reasoning — with conditions this bad, why would we stay if we could leave?— could apply all over the world to people who face no good alternatives for earning a living.

The court is confident that improvements in those wages and working conditions for many millions of people would make the world a better place. Yet federal courts in the United States must also keep in mind the *Sosa* Court's caution against having American courts decide and enforce limits on the power of foreign governments over their own citizens. How much more intrusive would American law be if American courts took it upon themselves to determine the minimum requirements for wages and working conditions throughout the world?

And to enforce those requirements here against any international business with property that could be found in the United States? Beyond situations presenting clear violations of specific, universal, and obligatory international law norms, these are matters left to diplomacy, legislation, publicity, and economic pressure from consumers, and not to the instincts of judges who would love to issue a writ to make the world a better place for some of the poorest and least fortunate members of the human family. The adult plaintiffs have pleaded circumstances in their Complaint that show they have no claim in Count One under the ATS for forced labor in violation of specific, universal, and obligatory norms of international law. Defendants' motion to dismiss is granted with respect to Count One, the adult plaintiffs' claims of forced labor under the ATS.

NOTES AND QUESTIONS

1. The *Roe* court took a rather restrictive view on the types of conditions that amounted to forced labor. The court explained that the *Roe* plaintiffs were not actually physically confined at the work premises nor did they suffer any direct threats of non-economic harm "deliberately inflicted" to compel them to work. Thus, the court concluded that the unfortunate economic circumstances of the workers and their inability to choose better employment could not provide the bases for an ATCA forced labor cause of action. Do you agree?

2. What concerns drove the *Roe* court's narrow definition of forced labor? What is the standard for forced labor under the TVPA? Is it similar or different from the *Roe* court's characterization of forced labor? What accounts for these differences?

3. Given that the TVPA provides a civil claim for forced labor, what is the benefit of an ATCA cause of action for forced labor, if any?

4. The text of the ATCA does not specify a statute of limitations. However, in *Papa v. United States*, 281 F.3d 1004, 1011–12 (9th Cir. 2002), the Ninth Circuit found that the 10-year statute of limitations of the Torture Victims Protection Act (TVPA) applies to ATCA claims. In *Manliguez v. Joseph*, 226 F. Supp. 2d 377, 386 (E.D.N.Y 2002), a human trafficking case, the Court also found that "[i]t is well-established that the ten-year statute of limitations of the [TVPA] applies to [the ATCA]." Further, the statute of limitations may be equitably tolled while the victim is unable to bring his claim. *See, e.g., Arce v. Garcia*, 434 F.3d 1254, 1265 (11th Cir. 2006).

5. While courts are not consistent in the method by which they determine the scope of damages, they have been consistent in allowing victims to receive both compensatory and punitive damages for infringement of the ATCA. *See Paul v. Avril*, 901 F. Supp. 330 (S.D. Fla. 1994) (awarding punitive damages in the amount of $4 million for torture and false imprisonment to Haitian citizens opposing the former Haitian military rule); *see also Filartiga v. Pena-Irala*, 577 F. Supp. 860, 867 (E.D.N.Y. 1984) (awarding plaintiffs $10 million in compensatory and punitive damages for the torture and murder of a 17-year-old member of their family).

VII. FEDERAL RACKETEER INFLUENCED AND CORRUPT ORGANIZATIONS ACT ("RICO")

The Federal Racketeer Influenced and Corrupt Organizations Act ("RICO"), 18 U.S.C. §§ 1960–1968, extends civil liability to any person, as defined in the act, who:

(a) . . . receive[s] any income derived . . . from a pattern of racketeering activity or through collection of an unlawful debt in which such person has participated as a principal . . . to use or invest . . . any part of such income, or the proceeds of such income, in acquisition of any interest in, or the establishment or operation of, any enterprise which is engaged in, or the activities of which affect, interstate or foreign commerce[; and/or][10]

(b) . . . through a pattern of racketeering activity or through collection of an unlawful debt [acquires or maintains] . . . any interest in or control of any enterprise which is engaged in, or the activities of which affect, interstate or foreign commerce[; and/or][11]

(c) . . . [is] employed by or associated with any enterprise engaged in . . . interstate or foreign commerce [and] conduct[s] or participate[s] . . . in the conduct of such enterprise's affairs through a pattern of racketeering activity or collection of unlawful debt[; and/or][12]

---

[10] 18 U.S.C. § 1962(a).

[11] *Id.* § 1962(b).

[12] *Id.* § 1962(c).

(d) . . . conspire[s] to violate any of [these provisions].[13]

Congress passed RICO in 1970 as part of the Organized Crime Control Act, aimed at strengthening legal mechanisms for combating organized crime. In particular, it broadened civil and criminal remedies and created evidentiary rules tailored to admitting evidence of organized crime.

A successful RICO civil claim must be based on a "pattern" of "racketeering activity." "Racketeering activity" is defined as behavior that violates certain other laws, either enumerated federal statutes or state laws addressing specified topics and bearing specified penalties. "Pattern" requires at least two predicate acts of racketeering activity, the last of which occurred within 10 years after the commission of a prior act of racketeering activity.[14]

The 2003 amendments to the TVPA added human trafficking crimes as predicate offenses for RICO charges and "trafficking in persons" is now included in the definition of a racketeering activity.[15] In 2011 the TVPA was further amended to include fraud in foreign labor contracting as a predicate act under RICO.[16]

Other racketeering activities that may qualify as criminal predicate acts for bringing a civil RICO claim in the trafficking context include:

- Mail and wire fraud
- Fraud in connection with identification documents
- Forgery or false use of passport
- Fraud and misuse of visas, permits, and other documents
- Peonage and slavery
- Activities prohibited under the Mann Act
- Importation of an alien for immoral use[17]
- Extortion (i.e., an employer threatening deportation when an employee complains about minimum wage or overtime amounts to unlawful extortion of employee's property interest in minimum wage or overtime)[18]

The RICO also requires the existence of an "enterprise" through which the defendant engages in racketeering activities.[19] An "association of fact" RICO enterprise is most common.[20] It has two key requirements:

- The defendant "person" must be separate from the "enterprise."[21]
- The "enterprise" must be a continuing unit and "separate and apart from

---

[13] *Id.* § 1962(d).

[14] *Id.* § 1961(5).

[15] *Id.* § 1961(1)(B).

[16] Violence Against Women Reauthorization Act of 2013 § 1211, 18 U.S.C. § 1597.

[17] 18 U.S.C. § 1961(1).

[18] Violation of state theft or extortion criminal laws is a RICO predicate act. *Id.* § 1961(1)(A).

[19] *Id.* § 1962(a)-c).

[20] *Id.* § 1961(4).

[21] *See* Bennett v. United States Trust Co. of New York, 770 F.2d 308, 315 (2d Cir. 1985).

the pattern of activity in which it engages."[22]

RICO does not specify a statute of limitations. However, the Supreme Court has applied a four-year statute of limitations. *See Agency Holding Corp. v. Malley-Duff & Associates, Inc.*, 483 U.S. 143, 155 (1987).

Plaintiffs in RICO civil actions are entitled to treble damages and recovery of reasonable attorney's fees and costs.[23] Other remedies include: "ordering any person to divest himself of any interest, direct or indirect, in any enterprise; imposing reasonable restrictions on the future activities or investments of any person, including, but not limited to, prohibiting any person from engaging in the same type of endeavor as the enterprise engaged in, the activities of which affect interstate or foreign commerce; or ordering dissolution or reorganization of any enterprise."[24] Any person whose business or property has been damaged as the result of proscribed racketeering activities may file a suit in federal court.[25]

In *Zavala v. Wal-Mart*, 393 F. Supp. 2d 295 (D.N.J. 2005) (internal citations omitted), a case that included allegations of human trafficking and involuntary servitude, the court dismissed the plaintiffs' RICO claims. The following excerpt from this opinion includes the background on the case and a portion of the court's analysis on the sufficiency of the plaintiffs' RICO claims:

> Defendant Wal-Mart, by its own account, is the nation's largest private employer. The named plaintiffs are undocumented immigrants who worked as janitors in various Wal-Mart retail store locations across the country.
>
> . . . .
>
> On October 23, 2003, four months before Plaintiffs filed their amended complaint in this Court, the United States Immigration and Customs Enforcement ("USICE") officers raided Wal-Mart retail stores in 21 states. Federal agents who conducted these raids as part of "Operation Rollback" arrested hundreds of janitors, including 12 of the named plaintiffs, for alleged immigration violations.
>
> . . . .
>
> The janitors arrested as part of Operation Rollback were undocumented immigrants from Mexico, the Czech Republic, Mongolia, Brazil, Uzbekistan, Poland, Russia, Georgia, and Lithuania. The named plaintiffs resided in New Jersey, Texas, Alabama, Florida, Virginia, Michigan, and Connecticut. At least 10 of the immigrants arrested in Arizona and Kentucky were employed directly by Wal-Mart. Others were employed through maintenance contractors. . . .
>
> Plaintiffs allege that, based on this history, Wal-Mart was aware that it was, and has been, employing unlawfully, hundreds of undocumented

---

[22] United States v. Turkette, 452 U.S. 576, 583 (1981).

[23] 18 U.S.C. § 1964(c) (2012)..

[24] *Id.* § 1964(a).

[25] *Id.* § 1964(c).

immigrants for janitorial positions, notwithstanding its frequent and nationwide use of maintenance contractors. Because of this alleged pattern of conduct, Wal-Mart has been under investigation by federal law enforcement authorities for over five years.

Plaintiffs allege that they were harmed by an ongoing "exploitative criminal enterprise" (herein the "Wal-Mart Enterprise") comprised of Wal-Mart and its various maintenance contractors, acting as Wal-Mart's co-conspirators or agents. Plaintiffs claim that the Wal-Mart Enterprise systematically employed, harbored, and trafficked in the labor of immigrants, aided and abetted violation of the immigration laws, failed to pay their wages and overtime and benefits as required, and concealed their profits and practices from detection.

More specifically, the Wal-Mart Enterprise operated as follows: participants in the Wal-Mart Enterprise violated the immigration laws to secure workers who could be exploited easily based on their undocumented status. It targeted, encouraged, harbored, trafficked, and employed undocumented aliens, specifically because they were a vulnerable population. The Wal-Mart Enterprise exploited them in any number of ways — by obligating them to work in excess of the statutory maximum number of hours, every day of the week, denying them of lawful pay and benefits under the FLSA, as well as time for sick leave, meals or breaks, and paying them in cash without withholding payroll taxes. The Wal-Mart Enterprise also easily could, and did, hide them from law enforcement authorities, by threatening them with deportation or locking them into the stores for the duration of their shifts.

Plaintiffs allege that, regardless of whether the janitors were hired directly by Wal-Mart or by a contractor, the terms of employment were illegal, and the same. Plaintiffs further allege that the Wal-Mart Enterprise used the mails and wire in order to operate the scheme, and concealed and prolonged the existence of the enterprise by money laundering. . . .

Plaintiffs allege that Wal-Mart and its contractors formed an unlawful "Wal-Mart Enterprise," in the form of an association-in-fact, for "the purpose of profiting from a systematic violation of immigration and labor, wage and hour laws and other laws." Plaintiffs assert that the members of the Wal-Mart Enterprise conducted the affairs of the enterprise "by employing, harboring, and trafficking in the labor of the plaintiff immigrants, failing to pay their wages and overtime and benefits as required by federal and state law, and concealing their profits and practices from detection." More specifically, they allege that Wal-Mart and its maintenance contractors engaged in, or aided and abetted, various racketeering activities, including: harboring, transporting, and encouraging undocumented aliens; conspiring to commit these immigration law violations; committing these immigration law violations for financial gain; involuntary servitude; money laundering; and mail and wire fraud. These activities are alleged to constitute a "pattern of racketeering" within the meaning of RICO, and since 1996 and continuing to the present, "were related to each other by virtue of" common participants, victims, method of commission, and purpose. The alleged result of these activities has been to deny Plaintiffs the protection of wage and hour laws and other laws in order to "enrich Wal-Mart" at Plaintiffs' expense.

[The court then provided a detailed examination of the plaintiffs' claims that the defendant engaged in the required predicate acts to state a claim for relief under RICO. The court began with the allegations of the immigration-related predicate acts. The court dismissed these claims, finding that even if Wal-Mart knew the plaintiffs were undocumented, this was not sufficient to show that Wal-Mart affirmatively engaged in immigration law violations for purposes of establishing RICO liability.]

Plaintiffs also allege that Wal-Mart violated the prohibition against involuntary servitude, which also constitutes a predicate act of racketeering. . . .

In *United States v. Kozminski*, 487 U.S. 931, 953 (1988), the Supreme Court, construing 18 U.S.C. § 1584, held that "involuntary servitude" meant "a condition of servitude in which the victim is forced to work for the defendant by the use of threat of physical restraint or physical injury, or by the use or threat of coercion through law or the legal process" and "encompasses those cases in which the defendant holds the victim in servitude by placing the victim in fear of such physical restraint or injury or legal coercion." The Court observed that it was "possible" that threatening an immigrant with deportation might amount to a "threat of legal coercion" that results in involuntary servitude, and that a person's special vulnerabilities may be a relevant consideration in determining whether a particular type of physical or legal coercion may be sufficient to hold a person in involuntary servitude. Id. at 948. At the same time, the Court also expressly endorsed Judge Friendly's observation in *United States v. Shackney*, 333 F.2d 475, 487 (2d Cir. 1964) (reversing convictions under § 1584):

> The most ardent believer in civil rights legislation might not think that cause would be advanced by permitting the awful machinery of the criminal law to be brought into play whenever an employee asserts that his will to quit has been subdued by a threat which seriously affects his future welfare but as to which he still has a choice, however painful.

Kozminski, 487 U.S. at 950, 108 S. Ct. 2751 (quoting *Shackney*).

In *Shackney*, the Court of Appeals concluded:

> . . . While a credible threat of deportation may come close to the line, it still leaves the employee with a choice, and we do not see how we could fairly bring it within § 1584 without encompassing other types of threat . . . . Friction over employment punctuated by hotheaded threats is well known and inevitable. But the subjugation of another's will is more easily accused than accomplished. There must be "law or force" that "compels performance or a continuance of the service" for the statute to be violated.

333 F.2d at 486–87 (internal citation omitted).

In the instant case, Plaintiffs allege that Wal-Mart's contractors threatened some of the undocumented janitorial workers with deportation. These allegations also include the claim that at least two plaintiffs were "abused" but do not identify who was directing or perpetrating the abuse, or the nature of the abuse that some of these plaintiffs may have endured. In addition, Plaintiffs allege that they were "forced to work" under threats of coercion.

These allegations of involuntary servitude are insufficient. . . . Plaintiffs have not alleged that they did not have any way to avoid "continued service or confinement." Thus, the complaint fails to allege the predicate act of involuntary servitude.

[The court also rejected the plaintiffs' claims that the defendants committed the predicate acts of mail and wire fraud, and money laundering.]

Plaintiffs have not alleged sufficient facts to state claims that Wal-Mart committed the predicate acts necessary to support a RICO claim.

NOTES AND QUESTIONS

1. Is the *Zavala* court's definition of involuntary servitude consistent with your understanding of its definition under the TVPA? What facts in the case are favorable to the plaintiffs' involuntary servitude claim? Unfavorable? Is there any argument that the TVPA expanded the definition of involuntary servitude as understood by the *Zavala* court, which relied on *Kozminski* and *Shackney*? Commentators have critiqued the *Zavala* court's narrow interpretation of involuntary servitude post-TVPA. *See* Kathleen Kim, *The Coercion of Trafficked Workers*, 96 IOWA L. REV. 409, 449 (2011); Jennifer M. Chacon, *Misery and Myopia: Understanding the Failures of U.S. Efforts to Stop Human Trafficking*, 74 FORDHAM L. REV. 2977 (2006).

2. What, if any, benefits does the RICO civil cause of action provide to plaintiffs in a human trafficking civil case? What are its challenges? *See* Kathleen A. McKee, *Modern-Day Slavery: Framing Effective Solutions for an Age-Old Problem*, 55 CATH. U. L. REV. 141 (2005) (examining the effectiveness of the civil component of RICO in trafficking cases, including its challenges and limitations). For an early view on the applicability of civil RICO in the forced prostitution context see Lan Cao, Note, *Illegal Traffic in Women: A Civil RICO Proposal*, 96 Yale L.J. 1297, 1309 (1987).

3. In another case alleging human trafficking, *Abraham v. Singh*, 480 F.3d 351 (5th Cir. 2007), the Fifth circuit reversed in part a district court dismissal of the plaintiffs' RICO claims. The plaintiffs, H-2B workers from India had paid thousands of dollars in recruitment fees to an agent of the defendant corporation. When the workers arrived, the defendants confiscated their passports, provided the workers with poor living conditions, and threatened the workers with punishment if they complained. The Fifth circuit found that the plaintiffs had adequately alleged a pattern of racketeering activity: "The Plaintiffs did not allege predicate acts

'extending over a few weeks or months and threatening no future criminal conduct.' . . . Rather, they alleged that the Defendants engaged in at least a two-year scheme involving repeated international travel. . . . " *Id.* at 356.

VIII. FAIR LABOR STANDARDS ACT ("FLSA")

The Fair Labor Standards Act ("FLSA") 29 U.S.C. §§ 201–219, is designed to alleviate "labor conditions detrimental to the maintenance of the minimum standard of living necessary for health, efficiency, and general well-being of workers." *Id.* § 202. The minimum wage and maximum hour protections offered by the FLSA provide trafficked workers with compensatory damages as well as liquidated damages for the willful wage and hour violations that occur in the context of forced labor.

A. Wage and Hour Protections

Any amount paid under minimum wage (currently $7.25/hour) will suffice for a claim of unpaid wages under the FLSA. Trafficked workers are often paid far less than federal minimum wage or are not paid at all. If the state minimum wage standard is higher, the Department of Labor ("DOL") will calculate unpaid wages according to federal and state standards, and inform the employer of their obligation under both. However, the DOL can *only* enforce requirements under the FLSA.[26] State labor commissioners will enforce state workplace standards. Trafficking civil complaints may include both FLSA and state labor code claims.

FLSA section 7(a)(1) states that:

> [N]o employer shall employ any of his employees who in any workweek is engaged in commerce or in the production of goods for commerce . . . for a workweek longer than forty hours unless such employee receives compensation for his employment in excess of the hours above specified at a rate not less than one and one-half times the regular rate at which he is employed.[27]

Trafficked workers are often forced to work far more than 40 hours per week. Exceedingly high hours can amount to significant damages in unpaid overtime. Some states provide more overtime protections than given by the FLSA. For example, California increases the overtime rate to two times the minimum wage for a workday of over 12 hours.

Hours worked are defined as "all time during which an employee is necessarily required to be on the employer's premises, on duty or at a prescribed work place."[28] Trafficked workers may be required to be "on-call" 24 hours a day without breaks or uninterrupted sleeping time. This "on call" time may constitute compensable work time.[29]

---

[26] *See* 29 U.S.C. § 216(c).

[27] *See Id.* § 207(a)(1).

[28] Anderson v. Mt. Clemens Pottery Co., 328 U.S. 680, 690–91 (1946).

[29] *See* 29 C.F.R. § 785.23 (2012).

The FLSA regulations provide guidelines for calculating hours worked and include specific interpretations for rest and meal breaks, sleep time and other periods of free time.[30] In general, if sleeping time, meal periods or other periods of free time is interrupted by a call to duty, the interruption must be counted as hours worked.

Actions for non-willful violations of the FLSA must be commenced within two years after the violation occurs. Actions for willful violations of the FLSA must be commenced within three years after they occur.[31] Still, there are several cases which suggest that if an employer fails to post notice of FLSA rights and/or promises to catch workers up in unpaid wages, the employer is estopped from later arguing statute of limitations. *See, e.g., United States v. Sabhnani*, 566 F. Supp. 2d 139, 145–46 (E.D.N.Y. 2008) (in forced labor criminal prosecution, FLSA statute of limitations equitably tolled because "not only was there no notice, but the women could not speak English. They were completely unaware of the FLSA or any of its minimum wage or overtime provisions").

An employer who violates the minimum wage and maximum hours provisions of the FLSA is liable to the employee for the amount of their unpaid wages and overtime. Additionally, the employer will almost always be liable for an additional, equal amount as liquidated damages. 29 U.S.C. § 216(b); *Chellen v. John Pickle Co.*, 446 F. Supp. 2d 1247, 1279–81 (N.D. Okla. 2006) (liquidated damages awarded in trafficking case, when defendants failed to show a reasonable and good faith belief that they were executing a "training program"). *But see* 29 C.F.R. § 790.22(b) (2012) (setting forth limited prerequisites for the court to exercise discretion in the award of liquidated damages).

Defendants in violation of the FLSA must also pay a plaintiff's reasonable attorney's fees in addition to any judgment awarded.[32] Civil penalties of up to $10,000 may be awarded in certain circumstances.[33] Injunctive relief is available to restrain violation of the minimum wages or overtime provisions of the Act, or the prohibition on engaging in transport of items produced in violation of such provisions.[34] Some courts have allowed the award of punitive damages.[35]

The FLSA prohibits an employer from firing or otherwise retaliating against an employee for exercising her rights under wage and hour laws.[36] An employer who violates the anti-retaliation provisions is liable for legal or equitable relief such as employment, reinstatement, promotion, and payment of wages lost plus an additional amount as liquidated damages.[37]

---

[30] *Id.* § 785.1.

[31] 29 U.S.C. § 255.

[32] 29 C.F.R. § 790.22(d).

[33] *See* 29 U.S.C. § 216(a); *see also* 29 U.S.C. § 216(e) (penalties arising from child labor violations).

[34] 29 U.S.C. § 217.

[35] *See* Sines v. Serv. Corp. Int'l., 2006 U.S. Dist. LEXIS 82164 (S.D.N.Y. Nov. 8, 2006).

[36] 29 U.S.C. § 215(a)(3).

[37] 29 U.S.C. § 216(b).

B. Employment Relationship

The FLSA affords protection to "any individual employed by an employer" who has "suffered or [is] permit[ted] to work."[38] The "economic reality" test is used to determine whether this employment relationship exists for purposes of FLSA enforcement. The test analyzes the circumstances of the whole activity to determine whether the individual is economically dependent on the supposed employer.[39] Some of the factors that may be considered in this analysis include: direct or indirect supervision of employees and direct or indirect authority to determine and modify employment terms.[40] Whether an individual meets the definition of an employee under the FLSA is not affected by factors such as the place where the work is performed, the absence of a formal employment agreement, the time or method of payment, or whether an entity is licensed by the state or local government.

While the FLSA applies to nearly every occupation and industry, special rules may modify or limit recovery in some situations. The rules that are particularly relevant to human trafficking cases are described below.

Commercial Sex: Although forced prostitution is not covered by the FLSA since it is considered illegal employment, other types of employment and legal commercial sex work may be covered. Congress intended the FLSA to apply to "labor conditions detrimental to the maintenance of the minimum standard of living necessary for health, efficiency, and general well-being of workers," so the FLSA presumably covers any work, including legal commercial sex work, that violates fair hours and pay standards.[41] For example, legal sex workers such as exotic dancers, who work irregular hours without a bona fide contract that specifies overtime pay, would have an actionable claim under the FLSA.[42] However, sex workers could be exempted from FLSA coverage if their place of work is considered a "recreational center" that does not operate for more than seven months of the year.[43] Even in the absence of an FLSA claim, victims of sex trafficking have many other causes of action available to them.

Relatives: When an enterprise's only regular employees are the owner and the owner's parent, spouse, child, brother, sister, grandchildren, grandparents, and in-laws, it is not a covered enterprise or part of a covered enterprise for purposes of FLSA.[44] While this exemption may preclude enforcement of the FLSA in cases of servile marriage or where certain family members are trafficked for forced labor, numerous other claims can be brought for both compensatory and punitive damages.[45]

---

[38] 29 U.S.C. § 203(e), (g).

[39] Goldberg v. Whitaker House Coop., 366 U.S. 28, 33 (1961).

[40] Rutherford Food Corp. v. McComb, 331 U.S. 722 (1947).

[41] 29 U.S.C. § 202.

[42] *Id.* § 207(f).

[43] *Id.* § 213(3)(A).

[44] *Id.* § 203(s)(2).

[45] *Singh*, 214 F. Supp. 2d at 1061.

Domestic Workers: The FLSA distinguishes between live-in and non-live-in domestic workers.[46] Domestic service employees[47] who reside in the household where they are employed are entitled to the same minimum wage as domestic service employees who work only during the day. However, the FLSA contains exemptions for domestic service employees who provide "companionship services for individuals who (because of age or infirmity) are unable to care for themselves."[48] The FLSA regulation interpreting the meaning of "domestic service employment" and therefore the extent of the exclusion includes only companionship services workers who are employed by the person they are providing services for (rather than those employed by a third party agency).[49] The Supreme Court has held that the 29 C.F.R. § 552.109(a) FLSA regulation in the "Interpretations" section is the controlling interpretation.[50] FLSA regulation 552.109(a) states that even companionship services workers who work for third-party agencies are included in "domestic service employment" and therefore exempted from the FLSA.[51]

Still, employers must pay live-in workers the applicable minimum wage rate for all hours worked. Many states provide overtime relief for live-in domestic workers. For example, California provides time and a half to live-in domestic workers after nine hours worked in a workday and two times the regular pay after nine hours worked on the sixth or seventh day worked in a workweek.[52] New York and New Jersey also give some overtime protections to live-in domestic workers under state law.[53]

The FLSA regulations provide for a special interpretation of calculating hours worked for live-in domestic workers, which differs from the general rule.[54] "In determining the number of hours worked by a live-in worker, the employee and the employer may exclude, by agreement between themselves, the amount of sleeping time, meal time and other periods of complete freedom from all duties when the employee may either leave the premises or stay on the premises for purely

---

[46] Workers such as "babysitters employed on a casual basis, companions for the aged and infirm, and domestic workers who reside in their employers' households" do not enjoy protection under FLSA. Deborah F. Buckman, *Validity and Construction of "Domestic Service" Provisions of Fair Labor Standards Act*, 165 A.L.R. Fed. 163 (2000); *see* 29 U.S.C. § 213(b)(21).

[47] "Domestic service employment refers to services of a household nature performed by an employee in or about a private home . . . . The term includes, but is not limited to, employees such as cooks, waiters, butlers, valets, maids, housekeepers, governesses, nurses, janitors, laundresses, caretakers, handymen, gardeners, footmen, grooms, and chauffeurs of automobiles for family use. It also includes babysitters employed on other than a casual basis." 29 C.F.R. § 552.3.

[48] 29 U.S.C. § 213(a)(15).

[49] *See* 29 C.F.R. § 552.3.

[50] Long Island Care at Home, Ltd. v. Coke, 551 U.S. 158 (2007).

[51] *See* 29 C.F.R. § 552.109(a).

[52] Cal. Code Regs. tit. 8, § 11150(3)(B).

[53] *See, e.g.*, N.Y. Lab. Law § 651; N.Y. Comp. Codes R. & Regs. tit.12, § 142-2.2; Topo v. Dhir, 2004 U.S. Dist. LEXIS 4134 (S.D.N.Y. Mar. 15, 2004).

[54] Note that the "casual babysitting" exception of the FLSA domestic worker coverage is narrowly construed and is intended for teenagers and others not dependent on the income. *See, e.g.*, *Topo*, 2004 U.S. Dist. LEXIS 4134, at *9–*10.

personal pursuits."[55] A copy of this agreement can be used to establish hours worked in the absence of a contemporaneous time record, allowing employers of live-in domestic workers to be exempt from the general FLSA record-keeping requirement.[56] However, the employer must still show that this agreement reflects actual hours worked.[57] The definition of free time for live-in domestic workers is the same as the general rule.[58] "For periods of free time (other than those relating to meals and sleeping) to be excluded from hours worked, the periods must be of sufficient duration to enable the employee to make effective use of the time."[59] "If the sleeping time, meal periods or other periods of free time are interrupted by a call to duty, the interruption must be counted as hours worked."[60]

Proving hours worked in domestic worker cases can be difficult since it is often the employer's word against the employee's. Evidence of the extent of the domestic worker's labor may be corroborated with witnesses or lists of tasks that the employer may have ordered the worker to complete. Domestic workers who were caring for children can corroborate their work schedule with the child's daily schedule.

Farmworkers — Agricultural workers[61] are entitled to the federal minimum wage. However, they are exempt from the FLSA's overtime requirements.[62] The FLSA definition of agriculture is fairly limited. Therefore, many packing shed workers, and any worker changing the raw, natural state of the agricultural product, *are* eligible for overtime.[63] Further exemptions apply to agricultural workers less than 16 years of age, particularly if employed by their parents. (*See* "Children" below.)

Joint employment liability almost always exists when agricultural employers utilize the services of farm labor contractors. In these situations, both the grower and the contractor are responsible for complying with the FLSA. Agricultural employers must also comply with the Migrant and Seasonal Agricultural Worker Protection Act ("AWPA"), which provides farmworkers with additional industry-specific protections. The AWPA imposes specific requirements for housing conditions, transportation safety and insurance, wage statements, payroll records, working arrangement enforcement, farm labor contractor registration, and disclosure of the terms and conditions of employment.

---

[55] 29 C.F.R. § 552.102(a).

[56] *Id.* § 552.102(b).

[57] *Id.*

[58] *Id.* § 552.102(a).

[59] *Id.*

[60] For domestic workers it can be argued that sleeping with a child is working because the worker is giving the employer the benefit of their services by comforting or tending to the child. *Id.*

[61] Agricultural work is defined as work performed on a farm as an incident to or in conjunction with farming operations. *See* 29 U.S.C. § 203(f). The U.S. Department of Labor regulations further refine this definition. *See generally* 29 C.F.R. § 780.

[62] 29 U.S.C. § 213.

[63] *See* 29 C.F.R. § 780.

Children — The FLSA provides both added protections and exemptions for children. The FLSA protects against oppressive child labor in three major areas: (1) hour regulation, (2) age limitations, and (3) regulation of hazardous occupations.[64] The FLSA provides that no producer, manufacturer, or dealer shall ship or deliver goods using oppressive child labor.[65] In addition, "[n]o employer shall employ any oppressive child labor in commerce or in the production of goods for commerce."[66] "Oppressive child labor" can occur when the employer violates the minimum age or hazardous job requirements.[67] The standard can vary greatly depending on the nature of the work (agriculture, non-agriculture or a job deemed particularly hazardous like mining and manufacturing), and whether the child is working for a parent.[68] The largest exemption in child minimum age and hazardous job restrictions occurs when the child is employed by his or her parent or by a person standing in the parent's place, except in manufacturing or mining occupations. These parental exceptions are particularly loose in the agricultural context.[69] Additional regulations granted to the Secretary of Labor under section 212(b) of the FLSA have added some substance to the FLSA guidelines. For example, youth under the age of 14 are not allowed to work any non-agricultural job with the exception of acting or delivering newspapers.[70]

NOTES AND QUESTIONS

1. FLSA claims are brought in virtually all civil trafficking cases. It provides an effective tool for recovering actual wage and hour losses, which in trafficking cases, because of egregious minimum wage and overtime violations, may amount to sizeable damage awards. Are there items of damages that are not covered by the FLSA? What are they?

2. Why are some categories of workers such as domestic workers and child workers treated differently under the FLSA? Does this differential treatment make sense? How might you reform the FLSA to better address the wage and hour issues that arise in human trafficking cases?

3. The FLSA may be enforced through private litigation or the Department of Labor (DOL). An aggrieved worker can bring a claim in federal district court under the FLSA. Or, if the worker chooses to file a complaint with the DOL, it will conduct an investigation into the wage/hour complaint and determine what wages are owed, if any. If the employer is unwilling to cooperate in the investigation and/or settle the amount in dispute, the DOL also has its own prosecutors, called solicitors, who may institute an action on behalf of one or more employees in federal court. If the DOL solicitors bring an action in court on the employee's behalf, the employee's right to

---

[64] 29 U.S.C. §§ 203(l), 212, 213(c).

[65] *Id.* § 212.

[66] *Id.* § 212(c) (basic child labor guidelines are found in this section).

[67] *Id.* § 203(l).

[68] *Id.*

[69] 29 C.F.R. § 570.2(a)(2); *see also* 29 U.S.C. § 213(c) (outlining particular tasks deemed unfit for youth).

[70] 29 C.F.R. §§ 570.124–125.

bring a separate action under the FLSA terminates.[71] What might be the benefits and drawbacks of private enforcement versus agency enforcement in human trafficking cases?

4. While *Zavala* described above dismissed the plaintiffs' RICO claims, the FLSA claims survived the motion to dismiss. In support of the plaintiffs' FLSA claim, the *Zavala* court found that the workers undocumented status did not preclude them from FLSA relief. The court also found that in addition to the contractor that recruited the plaintiffs, Wal-Mart was a joint employer and the plaintiffs had sufficiently alleged minimum wage and overtime violations under the FLSA:

> Wal-Mart . . . contends that the Supreme Court's decision in *Hoffman Plastic Compounds, Inc. v. NLRB*, 535 U.S. 137 (2002), casts substantial doubt on the notion that undocumented workers are entitled to seek back pay for minimum wage and overtime under the FLSA. . . . [For more information on *Hoffman*, see Chapter 14 *infra*.]
>
> Plaintiffs rebut this suggestion with several persuasive arguments. First, Plaintiffs correctly point out that, in contrast to the undocumented plaintiffs in *Hoffman* who sought back pay, in this case, they are seeking unpaid wages for work that already has been performed. In addition, the definition of "employee" under the FLSA is extremely broad, i.e., does not limit relief to citizens. Furthermore, the Department of Labor, which enforces the FLSA, interprets the FLSA to cover undocumented workers, even post-Hoffman. Finally, post-*Hoffman* decisions have construed the FLSA to cover undocumented workers. . . .
>
> This Court [also] concludes that Plaintiffs have alleged sufficient facts to suggest an employment relationship between Plaintiffs and Wal-Mart, and therefore, that Wal-Mart is a proper defendant to this action. Based on the Act's expansive definitions of the terms "employee" and "to employ" as well as the relevant regulations and case law governing whether an entity is a "joint employer" for purposes of stating an FLSA claim, Plaintiffs have alleged facts from which to infer that Wal-Mart qualifies as an "employer" under the Act.

393 F. Supp. 2d at 321–26 (citations omitted). Does this result help to inform how trafficked plaintiffs might choose and strategize the causes of action that they include in their complaints in the future? In what ways? How might defendants prepare and strategize their defense in trafficking civil cases?

---

[71] 29 U.S.C. § 216(b).

IX. ADDITIONAL CAUSES OF ACTION

A. Discrimination Claims

1. Title VII of the Civil Rights Act ("Title VII")[72]

Title VII of the 1964 Civil Rights Act prohibits employers from discriminating against employees on the basis of any of the following protected categories: race, color, religion, national origin, or sex. The 1978 Pregnancy Discrimination Act amended the Civil Rights Act Title VII to include pregnancy as a protected category.[73] Employers may not "fail or refuse to hire or to discharge any individual with respect to his compensation, terms, conditions, or privileges of employment because of such individual's race, color, religion, sex, or national origin."[74] Title VII violations in the human trafficking context are common, particularly in situations of sexual, racial or national origin harassment and other types of discriminatory treatment. However, Title VII only applies to employers with 15 or more employees.[75]

2. 42 U.S.C. § 1981

42 U.S.C. § 1981 is an additional discrimination cause of action. Section 1981 prohibits discrimination in the making, performance, modification, and termination of contracts, including enjoyment of all benefits, privileges, terms and conditions of contractual relationships, as well as terms and conditions of employment. The statute covers discrimination only on the basis of race.[76] This, in some circumstances, may also be extended to discrimination based on national origin. *See Chellen v. John Pickle Co.*, 434 F. Supp. 2d 1069, 1104 (N.D. Okla. 2006).

Section 1981 permits recovery of unlimited compensatory and punitive damages. Furthermore, it does not have the procedural filing requirements of Title VII and has a longer statute of limitations. It also allows a finding of liability against a defendant in his or her individual or personal capacity, which is not available under Title VII. Still, where § 1981 claims are brought arising out of the same facts as a Title VII claim, "[t]he elements of each cause of action have been construed as identical." *Chellen*, 434 F. Supp. 2d at 1103 (quoting *Skinner v. Total Petroleum, Inc.*, 859 F.2d 1439, 1444 (10th Cir. 1988)). Section 1981 also allows for attorney's fees and costs.[77]

---

[72] Title VII of the Civil Rights Act of 1964, 42 U.S.C. §§ 2000e–2000e17.
[73] 42 U.S.C. § 2000E(K).
[74] ID. § 2000E2.
[75] ID. § 2000E.
[76] *Id.* § 1981(b).
[77] 42 U.S.C. § 1988.

3. Conspiracy to Interfere with Civil Rights ("Section 1985")[78]

A claim may be brought under a provision of federal law emerged out of the Conspiracy Act of 1861[79] that was amended into its current form in 1871[80] for the purpose of enforcing Fourteenth Amendment protections. It provides as follows:

> If two or more persons in any State or Territory conspire, or go in disguise on the highway or on the premises of another, for the purpose of depriving, either directly or indirectly, any person or class of persons of the equal protection of the laws, or of equal privileges and immunities under the laws, [and] . . . in any case of conspiracy set forth in this section, if one or more persons engaged therein do, or cause to be done, any act in furtherance of the object of such conspiracy, whereby another is injured in his person or property, or deprived of having and exercising any right or privilege of a citizen of the United States, the party so injured or deprived may have an action for the recovery of damages, occasioned by such injury or deprivation, against any one or more of the conspirators.[81]

The U.S. Supreme Court has found that this provision allows for a private right of action.[82] What constitutes "class-based" discriminatory animus is an area of hot debate in the Courts. In *Deressa v. Gobena*, 2006 U.S. Dist. LEXIS 8659, at *16–*17 (E.D. Va. Feb. 13, 2006), a case involving a trafficked domestic worker, the court allowed the plaintiff to bring a § 1985(3) claim motivated by defendants' "desire to deprive Plaintiff [of] her rights to be free from slavery as a direct result of Plaintiff's being an alien, female, and of African descent." However, in *Zavala*, in which plaintiffs also brought a § 1985 claim, the court found that "recent immigrants, including undocumented persons" was not a "class of persons" subject to the protections of this Act. 393 F. Supp. 2d at 317–20.

B. Torts and Contracts Claims

Tort claims provide compensatory damages for the distress suffered by the employee, as well as punitive damages meant to punish the employer. The statute of limitations for common law torts in many states is *one year*. Since some human trafficking cases lead to successful criminal prosecutions, analogous torts may not have to be proven under the doctrine of collateral estoppel. A range of torts may arise in the trafficking context including: intentional infliction of emotional distress, false imprisonment, assault battery, fraudulent misrepresentation, negligence, negligent infliction of emotional distress, and conversion.

Trafficked plaintiffs may also have contract claims for breach of written or oral contracts. The award of contract remedies precludes tort remedies in a majority of states, and therefore punitive damages regardless of the willfulness of the breach.

---

[78] *Id.* § 1985(3).

[79] Conspiracies Act of 1861, ch. 33, 12 Stat. 284 (codified as amended at 42 U.S.C. § 1985(3)).

[80] Act to Enforce the Provisions of the Fourteenth Amendment, ch. 22, 17 Stat. 13 (1871) (codified as amended at 42 U.S.C. § 1985(3)).

[81] 42 U.S.C. § 1985(3).

[82] *See* Bray v. Alexandria Women's Health Clinic, 506 U.S. 263, 268 (1993).

NOTES AND QUESTIONS

1. Like the FLSA, enforcement of discrimination claims may be pursued individually or by a governmental agency, the Equal Employment Opportunity Commission (EEOC). The EEOC is charged with investigating discrimination complaints and may pursue discrimination lawsuits on behalf of the aggrieved worker. The EEOC has recently become involved in several large human trafficking lawsuits based on discrimination claims. In one case, the EEOC filed lawsuits against Global Horizons Inc., a Beverly Hills-based farm labor contractor, and eight farms. The complaint alleged that the defendant trafficked over 200 workers from Thailand to labor in farms in Hawaii and Washington where they were subjected to national origin and race discrimination, abuse and retaliation. In another case, the EEOC joined ongoing litigation against Signal International, LLC, a marine services company, which is claimed to have trafficked a class of approximately 500 Indian H-2B workers to work as welders and pipefitters in Mississippi and Texas. The original suit, *David v. Signal International, LLC*, still pending, was filed in the Eastern District of Louisiana by a team of civil rights lawyers from the Southern Poverty Law Center, the ACLU, the Asian American Legal Defense & Education Fund, the New Orleans Workers' Center for Racial Justice, the Louisiana Justice Institute, and *pro bono* law firms. What is the role of government enforcement in civil litigation on behalf of human trafficking victims? What should it be?

2. This chapter has introduced a range of claims that trafficked plaintiffs may bring in a civil case, in addition to 18 U.S.C. § 1595. Does the availability of causes of action covering wage and hour standards, discrimination, and torts, to name a few, render § 1595 moot? Recall the beginning of the chapter and the "expressive" force and "complete" relief provided by § 1595. Is the significance of § 1595 merely symbolic or also substantive and practical?

3. Some commentators have considered improvements and alternatives to trafficking civil litigation. *See* Shannon Lack, *Civil Rights for Trafficked Persons: Recommendations for a More Effective Federal Civil Remedy*, 26 J.L. & COM. 151 (2008) (discussing the infrequent use of § 1595 and suggesting amendments that would make it more useful to plaintiffs such as treble damage awards and securing the plaintiff's access to trafficker's seized assets); Jennifer S. Nam, *The Case of the Missing Case: Examining the Civil Right of Action for Human Trafficking Victims*, 107 COLUM. L. REV. 1655 (2007) (making policy recommendations that would increase the number of trafficking victims who would be able and willing to file civil actions including improved mechanisms to protect and empower victims, expanding the remuneration available, and increasing resources available to anti-trafficking NGO's and attorneys).

Chapter 12

IMMIGRATION RELATED PROTECTIONS FOR VICTIMS OF TRAFFICKING

The TVPA recognizes the unique vulnerability of foreign national victims of human trafficking, noting in its Purposes and Findings section that "because victims [of trafficking] are often illegal immigrants in the destination country, they are repeatedly punished more harshly than the traffickers themselves." To protect these victims the TVPA created a specific form of immigration relief: the T Nonimmigrant Visa (T Visa).

I. T VISA REQUIREMENTS

Foreign nationals who meet the following criteria are eligible to apply for a T Visa:

(I) [The foreign national] is or has been a victim of a severe form of trafficking in persons, as defined in section 7102 of Title 22;

(II) [The foreign national] is physically present in the United States, American Samoa, or the Commonwealth of the Northern Mariana Islands, or a port of entry thereto, on account of such trafficking, including physical presence on account of the [foreign national] having been allowed entry into the United States for participation in investigative or judicial processes associated with an act or a perpetrator of trafficking;

(III)

    (aa) [The foreign national] has complied with any reasonable request for assistance in the Federal, State, or local investigation or prosecution of acts of trafficking or the investigation of a crime where acts of trafficking are at least one central reason for the commission of that crime;

    (bb) [the foreign national is] in consultation with the Attorney General and, as appropriate, is unable to cooperate with a request described in item (aa) due to physical or psychological trauma; or

    (cc) [the foreign national] has not attained 18 years of age; and

(IV) [The foreign national] would suffer extreme hardship involving unusual and severe harm upon removal.[1]

---

[1] Immigration and Nationality Act, 8 U.S.C. § 1101(a)(15)(T) (2006) [hereinafter INA].

A. How to Apply for a T Visa

To apply for a T Visa a foreign national, or his or her representative, must fill out an I-914 application — also known as the "Application for T Nonimmigrant Status" — and submit the required supporting documentation. These documents are sent to the Vermont Service Center within the U.S. Citizenship and Immigration Services (USCIS) for adjudication. The first step in this adjudication process is an evaluation to determine if the application is "bona fide." An application is bona fide if it is complete, properly filed, no appearance of fraud exists, fingerprints and background checks are completed, and there is prima facie evidence of admissibility. If the application meets this standard, the final adjudication is then conducted de novo.[2]

All applicants for nonimmigrant visas must prove admissibility — but victims of human trafficking qualify for a special waiver, one which recognizes that victims will often become inadmissible while being exploited. There is no filing fee for the T Visa application, and, although there is a fee for the form required to waive inadmissibility, the fee may be waived.

The time it takes to prepare, submit, and adjudicate a T Visa application may be quite lengthy, and many foreign national victims are undocumented throughout this process — although some victims are granted an interim form of immigration relief during this time.[3] Continued presence (CP) is a form of immigration relief that federal law enforcement agents may apply for when a victim is a potential witness in the investigation or prosecution of a human trafficking case.[4] Federal officials from a variety of agencies may apply for CP, including those from Immigration and Customs Enforcement (ICE), the Federal Bureau of Investigation, and federal prosecutors from the U.S. Attorney's Offices within the Department of Justice. If a victim cooperates with state or local law enforcement, the officers involved with the case may request that a Federal official submit a CP application on their behalf.[5] USCIS recommends that applications for CP be initiated immediately upon identification of a victim of human trafficking.[6] After the law enforcement official has completed a CP application, it is submitted to the ICE Law Enforcement Parole Branch (LEPB). Approval is granted at LEPB's discretion.[7] CP lasts for up to one year and may be renewed in one-year increments.[8] Furthermore, individuals who receive CP usually receive

---

[2] 8 C.F.R. § 214.11(a) (2013).

[3] Victims of Trafficking and Violence Protection Act of 2000 § 107(c)(3), 22 U.S.C. § 7105(c)(3) (2006) [hereinafter TVPA].

[4] 28 C.F.R. § 1100.35(b)(1) (2012); *See* U.S. Immigration & Customs Enforcement, *Continued Presence: Temporary Immigration Status for Victims of Human Trafficking*, available at http://www.ice.gov/doclib/human-trafficking/pdf/continued-presence.pdf.

[5] *See* U.S. Dep't of Homeland Sec., *Information for Law Enforcement Officials: Immigration Relief for Victims of Human Trafficking and Other Crimes*, available at http://www.dhs.gov/xlibrary/assets/blue-campaign/ht-information-for-law-enforcement-officials-immigration-relief-for-victims-of-human-trafficking.pdf.

[6] *Continued Presence, supra* note 4.

[7] *Id.*

[8] *Id.*

I. T VISA REQUIREMENTS

authorization to work in the United States and are eligible for certain federal benefits.[9]

U.S. Citizenship and Immigration Services
Form I-914 - Application for T Nonimmigrant Status and Form I-918 - Petition for U Nonimmigrant Status
Service-wide Receipts, Approvals, and Denials
Fiscal Years: 2002 Through 2013 (October 2012)

Form I-914 – Application for T Nonimmigrant Status

T VISAS FISCAL YEAR	VICTIMS (T-1)			FAMILY OF VICTIMS (T-2,3,4,5)			I-914 TOTALS		
	Receipts	Approved	Denied	Receipts	Approved	Denied	Receipts	Approved	Denied
2002	163	17	12	234	9	4	397	26	16
2003	750	283	51	274	51	8	1,024	334	59
2004	566	163	344	86	106	11	652	269	355
2005	379	113	321	34	73	21	413	186	342
2006	384	212	127	19	95	45	403	307	172
2007	269	287	106	24	257	64	293	544	170
2008	408	243	78	118	228	40	526	471	118
2009	475	313	77	235	273	54	710	586	131
2010	574	447	138	463	349	105	1,037	796	243
2011	967	557	223	795	722	137	1,762	1,279	360
2012	885	674	194	795	758	117	1,680	1,432	311
2013	44	127	9	74	125	8	118	252	17

Form I-918 Petition for U Nonimmigrant Status

U VISAS FISCAL YEAR	VICTIMS (U-1)			FAMILY OF VICTIMS (U-2,3,4,5)			I-918* TOTALS		
	Receipts	Approved	Denied	Receipts	Approved	Denied	Receipts	Approved	Denied
2009	6,835	5,825	688	4,102	2,838	158	10,937	8,663	846
2010	10,742	10,073	4,347	6,418	9,315	2,576	17,160	19,388	6,923
2011	16,768	10,088	2,929	10,033	7,602	1,645	26,801	17,690	4,574
2012	24,768	10,122	2,866	15,126	7,421	1,465	39,894	17,543	4,331
2013*	2,199	1,999	177	1,538	2,161	159	3,737	4,160	336

*I-918 DATA COLLECTION DID NOT START UNTIL FY 2009 IN P4S
Data: Based on October 2012 Final Data
Source: Performance Analysis System (P4S)
Report Date: December 14, 2012
Report Frequency: Monthly
By: Office of Performance and Quality (OPQ), Data Analysis and Reporting Branch (DARB) - DMD
Parameters:
Date(s): Fiscal Years 2002 through 2013
Form Type(s): I-914, I-918
Data Type(s): Receipts, Approvals, Denials
USCIS Domestic Field Offices & Service Centers: Agency-wide

---

[9] 28 C.F.R. § 1100.35(b)(1) (2012); TVPA, 22 U.S.C. § 7105(b)(1)(A) (2006).

When an application for a T Visa is approved, the applicant is granted a four-year nonimmigrant visa. The visa can be beneficial to trafficking victims in a variety of ways. For instance, T Visa holders may work in the United States.[10] A T Visa holder is also allowed to travel, although many choose not to because of the risk of not being re-admitted to the United States due to inadmissibility concerns. Additionally, a T Visa holder may apply for legal permanent residence after three years or when the investigation or prosecution into acts of trafficking is complete, whichever comes first.[11]

B. Interpreting and Applying the T Visa Requirements

1. Interpreting Criteria One: Victim of a "Severe Form" of Human Trafficking

The first of the four eligibility criteria for T Visa applicants is that the individual must be a victim of a severe form of trafficking. The TVPA creates two categories of victims: an individual can be the "victim of a severe form of trafficking" or a "victim of trafficking."

> (9) Severe forms of trafficking in persons. The term "severe forms of trafficking in persons" means—
>
> > (A) sex trafficking in which a commercial sex act is induced by force, fraud, or coercion, or in which the person induced to perform such act has not attained 18 years of age; or
> >
> > (B) the recruitment, harboring, transportation, provision, or obtaining of a person for labor or services, through the use of force, fraud, or coercion for the purpose of subjection to involuntary servitude, peonage, debt bondage, or slavery.
>
> (10) Sex trafficking. The term "sex trafficking" means the recruitment, harboring, transportation, provision, or obtaining of a person for the purpose of a commercial sex act. . . .
>
> (14) Victim of a Severe Form of Trafficking— The term "victim of a severe form of trafficking" means a person subject to an act or practice described in paragraph (9).
>
> (15) Victim of Trafficking.— The term "victim of trafficking" means a person subjected to an act or practice described in paragraph (9) or (10).[12]

By definition, all victims of a severe form of trafficking are also victims of trafficking more generally. But the reverse is not true: all victims of trafficking are not victims of a severe form of trafficking. The difference only affects cases of sex trafficking, since the entirety of the definition for labor trafficking is contained within the severe forms of human trafficking definition.

---

[10] *Id.* § 7105(b)(1)(E)(i)(II)(bb).

[11] INA, 8 U.S.C. § 1255(l)(1)(A)(2006).

[12] TVPA, 22 U.S.C. § 7102.

To be a victim of a severe form of trafficking one must be subject to an act or practice described above in 9(A) or 9(B). These definitions create three categories of victims: (1) victims of sex trafficking who are under the age of 18, (2) victims of sex trafficking who are above the age of 18 and who are compelled into sex trafficking, and (3) victims of labor trafficking.

- *Victims of sex trafficking who are under the age of 18*: According to Section 103(8), anyone who has not attained 18 years of age and has been induced to perform a commercial sex act is a victim of a severe form of trafficking in persons. In other words, by definition, any child[13] who has been induced to perform a commercial sex act is a victim of a severe form of human trafficking.[14]

- *Victims of sex trafficking who are over the age of 18 and compelled into sex trafficking*: Unlike victims of sex trafficking who are under the age of 18, victims of sex trafficking who are age 18 and above must prove that force, fraud, or coercion was used to induce the performance of a commercial sex act.

- *Victims of Labor Trafficking*: Like victims of sex trafficking who are over the age of 18, victims of labor trafficking must prove force, fraud, or coercion. That is, they must show that they were (a) recruited, harbored, transported, provide, or obtained for labor or services (b) through the use of force, fraud, or coercion (c) for the purpose of involuntary servitude, peonage, debt bondage, or slavery.

As shown in the committee conference report that accompanied the passage of the TVPA in 2000, Congress intended for the phrases "victim of trafficking" and "victim of a severe form of trafficking" to differ substantively. In particular, legislators envisioned different levels of benefits for victims depending on which definition they satisfied.

> In various sections, the conference agreement uses more general terms such as "trafficking" or "trafficking in persons" rather than the more limited term "severe forms of trafficking in persons." In such contexts, these terms are intended to be used in a more general sense, giving the President and other officials some degree of discretion to apply the relevant provisions to a broader range of actions or victims beyond those associated with severe forms of trafficking in persons. Such discretion is particularly appropriate in assistance to and protection of victims, because trafficked women and children may have a compelling need for such assistance and protection even though they have not been subjected to severe forms of trafficking. In this connection, the conference agreement includes a definition of "victims of trafficking" that would encompass a broader class of victims in certain programs. Where, however, this Act uses the term "victims of severe forms of trafficking," even in provisions related to

---

[13] For purposes of this chapter the word "child" refers to anyone who has not yet attained the age of 18.

[14] This child would also be a victim of trafficking based on the definitions of TVPA § 7102.

protection and assistance, the application of such provisions is limited to such victims.[15]

A T Visa applicant must submit evidence that he or she is a victim of a severe form of trafficking. To satisfy this requirement an applicant may submit a law enforcement endorsement, evidence that the victim has received a grant of CP, or by supplying "sufficient credible secondary evidence describing the nature and scope" of the trafficking.[16] All applications must contain a statement by the applicant describing the applicant's victimization.

2. Interpreting Criteria Two: Physical Presence

The second criteria for T Visa eligibility is physical presence. An individual's entry into the United States does not have to be connected to his or her trafficking in order to qualify for a T Visa. Instead the individual's presence needs only to be "on account of" the trafficking. For individuals who remain in the United States:

> the physical presence requirement reaches [a] [foreign national] who: is present because he or she is being subjected to a severe form of trafficking in persons; was recently liberated from a severe form of trafficking in persons; or was subject to severe forms of trafficking in persons at some point in the past and whose continuing presence in the United States is directly related to the original trafficking in persons.[17]

When there is a gap between a victim's escape from a trafficking situation and their contact with law enforcement, the individual must show that "he or she did not have a clear chance to leave the United States in the interim."[18] The determination of whether an individual had a clear chance to leave will be based on the individual's circumstances. The lack of a clear chance can be established by a variety of evidence, including proof of "trauma, injury, lack of resources, or travel documents that have been seized by the traffickers."[19]

The regulations refer only to situations in which there is a gap between an individual's escape and contact with law enforcement. The regulations are silent on how to make a determination on an application in which there is no law enforcement involvement, which might occur, for example, on an application on behalf of a minor, or an adult who is not cooperating with law enforcement.[20]

If a victim has left the United States and returns, he or she may still qualify for relief. The 2008 reauthorization of the TVPA recognized that victims may need to return to the United States to participate in the trafficking investigation or

---

[15] 146 CONG. REC. H 8855 § 3 (2000).

[16] 8 C.F.R. § 214.11(f) (2013).

[17] *Id.* § 214.11(g).

[18] *Id.* § 214.11(g)(2).

[19] *Id.*; *see* Office On Violence Against Women, Legal Momentum: *Human Trafficking and the T-Visa*, available at http://www.vaw.umn.edu/documents/empoweringsurvivors/11humantraffickingtvisapdf.pdf.

[20] 8 C.F.R. § 214 (2013).

prosecution.[21] For individuals who are allowed to enter to participate in such processes, their presence is deemed to meet this requirement. For others who leave, either voluntarily or after having been removed, the victim is not considered to be present in the United States on account of such trafficking unless the individual's reentry "into the United States was the result of the continued victimization of the [foreign national] or a new incident of a severe form of trafficking in persons."[22]

3. Interpreting Criteria Three: Compliance with Law Enforcement

Under the third prong of the TVPA's eligibility criteria, to qualify for a T Visa a foreign national victim of a severe form of human trafficking must prove that he or she complied with all reasonable requests from law enforcement or meets one of the two exemptions from such compliance. Children under age 18 do not need to prove compliance with reasonable requests for cooperation. But they must prove their age, either with primary evidence like "a certified copy of their birth certificate, passport or certified medical opinion"[23] or secondary evidence such as "church or school records, or two sworn affidavits."[24]

Victims are also exempted from the compliance requirement if "physical or psychological trauma impedes their ability to cooperate with law enforcement."[25] This exemption is the result of changes made to the TVPA after the passage of the Violence Against Women Act of 2005.[26]

A variety of evidence can be used to establish trauma sufficient to justify an exemption. According to training materials published by the Women's Defense and Legal Education Fund, "[w]hile DHS has not yet issued regulations on this provision, possible evidence of physical trauma suffered includes photographs of bruises and injuries, police reports, medical reports and affidavits by witnesses. Evidence of psychological trauma suffered may include medical reports or affidavits by medical personnel."[27]

The reasonableness of a law enforcement request depends "on the totality of the circumstances taking into account general law enforcement and prosecutorial practices, the nature of the victimization, and the specific circumstances of the victim, including fear, severe traumatization (both mental and physical), and the age

---

[21] INA 8 U.S.C. § 1101(a)(15)(T)(i)(II) (2006); *see* U.S. Citizen & Immigration Serv., *Policy Memorandum: William Wilberforce Trafficking Victims Protection Reauthorization Act of 2008: Changes to T and U Nonimmigrant Status and Adjustment of Status Provisions* (July 21, 2010), *available at* http://www.uscis.gov/USCIS/Laws/Memoranda/2010/William%20Wilberforce%20TVPRAct%20of%202008%20July%2021%202010.pdf.

[22] 8 C.F.R. § 214.11(g)(3) (2013).

[23] *Id.*

[24] *Id.*; Submission and Adjudication of Benefit Requests, 8 C.F.R. § 103.2(b)(2)(i) (2012).

[25] INA § 1101(a)(15)(T)(iii).

[26] *See* Office On Violence Against Women, *supra* note 19.

[27] *Id.*

and maturity of young victims."[28] "Reasonableness," then, could vary widely from case to case.

The level of compliance required is also highly variable. There is no real guidance on the parameters of what qualifies as "reasonable cooperation" in the T-visa context.

A signed statement from officers involved in trafficking cases can be used as evidence of compliance with law enforcement requests. Form I-914 Supplement B is the "Declaration of Law Enforcement Officer for Victim of Trafficking in Persons" form and may be filed alongside the I-914 application. This is often referred to as a Supplement B or Law Enforcement Agency (LEA) endorsement. If USCIS is not in agreement with the Supplement B, USCIS will contact the law enforcement agency and work to reach an acceptable resolution, USCIS may interview the victim about his or her compliance, and additional evidence may be submitted by the victim. A Supplement B is considered to be primary evidence of compliance with law enforcement requests[29] — but it is not required:

> A signed I-914 Supplement B may be submitted with the petition to verify that he or she has complied with any reasonable request by law enforcement in the investigation or prosecution of the trafficking crime, but is not required. The certification is one of the pieces of evidence that USCIS will consider to grant or deny a T visa.[30]

Secondary evidence of compliance may be submitted instead. The secondary evidence must include an "original statement" by the victim explaining the absence of a completed Supplement B.

> The statement or evidence must show that an LEA [Law enforcement agency] that has responsibility and authority for the detection, investigation, or prosecution of severe forms of trafficking in persons has information about such trafficking in persons, that the victim has complied with any reasonable request for assistance in the investigation or prosecution of such acts of trafficking, and, if the victim did not report the crime at the time, why the crime was not previously reported. The statement or evidence should demonstrate that good faith attempts were made to obtain the LEA endorsement, including what efforts the applicant undertook to accomplish these attempts. In addition, applicants may also submit their own affidavit and the affidavits of other witnesses. The determination of what evidence is credible and the weight to be given that evidence shall be within the sole discretion of the Service. Applicants are encouraged to describe and document all applicable factors, since there is no guarantee that a particular reason will result in a finding that the applicant has complied with reasonable requests. An applicant who never has had contact with an

---

[28] 8 C.F.R. § 214.11(a) (2013).

[29] *Id.* § 214.11(h)(1).

[30] *See* U.S. Dep't of Homeland Sec., *U Visa Law Enforcement Certification Guide*, available at http://www.dhs.gov/xlibrary/assets/dhs_u_visa_certification_guide.pdf.

LEA regarding the acts of severe forms of trafficking in persons will not be eligible for T-1 nonimmigrant status.[31]

4. Interpreting Criteria Four: Extreme Hardship Involving Severe and Unusual Harm

The fourth criteria for T Visa eligibility is a showing of hardship. A T Visa applicant must prove that he or she would suffer extreme hardship involving severe and unusual harm if removed from the United States. This determination is made case by case and is based solely on the hardship facing the victim. Hardship to others, including family members, is irrelevant. 8 C.F.R. § 214.11 gives some guidance on how this standard is applied:

> Factors that may be considered in evaluating whether removal would result in extreme hardship involving unusual and severe harm should take into account both traditional extreme hardship factors and those factors associated with having been a victim of a severe form of trafficking in persons. These factors include, but are not limited to, the following:
>
> (i) The age and personal circumstances of the applicant;
>
> (ii) Serious physical or mental illness of the applicant that necessitates medical or psychological attention not reasonably available in the foreign country;
>
> (iii) The nature and extent of the physical and psychological consequences of severe forms of trafficking in persons;
>
> (iv) The impact of the loss of access to the United States courts and the criminal justice system for purposes relating to the incident of severe forms of trafficking in persons or other crimes perpetrated against the applicant, including criminal and civil redress for acts of trafficking in persons, criminal prosecution, restitution, and protection;
>
> (v) The reasonable expectation that the existence of laws, social practices, or customs in the foreign country to which the applicant would be returned would penalize the applicant severely for having been the victim of a severe form of trafficking in persons;
>
> (vi) The likelihood of re-victimization and the need, ability, or willingness of foreign authorities to protect the applicant;
>
> (vii) The likelihood that the trafficker in persons or others acting on behalf of the trafficker in the foreign country would severely harm the applicant; and
>
> (viii) The likelihood that the applicant's individual safety would be seriously threatened by the existence of civil unrest or armed conflict as demonstrated by the designation of Temporary Pro-

---

[31] 8 C.F.R. § 214.11(h) (2013).

tected Status, under section 244 of the Act, or the granting of other relevant protections.[32]

5. An Additional Consideration: Admissibility

In addition to satisfying the four criteria listed above, T Visa applicants must not be inadmissible.[33] All foreign nationals who seek admission to the United States must establish their admissibility; foreign nationals who are victims of human trafficking are not exempted from this requirement.

There are a number of inadmissibility grounds including criminal convictions, fraud and misrepresentation, and unlawful presence. The inadmissibility ground of being a public charge does not apply to T Visa applicants. In certain cases an inadmissibility ground can be waived. Many of the inadmissibility grounds can be waived for a victim of human trafficking if the reason for the inadmissibility is "caused by, or were incident to, the victimization."[34]

This waiver is crucial for many victims of human trafficking who were involved in the commercial sex industry. Many of these victims have criminal convictions or charges for prostitution or solicitation. Without this trafficking based waiver, many victims of human trafficking would not qualify for a T Visa.

II. DERIVATIVE VISAS

In addition to applying for a work permit and permission to remain in the United States, a T Visa applicant may also apply for something called "a derivative visa." A derivative visa allows the applicant to bring certain family members to the United States — their spouse, parents, children, or siblings under the age of 18 — so long as the applicant was under the age of 21 when the T Visa application was filed. Individuals who filed for their T Visa at age 21 or above may bring in their spouse or children. All T Visa applicants may bring parents, unmarried siblings under the age of 18, or adult or minor children of derivative beneficiaries — so long as these family members are facing "a present danger of retaliation" as a result of the T Visa's applicant's escape from the trafficking situation or his or her cooperation with law enforcement.[35]

To apply for a derivative T Visa, each family member must separately file an I-914 Supplement A form. The form requires derivative applicants to demonstrate both that they have the identified relationship to the principal applicant and that they would be admissible to the United States. The relationship element must be supported by documentation such as birth certificates, marriage licenses, or church records. Admissibility is addressed through questions on the form and a back-

---

[32] 8 C.F.R. § 214.11(i)(1) (2013).

[33] Inadmissibility grounds apply to non-citizens seeking admission to the United States. According to INA § 212(a), "aliens who are inadmissible under the following paragraphs are ineligible to receive visas and ineligible to be admitted to the United States." The full list of inadmissibility grounds can be found in the INA, 8 U.S.C. § 1182 (2006).

[34] INA § 1182(d)(13)(A)(2).

[35] INA § 1101(a)(15)(T).

ground check. The specific type of visa these relatives are eligible to receive depends upon which relationship category the applicant falls into: spouses of principal applicants receive T-2 Visas; children of principal applicants receive T-3 Visas; parents receive T-4 Visas; and siblings receive T-5 Visas. The principal applicant receives a T-1 Visa.

Derivative visa holders may work in the United States. They also qualify for certain benefits. Because a derivative T Visa holder's status is contingent on the principal applicant's status, derivative visas expire when the T-1 applicant's status ends.[36] Derivative visa holders may apply for legal permanent residence at the same time as the T-1 Visa holder. However, the derivative applicant will only be eligible for legal permanent residence if the T-1 applicant is eligible, and their application will be denied if the principal's application for adjustment is denied.[37]

III. CAPS ON T VISA AND DERIVATIVE VISAS

Only 5,000 T-1 Visas may be awarded each year.[38] If the annual cap were to be reached, a wait list would be created. However, this cap has never been reached; less than 500 T visas have been awarded each year since the TVPA came into effect in 2000.[39] See the table in Section I(A). There is no limit to the number of derivative visas that may be granted to qualifying spouses, children, or parents of trafficking victims.

NOTES AND QUESTIONS

"For a number of reasons, the T-Visa provision may be criticized as ineffective and a component of a larger restrictive immigration regime. First, the TVPA states that '[a]pproximately 50,000 women and children are trafficked into the United States each year.' If the authors of the TVPA believed this estimate, then limiting the number of T-Visa available per year to 5,000 is inadequate and morally objectionable. If lawmakers believed that 50,000 people were trafficked into the country annually or that the scope of the problem was unknown, then providing only 5,000 T-Visas each year indicates a broader push to restrict immigration into the country." Henry Andres Yoder, *Civil Rights for Victims of Human Trafficking*, 12 U. PA. J.L. & SOC. CHANGE 133, 152–53 (2008–2009).

IV. CHALLENGES TO OBTAINING A T VISA

One of the critiques of the TVPA is that, while it is ostensibly an act about victim protection, its true priority is prosecution. Consider, for example, the Purposes section of the TVPA as passed in 2000:

---

[36] *See* U.S. Citizenship and Immigration Services, *Policy Memorandum: Extension of Status for T and U Nonimmigrants* (Apr. 19, 2011) *available at* http://www.uscis.gov/USCIS/Laws/Memoranda/2011/April/exten.status-tandu-nonimmigrants.pdf.

[37] 8 C.F.R. § 245.23(b)(1) (2013); *see Policy Memorandum*, *supra* note 36.

[38] 8 C.F.R. § 214.11(m) (2013).

[39] INA § 1255(l)(4)(B); 8 C.F.R. § 214.11(m)(2) (2013).

Because victims of trafficking are frequently unfamiliar with the laws, cultures and languages of the countries into which they have been trafficked, because they are often subjected to coercion and intimidation including physical detention and debt bondage, and because they often fear retribution and forcible removal to countries in which they will face retribution or other hardship, these victims often find it difficult or impossible to report the crimes committed against them or to assist in the investigation and prosecution of such crimes.[40]

The realization that underreporting was hampering prosecution of traffickers prompted lawmakers to couple immigration relief with victim participation in law enforcement efforts. However, the tying of immigration relief to victim cooperation may be a barrier to victims in obtaining immigration relief — which means that this strategy may do more to aid law enforcement than it does to aid victims. As civil rights attorney Hussein Sadruddin explains in his article *Human Trafficking in the United States: Expanding Victim Protection Beyond Prosecution Witnesses*:

> [V]ictims who have been raped, tortured, or otherwise brutalized, as is common in human trafficking, often suffer severe psychological trauma, which may make them incapable of discussing the traumatic events. . . .
>
> Based on our knowledge of the experiences of trafficking victims and the psychological trauma they suffer, we can assume that the complexity of eligibility requirements as well as the linking of benefits to cooperation with law enforcement prevent many victims from coming forward. The powerful effects of psychological trauma on trafficking victims were forcefully laid out in the TVPA; yet Congress failed to recognize that many of the most traumatized victims might be physically or psychologically incapable of providing cooperation with law enforcement and would thus be ineligible for any benefits. The TVPA recognizes that trafficking victims are generally hidden, traumatized, or otherwise incapable of seeking assistance, and that many non-citizen victims live in fear of deportation Medical research shows that victims who are suffering from severe trauma will often be incapable of certain types of analytical thinking or remembering facts. Retelling their stories may cause additional trauma. The TVPA requirement of mandatory cooperation with law enforcement is another hurdle that many traumatized victims will not be able to overcome. The original TVPA standards required even children as young as fifteen to cooperate with law enforcement for access to protection. However, the 2003 TVPRA eliminated this requirement; children under eighteen no longer must cooperate in order to receive TVPA benefits. They are not exempt from contact with law enforcement, though, since the process continues to require the reporting of a trafficking crime for access to trafficking victim benefits.
>
> Even those victims willing and able to cooperate, however, may have difficulty understanding the complex regulations and complying with the burdensome paperwork required for immigration benefits. In addition, stiff eligibility standards may prevent many victims from having access to

---

[40] TVPA, 22 U.S.C. § 7101(20) (2006).

needed services, including immigration benefits.[41]

Although the reauthorization of the TVPA in 2005 added an exemption to the requirement for adults to provide assistance to law enforcement in certain cases of physical or psychological trauma, there are currently no standards for how this exemption should be implemented. Nor is there any requirement that the victim's needs be respected when there are significant prosecutorial interests. Professor Jayashri Srikantiah's article, *Perfect Victims and Real Survivors: The Iconic Victim in Domestic Human Trafficking Law* describes some of the complications of obtaining proof of cooperation from law enforcement officials:

> Through the LEA endorsement, DHS implements statutory language requiring that T Visa applicants be victims of a severe form of trafficking in persons and cooperate with any reasonable request from law enforcement. The LEA endorsement restriction goes beyond the language of the statute, which does not specify how such cooperation should be assessed, who should make such an assessment, or the level of cooperation sufficient for a T Visa. Individual law enforcement agents and prosecutors issue the endorsements, deciding whether a particular victim has suffered sufficiently severe trafficking and has cooperated sufficiently with law enforcement. DHS advises victims that these elements of their application "may be difficult to establish" without the endorsement, and 'strongly advise[s]' submission of the endorsement. A T Visa may be revoked if "[t]he LEA providing the LEA endorsement withdraws its endorsement." If a victim cannot obtain an LEA endorsement, she must provide "sufficient credible secondary evidence," which may include "trial transcripts, court documents, police reports, news articles, and copies of reimbursement forms for travel to and from court." A victim without an LEA endorsement must also provide a statement "describing what [she] has done to report the crime to an LEA," and must "demonstrate that good faith attempts were made to obtain the LEA endorsement, including what efforts the applicant undertook to accomplish these attempts."[42]

Furthermore, even when victims are cooperative, law enforcement officials are not obligated to return the favor. As discussed above, the determination of whether a victim has been sufficiently helpful is highly subjective. In certain cases, victims have cooperated with all requests. Yet law enforcement may still refuse to sign the Supplement B. These refusals can occur for a variety of reasons. Some refusals are based on misunderstandings of the role of the Supplement B, the definition of who is a victim of a severe form of human trafficking or even when a Supplement B can be signed. For example, in some cases law enforcement refuses to sign a Supplement B when there is no accompanying prosecution. Signing a Supplement B is not required even when victims are credible and cooperate with every request. Law enforcement may simply use their discretion and refuse to sign the form. Even when they choose to sign, law enforcement is under no requirement to supply a

---

[41] Hussein Sadruddin et al., *Human Trafficking in the United States: Expanding Victim Protection Beyond Prosecution Witness*, 16 STAN. L. & POL'Y REV. 379, 381–95 (2005) (internal citations omitted).

[42] Jayashri Srikantiah, *Perfect Victims and Real Survivors: The Iconic Victim in Domestic Human Trafficking Law*, 87 B.U. L. REV. 157, 176–77 (2007).

Supplement B form in a timely manner. Additionally, it is sometimes the case that a victim is unwilling to participate in the prosecution against their trafficker. As the article below, *Hidden Slaves: Forced Labor in the United States*, discusses, victims have a variety of reasons for not wishing to testify against their trafficker, ranging from fear of retaliation to a desire to put their trafficking experience behind them:

Yet for every victim who is willing to come forward and testify for prosecutors, there are many who are unable or unwilling to do so. As a result, the victims will not receive immigration relief or other benefits under the Trafficking Act. Jennifer Stanger, at [the Coalition to Abolish Slavery and Trafficking], estimates that only fifty percent of their clients wish to cooperate in the prosecution of their perpetrators. "Even though somebody has been beaten and abused," she says, "it may not be a priority for them to see . . . [the perpetrator] go to jail." Some survivors simply desire to return home and never see their traffickers again. Many advocates believe that immigration relief and permission to work should be granted to survivors automatically and not linked to cooperation with a prosecution.

Survivors of forced labor often fear pressing charges against their former captors because it could result in harm to themselves and their families. For example, after U.S. authorities arrested Lakireddy Bali Reddy in January 2000, journalists reported that many of the parents of Reddy's victims living in Velvadam, India were fearful of reprisals. In May 2000, a group of assailants attacked a long-time critic of Reddy and his family while they were asleep at their home in Velvadam and doused the residents with acid. Days later, the critic died from his injuries. A five-year-old victim was badly burned and the legs of the third victim, a woman, were also disfigured. Shortly after the Indian authorities launched an investigation into the attack, a key witness was killed. The motivation for the attack still remains unclear.

In July 2000, the United States immigration authorities took the unusual step of bringing some of the families of Reddy's victims to the United States for their protection. Yet in California, the Reddy victims were threatened. Soon after their liberation from their former captor, two men dressed as police officers — at least one of them carrying a gun — attempted to gain entry to the domestic violence shelter where two of Reddy's victims were housed. One of the women collapsed. Both women were then rushed to a local hospital for treatment. Authorities later moved them to a local Air Force base while service providers looked for suitable housing.

Even after conviction, survivors and their families may remain in danger, whether they return to their home countries or remain in the United States. Several of the perpetrators charged in the forced prostitution case escaped to Mexico, living in the same town as the victims and their families where they continued to threaten and harass their former captives. One witness testified: "They have even threatened to bring our younger sisters to the United States and force them to work in brothels as well." Similarly, in the case against R&A Harvesting, a witness stills feels that his life could be in danger. He believes there were more perpetrators involved than the three men arrested for the attack and that these men may harm him one day. "I still don't like to go out, like at night to the dances in town," he said. "I keep thinking that someone could be one of the Ramos guys looking for revenge. I live with that fear." Similarly, Khai, [a] Thai domestic worker, is desperate to have her son and daughter leave Thailand before her captor completes her sentence. "[My captor] is in prison now," she said. "After she is released, I believe something will happen because law enforcement is different in Thailand." Her former "employer" had once told Khai, perhaps as a warning, that a "hit man" could be hired in Thailand for $200–$300.

Vulnerability of family members abroad causes much anxiety and grief to forced labor victims in the United States. For victims, pursuing justice raises the stakes, and the threats of perpetrators — often powerful members of the communities in which they live and recruit — are quite credible. Several Indian workers who were trafficked for forced labor at John Pickle Company (JPC) reported that "Gulam" Pesh Imam, an executive with Al-Samit International, the company that had recruited them, had threatened their families. After the Indian workers began escaping the John Pickle Company factory, an Al-Samit agent reportedly phoned JPC to ask one of the Indian lead workers about the whereabouts of one of the escaped workers. The Al-Samit agent is alleged to have said that the police in India were looking for the escaped worker and that "[the worker's] brother had been taken by the police and beaten up." "If Gulam [Pesh Imam] knows I am coming [home], he will arrange to have someone meet me at the airport," one of the workers told the American court. "Gulam has shown that he is a violent man. . . . Many families in India have been threatened or contacted by Gulam or his agents. I have no doubt that if I were to return, my family and me would be in danger."

Despite these real dangers and the Trafficking Act's mandate to protect trafficking survivors, federal authorities have been unable to protect family members of survivors from retributions in their countries of origin. U.S. law enforcement has no authority to intervene directly when acts of retribution take place beyond its borders. While family members have the option of relocating to the United States through the T visa process, that process can take years and is not suited to addressing crisis situations. Emergency relocation is available but not routinely used. Unfortunately, help at the local level in the country of origin, where it could be most effective, is seldom an option. Corruption or indifference of local police and government authorities in the country of origin frequently leave family members and repatriated survivors with nowhere to turn for help. The influence of the perpetrator may hold sway over a survivor across international boundaries and across the span of years. Khai, the Thai woman forced to do domestic work, is painfully aware that her perpetrator's release date of 2006 is quickly approaching and that she only has a few years to arrange for family members to flee Thailand and seek safety in other countries. Thus, the inability to meet a global problem with a global response may leave victims of forced labor reluctant to step forward and thus jeopardize future arrests and prosecutions of perpetrators.

Police indifference and the victim's fear of retribution are compounded by the stature of traffickers in source countries. In at least five of the eight case studies researched for this report, the perpetrators held positions of great wealth and influence in home countries. The Reddy family in Velvadam, India, the Satia family in Cameroon, and the Cadena family in Veracruz, Mexico, are all very wealthy families who are well respected by economically and politically powerful sectors in their respective communities. Survivors reported that "Gulam" Pesh Imam, an executive of Al-Samit International, the recruitment company responsible for bringing the Indian men to work at John Pickle Company, was said to have connections to organized crime in India. Supawan Veerapool, who enslaved Khai, the Thai domestic worker, was the common law wife of Thailand's ambassador to Sweden and is thus politically connected at the highest levels of Thai government.[43]

A. Lack of Access to Legal Services

Historically, victims of human trafficking have not been provided with access to free legal services. And without access to an immigration lawyer, foreign national victims may not know they qualify for immigration relief. Moreover, applying for immigration relief as a trafficking victim without a lawyer is a daunting task; many victims will be unable to apply on their own even if they realize that they qualify for a visa.

But in 2006 the Department of Health and Human Services (HHS) began a new "per capita" system of distributing funds with a stated purpose "to more efficiently fund services to victims of human trafficking and to provide support for services to victims in any location within the United States."[44] This new regime reimburses government subcontractors for each trafficking victim who they aid. According to ORR, HHS's current system "streamlines support services in order to help victims of human trafficking gain timely access to shelter, legal assistance, job training and health care, enabling them to establish lives free of violence and exploitation."[45] These funds, then, may be available more readily to help trafficking victims obtain legal services.

---

[43] Free the Slaves & Human Rights Ctr., *Hidden Slaves: Forced Labor in the United States* 31–33 (2004), *available at* http://law.berkeley.edu/files/hiddenslaves_report.pdf (internal citations omitted).

[44] U.S. Conference of Catholic Bishops, *Reflections: HHS Service Mechanism for Foreign National Survivors of Human Trafficking* 3, *available at* http://www.usccb.org/upload/Reflections-HHS-Service-Mechanism-for-Foreign-National-Survivors-of-Human-Trafficking.pdf.

[45] Office of Refugee Resettlement, *Divisions — Anti-Trafficking in Persons* (Oct. 3, 2012), *available at* http://www.acf.hhs.gov/programs/orr/resource/divisions-anti-trafficking-in-persons.

B. Definitional Barriers

1. Are You a "Victim" if You Escape?

Under the TVPA a victim of human trafficking must be "in the United States on account of trafficking" or brought in for certain investigatory purposes.[46] This definition does not apply to individuals who were trafficked elsewhere and are now in the United States. There are also concerns that this provision might be used to deny individuals who were trafficked in the United States, escaped, but then remained in the United States for a period of time before contacting law enforcement.[47] As Professor Jayashri Srikantiah explains,

> Once a survivor escapes, she is expected to leave the United States. If she fails to leave, she must demonstrate why 'she did not have a clear chance to leave.' . . . To do so, she may provide information about 'circumstances attributable to the trafficking in persons situation, such as trauma, injury, lack of resources, or travel documents that have been seized by the traffickers. A survivor who is 'liberated' by law enforcement does not have to satisfy this requirement. . . . DHS regulations also go beyond the statute by preferring victims who await rescue from trafficking instead of escaping on their own. Unlike victims who are rescued by law enforcement, victims . . . , who escape their trafficker on their own, must meet a regulatory burden of demonstrating that they had no clear opportunity to have left the United States in the interim between escape and the moment they contacted law enforcement.[48]

2. Can an Individual Agree to be a Slave?

While the Palermo Protocol explicitly states that consent is irrelevant for the whether human trafficking has occurred,[49] there is no such explicit statement in the TVPA. As immigration scholar Jennifer Chacon points out, "It is an open question under the TVPA whether the consent of the individual to some element of the act of trafficking obviates the conclusion that the individual is a victim of a 'severe form of trafficking.'"[50]

---

[46] TVPA § 7105(e)(1)(C) (2006).

[47] *See* Supreme Court of the State of New York, *Lawyer's Manual on Human Trafficking: Pursuing Justice for Victims* (Jill Laurie Goodman & Dorchen A. Liedholdt eds. 2011), *available at* http://www.nycourts.gov/ip/womeninthecourts/LMHT.pdf

[48] Jayashri Srikantiah, *supra* note 42, at 176–77.

[49] United States Convention Against Transnational Organized Crime, Protocol to Suppress and Punish Trafficking in Persons, Especially Woman and Children art. 3(a), *opened for signature* Dec. 15, 2000, T.I.A.S. No. 13127, 2225 U.N.T.S. 209.

[50] Jennifer M. Chacn, *Misery and Myopia: Understanding the Failures of U.S. Efforts to Stop Human Trafficking*, 74 Fordham L. Rev. 2977, 2984 (2006). When drafting the TVPA the legislators on the conference committee weighed in on this issue by stating that "an applicant who voluntarily agrees to be smuggled into the United States in exchange for working to pay off the smuggling fee is not eligible for the 'T' visa, unless the applicant becomes a victim of a severe form of trafficking in persons . . . ." H.R. Rep. No. 106-939, at 95 (2000).

3. Does Human Trafficking Require Transportation?

Victims may not be categorized as victims if decision makers labor under common misconceptions about human trafficking. Many people believe that trafficking requires transportation — that it only happens to foreign nationals and it only happens to women and children. But in fact "Human trafficking does not require the crossing of an international border — it does not even require the transportation of victims from one locale to another. Victims of severe forms of trafficking are not all illegal aliens; they may, in fact, be U.S. citizens, legal residents, or visitors. Victims do not have to be women or children — they may also be adult males."[51]

V. BENEFITS FOR TRAFFICKING VICTIMS AND DERIVATIVES

The TVPA made a "[foreign national] who is a victim of a severe form of trafficking in persons" eligible for the same federal and state benefits received by refugees.[52] These benefits include, cash assistance, food stamps, health coverage, language training classes, and job training.[53] Adult victims must be certified by the Department of Health and Human Services (HHS) to be eligible for benefits. This certification occurs when the T Visa application is declared to be bona fide or when the adult is granted Continued Presence. Once the adult receives the certification letter from HHS, he or she may receive benefits for at least six months. These benefits can include cash, food stamps, housing assistance, job training, English language training, and medical services.[54]

Children who are foreign nationals and victims of a severe form of human trafficking do not have to be certified in order to receive benefits. They must, however, have an Eligibility Letter or Interim Assistance Letter issued by the Office of Refugee Resettlement (ORR).[55] To apply for benefits for a child, the child or someone on the child's behalf must submit a short form, which is available online, or talk with a Child Protection Specialist at the Office of Refugee Resettlement. For eligibility determination to be made, basic biographical information about the child must be provided as well as a narrative that describes the indicators of trafficking. This information may be submitted by anyone on behalf of a child and, unlike the certification process for adults, no law enforcement involvement is required. Children are eligible for interim assistance while their eligibility determination is pending if they have submitted "credible" information that they are a victim of a severe form of human trafficking. This interim assistance may last up to 90 days and

---

[51] U.S. Dep't of State, *Fact Sheet: Distinctions Between Human Smuggling and Human Trafficking 2006* (Jan. 1, 2006), *available at* www.state.gov/m/ds/hstcenter/90434.htm.

[52] TVPA, 22 U.S.C. § 7105 (2006).

[53] TVPA § 7105(b)(1)(E)(i)(II)(bb).

[54] *See* Office of Refugee Resettlement, *Fact Sheet: Victim Assistance (English)* (Aug. 7, 2012), *available at* http://www.acf.hhs.gov/programs/orr/resource/fact-sheet-victim-assistance-english.

[55] *See* Office of Refugee Resettlement, *Fact Sheet: Child Victims of Human Trafficking* (Aug. 7, 2012), *available at* http://www.acf.hhs.gov/programs/orr/resource/fact-sheet-child-victims-of-human-trafficking.

V. BENEFITS FOR TRAFFICKING VICTIMS AND DERIVATIVES

provides the same benefits and services available to refugees.[56]

Foreign national children who are unaccompanied[57] victims of human trafficking will be placed in either the Unaccompanied Refugee Minor Program (URM) or the Division of Unaccompanied Children's Services Program (DUCS). When a determination is made that a child is unaccompanied, he or she is usually referred to the URM program.[58] The URM was developed in 1979 and currently provides grants to 15 states. Those states, in turn, contract with private agencies that deliver services to eligible children with no parents or guardians. To date, about 13,000 unaccompanied foreign national children, some of whom are victims of trafficking, have been enrolled in the URM program.[59] A child is eligible for the URM if they have an Eligibility Letter from ORR. Again, this means that they have been certified as a victim of a severe form of human trafficking.[60] Once they are enrolled in the program, the URM will work to establish legal guardianship for the unaccompanied child. Usually this means placing the child in a foster home while efforts are made to reunify the child with relatives.[61] Children enrolled in the URM are eligible to receive both services that are generally available to foster children as well as specialized services geared towards helping them adjust to life in the United States. These services include things like housing allowances, food, clothing, medical services (including Medicaid), substance abuse, and mental health services.[62]

Children who have an Interim Assistance Letter and are awaiting a determination of their status may be eligible for the DUCS program.[63] DUCS was created in March 2003 to provide a safe environment for children waiting for reunification with family members or removal to the child's home country. DUCS also provides a wide variety of services for children enrolled in the program, such as classroom education, health care, mental health services, vocational training, and access to legal services. DUCS children are usually placed in shelters and group homes. Long-term foster care is also available for children who have special needs or who have no viable sponsor to reunite with. However, according to a 2009 study on the services provided to trafficking victims, "what typically occurs is that DUCS will screen children within its custody for trafficking, and those identified as trafficking

---

[56] TVPA § 7105(b)(1)(A), (F).

[57] An unaccompanied foreign national child is "a person under 18, who has no lawful immigration status in the United States; has not attained 18 years of age; and with respect to whom — there is no parent or legal guardian in the United States; or no parent or legal guardian in the United States is available to provide care and physical custody." 6 U.S.C. § 279(g) (2008).

[58] See Heather J. Clawson et al., U.S. Dep't of Health and Human Services, *Study of HHS Programs Serving Human Trafficking Victims: Final Report* (2009), *available at* http://aspe.hhs.gov/hsp/07/humantrafficking/final/index.shtml.

[59] *See* Elaine M. Kelley, Office of Refugee Resettlement, *ORR Programs for Vulnerable and Unaccompanied Children* (2009), *available at* http://icpc.aphsa.org/home/Doc/KelleyICPCReviewingPractices.pdf.

[60] *See Unaccompanied Refugee Minors*, Catholic Charities, *available at* http://www.catholiccharities.org/en/cms/74/ (last visited July 13, 2013).

[61] Clawson et al., *supra* note 58.

[62] See Office of Refugee Resettlement, *Fact Sheet: Child Victims of Human Trafficking* (Aug. 8, 2012), *available at* http://www.acf.hhs.gov/trafficking/about/child_victims.htm.

[63] *See Unaccompanied Refugee Minors, supra* note 60.

victims will receive an eligibility letter and be transferred to a URM program for long-term placement."[64] Approximately 8,000 children receive care in the DUCS program annually, with about 1,500 in care at any one time.[65]

Yet DUCS is far from a perfect program and has been highly criticized. A report on unaccompanied children in immigration custody found that "DUCS continues in some cases to rely on an institutional model of care that lacks appropriate monitoring and oversight and that fails to protect confidentiality or provide adequate services to all children consistent with child welfare principles"[66]; that "some children lack access to adequate medical, mental health care and legal services"[67]; and that "[b]oth care and safety are compromised by reliance on large facilities, as it is difficult for staff to give children the individualized attention necessary given their high level of trauma and vulnerability."[68]

Family members who are brought in as derivatives also qualify for benefits to the same extent as refugees. As ORR explains, "holders of a T-2, T-3, T-4 or T-5 visa (collectively referred to as 'Derivative T Visas') are eligible for federally funded or administered benefits and services (e.g., refugee cash and medical assistance, TANF, Medicaid and food stamps) provided they meet other program criteria (e.g., age or income levels)."[69]

VI. OTHER FORMS OF IMMIGRATION RELIEF

If a victim of human trafficking does not qualify for a T Visa, he or she may still qualify for other forms of immigration relief. The forms of immigration relief described below are not meant to be an exhaustive list but rather a brief introduction to other forms of relief a victim of trafficking might be eligible for. Family based immigration relief, such as marriage to a U.S. citizen, is not discussed.

A. U Visa

In addition to the T Visa the TVPA created another nonimmigrant visa category, the U Visa. A U Visa is for foreign national victims of certain serious crimes. The following criteria must be met to qualify for a U Visa:

> (I) the [foreign national] has suffered substantial physical or mental abuse as a result of having been a victim of criminal activity described in

---

[64] *See* Clawson et. al., *supra* note 58.

[65] Office of Refugee Resettlement, *Unaccompanied Children's Services* (Aug. 9, 2012), *available at* http://www.acf.hhs.gov/programs/orr/programs/unaccompanied_alien_children.htm.

[66] Women's Refugee Comm', *Halfway Home: Unaccompanied Children in Immigration Custody* 2 (2009).

[67] *Id.* at 14.

[68] *Id.* at 15.

[69] Office of Refugee Resettlement, *State Letter #04-12: The Trafficking Victims Protection Reauthorization Act of 2003 — Eligibility for Federally Funded or Administered Benefits and Services to the Same Extent as Refugees Extended to Certain Family Members of Victims of a Severe Form of Trafficking in Persons* (June 18, 2004) *available at* http://www.acf.hhs.gov/programs/orr/resource/state-letter-04-12.

clause (iii);

(II) the [foreign national] (or in the case of [a] [foreign national] child under the age of 16, the parent, guardian, or next friend of the [foreign national]) possesses information concerning criminal activity described in clause (iii);

(III) the [foreign national] (or in the case of [a] [foreign national] child under the age of 16, the parent, guardian, or next friend of the [foreign national]), has been helpful, is being helpful, or is likely to be helpful to a Federal, State, or local law enforcement official, to a Federal, State, or local prosecutor, to a Federal or State judge, to the Service, or to other Federal, State, or local authorities investigating or prosecuting criminal activity described in clause (iii); and

(IV) the criminal activity described in clause (iii) violated the laws of the United States or occurred in the United States (including in Indian country and military installations) or the territories and possessions of the United States;[70]

The Immigration and Nationality Act (INA) explicitly lists trafficking, prostitution, involuntary servitude, and the slave trade as qualifying crimes for a U Visa.[71] Applicants must be admissible to the United States and have a valid, unexpired passport.[72] The U Visa is a four-year nonimmigrant visa. Employment authorization is automatically granted when a U Visa is approved.[73]

To apply for a U Visa the I-918 form must be completed and submitted to the Vermont Service Center. A U Visa application must contain a I-918 Supplement B completed by a law enforcement officer. The Supplement B provides evidence of the victim's helpfulness in the investigation or prosecution of the criminal activity. The I-918 Supplement B may be signed by federal, state, or local law enforcement officials, judges, prosecutors, or "other authority that has the responsibility for the investigation or prosecution of a qualifying crime or criminal activity."[74] According to DHS, "[t]his includes agencies with criminal investigative jurisdiction in their respective areas of expertise, including but not limited to child and adult protective services, the Equal Employment Opportunity Commission, and Federal and State Departments of Labor."[75] Within each agency authorized to sign a I-918 Supplement B, only the head of the agency or a person in a supervisory role that has been specifically designated by the head of the agency may sign the Supplement B.[76] A

---

[70] INA, 8 U.S.C. § 1101(a)(15)(U) (2006).

[71] *Id.* § 1101(a)(15)(U)(iii).

[72] 8 C.F.R. § 214.1(a)(2) (2013); *see* INA § 1182 (inadmissibility grounds).

[73] 8 C.F.R. § 214.14(c)(7) (2013).

[74] *See* U.S. Dep't of Homeland Security, *U Visa Law Enforcement Certification Resource Guide: For Federal, State, Local, Tribal and Territorial Law Enforcement*, *available at* http://www.dhs.gov/xlibrary/assets/dhs_u_visa_certification_guide.pdf.

[75] *Id.*

[76] 8 C.F.R. § 214.14(a)(3) (2013).

U Visa may only be supported by a Supplement B that has been signed within the previous six months.[77]

An individual eligible for a U Visa may apply for derivative status for certain immediate family members. Individuals under 21 years of age may apply for their spouse, parents, children, and their unmarried siblings under the age of 18.[78] The siblings must be under the age of 18 at the time of the application for principal applicant's U Visa. Individuals 21 years of age or older may apply for visas for their spouse and children.

The number of U Visas that may be issued is statutorily limited to 10,000 per year.[79] But this cap does not apply to derivatives, meaning qualifying family members of the U Visa applicant. Instead it only applies to the principal U Visa applicant. On December 11, 2013, USCIS announced that the U Visa cap had been reached for fiscal year 2014, this announcement marked the fifth consecutive year in which all 10,000 available visas were issue.[80] If an eligible applicant is not granted a U Visa solely because of the cap, the applicant will be placed on a waiting list. An applicant's position on the waiting list is determined by the date of the filing of the U Visa petition; the oldest petitions receive the highest priority. U Visa petitioners and their derivatives on the waiting list will be granted deferred action or parole by USCIS. Employment authorizations may also be granted to such individuals at USCIS's discretion.[81]

U Visa holders may apply for legal permanent residence status. An eligible U nonimmigrant may also apply for legal permanent residence for his or her derivative family members.[82]

B. Asylum

The availability of a T Visa reduces the number of trafficking-based asylum claims in the United States. Still, individuals who are at risk of being persecuted if they return to their country of origin and who are in the United States may apply for asylum. Human trafficking can constitute persecution.

In the United States individuals who apply for asylum and are found eligible are granted asylee status. While the terms "asylee" and "refugee" are often used interchangeably, the DOJ distinguishes the two:

> The major difference between asylum and refugee applicants is that those seeking refugee status apply from outside the United States.

---

[77] 8 C.F.R. § 214.14(c)(2)(i) (2013).

[78] 8 C.F.R. § 214.11(a), (o) (2013).

[79] 8 C.F.R. § 214.14(d)(1) (2013).

[80] *See* U.S. Citizenship & Immigration Services, *USCIS Approves 10,000 U Visas for 5th Straight Fiscal Year* (Dec. 11, 2013), *available at* http://www.uscis.gov/news/alerts/uscis-approves-10000-u-visas-5th-straight-fiscal-year.

[81] 8 C.F.R. § 214.14(d)(2) (2013).

[82] 8 C.F.R. § 245.24(g) (2013).

Asylum-seekers must be in the United States or applying for admission at a port of entry.[83]

However, despite these definitional differences, asylee and refugee status are adjudicated under the same standard. To be granted asylee status, the petition must establish that the individual meets the definition of refugee under the The Refugee Act of 1980.[84] The act defines a refuge as a person

> who is outside any country of such person's nationality or, in the case of a person having no nationality, is outside any country in which such person last habitually resided, and who is unable or unwilling to return to and is unable or unwilling to avail himself or herself of the protection of that country because of persecution or a well-founded fear of persecution on account of race, religion, nationality, membership in a particular social group, or political opinion.[85]

Trafficking victims, or individuals at risk of being trafficked if forced to return to their countries of origin, may be eligible to apply for asylum in the United States under this definition. Victims must demonstrate that they were persecuted on account of one of the protected grounds: race, religion, nationality, particular social group, or political opinion, and that their home country is unable to protect them.

Although many trafficking victims will bring asylum claims under the "particular social group" prong of the refugee definition, other prongs may also apply. "Persecution under the refugee definition in 8 U.S.C.S. § 1101(a)(42)(A) does not encompass purely private actions. In order to demonstrate persecution or a well-founded fear of persecution, the petitioners must demonstrate that the threatening conduct is by the government, or that it is by private persons whom the government is unwilling or unable to control."[86]

Unlike victims seeking T and U Visas, victims seeking asylum do not need to submit any documents from law enforcement as part of their asylum claim. However, victims seeking asylum must file for asylum within one year of their arrival into the United States, unless they meet one of two exceptions: the "changed circumstances" exception or the "extraordinary circumstances" exception.[87] That is, asylum applications filed after the one year deadline may be considered if there are "changed circumstances" which materially affect the asylum seeker's eligibility to apply or if there are "extraordinary circumstances" relating to the delay in filing the petition.[88] The "changed circumstances" exception should apply if the trafficking victim's asylum claim is a direct result of their trafficking in the United States — for example, if a victim of sex trafficking is now at risk of persecution should he or she

---

[83] *See* U.S. Dep't of Justice, *News Release: Asylum Protection in the United States* (Apr. 28, 2005), *available at* http://www.justice.gov/eoir/press/05/AsylumProtectionFactsheetQAApr05.htm.

[84] *See Tapiero de Orejuela v. Gonzales*, 423 F.3d 666, 672 (7th Cir. 2005); *Galina v. INS.*, 213 F.3d 955, 958 (7th Cir. 2000).

[85] 8 U.S.C. § 1101(a)(42) (2012).

[86] *See Gonzales*, 423 F.3d at 672; *Galina*, 213 F.3d at 958.

[87] INA, 8 U.S.C. § 1158(a)(2)(B).

[88] INA § 1158(a)(2)(D).

be returned home — while the "extraordinary circumstance" exception should apply if the asylum seeker has been in the United States for more than one year since his or her arrival but has been a victim of trafficking during that time period. In 2005, a Ukrainian male victim of labor trafficking by an international trafficking ring was granted asylum and the one-year bar was excused. The bar was excused because the victim had been held against his will and thus met the extraordinary circumstances exception.[89]

C. Violence Against Women Act

Another form of immigration relief that might be available to victims of human trafficking is created by the Violence Against Women Act (VAWA). The VAWA was passed in 1994 and reauthorized in 2000, 2005, and 2013.[90] The act was designed to help battered immigrants who were being denied immigration benefits by abusive spouses and parents. The Purposes section of the 2000 reauthorization describes the legislative purposes behind the act, noting that the immigration provisions were

> [g]enerally designed . . . to prevent immigration law from being used by an abusive citizen or lawful permanent resident spouse as a tool to prevent an abused immigrant spouse from reporting abuse or leaving the abusive relationship. This could happen because generally speaking, U.S. immigration law gives citizens and lawful permanent residents the right to petition for their spouses to be granted a permanent resident visa, which is the necessary prerequisite for immigrating to the United States. In the vast majority of cases, granting the right to seek the visa to the citizen or lawful permanent resident spouse makes sense, since the purpose of family immigration visas is to allow U.S. citizens or lawful permanent residents to live here with their spouses and children. But in the unusual case of the abusive relationship, an abusive citizen or lawful permanent resident can use control over his or her spouse's visa as a means to blackmail and control the spouse. The abusive spouse would do this by withholding a promised visa petition and then threatening to turn the abused spouse in to the immigration authorities if the abused spouse sought to leave the abuser or report the abuse.

VAWA 1994 changed this by allowing immigrants who demonstrate that they have been battered or subjected to extreme cruelty by their U.S. citizen or lawful permanent resident spouses to file their own petitions for visas without the cooperation of their abusive spouse. VAWA 1994 also allowed abused spouses placed in removal proceedings to seek 'cancellation of removal,' a form of discretionary relief from removal available to individuals in unlawful immigration status with strong equities, after three years rather than the seven ordinarily required. Finally, VAWA 1994

---

[89] Center for Gender & Refugee Studies, http://cgrs.uchastings.edu/law/detail.php (last visited Oct. 12, 2012).

[90] *See* Nat'l Domestic Violence Hotline, *Violence Against Women Act (VAWA)*, *available at* http://www.thehotline.org/get-educated/violence-against-women-act-vawa/ (last visited Oct. 12, 2012).

granted similar rights to minor children abused by their citizen or lawful permanent resident parent, whose immigration status, like that of the abused spouse, would otherwise be dependent on the abusive parent.[91]

The passage of VAWA, then, created two new avenues of relief for victims of domestic violence. Usually, in order to obtain a visa, a spouse or parent with citizenship or legal permanent resident (LPR) status would have to petition for their immediate relative. In cases of abuse, the citizen or LPR often refused to file the petition, preventing their spouse or child from obtaining any legal immigration status in the United States. Without any legal status, the victim of abuse could more easily be kept dependent on their abuser.[92] After the passage of VAWA, however, an abused spouse or child who would otherwise be eligible for a visa can now petition for that visa without the aid of their abusive relative. This kind of relief is called a "VAWA self-petition." To be eligible for relief under VAWA, self-petitioners must prove:

1. That they have a qualifying relationship to the abuser. A self-petitioning spouse must show that they had a marital relationship with the citizen or LPR.[93] There are exceptions to this requirement in cases of bigamy, death or divorce.[94] Similarly, the self-petitioning child must show that they are the natural child, step-child, or adopted child of the citizen or LPR.[95]

2. That the abusive spouse or parent is a U.S. Citizen or Lawful Permanent Resident.[96] There is an exception to this requirement if the abuser lost or renounced his status within the past two years for a reason related to the abuse.[97]

3. They reside in the United States. This requirement will be waived if the abusive spouse or parent is an employee of the U.S. government, member of the U.S. armed forces, or committed the battery or extreme cruelty in the United States.[98]

4. That they resided with the abuser at some point.[99]

5. That there was battery or extreme cruelty.[100]

---

[91] Violence Against Women Act of 2000, Title V, Pub. L. No. 106-386, 114 Stat. 1464, *available at* http://www.acadv.org/VAWAbillsummary.html.

[92] *See* Moira Fisher Preda & Cecilia Olavarria, LEGAL MOMENTUM, *Preparing the VAWA Self-petition and Applying for Residence*, *available at* http://www.legalmomentum.org/assets/pdfs/www3_3_preparing_the_vawa_self-petition_and_applying_for.pdf (last visited Oct. 10, 2012).

[93] INA § 1154(a)(1)(A)(iii)(II)(aa)(AA), (B)(ii)(II)(aa)(AA).

[94] INA § 1154(a)(1)(A)(iii)(II)(aa)(BB), (A)(iii)(II)(aa)(CC), (B)(ii)(II)(aa)(BB), (B)(ii)(II)(aa)(CC).

[95] INA § 1154(a)(1)(A)(iv), (B)(iii)

[96] INA § 1154(a)(1)(A)(iii), (A)(iv), (B)(ii), (B)(iii).

[97] INA § 1154(a)(1)(A)(iii)(II)(aa)(CC)(bbb), (A)(iv), (B)(ii)(II)(aa)(CC)(aaa), (B)(iii).

[98] INA § 1154(a)(1)(A)(v), (B)(iv).

[99] INA § 1154(a)(1)(A)(iii)(II)(dd), (A)(iv), (B)(ii)(II)(dd), (B)(iii).

[100] INA § 1154(a)(1)(A)(iii)(I)(bb), (A)(iv), (B)(ii)(I)(bb), (B)(iii).

6. That they have good moral character.[101]

7. In the case of a self-petitioner who was married to the LPR or citizen: that the marriage was in good faith.[102] (Obviously, a self-petitioner who is the child of an LPR or citizen does not need to meet this requirement.[103])

A second form of relief created by the VAWA is "VAWA cancellation of removal." Like a VAWA self-petition, it allows a victim of abuse who otherwise would have been able to obtain a visa to obtain legal status, even if the abusive spouse or parent refuses to file a petition on their behalf. A VAWA self-petition is filed before the immigrant is placed into removal proceedings; however, cancellation of removal is only available after removal proceedings have been initiated.[104] The requirements to be eligible for cancellation or removal are similar to the requirements for a self-petition. Specifically, an immigration judge may grant cancellation of removal if applicants can prove:

1. That they have qualifying relationship to a U.S. Citizen or LPR abuser.[105]

2. That they have continuously resided in the U.S. for the three years immediately prior to filing for cancellation of removal.[106] Absences from the U.S. that are related to the domestic abuse will not break continuity of presence.

3. Battery or extreme cruelty at the hands of a U.S. citizen or LPR who is a parent or spouse.[107]

4. That they have good moral character.[108]

5. That they, their children, or their parents would suffer "extreme hardship" if the applicant was deported.[109] A finding of extreme hardship is made on a case-by-case basis.[110]

USCIS has issued memorandum to their field officers that victims of human trafficking may be eligible for relief under VAWA.[111] This is in line with language in

---

[101] INA § 1154(a)(1)(A)(iii)(II)(bb), (A)(iv), (B)(ii)(II)(bb), (B)(iii).

[102] INA § 1154(a)(1)(A)(iii)(I)(aa), (B)(ii)(I)(aa).

[103] INA § 1154(a)(1)(A)(vi).

[104] *See* Cecilia Olavarria & Moira Fisher Preda, Legal Momentum, *VAWA Cancellation of Removal*, available at http://www.legalmomentum.org/assets/pdfs/www3_4_vawa_cancellation_of_removal.pdf.

[105] INA § 1229b(b)(2)(A)(i).

[106] INA § 1229b(b)(2)(A)(ii).

[107] INA § 1229b(b)(2)(A)(i)

[108] INA § 1229(b)(2)(A)(iii).

[109] INA § 1229b(b)(2)(A)(v).

[110] *See Matter of Ige*, 20 I. & N. Dec. 880, 882 (BIA 1994); *Matter of Chumpitazi*, 16 I. & N. Dec. 629 (BIA 1978); *Matter of Kim*, 15 I. & N. Dec. 88 (BIA 1974); *Matter of Sangster*, 11 I. & N. Dec. 309 (BIA 1965); Cecilia Olavarria & Moira Fisher Preda, *supra* note 104.

[111] *See* U.S. Citizenship & Immigration Services, *Memorandum For: Field Office Directors and Special Agents in Charge* (Jan. 2, 2007), available at http://www.legalmomentum.org/assets/pdfs/ice_-_memo_2007__w-52_.pdf.

8 C.F.R. § 204.2(c)(1)(vi) (2004), which defines "battery and extreme cruelty" as

> Being the victim of any act of a threatened act of violence, including any forceful detention, which results or threatens to result in physical or mental injury. Psychological or sexual abuse or exploitation, including rape, molestation incest (if the victim is a minor) or *forced prostitution* shall be considered acts of violence. Other abusive actions may also be acts of violence under this rule. Acts or threatened acts that, in and of themselves, may not initially appear violent may be part of an overall pattern of violence. (emphasis added)

It seems that if trafficking victims can satisfy the other criteria for VAWA eligibility, they will most likely be found to be subject to "battery and extreme cruelty."

But as with other forms of relief, victims may have to overcome hurdles to obtain relief under VAWA. For example, VAWA is only available to victims who can demonstrate that they have good moral character.[112]

D. Special Immigrant Juvenile Status

Special Immigrant Juvenile Status (SIJS) was established to assist foreign national children in the United States who have been abused, abandoned, or neglected. SIJS was created in 1990 and was significantly expanded in 2008 by the reauthorization of the TVPA.[113] SIJS allows children who are unable to be reunited with their parents to obtain legal permanent residence so that they can live and work permanently in the United States.[114] This status could be used by minor victims of human trafficking who are separated from their parents. Yet unlike some forms of immigration relief discussed above, children who are granted SIJS may not petition for derivatives. And because SIJS focuses on helping abused children who cannot be reunited with their parents, children with SIJS may never petition for legal permanent residence for their parents. Furthermore, they must wait until they are citizens to petition on behalf of any siblings.[115] An application for SIJS requires the filing of an I-360 form ("Petition for Amerasian, Widow(er), or Special Immigrant").

To be eligible for SIJS, the state court that determines child custody cases must make a series of findings about the child's legal status. This state court order is then given to USCIS to be used in determining the child's immigration status.[116]

---

[112] INA § 1154(a)(II)(bb).

[113] Lisa Mendel-Hirsa, Empire Justice Ctr, *Understanding Special Immigrant Juvenile Status* (Jan. 16, 2010), *available at* http://www.empirejustice.org/issue-areas/immigrant-rights/access-to-status/understanding-special.html?print=t.

[114] *See* U.S. Citizenship & Immigration Services, *Special Immigrant Juvenile (SIJ) Status*, http://www.uscis.gov/portal/site/uscis/menuitem.eb1d4c2a3e5b9ac89243c6a7543f6d1a/?vgnextoid=3d8008d1c67e0310VgnVCM100000082ca60aRCRD&vgnextchannel=3d8008d1c67e0310VgnVCM100000082ca60aRCRD (last updated Sept. 6, 2011).

[115] *Id.*

[116] *See* U.S. Citizenship & Immigration Services, *Eligibility for SIJ*, http://www.uscis.gov/portal/site/uscis/menuitem.eb1d4c2a3e5b9ac89243c6a7543f6d1a/?vgnextoid=

That state court must:
1. Declare that the child is a dependent of the court OR legally place the child with a state agency, private agency, or private person.
2. Declare that it is not in the child's best interests to return to his home country (or, in some cases, that it is not in the child's best interests to return to the country he last lived in).
3. Declare that the child can't be reunited with a parent because of abuse, abandonment, neglect, or similar reason under state law.[117]

Once these findings have been made, the child still must additionally satisfy the following criteria in order to be granted SIJS:[118]
1. The applicant must be under the age of 21 on the day the I-360 petition is filed.
2. The state court order mentioned above must be in effect on the day the I-360 is filed AND on the day that USCIS makes a decision on the application. There is an exception to this requirement if the child "ages out" of the state court's jurisdiction through no fault of their own.
3. The applicant can't be married when they apply OR when the status is granted.
4. The applicant must be in the United States at the time the I-360 is filed.
5. The applicant must also show that they are eligible for legal permanent residency. Generally this means that the child must be admissible or have obtained a waiver for any inadmissibility.[119]

E. S Visa

Human trafficking victims who witnessed a crime may also be eligible for an S Visa. The visa is colloquially called the "snitch visa" because it allows witnesses to maintain a valid immigration status in the United States if they agree to help law enforcement in the investigation and prosecution of a crime.[120] As USCIS officials have commented, S Visas are "a powerful law enforcement tool because they allow investigators and prosecutors to work closely with foreign national witnesses and informants who provide continued cooperation in investigations and can supply

---

28f308d1c67e0310VgnVCM100000082ca60aRCRD&vgnextchannel=
28f308d1c67e0310VgnVCM100000082ca60aRCRD (last updated July 12, 2011).

[117] INA § 1101(a)(27)(J).

[118] 8 C.F.R. § 204.11(c) (2013).

[119] *See* U.S. Citizenship & Immigration Services, *Green Card Based on SIJ Status*, http://www.uscis.gov/portal/site/uscis/menuitem.eb1d4c2a3e5b9ac89243c6a7543f6d1a/?vgnextoid=b60508d1c67e0310VgnVCM100000082ca60aRCRD&vgnextchannel=
b60508d1c67e0310VgnVCM100000082ca60aRCRD (last updated July 12, 2011).

[120] *See* U.S. Citizenship & Immigration Services, *Green Card for an Informant (S Nonimmigrant)*, http://www.uscis.gov/portal/site/uscis/menuitem.eb1d4c2a3e5b9ac89243c6a7543f6d1a/?vgnextchannel=
af2b3a4107083210VgnVCM100000082ca60aRCRD&vgnextoid=
af2b3a4107083210VgnVCM100000082ca60aRCRD (last updated Sept. 3, 2009).

valuable information on criminal organizations and terrorist activities."[121] While this visa is not specific to victims of trafficking, advocates have recognized that "it may be an option for a victim of trafficking who for some reason cannot meet all the required elements for a T Visa."[122]

S nonimmigrant status[123] was first passed into law as part of the Violent Crime Control Act of 1994. It was largely seen as a response to the 1993 bombing of the World Trade Center in New York City.[124] The provision was originally set to expire, but after the terrorist attacks on September 11, 2001, Congress passed legislation that permanently incorporated the S Visa into the Immigration and Nationality Act.[125]

Because S nonimmigrant status was created with an eye towards prosecution, potential nonimmigrants are not permitted to self-petition for an S Visa. Instead, a law enforcement official must submit the S Visa application on behalf of the witness or a qualifying family member.[126] Under INA § 101(a)(15)(S) an individual may be eligible for one of three sub-categories of S visa:[127]

- S-5 visas are granted to an individual who "possesses critical, reliable information concerning a substantial criminal matter, is willing to supply such information to a federal or state law enforcement agency, and whose presence is essential to the success of an authorized criminal investigation or prosecution of an individual involved in the criminal organization or enterprise." A maximum of 200 S-5 Visas may be granted each fiscal year.

- S-6 Visas are granted to an individual who has "critical, reliable information concerning a terrorist organization, enterprise or operation, is willing to supply such information to a federal law enforcement agency, has been placed in danger or is in danger as a result of providing such information and is eligible to receive a reward under section 36(a) of the State Department Basic Authorities Act of 1956, 22 U.S.C. § 2708(a)." No more than 50 S-6 Visas may be granted in a given fiscal year.

- S-7 Visas may be granted to qualified dependents. This means derivative spouses, children or parents or S-5 or S-6 witnesses.

---

[121] See U.S. Citizenship & Immigration Services, *Protecting the Homeland: Tool Kit for Prosecutors* (Apr. 2011), *available at* http://www.ice.gov/doclib/about/offices/osltc/pdf/tool-kit-for-prosecutors.pdf [hereinafter Protecting the Homeland].

[122] See U.S. Dep't of Justice, *North Carolina Human Trafficking Taskforce* 58 (2007), *available at* http://humantrafficking.unc.edu/files/2011/03/NCHumanTraffickingTaskForceManual.pdf

[123] INA § 1101(a)(15)(S) (2006).

[124] Karma Ester, *Immigration: S Visas for Criminal and Terrorist Informants* (2005), *available at* http://www.fas.org/sgp/crs/terror/RS21043.pdf.

[125] *Id.*

[126] See *Protecting the Homeland*, *supra* note 121.

[127] *See id.*; INA § 1101(a)(15)(S).

All three types of S Visa expire three years after they are approved.[128] S visas cannot be extended,[129] but the law enforcement agency that originally sponsored the S visa can file an application for adjustment of status to legal permanent resident on behalf of the nonimmigrant.[130]

NOTES AND QUESTIONS

1. Do you think T Visas for victims of trafficking should have a numerical limit? What are the arguments in favor of a ceiling (such as the current limit of 5,000) and what are the arguments against?

2. What are the advantages and disadvantages of law enforcement's current role in whether adult victims of trafficking receive a T Visa? Do you think victims of human trafficking should be able to obtain temporary residency in the United States without relying on the discretion of a law enforcement official?

3. What do you think should constitute satisfactory cooperation with law enforcement to fulfill the "complied with any reasonable request for assistance" requirement to obtain a T Visa?

4. As discussed above, the TVPA does not include language making "consent" clearly irrelevant (as required by the Palermo Protocol for national laws). Are there situations in which you think it is possible to consent if the elements of a human trafficking crime exist?

---

[128] *Id.*

[129] *Id.*

[130] *See* U.S. Citizenship & Immigration Services, *Green Card for an Informant (S Nonimmigrant)*, available at http://www.uscis.gov/portal/site/uscis/menuitem.eb1d4c2a3e5b9ac89243c6a7543f6d1a/?vgnextchannel=af2b3a4107083210VgnVCM100000082ca60aRCRD&vgnextoid=af2b3a4107083210VgnVCM100000082ca60aRCRD (last updated Sept. 3, 2009).

Chapter 13

THEORETICAL AND DEFINITIONAL CHALLENGES

A number of theoretical and definitional challenges have emerged throughout the development of human trafficking-related legislation. Inspired by a range of morals and values, supported to varying degrees by empirical evidence, anti-trafficking laws and subsequent legal reforms have raised debates over, among other things, the definition of human trafficking, the scope of its beneficiaries, and the relevance of consent. Although domestic and international anti-trafficking policies have been enacted with wide support, disagreement over these issues persists.

This chapter sheds light on the background and substance of some of the most pressing theoretical and definitional difficulties that exist in human trafficking policy today. Each of the three parts included in this chapter address aspects of human trafficking doctrine that have raised conceptual challenges. Part I of this chapter examines the debate over the relationship between prostitution and sex trafficking. It highlights the range of positions within this debate and discusses some of the anti-trafficking policy implications that have followed. Part II departs from this debate to share alternative approaches to anti-trafficking policy that focus on labor, including a perspective that examines the sometimes blurred distinction between sex trafficking and labor trafficking. Part III discusses the difficult line-drawing problems between consent and coercion that have emerged in the implementation and interpretation of human trafficking laws.

There is no single answer to these issues and for each issue there is a spectrum of perspectives. Discussing all the possible viewpoints within each of these issues is beyond the scope of this book. Instead, the casebook authors have attempted to give readers a sense of the breadth of each issue in hopes that they will recognize that human trafficking is an incredibly complex and changing phenomenon, which has understandably elicited a wide range of perspectives.

I. SEX TRAFFICKING AND PROSTITUTION

A significant tension within the anti-trafficking movement relates to the debate over the role of prostitution in anti-trafficking policy. The definitions of human trafficking in both the Palermo Protocol and the TVPA acknowledge that the various purposes of trafficking in persons include exploitation specific to the commercial sex industry as well as many forms of forced labor in other industries, such as agricultural work, domestic servitude, sweatshop work, and begging. Yet heated discussion among scholars and activists has persisted over the place of prostitution in trafficking. While this debate often garners significant attention, it is important to note that the debate focuses only on a subset of the human trafficking definition.

Moreover, although a range of viewpoints exists as to the intersection of prostitution and sex trafficking, the viewpoints that have garnered the most attention exist at the outer ends of the spectrum. On one side, proponents of an "autonomy" view take the position that some trafficking — such as prostitution — is consensual and is based on self-determination of the trafficked person, who is in a situation of economic necessity. This position has also been referred to as the "individualist," "non-abolitionist," or "human rights approach" to trafficking. On the other side of the debate, proponents of the "abolitionist" approach — also referred to by some as a "structuralist" approach to trafficking — centers the sex trafficking discussion on prostitution and views prostitution as a violation of human rights. In this view, as well as under international law, "consent" in the context of trafficking is irrelevant. The excerpts below highlight these positions.

Catharine A. MacKinnon, *Trafficking, Prostitution, and Inequality*
46 Harv. C.R.-C.L. L. Rev. 271 (2011)[1]

No one defends trafficking. There is no pro-sex-trafficking position any more than there is a public pro-slavery position for labor these days. The only issue is defining these terms so nothing anyone wants to defend is covered. It is hard to find overt defenders of inequality either, even as its legal definition is also largely shaped by existing practices the powerful want to keep.

Prostitution is not like this. Some people are for it; they affirmatively support it. Many more regard it as politically correct to tolerate and oppose doing anything effective about it. Most assume that, if not exactly desirable, prostitution is necessary or inevitable and harmless. These views of prostitution lie beneath and surround any debate on sex trafficking, whether prostitution is distinguished from trafficking or seen as indistinguishable from it, whether seen as a form of sexual freedom or understood as its ultimate denial. The debate on the underlying reality, and its relation to inequality, intensifies whenever doing anything effective about either prostitution or trafficking is considered.

Wherever you are in the world, the debate, and usually the law as well, is organized by five underlying moral distinctions that divide the really bad from the not-so-bad. Adult is distinguished from child prostitution, indoor from outdoor, legal from illegal, voluntary from forced, and prostitution from trafficking. Child prostitution is always bad for children; adult prostitution is not always bad for adults. Outdoor prostitution can be rough; indoor prostitution is less so. Illegal prostitution has problems that legal prostitution solves. Forced prostitution is bad; voluntary prostitution can be not-so-bad. Trafficking is really, really bad. Prostitution — if, say, voluntary, indoor, legal, adult — can be a tolerable life for some people. Measured against known facts of the sex trade, these purported distinctions emerge as largely illusory, occupying instead points of emphasis on common

---

[1] Copyright © 2011 by Harvard Civil Rights Law Review and Catherine MacKinnon. Reprinted with permission. Internal citations omitted.

continua with convergence and overlap among the dimensions. These moral distinctions are revealed as ideological, with consequences for law, policy, and culture that are real.

Within or across nations, the fundamental positions in this debate — to polarize somewhat, but this debate is remarkably polarized — are the sex work model and the sexual exploitation approach. When prostitution is termed "sex work," it is usually understood as the oldest profession, a cultural universal, consensual because paid, stigmatized because illegal, a job like any other denied that recognition, love in public, a form of sexual liberation. Sex workers are expressing what its academic advocates term their "agency." Of the many meanings of this slippery piece of jargon that no one seems to think they have to define, agency here appears to mean freely choosing, actively empowering, deciding among life chances, asserting oneself in a feisty fashion, fighting back against forces of femininity, resisting moralistic stereotypes. Some who take this view see prostitution as an expression of agency, sometimes as potentially if not always actually a model of sex equality. The agentic actors, sex workers, most of them women, control the sexual interaction, are compensated for what is usually expected from women for free, and have independent lives and anonymous sex with many partners — behaviors usually monopolized by men, hence liberating for women. Some women graduate to the higher masculine role of selling other women to men for sex — which strains sisterhood, if perhaps less than women, who have never been and never will be part of the sex industry, effectively defending pimping, does.

By contrast, the sexual exploitation approach sees prostitution as the oldest oppression, as widespread as the institutionalized sex inequality of which it is analyzed as a cornerstone. Prostitute, the noun, is seen to misleadingly and denigratingly equate who these people are with what is being done to them; the past participle verb form, by contrast, highlights the other people and social forces who are acting upon them. Based on information from the women themselves, women in prostitution are observed to be prostituted through choices precluded, options restricted, possibilities denied. Although the full scope and prevalence of prostitution's arrangements, with all its varieties of transactional sex, is not known, use of this term reflects an evaluation of considerable information on the sex industry, not an a priori attribution of victim status. Prostitution here is observed to be a product of lack of choice, the resort of those with the fewest choices, or none at all when all else fails. The coercion behind it, physical and otherwise, produces an economic sector of sexual abuse, the lion's share of the profits of which goes to others. In these transactions, the money coerces the sex rather than guaranteeing consent to it, making prostitution a practice of serial rape. In this analysis, there is, and can be, nothing equal about it. Prostituted people pay for paid sex. The buyers do not pay for what they take or get. It is this, not its illegality, that largely accounts for prostitution's stigma. People in prostitution, in this view, are wrongly saddled with a stigma that properly belongs to their exploiters.

Each account has a corresponding legal approach. The sex work approach favors across-the-board decriminalization with various forms of legalization, usually with some state regulation, sometimes beginning with unionization. Its goal is to remove criminal sanctions from all actors in the sex industry so that prostitution becomes as legitimate as any other mode of livelihood. The Netherlands, Germany, New

Zealand, Victoria in Australia, as well as 10 counties in Nevada, United States, have adopted versions of this approach, although some are retreating from it.

The sexual exploitation approach seeks to abolish prostitution. The best way to end this industry is debated. But criminalizing the buyers — the demand — as well as the sellers (pimps and traffickers), while eliminating any criminal status for prostituted people — the sold — and providing them services and job training they say they want, is the approach being pioneered in Sweden, Iceland, and Norway, and recent changes in the U.K. that point in this direction. Movements in South Africa, which like South Korea recently expressly criminalized buyers, a bill in Israel, and debate in the Scottish Parliament involve steps along similar lines. For the Swedish model, at least as crucial as criminalizing the buyers and enforcing that prohibition is decriminalizing prostituted people, which seems even more difficult to achieve. In a growing list of jurisdictions, the Swedish model is one initiative that, having shown promise, is increasingly favored by abolitionists at the principled and practical forefront of this movement.

Each person who confronts this issue decides which approach best reflects the reality known and experienced and best promotes the world one wants to live in. But apart from preferences, commitments, values, and politics, each position can be measured against evidence of what is known about the sex industry, including conditions of entrance, realities of treatment, and possibilities for exit.

Everywhere, prostituted people are overwhelmingly poor, indeed normally destitute. There is no disagreement on this fact. Urgent financial need is the most frequent reason mentioned by people in prostitution for being in the sex trade. Having gotten in because of poverty, almost no one gets out of poverty through prostituting. They are lucky to get out with their lives, given the mortality figures. It is not unusual for the women in the industry to get further into poverty, deeper in debt. In India, not only do they have few if any options to start with, landlords who keep them in houses charge exorbitant rent, take chunks of their earnings, and refuse to let them leave the house or do anything else, although they would make and keep more money pumping gas.

Disproportionately, people in prostitution are members of socially disadvantaged racial groups or lower castes. In Vancouver, prostituted women are First Nations women in numbers that far exceed their proportion of the population. In India, although caste is illegal, there are still prostitute castes. Women members of the Nat caste, for example, are selected to prostitute by men in their families; men of this caste are supposed to prostitute women to higher caste men. As this example suggests, the structure of who is in prostitution often derives from colonialism and persists after it. No one chooses to be born into poverty or to stay in prostitution in order to stay poor. No one chooses the racial group or caste one is born into. No country freely chooses to be colonized or the post-colonial social pathologies that so often organize this industry. These circumstances, from the uncontested evidence of who the prostituted disproportionately are, most powerfully determine who is used in this industry. These circumstances are not chosen by any of them.

Another global commonality of prostitution — another that no one contests — is that people typically enter prostitution when they are young, often well below the age of majority. And the age of entry may be dropping. Most of the women and girls

I met in India were first prostituted at age 10. This is not a time when you are fully empowered to make a choice about the rest of your life. It is not a time when, if you decide not to let family members or other adults do something to you, you have much power to stop them. In most countries where prostituted people have been studied in any depth, sexual abuse in childhood prior to entry into prostitution is a major precondition. In many places, including the United States, you only very rarely meet a woman in prostitution who was not sexually or physically abused before, frequently in her intimate circle. In India, the women told me that their first sexual abuse — their first sexual experience period — occurred in prostitution, mind you at age 10. If they resisted then or later, they said they were gang-raped and tortured.

Depending, it seems, upon social and cultural circumstances — we really do not know what causes cultural variance in prevalence and incidence of sexual abuse in childhood, or even for certain if it does vary — children can be sexually abused prior to prostitution, or it can simply be socially assumed that a life of sexual use is your destiny. In this connection, caste functions in India like sexual abuse in childhood does in other places where it is documented: it tells you what you are for. In Kolkata, scores of girls around 13 years old line the streets of the red light areas I visited. Once, glancing down a narrow alley, I saw a tiny naked girl of about six with her legs being spread wide, crotch out. So when, exactly, does she choose? . . .

Slavery is internationally defined as the exercise of powers of ownership over a person. When pimps sell you for sex to johns who buy you, and you want to leave but cannot, you are a sex slave by international legal definition whether you have ever been beaten or crossed a border. That women who are pimped are exercising "agency" as independent entrepreneurs is a fantasy of privilege. Unless there is something biologically appropriate or existentially predestined about a life of sexual use by others for the benefit of third parties, these women — most of the industry — make the phrase "adult sex work that involves no victimization" largely a contradiction in terms. They are not being employed under some other name. They are being sexually exploited. To expand the language of two judges on the Constitutional Court of South Africa, arguing in dissent that criminalizing prostituted people and not buyers is sex discrimination, the differences between prostituted people and those who buy and sell them are that one is served, the other serves; one is bought, the other buys and sells them; one is stigmatized, the other retains respectability; one is a criminal, the others either are not, or the law against them is virtually never enforced. And the one is mostly women, the others overwhelmingly men. . . .

Proponents of the sex work model sometimes suggest that anyone who is against prostitution is against sex. The sex they are talking about is the reality I have been describing. It is like (indeed, it is) saying that being against rape is being against sex. The same group sometimes insists that all the abuse, rape, and beatings are invented or exaggerated by us ideologically motivated, repressed puritan sex-panicked whiners who just don't have what it takes to make it as whores. The pimps are invented too. These women are independent entrepreneurs — well, maybe some have managers. Then along came HIV/AIDS and even this crowd discovered a harm, along with a lucrative profit center in purporting to address it. Handy, this disease that harms the men who wipe themselves off on the women as well as the women whose faces they explode all over — how refreshingly gender neutral and symmetrical. So now the pernicious brothel system in India must stay in place, or where would we distribute the condoms? Who keeps track of whether the women can actually use them, or the skyrocketing prices for women who have no choice but not to? . . .

The second strategic concession of the sex work approach has been to criticize trafficking while defending prostitution. But what is trafficking? The Palermo Protocol definition, which is sweeping the world, includes being sexually exploited through force, fraud, or coercion for commercial sex, all of which indeed occurs in the sex industry. But that definition, and the industry's reality, also includes sexual exploitation through "abuse of power or a condition of vulnerability," elements often elided in this discussion. Caste, race, or age can be conditions of vulnerability, as is extreme poverty. So also, in reality, are sex and gender. Trafficking is transportation, transfer, harboring, or receipt of a human being for purposes of sexual exploitation: it is straight-up pimping. Movement across jurisdictional lines is not, and has not been, an element of the international definition of trafficking since at least 1949. The sine qua non of trafficking is thus neither border crossing nor severe violence. It is third-party involvement. This is why Sigma Huda, Special Rapporteur on Trafficking from 2004 to 2008 observed that, "prostitution as actually practised in the world usually does satisfy the elements of trafficking." You cannot traffic yourself, which separates it from prostitution. Sexual exploitation can also be slavery. Right there, in the international definition, is what is sometimes criticized as a "conflation" of slavery with trafficking. You cannot enslave yourself either. . . .

[A]lthough it may seem counterintuitive, experience shows that when prostitution is legalized, trafficking goes through the roof. This has been documented in the Netherlands, Germany, Victoria in Australia, and elsewhere. As a business decision, it makes sense to traffic women and children where business is legal because once you get them there, the risks to sellers are minimal even if trafficking is formally a crime, and the profits to be made from operating in the open are astronomical. Illegal prostitution more generally explodes under legalization. If authorities pursue harm reduction, legal brothels require condom and other restrictions; many johns (perhaps most, research is showing) do not want to use them, and they are there to do what they want. This raises the price on sex without condoms, a potentially lethal demand satisfied by the illegal industry, often populated largely by illegal immigrants, that springs up all around the legal ones. When men's belts and shoelaces and ties and cigarette lighters have to be confiscated at the door, when lamps and phones can't have cords, johns who want to use those for sex — and they do — go elsewhere. The upshot is, far from making life safer, across-the-board decriminalization can make it even more dangerous, and certainly no less so, for those women who have the fewest options to begin with.

In light of this investigation, the moral distinctions that organize the debate on prostitution, examined in light of reality, emerge as ideological, functioning to make more socially tolerable an industry of viciousness and naked exploitation. Most adult women in prostitution are first prostituted as girls and are just never able to escape. As they age out, they retain the adult vulnerabilities of class, sex, and often race. Traffickers are incentivized to grab girls when they are most desirable to the market; then, with each day that passes, their exploitation is more blamed on them.

When prostituted women are used indoors, they are industrially accessible to pimps and johns and invisible to everyone else. Legal and illegal regimes inflict the same harms and pathologies on prostituted people, many of which get worse with across-the-board legality. The forms of force that impel entrance into the sex industry, that are endemically visited upon those used in it, and that operate to keep them captive produce a circumstance that, once revealed, it is difficult to believe a free person with real options would voluntarily elect. Perhaps the deepest injury of prostitution, with material basis in the converging inequalities of which its unequal concrete harms are irrefutable evidence, is that there is no dignity in it. Attributing agency here as if it means freedom, ignoring the unequal and violent material conditions of the life, can be a desperate grab toward lost dignity, as well as a cooptation of the humanity that the exploited never lose.

Any adequate law or policy to promote the human rights of prostituted people has three parts: decriminalizing and supporting people in prostitution, criminalizing their buyers strongly, and effectively criminalizing third-party profiteers. This is what it takes to unlock the interlocked, often intergenerational discrimination to which people in situations of prostitution are subjected. As one Indian woman in prostitution put it to me: "[W]e don't understand why they say we are criminals but nobody does anything about the real criminals." She meant the men who buy them, as well as the goons and gangs who enforce prostitution on them, including often their fathers, and the police who collaborate. India's consideration of the Swedish model has resulted in proposed legislation to move toward equality by eliminating the criminal status of the prostituted and criminalizing the buyers who are the reason for their commercial sexual exploitation. The point is to call the criminals by their real name and to help dismantle the motive force driving this industry. . . .

Ann Jordan, *Sex Trafficking: The Abolitionist Fallacy*
Foreign Policy in Focus (Mar. 18, 2009), available at
http://fpif.org/sex_trafficking_the_abolitionist_fallacy/[2]

Economic hardship, discrimination, and violence have driven millions of women to work in the sex sector around the world, and their numbers will increase as a result of the current global economic crisis. Unless the underlying factors pushing women to opt for selling sex to support themselves and their families are remedied, many women will continue to have few other options.

Yet the Bush administration, supported by the evangelical right-wing and some radical feminists, spent eight years promoting laws to criminalize prostitution and clients as the means to abolish prostitution and stop human trafficking into the sex sector. The ideology-driven approach is notable for the absence of any concrete evidence that it works. Proponents of such an approach have also failed to demonstrate that it avoids harming women or provides other livelihoods for those it aspires to help. It reduces all adults in the sex sector (even highly paid "call girls" and those working legally) to victim status and considers all prostitution to be a form of trafficking.

---

[2] Copyright © 2009 by Foreign Policy in Focus IPS (FPIF). Reprinted with permission. Internal citations omitted.

Unfortunately for many of the women who are objects of this policy, the ensuing crackdowns have meant prison, violence, forced "rehabilitation" and no means to earn an adequate livelihood. At the same time, the policy has not achieved its goal of reducing the incidence of trafficking, prostitution, commercial sexual exploitation of children or HIV/AIDs. The only responses to date from the new administration are President Barack Obama's affirmation at the Saddleback Presidential Forum that human trafficking "has to be a top priority" and Secretary of State Hillary Clinton's statement at her confirmation hearing that she takes "very seriously the function of the State Department to lead our government through the Office on Human Trafficking to do all that we can to end this modern form of slavery."

The Abolitionists

The most politically active abolitionists in the United States are Michael Horowitz (Hudson Institute), Janet Crouse (Concerned Women for America), Donna Hughes (University of Rhode Island), Equality Now, and the Coalition Against Trafficking in Women. They have worked successfully over the last eight years to bring about many of the anti-prostitution legal and policy changes regarding human trafficking and HIV/AIDs.

The latest entrant to this crowded field of abolitionists is Siddharth Kara, a former investment banker and business executive who has written the book *Sex Trafficking: Inside the Business of Modern Slavery* (2008). Kara traveled to India, Nepal, Albania, Moldova, and elsewhere to research his book. But like his fellow abolitionists, he too falls short of producing evidence that criminalizing demand will stop trafficking or abolish prostitution. He supports criminalizing clients, in part, based on a visit to The Netherlands where prostitution is legal (but not to Sweden, where it is illegal and clients are criminalized). He quotes Suzanne Hoff of La Strada, an anti-trafficking organization, as reporting that the majority of the women selling sex in Amsterdam are trafficked. But, as Hoff told me, she did not and could not make such a statement "for the simple reason that there are not — and have never been — reliable figures on the number or percent of women being exploited or forced into the sex industry."

"If I had to choose a policy today," he writes, "I would choose the stance of the U.S. and Swedish governments: the criminalization of prostitution, including the purchase of sex acts and the owning, operating, or financing of sex establishments" because this approach "has a better chance of curtailing demand for sex slaves." Wishing won't make it so; neither is it a basis for sound policymaking.

Like similar travelers, Kara is deeply touched by the victims' stories and wants to mount a campaign to bring justice, assistance, and hope to the women and girls. The centerpiece of his campaign is the destruction of the economic basis of the trafficking business. The economic model he erects is built on several unexamined assumptions and unattributed statements of fact and data. The most seriously flawed assumption he makes is to equate human beings — trafficked persons and sex workers — with commodities. His economic model treats women as passive objects that are pushed and pulled by exploiters using forced labor to lower costs to meet demand, and ignores the poverty, discrimination, and violence that compel women to make risky decisions. Adults who make rational choices from among limited options are actors who don't fit a neat supply/demand economic model, and so they are factored out of the equation in order to situate trafficking as a commodity business.

Some of Kara's proposed solutions are dangerous, unworkable or unrealistic. For example, he advocates for private citizen community vigilance committees to go into brothels undercover to locate trafficked women and girls. But he was unsuccessful in going undercover and even chased away from one brothel area. He recognizes, on the one hand, that up to a third of victims are rescued by clients, and opines on the other that clients are looking "for a way to act out violent, racist, pedophiliac, or other antisocial traits." Yet, by opting to prosecute all clients, he ignores the fact that women and youth like those he met will continue to migrate and sell sex, no matter how many men are imprisoned. At the personal level, Kara also equivocates: While he advocates for raids to rescue trafficked women and girls, he nonetheless leaves a woman he believes has been trafficked in the United States to her fate because she "needed the money for her family and there was a threat of violence against her parents."

All of his proposed solutions suffer from a lack of input from the people who will be primarily affected: trafficked persons and adult sex workers. To develop effective, evidence-based, do-no-harm policies, advocates and policy makers must work collaboratively with persons who may be helped or harmed by the proposed laws and policies.

What Works

Effective change comes from the bottom up, within the affected community where the persons who are the most knowledgeable and motivated live and work. The only way to build sustainable movements for change is to empower and support a vibrant civil society. This is particularly important when the issues have social, cultural, and economic bases that are highly resistant to any attempt at regulation by criminal law. Sex worker organizations in the United States, India, Thailand, Cambodia, Mali, Brazil, South Africa, and elsewhere are the front-line actors, who have first-hand knowledge about how raids, anti-prostitution campaigns, "vigilance" committees, and law enforcement approaches impact their lives and undermine efforts to combat trafficking, child prostitution, and the spread of HIV/AIDs.

Instead of harassing and stigmatizing women in the sex sector, governments and civil society should recognize and value their accomplishments — such as removing children and trafficked women from brothels, creating adult literacy programs, organizing micro-enterprise programs so women can find other sources of income, setting up schools for their children, and raising awareness about HIV/AIDs and health issues.

The Obama administration should reject the ideology-driven policies, practices, and programs of the past eight years. Specifically, it should base all programs and policies on proven results and sound ideas derived from objective evidence. It should take into consideration the concerns and ideas of sex worker groups when developing new programs and policies. The administration should stop applying the anti-prostitution pledge in a way that prevents the funding of U.S. and foreign organizations that work with sex workers. Civil servants who have been trained to carry out the anti-prostitution agenda over the last eight years must abandon that agenda and operate under a new, more open and inclusive policy based on rights and evidence. And the government should remove all of its materials related to human trafficking, sex work, and/or HIV/AIDs that are inconsistent with the above recommendations from websites and distribution.

In this way, the new administration can create progressive, non-judgmental, rights-and evidence-based strategies in partnership with sex worker organizations and other experts to ensure that U.S. goals to stop human trafficking and the spread of HIV/AIDs are accomplished without causing further collateral harm.

NOTES AND QUESTIONS

1. What are the assumptions underlying each of these approaches? For additional perspectives on the debate over the relationship of prostitution and sex trafficking see, for example, Janet Halley, et al., *From the International to the Local in Feminist Legal Responses to Rape, Prostitution/Sex Work, and Sex Trafficking: Four Studies in Contemporary Governance Feminism*, 29 HARV. J.L. & GENDER 335 (2006) and Elizabeth Bernstein, *Militarized Humanitarianism Meets Carceral Feminism: The Politics of Sex, Rights, and Freedom in Contemporary Anti-trafficking Campaigns*, 36 SIGNS 45 (2010).

2. What is the relationship between criminal law enforcement responses and each of the approaches described above?

3. The domestic TVPA definition makes an explicit distinction between sex trafficking and other forms of trafficking. Professor Janie Chuang regards this as "a symbolic victory for the neo-abolitionists" because "the statute limited application of its key operational terms to severe forms of trafficking" which "does not criminalize 'sex trafficking' unless it involves 'trafficking of children' or is 'effected by force, fraud, or coercion.'" *Rescuing Trafficking from Ideological Capture: Prostitution Reform and Anti-Trafficking Law and Policy*, 158 U. PA. L. REV. 1655, 1679 (2010). Yet at least one commentator suggests that this has led "to an actual divergence in how the United States treats the different forms of trafficking, defin[ing] sex trafficking as a separate offense from every other form of trafficking, while lumping those other forms (such as domestic servitude, agricultural labor, debt bondage, and slavery) into one category." Rebecca Wharton, *A New Paradigm for Human Trafficking: Shifting the Focus from Prostitution to Exploitation in the Trafficking Victims Protection Act*, 16 WM. & MARY J. WOMEN & L. 753, 770 (2010). Does the TVPA's definition of human trafficking definition influence the way it has been implemented and enforced?

4. Does the Palermo Protocol adopt either approach outlined above? If so, how? If not, what approach does it take?

5. Can these two perspectives reach a compromise? Professor Shelley Cavalieri suggests such a compromise called "third-way feminism" that recognizes that "in the face of only unappealing options, a woman's choice to engage in sex cannot be termed a truly autonomous one." At the same time, the "third-way feminist" account also acknowledges that "because not all women experience each axis of oppression,

individuals' needs and responses will differ," giving individual women the opportunity "to name the sources of their own oppression, rather than defining the trafficking experience for them." Shelley Cavalieri, *Between Victim and Agent: A Third-Way Feminist Account of Trafficking for Sex Work*, 86 IND. L.J. 1409, 1439, 1448 (2011).

6. What is the relationship between child prostitution and child sex trafficking? *See* Cheryl Hanna, *Somebody's Daughter: The Domestic Trafficking of Girls for the Commercial Sex Industry and the Power of Love*, 9 WM. & MARY J. WOMEN & L. 1 (2002); Jonathan Todres, *Taking Prevention Seriously: Developing a Comprehensive Response to Child Trafficking and Sexual Exploitation*, 43 VAND. J. TRANSNAT'L L. 1 (2010); Wendi J. Adelson, *Child Prostitute or Victim of Trafficking?*, 6 U. ST. THOMAS L.J. 96 (2008).

7. Professor Janie Chuang argues that the debate over the role of prostitution in trafficking has had a strong impact on the approach taken by the U.S. government to trafficking. In *Rescuing Trafficking from Ideological Capture: Prostitution Reform and Anti-Trafficking Law and Policy*, 158 U. PA. L. REV. 1655 (2010), Chuang argues:

> The end of the Clinton Administration brought an opportunity for the neo-abolitionists to recalibrate U.S. anti-trafficking policy. The neo-abolitionist lobby found a powerful ally in President Bush, who came to champion the anti-prostitution cause at home and abroad. . . . [T]he Bush Administration took on anti-trafficking as a key humanitarian initiative. In National Security Presidential Directive 22 (NSPD-22), issued on December 16, 2002, President Bush made the neo-abolitionist position official U.S. policy. NSPD-22 states that U.S. anti-trafficking policy is based on an abolitionist approach to trafficking in persons, and our efforts must involve a comprehensive attack on such trafficking, which is a modern day form of slavery. In this regard, the United States Government opposes prostitution and any related activities, including pimping, pandering, or maintaining brothels, as contributing to the phenomenon of trafficking in persons. These activities are inherently harmful and dehumanizing. The United States Government's position is that these activities should not be regulated as a legitimate form of work for any human being. . . .
>
> The U.S. government's aim to eradicate prostitution writ large under the banner of anti-trafficking measures soon manifested in more explicit laws and regulations that were introduced and largely adopted in the 2003, 2005, and 2008 reauthorizations of the TVPA. Three initiatives in particular — each foreshadowed in earlier neo-abolitionist congressional testimony articulating an agenda for U.S. anti-trafficking policymaking — merit close attention: (1) anti-prostitution restrictions on federal-grant administration, (2) anti-prostitution restrictions on U.S. military personnel and government contractors, and (3) measures to end demand for prostitution and to federalize prostitution-related crimes. Through the first two measures, the neo-abolitionists have remapped the trafficking field, using the threatened withdrawal of U.S. funds to pressure foreign governments, civil-society organizations, and private-sector actors to adopt anti-prostitution mea-

sures. Though the third measure ultimately did not survive legislatively, that it was included in the House version of the 2008 reauthorization bill marks the tremendous inroads the neo-abolitionists have made in pursuit of their anti-prostitution agenda.

Do you agree with Chuang's view that the neo-abolitionist view of prostitution and trafficking has defined U.S. policy on sex trafficking?

The anti-prostitution restriction on federal grant administration referred to by Chuang was litigated in federal courts. This funding restriction — enacted pursuant to the 2003 Trafficking Victims Protection Reauthorization Act — prohibited international non-governmental organizations (NGO) receiving governmental funding from using the funds to "promote, support or advocate for the legalization or practice of prostitution." The specific rule required organizations to "state in either a grant application, a grant agreement, or both, that it does not promote, support or advocate the legalization or practice of prostitution." A similar rule applied to international organizations receiving governmental funding to combat HIV/AIDS. To get funding, these organizations needed "to have a policy explicitly opposing prostitution and sex trafficking."

Initially, the rule only applied to foreign NGOs. But in 2004, the Department of Justice issued an opinion letter supporting an extension of the restriction to U.S. grantees. Accordingly, in 2005, Congress again amended the TVPA — so now domestic NGOs are also required to adopt the anti-prostitution pledge.

Two lawsuits have challenged the constitutionality of the anti-prostitution pledge: *Alliance for Open Society International, Inc. and Open Society Institute v. United States Agency for International Development*, 430 F. Supp. 2d 222 (S.D.N.Y. 2006) and *DKT International, Inc. v. United States Agency for International Development*, 435 F. Supp. 2d 5 (D.D.C. 2006). Both lawsuits alleged a violation of the First Amendment right to free speech by requiring that they adopt the government's policy view to receive funding. The lawsuits also charged that the pledge was unconstitutionally vague, thereby permitting arbitrary enforcement. Finally, both suits argued that the pledge presented a public health danger because it undermined efforts to provide preventative health information and services to "sex workers" at high risk of contracting and spreading HIV/AIDS.

The district courts held that the pledge requirement was an unconstitutional violation of free speech rights under the First Amendment. Judge Victor Marrero of the Southern District of New York and Judge Emmet G. Sullivan of the District Court of Washington, D.C. granted the respective plaintiffs' preliminary injunctions against the enforcement of the pledge in order to prevent irreparable harm. Judge Sullivan wrote that the pledge implied a "demand that the organization become a mouthpiece for government policy," even if using its own funds. *DKT International, Inc.*, 435 F. Supp. 2d 5, 17 (D.D.C. 2006), and Judge Marrero of the Southern District explained that "[t]he Supreme Court has repeatedly found that speech, or an agreement not to speak, cannot be compelled or coerced as a condition of participation in a government program." *Alliance for Open Society International, Inc. and Open Society*, 430 F. Supp. 2d 222, 275 (S.D.N.Y. 2006).

While the Second Circuit affirmed Judge Marrero's finding for a preliminary injunction in the Southern District of New York, the DC Circuit overturned Judge Sullivan's ruling in the *DKT International v. United States Agency for International Development*, a case that appears below. In other words, at the time the constitutionality of the anti-prostitution pledge remained unresolved.

DKT INTERNATIONAL, INC., v. UNITED STATES AGENCY FOR INTERNATIONAL DEVELOPMENT
477 F.3d 758 (2007)

RANDOLPH, CIRCUIT JUDGE

The official position of the United States is that eradicating prostitution and sex trafficking is an integral part of the worldwide fight against HIV/AIDS. In awarding grants to private organizations for HIV/AIDS relief efforts, the government-through the U.S. Agency for International Development-only funds organizations that share this view. DKT International refused to certify that it has a policy opposing prostitution and sex trafficking, and therefore did not qualify for a grant. The district court struck down the funding condition on the ground that it violated DKT's freedom of speech under the First Amendment. We reverse.

In 2003 Congress enacted the United States Leadership Against HIV/AIDS, Tuberculosis, and Malaria Act, and the President proposed $15 billion for fighting the worldwide spread of HIV/AIDS. The Act directs the President to establish programs "to treat individuals infected with HIV/AIDS," to "prevent the further spread of HIV infections," and to "maximize United States capabilities in the areas of technical assistance and training and research, including vaccine research." The Act states that "the reduction of HIV/AIDS behavioral risks shall be a priority of all prevention efforts in terms of funding, educational messages, and activities by promoting abstinence from sexual activity and substance abuse, encouraging monogamy and faithfulness, promoting the effective use of condoms, and eradicating prostitution, the sex trade, rape, sexual assault and sexual exploitation of women and children."

Congress found that funding the relief efforts of private organizations was "critical to the success" of the international fight against HIV/AIDS. Congress thus authorized the President to "furnish assistance, on such terms and conditions as the President may determine," to nongovernmental organizations. The Act requires, however, that funds go only to organizations that share the Act's disapproval of prostitution and sex trafficking. Organizations may not use funds granted under the Act to "promote or advocate the legalization or practice of prostitution or sex trafficking." And under funds are unavailable "to any group or organization that does not have a policy explicitly opposing prostitution and sex trafficking," with the exception of four organizations, three of which are public organizations, and one of which deals only with vaccine research. It is the condition — that an organization have a policy opposing prostitution and sex trafficking to be eligible for funding — that DKT challenges.

Congress authorized the U.S. Agency for International Development to administer grants, cooperative agreements, and contracts pursuant to the Act. The Agency implemented [the Act] by requiring a boilerplate provision in grant contracts and cooperative agreements, and a certification that applicants are in compliance with the provision. The contractual provision states that recipient organizations and any sub-recipients "must have a policy explicitly opposing prostitution and sex trafficking," but does not specify any particular language or format. The certification requirement applies only to the prime recipient, which must include the boilerplate provision in all sub-agreements. Violation of the provision may be used as a ground for terminating the underlying agreement between the Agency and the prime recipient.

DKT International provides family planning and HIV/AIDS prevention programming in foreign countries, and receives about 16 percent of its total budget from Agency grants. DKT operates as a sub-grantee under Family Health International (FHI) in Vietnam, where it distributes condoms and condom lubricant. In June 2005, FHI provided DKT with a sub-agreement to run an Agency-funded lubricant distribution program. Included in the sub-agreement was a certification that DKT "has a policy explicitly opposing prostitution and sex trafficking." The sub-agreement stated that the certification requirement "is an express term and condition of the agreement and any violation of it shall be grounds for unilateral termination of the agreement by FHI or [the Agency] prior to the end of its term." DKT did not, and does not, have a policy for or against prostitution and sex trafficking. It therefore refused to sign the sub-agreement with the certification requirement. FHI then cancelled the grant and informed DKT that FHI was "unable to provide additional funding to DKT."

DKT alleged that it refuses to adopt a policy opposing prostitution because this might result in "stigmatizing and alienating many of the people most vulnerable to HIV/AIDS — the sex workers . . . ." It claims that the certification requirement violates the First Amendment because it constrains DKT's speech in other programs for which it does not receive federal funds and because it forces DKT to convey a message with which it does not necessarily agree.

The government may speak through elected representatives as well as other government officers and employees. Or it may hire private agents to speak for it, as in *Rust v. Sullivan*, 500 U.S. 173 (1991). When it communicates its message, either through public officials or private entities, the government can-and often must-discriminate on the basis of viewpoint. In sponsoring Nancy Reagan's "Just Say No" anti-drug campaign, the First Amendment did not require the government to sponsor simultaneously a "Just Say Yes" campaign. Or to repeat the example in *Rust:* "When Congress established a National Endowment for Democracy to encourage other countries to adopt democratic principles . . . it was not constitutionally required to fund a program to encourage competing lines of political philosophy such as communism and fascism." 500 U.S. at 194.

In this case the government's objective is to eradicate HIV/AIDS. One of the means of accomplishing this objective is for the United States to speak out against legalizing prostitution in other countries. The Act's strategy in combating HIV/AIDS is not merely to ship condoms and medicine to regions where the disease is rampant. Repeatedly the Act speaks of fostering behavioral change, and spreading "educational messages." The Act's stated source of inspiration is the success in Uganda, where President Yoweri Museveni "spoke out early, breaking long-standing cultural taboos, and changed widespread perceptions about the disease." The Act details the program Museveni instituted, which primarily involved a "message" about "a fundamental change in sexual behavior." "Uganda's success shows that behavior change . . . is a very successful way to prevent the spread of HIV." Spending money to convince people at risk of HIV/AIDS to change their behavior is necessarily a message.

Everyone, including DKT, agrees that the government may bar grantees from using grant money to promote legalizing prostitution. But DKT complains that [the Act] constrains its speech in other programs, for which it does not receive federal funds. That effect, DKT argues, makes the case like *FCC v. League of Women Voters of California*, 468 U.S. 364 (1984), and unlike *Rust v. Sullivan*. We think the opposite. The restriction struck down in *League of Women Voters* prohibited public broadcasting stations from editorializing. The Court pointed out that a public broadcasting station could not editorialize with its nonfederal funds even if its federal grants amounted to only a small fraction of its income. Therefore the restriction did not simply govern the use of federal funds. *Rust*, on the other hand, upheld regulations prohibiting federally funded family planning services from engaging in abortion counseling or in any way advocating abortion as a method of family planning.

The difference between the two decisions, as the Court later explained, is that in *Rust* "the government did not create a program to encourage private speech but instead used private speakers to transmit specific information pertaining to its own program. We recognized that when the government appropriates public funds to promote a particular policy of its own it is entitled to say what it wishes." *Rosenberger*, 515 U.S. at 833. Here too the government has not created "a program to encourage private speech," as it did in funding public broadcasting in *League of Women Voters*, and as it did in *Rosenberger* in funding student publications. In this case, as in *Rust*, "the government's own message is being delivered," *Legal Servs. Corp. v. Velazquez*, 531 U.S. 533 (2001).

Under *Rust*, as interpreted in *Rosenberger* and *Velazquez*, the government may thus constitutionally communicate a particular viewpoint through its agents and require those agents not convey contrary messages. We think it follows that in choosing its agents, the government may use criteria to ensure that its message is conveyed in an efficient and effective fashion. The Supreme Court has also recognized that the government may take "appropriate steps" to ensure that its message is "neither garbled nor distorted." *Rosenberger*, 515 U.S. at 833. This is particularly true where the government is speaking on matters with foreign policy implications, as it is here. The government's brief summarizes these points: "It would make little sense for the government to provide billions of dollars to encourage the reduction of HIV/AIDS behavioral risks, including prostitution and sex trafficking, and yet to engage as partners in this effort organizations that are neutral toward or even actively promote the same practices sought to be eradicated. The effectiveness of the government's viewpoint-based program would be substantially undermined, and the government's message confused, if the organizations hired to implement that program by providing HIV/AIDS programs and services to the public could advance an opposite viewpoint in their privately-funded operations."

The Act does not compel DKT to advocate the government's position on prostitution and sex trafficking; it requires only that if DKT wishes to receive funds it must communicate the message the government chooses to fund. This does not violate the First Amendment. We therefore reverse the district court.

So ordered.

NOTES AND QUESTIONS

1. As noted above, the Second Circuit in *Alliance for Open Society International, Inc*, 651 F.3d 218 (2d Cir. 2011) declined to follow the DC Circuit's decision in *DKT International*, 477 F.3d 758 (D.C. Cir. 2007):

> [W]e conclude that [the Act] as implemented by the Agencies, falls well beyond what the Supreme Court and this Court have upheld as permissible conditions on the receipt of government funds. [The Act] does not merely require recipients of [its] funds to refrain from certain conduct, but goes substantially further and compels recipients to espouse the government's viewpoint. Consequently, we agree with the district court that Plaintiffs have demonstrated a likelihood of success on the merits. Finding no abuse of discretion by the district court, we affirm.
>
> The Policy Requirement goes well beyond the funding condition upheld in *Rust* because it compels Plaintiffs to voice the government's viewpoint and to do so as if it were their own. Indeed, the *Rust* Court expressly observed that "[n]othing in [the challenged regulations] *requires a doctor to represent as his own any opinion that he does not in fact hold."* 500 U.S. at 200 (emphasis added). Rather, the grantee's staff could remain "silen[t] with regard to abortion," and, if asked about abortion, was "free to make clear that advice regarding abortion is simply beyond the scope of the program." Here, on the other hand, Plaintiffs do not have the option of remaining silent or neutral. Instead, they must represent as their own an opinion — that they affirmatively oppose prostitution — that they might not categorically hold. Suffice it to say that *Rust* would have been a very different case had the government gone as far as requiring Title X recipients to affirmatively adopt a policy statement opposing abortion, in the way the Leadership Act mandates the adoption of a policy statement opposing prostitution. The government has, by compelling NGOs to affirmatively pledge their opposition to prostitution, stepped beyond what might have been appropriate to ensure that its anti-prostitution message would not be "garbled" or "distorted," *Rosenberger*, 515 U.S. at 833. *Alliance for Open Society International, Inc*, 651 F.3d 218, 237 (2d Cir. 2011).

The Agency for International Development appealed the Second Circuit decision to the Supreme Court. The Supreme Court granted the petition for certiorari and on June 20, 2013 rendered a 6-2 decision affirming the Second Circuit decision in holding the policy requirement unconstitutional. The majority opinion authored by Chief Justice John Roberts found that "the policy requirement violates the First Amendment by compelling as a condition of federal funding the affirmation of a belief that by its nature cannot be confined within the scope of the Government program." 570 U.S. __ (2013). The Court held that the government cannot force a non-governmental organization to state a governmental viewpoint that is not held by the organization itself. Such a requirement was a form of "leveraging" and violated the free speech protection's of the First amendment. Justices Antonin Scalia and Clarence Thomas joined in dissent. What accounted for the circuit court split? What are the arguments in support of the funding restrictions? Against? How did the Supreme Court resolve this debate?

2. What is the relationship between HIV/AIDS prevention efforts, prostitution, and trafficking? Do policies like the Leadership Act's funding restriction or NSPD 22 link prostitution, trafficking, and health care? If so, is that the correct approach to confronting each issue?

3. In an article by Professors Grace Chang and Kathleen Kim, *Reconceptualizing Approaches to Human Trafficking: Perspectives from the Field(s)*, 3 STAN. J. CIV. R. C. L. 317 (2007), the authors note that "organizations in Brazil rejected $40 million of U.S. global AIDS funds, declaring that the [funding] restrictions would counter the very programs that have proven effective in reducing the spread of HIV in Brazil. Such programs include rights-based and harm reduction approaches to prostitution that are designed to de-stigmatize and empower women as they move towards better health and self-sufficiency."

4. What is the impact of refusal of U.S. government AIDS funding? Both on countries that accept the funding and those that do not?

II. LABOR-FOCUSED APPROACHES

Many scholars and advocates have sought approaches to anti-trafficking policy that, by focusing on labor rights, tend to avoid debates over the relationship of prostitution with trafficking. As Professor Jane Larson has suggested, by determining what legal standards define "just and favourable" free labor conditions that are "worthy of human dignity," human rights and labor rights can be brought together in a way that obviates what she describes as "fruitless debates" over consent and prostitution in the context of trafficking. *See* Jane E. Larson, *Prostitution, Labor, and Human Rights*, 37 U.C. DAVIS L. REV. 673, 698–99 (2004). Such a view bypasses questions of trafficked persons' consent to engage in risky activities that led to being trafficked and thereby exculpates them from being accomplices in their own victimization. Based on scrutinizing workplace conditions, this framework privileges the person who has been in the exploitative situation. It also prioritizes enforcement of individual rights and measures the successfulness of anti-trafficking legislative policy not only by its effectiveness in addressing crimes against the state through public prosecution but also by its effectiveness in enabling trafficked persons to obtain protection and remedies.

Professor Melynda Barnhart echoes this labor focus in the following excerpt in which she blurs the distinction between sex trafficking and labor trafficking:

Melynda Barnhart, *Sex and Slavery: An Analysis of Three Models of State Human Trafficking Legislation*
16 William & Mary J. W. L. 83 (2009)[3]

The separation of labor and sex trafficking into distinct crimes is normatively obvious at first blush. Sex trafficking involves forced sex, i.e., rape, and thus constitutes one of the most egregious crimes that humans can inflict upon one another. Labor trafficking involves forced labor, i.e., someone being forced to perform work that thousands of other people legally and voluntarily perform on a daily basis. Thus sex trafficking appears far worse for victims than labor trafficking, and legal distinctions between them appear to reflect common sense. These distinctions track expectations regarding harms to the victims involved. "Good" women forced into sex work are far more deserving of governmental assistance and rescue than "bad" undocumented low-wage immigrant workers whose labor is expected to be exploited. Performing tasks that one would not otherwise consider performing in exchange for a paycheck, which is usually smaller than one wants, is par for the course in regular employment, and only a lucky few are able to describe their work as a labor of love rather than wage slavery. However, upon examination of cases in context, sex and labor trafficking are not actually so far apart.

Distinctions between sex and labor exploitation are generally difficult to draw in actual cases because the actions of the traffickers are so similar. Many trafficking cases, technically considered labor trafficking, involve egregious sexual violations as a part of the physical and psychological coercion the victims endure. Cases are often difficult to classify as purely sex or labor, because when women are trafficking victims, they are often "sexually abused and forced to work." For example, in the Lakireddy Bali Reddy case from California, the trafficker blurred the line between labor exploitation and sexual exploitation by using "whatever means [were] necessary to ensure the confinement and cooperation of [his] victims, including sexual assault." Victims in many high profile federal labor trafficking cases were also sexually exploited by their abusers. In the Soto case, the women were raped almost nightly by captors who forced them to cook and clean smuggling safe houses during the day. The victim in the Tecum case was forced to perform sexual acts at night after days of backbreaking farm labor. The Department of Justice Office for Victims of Crime recognizes this common problem by collecting data on sex and labor trafficking victims in three categories: sex, labor, and sex and labor. Traffickers use whatever coercive tools they have at their disposal, and sexual abuse is common.

When sex trafficking and labor trafficking are distinguished at law, traffickers are charged, convicted, and sentenced not based on their exploitative actions, but on the end result of their coercion. This leads to unpredictable results. Without "prostitution" or a commercial sexual act to define the crime as sex trafficking, the abuse becomes labor trafficking whether or not sexual abuse was involved. Cases are often categorized criminally as labor trafficking, even those encompassing clear sexual exploitation in the sex industry, if the case does not involve an exchange of sex for money. Several federal cases involving women trafficked for work in strip

---

[3] Copyright © 2009 by William & Mary Journal of Women and the Law. Reprinted with permission. Internal citations omitted.

clubs have been prosecuted as labor trafficking crimes, although the underlying exploitation was certainly sexual in nature. In practice, the theoretical designation of labor trafficking as inherently less sexually exploitative than sex trafficking is false.

Sex trafficking can be seen normatively as more inherently harmful, because it violates a woman's bodily integrity in a manner that labor trafficking apparently does not. Sexual abuse and exploitation may be assumed to cause higher levels of trauma to victims. Thus, higher penalties for sex trafficking seem a common sense response to different harms. However, this distinction does not hold true. Victims of labor trafficking often present forms of psychological trauma similar to those of sex trafficking victims, largely because both are subjected to performing demeaning and often degrading tasks against their will by similarly coercive abusers. Losing the ability to control what happens to one's body leaves similar psychological damage, whether one is forced to clean toilets or to provide sexual services. Victims also tend to emotionally react to their experiences individually. Such factors as the length of time in the trafficking situation, the relationship of the victim to the trafficker, and the expectations the victim held prior to the trafficking situation all affect the level of harm the individual victim experiences. A sex trafficking victim who knew she would be performing sexual labor but did not expect to be in debt bondage may weather her abuse fairly well. A labor trafficking victim in a purportedly romantic relationship with a trafficker who forces her to clean houses may be completely devastated. Further, offenses against the right to bodily integrity should surely include any services a person is forced to perform for another, even if those services are not of a sexual nature. Since victims show differing levels of trauma based on their individual circumstances, and not based on the type of exploitation they experience, violation of bodily integrity cannot serve as the marker of difference between sex and labor trafficking.

The distinctively gendered nature of most sex work, i.e., women paid to provide services to male clients, is an oft-cited reason for why sex trafficking is worthy of greater prosecution and punishment. There is no question that abuse and exploitation of women occurs in all areas of the sex industry, whether that abuse rises to the level of sex trafficking or not. However, trafficking in the sex industry is not the exclusive way that women as women are targeted for exploitation. Most trafficking victims in the United States are victims of labor trafficking, and most victims of trafficking are women. The second largest percentage of human trafficking cases are domestic servitude cases, an almost exclusively female occupation. While these numbers could reflect a law enforcement bias towards prosecuting cases that involve a traditionally female victim of male aggression, there may simply be more women targeted for trafficking. Trafficking in the United States is clearly a gendered crime, as the majority of victims in both sex and labor trafficking are women.

Once the usual distinctions between sex and labor trafficking based on sexual and gendered exploitation are proven false by practical experience, what remains of this distinction lies in the field of moral disapproval. Sex trafficking is simply considered more morally repugnant than labor trafficking. Anti-trafficking statutes strongly distinguishing sex and labor trafficking reflect this moral disapproval of the sex industry and give labor exploitation a free pass. Dividing sex and labor trafficking along moral lines underplays the actual harms of labor trafficking, "marginalizes persons trafficked in non-sex related industries," and erases the gendered nature of labor trafficking.

The underlying exploitation involved in sex trafficking, prostitution, pimping, or patronizing a prostitute, is already criminalized as morally repugnant. Without any type of force or coercion, pimping or patronizing a prostitute are also illegal activities in most jurisdictions. In contrast, most states and the federal government leave regulation of the labor sector to civil regulation rather than criminal. Very few, if any, jurisdictions criminalize the hiring of undocumented workers or the underpayment of workers. Prostitution is almost universally illegal, while working without legal authorization is barely a civil violation. Thus, it seems to be common sense that sex trafficking should be punished at a higher level than labor trafficking, because the underlying exploitation in sex trafficking is already subject to criminal penalties.

Yet, this only makes sense if we assume that labor exploitation is not morally reprehensible. Labor exploitation could be considered criminal if society chooses to recognize it as such. Not paying workers for their work or underpaying them may be considered just as morally wrong in some circles as paying someone for sexual services. Even if labor regulation remains civil, lax enforcement gives a free pass to those who choose to exploit vulnerable labor. The lack of enforcement leads to the perception that labor exploitation is acceptable. This acceptance of the status quo makes labor trafficking seem to be the lesser moral harm.

NOTES AND QUESTIONS

1. In what ways is sex trafficking similar to labor trafficking? Different? Do you agree with Barnhart's assessment? Should the similarities and differences between sex trafficking and labor trafficking inform anti-trafficking policies and practices? How so?

2. Barnhart suggests that the criminality of prostitution has supported a strong criminal enforcement approach to sex trafficking, while the absence of criminal sanction for labor exploitation has resulted in the under enforcement of labor trafficking crimes. Should labor exploitation be considered a crime on par with sexual exploitation? Does the absence of criminal sanction for labor exploitation suggest that it is less morally reprehensible than sexual exploitation?

3. Barnhart like many scholars have focused on the "gendered" nature of human trafficking, which primarily victimizes women, yet men and boys are also trafficked. *See* Samuel Vincent Jones, *The Invisible Man: The Conscious Neglect of Men and Boys in the War on Human Trafficking*, 4 UTAH L. REV. 1143 (2010); Cynthia L. Wolken, *Feminist Legal Theory and Human Trafficking in the United States: Towards a New Framework*, 6 U. MD. L.J. RACE, RELIGION, GENDER & CLASS 407 (2006) (arguing that the dominant human trafficking discourse has marginalized and neglected many trafficking victims, especially men).

Other labor-focused approaches to human trafficking policy have centered on structural perspectives of the systemic forces that cause trafficking, such as global labor migration, weak labor protections, and immigration restrictions. These approaches suggest that anti-trafficking policy should reflect a better understanding of how sociological phenomena perpetuate trafficking and how governmental polices might be reformed to prevent trafficking. One such approach has been proffered by Professors Chang and Kim in *Reconceptualizing Approaches to Human Trafficking: Perspectives from the Field(s)*, 3 STAN. J. CIV. R. C. L. 317 (2007). Chang and Kim argue that:

> Anti-trafficking and human rights advocates now consider it absolutely essential for anti-trafficking service providers to expand their work beyond the "3 Ps" of prevention, prosecution and protection. While the "3 Ps" approach assisted many potential and actual lives of victims, it does not address underlying social structures that facilitate human trafficking. . . .
>
> This new discourse must be grounded in understandings of the processes of globalization, and the coercive nature of most migration within this context. The new discourse supports a framework that views trafficking as coerced migration or exploitation of migrant workers for all forms of labor, including a broad spectrum of work often performed by migrants, such as manufacturing, agriculture, construction, service work, servile marriage and sex work. This definition of trafficking rests upon an understanding that many migrant workers are coerced to migrate because of economic devastation caused by neoliberal policies in their home countries. While this displacement does not imply physical force or deception, it recognizes coercion created by the destruction of subsistence economies and social service states through neoliberal policies imposed on indebted sending countries by wealthy creditor nations. . . .
>
> [T]he underlying root causes for rendering human beings vulnerable to human trafficking are complex and regionally diverse and cannot be addressed by a "one size fits all" strategy. The development of a new discourse on trafficking, therefore, requires a critical analysis of the current U.S. policy and its consequences that integrates multiple perspectives from varied fields of human rights, women's rights, labor rights and health rights. An integrated and cross-disciplinary framework launches a reconceptualization of trafficking that considers root causes and the role of U.S. policies in hampering efforts to combat trafficking.

NOTES AND QUESTIONS

1. Do you agree with Chang and Kim? How might these other areas be integrated into human trafficking policy today? Chang and Kim suggest a multi-disciplinary anti-trafficking approach that aims to build a movement across many rights-based constituencies. What should an anti-trafficking movement look like? What are its goals? Who are the stakeholders?

2. What would constitute an effective anti-trafficking strategy? What are the components? Is it necessary to go beyond the "3Ps" of prosecution of traffickers, protection of victims, and prevention of trafficking? Why or why not?

3. Additional structural approaches have been suggested by James Gray Pope, *A Free Labor Approach to Human Trafficking*, 158 U. PA. L. REV. 1849 (2010)

(discussing labor organizing as a strategy to secure rights for trafficked workers), Karen E. Bravo, *Free Labor! A Labor Liberalization Solution to Modern Trafficking in Humans*, 18 TRANSNAT'L L. & CONTEMP. PROBS. 545 (2009) (proposing the free movement of migrant labor as a human trafficking prevention strategy) and Hila Shamir, *A Labor Paradigm for Human Trafficking*, 60 UCLA L. REV. 76 (2012). Shamir rejects a focus on individual victims' remedies and rights in favor of a labor rights paradigm:

> Adopting a labor approach to anti-trafficking would shift the focus away from individual harms to the power disparities between victims and traffickers and the economic and social conditions that make individuals vulnerable to trafficking. This approach understands workers as agents and rests on the possibility of an ongoing employment relationship and bottom-up change that can occur only by remedying the structural causes of power disparities. The outcome it seeks, therefore, is the ex ante transformation of the economic conditions and legal rules that enable severe forms of labor exploitation. A labor approach, accordingly, turns to strategies of collective action and bargaining, protective employment legislation, and contextual standard setting, in its attempt to remedy the unequal power relations in labor sectors susceptible to trafficking.

How might this approach play out in practice?

III. CONSENT vs. COERCION

Another difficult conceptual issue within human trafficking law and policy is the meaning of consent and coercion and the complex line-drawing problems that these concepts raise in the implementation and the interpretation of human trafficking laws. Under the TVPA, a legal violation of human trafficking requires evidence of "force, fraud, or coercion" (except for minor victims of sex trafficking). In theory, such conduct in perpetrating forced labor or commercial sex services renders any initial consent that the trafficked person provided meaningless. Although evidence of "force" may be apparent through physical restraint — and evidence of "fraud" equally apparent through false promises — coercion has persisted as a murky concept in human trafficking law and policy.

The ambiguity of coercion as a legal concept was first noted by the *Kozminski* Court, which narrowly defined coercion as direct or threatened physical force or legal restraint. In rejecting the *Kozminski* standard, the TVPA aimed to broaden the legal standard for coercion to include psychological and indirect means of effectuating servitude. While this broadened definition better captures the actual dynamics of human trafficking, which often involve non-overt and subtle means of forcing labor, its open-endedness has lent itself to a wide range of views both on what constitutes a "victim of human trafficking" and whether he or she was sufficiently coerced.

According to a report by the Institute Race and Justice at Northeastern University on the way law enforcement officials respond to trafficking, definitional inconsistencies make it difficult for them to implement the TVPA:

> Internal disagreements among task force members about the definition, elements and nature of this crime increase the challenges of multi-agency task force responses. . . . In human trafficking cases the situation is much more ambiguous. In the task forces we observed there were situations where members of the group did not agree about whether or not someone was in an exploitive situation freely or whether they were a victim of force, fraud or coercion.

INST. ON RACE & JUSTICE, NE. UNIV., UNDERSTANDING AND IMPROVING LAW ENFORCEMENT REPONSES TO HUMAN TRAFFICKING 104 (2008). The report further noted that such "[d]efinitional disagreements often have serious consequences for potential victims, such as determining whether or not they will receive benefits that allow them to receive medical and cash assistance and to stay in the country lawfully for some time." *Id.*

In her article, *Trafficking, Migration, and the Law: Protecting Innocents, Punishing Immigrants*, Wendy Chapkis addressed the role that definitional differences can play in the assessment of who is a trafficking victim and whether he or she "consented" to exploitation. She points out the difficult line-drawing problems in determining who is trafficked and who is not. Although written at a time when the TVPA was first enacted, Chapkis' observations continue to have relevance today:

> The Trafficking Victims Protection Act helps to define "compassionate conservatism": a willingness to provide assistance and protection for a few by positioning them as exceptions, proving the need for punitive measures used against the many. The law thus symbolically and legally separates trafficking victims from economic migrants who are understood to have unfairly benefited from facilitated migration. But, in fact, making such distinctions is difficult at best. Amy O'Neill Richards, a State Department analyst with the Bureau of Intelligence and Research, noted that more than a million people are arrested each year by the U.S. Immigration and Naturalization Service (INS). She argued that, among this group, "it is tough to determine who has been severely victimized and trafficked." Indeed, according to O'Neill Richards, the INS "finds it is hard to 'play favorites' because there are countless other illegal aliens who are exploited by unscrupulous employers, and it is not easy to know where you draw the line in terms of who is being exploited." The need to "draw the line" at all is justified by the belief that not all can be deserving victims: "Protection and assistance afforded the victims differ depending upon where the victims fall within the spectrum." . . .
>
> Innocence becomes a key element in separating the violated from violators, but convincing the INS that any migrant is innocent may be an uphill battle: Distinctions regarding trafficking in women, alien smuggling, and irregular migration are sometimes blurred with INS predisposed to jump to the conclusion that most cases involving illegal workers are alien smuggling cases instead of trafficking cases. One INS agent recently stated that there are no innocent victims, they are all willing participants. Consequently, their focus is on deporting the women once they are

discovered. [The TVPA] then, attempts to counter the expectation that all migrants are guilty by creating an utterly passive, entirely pure, and extremely vulnerable victim who is above reproach. Victims are portrayed as no more than unwilling goods exchanged between unscrupulous men. In the words of one anti-trafficking activist, they are just "commodities, they are nothing more than commodities . . . bodies exchanged on a market." Another anti-trafficking activist echoed this description, arguing that trafficked women are "goods and services in an industry without borders." "Innocent victims," in other words, are much more likely to be depicted as objects of exchange than as exploited workers. As such, they are not even guilty of ambition. . . .

The line drawn between the innocent victim and the willful illegal immigrant used to determine punishment and protection is not only a dangerous one, but it is also a distinction that does not hold. Most trafficking victims are also economic migrants. Their victimization most often involves high debts and abusive working conditions, not outright kidnapping and imprisonment. O'Neill Richards noted that many victims even of serious abuse actually resist assistance, distrusting law enforcement and fearing deportation even more than continued exploitation.

In light of the line-drawing difficulties that may result from varied interpretations on the meaning of coercion, one scholar has attempted to delineate a specific legal framework for coercion in the trafficking context. Called "situational coercion," this framework "evaluates all the circumstances surrounding the alleged trafficking scenario, paying special attention to power inequalities and the workers' individual characteristics that may render them vulnerable to exploitation":

Kathleen Kim, *The Coercion of Trafficked Workers*
96 IOWA L. REV. 409 (2011)[4]

[W]hat sets the TVPA apart from its predecessors is its expansive notion of "serious harm," which includes "psychological, financial, or reputational harm"; its emphasis on the "circumstances" of the trafficked victim to determine the seriousness of the threatened harm; and its inclusion of an indirect "scheme, plan, or pattern" of coercion as a sufficient basis for a forced-labor violation. These latter provisions codify portions of the TVPA's original conference report that emphasized an open-ended approach to coercion, responsive to the wide variability in means of coercion depending on the characteristics of individual cases.

For example, in determining the degree of coercion that is legally actionable, the 2008 TVPA incorporates the conference report's instruction that courts take into account the victim's individual circumstances, such as age and background. Furthermore, the 2008 TVPA's reference to "psychological, financial, or reputational harm" as forms of serious harm reflects the conference report's three case examples involving subtle, nonphysical coercion. In one case example, the conference report states that a trafficked domestic worker suffers a threat of serious harm when a trafficker leads her "to believe that children in her care will be harmed if she leaves

---

[4] Copyright © 2011 by Iowa Law Review. Reprinted with permission. Internal citations omitted.

the home." In another scenario, a trafficker subjects a worker to a "scheme, plan, or pattern" when the worker is caused "to believe that her family will face harms such as banishment, starvation, or bankruptcy in their home country." In a third example, individuals traffic children into forced labor by means of "nonviolent and psychological coercion," including "isolation, denial of sleep, and other punishments." These examples describe broader conduct, rather than specific threats, where individuals are coerced into submission by fear of negative consequences other than bodily harm. Additionally, these examples encompass not only a trafficker's directly coercive conduct, but also contemplate the worker's individualized economic and social pressures. For instance, in the scenario of the domestic worker who faces her family's banishment, starvation, or bankruptcy, one can imagine such a consequence for many workers who must migrate for work to sustain their families in their countries of origin. Economically dependent on his or her job, the worker may feel indirectly forced to endure exploitative labor conditions to send money to his or her family to prevent their destitution.

Distinct from the no reasonable alternative framework for coercion, which sets the relevant baseline at physical or legal harm, the TVPA does not limit the range of conceivable possibilities within the realm of nonphysical coercion. Instead, the TVPA's coercion standard depends on the particular circumstances of the trafficking victim. Threatened "harm," whether explicit or implied, is determined according to an assessment of the alleged victim's "background" and "surrounding circumstances"; in other words, the TVPA recognizes that coercion can operate *situationally*. . . .

Is this framework applied subjectively or objectively? The 2008 TVPA indicates that the evaluation of "serious harm" must be "reasonable," connoting an objective standard. Yet, the 2008 TVPA also states that reasonableness should be judged against the victim's background and all the surrounding circumstances, contemplating the victim's particularized traits, which connotes a subjective analysis. . . .

[I]n the trafficking realm, coercion is highly contextualized. The trafficked victim's subjective feelings of being coerced must be objectively reasonable when considering the trafficked victim's circumstances. "Circumstances" include both the victim's particular vulnerabilities as well as the specific facts surrounding the case. As the *Bradley* court stated, "Viewed with the rest of the charge, the district court's instruction makes clear that any fear of serious harm on the part of Hutchinson or Flynn needed to be reasonable for an individual with his special vulnerabilities."

A similar dichotomous analysis takes place in *United States v. Farrell*. In this case, the defendants recruited individuals from the Philippines to work as housekeepers in their hotels in South Dakota. The defendants subjected the workers to harsh working conditions and coerced the workers' compliance through threats of violence, deportation, and social isolation. The court determined that the evidence established sufficient coercion for a finding of forced labor. The workers "subjectively feared" the defendants because they believed that the defendants were capable of "hunt[ing] them down . . . if they were not able to meet their debt obligations or left the Farrells' employment." Furthermore, the court found that the victims' subjective fears were reasonable and supported by objective evidence. For example, the evidence showed that one of the defendants "regularly lost his temper during meetings at the hotel, revealing to the workers his volatile temper and sparking fears that he would resort to physical violence." The victims also reasonably believed that the defendants were "'powerful people'" because they showed the workers a letter from South Dakotan congresspersons "fixing" the workers' visas: "The visas were subsequently approved, leading the workers to believe that the Farrells were well connected politically." . . .

[A] situational coercion theory better accommodates the empirical realities of trafficking cases. In actuality, many human-trafficking cases appear to fall somewhere between consent and coercion. Those who are willing are easier to coerce. Thus, trafficked persons often begin as voluntary migrants who seek economic opportunity. Subsequent to arrival, the trafficked worker, legally disenfranchised and culturally alienated, is far more vulnerable to exploitation. Workers may receive compensation. They may even be free to run errands or move throughout their neighborhood. However, they may not have the freedom to leave their work situation because of a mix of the employers' intimidating conduct with the workers' own economic or social circumstances.

Like the no reasonable alternative framework, situational coercion is also a phenomenon of constrained choice sets, which limit an individual's freedom, but its sufficiency does not rely on violation of that individual's moral baseline. Instead, the constraints on a worker's alternatives depend on all the circumstances of the case, including the worker's vulnerabilities and the power inequality between the worker and the employer. Vulnerabilities can include such things as irregularized immigration status, cultural and linguistic isolation, poverty and impoverished dependent family members, youth, and illiteracy. Differentials in power are characterized by the worker's dependency on the employer and the employer's ability to inflict some type of harm on the worker. The situational coercion framework asks whether the alleged trafficker took advantage of these vulnerabilities and power imbalances to obtain labor or services at an exploited price. Thus, as described in *Garcia v. Audubon*, the undocumented status of the workers and their dependency on their employer for housing provided the employer with enormous power over them. The employer exercised this power and forced the workers to comply with the exploitive working conditions by "taking advantage of the [workers'] undocumented immigration status" and threatening the workers with eviction when they complained about the substandard working conditions. The court determined that the workers established a prima facie case for coercion under the TVPA. . . .

The relevance of power and vulnerability in the determination of a trafficking violation has been recognized by a number of psychological and sociological studies. A recent report explains that the "most common and perhaps the most problematic" means of coercing labor is through the "abuse of power or of a position of vulnerability." The characteristics that render victims vulnerable to coercion are wide ranging, including "insecurity or illegality of the victim's administrative status, economic dependence or fragile health." Vulnerability may be "physical, psychological, emotional, family-related, social or economic." The presence of vulnerabilities facilitates coercion. Explicit threats are not needed when the workers, because of their desperate situations, must depend on their employer for basic essentials: "Economic deprivation creates dependence on the trafficker for food and shelter, with victims unable to find other viable options." These "multiple dependenc[ies]" exacerbate power differentials, allowing for increased opportunity to manipulate and control the insecure workers.

NOTES AND QUESTIONS

1. How do both the Palermo Protocol and the TYPA address the issues of consent and coercion? How do each of them differentiate between consent and coercion, if at all? *See also* Marisa Silenzi Cianciarulo, *What Is Choice? Examining Sex Trafficking Legislation Through the Lenses of Rape Law and Prostitution*, 6 U. St. Thomas L.J. 54 (2008) (discussing the meaning of consent in the context of sex trafficking and prostitution).

2. Chapkis suggests that the TVPA creates a line between trafficking victims, who receive legal protections, and undocumented workers subjected to labor exploitation, who do not. She characterizes this divide as one of innocent victim versus illegal migrant. Do you agree? Should victims of labor exploitation be given legal protections? Is there a distinction between victims of trafficking and victims of other types of exploitation? What is it? *See also* Dina Francesca Haynes, *Exploitation Nation: The Thin and Grey Legal Lines Between Trafficked Persons and Abused Migrant Laborers*, 23 Notre Dame J.L. Ethics & Pub. Pol'y 1 (2009) (drawing from migration theory to argue for expanded legal protections for exploited migrant workers).

3. What legal elements are required to establish "coercion" sufficient for a violation under the TVPA? Is Kim's "situational" framework helpful in elucidating the TVPA's coercion standard or does it further muddy the already nebulous concept of coercion?

4. What factors should be relevant in determining whether an individual meets the legal standard of human trafficking victim? To what extent should the vulnerable circumstances of a worker such as poverty, noncitizen status, race, class and gender, be relevant to the determination of whether the worker was coerced into forced labor or services under the TVPA?

5. The United Nations Office of Drugs and Crimes recently issued a report intended to highlight the concept of "abuse of a position of vulnerability" as a legally recognized means of committing the crime of human trafficking as contained in Article 3 of the Palermo Protocol. The report explains that legal practitioners who were surveyed "generally agreed that the use of . . . [abuse of a position of vulnerability] must be of a sufficiently specific and serious nature as to vitiate the consent of the victim." U.N. Office on Drugs and Crimes, Issue Paper: Abuse of a Position of Vulnerability and other "Means" Within the Definition of Trafficking in Persons, at 9 (2012). How might the concept of "abuse of position of vulnerability" be applied in trafficking cases?

IV. CONCLUSION

This chapter has presented a diverse range of theoretical and policy perspectives on anti-trafficking frameworks. There are many varied approaches and new approaches continually emerge. Attention to these issues and related concepts are highly relevant and meaningful in the context of human trafficking as line drawing and ambiguity in "blurry line" trafficking cases persists. As a result, inquiry into and discussion of these issues will certainly continue on for some time.

Chapter 14
SPECIAL ISSUES RELATED TO SPECIFIC TRAFFICKED POPULATIONS

It is beyond the scope of this book to discuss every type of trafficking situation and the unique issues faced by each victim. However, it is often the case that similarly situated trafficking victims face similar obstacles and barriers to identification and protection — and that these groups are particularly vulnerable to being exploited by traffickers. In this chapter we focus on the special issues faced by a few of these groups in the United States: undocumented workers, victims of sex trafficking, domestic workers for diplomats, and agricultural workers.

I. IMMIGRATION ENFORCEMENT AND UNDOCUMENTED WORKERS

A. Undocumented Workers

The Supreme Court in *United States v. Kozminksi* recognized that the unique vulnerabilities of certain workers could be taken into account when considering violations of involuntary servitude. In particular, the majority stated that threatening immigrant workers "with deportation could constitute the threat of legal coercion that induces involuntary servitude, even though such a threat made to an adult citizen of normal intelligence would be too implausible to produce involuntary servitude." In doing so, the *Kozminski* majority contemplated the role that a worker's immigration status or lack of immigration status might play in facilitating his or her exploitation. More recently, modern human trafficking cases have highlighted that a violation of forced labor may be established where an employer takes advantage of a worker's undocumented status to compel labor. For example, the court in *Garcia v. Audobon* explained that the defendants engaged in a "pattern of conduct . . . to force the plaintiff-employees to work by taking advantage of [their] undocumented immigration status." Similarly, in *United States v. Calimlim*, 538 F.3d 706 (7th Cir. 2008), the Seventh Circuit stated that "[t]he Calimlims [] warned Martinez about her precarious position under the immigration laws" in order to instill fear in their domestic worker that detrimental immigration consequences would result if she failed to comply with the work situation. Because of the vulnerability to both human trafficking and labor exploitation that noncitizen, particularly undocumented, workers face, this part provides an overview of the workplace conditions and immigration-related legal issues that affect them.

According to experts on the intersection of immigration and workers' rights, undocumented workers experience a greater number of unlawful working conditions such as substandard wages, overtime violations, and health and safety violations. *See* Annette Bernhardt, Siobhán McGrath & James DeFilippis, *Report: Unregulated Work in the Global City: Employment and Labor Law Violations in New York City* (Brennan Center for Justice at NYU Law School 2007), *available at* http://nelp.3cdn.net/cc4d61e5942f9cfdc5_d6m6bgaq4.pdf. Many undocumented workers are found in low-wage occupations such as agriculture, construction, manufacturing, and service industries, where workers face the greatest risk of exploitation. *Id.* While there is little comprehensive national data, due to the hidden nature of the undocumented workers' employment, a recent study of Los Angeles low-wage workers found that 76 percent of undocumented workers in Los Angeles worked off-the-clock without pay and over 85 percent did not receive overtime pay. Ruth Milkman et al., *Wage Theft and Workplace Violations in Los Angeles: The Failure of Employment and Labor Law for Low-Wage Workers*, 46–48 (2010). The day laborer population, 75 percent of which has been estimated as undocumented, may also face employment abuses. Almost half of this population reports wage theft and denial of food and water while on the job. Many of these workers also reported verbal and physical harassment by their employers including threats of deportation. Abel Valenzuela, Jr. et al., *On the Corner: Day Labor in the United States*, 17 (UCLA Center for the Study of Urban Poverty Jan. 2006), *available at* http://www.sscnet.ucla.edu/issr/csup/uploaded_files/Natl_DayLabor-On_the_Corner1.pdf.

For undocumented workers who complain about substandard working conditions, employers may retaliate by reporting the workers' unauthorized status to immigration authorities. *See, e.g., Rivera et al. v. Nibco, Inc.*, 364 F.3d 1057, 1064 (9th Cir. 2004) ("While documented workers face the possibility of retaliatory discharge for an assertion of their labor and civil rights, undocumented workers confront the harsher reality that, in addition to possible discharge, their employer will likely report them to the INS and they will be subjected to deportation proceedings or criminal prosecution."). Employer retaliation, while unlawful under employment and labor laws, such as the FLSA, Title VII, and the NLRA, may still provide a legitimate basis for removal. *See Montero v. INS*, 124 F.3d 381, 384–85 (2d Cir. 1997) (reasoning that "[w]hether or not an undocumented alien has been the victim of unfair labor practices, such an alien has no entitlement to be in the United States," and holding that information about immigration status from employers in violation of labor laws can form a basis for deportation). This may reduce employer accountability for workplace violations against undocumented immigrants, thereby producing additional incentives for unscrupulous employers to employ and to exploit undocumented workers. In some instances, as noted above in *United States v. Calimlim* and *Garcia v. Audobon*, this may lead to exploitation that constitutes forced labor and human trafficking.

Rampant abuses against temporary workers have also been documented. In particular, the H-2A nonimmigrant visa program has been characterized by Mary Bauer, the Legal Director of the Southern Poverty Law Center, as akin to slavery because workers are especially vulnerable to employment abuses due to the restrictive terms of their visa status. Mary Bauer, *Close to Slavery: Guestworker Programs in the United States* (Southern Poverty Law Center Feb. 2007), *available at* http://www.splcenter.org/pdf/static/SPLCguestworker.pdf; *Litany of Abuses: More — Not Fewer — Labor Protections Needed in the H-2A Guestworker*

Program (Farmworker Justice Dec. 2008), *available at* http://www.fwjustice.org/Immigration_Labor/H2abDocs/LitanyofAbuseReport12-09-08.pdf.

Moreover, discrimination against immigrants, even those who have legal permanent residency, has been documented to have an overall impact on working conditions. *See* Leticia M. Saucedo, *The Employer Preference for the Subservient Worker and the Making of the Brown Collar Workplace*, 67 Ohio St. L.J. 961, 962 (2006) (arguing that the "brown collar [Latino] labor pool is presumed to be undocumented," and low-wage Latino workers face negative employment treatment "regardless of documentation status").

B. Immigration Reform and Control Act

The chief law regulating immigration enforcement in the workplace is the Immigration Reform and Control Act of 1986 ("IRCA"), which as discussed below has been cited as sometimes facilitating the exploitation of undocumented workers, rather than preventing it. Previous to the passage of the IRCA, employers could hire undocumented immigrants without sanction. With the objective to eliminate unauthorized migration — which was thought to be driven largely by employment opportunities in the United States — Congress passed IRCA in 1986, reversing this implicit federal policy by transferring immigration enforcement to the workplace. Employers who knowingly hire unauthorized aliens can be sanctioned under IRCA's immigration regulatory regime. 8 U.S.C. § 1324(a). Employers must therefore verify the legal immigration status of their employees upon hiring. In theory, immigration status verification and the threat of sanctions provide an incentive to employers to identify potential immigration violators as employees, thereby deterring illegal immigration. Richard M. Stana, Director, Homeland Security and Justice, Statement, *Immigration Enforcement: Preliminary Observations on Employment Verification and Worksite Enforcement Efforts*, at 1 (GAO 2005) ("As we and others have reported in the past, the opportunity for employment is one of the most important magnets attracting illegal aliens to the United States. To help address this magnet, in 1986 Congress passed the Immigration Reform and Control Act (IRCA), which made it illegal for individuals and entities to knowingly hire, continue to employ, or recruit or refer for a fee unauthorized workers.").

In addition to its enforcement provisions, IRCA implemented a broad amnesty to certain undocumented immigrants who had resided continuously in the United States for a number of years. INA § 245A. IRCA also included provisions against national origin and alienage discrimination to protect lawful workers from adverse employment decisions based on a worker's foreign appearance. INA § 274B. However, IRCA did not contemplate substantive civil rights protections for undocumented workers, since its chief goal was to bring an end to unauthorized migration.

In the years that followed IRCA's passage, the demand of the U.S. economy has perpetuated the hiring of undocumented labor. Moreover, commentators and advocates have argued that IRCA's enforcement framework has facilitated the exploitation of undocumented workers by empowering employers to act as immigration enforcers, who are required to investigate the immigration status of their workers. In doing so, at least one scholar has contended that IRCA confers "a broad coercive power on employers," which allows them to threaten workers with the verification of their immigration status or reporting workers' unauthorized status to ICE when immigrant workers "seek to form a union, demand overtime pay, resist sexual harassment, or otherwise defend their interests in the workplace." Michael Wishnie, *Prohibiting the Employment of Unauthorized Immigrants: The Experiment Fails*, 2007 U. CHI. LEGAL F. 193 at 215; *see also* Stephen Lee, *Private Immigration Screening in the Workplace*, 61 STAN. L. REV. 1103 (2009).

In addition to the role that employers play in implementing IRCA's provisions, recent governmental enforcement of IRCA has been characterized as having detrimental consequences on undocumented workers who may have experienced workplace exploitation. Under the Bush Administration, the enforcement of IRCA was primarily exercised through ICE's deployment of worksite raids, large-scale investigations of immigration violations in the workplace. ICE swept and raided workplaces populated by undocumented immigrants, enforced employment verification laws, and arrested those who failed to comply. These raids led to the mass firing and deportation of unauthorized workers without regard to whether they had been trafficked or exploited in their work situations:

> [I]n the aftermath of the raids, numerous employment abuses have been uncovered.... For example, an ICE warrant for the Agriprocessors raid states that a witness observed a "floor supervisor blindfolded an immigrant with duct-tape" and then "took one of the meat hooks and hit the Guatemalan with it." According to an attorney who interviewed some of the detained Agriprocessors' workers, the company consistently underpaid the workers claiming that the workers owed debts of immigration fees. The company also denied the workers breaks and prohibited them from using restrooms during ten-hour shifts. Workers reported physical abuse and female workers reported sexual abuse by company supervisors. Agriprocessors also allegedly violated numerous child labor laws by forcing under-age employees to labor up to seventeen hours per day in prohibited occupations and under dangerous conditions....

> ... In a similar scenario, in June 2007, ICE raided three Fresh Del Monte Produce plants in Portland, Oregon, taking into custody one hundred sixty-seven workers for the administrative violation of unlawful presence. After the raid, it was revealed that the "Oregon Occupational Safety and Health Division had opened two separate investigations into safety practices at the plant." In retaliation, employers fired the workers who had made the complaints. The health and safety violations included unsanitary living and working conditions on the farms, such as a lack of bathrooms and drinking water and improper exposure to pesticides. Complaints to the Oregon Bureau of Labor also revealed minimum wage and overtime violations, unconscionably long work shifts, and denial of rest breaks. Despite these allegations, "none of the workers detained in the ICE raids were allowed to file or pursue claims against their employer."

Kathleen Kim, *The Trafficked Worker as Private Attorney General: A Model for Enforcing the Civil Rights of Undocumented Workers*, 2009 U. CHI. LEGAL F. 247.

Those who employed the workers remained largely unaffected. Even as late as 2008, when ICE stated a commitment to targeting employers and protecting workers, less than 2.5 percent of the individuals arrested as a result of ICE work-site enforcements were employers. Fact Sheet, Worksite Enforcement Strategy, U.S. Dep't of Homeland Security (Apr. 30, 2009), *available at* http://www.ice.gov/doclib/news/library/factsheets/pdf/worksite-strategy.pdf.

In response to criticisms of high visibility raids and with an increased ICE budget, the current administration reduced the number of "headline-making factory raids" and replaced them with workplace audits or so-called "silent raids." Julia Preston, *Illegal Workers Swept from "Silent Raids,"* N.Y. TIMES, July 10, 2010, at A1. During workplace audits ICE conducts lengthy investigations of employers and their employment records to verify that the immigration status and identification documents of all their employees are available and correct. Though the Administration states that audits discourage employers from hiring undocumented immigrants whom they might exploit and victimize, statistics from audits demonstrate that a large number of discharges of undocumented workers frequently occurs. In 2011, ICE conducted audits of employee files at almost 2,500 companies. As a result of these inspections, there were 713 criminal arrests made: 221 were owners, managers or supervisors facing charges such as harboring or knowingly hiring unauthorized workers. The remaining 492 criminal arrests made were workers, who faced charges of aggravated identity theft and Social Security fraud. Immigration and Customs Enforcement, *Fact Sheet: Worksite Enforcement* (May 23, 2012), *available at* http://www.ice.gov/news/library/factsheets/worksite.htm.

NOTES AND QUESTIONS

1. Are these immigration workplace enforcement measures a positive preventive strategy for human trafficking? Or does heightened immigration enforcement in the workplace facilitate trafficking? What kinds of reforms to IRCA and its implementation strategy might reduce human trafficking and protect and assist human trafficking survivors?

2. Do audits increase or decrease the likelihood that employers will take advantage of undocumented workers? Do audits or raids impact the likelihood of an undocumented worker to be trafficked? If so, how?

* * *

The Supreme Court interpreted IRCA's prohibition against the hiring of unauthorized workers in *Hoffman Plastic Compounds, Inc. v. NLRB*. In a five to four opinion authored by Justice Rehnquist, the Court determined that an undocumented worker, wrongfully terminated from his job for union organizing, was not entitled to the traditional remedy of back pay and reinstatement under the National Labor Relations Act. As discussed below, this decision has been cited by commentators and advocates as chilling undocumented workers from complaining about substandard working conditions, which in turn, has been linked to increasing the vulnerability of these workers' more severe exploitation. The following excerpt describes the *Hoffman* majority's reasoning:

> Under the IRCA regime, it is impossible for an undocumented alien to obtain employment in the United States without some party directly contravening explicit congressional policies. Either the undocumented alien tenders fraudulent identification, which subverts the cornerstone of IRCA's enforcement mechanism, or the employer knowingly hires the undocumented alien in direct contradiction of its IRCA obligations. The Board asks that we overlook this fact and allow it to award backpay to an illegal alien for years of work not performed, for wages that could not lawfully have been earned, and for a job obtained in the first instance by a criminal fraud. We find, however, that awarding backpay to illegal aliens runs counter to policies underlying IRCA, policies the Board has no authority to enforce or administer. Therefore, as we have consistently held in like circumstances, the award lies beyond the bounds of the Board's remedial discretion.
>
> The Board contends that awarding limited backpay to Castro "reasonably accommodates" IRCA, because, in the Board's view, such an award is not "inconsistent" with IRCA. The Board argues that because the backpay period was closed as of the date Hoffman learned of Castro's illegal status, Hoffman could have employed Castro during the backpay period without violating IRCA. The Board further argues that while IRCA criminalized the misuse of documents, "it did not make violators ineligible for back pay awards or other compensation flowing from employment secured by the misuse of such documents." This latter statement, of course, proves little: The mutiny statute in *Southern S.S. Co.*, and the INA in *Sure–Tan*, were likewise understandably silent with respect to such things as backpay awards under the NLRA. What matters here, and what sinks both of the Board's claims, is that Congress has expressly made it criminally punishable for an alien to obtain employment with false documents. There is no reason to think that Congress nonetheless intended to permit backpay where but for an employer's unfair labor practices, an alien-employee would have remained in the United States illegally, and continued to work illegally, all the while successfully evading apprehension by immigration authorities. Far from "accommodating" IRCA, the Board's position, recognizing employer misconduct but discounting the misconduct of illegal alien employees, subverts it.
>
> Indeed, awarding backpay in a case like this not only trivializes the immigration laws, it also condones and encourages future violations. The Board admits that had the INS detained Castro, or had Castro obeyed the law and departed to Mexico, Castro would have lost his right to backpay. Castro thus qualifies for the Board's award only by remaining inside the United States illegally. Similarly, Castro cannot mitigate damages, a duty our cases require, without triggering new IRCA violations, either by tendering false documents to employers or by finding employers willing to ignore IRCA and hire illegal workers. The Board here has failed to even consider this tension.

The following excerpt provides a glimpse of Justice Breyer's dissent:

> I cannot agree that the backpay award before us "runs counter to," or "trenches upon," national immigration policy. As *all* the relevant agencies (including the Department of Justice) have told us, the National Labor Relations Board's limited backpay order will *not* interfere with the implementation of immigration policy. Rather, it reasonably helps to deter unlawful activity that *both* labor laws *and* immigration laws seek to prevent. Consequently, the order is lawful.
>
> The Court does not deny that the employer in this case dismissed an employee for trying to organize a union — a crude and obvious violation of the labor laws. And it cannot deny that the Board has especially broad discretion in choosing an appropriate remedy for addressing such violations. Nor can it deny that in such circumstances backpay awards serve critically important remedial purposes. Those purposes involve more than victim compensation; they also include deterrence, *i.e.*, discouraging employers from violating the Nation's labor laws.
>
> Without the possibility of the deterrence that backpay provides, the Board can impose only future-oriented obligations upon law-violating employers — for it has no other weapons in its remedial arsenal. And in the absence of the backpay weapon, employers could conclude that they can violate the labor laws at least once with impunity. See *A.P.R.A. Fuel Oil Buyers Group, Inc.*, 320 N.L.R.B. 408, 415, n. 38 (1995) (without potential backpay order employer might simply discharge employees who show interest in a union "secure in the knowledge" that only penalties were requirements "to cease and desist and post a notice"); *EEOC v. Waffle House, Inc.*, 534 U.S. 279, 296, n. 11, 122 S.Ct. 754, 151 L.Ed.2d 755 (2002) (backpay award provides important incentive to report illegal employer conduct); *Albemarle Paper Co. v. Moody*, 422 U.S. 405, 417–418, 95 S.Ct. 2362, 45 L.Ed.2d 280 (1975) ("It is the reasonably certain prospect of a backpay award" that leads employers to "shun practices of dubious legality"). Hence the backpay remedy is necessary; it helps make labor law enforcement credible; it makes clear that violating the labor laws will not pay.

NOTES AND QUESTIONS

1. By denying backpay and reinstatement to Jose Castro, the Court prioritized IRCA's immigration enforcement goals over the NLRA's protection of organizing activity from employer retaliation. Yet, most remedies for undocumented workers under federal anti-discrimination laws and FLSA remain intact. *Rivera v. Nibco, Inc.*, 364 F.3d 1057 (9th Cir. 2004) (upholding a protective order against discovery into a plaintiff's immigration status and finding that even in light of *Hoffman*, immigration status is not relevant to determining whether an employer engaged in national origin discrimination under Title VII); *Liu, et al v. Donna Karan Intl, Inc*, 207 F. Supp. 2d 191 (S.D.N.Y. 2002) (holding that the Hoffman decision had no bearing on the recovery of backpay for undocumented plaintiffs filing suit under the FLSA).

Despite the continued existence of potential remedies for undocumented workers, *Hoffman* has had a lasting impact on the immigrant community. Advocates argue that *Hoffman* has chilled immigrant workers, even those with legal status, from reporting workplace violations, thereby permitting employers to exploit workers with impunity. Amy Sugimori, et al., *Assessing the Impact of the Supreme Court's Decision in* Hoffman Plastic Compounds v. NLRB *on Immigration Workers and Recent Developments* (Nat'l Employment Law Project and Nat'l Immigration Law Center), *available at* http://blogs.umass.edu/ulaprog/files/2008/06/assessing-the-impact-of-hoffman-plastics.pdf; *see also* Wishnie, 2007 U. CHI. LEGAL F. at 213 (citing a broad consensus of labor, civil, and immigrants' rights groups opposed to IRCA's sanctioning regime).

Do you agree? After *Hoffman*, do employers have incentives to comply with the NLRA and other worker protection statutes? Do employees have any incentive to assert the NLRA's protections?

2. Professor Maria Ontiveros examines the Thirteenth Amendment implications of *Hoffman* in *Immigrant Workers' Rights in a Post-Hoffman World — Organizing Around the Thirteenth Amendment*, 18 GEO. IMMIGR. L.J. 651 (2004).

> By legally sanctioning and creating a class of workers that labor in conditions below the floor which has been established for free labor, *Hoffman* and its progeny would violate the Thirteenth Amendment. A two-tiered system of labor, with the lower tier composed primarily of workers of color, violates . . . the purpose of the Thirteenth Amendment.
>
> A broad reading of *Hoffman* violates the doctrine developed in the involuntary servitude line of cases because it depresses the working and living conditions of both undocumented workers and those not involved in the system. The creation of a class of workers laboring below the statutory minimum will depress the wages and working conditions of all workers. *Hoffman* has the potential to create a semi-free caste of workers that will drag down the protection of all workers. [The involuntary servitude cases] provide support for the proposition that treating some workers as less than free violates the Thirteenth Amendment.
>
> This racially based two-tiered system of labor is also a slavery-like system prohibited by the Thirteenth Amendment. Undocumented workers are in a separate tier because, as a matter of law, they are not effectively protected by the labor laws. Without protection and without the ability to seek legal recourse, they labor in conditions that are below the floor set for free labor. No new floor, other than that offered by the market, is created in its place. This is the type of system which, in practical operation, tends to produce undesirable results approaching those found in African-American slavery for several reasons. First, these workers are primarily racial minorities, who are laboring in dangerous and oppressive conditions similar to those who were enslaved. Like slaves, undocumented workers are also excluded from the political process so they cannot improve their situation in traditional ways. Second, the inability to appeal to statutorily provided labor rights is a "badge[] and incident" of slavery that violates the Thirteenth Amendment. Because they lack legal recourse and remedy, they

are within the absolute control of their employers, in the same way that slaves were in *Mann*. Finally, if courts find that the labor laws do not cover these workers, it defines them as not qualifying as "individuals," which harkens back to language that found slaves were not "persons."

Viewing an unprotected tier of labor as a violation of the Thirteenth Amendment has other implications. For example, the exclusion of certain industries from our labor laws is problematic. Two industries in particular have been excluded: the agricultural industry and the domestic industry. Both of these tend to have a majority of workers who are people of color. There is also compelling evidence that these industries were excluded from New Deal labor legislation for racial reasons — to perpetuate the use of African Americans in the two areas where they labored as slaves and on which the South was dependent. This challenge has force because they are completely excluded from coverage under our laws, rather than merely being afforded lower or different protections.

Most importantly, a Thirteenth Amendment challenge to *Hoffman* can be based on the broader understanding of the purpose of the Thirteenth Amendment, rather than the textual approaches that focus on "involuntary servitude" or "slavery." By harkening back to the legislative history and social understanding of the Amendment, Thirteenth Amendment doctrine can tackle a broader range of race, labor and class issues. The evil of slavery was not just that people were not allowed to quit. It was the treatment of people as less than human and as property. The wrong of slavery was the commodification and dehumanization of a racially defined group of workers. The current treatment of undocumented immigrant workers mirrors this commodification and dehumanization.

Some people object to the extension of labor protection to undocumented workers because they believe that, being in this country illegally, these workers do not deserve any benefits or protection. Although that argument may have some intuitive appeal, it does not foreclose the Thirteenth Amendment analysis. As previously discussed, the text of the statute and the early cases are concerned not only with the moral claims of slaves, but also with the effects of slavery on other workers and on the country as a whole. Thus, Section 1 of the Amendment states simply, "[n]either slavery nor involuntary servitude . . . shall exist within the United States." The narrowest, most textual reading of the Amendment prohibits involuntary servitude, slavery and slavery-like systems, regardless of who is being enslaved. The social understanding of the Amendment brings in the moral claims both of slaves and former slaves to connect the economic and labor market aspects of the Amendment to the notion of workers rights as human rights.

Professor Ontiveros suggests that the *Hoffman* decision violates the Thirteenth Amendment by relegating undocumented workers to a second tier status that labors below the minimum floor of acceptable labor standards. Do you agree? What are the implications of *Hoffman* for trafficked workers?

3. At the time of the writing of this casebook, a bipartisan group of legislators recently introduced the much anticipated comprehensive immigration reform bill, Border Security, Economic Opportunity, and Immigration Modernization Act of 2013 (S. 744). The bill proposes to repeal the *Hoffman* decision by providing that workers may not be denied backpay or other remedies based on their immigration status. The bill also provides expanded U-visa relief for workers who pursue civil claims against their employers for serious workplace exploitation or retaliation. Yet, the bill also makes mandatory, E-Verify, an electronic database verification system that employers would be required to use to check the immigration status of their workers. Critics of E-Verify have raised issues related to errors in the current E-Verify system and the heightened role of employers as immigration enforcers. *See* Juliet Stumpf, *Getting to Work*, 2 U.C. IRVINE L. REV. 381 at 395 (Feb. 2012). Do these immigration reform measures achieve the right balance in decreasing the vulnerability of undocumented workers to exploitation and trafficking while maintaining the enforcement of IRCA through E-Verify? Why or why not?

II. VICTIMS OF SEX TRAFFICKING

Federal prosecutions of sex trafficking cases far outpace the number of labor trafficking cases prosecuted. "In fiscal year 2010, federal law enforcement officials filed 32 labor trafficking cases against a total of 68 defendants, and 71 cases against 113 total defendants under the sex trafficking provision at 18 U.S.C. § 1591."[1] Increased familiarity with sex trafficking cases however has not led to sex trafficking victims consistently being treated as victims. Victims of sex trafficking are at risk of being treated as criminals, particularly at the state level, where victims of sex trafficking, including minors, are often arrested and charged with prostitution and related crimes. The State Department's 2012 Trafficking in Persons (TIP) report specifically addressed this issue and noted that "[T]he TVPA provides that victims should not be incarcerated, fined, or otherwise penalized for unlawful acts committed as a direct result of being trafficked. [Yet] NGOs reported some cases of prosecutions of trafficking victims. In 2010, the most recent year for which data are available, 112 males and 542 females under 18 years of age — some of whom were likely trafficking victims — were reported to the FBI as having been arrested for prostitution and commercialized vice."[2]

Such treatment is surprising given the TVPA's definition of sex trafficking. The aim of this definition was highlighted in the purposes and findings of the TVPA which explained that: "[t]rafficking includes all the elements of the crime of forcible rape when it involves the involuntary participation of another person in sex acts by means of fraud, force, or coercion."[3] Yet despite this recognition, victims of sex trafficking are not treated as victims of forcible rape or even in many cases even

---

[1] *See* U.S. DEP'T OF JUSTICE, ATTORNEY GENERAL'S ANNUAL REPORT TO CONGRESS AND ASSESSMENT OF U.S. GOVERNMENT EFFORTS TO COMBAT TRAFFICKING IN PERSONS 62 (2011); Jayashri Srikantiah, *Perfect Victims and Real Survivors: The Iconic Victim in Domestic Human Trafficking Law*, 87 B.U. L. REV. 157, 177 (2007) (citations omitted).

[2] UNITED STATES DEPARTMENT OF STATE, *2012 Trafficking in Persons Report — United States of America*, June 2012.

[3] 22 U.S.C. § 7101(9) (2012).

viewed as victims of sexual abuse. For victims of sex trafficking it is often their cooperation with the prosecution and not the reality of what has happened to them that determines whether they are treated as a victim and in some cases whether they have access to benefits.[4] For example a U.S. citizen victim of sex trafficking who refuses to cooperate with law enforcement may be charged with prostitution, for adult foreign national victims failure to cooperate may result in criminal charges, deportation, or an inability to receive federal benefits. The risk of failing to identify victims when cooperation is required is discussed by Professor Jayashri Srikantiah in which she points out that, "[t]he decision by a victim to cooperate does not necessarily correlate to her authenticity as a victim. The victims we might characterize as most worthy of relief — those most under the control of the trafficker, or those subjected to the most horrific abuse — may in fact be the least likely to cooperate with law enforcement." See *Perfect Victims and Real Survivors: The Iconic Victim in Domestic Human Trafficking Law*, 87 B.U. L. REV. 157, 201 (2007).

NOTES AND QUESTIONS

1. The TVPA defines an individual to be a victim of a "severe form of human trafficking" if the individual has been subjected to the following: "a commercial sex act [which] is induced by force fraud or coercion, or in which the person induced to perform such act has not attained 18 years of age." 22 U.S.C. § 7102 (14) (2012). An individual's cooperation with law enforcement is irrelevant under this definition. Why then does the issue of whether an individual cooperates with law enforcement arise in sex trafficking cases? Is this a legacy of the Mann Act's early approach of charging victims that refuse to cooperate? Is this a blurring of the lines between whether an individual is a victim of trafficking and whether the individual is eligible for immigration relief?

2. If cooperation is used, in practice, as a way to decide who is a victim and who is not, how might that impact the prosecution of traffickers? For example, are prosecutions at risk if defense attorneys can suggest that victim testimony was only provided so that the victim would not be charged or so the victim could obtain immigration benefits?

3. Does the use of the phrase "victim of sex trafficking" impact the analysis of whether someone must cooperate to be a victim? For example what if we used the language from the purposes and findings of the TVPA and called victims of sex trafficking victims of forcible rape, would there still be a connection between whether an individual cooperated and whether or not the individual was a victim? If there is an impact, what accounts for this impact? Is it the long history of criminalizing prostitution in the United States? Is it because sex trafficking involves a commercial sex act? Other reasons?

---

[4] For adult foreign national victims benefits will be difficult if not impossible to obtain without cooperation. See the Benefits section in Chapter 12.

A. Reconciling State Laws on Sex Trafficking and Prostitution

Treating all victims of sex trafficking as crime victims will require the criminal justice system in the United States to resolve inconsistencies and conflicts between human trafficking and prostitution laws. This is especially true for state level criminal justice systems that protect victims of sexual abuse but rarely consider victims of sex trafficking as victims of sexual abuse.

That said, a few states have statutorily amended their child protections systems to include victims of sex trafficking as victims of sexual or child abuse.[5] Absent such legislative reform, some state courts have attempted to resolve the issue by reconciling prostitution laws with consent and human trafficking laws. A case excerpted below, *In re B.W.* from the Texas Supreme Court, illustrates one such attempt at this type of reconciliation.

IN RE B.W.
313 S.W.3d 818 (Tex. 2010)

JUSTICE O'NEILL delivered the opinion of the Court, in which CHIEF JUSTICE JEFFERSON, JUSTICE HECHT, JUSTICE MEDINA, JUSTICE GREEN, and JUSTICE GUZMAN joined.

In this case we must decide whether the Legislature, by its wholesale incorporation of Penal Code offenses into the juvenile justice provisions of the Family Code, intended to permit prosecution of a thirteen-year-old child for prostitution considering its specific pronouncement that a child under fourteen is legally incapable of consenting to sex with an adult. We conclude that transforming a child victim of adult sexual exploitation into a juvenile offender was not the Legislature's intent, and reverse the court of appeals' judgment.

BACKGROUND

B.W. waved over an undercover police officer who was driving by in an unmarked car and offered to engage in oral sex with him for twenty dollars. The officer agreed. When B.W. entered the officer's car, he arrested her for the offense of prostitution. B.W. was originally charged in criminal court, but when a background check revealed that she was only thirteen the case was dismissed. Charges were then refiled under the Family Code, which governs juvenile proceedings.

---

[5] For example, The Building Child Welfare Response to Child Trafficking in Illinois is "designed to increase identification of cases, ensure that child trafficking victims receive full access to the legal and human rights afforded to them under law, and ultimately to prevent further trafficking." Additionally, the project is focused on "enabling child protection staff to identify and access key protections and services for victims, including special visas for undocumented victims, public benefits, job training programs, foster care, assistance in the criminal justice system and mandatory restitution offered under the Trafficking Victims Protection Act (2000) and applicable state laws." LOYOLA UNIVERSITY CHICAGO, CENTER FOR THE HUMAN RIGHTS OF CHILDREN AND THE INTERNATIONAL ORGANIZATION FOR ADOLESCENTS (IOFA), BUILDING CHILD WELFARE RESPONSE TO CHILD TRAFFICKING, *available at* http://www.luc.edu/chrc/pdfs/BCWR_Handbook_Final1_for_posting_1.pdf. (*See also* Appendix 1 by Mary Ellison).

Before trial, a State psychologist examined B.W. During the examination, B.W. related a history of sexual and physical abuse. The psychologist concluded that B.W. was "emotionally impoverished, discouraged and dependent." The psychologist noted that the report should be viewed with caution given that some of B.W.'s statements were inconsistent with probation records, but expressed concern over B.W.'s untreated substance abuse and her report that she had been living, and having sex, with her thirty-two-year-old "boyfriend" for the last year and a half.

At trial, pursuant to an agreed recommendation, B.W. pleaded true to the allegation that she had "knowingly agree[d] to engage in sexual conduct . . . for a fee." Following her plea, the trial court found that B.W. had engaged in delinquent conduct constituting a Class B misdemeanor offense of prostitution as defined by section 43.02 of the Penal Code, and placed her on probation for eighteen months. The trial court denied B.W.'s motion for new trial and granted her permission to appeal. The court of appeals affirmed. We granted B.W.'s petition for review to consider the challenges she raises to her adjudication of delinquency for the offense of prostitution.

Discussion

The statute proscribing prostitution is found in the Texas Penal Code, which does not generally apply to juveniles under the age of seventeen. Instead, the Legislature made a blanket adoption of the Penal Code into the Texas Family Code, which provides that the juvenile justice courts have jurisdiction in all cases involving delinquent conduct of children between the ages of ten and seventeen. The Family Code defines "[d]elinquent conduct" as "conduct, other than a traffic offense, that violates a penal law of this state or of the United States punishable by imprisonment or by confinement in jail." One of the purposes of placing such jurisdiction in civil courts under the Family Code is to "provide for the care, the protection, and the wholesome moral, mental, and physical development of children coming within its provisions."

The offense of prostitution is punishable by confinement in jail, and therefore falls under the Family Code's definition of "delinquent conduct." Under the Texas Penal Code, a person commits prostitution if the person "knowingly offers to engage, agrees to engage, or engages in sexual conduct for a fee." "A person acts knowingly, or with knowledge, with respect to the nature of his conduct . . . when he is aware of the nature of his conduct." Thus, "knowing agree[ment]" suggests agreement with an understanding of the nature of what one is agreeing to do. B.W. contends the Legislature cannot have intended to apply the offense of prostitution to children under fourteen because children below that age cannot legally consent to sex. The State, on the other hand, claims that consent by a child under the age of fourteen is a shifting concept designed to protect victims of sex crimes rather than juvenile offenders like B.W. We agree with B.W.

The notion that an underage child cannot legally consent to sex is of longstanding origin and derives from the common law. While at the time of Blackstone this age was set at ten, every state in the United States has raised this age by statute. Texas follows the majority of states which have established a two-step scheme that differentiates between sex with a younger child and sexual relations with an older teen. The rule's underlying rationale is that younger children lack the capacity to appreciate the significance or the consequences of agreeing to sex, and thus cannot give meaningful consent.

Our Legislature has incorporated this rationale into the Texas Penal Code. In enacting the sexual assault statute, section 22.011 of the Texas Penal Code, the Legislature made it a crime to intentionally or knowingly have non-consensual sex with an adult, or sex under any circumstances with a child (a person under seventeen). There are defenses available if the child is at least fourteen, such as when the accused is no more than three years older than the child, or when the accused is the child's spouse. In those instances, the child's subjective agreement or assent becomes the main issue in determining whether or not a crime has been committed. There are no such defenses, however, when the child is under fourteen, irrespective of the child's purported willingness. Thus, in Texas, "a child under fourteen cannot legally consent to sex."

The Legislature has passed a number of statutes providing greater protection against sexual exploitation for underage children. For example, promotion of prostitution involving an adult, without the use of force, threat, or fraud, is a misdemeanor. Compelling a child under eighteen to commit prostitution, however, is treated as a crime equivalent to using "force, threat, or fraud" to compel an adult to commit prostitution, and is a second-degree felony. Similarly, sexual assault of a child under fourteen is considered "aggravated sexual assault" and is subject to the same consequences as the rape of an adult involving serious bodily injury or other aggravating circumstances. In passing these statutes, the Legislature has expressed both the extreme importance of protecting children from sexual exploitation, and the awareness that children are more vulnerable to exploitation by others even in the absence of explicit threats or fraud.

It is difficult to reconcile the Legislature's recognition of the special vulnerability of children, and its passage of laws for their protection, with an intent to find that children under fourteen understand the nature and consequences of their conduct when they agree to commit a sex act for money, or to consider children quasi-criminal offenders guilty of an act that necessarily involves their own sexual exploitation. In the context of these laws, and given the blanket adoption of the Penal Code into the Family Code, it is far more likely that the Legislature intended to punish those who sexually exploit children rather than subject child victims under the age of fourteen to prosecution. Given the longstanding rule that children under fourteen lack the capacity to understand the significance of agreeing to sex, it is difficult to see how a child's agreement could reach the "knowingly" standard the statute requires. Because a thirteen-year-old child cannot consent to sex as a matter of law, we conclude B.W. cannot be prosecuted as a prostitute under section 43.02 of the Penal Code.

The dissent contends Texas' statutory rape statutes do not render all minors under the age of fourteen incapable of consenting to sex with an adult as a matter of law. In the dissent's view, the statutes merely eliminate consent as an affirmative defense to the offense of child rape. But the very purpose of the Legislature's abrogation of the consent defense was its determination that underage children cannot meaningfully consent to sex. While no statute explicitly states that children under fourteen are unable to provide consent for all purposes, the inability of children to consent to sex as a matter of law is both part of the common law and a necessary inference from section 22.021 and the other statutes dealing with sexual exploitation of a child.

The dissent concedes that children below a certain age lack the mental capacity to consent to certain actions, and that the law reflects that inability to consent. Nonetheless, the dissenting justices would themselves allow children as young as ten to be prosecuted for prostitution. By contrast, our conclusion that children under a certain age lack the legal capacity to consent to sex rests on the legislative policy determination expressed in the statutory rape statute that children under the age of fourteen are legally incapable of consenting to sex.

Courts around the country have long recognized that children lack the experience and mental capacity to appreciate the nature and consequences of sex, and therefore cannot knowingly consent to sex. As Justice Kogan noted in his concurrence in Jones v. State:

> I cannot believe, for example, that any responsible adult seriously thinks a six-year-old legally could consent to sex. Children of that age always lack the experience and mental capacity to understand the harm that may flow from decisions of this type. They may unwittingly "consent" to something that can ruin their lives, jeopardize their health, or cause emotional scars that will never leave them. I think most concerned adults and experts in the field would agree that this lack of prudent foresight continues in youths well into the teen years.

640 So.2d at 1089 [Fla. 1994]. By unequivocally removing the defense of consent to sexual assault, the Texas Legislature has drawn this line at the age of fourteen.

Nor is this the only area in which the law recognizes that minors of a certain age have a reduced or nonexistent capacity to consent, no matter their actual agreement or capacity. A minor under the age of sixteen cannot consent to be married without a court order finding the marriage to be in the child's best interest, no matter how mature the child appears or how earnestly the child might mouth the words "I do." Similarly, a minor's contracts are voidable at the minor's election, even if the minor knew what he or she was doing and innocent people are prejudiced. When it comes to a child under fourteen consenting to sex, the Legislature has made it clear that the child's consent is void rather than voidable. To engage in an individualized determination of a child's capacity to knowingly consent to sex is contrary to the Legislature's pronouncement that all minors under fourteen lack the capacity to give that consent. . . .

We also reject the State's argument that exempting children under fourteen from prosecution for prostitution will somehow undermine the State's ability to protect children and encourage the sexual exploitation of minors. The State claims that under our interpretation, an adult male who agreed to pay a thirteen-year-old girl for sex could claim that he did not commit the offense of prostitution because the sex would not have been consensual. But section 43.02 expressly allows for the prosecution of a person who "solicits another in a public place to engage with him in sexual conduct for hire," regardless of the solicitee's consent. Similarly, pimps and other sexual exploiters of children may still be prosecuted for compelling prostitution and other crimes of sexual exploitation even though the child herself may not be prosecuted for prostitution.

Similarly unavailing is the State's argument that our reading of the law will encourage pimps to seek out young children because they would be immune from criminal liability. The sexual exploitation of children under fourteen is already a crime. It is unclear how the prosecution of a child for prostitution would serve as any further deterrent, especially in the case of children on the streets. *See* Roper, 543 U.S. at 571, 125 S.Ct. 1183 ("[T]he same characteristics that render juveniles less culpable than adults suggest as well that juveniles will be less susceptible to deterrence.") Most of these children are controlled by their pimps through a combination of emotional and financial security mixed with violence and drugs, and are unaware that the treatment they are receiving is against the law.

The State has broad power to protect children from sexual exploitation without needing to resort to charging those children with prostitution and branding them offenders. . . . The dissent suggests that our decision bars the State from providing treatment, confinement, probation, counseling or any other rehabilitation, implying that the juvenile justice system is the only portal to such services for children like B.W. That is simply not true. Even absent a report or investigation, a law enforcement officer may take possession of a child without a court order if a person of ordinary prudence and caution would believe there is an immediate danger to the physical health or safety of the child, or that the child has been the victim of sexual abuse. Presumably a thirteen-year-old girl walking the streets offering sex for money would meet this standard. The State may also seek a court order to take possession of a child to protect the child's health and safety. Thus, the suggestion that lack of criminal prosecution would somehow mean the State would have no option but to put the exploited child back on the streets is entirely without merit. While in CPS [Child Protective Services'] custody, a child has access to a full range of counseling and treatment options, including 24-hour supervision and one-on-one monitoring. CPS provides these services within a purely rehabilitative setting, and without the permanent stigma associated with being adjudged a prostitute. Furthermore, while the trial court in this particular case may have exercised good judgment in adjudicating treatment and rehabilitation, there is no guarantee that a another judge would do the same, nor would the dissent's opinion protect a thirteen-year-old, or even a ten-year-old, from being subjected to a harsh and punitive sentence.

The dissent emphasizes B.W.'s "long and sad history of delinquent behavior," presumably suggesting that her bad behavior is indicative of her mental capacity to commit this crime. The United States Supreme Court has recognized that juveniles "are more vulnerable or susceptible to negative influences and outside pressures," and that "[i]t is difficult even for expert psychologists to differentiate between the juvenile offender whose crime reflects unfortunate yet transient immaturity, and the rare juvenile offender whose crime reflects irreparable corruption." Roper, 543 U.S. at 569, 573, 125 S.Ct. 1183. Notwithstanding that fact, B.W.'s behavior is sadly in keeping with many children who have been abused or neglected at home. This dysfunctional family life leads to problems with discipline and fighting, and often results in the child running away, just as B.W. did. These children are also the ones most at risk of being victimized by pimps and exploited as prostitutes, and are the most in need of serious treatment. . . .

Children are the victims, not the perpetrators, of child prostitution. Children do not freely choose a life of prostitution, and experts have described in detail the extent to which they are manipulated and controlled by their exploiters. . . . Drawing a distinction between consensual sex with a child and exploitation simply blinks reality.

Our Legislature has passed laws recognizing the vulnerability of children to sexual exploitation, including an absolute prohibition of legal consent for children under fourteen. In the absence of a clear indication that the Legislature intended to subject children under fourteen to prosecution for prostitution when they lack the capacity to consent to sex as a matter of law, we hold that a child under the age of fourteen may not be charged with that offense. Accordingly, we reverse the court of appeals' judgment, and remand the case to the trial court for an appropriate disposition.

JUSTICE WAINWRIGHT, joined by JUSTICE JOHNSON and JUSTICE WILLETT, dissenting.

The Court holds that a thirteen-year-old minor cannot be adjudicated under the Juvenile Justice Code for prostitution, despite a clear statutory charge to address such distressing conduct by treatment and rehabilitation of the minor and protection of the public through the juvenile justice system. The text of the Juvenile Justice and Penal Codes does not support the Court's result. The language of the prostitution statute includes thirteen-year-olds, and the Juvenile Justice Code makes them subject to juvenile delinquency proceedings for committing that offense; and neither the Court nor B.W. point to any language in the Juvenile Justice or des that changes the prostitution statute to mean something other than what it says. The Court attempts to justify this infirmity through a narrow exception found in a criminal statute unrelated to the provision proscribing prostitution, even though the circumstances of this case support the juvenile court order of rehabilitation and treatment. The minor's probation report states that B.W. was convicted "for Assault Causes Bodily Injury" and "for Possession of a Controlled Substance." She also pulled a knife on her school principal, threatening to kill him, and seriously assaulted a fellow resident of a group home. Her caseworker explained that she is "violent" and a "chronic runaway." Placed in foster care by Child Protective Services, she ran away from a group home in Harris County the day after her placement there and was missing for over a year before an undercover police officer arrested her for soliciting sex for a fee. After B.W. pled true to commission of prostitution, the juvenile court judge found that she had engaged in delinquent conduct (prostitution) and that rehabilitation was in her best interest and necessary to protect the public. The court ordered probation, treatment, and counseling for the wayward teen under the auspices of the Harris County Juvenile Probation Department, and the court of appeals affirmed the ruling. This Court, however, overturns the treatment order and bars juvenile courts from ordering treatment, confinement, probation, counseling, or any other rehabilitation under the Juvenile Justice Code for minors of age thirteen who commit the charged sex crime. . . .

Notwithstanding the Court's use of the term "prosecute" repeatedly in its opinion, there is no dispute that in the juvenile court proceeding B.W. was not convicted of a crime. She was adjudicated delinquent as a juvenile, and the juvenile court ordered rehabilitation, counseling, and treatment. In fact, the juvenile court ordered only probation for B.W. with no term of juvenile confinement. The Court fails to credit the purpose of the juvenile justice system as distinct from the criminal justice system. Its holding precludes juvenile courts from adjudicating and then ordering counseling and treatment as the Legislature intended for minors like B.W. who commit prostitution. The Legislature enacted the Juvenile Justice Code for various public purposes, including: "to provide for the protection of the public and public safety"; "to promote the concept of punishment for criminal acts"; "to remove, where appropriate, the taint of criminality from children committing certain unlawful acts"; "to provide treatment, training, and rehabilitation that emphasizes the accountability and responsibility of both the parent and the child for the child's conduct"; "to provide for the care, the protection, and the wholesome moral, mental, and physical development of children coming within its provisions"; and "to protect the welfare of the community and to control the commission of unlawful acts by children." . . .

The Legislature decided to subject minors ten or older and younger than seventeen to civil adjudication as opposed to generally subjecting them to the same criminal laws as adults. The Juvenile Justice Code provides a civil means for effectuating its stated purposes to avoid subjecting minors, who might be headed down a treacherous path, to criminal proceedings. Sadly, many minor prostitutes are exploited by others who take advantage of their vulnerability. Those exploiters deserve criminal punishment. However, the Legislature enacted the Juvenile Justice Code not merely as a means of punishment, but also for treatment and rehabilitation in order "to provide for the care, the protection, and the wholesome moral, mental, and physical development of children coming within its provisions." . . .

The Legislature recognizes the problem of prostitution committed by minors, and it continues to work on solutions to address it. Instead of exempting minors from adjudication in the statute, the Legislature requested the committee to study and evaluate the effectiveness of alternative treatment options outside the justice system. In the same September 2009 bill, the Legislature added a defense to prosecution for victims of human trafficking, acknowledging in the bill analysis that trafficked minors are often arrested for committing prostitution. Nonetheless, the Legislature did not modify the Family Code to exempt teenagers from delinquency adjudication for prostitution. But the Court's opinion today does just that and removes the juvenile justice system as a viable alternative to CPS and other treatment programs for minors younger than fourteen who are accused of prostitution. This is an unnecessary and intrusive limitation on the Legislature's discretion to address an important social policy issue.

NOTES AND QUESTIONS

1. *Influence of the TVPA.* The court in *In re B.W.* references a Texas statute that follows the federal approach of the TVPA.[6] The statute, like the TVPA, criminalizes compelled prostitution of adults, and any prostitution of children.

> The Legislature has passed a number of statutes providing greater protection against sexual exploitation for underage children. For example, promotion of prostitution involving an adult without the use of force, threat, or fraud, is a misdemeanor. Compelling a child under eighteen to commit prostitution, however, is treated as a crime equivalent to using "force, threat, or fraud" to compel an adult to commit prostitution, and is a second-degree felony.[7]

Do you think this statute helped sway the majority?

2. *Boyfriends, Pimps, and Traffickers.* Did B.W. have a trafficker? If the answer is no, would it change the court's decision? Note the reference to a "boyfriend." Do you think the court is assuming her boyfriend is her trafficker? Or is this a case about "survival sex"?

Survival sex "refers to the selling of sex to meet subsistence needs. It includes the exchange of sex for shelter, food, drugs, or money." Jody M. Greene, Susan T Ennett & Christopher L. Ringwalt, *Prevalence and Correlates of Survival Sex Among Runaway and Homeless Youth*, 89 AM. J. PUB. HEALTH 1406, 1406 (1999).

As was the case *In re B.W.*, many children who run away from home are forced to turn to selling sex to survive. In 2009, *The New York Times* chronicled the story of one 14-year-old girl who ran away from a group home and spent weeks sleeping in parks and under bridges until a man approached her and offered her a place to stay. She had sex with the man, and he soon became her "boyfriend." The man then threatened to kick her out if she did not have sex with a number of his friends in exchange for money. Fearing that she had no choice, she agreed. For the next 14 months, she lived with the man and was forced to prostitute herself, until eventually escaping. As the article states, "[m]ost of the estimated 1.6 million children who run away each year return home within a week. But for those who do not, the desperate struggle to survive often means selling their bodies." Ian Urbina, *For Runaways, Sex Buys Survival*, N.Y. TIMES, Oct. 26, 2009.

Should the outcome of the case depend on whether there was a boyfriend, pimp, or trafficker involved?

3. *Framing the Victim.* In the dissent, B.W. is framed as "violent and a chronic runaway." She is said to have pulled a knife on her school principal, threatened to kill him, and seriously assaulted a fellow resident of a group home. Would these facts be used if B.W. were viewed as a victim of sexual abuse? More broadly, do sex trafficking victims have to be what Robert Uy calls "perfect victims"? "[The] perfect trafficking victim in the eyes of many . . . is that of a third world woman or child, hiding in a closet, disheveled, fearful shivering, and sexually abused. . . . The idea

---

[6] TEX. PENAL CODE ANN. § 20A.02 (West 2011).

[7] *In re B.W.*, 313 S.W.3d 818, 821 (Tex. 2010).

of saving this victim is 'uncontroversial,' . . . . Unfortunately, the reality is that while many of these victims do exist many other victims exist as well: from men laboring in forced labor camps to women and men working in sweatshops to persons working as caregivers, teachers, and domestic servants. Many of these victims do not fit the 'perfect victim' archetype. As a consequence, many of these people do not get the help that they need and remain in the shadows."

4. *Sex Trafficking and Stockholm Syndrome.* Victims of sex trafficking often have attachments to their traffickers. Traffickers often employ abusive methods of control to impact the victims both physically and mentally. Similar to cases involving Stockholm Syndrome, these victims, who have been abused over an extended period of time, begin to feel an attachment to the perpetrator. This paradoxical psychological phenomenon makes it difficult for law enforcement to breach the bond of control, albeit abusive, the trafficker holds over the victim." Federal Bureau of Investigation, Human Trafficking Bulletin, *available at* http://www.fbi.gov/stats-services/publications/law-enforcement-bulletin/march_2011/march-2011-leb.pdf (last accessed Nov. 5, 2012).

III. DOMESTIC WORKERS

In homes across the United States, foreign nationals are often forced into domestic servitude. These "domestics" may represent one-fourth of all human trafficking victims in the United States.[8]

The plight of these victims was not lost on Congress when it passed the TVPA, as the House Conference Report shows. According to that report, Section 1589 of the TVPA was written so "prosecutors will be able to bring more cases in which individuals have been trafficked into domestic service, an increasingly common occurrence, not only where such victims are kept in service through overt beatings, but also where the traffickers use more subtle means designed to cause their victims to believe that serious harm will result to themselves or others if they leave."[9]

Yet, despite this congressional concern, many barriers to prosecuting domestic service cases still exist. First, these cases often only involve a single victim, with whom few individuals interact other than the victim's trafficker and the trafficker's family members. This makes finding evidence to corroborate any of the victim's allegations against the trafficker more difficult.[10] Second, trafficking victims frequently believe, and are often also told by their traffickers, that U.S. law enforcement officials are corrupt based on their experiences with law enforcement officials in their country of origin — so they are less likely to bring allegations to these officials in the first place.[11] Relatedly, trafficking victims from foreign nations are often told by their traffickers that they are unlawfully in the United States and will be jailed and prosecuted if found by U.S. law enforcement. Third, the TVPA

---

[8] *See* KEVIN BALES & RON SOODALTER, THE SLAVE NEXT DOOR: HUMAN TRAFFICKING AND SLAVERY IN AMERICA TODAY 12 (2009).

[9] H.R. REP. No. 106-939, at 101 (2000) (Conf. Rep.)

[10] *See* Srikantiah, *supra* note 1, at 182.

[11] *Id.* at 186.

"provides few tools for law enforcement agents to ensure the safety of victims' families abroad," which may hamper a victim's willingness to cooperate with law enforcement.[12] And finally, cases of labor trafficking are sometimes incorrectly classified as labor disputes such as demands for payment of wages, rather than complaints relating to violating anti-trafficking statutes.[13]

Because domestic servant cases routinely involve foreign nationals whose job prospects in their home country are bleak, rationalizations are sometimes used to explain why it is acceptable for them to do their labor for little or no pay: the argument that is often made is that these individuals are making more money than they would have made had they remained in their home country. The defendants in *United States v. Djoumessi* used such an argument. That case is excerpted below, although note the victim's name has been changed to "P" to protect her identity.

UNITED STATES v. DJOUMESSI
538 F.3d 547 (6th Cir. 2008)

SUTTON, CIRCUIT JUDGE.

The federal government successfully prosecuted Joseph Djoumessi for violating one (happily) obscure statute — holding someone in involuntary servitude—and for violating another less obscure statute — harboring an alien for private financial gain. Djoumessi claims that the charges violated his rights under the Double Jeopardy Clause and that the government failed to support the involuntary-servitude conviction (and a related conspiracy conviction) with sufficient evidence. We affirm.

In 1996, Joseph and Evelyn Djoumessi, immigrants from Cameroon living in a Detroit suburb, arranged for then-fourteen-year-old "P" to immigrate to the United States from Cameroon under a false name and with a fraudulent passport. The idea behind the arrangement was that P would perform housekeeping tasks for the Djoumessis and look after their two young children, in exchange for which they would provide for her and send her to school.

The arrangement did not work out that way during the next three years, years that P will not soon forget. The Djoumessis required P to perform substantially all of their housework and to provide essentially all of the care for their children. She worked every day from 6:00 a.m. to 10:00 p.m. for no compensation other than room and board, and the Djoumessis never sent her to school. Her housing consisted of a dilapidated, dark and sometimes-flooded space in the Djoumessis' basement. The Djoumessis did not allow her to use any of the working showers in the home, reducing her to collecting hot water from the basement sink in a bucket to clean herself. When P started her menstrual cycle, Evelyn refused to give her sanitary pads, leaving her to use her clothing instead. The Djoumessis also closely controlled P's contact with outsiders, rarely allowing her to leave the property except to take the Djoumessis' children to the bus stop or to other events, and telling her that if she

---

[12] *See id.* at 181.

[13] *See id.* at 186.

ever contacted the police she would go to jail because she was in the country illegally. When the Djoumessis were not satisfied with P's work, they beat her and threatened her. And on top of all of this, Joseph Djoumessi sexually abused P on three occasions.

In February 2000, a neighbor contacted the police about P's situation, after which the police removed her from the home. Later that year, Michigan charged Joseph Djoumessi with kidnapping, conspiracy to kidnap, first-degree criminal sexual conduct, third-degree criminal sexual conduct and third-degree child abuse. *See People v. Djoumessi*, No. 238631, 2003 Mich. App. LEXIS 2746, 2003 WL 22439688, at *1 (Mich. Ct. App. Oct. 28, 2003). A jury convicted him of third-degree criminal sexual conduct and third-degree child abuse and acquitted him of the other charges. *See id.* The court sentenced him to 9-15 years for the sexual-conduct conviction and a concurrent 1-year prison term for the child-abuse conviction. *See id.*

In 2005, a federal grand jury indicted Joseph and Evelyn Djoumessi for holding P in involuntary servitude, *see* 18 U.S.C. § 1584, conspiring to hold P in involuntary servitude, *see id.* §§ 371, 1584, and harboring an alien for private financial gain, *see* 8 U.S.C. § 1324. After a bench trial, the judge found Joseph guilty on all three counts, sentenced him to 204 months' imprisonment (to run concurrently with his state sentence) and ordered him to pay $100,000 in restitution to P. (A jury, who heard the same evidence at the same trial, convicted Evelyn only of conspiracy.)

[The Double Jeopardy argument is omitted.]

Djoumessi's evidentiary challenge to his involuntary-servitude convictions fares no better [than the double jeopardy claim]. In reviewing a sufficiency-of-the-evidence challenge, the issue is not whether *we* "believe [] that the evidence at the trial established guilt," but instead "whether, after viewing the evidence in the light most favorable to the prosecution, *any* rational trier of fact could have found the essential elements of the crime beyond a reasonable doubt." *Jackson v. Virginia*, 443 U.S. 307, 318-19, 99 S. Ct. 2781, 61 L. Ed. 2d 560 (1979) (internal quotation marks omitted). Djoumessi has not made that showing. Section 1584 prohibits a person from "knowingly and willfully hold[ing] to involuntary servitude . . . any other person for any term." 18 U.S.C. § 1584. As used in this section, the term "involuntary servitude" necessarily means a condition of servitude in which the victim is forced to work for the defendant by the use or threat of physical restraint or physical injury, or by the use or threat of coercion through law or the legal process. This definition encompasses those cases in which the defendant holds the victim in servitude by placing the victim in fear of such physical restraint or injury or legal coercion. *United States v. Kozminski*, 487 U.S. 931, 952, 108 S. Ct. 2751, 101 L. Ed. 2d 788 (1988). A § 1584 conviction thus requires proof that the defendant intentionally held the victim in service against her will in one of three ways: (1) by physical restraint or force, (2) by legal coercion or (3) by threats of physical force or legal coercion. *See United States v. Alzanki*, 54 F.3d 994, 1001 (1st Cir. 1995). In assessing whether these things happened, the trier of fact may consider "the vulnerabilities of the victim" as well as "evidence of other means of coercion or of extremely poor working conditions." *Kozminski*, 487 U.S. at 952.

In this case, a rational trier of fact could find beyond a reasonable doubt that the government satisfied these requirements. At trial, P testified not only about her extremely poor working and living conditions but also about Djoumessi's physical abuse and threats of further abuse. Explaining why she never objected to her assigned tasks, P said she had no choice because she was afraid that the Djoumessis would hit her if she did not work. Those fears were not unfounded. Djoumessi once beat her with a belt — severely enough to draw blood — because P failed to make him breakfast, change the sheets and turn off the Christmas lights. He beat her again on two separate occasions when she called a family friend without his permission. And he sexually abused P three times, two of those times by forcing her to engage in sexual intercourse. . . .

Djoumessi also threatened P with imprisonment, telling her that she would go to jail if she contacted the police because he would tell the police that she had entered the country illegally. *Cf. Alzanki*, 54 F. 3d at 1004 ("[T]he evidence must establish that the victim reasonably believed she was left with no alternative to continued servitude that was not the equivalent of imprisonment or worse.") (internal quotation marks omitted). In view of her illegal status and in view of Djoumessi's and Evelyn's threats to send her back to Cameroon, P also described living and working in fear of deportation. *Cf. Kozminski*, 487 U.S. at 948 ("[I]t is possible that threatening . . . an immigrant with deportation could constitute the threat of legal coercion that induces involuntary servitude . . . .").

P's "special vulnerabilities," *id.* at 952, complete this grim picture. Just fourteen years old when the Djoumessis brought her to the United States, she was here illegally, she had no money or other means of support and she had no substantial contact with anyone other than these modern-day Thenardiers. These realities made her more susceptible to the Djoumessis' threats of imprisonment and deportation, even if "such a threat made to an adult citizen of normal intelligence" might be "too implausible to produce involuntary servitude." *Id.* at 948.

Djoumessi first resists this conclusion on the ground that P voluntarily chose to stay. As Djoumessi reads the record, it shows that P did not want to return to Cameroon, *see* JA 138 ("My [greatest] threat was [that] they had the power to send me home. And everything I have done, and being close to going to school, being close to having a life, was for nothing."), and that she wanted to help her family by coming to this country, *see* JA 137 ("I wanted to help my family . . . So, by me staying there, someday I will go to school and someday I will have a career and someday I will be able to help them. So, putting up with it is not going to kill me."). Voluntariness is of course a defense to this charge, and Djoumessi offers one way to read the record so that it supports this defense. But it is not the only way to read the record, and that makes all the difference. Even if P had independent reasons for staying in this country, a rational trier of fact could conclude that it was the Djoumessis' acts of physical abuse and restraint, their threats of more to come and their threats of legal coercion, not P's innocent hopes and dreams, that reasonably made her feel compelled to serve.

Even assuming there were moments during P's stay when she had an opportunity to escape (without risking imprisonment or worse), moreover, Djoumessi's argument still falls short because a rational trier of fact could conclude that P's labor was involuntary for at least *some* portion of her stay. And that involuntary portion would suffice to sustain the conviction. *See* 18 U.S.C. § 1584 (requiring the involuntary servitude to be for "any term"); *see also United States v. Pipkins*, 378 F.3d 1281, 1297 (11th Cir. 2004) ("Section 1584 requires that involuntary servitude be for 'any term,' which suggests that the temporal duration can be slight."), *reinstated by* 412 F.3d 1251 (11th Cir. 2005).

Djoumessi next points out that P's parents placed her in his care under a Cameroonian tradition known as "take my child," by which a poor family entrusts its child to a wealthier one who pledges to care for the child as its own. JA 192-93, 217. Once that tradition is accounted for, Djoumessi argues, it is clear either that P became his adopted daughter as a matter of law or that he at a minimum had the consent of P's parents, both of which would permit him to require her to perform chores around the house. In one sense, Djoumessi is right. Section 1584 does not restrict parents' (or guardians') rights to require their children (or wards) to help with household chores. *See Kozminski*, 487 U.S. at 944 (stating that § 1584 does not interfere with "the right of parents and guardians to the custody of their minor children or wards"). But in at least two material ways, Djoumessi is wrong. The record offers no evidence that Djoumessi was P's legal guardian. And even if Djoumessi had the consent of P's parents to treat her the way he did (something the record also does not support), that would not do the trick. "When parents explicitly renounce their parental relationship — by selling a child into slavery or abandoning [her] to involuntary servitude — parental consent cannot provide a subsequent defense for the third party." *United States v. King*, 840 F.2d 1276, 1283 (6th Cir. 1988). "[A] parental consent defense is particularly inappropriate on the facts of this case" because P's parents "abdicated any semblance of parental supervision and control." Id. at 1282.

Also unavailing is Djoumessi's contention that P necessarily remained voluntarily at his home because he never physically restrained her (in the sense of placing a lock on her door) and she never attempted to escape. But opportunities for escape mean nothing if Djoumessi gave her reasons to fear leaving the house — as indeed he did when he told this fourteen-year-old girl that she would either go to jail or be deported because she had entered the country illegally. *See Kozminski*, 487 U.S. at 948, 952; *see also United States v. Warren*, 772 F.2d 827, 834 (11th Cir. 1985) ("That the worker had the opportunity to escape is of no moment, if the defendant has placed him in such fear of physical harm that he is afraid to leave.").

Bad as P's life in the United States may have been, Djoumessi claims, it was better than what she would have faced had she returned to Cameroon (or stayed there), proving that there was nothing involuntary about her circumstances. Even if we grant the factual premise of Djoumessi's contention (we have no way of knowing), that does not help him: A slave master cannot escape the clutches of § 1584 by contending that he subjected the servant to slightly less wretched conditions than she would have experienced elsewhere. Involuntary servitude is a fixed prohibition, not a relative one. It thus sweeps up all forced labor, even when the victim is freed from the bondages of one bad relationship and placed in another.

A final point deserves mention. "Involuntary servitude" at first blush might seem like strong medicine for what could (charitably) be described as an au pair relationship gone awry. The first answer is that P's circumstances bear an unfortunate resemblance to the conditions that victims of the "padrone system" faced, a system outlawed by one of the two predecessors of § 1584. *See Kozminski*, 487 U.S. at 945-46 (explaining that the passage of § 1584 resulted from the consolidation "of two earlier statutes: the Slave Trade statute . . . and the Padrone statute" and that the histories of those statutes "inform [the] construction of § 1584"). Under the padrone system, children were taken from their families in Italy and brought to the United States to work as street musicians or beggars in large cities. *See id.* at 947. Upon their arrival, the children were literally stranded in large, hostile cities in a foreign country. They were given no education or assistance toward self sufficiency. Without such assistance, without family, and without other sources of support, these children had no actual means of escaping the padrones' service; they had no choice but to work for their masters or risk physical harm. The padrones took advantage of the special vulnerabilities of their victims, placing them in situations they were physically unable to leave. *Id.* at 947-48. It is difficult to see any meaningful difference between the Italian victims of the padrone system and the Cameroonian victim of Joseph Djoumessi.

Another answer is that, even on its own terms, involuntary servitude is not too strong a phrase to describe what Djoumessi and his wife did to this fourteen-year-old girl. "In the jury's view, [the defendant] was part of a conspiracy that substituted for a promised education and compensation a regime of psychological cruelty and physical coercion that took some of the best years of a young girl's life. For that, involuntary servitude is not too strong a term." *United States v. Udeozor*, 515 F.3d 260, 272 (4th Cir. 2008).

NOTES AND QUESTIONS

1. Djoumessi argues that P was better off in the United States: "Bad as P's life in the United States may have been, Djoumessi claims, it was better than what she would have faced had she returned to Cameroon (or stayed there), proving that there was nothing involuntary about her circumstances." Does this argument have merit? Consider the opposite view: perhaps P's economic disadvantage warrants greater protection from the court, since she is even more vulnerable to exploitation?

2. The court comments on the use of the involuntary servitude statute by saying it is a "happily" obscure statute. What do you think of this comment? Does it imply that the incidence of involuntary servitude is low in the United States? If so, do you agree? Or does it assume that the use is low because identification of victims is rare?

3. Note that the victim in this case was found only because a neighbor called the police.

IV. AGRICULTURAL WORKERS

Victims of human trafficking exploited in the agricultural industry are at risk of being identified as unauthorized immigrants rather than victims of human trafficking. When victims of trafficking within the agricultural industry come in contact with law enforcement officials, they may not be screened to see if they are victims — even when officials have been alerted to potential worker violations. As a result, we get situations like the 2008 workplace raid in Postville, Iowa, which Professor

Britta Loftus chronicles below:

On May 12, 2008, the largest single-site workplace raid in U.S. history occurred at the Agriprocessors Inc. meatpacking plant in Postville, Iowa. Two law enforcement helicopters hovered over the plant as federal agents arrested more than three hundred people for crimes involving reporting false Social Security numbers. After being arrested, the workers were detained at a hall at the National Cattle Congress and local jails. Some of the detainees were asked about "caregiver situations" and released "on humanitarian grounds." However, the questioning was limited to issues involving separation of parents and children or others in need — not broader issues intended to identify human trafficking victims. The majority of the detainees were jailed for five months and then deported.

Though no effort to identify human trafficking victims was made during the Postville raid, critics of the raid have argued that some of the laborers may have been victims of human trafficking. Before the raid, a labor union had alerted government investigators that the plant was exploiting underage workers and paying them off the books, and the union had asked the investigators not to raid the plant until a labor investigation had been completed. Nevertheless, the raid went forward. Through her representation of some laborers affected by the raid, Iowa attorney Sonia Parras Konrad found that the child labor law violations involving young Guatemalan workers were "classic examples of human trafficking."

The allegations involving child labor and possible trafficking of children were not the only troubling aspects of the plant. The treatment of adult workers also had characteristics of human trafficking. For example, one source alleged that a supervisor had covered an employee's eyes with duct tape and struck him with a meat hook. Another worker, Mardoqueo Valle-Callejas, said that he was forced to work without pay, was forced to work when injured, and had questionable fees deducted from his earnings.

While it may be true that there is "a fairly thin line between getting shorted on your paycheck and in the end being held, in a sense, in bondage," the enforcement officials in the Postville case did not make any attempt to determine on which side of that thin line the Postville workers fell. Despite facts showing that some of the laborers may have been victims of human trafficking, they did not receive protections afforded to trafficking victims but rather were simply arrested and detained.

The 2010 TIP Report identified raids such as the Postville raid as "blind" raids. Blind raids are characterized by investigators not knowing before the operation whether the workers at the sites may be trafficking victims. Grounded in "assumptions" rather than "evidentiary basis," these blind raids are particularly devastating for human trafficking victims because they "do not include victim identification processes." As a result, blind raids "[hinder] the effectiveness of anti-trafficking efforts" and "can contribute to new cases of human trafficking." The 2010 TIP Report confirmed the existence of blind raids, finding that although the Department of Labor targets civil law enforcement at industries that employ at-risk workers and thus "DOL inspectors and investigators are often in a position to identify exploitive labor practices, which may be indicative of trafficking," "investigators did not receive trafficking-specific training."

Britta S. Loftus, *Coordinating U.S. Law on Immigration and Human Trafficking: Lifting the Lamp to Victims*, 43 COLUM. HUM. RTS. L. REV. 143, 179–81 (2011) (internal citations omitted).

NOTES AND QUESTIONS

1. During a congressional hearing on human trafficking in 2010, Chairman Berman stated that there is "a fairly thin line between getting shorted on your paycheck and in the end being held, in a sense, in bondage."[14] Do you agree? Does this line depend on the economic opportunities in your home country? Should it?

2. Prof. Lotus notes that "[t]he incidence of blind raids is not limited to the factory or agricultural context, but also extends to raids conducted at brothels. In such a federal raid of the Cadena brothels in November 1997, victims were held in detention, but many of the perpetrators evaded arrest. Blind raids can affect both victims of sex trafficking and victims of labor trafficking." Britta S. Loftus, *Coordinating U.S. Law on Immigration and Human Trafficking: Lifting the Lamp to Victims*, 43 COLUM. HUM. RTS. L. REV. 143, 181 (2011).

3. What type of screening should have been done during the Postville raids? Will screening only by law enforcement officials result in victim identification? Is one screening — essentially taking a "snapshot" — enough to decide whether someone is a victim of human trafficking? Professor Bridgette Carr argues for lengthening these "snapshot moments" when decision makers categorize someone as a victim or unauthorized immigrant: "The critical determination of whether [an individual] is a victim of human trafficking or a noncitizen living in the United States without permission should not be left to a law enforcement agent in the heat of a rescue or raid."[15]

---

[14] *Out of the Shadows: The Global Fight Against Human Trafficking: Hearing Before the Subcomm. On Immigration, Citizenship, Refugees, Border Security, and International Law of the H. Comm. on Foreign Affairs*, 111th Cong 104 (2010), *available at* http://foreignaffairs.house.gov/hearing_notice.asp?id=1198.

[15] Bridgette Carr, *Examining the Reality of Foreign National Child Victims of Human Trafficking in the United States*, 37 WASH. U. J.L. & POL'Y 183, 201 (2011) (internal citations omitted).

APPENDIX 1

STATE AND LOCAL HUMAN TRAFFICKING LAWS AND PROSECUTIONS

By Mary C. Ellison, J.D.[1]

As discussed in Chapter 5, the United States enacted the Trafficking Victims Protection Act in 2000 establishing the first comprehensive federal legislation addressing human trafficking in the United States. A few years later, individual states began to enact their own state human trafficking laws. In 2003, Washington was the first state to enact a state anti-trafficking law, followed closely by Texas. Florida and Missouri enacted state anti-trafficking laws in 2004. Between 2005 and 2013, all fifty states and the District of Columbia have enacted labor trafficking criminal laws and 48 states and the District of Columbia have enacted sex trafficking criminal laws. Numerous states have also enacted laws to provide a lower burden of proof for sex trafficking of minors, "safe harbor" for sex trafficked minors, victim assistance, asset forfeiture, wiretapping, civil remedies, training for law enforcement, task forces, hotline posting, and the ability for sex trafficking victims to vacate criminal convictions.

While most states have made good progress in enacting state laws to address human trafficking, the implementation of these laws lags behind with few cases of human trafficking identified and prosecuted by state and local law enforcement and prosecutors. There are a number of factors for the gaps in implementation of these laws include a lack of awareness of human trafficking, insufficient knowledge to identify human trafficking cases, low prioritization of such cases, the complexity of these cases, and challenges in presenting such cases to the court and receiving favorable verdicts.

This chapter will explore the history of state anti-trafficking legal reform, a state-by-state analysis of human trafficking laws, a discussion of the implementation of these laws, and finally, make recommendations for fulfilling the promise of state and local laws to address this heinous crime and grave human rights violation to ensure these laws not only live in state statutes, but also in the lives of all those victimized and enslaved by human trafficking.

---

[1] Mary Ellison is currently a Public Engagement Officer at the Office to Monitor & Combat Trafficking in Persons, U.S. Department of State. The views expressed in this appendix are her own and do not necessarily reflect those of the Department of State or the United States Government. Previously Ms. Ellison served as the Director of Policy for the Polaris Project. The authors would like to thank Ms. Ellison for her contribution to this book.

I. THE HISTORY OF STATE AND LOCAL HUMAN TRAFFICKING LAWS

In the 21st century, legal scholars, human rights advocates, and practitioners alike often conclude that they saw evidence of human trafficking long before the crime was defined in international, federal, and state law but often viewed this evidence as stand-alone criminal activity rather than a cluster of related crimes that constitute what we now know to be human trafficking also known as trafficking in persons or modern-day slavery. For example, professionals working in the field of runaway and homeless youth tell us that they were seeing youth bought and sold for commercial sex acts in the decades of the 1980s and 1990s. Labor unions and immigrant rights groups acknowledge that they too had been seeing labor exploitation rising above wage and hour violations to false imprisonment, illegal restraint, and debt bondage.

As we are painfully aware, during the 18th, 19th, and 20th centuries, the slave trade flourished on both sides of the Atlantic Ocean and even reached as far back as 1502.[2] While the abolition of the British and American slave trade took effect in 1808, it was not until 1865 that the United States abolished slavery within the country through the Thirteenth Amendment to the U.S. Constitution. While the Thirteenth Amendment technically prohibited slavery and involuntary servitude, modern-day purveyors of human trafficking have continued to subvert the Thirteenth Amendment and its enforcing federal and state legislation and to thrive upon the low-risk, high-profit nature of human trafficking making it a multi-billion dollar business today.

While those who profit from human trafficking and modern-day slavery continue to evade accountability, those responsible for enacting and enforcing the laws continue to proceed much too slowly allowing this heinous crime and grave human rights abuse to enslave more than 20 million around the globe. Prior to the enactment of the Trafficking Victims Protection Act (TVPA) in 2000, trafficked persons were more often arrested or deported, charged, prosecuted, and convicted because first responders failed to recognize them as victims of a heinous crime. In addition, traffickers were only sometimes arrested, charged, prosecuted, and convicted but often under state laws other than human trafficking laws.

The TVPA began to shift this paradigm, defined the national response, and created a new framework which elevated the country's and the world's consciousness about a previously misunderstood and unrecognized human rights abuse. In her comments at the launch of the 2012 U.S. *Trafficking in Persons Report*, Secretary of State Hillary Rodham Clinton said:

> I've worked on this issue now for more than a dozen years. And when we started, we called it trafficking. And we were particularly concerned about what we saw as an explosion of the exploitation of people, most especially women, who were being quote, "trafficked" into the sex trade and other

---

[2] Hilary McDonald Beckles, *Slave Voyages: The Transatlantic Slave Trade in Enslaved Africans* (UNESCO, 2002), *available at* http://unesdoc.unesco.org/images/0012/001286/128631eo.pdf.

I. STATE AND LOCAL HUMAN TRAFFICKING LAWS AND PROSECUTIONS

forms of servitude. But I think labeling this for what it is, slavery, has brought it to another dimension.[3]

While the federal government began to shift the paradigm in the early 2000s, most state governments held fast to the belief that each of the stand-alone activities that make up human trafficking was already criminalized. These beliefs created reluctance in many state legislatures when challenged to enact specific anti-trafficking laws. In fact, while states like Washington, Texas, Florida, and Missouri recognized early on that state laws were needed to complement the Trafficking Victims Protection Act of 2000, many states hesitated to pass laws claiming in part that other criminal laws like kidnapping, false imprisonment, felonious restraint, involuntary servitude, promoting prostitution, sexual assault, harboring of aliens, among others were adequate to address the problem. The 1962 Model Penal Code had even provided for a crime of felonious restraint defined as holding another in a condition of involuntary servitude or interfering with a person's liberty as a lesser included crime of kidnapping. As of 2012, Wyoming still had such a statute on the books, and was the last state to enact a comprehensive human trafficking statute in 2013.[4] Several other states had also enacted such statutes in the late 1970s (Missouri § 565.120.1, Nebraska § 28-314; and North Carolina § 14-43.3 to name a few). But anti-trafficking advocates and service providers among other stakeholders and courageous leaders found those laws wanting and slowly chipped away at this resistance in subsequent years buoyed not only by the advances in other states, but also by the development of a number of state model anti-trafficking laws.

On May 14, 2003, Washington State became the first state to enact a state human trafficking criminal law followed by Texas. Both states cited their international borders and occurrences of labor and sex trafficking as factors that contributed to the enactment of such legislation. However, as early as 2001, the media in Washington addressed human trafficking in its state, recognizing that human trafficking occurred within the state's borders.[5] Sex trafficking of women and children and labor trafficking, especially through false promises of marriage[6] or a better life, were cited as key examples of the types of trafficking happening in Washington. Particularly due to Washington's border with Canada and extensive ports, the *Seattle Times* published data in July 2004 that Washington was a "hot bed" for both sex trafficking (e.g., through mail-order brides) and labor trafficking (e.g., agricultural workers).[7]

Meanwhile, in Texas the Committee Report from the House Research Organization cited the border between Texas and Mexico as a critical factor in high rates

---

[3] U.S. Dep't of State, Secretary's Remarks Section, *Release of the 2012 Trafficking in Persons Report*, available at http://www.state.gov/secretary/rm/2012/06/193368.htm.

[4] Wyo. Stat. Ann. § 6-2-7 (2013).

[5] Robert L. Jamieson, *New Law Would Help Stop Tragedy of People Trafficking*, Seattle Post-Intelligencer, Nov. 7, 2001, http://www.seattlepi.com/default/article/New-law-would-help-stop-tragedy-of-people-1071095.php.

[6] *History of our Movement*, Univ. of Wash. Women's Center, http://depts.washington.edu/womenctr/events/human-trafficking-conference-2013/history-of-our-movement/ (last visited Dec. 28, 2012).

[7] Florangela Davila, *Washington State a Hotbed for Human Trafficking, Report Says*, The Seattle Times, July 14, 2004, http://209.157.64.200/focus/f-news/1171283/posts.

of human trafficking in the state.[8] Smuggling can transform into human trafficking, especially of undocumented workers, from Mexico into Texas, and these individuals can be abused during their journey.[9] Media reports also revealed that a key concern for Texas lawmakers were traffickers preying on undocumented workers seeking a better life in the United States, especially after 19 illegal immigrants were found dead in an abandoned trailer.[10] Smuggling-turned-trafficking and abuse of migrants from Mexico into Texas at the hands of traffickers is well documented in Texas news reports.[11] Trafficking of women (especially Latina women) into Texas for commercial sex was also reported.[12]

Florida and Missouri joined Washington and Texas in 2004. At the time, the Center for the Advancement of Human Rights at Florida State University reported that human traffickers were bringing thousands of people into the United States each year and Florida was believed to be one of the top three destinations, along with New York and Texas.[13] In South Florida, federal prosecutions indicated hundreds of farmworkers were victims of human trafficking, and a forced prostitution ring identified as many as 40 young women and girls brought from Mexico. The center also cited a case of "domestic servitude" in Southwest Florida.[14] According to the Florida Criminal Justice Executive Institute, the state legislature adopted Florida Statute 787.06 in response to the widespread problem throughout the state.[15]

Also in 2004, both governmental and non-governmental entities began to develop model anti-trafficking laws to serve as springboards for the drafting and passage of state laws. The U.S. Department of Justice promulgated its Model State Anti-Trafficking Criminal Statute (hereinafter DOJ Model Law) in 2004, billed as the first model state law. The DOJ Model Law covered both "labor," which absent coercion or force would normally be lawful employment, and "services," which

---

[8] Texas State Legislature, House Research Service, *Bill Analysis of Offense for Transporting People in Truck Trailers or Semitrailers*, Apr. 10, 2003, http://www.lrl.state.tx.us/scanned/hroBillAnalyses/78-0/HB2096.PDF.

[9] *Id.*

[10] Jim Vertuno, *Bill Would Ban Human Trafficking in Texas*, VICTORIA ADVOCATE, May 22, 2003, at 9A, http://news.google.com/newspapers?id=nBxZAAAAIBAJ&sjid=h0YNAAAAIBAJ&pg=7040,5344220&dq=texas+human+trafficking&hl=en.

[11] Mark Stevenson, *Mexican Families Bury Victims of Texas Smuggling Tragedy*, ASSOCIATED PRESS, May 24, 2003, *available at* http://news.google.com/newspapers?id=UWNJAAAAIBAJ&sjid=UwoNAAAAIBAJ&pg=1198,4049440&dq=texas+human+trafficking&hl=en.

[12] *Honduran Women Freed in Texas Prostitution Ring Raid*, THE MIAMI HERALD, May 18, 2002, http://nl.newsbank.com/nl-search/we/Archives?p_product=MH&s_site=miami&p_multi=MH&p_theme=realcities&p_action=search&p_maxdocs=200&p_topdoc=1&p_text_direct-0=0F3A83414E4D17B2&p_field_direct-0=document_id&p_perpage=10&p_sort=YMD_date:D&s_trackval=GooglePM.

[13] *Id.*

[14] *Id.*

[15] Sonide Simon, *Human Trafficking and Florida Law Enforcement*, FLA. CRIMINAL JUSTICE EXEC. INST., Mar. 2008, at 5, http://www.google.com/url?sa=t&rct=j&q=&esrc=s&source=web&cd=3&ved=0CDkQFjAC&url=http%3A%2F%2Fwww.fdle.state.fl.us%2FContent%2Fgetdoc%2Fe77c75b7-e66b-40cd-ad6e-c7f21953b67a%2FHuman-Trafficking.aspx&ei=WvTBUI--Boe70QGVyYGoAg&usg=AFQjCNEn_Z7xssVxsjfDolOoEM8IVd9llw.

include "unlawful activities such as prostitution."[16] The explanatory notes acknowledged that:

> Many trafficking-like crimes may be codified in seemingly-unrelated parts of a state code, such as the kidnapping or prostitution sections. Unfortunately, by being codified in disparate parts of the criminal code, it may be unclear to prosecutors that the behaviors are trafficking in persons crimes and may be charged as such. Research into these existing state statutes revealed that they are often archaic, little-known, or underutilized, and do not necessarily reflect the current understanding of slavery and trafficking in persons.[17]

In addition, the drafters of the DOJ Model Law recognized that the enactment of state anti-trafficking laws would allow for greater numbers of prosecutions by state and local prosecutors responding to the problem in their own jurisdictions.[18] The goal for the DOJ Model Law was to create "uniformity in definitions and concepts across state lines to minimize confusion as trafficking victims in state prosecutions begin to seek the victim protections available through the federal Departments of Health and Human Services and of Homeland Security."[19] By December 2005, 13 states had adopted part of the DOJ Model Law.[20]

Anti-trafficking organizations responded by developing alternative model laws to address gaps related to victim assistance and protection. In 2004 Polaris Project published its first Model Provisions of Comprehensive State Legislation (hereinafter Polaris Project Model Law) addressing all forms of human trafficking to "assist state legislators and anti-trafficking activists who wanted to improve their state's strategy to fight human trafficking — a modern form of slavery."[21]

In June 2005, the Center for Global Rights published a State Model Law on Protection for Victims of Human Trafficking (hereinafter Global Rights Model Law) in direct response to the Department of Justice Model Law to also "fill in the gaps and inconsistencies of the DOJ model Criminal Statute."[22] The Global Rights Model Law was guided in large part by the Freedom Network whose members provide direct service to human trafficking victims in the United States. Like the Department of Justice, Global Rights recognized the need for state laws to complement the TVPA. In fact, the drafters wrote:

---

[16] Farrell, Amy; McDevitt, Jack; Pfeffer, Rebecca; Fahy, Stephanie; Owens, Colleen; Dank, Meredith; and Adams, William, *Identifying Challenges to Improve the Investigation and Prosecution of State and Local Human Trafficking Cases*, Apr. 2012, http://www.urban.org/UploadedPDF/412592-State-and-Local-Human-Trafficking-Cases.pdf.

[17] U.S. Dep't. of Justice, *Model State Anti-Trafficking Criminal Statute* (Feb. 4, 2006), http://www.csg.org/knowledgecenter/docs/pubsafety/ModelStateAnti-TraffickingCriminalStatute.pdf.

[18] *Id.*

[19] *Id.*

[20] *Id.*

[21] Polaris Project, *Model Comprehensive State Legislation to Combat Trafficking in Persons* (Nov. 2006), http://www.markwynn.com/trafficking/model-comprehensive-state-legislation-to-combat-trafficking-in-persons-2006.pdf.

[22] Global Rights, *State Model Law on Protection for Victims of Human Trafficking* (June 2005), http://www.globalrights.org/site/DocServer/StateModelLaw_9.05.pdf.

However, the federal government alone cannot uncover and prosecute all of the large and small trafficking rings operating within the United States. State and local authorities are often more likely to encounter victims of trafficking while conducting routine arrests, inspecting buildings, factories and farms, operating fire, rescue and medical emergency services and working with child abuse and neglect cases. For this reason, it is necessary for state legislators and officials to learn more about human trafficking and to consider adopting laws that will allow local and state officials to investigate, prosecute and punish human traffickers and to provide appropriate and adequate services for, and to protect the rights of, trafficked persons.[23]

The drafters of the Global Rights Model Law set out to ensure that psychological coercion, an element left out of the DOJ Model Law, constituted an element of the definition of "forced labor" given that traffickers "routinely avoid force and use psychological coercion to hold their victims in captivity."[24] Other significant inclusions in the Global Rights Model Law were a crime of "Unlawful Conduct with Respect to Documents in Furtherance of Trafficking or Involuntary Servitude," a sentencing enhancement for "vulnerable victims" and "minors involved in involuntary servitude or forced labor or services," important non-detention and non-referral for removal or deportation inappropriate for trafficked persons, and several strong provisions related to services and benefits for trafficked persons.[25]

Only a month later, in July 2005, the Center for Women Policy Studies published a Resource Guide for State Legislators: Model Provisions for State Anti-Trafficking Laws (hereinafter CWPS Model Law) having begun their work on trafficking in women and girls in 1999 when they convened a workshop on the subject at the National Conference of State Legislatures.[26] The CWPS Model Law took a slightly different tact than the Polaris Project Model Law and the Global Rights Model Law and focused on criminalization of human trafficking, "bride trafficking," and sex tourism.

In 2006, Polaris Project published the second edition of the Polaris Project Model Law, clearly reflecting much of the development from 2004 to 2006. The drafters noted that as of November 2006, when the second edition was published, 25 states and one U.S. territory had some form of trafficking law.[27] The drafters drew upon enacted state laws to date as well as the TVPA of 2000, the PROTECT Act of 2003, and the DOJ Model Law of 2004.[28] This new Polaris Project Model Law added a crime of involuntary servitude whereas the previous version had only defined

---

[23] *Id.*

[24] *Id.*

[25] *Id.*

[26] *National Institute on State Policy on Trafficking of Women and Girls, Resource Guide for State Legislators: Model Provisions for State Anti-Trafficking Laws*, Center for Women Policy Studies (July 2005), http://www.centerwomenpolicy.org/pdfs/TraffickingResourceGuide.pdf.

[27] Polaris Project, *Model Comprehensive State Legislation to Combat Trafficking in Persons* (Nov. 2006), http://www.markwynn.com/trafficking/model-comprehensive-state-legislation-to-combat-trafficking-in-persons-2006.pdf.

[28] *Id.*

involuntary servitude, but had not criminalized it.

Perhaps ignited in part by the guidance of these model laws, momentum began to grow in 2005, when seven additional states enacted human trafficking criminal laws: Arizona, Arkansas, California, Kansas, Louisiana, Minnesota, and New Jersey. The next two years — 2006 and 2007 — saw the most legislative activity when 22 states each of those years enacted laws: Alaska, Connecticut, Idaho, Illinois, Indiana, Iowa, Michigan, Mississippi, Nebraska, North Carolina, and South Carolina in 2006; and Delaware, Georgia, Kentucky, Maine, Maryland, Montana, Nevada, New York, Oregon, Pennsylvania, and Rhode Island in 2007. All told, the years of 2003 to 2007 saw 33 states join the wave of anti-trafficking criminal law reform and created a tipping point.

From 2008 to 2013, eighteen (18) additional states have joined to nearly complete the map of anti-trafficking criminal law reform. In 2008, five states enacted laws: New Mexico, Oklahoma, Tennessee, Utah, and Wisconsin. In 2009, two states enacted laws: New Hampshire and North Dakota. In 2010, four states enacted laws: Alabama, Colorado, the District of Columbia, and Ohio.

In 2010, Polaris Project published the third edition of the Polaris Project Model Law, the latest model law to comprehensively address all forms of human trafficking. Noting that the organization had published previous editions in 2004 and 2006, the authors suggest that the criminal provisions were revised and new provisions were added addressing "prevention of human trafficking and protection and services to survivors."[29] Given the development of state laws on the subject during the preceding seven years, the authors also acknowledged that "state legislatures will not pass all provisions as one large, single piece of legislation. Instead, state legislators and anti-trafficking advocates may select and adapt those provisions that are best suited to their states' needs and political realities."[30]

In 2011, five states enacted laws: Hawaii, Massachusetts, South Dakota, Vermont, and Virginia and in 2012, West Virginia enacted a human trafficking criminal law. Most notably, Massachusetts and Vermont enacted comprehensive anti-trafficking laws which arguably now represent two of a half dozen of the country's strongest state laws. While legislators had worked for years to pass an anti-trafficking law in Massachusetts, they began in 2011 as one of only three states without such legislation. The legislation carries a potential 20-year sentence for human trafficking, and traffickers of children could face life in prison. It also establishes fines of up to $1 million on businesses who engage in human trafficking and increases funding for social services for victims of sex and labor trafficking. Two other provisions significantly target traffickers' profits: the state may forfeit traffickers' assets and put them into a victims' trust fund and trafficking victims may also sue their traffickers.[31] The law also created what has been called a "safe harbor" for sexually exploited and sexually trafficked children ensuring that these

---

[29] Polaris Project, *Model Provisions of Comprehensive State Legislation to Combat Human Trafficking* (Aug. 2010), http://www.polarisproject.org/storage/documents/policy_documents/state_policy/Final_Comprehensive_ModelLaw_8_2010.pdf.

[30] *Id.*

[31] Polaris Project, *Massachusetts Passes Its First Human Trafficking Bill* (Nov. 15, 2011), http://

children are provided with comprehensive services through the Department of Children and Families.[32]

The Vermont law was passed with the acknowledgement that "Vermont and all of its bordering states have seen elements of human trafficking, yet Vermont is the only remaining state in the Northeast and one of the remaining five in the nation lacking legislation on this issue. Vermont's geographical location bordering Canada makes it susceptible to human trafficking activity."[33] The law created human trafficking and aggravated human trafficking criminal offenses, a "safe harbor" for sexually exploited and sexually trafficked children, patronizing a human trafficking victim, business liability for human trafficking, restitution, posting of the National Human Trafficking Resource Center hotline, a private cause of action for trafficking victims to sue their traffickers, and the development of a statewide victim services protocol.[34]

Also in 2011, in response to a growing wave of concern about child sex trafficking in the United States, Shared Hope International published the Protected Innocence Framework (hereinafter Shared Hope DMST Framework) in 2011 to specifically address "domestic minor sex trafficking," which is defined as "the commercial sexual exploitation of American children within U.S. borders and is synonymous with child sex slavery, child sex trafficking, prostitution of children, and commercial sexual exploitation of children (CSEC)."[35] As such, the Shared Hope Legislative DMST Framework provides legislative recommendations related to the sex trafficking of U.S. citizen children, a concern to all those working to combat human trafficking. At the same time, the Shared Hope DMST Framework addresses only one category of trafficked persons in the United States and utilizes a definition of child sex trafficking that diverges from the federal definition. The state report cards that accompany the Shared Hope DMST Framework grade each state on 41 key legislative components judged to be necessary to respond effectively to the crime of domestic minor sex trafficking, including provisions addressing the purchase of commercial sex, and offer recommendations for improvement.[36] Shared Hope updated these report cards in 2012 and 2013, noting in 2013 that twenty-nine states had raised their grade.[37]

The Uniform Law Commission (hereinafter ULC) launched the most recent effort to bring together almost a decade of legal development in the area of state

---

www.polarisproject.org/media-center/news-and-press/press-releases/524-massachusetts-passes-first-ever-human-trafficking-bill-nov-15-2011.

[32] Mass. Gov, *Governor Patrick Signs Anti-Human Trafficking Legislation* (Nov. 21, 2011), http://www.mass.gov/governor/pressoffice/pressreleases/2011/111121-antihuman-trafficking-bill.html.

[33] The law is called An Act Relating to Human Trafficking, and is available at http://www.leg.state.vt.us/docs/2012/Acts/ACT055.PDF.

[34] *Id.*

[35] Shared Hope International, *Protected Innocence Legislative Framework* (2011), http://sharedhope.org/wp-content/uploads/2012/09/SHI_ProtectedInnocence_Methodology_FINAL.pdf.

[36] Shared Hope International, *Policy Development: Protected Innocence Challenge*, http://sharedhope.org/what-we-do/bring-justice/state-by-state-grades/ (last visited Dec. 28, 2012).

[37] Shared Hope International, *Policy Development: Protected Innocence Challenge*, http://sharedhope.org/what-we-do/bring-justice/reportcards/ (last visited Jan. 25, 2013).

I. STATE AND LOCAL HUMAN TRAFFICKING LAWS AND PROSECUTIONS 417

anti-trafficking legal reform. In July 2010, the American Bar Association (ABA) Center for Human Rights, Lexis Nexis, and Reed Elsevier (Lexis Nexis' parent company) proposed that the Uniform Law Commission consider whether to draft a uniform state law on human trafficking and the ULC appointed a study commission. The study commission met several times between October 2010 and January 2011 and issued an interim report in February 2011 recommending that the ULC appoint a drafting committee to develop a Uniform State Statute on the Prevention of and Remedies for Human Trafficking (hereinafter ULC Uniform Statute).

The goal of the ULC in drafting the ULC Uniform Statute is to bring uniformity among state laws and fill in gaps in state laws particularly in the area of victim protection. The drafting committee, reporter and associate reporter, and many observers representing anti-trafficking organizations engaged in direct service provision, legal representation, and advocacy as well as observers representing law enforcement, prosecution, defense, business, and the federal government have engaged in drafting, re-drafting, and discussion. In addition, drafters of the ULC Draft Uniform State Statute consulted five model laws for breadth of necessary provisions, topics, and effective language: DOJ Model Law (2005); Global Rights Model Law (2005); CWPS Model Law (2005); Model Law Against Trafficking In Persons (2009) (UN Office on Drugs and Crimes); and the Polaris Project Model Law (2010).[38] The ULC Uniform Statute received a first reading in July 2012, and its second and final reading in July 2013 before the Uniform Law Commission of approximately 350 members from every U.S. state and territory at which point it was approved and promulgated.

The final Uniform Act on the Prevention of and Remedies for Human Trafficking addresses the components of the three-P framework: Prosecution, Protection, and Prevention by criminalizing the acts that comprise human trafficking, providing key protections for victims, and mandating public awareness efforts.[39] The ULC Uniform Statute builds upon and goes beyond previous model laws in bringing together a number of victim-centered practices such as immunizing those under 18 for non-violent offenses committed as a result of being trafficked, providing adults with an affirmative defense for prostitution or non-violent offenses committed as a result of being trafficked, allowing human trafficking victims the ability to seek vacation of convictions for prostitution or other non-violent offenses, and directing law enforcement to the forms necessary to certify a victim as eligible for immigration relief. The ULC Uniform Statute also includes a provision that provides the ability to hold accountable business entities and employees acting on behalf of and for the benefit of the business entity for engaging in human trafficking, a provision that builds upon and goes beyond advocacy efforts to ensure that businesses do not unwittingly contribute to human trafficking such as the California Supply Chain Transparency Act of 2010.

---

[38] Uniform Law Commission, *Section on Prevention of and Remedies for Human Trafficking*, December 2011 Post Cmte. Meeting Draft with Comments, http://www.uniformlaws.org/shared/docs/Human%20Trafficking/prht_postcmtemtg_draft_dec11.pdf.

[39] Uniform Law Commission, *Uniform Act on the Prevention of and Remedies for Human Trafficking* (2013), http://www.uniformlaws.org/shared/docs/prevention%20of%20and%20remedies%20for%20human%20trafficking/2013am_uprht_as%20approved.pdf.

Today, nearly every state has realized that state laws could and should be enacted to respond to human trafficking because the federal response is not sufficient, but state laws do vary in their breadth, depth, and focus requiring a more in-depth look at their laws.

II. STATE-BY-STATE ANALYSIS OF HUMAN TRAFFICKING LAWS[40]

As of the end of 2013, fifty (50) states and the District of Columbia have enacted labor trafficking criminal laws and forty-eight (48) states and the District of Columbia have enacted sex trafficking criminal laws.[41]

With the exception of Colorado and Pennsylvania, every state plus the District of Columbia has criminalized sex trafficking in some form. Most states have defined sex trafficking as a distinct crime, although some states (like Montana and New Hampshire) have instead recognized sex trafficking as another form of "labor" trafficking that ultimately involves the exploitation of "services" or included both sexual and labor servitude within the same criminal statute (Georgia). While the specifics of state statutes vary, each such statute: (i) defines the nature of the crime — including what constitutes a commercial sex act and force, fraud, or coercion; (ii) identifies which persons are subject to prosecution for their participation in such activity; and (iii) imposes fines and penalties, with varying degrees of severity.

Most state statutes define sex trafficking as trafficking for the purpose of compelling a commercial sex act — a term that generally is defined to include prostitution, sexual servitude, or a sex act that is given in exchange for anything of value. Most, but not all, state statutes provide that the means of force, fraud, and coercion must be used to prove sex trafficking of an adult whereas these means are not typically required for those under 18 years of age with some exceptions.

Twenty-six (26) states — Arizona, California, Connecticut, Florida, Georgia, Illinois, Indiana, Louisiana, Maryland, Michigan, Missouri, Mississippi, Montana, Nebraska, New Hampshire, New Jersey, New York, North Carolina, North Dakota, Oregon, Rhode Island, Texas, Utah, Virginia, Washington, and Wisconsin — and the District of Columbia have enacted statutes that specifically define what constitutes force, threat, or coercion in the context of sex trafficking. The relevant definitions typically encompass not only physical restraint or physical harm, but also various acts or omissions (or threats thereof) that, individually or collectively, could create a context of coercion. Such acts or omissions include: the confiscation of government identification documents or visas, threats of deportation, threats of harm to family members, withholding of necessities (e.g., food, clothes, and shelter), damage to personal property, and threats to expose secrets and other forms of blackmail.

Minnesota has taken a different approach, and does not require force, fraud, or coercion as an element of sex trafficking. Rather, Minnesota's sex trafficking statute

---

[40] Parts of this state-by-state analysis was previously published as Polaris Project's 2013 Analysis of State Human Trafficking Laws, which Ms. Ellison contributed to while Director of Policy.

[41] POLARIS PROJECT, *Annual State Ratings*, http://www.polarisproject.org/what-we-do/policy-advocacy/national-policy/state-ratings-on-human-trafficking-laws/2012-state-ratings (last visited Dec. 28, 2012).

simply defines sex trafficking as the "receiving, recruiting . . . or obtaining by any means an individual to aid in the prostitution of the individual." The use by a perpetrator of physical force or threat is simply treated as an aggravating factor that could result in more severe fines or imprisonment.

Every state has enacted a statute criminalizing labor trafficking in some form. While the specifics vary, each statute: (i) defines the nature of the crime — including what constitutes labor or involuntary servitude, as well as force, fraud, or coercion; (ii) identifies which persons are subject to prosecution for their participation in such activity; and (iii) imposes fines and penalties, with varying degrees of severity. Many states — including Alabama Alaska, Arizona, California, Connecticut, Florida, Indiana, Maine, Nevada, New Mexico, New York, Ohio, Pennsylvania, Rhode Island, South Carolina, South Dakota, Tennessee, and Virginia — have enacted statutes defining labor trafficking as trafficking for the purpose of exploiting a person's "labor or services" under threats, violence, or coercion. The term coercion is meant to be kept fairly broad and includes both physical, as well as psychological harm to better enable law enforcement and prosecutors to target a broad range of actors who are obtaining forced labor. The more expansive use of the term "coercion" is in harmony with federal law, which adopts a broad interpretation of the criminal elements of forced labor, as evidenced by the inclusion of the term "serious harm," which is defined as "any harm, whether physical or nonphysical, including psychological, financial, or reputational harm, that is sufficiently serious, under all the surrounding circumstances, to compel a reasonable person of the same background and in the same circumstances to perform or to continue performing labor or services in order to avoid incurring that harm."[42]

States typically have defined labor trafficking to require elements of force, fraud, or coercion. These terms are evolving to fit the subtle means often used by traffickers and to take the trafficking victim's particular vulnerability and to view force, fraud, and coercion not from the perspective of a "reasonable person" but from the particular subjective experience of a trafficking victim in the same or similar circumstances. Twenty-nine (29) states — Arizona, California, Colorado, Connecticut, Florida, Georgia, Illinois, Indiana, Louisiana, Maryland, Michigan, Missouri, Mississippi, Montana, Nebraska, New Hampshire, New Jersey, New York, North Carolina, North Dakota, Oregon, Rhode Island, Texas, Utah, Virginia, Washington, West Virginia, Wisconsin, and Wyoming — and the District of Columbia provide additional guidance on what would constitute force, fraud, deception, or coercion in the context of labor trafficking. The relevant definitions typically encompass not only physical restraint or physical harm, but also various acts or omissions (or threats thereof) that, individually or collectively, could create a context of coercion. Such acts or omissions include: the confiscation of government identification documents or visas, threats of deportation, threats of harm to family members, withholding of necessities (e.g., food, clothes, and shelter), damage to personal property, and threats to expose secrets and other forms of blackmail.

In addition to enacting basic criminal statutes, many states have enacted one or more of 10 additional basic categories of anti-trafficking laws to combat human trafficking such as asset forfeiture, wiretapping, training, task force, hotline

---

[42] 18 U.S.C. § 1591 (2012).

posting, lower burden of proof for sex trafficking of minors, victim assistance, civil remedies, and vacating convictions. As of August 2013, more than half of the states had enacted laws to provide a lower burden of proof for sex trafficking of minors, victim assistance, asset forfeiture, and wiretapping.

Forty-two (42) states and the District of Columbia have enacted statutes to ensure that the elements of force, fraud, or coercion are not required for a trafficker to be prosecuted for the sex trafficking of a minor. These states include: Alabama, Alaska, Arizona, Arkansas, California, Delaware, Florida, Georgia, Hawaii, Idaho, Illinois, Indiana, Iowa, Kansas, Kentucky, Louisiana, Maine, Maryland, Massachusetts, Michigan, Minnesota, Mississippi, Missouri, Montana, Nevada, Nebraska, New Jersey, New Mexico, North Carolina, North Dakota, Oklahoma, Oregon, Rhode Island, South Carolina, Tennessee, Texas, Vermont, Washington, West Virginia, Wisconsin, and Wyoming. The laws of these states recognize that children have diminished capacity to grant their consent to participate in certain activities — including sexual activities. In cases of statutory rape, prosecutors generally are not required to show that sexual activity was compelled through force or coercion. Requiring prosecutors to show that a trafficker has induced a child to perform a sexual act through force, fraud, or coercion is incongruent with the notion that a minor is inherently unable to consent to sexual activity. By eliminating the need to prove force, fraud, or coercion in cases involving the sex trafficking of minors, a state can eliminate this incongruity. Other states may have statutes with lower burdens that are found within their prostitution or promoting prostitution statutes — especially those that deal with the exploitation of minors.

Thirty-five (35) states and the District of Columbia have enacted statutory provisions which provide courts with the authority to seize assets of convicted human traffickers either gained due to human trafficking crimes or used to facilitate human trafficking: Alaska, Alabama, Arkansas, California, Colorado, Connecticut, Florida, Georgia, Hawaii, Idaho, Illinois, Indiana, Iowa, Kansas, Kentucky, Louisiana, Maine, Massachusetts, Michigan, Minnesota, Mississippi, Missouri, Nevada, New Hampshire, New Jersey, North Carolina, Ohio, Oklahoma, Oregon, Pennsylvania, Rhode Island, South Carolina, Texas, Tennessee, and Washington. While the exact language of these statutes varies, the relevant provisions can be grouped into a few broad categories.

Six states — Alabama, Indiana, Michigan, Minnesota, North Carolina, and Rhode Island — allow forfeiture only of the proceeds of human trafficking. These statutes generally also permit the forfeiture of real and personal property purchased using such proceeds. Seven states — Arkansas, Colorado, Florida, Louisiana, Maryland, Mississippi, and New Hampshire — allow forfeiture only of assets used in the commission of human trafficking offenses (e.g., real estate used to house and vehicles used to transport human trafficking victims). Twenty-one states and the District of Columbia allow both the forfeiture of the proceeds of human trafficking *and* assets used to commit human trafficking offenses. These states are: Alaska, Connecticut, Georgia, Hawaii, Idaho, Illinois, Iowa, Kansas, Kentucky, Maine, Massachusetts, Missouri, Nevada, New Jersey, Ohio, Oregon, Pennsylvania, South Carolina, Tennessee, Texas, and Washington. Where used effectively, these provisions can be used to both: (i) limit the ability of human traffickers to profit from their illicit activities and (ii) undermine the ongoing operations of human trafficking networks.

Thirty-eight (38) states and the District of Columbia have enacted wiretapping statutes which provide law enforcement with an exemption to any prohibition on one-party wiretapping during investigations of human trafficking and/or "RICO" statutes that treat human trafficking as a predicate "racketeering" activity sufficient to sustain a conviction. At least fourteen states have enacted statutes authorizing law enforcement personnel to intercept electronic communications in the course of investigating human trafficking offenses, with a duly authorized court order. These states include: Arizona, Arkansas, Connecticut, Florida, Hawaii, Illinois, Indiana, Kansas, Louisiana, Maryland, New York, Texas, Washington, and Wisconsin. Generally, these states have enacted statutes that enumerate a list of offenses, including human trafficking offenses, for which intercepts may be authorized. Florida, Illinois, and Indiana permit the use of intercepts in cases of human trafficking broadly defined, including both sex and labor trafficking. Hawaii and New York restrict the use of intercepts to cases of labor trafficking — although the underlying labor trafficking statutes could be read to encompass some forms of sex trafficking as well. In contrast, Washington restricts the use of intercepts to cases involving the commercial sexual abuse of a minor. The lone outlier is Arizona, which has enacted a statute authorizing the use of wiretapping and similar techniques in investigating of any type of criminal activity.

Thirty-one (31) states have enacted "RICO" statutes that treat human trafficking as a predicate "racketeering" activity sufficient to sustain a conviction under such statutes. These states include: Arkansas, California, Colorado, Connecticut, Delaware, Florida, Georgia, Hawaii, Idaho, Illinois, Indiana, Kentucky, Louisiana, Maryland, Massachusetts, Michigan, Mississippi, Nebraska, Nevada, New Jersey, New York, North Carolina, North Dakota, Ohio, Oklahoma, Oregon, Pennsylvania, Tennessee, Utah, Virginia, and Wisconsin. In addition, Minnesota's "RICO" statute treats sex trafficking — but not other types of human trafficking offenses — as sufficient to sustain a conviction under the statute. Similarly, Rhode Island's "RICO" statute is implicated only in cases of "child exploitation for commercial or immoral purposes" — a category that certainly could encompass sex trafficking of minors.

Thirty-three (33) states and the District of Columbia have enacted statutes to provide assistance, mandate the creation of a victim services plan, or fund programs to help victims of human trafficking. These states are: Arkansas, California, Connecticut, Florida, Georgia, Idaho, Illinois, Indiana, Iowa, Kansas, Kentucky, Louisiana, Massachusetts, Minnesota, Mississippi, Missouri, Nebraska, Nevada, New Jersey, New Mexico, New York, North Carolina, Ohio, Oklahoma, Oregon, Pennsylvania, South Carolina, Tennessee, Texas, Vermont, Virginia, Washington, and Wyoming. Each of these state statutes addresses one or more of the following types of assistance critical to a victim's ability to adjust to life after trafficking:

- *Financial assistance.* Several states — including California, Florida, Georgia, Iowa, Illinois, Minnesota, New Mexico, South Carolina, Texas, and Virginia — provide direct financial assistance to trafficking victims. New Jersey's statute limits financial assistance to victims who have suffered personal injury. Other states, such as Massachusetts, Missouri, North

Carolina, and New York, provide financial assistance indirectly by giving funds to local non-profit organizations and/or community-based programs, which then provide funds to victims.

- *Medical services.* A number of states have enacted statutes that facilitate the provision of physical and/or psychological medical services to victims of human trafficking. These states include: Florida, Minnesota, North Carolina, New Jersey, Oklahoma, Virginia, and Washington. New Mexico also provides such benefits, but only after the victim has become eligible for similar federal benefits. Missouri provides medical benefits indirectly by funding local non-profit and community-based centers which provide such services to trafficking victims.

- *Assistance securing housing and/or food.* Six states — Florida, Ohio, Oklahoma, South Carolina, Virginia, and Washington — help victims to secure food and/or housing, sometimes through shelters. Missouri and Texas provide such benefits indirectly by providing funds to local non-profit and community-based centers, while New Mexico provides such benefits only until federal assistance is made available to victims.

- *Employment and/or educational services.* Several states provide job placement, job training, and/or educational services to trafficking victims. These states include: California, Florida, Minnesota, New Mexico, Ohio, and Washington. Missouri provides these services indirectly through community groups.

- *Legal services.* Some states, such as Minnesota, New Jersey, Oklahoma, and New Mexico, offer various legal services to trafficking victims.

- *Access to Information about traffickers.* Many victims of human trafficking fear for their safety or that of their family members, even after their traffickers have been arrested. As a result, several states have enacted laws that facilitate the provision to victims of information about the status of legal proceedings against their traffickers. For example, Georgia, North Carolina, and New Jersey have enacted statutes that provide victims with access to information about a trafficker's possible pretrial release, and/or educate victims about their rights and roles in the state criminal justice process. Such provisions help to empower victims of human trafficking offenses.

- *Protection from traffickers.* A number of states have enacted laws that are meant to provide additional protections to trafficking victims. For example, Indiana's statute ensures that the names and identifying information of victims and victims' families are not disclosed to the public. Similarly, South Carolina's statute punishes, by fine and/or imprisonment, persons who publish, disseminate, or otherwise disclose the location of a trafficking victim or trafficking shelter without authorization. Furthermore, South Carolina requires that trafficking shelters post signs stating that trespass is forbidden. Vermont's statute also allows victims to enter into an address confidentiality program run by the Secretary of State.

- *Education about rights and benefits.* A number of states — including North Carolina, New Jersey, Oregon, Tennessee, Texas, and Virginia —

have enacted statutes providing for victims of human trafficking to be informed about benefits available through the state or through community-based centers, and/or their rights under the state legal system. For example, a Texas statute provides for the creation of a searchable database to include assistance and grant programs.

- *Public awareness.* Several states — including Connecticut, Missouri, Ohio, Tennessee, and Texas — disseminate information to various state agencies and/or their state legal systems regarding the rights of, and ways to assist, victims of human trafficking. Some states also focus on disseminating information to local centers and organizations to improve their public services. Other states, such as Florida, Virginia, and Washington, work to educate the general public to raise awareness about human trafficking with the hope of protecting potential victims, identifying current victims, and providing assistance to freed victims.
- *Family reunification.* An important but rarely supplied service is assistance locating and reuniting with family members. Tennessee's statute offers such assistance.

A number of state statutes provide access to state benefits and services regardless of the immigration and/or citizenship status of victims of human trafficking. Many victims enter the United States without identifying legal documentation, which may prevent them from being eligible for federal or state benefits and protections. Approximately, a dozen states have enacted statutes to address this issue. For example, California, Florida, and Missouri have enacted statutes establishing that non-citizen victims of human trafficking are entitled to receive the same benefits and services as refugees. Similarly, Iowa, New Mexico, and North Carolina have enacted statutes providing victims of human trafficking with the same rights as other victims of a crime, regardless of their immigration status. Other states, such as Louisiana, Minnesota, New Jersey, New York, and Vermont, have enacted statutes providing immigration and/or translation services to victims. Virginia's statute offers victims assistance in returning to their places of origin if they so desire.

In addition to enumerating the availability of the benefits described above, some state statutes discuss the logistics of how such assistance is provided and accessed. A number of states — including Connecticut, Georgia, Missouri, North Carolina, Ohio, Tennessee, Texas, Virginia, and Washington — have enacted statutes providing for coordination among various state departments to improve the success of victim assistance programs. For example, Connecticut's statute provides for a "coordinated response system" to assist victims. Similarly, Georgia has tasked its Criminal Justice Coordinating Council with coordinating the activities of "various law enforcement agencies, the courts, and social service delivery agencies."

While the majority of states have enacted laws to provide a lower burden of proof for sex trafficking of minors, victim assistance, asset forfeiture, and wiretapping; less than half of the states have enacted laws to provide civil remedies, train law enforcement, create a task force, post a hotline, provide "safe harbor" for sex trafficked minors, or enable sex trafficking victims to vacate criminal convictions.

Twenty-nine (29) states and the District of Columbia have enacted a statute to provide victims of human trafficking access to seek civil damages from their traffickers. These states are: Alabama, Arkansas, California, Colorado, Connecticut, Florida, Hawaii, Illinois, Indiana, Kentucky, Louisiana, Maine, Massachusetts, Minnesota, Mississippi, Missouri, Nevada, New Jersey, New Mexico, Ohio, Oklahoma, South Carolina, Tennessee, Texas, Vermont, Washington, West Virginia, and Wisconsin. Two critical issues discussed by these statutes are: (i) the types and amount of damages available; and (ii) the periods within which a civil action must be brought so as not to be time-barred. Nearly all of the states that have enacted statutes enabling victims to pursue civil remedies allow for the award of actual damages. Yet only about one-third of these states allow victims to pursue compensatory damages, and only about half have enacted statutes allowing victims to pursue injunctive relief, punitive damages, attorney's fees, or costs. Alabama, Arkansas, California, Florida, Louisiana, Massachusetts, Mississippi, Nevada, New Mexico, South Carolina, Washington, West Virginia, and Wisconsin have each enacted statutes permitting a court to award treble damages where the defendant's acts were demonstrably willful and malicious. Texas' statute is unique in that it explicitly permits an award of damages based on a victim's mental anguish, even in the absence of other injury.

Interestingly, Minnesota's statute permits damages to be assessed against business entities, in addition to individual defendants. More specifically, the statute allows victims to seek civil damages from business entities, and provides that a court may order, when appropriate: (i) the dissolution or reorganization of a business entity; (ii) the suspension or revocation of any license, permit, or prior approval granted to the business entity by a state agency; or (iii) the surrender of the business entity's charter (if it is organized under Minnesota law) or the revocation of the business entity's certificate to conduct business in Minnesota (if it is not). Washington's statute similarly permits victims to seek civil damages from business entities involved in human trafficking, while Illinois' statute permits the same with respect to entities that have recruited, harmed, profited from, or maintained a victim in the sex trade.

In contrast, a number of states have enacted statutes that explicitly limit the damages that may be awarded to trafficking victims. For example, Connecticut, Missouri, and Washington have enacted statutes that explicitly cap the amount of civil damages that may be awarded to a victim; Connecticut's statute limits damages to $1,000 for each day the victim was held; Missouri's statute limits damages to $50,000 for each offense; and Washington's statute limits damages to $250,000 (plus costs and attorney's fees). Hawaii's statute restricts the damages that may be awarded to economic damages proximately caused by trafficking activity. Florida's statute is more restrictive and explicitly bans punitive damages, and further provides that a *victim* must pay the reasonable attorney's fees and costs of the defendant if the court finds that the victim raised a claim, which lacked substantial factual or legal support.

Although most of the states identified above have not explicitly limited the period within which a victim may bring a civil suit against a trafficker, the following states have imposed such limitations periods. In California, a victim must bring a civil suit within five years of the date on which he or she was freed from the trafficking situation, or, if the victim was a minor at such time, within eight years after the date he or she attains the age of majority. Indiana requires a victim to bring a civil suit not more than two years after the date on which the perpetrator was convicted of the underlying human trafficking offense. In Maine, a victim must commence the civil suit within 10 years of the date on which he or she was freed from the trafficking situation.

Massachusetts requires a victim to commence a civil suit within three years of the date on which he or she was freed from the trafficking situation or, if the victim was a child during the commission of the offense, within three years of the date on which he or she attains the age of 18. In Missouri, a victim must bring suit within 10 years of the later of: (i) the issuance of a final order in the related criminal case; (ii) the victim's emancipation from the trafficking situation; or (iii) the victim's 18th birthday. Finally, Washington requires a victim (or the state) to commence civil proceedings within three years after discovering that a perpetrator has been engaged in a pattern of criminal profiteering activity, or after such pattern should reasonably have been discovered, or within three years of the final disposition of any criminal charges relating to the underlying human trafficking offense (whichever is later). Several of these statutes explain that the limitations period may be tolled by a victim's disability, other circumstances resulting from the trafficking situation (such as psychological trauma or cultural or linguistic isolation), or the victim's status as a minor.

Twenty-nine (29) states have enacted a statute to mandate or encourage law enforcement to receive training with respect to human trafficking-related matters. While the specifics vary, the approaches taken by these states can be grouped into several categories. Twelve states — Arkansas, California, Georgia, Indiana, Kentucky, Minnesota, Nebraska, Ohio, and Wyoming — have enacted statutes: (i) requiring that a state agency or task force train law enforcement personnel with respect to human trafficking-related matters; and (ii) specifying topics to be covered in the course of such training. Typical of this approach is Indiana's statute, which requires that law enforcement personnel receive training with respect to: (i) human and sexual trafficking laws; (ii) identification of human and sexual trafficking; (iii) communicating with traumatized persons; (iv) therapeutically appropriate investigative techniques; (v) collaboration with federal law enforcement officials; (vi) rights of and protections afforded to victims; (vii) the provision of documentation satisfying federal legal requirements; and (viii) community resources available to assist human and sexual trafficking victims. California, Georgia, Nebraska, and Ohio have adopted similar approaches.

Minnesota's statute also establishes a detailed curriculum for training with respect to human trafficking-related matters, but goes further in two important respects. First, Minnesota requires state officials to develop training curricula in light of human trafficking data collected in the state. Second, Minnesota requires that such data be used to inform not only *law enforcement* training, but also a public awareness campaign (i.e., "training" for the general public).

Nine states — Alaska, Connecticut, Florida, Iowa, Mississippi, Missouri, New Mexico, Texas, and Washington — have enacted statutes that require a state agency or task force to train law enforcement personnel with respect to human trafficking-related matters, but that do not identify specific topics to be covered in the course of such training. Instead, the relevant state agency or task force is afforded discretion to develop a training program that it deems appropriate.

Only twenty states have enacted a statute to create, establish, or encourage a task-force, commission, or advisory committee dedicated to addressing human trafficking. These states are: Alaska, Arkansas, Colorado, Connecticut, Kansas, Louisiana, Massachusetts, Mississippi, Nebraska, New Jersey, New Mexico, New York, North Carolina, Pennsylvania, Rhode Island, South Carolina, Tennessee, Texas, Utah, Vermont, and Washington. The statutes normally prescribe the mandatory and voluntary duties of the task force, as well as its membership. The substantive mandates of these state task forces vary, but tend to fall into a few broad categories.

A number of states — including Arkansas, Connecticut, Louisiana, Massachusetts, Nebraska, New Jersey, New York, North Carolina, Pennsylvania, Tennessee, and Washington — have created task forces designed to evaluate human trafficking-related issues and formulate state-specific recommendations as to how those issues could be addressed more effectively. Several states — including New Mexico, New York, North Carolina, Texas, and Utah — use their human trafficking task forces to coordinate and improve law enforcement efforts. New York's task force has a broad mandate and its responsibilities include: (i) coordinating with other bodies to strengthen state and local efforts to prevent trafficking; (ii) establishing interagency protocols and collaboration between federal, state, and local law enforcement; and (iii) evaluating the effectiveness of training programs on human trafficking that have been designed for law enforcement personnel. Similarly, the Texas legislature has directed its task force to collaborate with U.S. attorneys and agents from the Federal Bureau of Investigation, the Drug Enforcement Administration, the Bureau of Alcohol, Tobacco, Firearms and Explosives, the Immigration and Customs Enforcement Agency, and the Department of Homeland Security in order to improve efforts to combat human trafficking.

Several states — including Connecticut, Louisiana, Massachusetts, Texas, Vermont — have directed their task forces to work to improve the provision of social services to human trafficking victims. For example, Vermont's statute authorizes the creation of a task force to assist "social service providers, victim service providers, state agencies, law enforcement agencies, state's attorneys' offices, the office of the attorney general, and other agencies and nongovernmental organizations as necessary to develop a statewide protocol to provide services for victims of human trafficking in Vermont," and to contract with third parties for the provision of victim services, including: (i) case management; (ii) emergency temporary housing; (iii) health care; (iv) mental health counseling; (v) drug addiction screening and treatment; (vi) language interpretation and translation services; (vii) English language instruction; (viii) job training and placement assistance; (ix) post-employment services for job retention; and (x) immigration services. Massachusetts, while not going quite so far, has charged its task force with evaluating whether existing health, education, job training and legal services and facilities meet the needs of victims of human trafficking, as well as approaches to increase public awareness of human trafficking.

Several states — including Massachusetts, New York, South Carolina, and Texas — have directed their task forces to coordinate the collection, analysis, and dissemination of data with respect to human trafficking issues. For example, New York's statute directs its task force to "collect and organize data on the nature and extent of trafficking in persons in the state" and to "measure and evaluate the progress of the state in preventing trafficking, protecting and providing assistance to victims of trafficking, and prosecuting persons engaged in trafficking." Similarly, Texas has directed its task force to "collect, organize, and periodically publish statistical data on the nature and extent of human trafficking in this state," while Massachusetts has directed its task force to "coordinate the collection and sharing of human trafficking data among government agencies."

In addition to the statutory task forces discussed above, many states have established "ad hoc" task forces to address human trafficking-related issues. Typically, these task forces are formed at the instigation of one or more state agencies, as opposed to the legislature. These task forces can lack the same level of permanence and resource commitment enjoyed by statutorily authorized task forces; however, this is not always the case, especially for those task forces that have acquired an independent funding stream.

Twenty-two (22) states have enacted a statute to mandate or encourage the public posting of a human trafficking hotline such as the National Human Trafficking Resource Center (NHTRC) Hotline (888-373-7888) or a state human trafficking hotline. In 2007, Texas became the first state to mandate the posting of the NHTRC hotline in establishments with a liquor license and in lodging establishments cited for nuisance violations. Now, more than 35,000 establishments in Texas post materials relating to the hotline. In subsequent years, twenty-one additional states have enacted legislation providing for the posting of information about the NHTRC hotline. These states are: Alabama, Arkansas, California, Connecticut, Georgia, Hawaii, Kansas, Louisiana, Maryland, Minnesota, Mississippi, Montana, Nebraska, New Jersey, Ohio, Oklahoma, Pennsylvania, Tennessee, Virginia, Vermont, and Washington.

Of these states, only Alabama, Arkansas, California, Connecticut, Georgia, Hawaii, Louisiana, Maryland, Virginia, Pennsylvania, and Texas *require* that certain establishments actually post hotline information. Typically, such a requirement extends to establishments likely to be frequented by victims of human trafficking or those with whom they have contact (e.g., bars, hotels found to be prostitution and drug nuisances, strip clubs, rest stops, bus depots, and train stations). For example, Maryland requires all lodging establishments "where arrests leading to convictions of prostitution, solicitation of a minor, or human trafficking" have occurred, as well as all truck and rest stops to display a state created poster providing information about the NHTRC hotline.

Similarly, Alabama, Georgia, and Pennsylvania require all strip clubs, truck and rest stops, airports, train stations, bus stations, hotels, and personal service establishments cited as a nuisance for prostitution, and some establishments with a wine, beer, or liquor license to display a sign with information about the NHTRC hotline in English and Spanish. Other states rely on the willingness of business owners to post information about the NHTRC hotline voluntarily — an approach that may be of limited value where a business owner himself or herself is engaged in human trafficking activity. Three states — Minnesota, Tennessee, and Oklahoma — have not established any requirement with respect to the posting of hotline information, but have enacted legislation addressing the creation of a state human trafficking hotline.

Twelve states have enacted robust "safe harbor" laws that recognize sex trafficked individuals under 18 years of age as victims of a crime in need of protection and services by granting immunity from prosecution or diverting the child from juvenile delinquency proceedings, and instead directing them to specialized services. These states are: Connecticut, Florida, Illinois, Massachusetts, Minnesota, Nebraska, New Jersey, New York, Ohio, Tennessee, Vermont, and Washington. In 2013, Minnesota secured $2.8 million in funding from the legislature for housing, shelter, and training; representing the largest state investment to-date. Although each of these states has approached the idea of protecting sex trafficked minors differently, they have signaled that policy-makers, law enforcement, and the criminal justice system should shift their response from one of criminalization to restoration.

Laws to protect minor victims of sex trafficking should strive to include the following general principles: (1) Prevent minor victims of sex trafficking from being prosecuted for prostitution including immunity for individuals under 18 years of age from prosecution for prostitution; define trafficked children as victims of abuse and neglect; and divert arrested children to child protection rather than juvenile delinquency proceedings; (2) Protect minor victims of sex trafficking by providing them with specialized services; and (3) Ensure that coercion is not required to prosecute sex trafficking of children, including severely penalizing child predators without requiring evidence that they used force or coercion to induce the child victim to engage in commercial sex acts, and viewing purchasers of commercial sex acts with children as child sexual predators to be punished as severely as other forms of child sexual abuse.

Illinois, Nebraska, and Tennessee have enacted the most protective statutes in regard to immunity from prosecution. Both state statutes provide prosecutorial immunity to minors under the age of 18. In Illinois, as soon as an officer realizes that a person charged with prostitution is a minor, the officer must refer the case to the Illinois Department of Children and Family Services. In Nebraska, the officer must report the alleged crime to the Department of Health and Human Services to open an investigation under the Child Protection Act. In Tennessee, the officer must provide the minor with the telephone number for the National Human Trafficking Resource Center hotline, and then release the victim into the custody of his or her parent or legal guardian.

A number of states have taken a moderated approach. Connecticut's statute prohibits the prosecution of minors under the age of 15, but also establishes a rebuttable presumption that 16- and 17-year-olds were coerced into prostitution — and thus lack the *mens rea* necessary to support a finding of criminal culpability. Michigan, while technically not having a safe harbor law, offers some protection to minors by setting a minimum age of 16 for someone to be charged with a prostitution-related offense. In other states, age is an important factor, but does not provide complete immunity from prosecution. For example, statutes in Minnesota and New York make children under the age of 16 who are engaged in or have engaged in prostitution eligible for conditional diversion programs (discussed below), but do not provide automatic immunity. Similarly, in Massachusetts, a child who engages in prostitution is recognized under the law as a "sexually exploited child" eligible to participate in certain diversion programs and entitled to access to an advocate.

Texas has not enacted a statute establishing a "safe harbor" for children engaged in prostitution, although one has been established by case law. The Texas Supreme Court has held that a child under the age of 14 may not be charged with prostitution because, under statutory rape laws, children may not legally consent to sex. This ruling represents a victory for child trafficking victim advocates — although children aged 14 and older remain completely vulnerable in Texas to prosecution for prostitution-related offenses.

Ideally, a "safe harbor" law would completely protect any minor who is engaged in prostitution; however, most state statutes that provide some measure of "safe harbor" protection to minors seek to divert them from prosecution if certain conditions are satisfied. For example, in Ohio, diversion is available if the minor first completes "diversion actions" (e.g., treatment) established by a court. In such a case, the court will dismiss and expunge the underlying criminal charge. Massachusetts similarly requires that the minor complete certain court-ordered programs before criminal charges will be dismissed.

In other states, diversion programs may be unavailable to a minor that is a prior offender. New York's statute *allows* diversion in such cases — at the discretion of the sitting judge — but does not *require* such diversion. Similarly, Washington's statute permits the prosecutor to determine whether diversion is appropriate in a given case. Finally, Vermont's statute provides even greater discretion to the state, establishing that it *may* divert *any* minor away from juvenile delinquency and into a Child in Need of Supervision program, despite the fact that children are granted immunity from prosecution under its criminal statutes.

In 2013, several state legislatures considered legislation to increase penalties for purchasing sex from minors. Hawaii, Idaho, Oregon, Utah, and Virginia have made buying sex with a minor a felony offense carrying severe penalties while at least two states (Washington and Tennessee) amended human trafficking laws to encompass buyers.[43] Other states continue to amend existing prostitution laws to increase penalties for buyers of commercial sex. Although the passage of such laws signals an increasing interest in holding sex purchasers accountable, whether the laws will be implemented remains to be seen.

Fourteen states have enacted a law to permit sex trafficking victims to have convictions for prostitution-committed incident to being trafficked vacated from their criminal records. These states are: Connecticut, Florida, Hawaii, Illinois, Maryland, Mississippi, Montana, Nevada, New Jersey, New York, North Carolina, Vermont, Washington, and Wyoming. New York was the first state to enact such

---

[43] Shared Hope International, *2013 National Legislative Progress Report*, http://sharedhope.org/wp-content/uploads/2013/10/PIC_2013-End-of-Year-Report.pdf (last visited Jan. 25, 2013).

legislation in 2010, which permits a victim of sex trafficking to file a motion in state court seeking to vacate his or her conviction for prostitution-related offenses where the victim's participation in the underlying illicit activity resulted from his or her status as a victim of sex trafficking. The Criminal Court of the City of New York, Queens County, decided such a motion in *New York v. G.M.* In that case, the court found that the victim had provided "a very compelling narrative of the circumstances surrounding all of her arrests, demonstrating that they were the product of years of brutal physical, psychological and sexual violence by her husband, which resulted in having been trafficked by him." The court therefore vacated the victim's criminal convictions.

The other states identified above have enacted statutes that mirror New York's statutes in important respects, but also differ in the time period to file a motion. For example, Hawaii's statute gives victims six years after the date on which the victim ceased being held to file a motion to vacate his or her conviction. The Maryland statute similarly requires that a motion to vacate be filed "within a reasonable period of time after the conviction." In contrast, the statutes enacted in New York and Illinois allow victims to file motions to vacate convictions "at any time" after the entry of a judgment.

State statutes also vary with respect to the burden of proof they impose and other obstacles to relief. Hawaii and Maryland both have enacted statutes that explicitly place the burden of proof on the victim seeking to vacate a prior conviction. Washington's statute goes further and does not permit a victim to have his or her record for conviction for prostitution vacated if: (i) there are any criminal charges pending against him or her in any court; (ii) the victim has been convicted of another crime since the date of the conviction at issue; or (iii) the victim has ever had the record of another prostitution conviction vacated.

The statutes enacted by Vermont and Maryland require that a victim's motion to vacate a conviction describe supporting evidence with particularity, and provide documentary evidence showing that the victim is entitled to relief.

Clearly, state legislative and executive branches have worked successfully across political party lines to enact all of the categories of anti-trafficking laws discussed. The legislative trends demonstrate that the paradigm is indeed beginning to shift at least as laws are written on paper. Trafficked persons are still sometimes arrested, charged, prosecuted, and convicted for crimes or administrative violations incident to their trafficking situation. Traffickers are often arrested, charged, prosecuted, and convicted. Finally, purchasers are sometimes arrested, charged, prosecuted, and convicted.

However, more must still be done to fill in the gaps particularly in states in the Western and mid-Western region of the country. It is striking to note that state courts have seen very few cases come before them. As of January 1, 2013 the Federal Bureau of Investigation launched a new effort to collect human trafficking offense and arrest data under its Uniform Crime Reporting Program.[44] Such

---

[44] Federal Bureau of Investigation, *UCR Program Adds Human Trafficking Offenses to Data Collection*, (May 2013), http://www.fbi.gov/about-us/cjis/cjis-link/may-2013/ucr-program-adds-human-trafficking-offenses-to-data-collection-includes-more-specific-prostitution-offenses.

statistics and further research on the use of state human trafficking laws are needed to measure progress in holding traffickers accountable. In fact, the lack of data has caused many lawyers, law enforcement, service providers, academics, researchers, and policy advocates to question what it might take to ensure that these laws are implemented, and what might be done to monitor the implementation of laws and hold state governments responsible under international human rights principles of due diligence among other international human rights standards.[45]

III. IMPLEMENTATION OF STATE AND LOCAL LAWS TO COMBAT HUMAN TRAFFICKING

States have clearly become more sophisticated in their approaches to enacting and amending anti-trafficking laws over time, but very few states have focused on an effective implementation of these laws. Until the criminal justice systems effectively uses these laws victims will not be protected, traffickers will not be held accountable, and human trafficking will not be prevented. State and local law enforcement and prosecutors, national and state hotlines, local service providers, and the public play an important role in ensuring this occurs. In a comprehensive study of state and local human trafficking prosecutions, researchers at Northeastern University and the Urban Institute stated that:

Despite the TVPA's focus on federal prosecution of human trafficking, the federal criminal justice system cannot effectively prosecute all incidents of human trafficking occurring throughout the U.S. Local, and state governments have traditionally been responsible for crime control in the United States. As an illustration of this division of responsibility, the federal courts handle only a small proportion of all criminal offenses. In 2008, approximately 80,000 criminal cases were filed in U.S. federal courts compared to over 21 million criminal cases filed in state courts (U.S. Census Bureau, 2011). State and local authorities will encounter and must identify trafficking incidents occurring in local communities and as a result, they need to have the adequate authority through statute and institutional capacity to prosecute human trafficking cases locally.[46]

Not only should states be moved by a practical argument to push for stronger implementation of state anti-trafficking laws, but they should also be compelled by obligations under international law as one constituent part of the United States. As a nation state, the United States is obligated to guarantee freedom from slavery and institutions and practices similar to slavery; the individual rights to life, security of

---

[45] The duty of due diligence under international law evolved from the principles of diplomatic protection whereby a state incurs international responsibility for the commission of an international wrongful act against a non-national person. It has been applied in the context of human rights violations since the landmark case of *Velasquez Rodriguez v. Honduras* (1989). In this case (which concerned disappearances), the Inter-American Court of Human Rights held that a state must take action to prevent human rights violations, and to investigate, prosecute, and punish them when they occur. The Court determined that the state's failure or omission to take preventive or protective action "itself represents a violation of basic rights on the State's part. This is because the state controls the means to verify acts occurring within its territory." *Velasquez Rodriguez v. Honduras*, Inter-American Court of Human Rights (July 21, 1989), http://www.corteidh.or.cr/docs/casos/articulos/seriec_07_ing.pdf.

[46] Farrell, Amy; McDevitt, Jack; Pfeffer, Rebecca; Fahy, Stephanie; Owens, Colleen; Dank, Meredith; and Adams, *supra*, note 16.

person, and freedom from torture; freedom from discrimination; equal protection of the laws; and the right to an effective remedy. This is true because we have ratified and are bound by a number of international treaties such as the International Covenant on Civil and Political Rights ("ICCPR"), the International Convention on the Elimination of All Forms of Racial Discrimination ("CERD"), and the Convention Against Torture, and Other Cruel, Inhuman or Degrading Treatment or Punishment ("CAT"), the United Nations Optional Protocol to Prevent, Suppress and Punish Trafficking in Persons, Especially Women and Children, Supplementing the United Nations Convention against Transnational Organized Crime("U.N. Trafficking Protocol"), and the Optional Protocol to the Convention of the Rights of the Child on the Sale of Children, Child Prostitution and Child Pornography.[47]

Failure to take steps to prosecute traffickers, protect trafficked persons, and prevent trafficking by the United States or any of the states within it would constitute non-compliance with international human rights standards.[48] As the global standard-bearer of success when it comes to combatting trafficking in persons, the United States must do all it can to model, both at the federal level and within the states, the most effective implementation of anti-trafficking laws.

Despite the practical and international human rights arguments for more effective implementation, most states have failed to use their relatively recent human trafficking statutes to prosecute traffickers or protect victims. According to the recent study undertaken by Northeastern University and the Urban Institute, challenges to the implementation of laws include: (1) ambiguity in the elements of the newly established criminal offenses which are untested in state courts; (2) victim reluctance to testify, credibility of victim witnesses, specialized services for victims, and overcoming prejudice by courts and juries; and (3) the lack of institutionalized training, policies, procedures, and funding to assist law enforcement and prosecu-

---

[47] U.N. Children's Protocol, *see also* Convention Concerning the Prohibition and Immediate Actions for the Elimination of the Worst Forms of Child Labour, June 17, 1999, 38 I.L.M. 1207, art. 3(b), *available at* http://www.ilo.org/public/english/standards/relm/ilc/ilc87/com-chic.htm (ratified by United States Dec. 2, 1999) (hereinafter Convention Concerning the Worst Forms of Child Labour); *see also* CEDAW, art. 6; *General Recommendation No. 19, Violence against Women*, Committee on the Elimination of Discrimination against Women, 11th Sess., U.N. Doc. CEDAW/C/1992/L.1/Add.15 (1992).

[48] RESTATEMENT (THIRD) OF THE FOREIGN RELATIONS LAW OF THE UNITED STATES § 321 cmt. b (1987) ("A state is responsible for carrying out the obligations of an international agreement. A federal state may leave implementation to its constituent units but the state remains responsible for failures of compliance.") (hereinafter RESTATEMENT); *see also* International Covenant on Civil and Political Rights, Dec. 16, 1966, art. 50, 999 U.N.T.S. 171, TIAS (the Covenant's provisions "shall extend to all parts of federal states without any limitations or exceptions") (hereinafter ICCPR); *Nature of the General Legal Obligation on States Parties to the Covenant*, Human Rights Committee, General Comment 31, U.N. Doc. CCPR/C/21/Rev.1/Add.13 (2004) (government "may not point to the fact that an action incompatible with the provisions of the Covenant was carried out by another branch of government as a means of seeking to relieve the State Party from responsibility for the action and consequent incompatibility"); Vienna Convention on the Law of Treaties, May 23, 1969, art. 27, 1155 U.N.T.S. 331, *reprinted in* 25 I.L.M. 543 (a state "may not invoke the provisions of its internal law as justification for its failure to perform a treaty") (hereinafter Vienna Convention). *Also see* RESTATEMENT, *supra* note 1270 ("Every international agreement in force is binding upon the parties to it and must be performed by them in good faith.").

III. STATE AND LOCAL HUMAN TRAFFICKING LAWS AND PROSECUTIONS

tors in using the laws.[49] In fact of the 140 cases surveyed, 33% were prosecuted in state courts, but only 7% of that 33% were pursued as adult sex trafficking offenses under state human trafficking laws, 9% as minor sex trafficking offenses, and 2% as labor trafficking offenses.[50]

While less than two dozen states have used their laws to convict traffickers, those that have been successful have obtained sentences of up to 25 years. In Iowa, state prosecutors convicted Leonard Russell of two counts of human trafficking under Iowa Code § 710a.1(1) (2007), two counts of pandering and a count of ongoing criminal conduct for recruiting Nebraska runaways and compelling them into prostitution with a sentence of 25 years.[51]

The New Jersey Attorney General's office secured a successful human trafficking conviction of Allen Brown, aka "Prince," who ran "prostitution rings" for over two decades using drugs to control and exploit women, confiscating their identification documents and cell phones, employing others to enforce, beat, and transport the women to various locations in New Jersey.[52] In July 2012, the Cook County Illinois State's Attorney secured the first successful prosecution under the state human trafficking law when Troy Bonaparte was sentenced to 18 years in prison for involuntary servitude, trafficking in persons for forced labor or services, and pandering.[53]

In the first case to be prosecuted under the 2011 Massachusetts human trafficking law, Rafael Henriquez and his wife Ramona Carpio Hernandez were indicted May 24, 2012 by a Special Statewide Grand Jury each on one count of Trafficking in Persons for Sexual Servitude, Conspiracy to Traffic Person for Sexual Servitude, Owner of a Place Inducing or Suffering a Person to Resort in Such Place for Sexual Intercourse, Deriving Support from Prostitution, and Keeping a House of Ill Fame. The couple, along with two other defendants, ran a sophisticated human trafficking operation that transported numerous women into the area, housed them in deplorable conditions for a week at a time for the purpose of engaging in sexual acts with "johns," sometimes up to 15 times a day.[54]

In early 2013, a New York District Court convicted four family members of various crimes, including labor trafficking, for forcing a 20 year-old Indian citizen to work as a domestic servant from 2008 to 2010 in a scheme that involved an arranged

---

[49] Farrell, Amy; McDevitt, Jack; Pfeffer, Rebecca; Fahy, Stephanie; Owens, Colleen; Dank, Meredith; and Adams, William, *supra*, note 16.

[50] *Id.*

[51] *State v. Russell*, 781 N.W.2d 303 (Iowa Ct. App. 2010).

[52] Office of the Attorney General of New Jersey, *Woman Sentenced to Prison for Acting as Boss over Prostitutes in Jersey City Human Trafficking Ring* (May 21, 2010), http://www.nj.gov/oag/newsreleases10/pr20100521b.html.

[53] Cook County State's Attorney, *Cook County State's Attorney Secures Significant Sentence in First Ever Human Trafficking Conviction* (July 12, 2011), http://www.statesattorney.org/index2/press_humantrafficking03.html.

[54] Office of the Attorney General of Massachusetts, *Four Indicted in Connection with Human Trafficking Operation* (May 25, 2012), http://www.mass.gov/ago/news-and-updates/press-releases/2012/2012-05-25-human-trafficking-indictments.html.

marriage, physical and sexual abuse, and forced labor.[55]

While each of the states mentioned here have been successful, much more needs to be done to ensure that all governments utilize their laws to hold traffickers accountable and protect victims. The question is: "What tools would provide governments with the ability to more effectively implement their laws?" The U.S. State Department's *Annual Trafficking in Persons Report* is the U.S. government's principal diplomatic tool to engage foreign governments in addressing human trafficking, and contains a methodology to assess government's efforts. A few non-governmental organizations have attempted to provide tools as well — The American Bar Association Rule of Law Initiative and The Advocates for Human Rights. The former organization developed a human trafficking assessment tool (HTAT) in 2005 and has used the HTAT to:

> Assess countries' de jure and de facto compliance with the Protocol to Prevent, Suppress and Punish Trafficking in Persons, Especially Women and Children, Supplementing the United Nations Convention against Transnational Organized Crime (Trafficking Protocol), which is one of the most important international tools aimed at combating trafficking in persons. The primary purpose of the HTAT is to enable technical assistance providers, donors, and local stakeholders to design and implement more effective national and regional counter-trafficking strategies, to enhance countries' compliance with the Trafficking Protocol, and to monitor progress in the fight against human trafficking.[56]

The tool asks questions such as whether the country has strong laws to effectively address human trafficking, and whether the country has made a financial commitment to protect victims and prevent human trafficking. In all, the researchers identified the gaps and made recommendations related to several areas including (1) Scope and Nature of Trafficking in Persons in Nepal; (2) Legal Framework; (3) Institutional Framework; (4) International Collaboration; (5) Prevention of Trafficking in Persons; (6) Protection; and (7) Prosecution[57]. The recommendations included but were not limited to:

- Ratifying and promptly implementing the UN Trafficking Protocol;
- Creating a national (human trafficking) victim referral system;
- Committing more financial and human resources to preventing trafficking in persons and eliminating the worst forms of child labor;
- Developing more robust national and local prevention campaigns in cooperation with civil society, the media, and the private sector. Institute fully operational protocols for victim identification, screening, rescue, repatriation, as well as victim and witness protection;

---

[55] *Labor Trafficker Parveen Jogota receives 1-3 years* (Jan. 30, 2013), http://www.lohud.com/article/20130130/NEWS03/301300076/Labor-trafficker-Parveen-Jagota-receives-1-3-years.

[56] ABA RULE OF LAW INITIATIVE, HUMAN TRAFFICKING ASSESSMENT TOOL REPORT FOR NEPAL, INTRODUCTION (July 2011), http://www.americanbar.org/content/dam/aba/directories/roli/nepal/nepal_human_trafficking_assessment_report_2011.authcheckdam.pdf.

[57] *Id.*

- Refraining from arresting and criminalizing human trafficking victims;
- Enhancing victims' access to justice and essential services;
- Conducting mandatory, multi-sectoral trainings on trafficking in persons for justice system actors; and
- Creating and adopting a universal protocol for interviewing human trafficking victims.[58]

Recommendations such as these and those of other reports such as the U.S. State Department's *Annual Trafficking in Persons Report* provide leverage and a rallying point for non-governmental organizations and civil society in holding a national government accountable for properly implementing its anti-trafficking law.

In 2008, the Advocates for Human Rights developed a methodology akin to the HTAT to assess the implementation of a state anti-trafficking law, which resulted in the publication of the Sex Trafficking Needs Assessment for the State of Minnesota (2008) (hereinafter "Minnesota Assessment").[59] This needs assessment was designed to evaluate the government response to sex trafficking in Minnesota at the local, tribal, and federal levels.[60] Like the HTAT, the Minnesota Assessment sought to identify gaps and make recommendations to better address the three P's of a successful human trafficking response: Prevention, Protection, and Prosecution. Researchers engaged in the following steps:

- Review of local, national, and international research on sex trafficking;
- Review of relevant laws, policies, regulations, and legal precedent;
- Review of media accounts of sex trafficking;
- Review of training and outreach materials;
- Discussions with 32 focus group participants consisting of legal, healthcare, and service providers who work with trafficked persons;
- Interviews with judges, prosecutors, attorneys, service providers, immigration officials, social service providers, healthcare providers, mental healthcare providers, chemical dependency providers, and other stakeholders; and
- Interviews with survivors of sex trafficking interested in telling their story, as referred by service providers.[61]

The recommendations of the Minnesota Assessment provided directives for state anti-trafficking advocates and the government to take action. These recommendations included, but were not limited to:

- Law enforcement officers, prosecutors, judges, immigration officials, social service workers, healthcare providers, non-profit organizations, and others

---

[58] *Id.*

[59] Angela Bortel, Mary Ellingen, Mary C. Ellison, Robin Phillips & Cheryl Thomas, *Sex Trafficking Needs Assessment for the State of Minnesota*, THE ADVOCATES FOR HUMAN RIGHTS MINNEAPOLIS (Oct. 2008), http://www.theadvocatesforhumanrights.org/uploads/report_final.10.13.08.pdf.

[60] *Id.*

[61] *Id.*

responding to trafficking cases should receive training relevant to their profession on properly identifying and assisting trafficked persons as defined by federal and state law.

- The Legislature should appropriate funding for services. Community leaders should work together to ensure there are adequate services for trafficked persons that are tailored to meet their specific needs. These services should include case management, housing, healthcare, language interpretation, and legal services.
- Law enforcement agencies, healthcare providers, service providers, and other first responders to sex trafficking cases should develop screening protocols based on model practices to identify trafficked persons and to screen for risk factors for sex trafficking.
- Federal law enforcement agencies, prosecutors, and immigration officials should institute policies and procedures that ensure that trafficked persons, including those defined as victims under Minnesota law, are not detained, charged, prosecuted, or removed from the country for the illegality of their entry into or residence in the United States.
- The Legislature should amend state law to ensure that sentences for sex trafficking are proportionate to other felony offenses for crimes against persons. The law should also be amended to allow for sentence enhancements.[62]

While the HTAT and Minnesota Assessment were designed on the one hand to evaluate a national government's response to human trafficking and on the other hand to evaluate a state government's response to human trafficking, the recommendations issued bear a striking resemblance. Whether national, state, or local government response is being evaluated, anti-trafficking advocates should begin by looking at the legal framework; the institutional framework namely the criminal justice and social service system, and the link between them in the form of a national referral mechanism; specific efforts aimed at the three P's of prosecution, protection, and prevention; and finally, efforts at multi-disciplinary and multi-sector collaboration and cooperation.

States desperately need a model implementation and assessment tool (not unlike a model law) and advocates need to actively assess the states' use of its laws. This tool should enable states to assess the effectiveness of services, laws, and highlight the gaps in addressing human trafficking with the ultimate goal of prosecuting traffickers, protecting victims, and preventing human trafficking. Finally, advocates should use the assessments of the states to hold decision makers accountable through the use of mainstream media and online outreach platforms. Advocates should also educate the public on the impact of failing to implement these laws. Ultimately, the implementation of state anti-trafficking laws must fulfill the promise of our state and federal constitutions, and obligations under international law to address this heinous crime and grave human rights violation. As we enter the second decade of the development of state laws to address human trafficking and modern-day slavery, we must ensure these laws not only live in state statutes, but

---

[62] *Id.*

also in the lives of all those victimized and enslaved by what President Obama described as "the injustice, the outrage, of human trafficking, which must be called by its true name — modern slavery.[63]"

---

[63] *Remarks by the President to the Clinton Global Initiative* (Sept. 25, 2012), http://www.whitehouse.gov/the-press-office/2012/09/25/remarks-president-clinton-global-initiative.

APPENDIX 2

18 USCS § 1589

§ 1589. Forced labor

(a) Whoever knowingly provides or obtains the labor or services of a person by any one of, or by any combination of, the following means—

(1) by means of force, threats of force, physical restraint, or threats of physical restraint to that person or another person;

(2) by means of serious harm or threats of serious harm to that person or another person;

(3) by means of the abuse or threatened abuse of law or legal process; or

(4) by means of any scheme, plan, or pattern intended to cause the person to believe that, if that person did not perform such labor or services, that person or another person would suffer serious harm or physical restraint, shall be punished as provided under subsection (d).

(b) Whoever knowingly benefits, financially or by receiving anything of value, from participation in a venture which has engaged in the providing or obtaining of labor or services by any of the means described in subsection (a), knowing or in reckless disregard of the fact that the venture has engaged in the providing or obtaining of labor or services by any of such means, shall be punished as provided in subsection (d).

(c) In this section:

(1) The term "abuse or threatened abuse of law or legal process" means the use or threatened use of a law or legal process, whether administrative, civil, or criminal, in any manner or for any purpose for which the law was not designed, in order to exert pressure on another person to cause that person to take some action or refrain from taking some action.

(2) The term "serious harm" means any harm, whether physical or nonphysical, including psychological, financial, or reputational harm, that is sufficiently serious, under all the surrounding circumstances, to compel a reasonable person of the same background and in the same circumstances to perform or to continue performing labor or services in order to avoid incurring that harm.

(d) Whoever violates this section shall be fined under this title, imprisoned not more than 20 years, or both. If death results from a violation of this section, or if the violation includes kidnaping, an attempt to kidnap, aggravated sexual abuse, or an attempt to kill, the defendant shall be fined under this title, imprisoned for any term of years or life, or both.

TABLE OF CASES

[References are to pages]

A

Abraham v. Singh 285; 312
Abrorkhodja Askarkhodjaev; United States v. . . 254
Adhikari v. Daoud & Partners 198, 199
Ae Soon Cho; United States v. 270
Agency Holding Corp. v. Malley-Duff & Associates, Inc. 309
Aguilar v. Imperial Nurseries 285
Ah Sou; United States v. 18
Albemarle Paper Co. v. Moody 387
Alliance for Open Society International, Inc. and Open Society Institute v. United States Agency for International Development 364; 368
Alzanki; United States v. 236; 402; 403
Ancarola; United States v. 80
Anderson v. Mt. Clemens Pottery Co. 313
Arce v. Garcia 307
Aronov; United States v. 244; 254

B

B.W., In re 392; 399
Bailey v. Alabama 33; 40; 61; 72; 118; 243
Bailey v. State 34
Bank; United States v. 104
Baoanan v. Baja 255
Bass; United States v. 86
Bate Refrigerating Co. v. Sulzberger 104
Beebe; United States v. 241
Bell v. United States 57
Bennett v. United States Trust Co. of New York . 308
Bibbs; United States v. 59
Bifulco v. United States 86
Bitty; United States v. 105
Bohonus; United States v. 64
Booker; United States v. 59; 61
Bowman; United States v. 291; 294
Boyce Motor Lines, Inc. v. United States 64
Bradley; United States v. 118; 233; 253; 254
Bray v. Alexandria Women's Health Clinic 321
Buchanan v. City of Bolivar 280; 281; 285
Bureerong v. Uvawas 282, 283
Butler v. Perry 55; 57; 71; 72; 82

C

Calimlim; United States v. 239; 242; 247; 381
Camayo v. John Peroulis & Sons Sheep 242
Caminetti v. United States 104
Champion v. Ames 100
Chatwin v. United States 84
Chellen v. John Pickle Co. 314; 320
Cherry; United States v. 249
Cintolo; United States v. 238
City of (see name of city)
Clark; United States v. 271, 272
Clyatt v. United States . . 29; 35; 36; 54; 57; 62; 72; 78
Coates v. City of Cincinnati 65
Colautti v. Franklin 65
Connally v. General Construction Co. 52
Cortes-Meza; United States v. 257
Craine v. Alexander 280, 281

D

Dann; United States v. 239
Davis v. United States 56
Dawn; United States v. 290
Delaware & Hudson Co.; United States v. 57
Deressa v. Gobena 321
Deutsch v. Turner Corp. 303
Djoumessi; United States v. . . 239; 251; 254; 401; 402
DKT International, Inc. v. United States Agency for International Development 364; 365; 368
Dunn v. United States 64

E

EEOC v. Arabian Am. Oil Co. 290
EEOC v. Waffle House, Inc. 387
Elbert; United States v. 268
Estate of (see name of party)
Evans; United States v. 267
Ex parte (see name of relator)

F

Farrell; United States v. 242; 253
FCC v. League of Women Voters of California . . 367
Filartiga v. Pena-Irala 302; 307
Flores Carreto; United States v. 257
Foley Bros., Inc. v. Filardo 292
Forti v. Suarez Mason 302
Fu Sheng Kuo; United States v. 269

[References are to pages]

Fujii; United States v. 251

G

Galina v. INS. 345
Garcia v. Audubon Cmtys. Mgmt., LLC 295
Garcia; United States v. 242
Gaskin; United States v. 54
Gloucester Ferry Co. v. Pennsylvania. 102
Goldberg v. Whitaker House Coop. 315
Grayned v. City of Rockford 64

H

Hackwell v. United States 117
Hamilton v. Rathbone 104
Harris; United States v. 59; 231
Henderson v. Mayor of New York 36
Hernandez v. Attisha. 279
Hernandez; U.S. v. 108
Hipolite Egg Co. v. United States. 101
Hodges v. United States 46; 55; 56
Hoffman Plastic Compounds, Inc. v. NLRB . . . 319
Hoke v. United States 100
Hollman, Ex parte 40

I

In re Estate of (see name of party)
In re (see name of party)
Ingalls; United States v. 43; 58; 79
Iwanowa v. Ford Motor Co.. 303

J

Jackson v. Virginia. 402
Jane Doe I v. Reddy 303
Jaremillo v. Romero. 22
Jimenez-Calderon; United States v. 245; 261
Jones v. Blanas. 283
Jones v. State. 395

K

Kadic v. Karadzic. 301, 302
Karadzic v. Kadic 301
Kaufman; United States v. 115; 240; 241
Keller v. United States 96; 99
King; United States v. 404
Kolender v. Lawson 64; 249
Kozminski; United States v.. 67; 69; 80; 84; 86; 117; 232; 235; 236; 243; 311; 402; 403; 404; 405

L

Lake County v. Rollins 104
Legal Servs. Corp. v. Velazquez. 367
Lewis v. Super. Ct.. 283
Lexington Mill and Elevator Co; United States v.. 104
Liu, et al v. Donna Karan Intl, Inc 387
Long Island Care at Home, Ltd. v. Coke. 316
Lopez; United States v. 266

M

Maksimenko; United States v. 244; 254
Manliguez v. Joseph 284; 307
Marcos, Estate of v. Hilao. 301
Marcos Human Rights Litig., In re Estate of. . .301
Marcus; United States v. 119; 241; 244; 245
Mazengo v. Mzengi 285
Mazurie; United States v. 64
McBoyle v. United States 86
Memphis, City of v. Greene. 284
Mendez; United States v. 257
Meyers v. Meyers 288
Mincey v. Arizona. 85
Mondragon; United States v.. 254
Montero v. INS. 382
Mortensen v. United States. 102, 103
Moskal v. United States 86
Murphy v. Ramsey. 105
Mussry; United States v. 60; 70; 79

N

Nash v. United States 83

O

O'Connor; United States v. 245

P

Papa v. United States. 307
Paris; United States v. 265, 266; 267
Paul v. Avril 307
People v. (see name of defendant)
Pierce v. United States 62
Pipkins; United States v. 263; 267; 404
Plessy v. Ferguson. 31
Pollock v. Williams 53; 61; 118
Presbyterian Church of Sudan v. Talisman Energy, Inc. 301

TABLE OF CASES

[References are to pages]

Prueitt; United States v. 65

R

Ramos v. Hoyle. 240; 242
Reid v. Colorado. 100
Reynolds; United States v. 39; 54; 72
Rivera et al. v. Nibco, Inc. 382; 387
Robertson v. Baldwin. 72
Robinson; United States v. 268
Roe v. Bridgestone Corp. 286
Roper v. Simmons 396
Rosenberger v. Rector & Visitors of the Univ. of Va. 367, 368
Royal Dutch Petroleum Co. v. Wiwa. 301
Rust v. Sullivan 366
Rutherford Food Corp. v. McComb. 315

S

Sabhnani; U.S. v. 123; 253
Sabhnani; United States v. 314
Scott v. Sandford. 4; 7
Screws v. United States 76
Serino; United States v. 235
Shackney; United States v. . .48; 62; 69; 73; 76; 311
Siderman de Blake v. Republic of Argentina. . .302
Sines v. Serv. Corp. Int'l. 314
Singh v. Jutla. 315
Skinner v. Total Petroleum, Inc. 320
Slaughter-House Cases 31; 55; 61; 81
Sosa v. Alvarez-Machain 301, 302; 304
Sotomayor-Vazquez; United States v. 236
Spinosa; United States v. 238
Standard Oil Co. v. United States. 76
Stoll v. Runyon. 282, 283
Subpoena of Persico, In re 65
Swarna v. Al-Awadi 255

T

Tapiero de Orejuela v. Gonzales. 345
Telichenko; United States v. 270
Tel-Oren v. Libyan Arab Republic. 301
Temple v. United States. 65
Turkette; United States v. 309
Turner v. Unification Church 285

U

U.S. v. (see name of defendant)
Udeozor; United States v. 119; 241; 252; 405
United States v. (see name of defendant)

V

Valenzuela; United States v. 269, 270
Van Horn; United States v. 238
Virginia v. Hicks. 250

W

Warren; United States v. 66; 79; 240; 404
Wilson v. United States 102
Wilson; United States v. 267
Wood; United States v. 238
World War II Era Japanese Forced Labor Litigation, In re 303

Y

Yick Wo v. Hopkins. 37

Z

Zavala v. Wal-Mart Stores, Inc. 309; 319; 321

INDEX

[References are to sections.]

A

ABOLITION OF SLAVERY
Generally . . . 1[V]
Ah Sou, Thirteenth Amendment and . . . 1[VI]

AGRICULTURAL WORKERS
Generally . . . 14[IV]

ALIEN TORT CLAIMS ACT (ATCA)
Generally . . . 11[VI]

ANTI-PEONAGE ACT OF 1867
Generally . . . 2[IV][A]

ANTI-TRAFFICKING AGENCIES AND ORGANIZATIONS
Generally . . . 9[I]; 9[V]
Anti-trafficking task forces . . . 9[II][C][2]
Congress, Department of Justice annual report to . . . 9[II][C][3]
Department of Health and Human Services (HHS)
    Generally . . . 9[II][F]
    Certification for foreign victims of trafficking . . . 9[II][F][1]
    Foreign victims of trafficking, certification for . . . 9[II][F][1]
    Public-awareness and victim-identification efforts . . . 9[II][F][3]
    Services grants . . . 9[II][F][2]
    Victim-identification efforts, public-awareness and . . . 9[II][F][3]
Department of Homeland Security (DHS) . . . 9[II][E]
Department of Justice (DOJ)
    Generally . . . 9[II][B]; 9[II][G]
    Annual report to congress . . . 9[II][C][3]
    Coordinated prosecution efforts, partnerships and . . . 9[II][B][1][c]
    Criminal prosecutions
        Child exploitation section . . . 9[II][B][1][a]; 9[II][B][1][a][ii]
        Section, criminal . . . 9[II][B][1][a]; 9[II][B][1][a][i]
    Partnerships and coordinated prosecution efforts . . . 9[II][B][1][c]
    United States attorneys' offices . . . 9[II][B][1][b]
Department of State
    Generally . . . 9[II][D]
    Awareness, public engagement and . . . 9[II][D][3]
    Foreign financial assistance grants . . . 9[II][D][2]
    Offices and efforts, additional state department . . . 9[II][D][4]
    Public engagement and awareness . . . 9[II][D][3]

ANTI-TRAFFICKING AGENCIES AND ORGANIZATIONS—Cont.
Department of State—Cont.
    Report on trafficking in persons . . . 9[II][D][1]
Federal agencies, other . . . 9[II][H]
Federal Bureau of Investigation (FBI) (See FEDERAL BUREAU OF INVESTIGATION (FBI))
Federal law enforcement
    Generally . . . 9[II][C]
    Anti-trafficking task forces and . . . 9[II][C][2]
    Department of Justice annual report to congress . . . 9[II][C][3]
    Federal Bureau of Investigation (FBI) (See FEDERAL BUREAU OF INVESTIGATION (FBI))
International organizations (See INTERNATIONAL ORGANIZATIONS)
Non-governmental organizations . . . 9[III]
U.S. government
    Generally . . . 9[II]
    Department of Health and Human Services (HHS) (See subhead: Department of Health and Human Services (HHS))
    Department of Homeland Security (DHS) . . . 9[II][E]
    Department of Justice (DOJ) (See subhead: Department of Justice (DOJ))
    Department of Labor (DOL) . . . 9[II][G]
    Department of state (See subhead: Department of State)
    Federal law enforcement forces (See subhead: Federal law enforcement)
    President, the . . . 9[II][A]

ATCA (See ALIEN TORT CLAIMS ACT (ATCA))

C

CAATH (See COUNCIL OF EUROPE CONVENTION ON ACTION AGAINST TRAFFICKING IN HUMAN BEINGS (CAATH))

CIVIL LITIGATION
Generally . . . 11[I]
Alien Tort Claims Act (ATCA) . . . 11[VI]
Causes of action, additional
    Contracts claims . . . 11[IX][B]
    Discrimination claims (See subhead: Discrimination claims)
    Torts and contracts claims . . . 11[IX][B]
Civil remedies, state trafficking . . . 11[V]
Contracts claims . . . 11[IX][B]
Discrimination claims
    Civil rights, conspiracy to interfere with . . . 11[IX][A][3]
    Conspiracy to interfere with civil rights . . . 11[IX][A][3]

I-1

CIVIL LITIGATION—Cont.
Discrimination claims—Cont.
    42 U.S.C. Section 1981 . . . 11[IX][A][2]
    Section 1985 . . . 11[IX][A][3]
    Title VII of Civil Rights Act
        . . . 11[IX][A][1]
18 U.S.C. Section 1595: trafficking private right of action
    Generally . . . 11[II]
    Defendants under Section 1595, scope of
        . . . 11[III]
    Immigration relief under Section 1595
        . . . 11[IV]
Fair Labor Standards Act (FLSA) (See FAIR LABOR STANDARDS ACT (FLSA))
Racketeer Influenced and Corrupt Organizations Act (RICO) . . . 11[VII]
Torts and contracts claims . . . 11[IX][B]

CIVIL WAR
Emancipation Proclamation, and . . . 1[IV]

COERCION
Consent versus . . . 13[III]

CONSENT
Coercion, versus . . . 13[III]

CONTRACTS CLAIMS
Generally . . . 11[IX][B]

CORPORATE ACCOUNTABILITY AND FEDERAL CONTRACTORS
Council of Europe Convention on Action Against Trafficking in Human Beings (CAATH) . . . 8[II]
Department of Defense (DoD) . . . 8[V]
Federal acquisitions regulations . . . 8[IV]
Labor recruiter in human trafficking, role of
    . . . 8[VI]
Liability for companies, legal . . . 8[I]
Sub-group of corporate accountability . . . 8[III]

COUNCIL OF EUROPE
Generally . . . 9[IV][B][2]

COUNCIL OF EUROPE CONVENTION ON ACTION AGAINST TRAFFICKING IN HUMAN BEINGS (CAATH)
Generally . . . 8[II]

CRIMINAL PROSECUTIONS, FEDERAL (See FEDERAL CRIMINAL PROSECUTIONS)

D

DEPARTMENT OF DEFENSE (DOD)
Generally . . . 8[V]

DEPARTMENT OF HOMELAND SECURITY (DHS)
Generally . . . 9[II][E]

DEPARTMENT OF JUSTICE (DOJ) (See ANTI-TRAFFICKING AGENCIES AND ORGANIZATIONS, subhead: Department of Justice (DOJ))

DEPARTMENT OF LABOR (DOL)
Generally . . . 9[II][G]

DERIVATIVE VISAS
Generally . . . 12[II]
Caps on . . . 12[III]

DHS (See DEPARTMENT OF HOMELAND SECURITY (DHS))

DIPLOMATIC IMMUNITY
Domestic servitude and . . . 10[III][C][5]

DISCRIMINATION CLAIMS (See CIVIL LITIGATION, subhead: Discrimination claims)

DOD (See DEPARTMENT OF DEFENSE (DOD))

DOL (See DEPARTMENT OF LABOR (DOL))

DOMESTIC SERVITUDE (See FORCED LABOR, subhead: Domestic servitude)

DOMESTIC SEX-TRAFFICKING (See SEX TRAFFICKING, subhead: Domestic sex-trafficking)

DOMESTIC WORKERS
Generally . . . 14[III]

E

EMANCIPATION PROCLAMATION
Civil war and . . . 1[IV]

F

FAIR LABOR STANDARDS ACT (FLSA)
Generally . . . 11[VIII]
Employment relationship . . . 11[VIII][B]
Wage and hour protections . . . 11[VIII][A]

FBI (See FEDERAL BUREAU OF INVESTIGATION (FBI))

FEDERAL BUREAU OF INVESTIGATION (FBI)
Generally . . . 9[II][C][1]
Child sex tourism initiative . . . 9[II][C][1][a]
Lost initiative, innocence . . . 9[II][C][1][b]

FEDERAL CRIMINAL PROSECUTIONS
Generally . . . 10[I]; 10[V]
Forced labor (See FORCED LABOR)
Sex trafficking (See SEX TRAFFICKING)
Trafficking Victims Protection Act (TVPA), under (See TRAFFICKING VICTIMS PROTECTION ACT (TVPA), subhead: Criminal prosecutions under)

[References are to sections.]

FLSA (See FAIR LABOR STANDARDS ACT (FLSA))

FORCED LABOR
Generally . . . 10[I][A][1]; 10[III]
Compelled sexualized labor . . . 10[III][B][2][d]
Domestic servitude
    Generally . . . 10[III][C]
    Diplomatic immunity, and . . . 10[III][C][5]
    Involuntary servitude and . . . 10[III][C][2]
    Knowledge requirement under forced labor and restitution . . . 10[III][C][4]
    Restitution, knowledge requirement under forced labor and . . . 10[III][C][4]
    Sexual abuse, and . . . 10[III][C][3]
    United States v. Calimlim . . . 10[III][C][1]
Legal process as form of coercion, abuse of . . . 10[III][B][2][b]
Military contractors, forced labor by . . . 10[III][B][2][e]
Non-economic labor or services . . . 10[III][B][2][a]
Peonage . . . 10[III][B][2][c]
Post-Trafficking Victims Protection Act forced labor cases
    Section 1589
        Generally . . . 10[III][B][2]
        Compelled sexualized labor, forced labor involving . . . 10[III][B][2][d]
        Legal process as form of coercion, abuse of . . . 10[III][B][2][b]
        Military contractors, forced labor by . . . 10[III][B][2][e]
        Non-economic labor or services . . . 10[III][B][2][a]
        Peonage . . . 10[III][B][2][c]
        United States v. Bradley . . . 10[III][B][1]
Pre-Trafficking Victims Protection Act forced labor cases
    Generally . . . 10[III][A]
    Paoletti case . . . 10[III][A][2]
    United States v. Harris . . . 10[III][A][1]
    United States v. Kozminski . . . 10[III][A][3]

H

HUMAN TRAFFICKING (GENERALLY)
Agricultural workers . . . 14[IV]
Anti-trafficking agencies and organizations (See ANTI-TRAFFICKING AGENCIES AND ORGANIZATIONS)
Challenges
    Generally . . . 13[III]
    Coercion, consent versus . . . 13[III]
    Consent versus coercion . . . 13[III]
    Labor-focused approaches . . . 13[II]
    Prostitution . . . 13[I]
    Sex trafficking and prostitution . . . 13[I]
Civil litigation (See CIVIL LITIGATION)
Coercion, consent versus . . . 13[III]
Consent versus coercion . . . 13[III]

HUMAN TRAFFICKING (GENERALLY)—Cont.
Contractors, corporate accountability and federal (See CORPORATE ACCOUNTABILITY AND FEDERAL CONTRACTORS)
Corporate accountability and federal contractors (See CORPORATE ACCOUNTABILITY AND FEDERAL CONTRACTORS)
Federal criminal prosecutions (See FEDERAL CRIMINAL PROSECUTIONS)
Immigration protections for trafficking victims (See IMMIGRATION PROTECTIONS FOR TRAFFICKING VICTIMS)
Immigration Reform and Control Act (IRCA) . . . 14[I][B]
International legal and policy framework (See INTERNATIONAL LEGAL AND POLICY FRAMEWORK)
Involuntary servitude (See INVOLUNTARY SERVITUDE)
Issues related to
    Agricultural workers . . . 14[IV]
    Immigration Reform and Control Act (IRCA) . . . 14[I][B]
    Prostitution, reconciling state laws on sex trafficking and . . . 14[II][A]
    Sex trafficking, victims of (See SEX TRAFFICKING, subhead: Victims of sex trafficking)
    Undocumented workers . . . 14[I][A]
    Victims of sex trafficking (See SEX TRAFFICKING, subhead: Victims of sex trafficking)
Labor-focused approaches . . . 13[II]
Palermo protocol (See PALERMO PROTOCOL)
Peonage (See PEONAGE)
Policy framework, international legal and (See INTERNATIONAL LEGAL AND POLICY FRAMEWORK)
Prostitution (See PROSTITUTION)
Sex trafficking (See SEX TRAFFICKING)
Slavery (See SLAVERY)
State and local human trafficking laws and prosecutions . . . App. 1
Trafficking Victims Protection Act (TVPA) (See TRAFFICKING VICTIMS PROTECTION ACT (TVPA))
Undocumented workers . . . 14[I][A]

I

ILO (See INTERNATIONAL LABOR ORGANIZATION (ILO))

IMMIGRATION PROTECTIONS FOR TRAFFICKING VICTIMS
Asylum . . . 12[VI][B]
Derivative visas
    Generally . . . 12[II]
    Caps on . . . 12[III]
Relief, immigration
    Generally . . . 12[VI]
    Asylum . . . 12[VI][B]

[References are to sections.]

IMMIGRATION PROTECTIONS FOR TRAFFICKING VICTIMS—Cont.
Relief, immigration—Cont.
    Special Immigrant Juvenile Status (SIJS) . . . 12[VI][D]
    S visa . . . 12[VI][E]
    U visa . . . 12[VI][A]
    Violence Against Women Act (VAWA) . . . 12[VI][C]
Special Immigrant Juvenile Status (SIJS) . . . 12[VI][D]
Statutes . . . 4[I]
S visa . . . 12[VI][E]
Trafficking victims and derivatives, benefits for . . . 12[V]
T visa requirements (See T VISA, subhead: Requirements)
U visa . . . 12[VI][A]
Violence Against Women Act (VAWA) . . . 12[VI][C]

IMMIGRATION REFORM AND CONTROL ACT (IRCA)
Generally . . . 14[I][B]

IMMUNITY, DIPLOMATIC
Domestic servitude and . . . 10[III][C][5]

INTERNATIONAL LABOR ORGANIZATION (ILO)
Generally . . . 9[IV][A][2]

INTERNATIONAL LEGAL AND POLICY FRAMEWORK
Anti-trafficking obligations of nations . . . 7[VI]
Assistance . . . 7[III]; 7[II][B]
International courts and anti-trafficking obligations of nations . . . 7[VI]
Prevention . . . 7[I]
Prosecution . . . 7[III]
Protection
    Generally . . . 7[II]
    Physical safety . . . 7[II][A]
Protocol
    Generally . . . 7[IV]
    Assistance, strengthening protections and . . . 7[V]
    Protections and assistance, strengthening . . . 7[V]

INTERNATIONAL ORGANIZATION FOR MIGRATION (IOM)
Generally . . . 9[IV][B][1]

INTERNATIONAL ORGANIZATIONS
Generally . . . 9[IV]
Non-United Nations organizations
    Council of Europe . . . 9[IV][B][2]
    International Organization for Migration (IOM) . . . 9[IV][B][1]
    Organization for Security and Cooperation in Europe . . . 9[IV][B][3]
United Nations
    Generally . . . 9[IV][A]

INTERNATIONAL ORGANIZATIONS—Cont.
United Nations—Cont.
    International Labor Organization (ILO) . . . 9[IV][A][2]
    United Nations Office on Drugs and Crime (UNODC) . . . 9[IV][A][1]

INTERNATIONAL SEX TRAFFICKING
Generally . . . 10[IV][A]
Mexican sex trafficking rings . . . 10[IV][A][1]

INVOLUNTARY SERVITUDE
Generally . . . 3[I]
Circuit court split . . . 3[III]
Domestic servitude, and . . . 10[III][C][2]
18 U.S.C. Section 1584 . . . 3[III]
Statute . . . 3[II]

IOM (See INTERNATIONAL ORGANIZATION FOR MIGRATION (IOM))

IRCA (See IMMIGRATION REFORM AND CONTROL ACT (IRCA))

L

LABOR-FOCUSED APPROACHES
Generally . . . 13[II]

M

MANN ACT
Constitutionality of . . . 4[II][C]
Decline of . . . 4[II][E]
Legislative history . . . 4[II][A]
Modern-day Mann Act . . . 4[III]
Passed in 1910, as . . . 4[II][B]
Scope of . . . 4[II][D]

MEXICAN SEX TRAFFICKING RINGS
Generally . . . 10[IV][A][1]

O

ORGANIZATIONS, ANTI-TRAFFICKING AGENCIES AND (See ANTI-TRAFFICKING AGENCIES AND ORGANIZATIONS)

P

PALERMO PROTOCOL
Generally . . . 6[I]; 6[II][A]
Anti-trafficking legislation principles
    Generally . . . 6[VII]
    Address all forms of human trafficking . . . 6[VII][C]
    Address root causes/contributing factors . . . 6[VII][E]
    Best interest of child, act in . . . 6[VII][F]
    Comprehensive and integrated response . . . 6[VII][D]
    Cooperation, international and domestic . . . 6[VII][G]

[References are to sections.]

PALERMO PROTOCOL—Cont.
Anti-trafficking legislation principles—Cont.
    Integrated response, comprehensive and
        . . . 6[VII][D]
    Remedies, legal . . . 6[VII][H]
    Root causes/contributing factors, address
        . . . 6[VII][E]
    Victim care and protection to need in individual cases . . . 6[VII][B]
    Victim-centered responses . . . 6[VII][A]
Children
    Domesticity, in . . . 6[IV][B]
    Forced marriage, child brides and
        . . . 6[IV][C]
Consent . . . 6[IV][G]
Countries to criminalize, obligation by . . . 6[VI]
Criminal, extending scope of . . . 6[IV][F]
Definitional issues
    Generally . . . 6[IV]
    Children
        Domesticity, in . . . 6[IV][B]
        Forced marriage, child brides and
            . . . 6[IV][C]
        Consent . . . 6[IV][G]
    Domesticity, children in . . . 6[IV][B]
    Forced marriage . . . 6[IV][C]
    Fostering . . . 6[IV][B]
    Guise of adoption, human trafficking under
        . . . 6[IV][A]
    Labor migration . . . 6[IV][D]
    Organs, removal of . . . 6[IV][F]
    Prostitution of others, exploitation of
        . . . 6[IV][E]
    Removal of organs . . . 6[IV][F]
Domesticity, children in . . . 6[IV][B]
Elements
    Generally . . . 6[II][B]
    "Means" : person coerces or controls another person . . . 6[II][B][2]
    Purpose of exploitation . . . 6[II][B][3]
    "Recruitment, transportation, transfer, harbouring or receipt of persons" . . . 6[II][B][1]
Forced marriage . . . 6[IV][C]
Fostering . . . 6[IV][B]
Guise of adoption, human trafficking under
    . . . 6[IV][A]
Issues, definitional (See Definitional issues)
Labor migration . . . 6[IV][D]
Organs, removal of . . . 6[IV][F]
Prostitution of others, exploitation of . . . 6[IV][E]
Removal of organs . . . 6[IV][F]
Umbrella term . . . 6[III]

PEONAGE
Generally . . . 2[VI]
American South
    Generally . . . 2[III]; 2[III][B]
    Peonage system . . . 2[III][A]
Challenges to peonage
    Bailey case . . . 2[V][A]
    Federal law, finding and enforcing (See subhead: Federal law, finding and enforcing)
    Reynolds case . . . 2[V][B]

PEONAGE—Cont.
Federal law, finding and enforcing
    Generally . . . 2[IV]
    Anti-Peonage Act of 1867 . . . 2[IV][A]
    First court test — *US v. Clyatt* . . . 2[IV][B]
Forced labor . . . 10[III][B][2][c]
Proclamation to peonage . . . 2[I]
Southwest, in . . . 2[II]

POLICY FRAMEWORK, INTERNATIONAL LEGAL AND (See INTERNATIONAL LEGAL AND POLICY FRAMEWORK)

POST-TRAFFICKING VICTIMS PROTECTION ACT FORCED LABOR CASES (See FORCED LABOR, subhead: Post-Trafficking Victims Protection Act forced labor cases)

PRE-TRAFFICKING VICTIMS PROTECTION ACT FORCED LABOR CASES (See FORCED LABOR, subhead: Pre-Trafficking Victims Protection Act forced labor cases)

PROCLAMATION
Peonage, to . . . 2[I]

PROSTITUTION
Generally . . . 13[I]
Prostitution of others, exploitation of . . . 6[IV][E]
State laws on sex trafficking and, reconciling
    . . . 14[II][A]

PROTECT ACT OF 2003
Generally . . . 10[IV][D]

R

RACKETEER INFLUENCED AND CORRUPT ORGANIZATIONS ACT (RICO)
Generally . . . 11[VII]

S

SERVITUDE
Document servitude . . . 5[II][A][3]
Domestic servitude (See FORCED LABOR, subhead: Domestic servitude)
Involuntary servitude (See INVOLUNTARY SERVITUDE)

SEX TRAFFICKING
Generally . . . 10[I][A][2]; 10[IV]; 13[I]
Constitutionality of Section 2423(c) . . . 10[IV][D]
Domestic servitude and sexual abuse
    . . . 10[III][C][3]
Domestic sex-trafficking
    Generally . . . 10[IV][B]
    Commercial sex act . . . 10[IV][B][2]
    Conspiracy . . . 10[IV][B][2]
    Interstate commerce . . . 10[IV][B][2]
    Opportunity to observe, reasonable
        . . . 10[IV][B][3]
    Prior sexual behavior, exclusion of victims'
        . . . 10[IV][B][4]
    United States v. Pipkins . . . 10[IV][B][1]

[References are to sections.]

SEX TRAFFICKING—Cont.
International sex trafficking
    Generally . . . 10[IV][A]
    Mexican sex trafficking rings
        . . . 10[IV][A][1]
PROTECT Act of 2003 . . . 10[IV][D]
United States, in . . . 10[IV][C]
Victims of sex trafficking
    Generally . . . 14[II]
    Prostitution, reconciling state laws on sex trafficking and . . . 14[II][A]
    State laws on sex trafficking and prostitution, reconciling . . . 14[II][A]

SIJS (See SPECIAL IMMIGRANT JUVENILE STATUS (SIJS))

SLAVERY
Generally . . . 1[I]; 1[VII]
Abolition of slavery
    Generally . . . 1[V]
    Ah Sou, Thirteenth Amendment and . . . 1[VI]
Ah Sou, Thirteenth Amendment and . . . 1[VI]
Citizenship question, *Dred Scott* and . . . 1[III]
Civil war and Emancipation Proclamation
    . . . 1[IV]
Colonies and early republic, in . . . 1[II]
Dred Scott and citizenship question . . . 1[III]
Emancipation Proclamation, civil war and
    . . . 1[IV]
Thirteenth Amendment: abolition of slavery
    Generally . . . 1[V]
    Ah Sou, and . . . 1[VI]

SPECIAL IMMIGRANT JUVENILE STATUS (SIJS)
Generally . . . 12[VI][D]

S VISA
Generally . . . 12[VI][E]

T

THIRTEENTH AMENDMENT
Generally . . . 1[V]
Ah Sou, and . . . 1[VI]

TORTS CLAIMS
Generally . . . 11[IX][B]

TRAFFICKING VICTIMS PROTECTION ACT (TVPA)
Civil relief, restitution and . . . 5[II][B]
Criminal prosecutions under
    Generally . . . 10[I][A]
    Evolution of criminal prosecutions
        . . . 10[I][B]
    Forced labor (See FORCED LABOR)
    Offenses, other . . . 10[I][A][3]
    Principles for criminal offenses under TVPA
        . . . 10[II]
    Sex trafficking (See SEX TRAFFICKING)
Criminal provisions
    Generally . . . 5[II][A]
    Attempt . . . 5[II][A][3]

TRAFFICKING VICTIMS PROTECTION ACT (TVPA)—Cont.
Criminal provisions—Cont.
    Document servitude . . . 5[II][A][3]
    Forced labor . . . 5[II][A][1]
    Sex trafficking . . . 5[II][A][2]
    Trafficking, document servitude, and attempt
        . . . 5[II][A][3]
Forced labor (See FORCED LABOR)
Legislative history
    Generally . . . 5[II]
    Civil relief, restitution and . . . 5[II][B]
    Criminal provisions (See subhead: Criminal provisions)
    Restitution and civil relief . . . 5[II][B]
    Social service provisions . . . 5[II][C]
Policy history
    Generally . . . 5[I]
    El Monte
        Generally . . . 5[I][A]
        Multi-pronged approach, from El Monte to . . . 5[I][B]
    Multi-pronged approach, from El Monte to
        . . . 5[I][B]
Principles for criminal offenses under . . . 10[II]
Restitution and civil relief . . . 5[II][B]
Sex trafficking (See SEX TRAFFICKING)
Social service provisions . . . 5[II][C]

T VISA
Admissibility . . . 12[I][B][5]
Application process . . . 12[I][A]
Caps on . . . 12[III]
Challenges to obtaining T visa
    Generally . . . 12[IV]
    Access to legal services, lack of
        . . . 12[IV][A]
    Escaping victims . . . 12[IV][B][1]
    Legal services, lack of access to
        . . . 12[IV][A]
    Slave, individual agree to be
        . . . 12[IV][B][2]
    Transportation for human trafficking
        . . . 12[IV][B][3]
Criteria, interpreting
    Compliance with law enforcement
        . . . 12[I][B][3]
    Hardship involving severe and unusual harm
        . . . 12[I][B][4]
    Law enforcement, compliance with
        . . . 12[I][B][3]
    Physical presence . . . 12[I][B][2]
    Severe form of human trafficking, victim of
        . . . 12[I][B][1]
    Victim of severe form of human trafficking
        . . . 12[I][B][1]
Requirements
    Generally . . . 12[I]
    Admissibility . . . 12[I][B][5]
    Application process . . . 12[I][A]
    Criteria, interpreting (See subhead: Criteria, interpreting)

[References are to sections.]

TVPA (See TRAFFICKING VICTIMS PROTECTION ACT (TVPA))

U

UNDOCUMENTED WORKERS
Generally . . . 14[I][A]

UNITED NATIONS OFFICE ON DRUGS AND CRIME (UNODC)
Generally . . . 9[IV][A][1]

UNODC (See UNITED NATIONS OFFICE ON DRUGS AND CRIME (UNODC))

U VISA
Generally . . . 12[VI][A]

V

VAWA (See VIOLENCE AGAINST WOMEN ACT (VAWA))

VICTIMS
Immigration protections for trafficking victims (See IMMIGRATION PROTECTIONS FOR TRAFFICKING VICTIMS)

VICTIMS—Cont.
Sex trafficking, of (See SEX TRAFFICKING, subhead: Victims of sex trafficking)
Trafficking Victims Protection Act (TVPA) (See TRAFFICKING VICTIMS PROTECTION ACT (TVPA))

VIOLENCE AGAINST WOMEN ACT (VAWA)
Generally . . . 12[VI][C]

VISAS
Derivative visas
    Generally . . . 12[II]
    Caps on . . . 12[III]
S visa . . . 12[VI][E]
T visa (See T VISA)
U visa . . . 12[VI][A]

W

WORKERS
Agricultural workers . . . 14[IV]
Domestic workers . . . 14[III]
Undocumented workers . . . 14[I][A]